Advancements in Cybersecurity

This book offers a comprehensive exploration of cutting-edge research and developments in the field of cybersecurity. It presents a curated collection of chapters that reflect the latest in empirical data approximation, malware recognition, information security technologies, and beyond.

Advancements in Cybersecurity: Next-Generation Systems and Applications offers readers a broad perspective on the multifaceted challenges and solutions in contemporary cybersecurity through topics ranging from the application of blockchain technology in securing information systems, to the development of new cost functions for the iterative generation of cryptographic components. The book not only addresses technical aspects but also provides insights into the theoretical frameworks and practical applications that underpin the development of robust cybersecurity systems. It explores the optimization of algorithms for generating nonlinear substitutions, the application of machine learning models for security evaluation, and the implementation of deep learning techniques for detecting sophisticated cyber-attacks. Through its in-depth analysis and forward-looking perspectives, this book contributes significantly to advancing cybersecurity research and practice, paving the way for a safer digital future.

This book is designed to serve as an essential resource for researchers, practitioners, policymakers, and engineers in the fields of ICT, next-generation computing and IT security, including cryptography, AI/ML/DL, cyber resilience, network security, threat modeling and risk assessment, digital forensics, secure software development, hardware security, and human-centric security.

Advancements in Cybersecurity

Next-Generation Systems and Applications

Edited By
Agbotiname Lucky Imoize,
Oleksandr Kuznetsov, Oleksandr Lemeshko,
and Oleksandra Yeremenko

CRC Press
Taylor & Francis Group
Boca Raton London New York

CRC Press is an imprint of the
Taylor & Francis Group, an **informa** business

Designed cover image: © Getty

First edition published 2025
by CRC Press
2385 NW Executive Center Drive, Suite 320, Boca Raton FL 33431

and by CRC Press
4 Park Square, Milton Park, Abingdon, Oxon, OX14 4RN

CRC Press is an imprint of Taylor & Francis Group, LLC

ISBN: 978-1-032-90099-5 (hbk)
ISBN: 978-1-032-90101-5 (pbk)
ISBN: 978-1-003-54615-3 (ebk)

DOI: 10.1201/9781003546153

Typeset in Times
by Apex CoVantage, LLC

Contents

About the Editors

Agbotiname Lucky Imoize (senior member, IEEE; B.Eng. (Hons.), M.Sc.) is a lecturer in the Department of Electrical and Electronics Engineering at the University of Lagos, Nigeria. Before joining the University of Lagos, he was a lecturer at Bells University of Technology, Nigeria. He is a research scholar at the Ruhr University Bochum, Germany, under the sponsorship of the Nigerian Petroleum Technology Development Fund (PTDF) and the German Academic Exchange Service (DAAD) through the Nigerian-German Postgraduate Program. He was awarded the Fulbright fellowship as a visiting research scholar at the Wireless@VT Laboratory, Bradley Department of Electrical and Computer Engineering, Virginia Tech, USA, where he worked under the supervision of Professor R. Michael Buehrer from 2017 to 2018. He previously worked as a core network products manager at ZTE, Nigeria, and as a network switching subsystem engineer at Globacom, Nigeria. His research interests cover the fields of 6G wireless communications, wireless security systems, and artificial intelligence. He is the Vice Chair of the IEEE Communication Society Nigeria chapter, a registered engineer with the Council for the Regulation of Engineering in Nigeria, and a member of the Nigerian Society of Engineers.

Oleksandr Kuznetsov (member, IEEE; D.Eng.Sc.) is an Academician at the Academy of Applied Radioelectronics Sciences and the recipient of the Boris Paton National Prize of Ukraine in 2021. Additionally, he serves as a professor at the Department of Theoretical and Applied Sciences, eCampus University, Italy. He is also a professor in the Department of Security Information Systems and Technologies at the V. N. Karazin Kharkiv National University, Ukraine. With a distinguished career as a scientific researcher, Professor Kuznetsov has demonstrated exemplary leadership and a hands-on approach to research and development across various sectors, including state defense, private organizations, international IT companies, and industry consortiums. His involvement in numerous pivotal projects has significantly contributed to the advancement of the scientific domain. A recognized expert in computer science, his expertise spans numerous subdisciplines, including information and cybersecurity, applied cryptography, information and coding theory, steganography, authentication, and the modeling and evaluation of complex technical systems, among others. His knowledge encompasses the theoretical underpinnings as well as models, methods, and algorithms of information processing and transmission. As a cryptographic technologist, Professor Kuznetsov has significantly contributed to the development and implementation of advanced cryptographic information protection technologies, co-authoring several national cryptographic standards for Ukraine. These contributions have been successfully integrated into current information systems and IT networks.

Oleksandr Lemeshko (senior member, IEEE; Ph.D. 1999, D.Eng.Sc. 2005) is a professor and the Head of V.V. Popovskyy Department of Infocommunication Engineering at the Kharkiv National University of Radio Electronics in Kharkiv, Ukraine. Previously, he worked as a professor of the Department of Combat Application of Automated Aviation Control Systems at the Ivan Kozhedub Kharkiv University of Air Force and National Technical University "Kharkiv Polytechnic Institute" (Kharkiv, Ukraine). He was awarded the Georgy Proskura Academic Scholarship of Kharkiv Regional State Administration in 2003 and won the Kharkiv Region High School—Best Names contest in the "Young Scientists" category in 2006. He received state awards such as the 15 Years of Ukraine Military Force medal and accolade from the Ministry of Defense of Ukraine "For the Conscientious Service" II degree medal in 2006. In 2018–2021, he won the annual competition The Best Scientific and Pedagogical Worker of the Kharkiv National University of Radio Electronics in the category of doctors' professors. He has participated in national research projects in different capacities, such as proposer, researcher, and principal researcher, mostly in networking and information security. He was the local researcher of the National Research Foundation of Ukraine project. He is a chief editor of the electronic journal *Problems of Telecommunications* and an editorial board member of the *International Journal of Wireless and Microwave Technologies* (Hong Kong). He has served as organizing committee member, executive co-chair, and program committee member of numerous IEEE conferences, among them the IEEE Conference on Problems of Infocommunications, Science and Technology (PIC S&T), IEEE International Conference on Advanced Information and Communication Technologies, IEEE International Conference on Advanced Trends in Information Theory (ATIT), and others. He has supervised over 17 Ph.D. theses and four D.Eng.Sc. theses. He has been a reviewer for European high-impact scientific journals. The fields of scientific interest are cyber-resilience networks, incident response, communication network resilience, network security, fault-tolerant networks, future networks, software-defined networking, and cloud computing. He participated in international projects: TEMPUS/ERASMUS+ 544455-TEMPUS-1-2013-1-SE-TEMPUS-JPCR "Educating the Next Generation Experts in Cyber Security: the New EU-Recognized Master's Program" (ENGENSEC); Project №: 101085825—ERASMUS-JMO-2022-MODULE Erasmus + project Jean Monnet module: «The European experience for enhancement the resilience of critical entities in Ukraine»; and German-Ukrainian Project "DigiJED-2: Digital Education with Joined Efforts." He represents NURE in the project COST CA22104—Behavioral Next Generation in Wireless Networks for Cyber Security (BEiNG-WISE) since 2024. Scientific publications: more than 300 articles and papers. Monographs, textbooks, and teaching aids: four textbooks, 15 monographs, and nine teaching aids. Patents: 19 patents.

Oleksandra Yeremenko (senior member, IEEE; Ph.D. 2008, D.Eng.Sc. 2018) is a professor of V.V. Popovskyy Department of Infocommunication Engineering at the Kharkiv National University of Radio Electronics (NURE) in Kharkiv, Ukraine. She was awarded by Commendations from the Head of Kharkiv Regional Council (Kharkiv, Ukraine) in 2018 and the Ministry of Education and Science of Ukraine in 2020. She won the XXI regional contest Higher School of Kharkiv region—Best Names in the "Young Scientists" category in 2019. She received a scholarship from the Cabinet of Ministers of Ukraine for young scientists (2018–2020), a personal scholarship from the Verkhovna Rada of Ukraine for Young Scientists—Doctor of Sciences (2020), and a state nominal scholarship for the best young scientists to commemorate the events of the Revolution of Dignity (2022). In 2019–2021, she won the annual competition The Best Scientific and Pedagogical Worker of the Kharkiv National University of Radio Electronics for young scientists and doctors of sciences up to 40 years old. She has participated in national research and international projects as a researcher, mainly in the network resilience field. She is the researcher of the Erasmus+ project Jean Monnet modules: "Integrating the EU cybersecurity framework and policies in Ukraine" (Project № 621250-EPP-1-2020-1-UA–EPPJMO–MODULE at 09/01/20-08/31/2023) and "The European experience for enhancement the resilience of critical entities in Ukraine" (Project №: 101085825—ERASMUS-JMO-2022-MODULE). She represented NURE in the project COST CA15127—Resilient Communication Services Protecting End-user Applications from Disaster-based Failures (RECODIS) in 2019–2020, and CA22104—Behavioral Next Generation in Wireless Networks for Cyber Security (BEiNG-WISE) since 2024. She is a secretary in charge of the electronic journal *Problems of Telecommunications* (Ukraine) and an editorial board member of the *International Journal of Mathematical Sciences and Computing* (Hong Kong). She served as the Organizing and Program Committee Member of IEEE conferences, among them the IEEE Conference on Problems of Infocommunications, Science, and Technology (PIC S&T); IEEE 5th International Conference on Advanced Information and Communication Technologies (AICT-2023); IEEE 16th International Conference on Advanced Trends in Radioelectronics, Telecommunications and Computer Engineering (TCSET 2022, 2024); and others. She has supervised over 15 M.Sc. projects. She has been a reviewer for European high-impact scientific journals. The fields of scientific interest are cyber-resilience, communication network resilience, network security and fault tolerance, future networks, software-defined networking, and cloud computing.

Contributors

Bayan Abduraimova
L.N. Gumilyov Eurasian National University
Astana, Republic of Kazakhstan

Bakhytzhan Akhmetov
Kazakh National Pedagogical University
Abai, Almaty, Kazakhstan

Zhuldyz Alimseitova
Kazakh National Research University K.I. Satpayev
Almaty, Kazakhstan

Marco Arnesano
eCampus University
Novedrate, Italy

Oleksii Baranovskyi
National Technical University of Ukraine Igor Sikorsky Kyiv Polytechnic Institute
Kyiv, Ukraine

Gulvira Bekeshova
L.N. Gumilyov Eurasian National University
Astana, Republic of Kazakhstan

Yuriy Bobalo
Rector of Lviv Polytechnic National University
Lviv, Ukraine

Andrii Davydiuk
G.E. Pukhov Institute for Modelling in Energy Engineering National Academy of Sciences of Ukraine
Kyiv, Ukraine

Yaroslav Derevianko
V. N. Karazin Kharkiv National University
Kharkiv, Ukraine

Valeriy Dudykevych
Lviv Polytechnic National University
Lviv, Ukraine

Frederick Obataimen Edeko
University of Benin
Benin City, Nigeria

Emanuele Frontoni
University of Macerata
Macerata, Italy

Emanuele Gennuso
eCampus University
Novedrate, Italy

Oleh Harasymchuk
Lviv Polytechnic National University
Lviv, Ukraine

Olena Harkusha
Poltava University of Economics and Trade
Poltava, Ukraine

Serhii Harkusha
Poltava University of Economics and Trade
Poltava, Ukraine

Serhii Hilgurt
G.E. Pukhov Institute for Modelling in Energy Engineering of the National Academy of Sciences of Ukraine
Kyiv, Ukraine

Viktor Hnatiuk
State University "Kyiv Aviation Institute"
Kyiv, Ukraine

Maksim Iavich
Caucasus University
Tbilisi, Georgia

Augustus Ehiremen Ibhaze
University of Lagos
Akoka, Lagos, Nigeria

Aisha Glory Ibhaze
Petinence Group
Akowonjo, Lagos, Nigeria

Azamat Zhanatuly Imanbayev
Kazakh National University
al-Farabi, Almaty, Kazakhstan

Agbotiname Lucky Imoize
University of Lagos
Akoka
Lagos, Nigeria
Ruhr University
Bochum, Germany

Boris Khruskov
University of Customs and Finance
Dnipro, Ukraine

Mykola Khudyntsev
G.E. Pukhov Institute for Modelling in Energy Engineering
National Academy of Sciences of Ukraine
Kyiv, Ukraine

Dinara Kozhakhmetova
Shakarim University
Semey, Republic of Kazakhstan

Oleksandr Kuznetsov
V. N. Karazin Kharkiv National University
Kharkiv, Ukraine
eCampus University
Novedrate, Italy

Oleksandr Lemeshko
Kharkiv National University of Radio Electronics
Kharkiv, Ukraine

Francis Masi
Malawi University of Business and Applied Sciences
Blantyre, Malawi

Amal Mersni
International University of Sarajevo
Sarajevo, Bosnia and Herzegovina

Viacheslav Moskalenko
Sumy State University
Sumy, Ukraine

Olha Mykhaylova
Lviv Polytechnic National University
Lviv, Ukraine

Halyna Mykytyn
Lviv Polytechnic National University
Lviv, Ukraine

Roman Odarchenko
State University "Kyiv Aviation Institute"
Kyiv, Ukraine

Ivan Opirskyy
Lviv Polytechnic National University
Lviv, Ukraine

Patience Ebehiremen Orukpe
University of Benin
Benin City, Nigeria

Aleksandra Pauls
Marche Polytechnic University
Ancona, Italy

Anatoliy Persikov
Kharkiv National University of Radio Electronics
Kharkiv, Ukraine

Alla Pinchuk
State University "Kyiv Aviation Institute"
Kyiv, Ukraine

Oleh Polihenko
State University "Kyiv Aviation Institute"
Kyiv, Ukraine

Nikolay Poluyanenko
V. N. Karazin Kharkiv National University
Kharkiv, Ukraine

Volodymyr Porokhniak
Kharkiv National University of Radio Electronics
Kharkiv, Ukraine

Cristian Randieri
eCampus University
Novedrate, Italy

Luca Romeo
Marche Polytechnic University
Ancona, Italy

Riccardo Rosati
Marche Polytechnic University
Ancona, Italy

Aigul Shaikhanova
L.N. Gumilyov Eurasian National University
Astana, Republic of Kazakhstan

Oleksii Smirnov
Central Ukrainian National Technical University
Kropyvnytskyi, Ukraine

Yaroslav Sovyn
Lviv Polytechnic National University
Ukraine

Taras Stosyk
Lviv Polytechnic National University
Lviv, Ukraine

Vitaliy Susukailo
Lviv Polytechnic National University
Lviv, Ukraine

Meruert Arynkazievna Tastandiyeva
Kazakh-British Technical University
Almaty, Kazakhstan

Nurzhigit Zauirbekuly Tolendi
Kazakh-British Technical University
Almaty, Kazakhstan

Claudio Tomazzoli
University of Verona
Strada Le Grazie, Verona, Italy

Ivan Tyshyk
Lviv Polytechnic National University
Ukraine

Sviatoslav Vasylyshyn
Lviv Polytechnic National University
Lviv, Ukraine

Oleksandra Yeremenko
Kharkiv National University of Radio Electronics
Kharkiv, Ukraine

Maryna Yevdokymenko
Kharkiv National University of Radio Electronics
Kharkiv, Ukraine

Igor Zakutynsky
State University "Kyiv Aviation Institute"
Kyiv, Ukraine

Giordano Zannoni
eCampus University
Novedrate, Italy

Artem Zhylin
The State Cyber Protection Centre State Service of Special Communications and Information Protection of Ukraine
Kyiv, Ukraine

Primo Zingaretti
Marche Polytechnic University
Ancona, Italy

Vitalii Zubok
G.E. Pukhov Institute for Modelling in Energy Engineering National Academy of Sciences of Ukraine
Kyiv, Ukraine

Preface

In the rapidly evolving cybersecurity domain, the advent of next-generation systems and applications heralds a new era of sophisticated defense mechanisms against an increasingly complex landscape of cyber threats. *Advancements in Cybersecurity: Next-Generation Systems and Applications* offers a comprehensive exploration of cutting-edge research and developments in the field, presenting a curated collection of chapters that reflect the latest in empirical data approximation, malware recognition, information security technologies, and beyond. This book delves into a wide array of topics, beginning with innovative approaches to empirical data approximation and extending through the latest methodologies for malware detection in IoT devices, optimization of information security in data centers, and advanced clustering techniques for multidimensional threats in heterogeneous networks.

Each chapter presents a unique study, ranging from the application of blockchain technology in securing information systems to the development of new cost functions for the iterative generation of cryptographic components, offering readers a broad perspective on the multifaceted challenges and solutions in contemporary cybersecurity. The book addresses technical aspects and provides insights into the theoretical frameworks and practical applications that underpin the development of robust cybersecurity systems. It explores the optimization of algorithms for generating nonlinear substitutions, the application of machine learning models for security evaluation, and the implementation of deep learning techniques for detecting sophisticated cyber-attacks.

The book *Advancements in Cybersecurity* is designed to serve as an essential resource for cybersecurity researchers, practitioners, and policymakers. It aims to foster an understanding of the current state of cyber defense technologies, encourage the exchange of ideas among experts, and inspire the development of innovative solutions to secure the cyber landscape of tomorrow. Through its in-depth analysis and forward-looking perspectives, this book contributes significantly to advancing cybersecurity research and practice, paving the way for a safer digital future. The book is structured into 23 chapters outlined as follows.

Chapter 1 introduces a novel hybrid method for randomness extraction. Chapter 2 exploits blockchain technology as the new defense of information systems and networks in cyber-spheres. Chapter 3 highlights innovative cost functions for optimizing cryptographic s-box generation. Chapter 4 employs enhanced cryptographic security through advanced s-box optimization, leveraging a hybrid heuristic approach. Chapter 5 dwells on enhancing cryptographic strength, exploring a novel approach to s-box generation using modified simulated annealing. Chapter 6 examines a factorial representation of s-boxes, employing a novel cryptographic analysis and optimization. Chapter 7 optimizes simulated annealing for efficient generation of highly nonlinear s-boxes. Chapter 8 analyzes the security mechanisms of new-generation cellular networks.

Chapter 9 discusses deep learning frontiers in copy-move forgery detection, considering advances, challenges, and future directions. Chapter 10 provides a deep learning model for detecting copy-move attacks in images, emphasizing testing and verification. Chapter 11 deploys a system of routing solutions based on security-aware traffic engineering models. Chapter 12 offers an information technology security platform for intellectualization. Chapter 13 explores a robust model and training method for malware recognition in IoT devices. Chapter 14 focuses on the detection of network attacks based on the RedHunt virtual machine. Chapter 15 provides a secure 5G network for monitoring the state of critical infrastructure facilities. Chapter 16 investigates the cybersecurity and resilience of data centers designed in wartime.

Chapter 17 indexes the state of military cyber defense and hacktivism in wartime Ukraine. Chapter 18 examines fast quantification methods for reconfigurable cybersecurity systems using multi-pattern matching. Chapter 19 projects the research and development of normalized link-blocking models in secure traffic engineering routing for programmable networks. Chapter 20 presents AI-driven content optimization and generation with integrated digital forensics for authentic and secure media. Chapter 21 elucidates the deployment of visible light communication, enabling next-generation wireless networks. Chapter 22 leverages the integrated decision model for the emerging visible light communication market. Finally, Chapter 23 concludes the book with advancing cyber defense with artificial intelligence, emphasizing state-of-the-art techniques and future directions.

The book is an ideal reference for practitioners, researchers, scientists, and engineers in the fields of information and communication technology (ICT), next-generation computing, and IT security (cybersecurity, cryptography, artificial intelligence, machine learning, deep learning, cyber resilience, cyber defensive walls, network security, threat modeling, risk assessment, digital forensics, secure software development, hardware security, and human-centric security). It is also a good textbook for graduate and senior undergraduate courses in next-generation computing, security and privacy, cybersecurity, cryptography, artificial intelligence, machine learning, deep learning, cyber resilience, cyber defensive walls, network security, threat modeling, risk assessment, digital forensics, secure software development, hardware security, and human-centric security.

We would like to thank the reviewers of the original book proposal for their constructive suggestions, all the authors of the chapters for their insightful contributions, and the editors and editorial assistants for their cooperation and support.

Gelsenkirchen, North Rhine-Westphalia, Germany
Agbotiname Lucky Imoize
Kharkiv, Ukraine
Oleksandr Kuznetsov
Kharkiv, Ukraine
Oleksandr Lemeshko
Kharkiv, Ukraine
Oleksandra Yeremenko

1 A Novel Hybrid Method for Randomness Extraction

Maksim Iavich and Roman Odarchenko

1.1 INTRODUCTION

Random numbers have many uses, such as cryptography, science, statistics, and simulation. Unfortunately, finding true coincidence is incredibly difficult [1, 2]. There are algorithmically generated numbers that are similar to random distributions but are not actually random, called pseudo-random number generators [3, 4]. They can generate random numbers at high speeds but with little resource utilization. In many cases, the tasks to be solved are based on the unpredictability of random numbers, which cannot be guaranteed in the case of pseudo-random number generators; true randomness is required. In such situations, we use real random number generators whose source of randomness is unpredictable random events.

Quantum random number generators (QRNGs) generate real random numbers based on the inherent randomness of quantum measurements. Through quantum mechanics, we can obtain true numbers using the unpredictable behavior of a photon, which is the basis of many modern cryptographic protocols [5]. A QRNG can theoretically generate random numbers with reasonable randomness. In practice this is not the case, as quantum signals (a source of true randomness for us) are necessarily mixed with classical noise [6]. Therefore, it is necessary to use a further processing procedure to reveal a true randomness. This procedure is called randomness extraction, which is performed using randomness extractors. In other words, randomness extractors are used to extract true randomness and eliminate the effects of classical noise.

Standard random number generators are designed to produce an equal random string. The post-processing phase then processes the resulting raw bits sequence and converts them to good quality output values that are as close to equal distribution as possible. The processing period may include tasks that check that the generator is working properly or that test values are being generated before generating the final strings.

The major purpose of the post-processing phase is randomness extraction, in addition to these tasks, which are varied for different generators. To correct biases and correlations, most physical RNGs include some sort of random extractor. Even if we have good random sources with high entropy, they originate from flaws in measurement and generation equipment.

DOI: 10.1201/9781003546153-1

An entropy source and a randomness extractor are the two most common components of a Random Number Generator. The entropy source in a QRNG could be a physical device with inherently unpredictable output, whereas the randomness extractor could be an algorithm that generates nearly perfect random numbers from the output of the previous entropy source, which could be imperfectly random. By measuring the randomness with min-entropy, the two components of QRNG are linked. The entropy source's min-entropy is calculated first and then used as an input parameter in the randomness extractor.

In information theory, min-entropy is the smallest family of Rényi entropies. Minimal entropy describes the unpredictability of the result, which is determined only by the probability of the most probable outcome. This is a conservative measure that is good for describing passwords and other heterogeneous distributions of secrets. The min-entropy of a random variable is the lower limit of its entropy. Min-entropy is never greater than normal or Shannon entropy (which measures the average unpredictability of results), and it, in turn, is never greater than Hartley or maximum entropy, which is defined as the logarithm of the number of outcomes with non-zero probability. Minimal entropy is widely used to measure the randomness of the probability distribution [7].

The probability distribution X's min-entropy at $\{0, 1\}^n$ is defined as (1.1):

$$\mathrm{H}\infty(\mathrm{X}) = \begin{array}{c} -\log\left(\max Prob\left[X = v\right]\right) \\ v \in \{0,1\}^n \end{array} \tag{1.1}$$

High entropy is no guarantee that the resulting random sequence will be suitable in any case. While there are methods that can detect weak sources for use in randomized algorithms, not all protocols work in perfect imperfection. In particular, many cryptographic protocols for tasks such as: Bit binding, encryption, zero knowledge, or secret sharing are not secure unless we use an almost equal random sequence.

Some hardware random number generators mix different sources of randomness by taking a logical XOR of their bits or delivering the function of cryptographic hashing to strings.

One of the first cases of a random extractor is the von Neumann extractor. He proposed a simple debiasing method in which, for each pair of bits generated, we could cancel out the 00 and 11 results, assigning 0 to 0 and even 1.

If there is systemic bias, this method will eliminate it, but at the cost of discarding half of the bits and reducing the bit rate by at least a quarter.

The more bits we throw, the more biased the original sequence is [8].

Even if the distribution of input bits is not uniform, the Von Neumann extractor may be proved to create a uniform output as long as each bit has the same probability of being one and there is no connection between successive bits. This method, of course, has been refined and made more effective. Before we go into further detail about random extractors, we need to figure out what qualifies as an equal result. The distance between distributions is a key notion for us. These are the statistical probabilities of two distributions, *X* and *Y*, defined in the same framework as (1.2):

$$d(X,Y) = \max_{a \in A} \left| P_X(a) - P_Y(a) \right|, \tag{1.2}$$

They can take the same values in the finite alphabet *A*. This metric gives us the maximum difference in the probability of obtaining a particular result in comparative distributions. Assume that the two distributions *X* and *Y* are ϵ-close if (1.3) holds.

$$d(X, Y) \leq \in \tag{1.3}$$

Random extraction's purpose is to produce a sequence that is as near to an equal as possible. Depending on our goals, this usually entails extracting *n* bits from the raw output values and turning them into a string of *m* bits, whose distribution ϵ is close to U^m, depending on our needs. $\{0, 1\}^m$ is an equal distribution, and ϵ is of minimal significance.

Ideally, we want extractors that give us as many output bits as possible, using small additional resources such as computation time or extra randomness. The minimum entropy of the raw distribution gives us a limit on how many bits can be extracted.

If we take an *n*-bit string from a raw bit sequence that has a minimum entropy of $H_\infty(x) = k$ in the *X* distribution, we can get a maximum of *k* random bits that are close to equal. The original length does not matter. A random source is called (*n*, *k*)—a source if it produces *n* bits with $H_\infty(x) = k$ with minimal entropy from the *X* distribution.

We discuss the different methods of generating a sequence of bits that give us an approximate sequence close to the minimum entropy limit. We also discuss the advantages and limitations of different random extractor approaches.

1.1.1 Key Contributions of the Chapter

The following are the significant contributions of this chapter:

i. Innovative Methodology for Quantum Randomness Extraction: The chapter presents a novel methodology aimed at enhancing the effectiveness of quantum random number generators (QRNGs) through advanced randomness extraction techniques. This methodology integrates various extraction methods—such as seeded and deterministic extractors—to effectively address the challenges posed by classical noise, resulting in improved quality of the generated randomness.
ii. Comprehensive Framework for Evaluating Randomness Extractors: A detailed framework for evaluating different randomness extractors is outlined, analyzing their performance and security features. The chapter emphasizes deterministic extractors that are resilient to quantum attacks and discusses

the conditions under which seeded extractors can provide additional randomness, ensuring the output values approach uniform distributions.

iii. Implementation and Comparison of Strong Randomized Extractors: The chapter implements and compares two robust randomized extractors: Toeplitz-hashing and Trevisan's extractors. It highlights their individual advantages and demonstrates how combining these extractors enhances the overall randomness extraction process. The results indicate that the generated sequences closely approximate uniform distributions, fulfilling the rigorous demands of cryptographic applications.

1.1.2 Chapter Organization

Section 1.2 offers a comprehensive literature review of recent advancements in quantum computing and random number generation. Section 1.3 discusses randomness extractors, which are functions designed to convert weak sources of entropy into uniform bit generators. Initially developed for studying randomized algorithms, these extractors have become essential tools in theoretical computer science, facilitating the transformation of weak randomness into nearly uniform distributions. They are utilized in various applications, including pseudo-random number generators, error correction codes, and expansion graphs. In section 1.4, we examine different types of extractors: Deterministic extractors produce outputs from inputs but are limited by their reliance on intrinsic entropy, making them unsuitable for all distributions. Section 1.5 introduces seeded extractors, which enhance weak sources by using a small additional sequence of true random bits (the seed) to achieve near-uniform outputs. Section 1.6 explores novel randomness extractors that process outputs from multiple weak sources to generate sequences that closely approximate uniformity. The analysis in section 1.7 underscores that without proper post-processing, generated data cannot pass statistical tests, highlighting the necessity of effective randomness extraction methods. This chapter evaluates various techniques, including both deterministic and seeded extractors, and employs strong randomized extractors like Toeplitz-hashing and Trevisan's extractors, which are information-theoretically proven to enhance the quality of randomness in QRNGs.

1.2 LITERATURE REVIEW

The authors of paper [2] are working on the creation of quantum computers, which can easily solve the problem of factoring large numbers, and they are able to crack the crypto RSA system. In [3, 4, 9], several pseudo-random number generators are considered that use a different method to ensure the randomness of the sequences and a higher level of security. Random numbers are widely used in different applications. The paper [5] presents the different technologies in quantum random number generation and the multiple ways to use them to gather entropy from a quantum origin. The authors of the paper [6] propose a generic framework for evaluating quantum randomness QRNGs and apply it to two different existing quantum random-number systems. Paper [7] describes the measurement of quantum randomness.

The paper [8] presents one of the first cases of a deterministic extractor, a von Neumann extractor, and propose different variations of this extractor. In [10–12] authors present a study of efficient deterministic extractors.

Previously, deterministic extraction procedures were known only for sources satisfying strong independence requirements. The paper [10] looks at sources that can be generated by an efficient sampling algorithm and seeks an efficient deterministic procedure that gives an almost uniformly distributed output. The authors explore the conditions under which such deterministic extractors exist.

Different seeded extractors are introduced in [13–15], which are effective against quantum attacks. Papers [16, 17] describe two universal hashing, extraction methods, where universal hashes with high entropy input values are almost equally random. In the presence of an adversary, two universal hashing methods are capable of successfully eliminating a weak source at random.

1.3 RANDOMNESS EXTRACTORS

Randomness extractors are functions that convert a weak source of entropy into an equal bit generator. These functions were originally introduced to study randomized algorithms but have become a major tool in many areas of theoretical computer science. The standard notion of a random extractor is a procedure that transforms a weak source of randomness into an almost uniform distribution. The procedure is illustrated in Figure 1.1. Randomness extractors and related concepts such as dispersions, capacitors, and expansion graphs have a variety of uses and are found in many areas of pseudo-random number generators, including error correction codes, samples, expansion graphs, and hardness amplifiers [10].

We discuss some of the most suitable extractor concepts for QRNG, as well as some interesting extractors. There are many options for obtaining randomness and the final choice is influenced by the speed and technique of each method.

In order to have an efficient method and maintain as many bits as possible, we need to well define the entropy available to us and then choose an adequate random extractor. Otherwise, the output values of the extractor function will not have the desired properties.

We assume we have a well-described source of randomness. We assume that the raw sequence has a familiar minimum entropy or, in some cases, at least such known properties as independence between bits or that this sequence is derived from the Markov process.

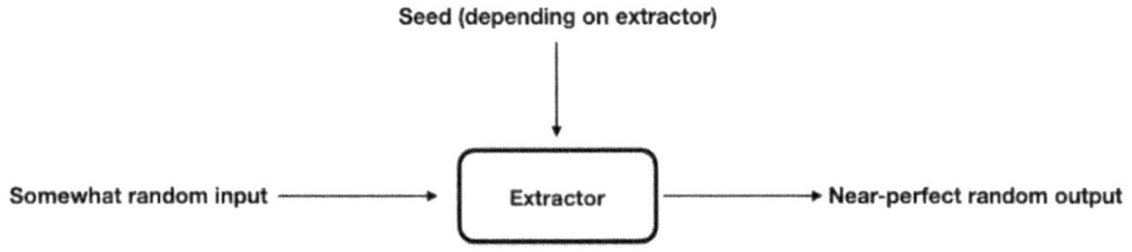

FIGURE 1.1 Randomness Extractors.

We assume that by default, we want (n, m, k, ϵ) - extractor: A function that converts (n, k) - a source n bits into output bits whose distribution is ϵ-close to equal and m is as close as possible to k.

1.4 DETERMINISTIC EXTRACTORS

Deterministic extractors are functions

$$Ext\colon \{0,1\}^n \rightarrow \{0,1\}^m \tag{1.4}$$

They take n bits of $\{0, 1\}n$ input strings and give us m output bits. These functions are particularly attractive because they are deterministic algorithms that require only an input sequence to work. However, they do have some limitations that prevent them from being used for certain sources of randomness.

If the input sequence has enough intrinsic entropy, we can calculate the equation as we can with all extractors. The requirement for obtaining an approximation is $m \geq k$ if the entered sequence (n, k) is a source. Unfortunately, the required ones are insufficient. Thus, we can only find deterministic extractors for a limited set of input distributions.

The basic argument establishes that general deterministic extractors are not feasible. We do not have a single general deterministic extractor that would be appropriate for all forms of input distributions. Imagine the function from $\{0, 1\}n$ to $\{0, 1\}$. We can denote all possible input values of n-bit strings in one set that gives us a value of 0, $\text{Ext}^{-1}(0)$, and we have a second set that gives us 1, $\text{Ext}^{-1}(1)$. At least one of them has a size of $2n^{-1}$ or more. The input value, which is a uniform distribution in a larger set, has $n - 1$ minimum entropy but always gives us the same output values, indicating that there is no one-size-fits-all extractor that is valid for any type of input distribution.

However, there are working extractors for the input distributions of specific process families that characterize acceptable sources. In addition, for fixed sources of bits, there are feasible determinant extractors for selective distribution. The opponent can adjust a portion of the bits in these extractors and generalize for affine sources or sources with output values uniformly distributed over an unknown algebraic diversity.

Variable-length deterministic extractors form another interesting group of deterministic extractors that deviate slightly from the given equation of the deterministic extractor

$$Ext\colon \{0,1\}^n \rightarrow \{0,1\}^m \tag{1.5}$$

This is demonstrated by von Neumann's approach, which is a deterministic method that works for an unknown distribution and returns an output value of a length that is unknown prior to extraction. Each input bit must be independent of the previous and following bits, which is the only requirement of the von Neumann random extractor described. Advanced versions of Von Neumann's approach minimize discarded entropy and enable efficiency close to Shannon's entropy, which represents the theoretical limit of information theory. We found algorithms that construct unbiased sequences under more broad conditions as a consequence of further changes, with the input sequence coming from a Markov chain.

The original method's greatest appeal is its simplicity. It takes the least amount of calculated energy. It may be done with very basic equipment and does not require a thorough understanding of the source distribution. The original system, however, has some significant drawbacks. The von Neumann extractor will no longer work if an external attacker can modify the bias from bit to bit, even minimally.

In reality, if the bias of the input bits changes so that the chance of finding 1 for the n-th bit depends on the value of the prior bit s, there is no deterministic algorithm that yields a variable of n bits of equal value for the variable $X = (X_1, X_2, \dots X_n)$.

$$\delta \leq P_{X_i}\left(1 \mid x_1 x_2 \dots x_{n-1} = s\right) \leq 1-\delta, \tag{1.6}$$

$$\text{where } 0 < \delta \leq \frac{1}{2}, \tag{1.7}$$

This is known as the Santha-Vazirani source. Santha and Vazirani described it as a model of weak random sources with evidence for the impossibility of a deterministic extractor [11].

Despite this limitation, there are deterministic algorithms that allow us to use a weak Santha-Vazirani source to simulate random algorithms. Randomization requirements are less stringent than for other uses, such as cryptography. Sometimes, weak sources that fail to produce almost identical results are valid in some cases [12].

Even if we use a deterministic extractor, one weak source is not enough for many cryptographic protocols. While weak randomness can be safely used in signature schemes, high quality keys are required in encryption and other related protocols, otherwise they will become vulnerable.

For devices where it is necessary for the output values to be close to equal, Santha and Vazirani offer a simple solution. Combine the results of two independent, weak Santha-Vazirani sources to derive an output sequence that we can not distinguish from an equal distribution by a polynomial time algorithm. As long as we have access to a physical method that generates some randomness, we can generate bit strings that we can not distinguish from random strings by any efficient algorithm. This is as good as true randomness in many implementations of randomness, including cryptography.

All the methods described earlier take values from a single source. Multiple source extractors follow this model and obtain results from two or more weak sources. Cultivate them and a sequence is created that is close to equal. There are many methods depending on the distribution of specific input values, the number of sources, and the desired properties of the output sequence.

A simple extractor valid for two n-bit blocks from two independent, weak sources receives the GF (2) internal product of the n-bit blocks, which reduces the computation of the two-sequence bit AND. The minimum entropy of both should be at least $n / 2$. Of course, different sources of randomness can be combined in different ways.

Combining sources is also used in the second major group of random extractors, seeded extractors. They can represent a special case of multiple source extractors, with a single weak source and a perfectly equal source generating only a small number of bits.

1.5 SEEDED EXTRACTORS

We need a weaker concept of extractors. For the distribution of many raw bits, we can only produce a near-uniform output by adding some additional randomness. In some cases, deterministic randomness is not enough and requires a small additional sequence of true random bits. We hope that by using a small number of random bits representing the additional input value, the output value of the extractors will be ε-close to the uniform distributions [13].

Seeded extractors use an additional number of really random bits, called seed, to try to extract pure randomness from a single weak source. Obviously, this is interesting primarily when the seed's length is less than the weak source's and output's combined lengths. A seeded extractor is strong if its output values are almost independent of the seed. Formally, a seed extractor can be represented as a two-source extractor, with the first source's min-entropy equal to its length.

As we have said, for the many distributions of raw bits, we can only achieve a uniform result, only with the help of any additional randomness. In seeded extractors, we have a function

$$Ext : \{0,1\}^n \times \{0,1\}^m \rightarrow \{0,1\}^m \tag{1.8}$$

This function includes n bits of raw sequence and uniform random bit seed d, which generate m output bits. We assume that d is much smaller than m. In addition to the seeds, we have a guarantee that there are extractors that produce almost equal output values whose length is close to the maximum length. These seeds play a similar role as seeds in pseudo-random number generators. $(k, \in)$ extractor is a function for any input source k (raw sequence, minimum entropy k at least) that produces an output sequence that is ϵ-close to the uniform. The seed acts as a catalyst, allowing us to find general methods that will always work.

In the case of a seeded extractor, each extractor has values: Input length - n, output value length m, seed length d, minimum entropy threshold k, extractor error ε. In the case of a good extractor, it is necessary to reduce the seed d and increase the obtained values m.

Random-seeded extractors were developed originally in the context of randomized algorithms. Using probabilistic approaches, it has been proven that there are always extractors that include practically all existing latent entropies from the raw sequence of the input k source. To insert n block bits of the source k, we can construct extractors of size $m \approx k + d$ that is ϵ-close to the uniform, using seeds of length d of the order $\log_2 n$. There are various constructions for these seeded extractors.

The requirement for uniform seeds appears paradoxical: We demand the resources we are attempting to generate. The seeds' specifications, on the other hand, are less restricted than they appear. The seed length measure is logarithmic to the length of the input string in several apparent extractors. For a sufficiently small d, we can adjust the needed randomness condition to include all possible $2d$ sequences. The report, followed by majority voting permissions, is good for modeling a uniform source in randomized algorithms. However, in cryptography, where unpredictability is required, this strategy is obviously ineffective. Seeded extractors also protect us from external attackers in quantum random number generators. There are some constructions for which there is proof of safety against various quantum attackers.

The Trevisan's extractor is the first noticeable outcome. It sparked a lot of theoretical curiosity because of the scarcity of its data and because this extractor was protected from quantum enemies [14]. The Trevisan extractor's seed length is a poly-logarithm of the input value's length and has been shown to be a strong extractor [15]. Also, Trevisan's extractor's random seeds can be reused. This is especially crucial for features like Toeplitz-hashing, which are popular universal hashing features [18].

The Trevisan's extractor is built on a Nisan-Widgerson pseudo-random number generator. This can be compared to a random function whose truth table is determined by a small number of bits. The random function expands equal random seed d bits to both PRNG and extractor values. Various variations of Trevisan's extractor were implemented with quantum random number generators and quantum key distributions. Their main advantage is that the random, equal seed size is only poly-logarithmic to the size of the input blocks. However, practical implementation can slow down the bit generation process as calculations are required during extraction.

As we have said, Trevisan's extractor is safe from quantum opponents, protecting us from quantum attacks. Moreover, it is a powerful extractor (its seeds can be reused), and its seed length is a poly-logarithmic function of the input. The Trevisan's extractor consists of two main parts: A single-bit extractor and a combinatorial design. The Toeplitz-hashing extractor was well developed in the QKD system privacy enhancement procedure. This type of extractor is also a powerful extractor. Using the fast Fourier transform technique, the working time of the Toeplitz-hashing extractor can be improved to O (n log n).

Two-universal hashing is the second approach. The Leftover Hash Lemma demonstrates that the functions of two universal hashes with high entropy input values are almost equally random [16]. In the presence of an adversary, two universal hashing methods are capable of successfully eliminating a weak source at random. It is necessary to utilize the Lemma generalization employing conditional entropies, leveraging lateral information, if we have a decent estimate or a conservative constraint on associating our weak random source with the listener [17]. Lateral information can be quantum in a broad sense. We can suppose that all the randomness that arises from imperfection or otherwise does not fit our model of the quantum system that produces the raw bit is due to an intruder in a quantum random number generator with technical noise. It is still possible to design a seeded extractor that produces nearly identical results while being independent of external systems under these conditions. These techniques are also used to improve privacy in quantum key distribution.

A randomness extractor with two universal or, more generally, n-universal hashing forces us to use a relatively long seed equivalent to n block size but capable of recycling [19, 20]. Randomly selected equal seeds can also be reused. Randomly selected uniform seeds can also be reused. Unlike Trevisan's extractor, this approach provides a rapid extraction feature that consumes fewer computational resources at the cost of larger seeds. Some implementations, such as Toeplitz random binary matrix hashing, are particularly effective [21, 22]. One such extractor can be defined as a rectangular matrix that multiplies on n-vectors from the source to produce nearly independent bits. This approach is used in some commercial devices that contain the extraction function as a pre-calculated random matrix that acts as a seed and is distributed in the device encoded. Although high-quality seed randomness is a difficult process, it only needs to be done once. Long, non-sophisticated methods, such as repeating the XOR of multiple independent generators, are acceptable.

1.6 NOVEL RANDOMNESS EXTRACTOR

Table 1.1 summarizes three types of extractors used in randomness extraction: Seeded extractors, deterministic extractors, and randomness extractors. Each extractor type is defined, highlighting its key features and common applications. Seeded extractors utilize a seed to extract uniform randomness from weak sources, deterministic extractors guarantee uniform output without randomness, and randomness extractors work with noisy random sources to produce uniform randomness.

A QRNG can theoretically generate random numbers with reasonable randomness. In practice, this is not the case; quantum signals (a source of true randomness for us) are necessarily mixed with classical noise. Therefore, it is necessary to use a further processing procedure to reveal a true randomness. This procedure is called randomness extraction, which is performed using randomness extractors. In other words, randomness extractors are used to extract true randomness and eliminate the effects of classical noise.

We use multiple source extractors whose model is similar to single source extractors. We derive results from several weak sources, process them, and generate a sequence that is close to equal.

TABLE 1.1
Comparison of Seeded, Deterministic, and Randomness Extractors

Extractor Type	Definition	Key Features	Applications
Seeded extractor	A function that extracts nearly uniform randomness from a weak random source using a short seed	- Requires seed	Cryptography, random number generation
Deterministic extractor	A function that deterministically produces uniform randomness from a weak random source	- No randomness used - Guaranteed output	Complexity theory, derandomization
Randomness extractor	A function that extracts uniform randomness from a source that has some randomness, possibly with noise	- Works with random sources - May require additional randomness	Cryptographic protocols, simulation

The two-source extractor attempts to extract true randomness from two independent weak sources. Consider a class of X random variables consisting of two independent random variables X_1 and X_2, such that $H_\infty(x_1) \geq k_1$ and $H_\infty(x_2) \geq k_2$.

We get the function

$$Ext: \{0,1\}n_1 \times \{0,1\}n_2 \rightarrow \{0,1\}^m \tag{1.9}$$

which is an extractor of two sources $(k_1, k_{2,} \in)$. For each independent random variable X_1 and X_2, for which $H_\infty(x_1) \geq k_1$ and $H_\infty(x_2) \geq k_2$: $Ext(x_1, x_2)$ are ϵ-close to the uniform distribution of m bits.

We use two strong randomized extractors, Toeplitz-hashing and Trevisan's extractors. Both of them are information-theoretically proven extractors. The Trevisan's extractor is safe from quantum attacks, as well as its seed length is polylogarithmic to the length of the input value. It is a powerful extractor; we can reuse random seeds.

Toeplitz-hashing, among the universal-hashing functions, has the advantage of a shorter random seed length (the random bits used to generate a hashing function) and hardware processing simplicity. The random seed used to generate a Toeplitz matrix is longer than the output string in Toeplitz-hashing.

Toeplitz matrices are used to create universal hashing functions. Only the first row and column of a Toeplitz matrix of dimension $n \times m$ must be specified, and the remaining elements of the matrix are calculated by going diagonally down from left to right. As a result, the total number of random bits necessary to build a Toeplitz matrix is $n + m - 1$.

In the Toeplitz-hashing extractor, we have n-size raw data with the min-entropy of k and a security parameter ε, the output length will be

$$m = k - 2log\varepsilon \tag{1.10}$$

Toeplitz matrix is constructed with $n + m - 1$ random seed. The extracted random bit string is obtained by multiplying the raw data with the Toeplitz matrix. We use an improved version of the Trevisan extractor, which is composed of two main parts: The error correction code and the combinatorial design. For the combinatorial design part, we use a sophisticated version of the Nisan-Wigderson design. The advantage is that the random, uniform seed size is only poly-logarithmic to the size of the input blocks. However, practical implementation can slow down the bit generation process as calculations are required during extraction. Nevertheless, we have better results in statistical tests through it.

Although Travisan's extractor is more secure than Toeplitz-hashing, strict speed limits reduce the use of this extractor in real-time applications. Therefore, hashing can be used in speed-critical applications, and Travisan's extractor can be used in applications where enhanced security is required. In this case, we choose an intermediate based on our usage needs. Furthermore, introducing parallelism allows us to use the extractors more efficiently, allowing us to do multiple extractions in parallel.

1.7 CONCLUSIONS

The generated data cannot pass statistical tests without further processing, given the fact that the output randomness is mixed with unclassified classical noise, making it impossible to create a uniform distribution. This demonstrates the requirement for appropriate QRNG post-processing. The extractors' results pass all standard statistical tests. In this chapter we explored different randomness extraction methods. First, variety of deterministic extractors are analyzed, which are secure against quantum attacks. Then, seeded extractors are discussed; they are based on the assumption that, in some cases, a deterministic extractor is not enough and requires a small additional sequence of true random bits. We hope that by using a small number of random bits representing the additional input value, the output value of the extractors is close to the uniform distributions. We used multiple source extractors whose model is similar to single source extractors. We obtained results from several weak sources, processed them, and generated a sequence that is close to equal. We used two strong randomized extractors, Toeplitz-hashing and Trevisan's extractors. Both of them are information-theoretically proven extractors. We combined these extractors.

1.8 ACKNOWLEDGMENTS

This work was supported by the Shota Rustaveli National Foundation of Georgia (SRNSFG) (NFR-22-14060).

REFERENCES

[1] Naik, Rasika B., and Singh, Udayprakash. "A review on applications of chaotic maps in pseudo-random number generators and encryption." *Annals of Data Science*, vol. 11, no. 1 (2024): 25–50.

[2] Gagnidze, Avtandil, Iavich, Maksim, and Iashvili, Giorgi. "Novel version of Merkle cryptosystem." *Bulletin of the Georgian National Academy of Sciences*, vol. 11, no. 4 (2017): 28–33.

[3] Lewis, P. A. W., Goodman, A. S., and Miller, J. M. "A pseudo-random number generator for the System/360." *IBM Systems Journal*, vol. 8, no. 2 (1969): 136–146. https://doi.org/10.1147/sj.82.0136.

[4] Mcginthy, J. M., and Michaels, A. J. "Further analysis of PRNG-based key derivation functions." *IEEE Access*, vol. 7 (2019): 95978–95986. https://doi.org/10.1109/ACCESS.2019.2928768.

[5] Herrero-Collantes, Miguel, and Garcia-Escartin, Juan Carlos. "Quantum random number generators." *Reviews of Modern Physics*, vol. 89 (2016). https://doi.org/10.1103/RevModPhys.89.015004.

[6] Ma, Xiongfeng, Xu, Feihu, Xu, He, Tan, Xiaoqing, Qi, Bing, and Lo, Hoi-Kwong. "Postprocessing for quantum random- number generators: Entropy evaluation and randomness extraction." *Physical Review A*, vol. 87, no. 6 (2013): 062327.

[7] Ma, Xiongfeng, et al. "Quantum random number generation." *npj Quantum Information*, vol. 2, no. 1 (2016): 1–9.

[8] Rožić, Vladimir, Yang, Bohan, Dehaene, Wim, and Verbauwhede, Ingrid. "Iterating von Neumann's post-processing under hardware constraints." In *2016 IEEE international symposium on hardware oriented security and trust (HOST)*, pp. 37–42. IEEE, 2016.

[9] Lambić, D., and Nikolić, M. "Pseudo-random number generator based on discrete-space chaotic map." *Nonlinear Dynamics*, vol. 90 (2017): 223–232. https://doi.org/10.1007/s11071-017-3656-1

[10] Trevisan, L., and Vadhan, S. "Extracting randomness from samplable distributions." In *Proceedings 41st annual symposium on foundations of computer science*, pp. 32–42. Redondo Beach, CA, USA, 2000. https://doi.org/10.1109/SFCS.2000.892063.

[11] Santha, M., and Vazirani, U. V. "Generating quasi-random sequences from semi-random sources." *Journal of Computer and System Sciences*, vol. 33, no. 1 (1986): 75–87.

[12] Vazirani, U. V. "Towards a strong communication complexity theory or generating quasi-random sequences from two communicating slightly-random sources." In *Proceedings of the seventeenth annual ACM symposium on theory of computing*, pp. 366–378. 1985, December, 01.

[13] Raz, R. "Extractors with weak random seeds." In *Proceedings of the thirty-seventh annual ACM symposium on theory of computing*, pp. 11–20. 2005, May. Retrieved October 14, 2024, from https://dl.acm.org/doi/10.1145/1060590.1060593.

[14] De, Anindya, Portmann, Christopher, Vidick, Thomas, and Renner, Renato. "Trevisan's extractor in the presence of quantum side information." *SIAM Journal on Computing*, vol. 41, no. 4 (2012): 915–940.

[15] Raz, Ran, Reingold, Omer, and Vadhan, Salil. "Extracting all the randomness and reducing the error in Trevisan's extractors." *Journal of Computer and System Sciences*, vol. 65, no. 1 (2002): 97–128.

[16] Stinson, Douglas Robert. *Universal hash families and the leftover hash lemma, and applications to cryptography and computing.* Faculty of Mathematics, University of Waterloo, 2001.

[17] Tsurumaru, Toyohiro, and Hayashi, Masahito. "Dual universality of hash functions and its applications to quantum cryptography." *IEEE Transactions on Information Theory*, vol. 59, no. 7 (2013): 4700–4717.

[18] Trevisan, L. "Extractors and pseudorandom generators." *Journal of the ACM*, vol. 48, no. 4 (2001): 860–879.

[19] Doron, Dean, Pyne, Edward, and Tell, Roei. "Opening up the distinguisher: A hardness to randomness approach for BPL= L that uses properties of BPL." In *Proceedings of the 56th annual ACM symposium on theory of computing*. 2024, June, 11.

[20] Cachet, Chloe, et al. "Upgrading fuzzy extractors." In *International conference on applied cryptography and network security.* Cham, Switzerland: Springer Nature, 2024.

[21] Lin, Fading, et al. "Seed renewable parallel and real-time Toeplitz post-processing for QRNG." *Journal of Lightwave Technology*, (2024). https://doi.org/10.1109/JLT.2024.3445327.

[22] Ng, H. J., Kon, W. Y., Primaatmaja, I. W., Wang, C., and Lim, C. "Sampled subblock hashing for large-input randomness extraction." *Physical Review Applied*, vol. 21, no. 3 (2024): 034005.

2 Blockchain Technology as the New Defense of Information Systems and Networks in Cyber-Spheres

Sviatoslav Vasylyshyn, Ivan Opirskyy, Vitaliy Susukailo, and Olha Mykhaylova

2.1 INTRODUCTION

While hackers are constantly improving in their jobs, ways to defend ourselves from them are also improving super-fast. In fact, today, already in our hands is almost impenetrable technology known as the blockchain, which can be used to protect different types of data from cyberattacks and overall improve the cybersecurity layer in various spheres, including infrastructure in Ukraine, special information networks, and networks where confidential information, such as medical and banking secrecy, is transmitted. Blockchain technology has existed for a little less than ten years and was originally introduced as a way to store or send the first cryptocurrency, Bitcoin. However, as this technology gradually spread around the world, people began to use it in various ways in many industries, including as a means of improving cybersecurity [1]. The aim of this chapter is to analyze the use of blockchain technology in cyber areas of information protection and consider the use of this technology as a tool to protect special information systems and networks.

2.1.1 Formulation of the Problem

Building a network based on the principles of blockchain technology is a very difficult task and requires considerable knowledge and experience in this field. It follows from the previous statement that this process is also not one of the cheapest. Good specialists in the market who work in this field are very expensive, and besides that, there are not too many of them. An additional complication is that the use of ready-made solutions, such as branching from a first-tier network such as Ethereum, is not suitable for information security systems, especially for special information systems or critical infrastructure. You need to develop your own first-class blockchain along with security policies, user authorization, and authentication protocols, and add and

 DOI: 10.1201/9781003546153-2

disconnect nodes (users) to the system. When it comes to important and strategic objects, there should not be such words as "savings on security" because in 80% of cases an attacker gains access to the internal network or successfully carries out DDoS and other attacks on objects precisely because of security savings on measures of defense. The remaining 20% includes the human factor, which can include both the incompetence of system operators (social engineering) and its developers. This chapter highlights all the advantages and disadvantages of protecting cyber systems based on blockchain technology in order to demonstrate the importance and feasibility of switching to this technology in the future, taking into account the risks.

The aim of the work is to study the cyber-spheres of using blockchain technology for the defense of information systems and networks. In this chapter we analyze the blockchain functionality, data encryption, give overall view on the spheres where the blockchain network can be applied, define pros and cons of using it via collected information, and compare blockchain effectiveness by using its dynamic attributes to non-dynamic honeypot while performing the DoS attack.

2.1.2 Key Contributions of the Chapter

The following are the significant contributions of this chapter:

i. The chapter examines some of the key blockchain technology attributes that can be used in various cyber-spheres as the new defense technology.
ii. The significant challenges and the prospects of using blockchain technology, in general, have been discussed.
iii. The pros and cons of using systems based on blockchain technology to protect them are defined and analyzed.

2.1.3 Chapter Organization

Section 2.2 presents related works on blockchain technologies and how they can be related to the defense of information systems. Section 2.3 analyzes cyber-spheres where blockchain can be used to protect data in organization infrastructure. Section 2.4 defines and analyzes the pros and cons of using systems based on blockchain technology to protect them. Section 2.5 concludes the chapter.

2.2 RELATED WORK

Blockchain technology has been extensively studied and implemented across various domains for its potential to enhance cybersecurity and ensure data integrity. Several notable works have contributed to understanding how blockchain can be effectively used to defend information systems and networks. Blockchain technology's potential to secure IoT devices has been a significant area of research. Surajdeep (2021) [2] examined various cases of blockchain use in cybersecurity, particularly focusing on IoT devices. The decentralization attribute of blockchain helps in protecting these devices by removing central points of failure, thereby making it difficult for attackers to gain control over the entire system. Yogesh (2021) [3] explored how blockchain can be used to rethink cybersecurity, emphasizing its role in maintaining data integrity and securing communication channels. The study demonstrates how blockchain's cryptographic features can protect data during transmission and ensure that any unauthorized access or modification is easily detectable. The potential for blockchain to secure private communications, particularly in social networks, is also examined. Blockchain can provide a higher level of security than traditional end-to-end encryption by creating immutable records of all communications and interactions within a network. Multiple studies have discussed the ability of blockchain to provide decentralized storage solutions. This method ensures that data are not stored in a single location, reducing the risk of data breaches and leaks. For example, the Apollo Currency Team has actively utilized blockchain to enhance its security levels by implementing decentralized storage.

2.2.1 Blockchain Mechanism Overview

Blockchain is a distributed network that can connect millions of users on the world wide web. Each user can add any kind of information to the blockchain knowing that all data in the chain are protected by cryptography. Every member of the designed and active network is responsible for verifying the data added to the chain are eligible and valid. This is done in a way that is designed to use a system of three keys (private, public, and user key), which allow valid users to verify the data, as well as confirm who they are and from where they come, as shown in Figure 2.1.

The verified part of data about to enter the chain forms a block, which will then be added to the network. In order to make this happen, blockchain participants must use appropriate keys and their computing systems to execute algorithms that solve mathematical problems of different complexity. When the problem is about to be resolved, the block is added to the network chain, and all the data it contains on the network will be recorded and exist forever in this chain, which means that it cannot be changed, deleted, or modified in any way.

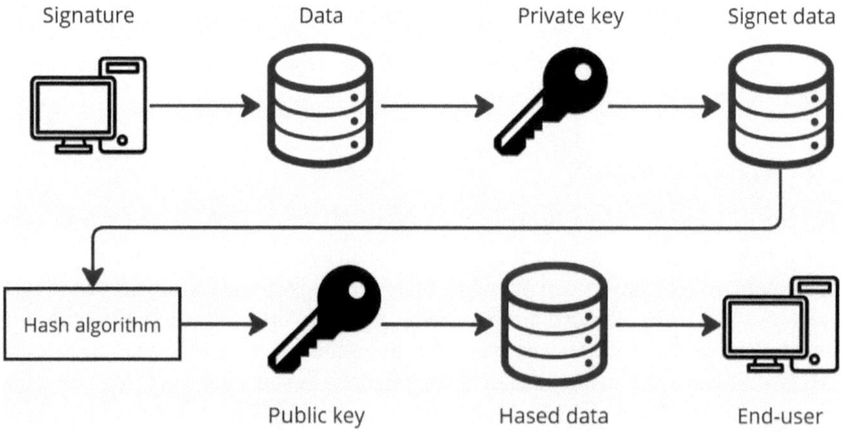

FIGURE 2.1 Encryption of data transmission in the blockchain.

In order to modify any data, the owner of this piece of data should add a new block on top of the previous block in the network, and by doing this, he will create a specific string of information. Even if something as small as, for example, a comma requires to be changed from how it was displayed in the previous block, the whole chain also changes accordingly, and this action is transmitted to every other user in this chain. Every single change is tracked, and no data are lost or deleted in any possible way, as blockchain participants can always view the previously modified versions of any block to define what is different from the latest version they were using or observing. Using this system allows us to easily detect any blocks that can contain incorrect or damaged data, preventing data loss and damage, as shown in Figure 2.2 [4].

So after all that was said, another important point to take in mind about blockchain is that the chain participants can store all the data located on the network on personal computers if there is a demand or users simply want to do so. This action leads to two interesting things. Firstly, the participants of the chain can receive extra rewards, as defined by the network design, by renting computer storage space. Secondly, the network users can verify that the chain is not modified or broken. For example, if anyone who does not have the right to own a piece of particular data tries to intrude in a block, the whole designed system analyzes every block to find the one that is different from the rest or that is not aligned with others. When the system finds this modified or damaged block, it excludes this block from the circuit [3].

Blockchain is designed using unique technology in a way that there is no central operational center or storage space defined. Each chain participant plays a role in kind of saving a particular part or even all of them from the blockchain. Every user is responsible for checking and authorizing the data stored or transferred in order to

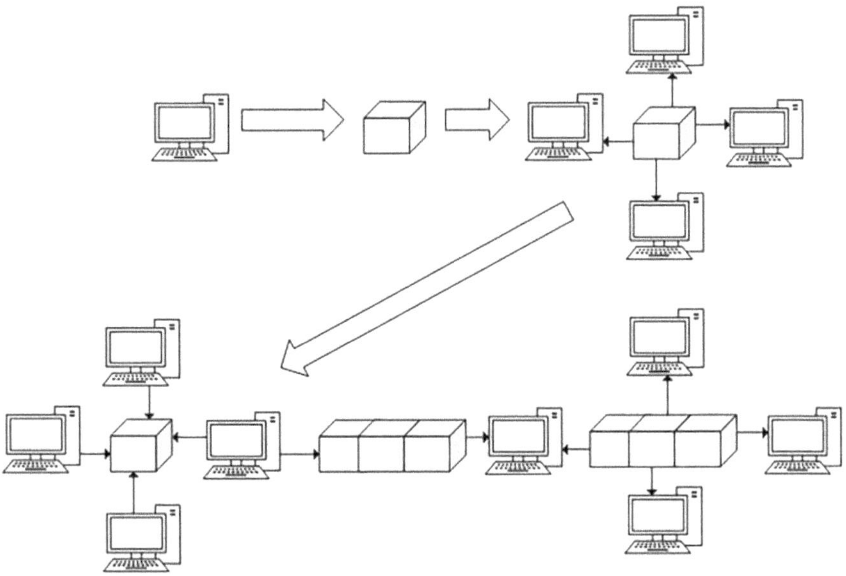

FIGURE 2.2 The scheme of check of the block on knots.

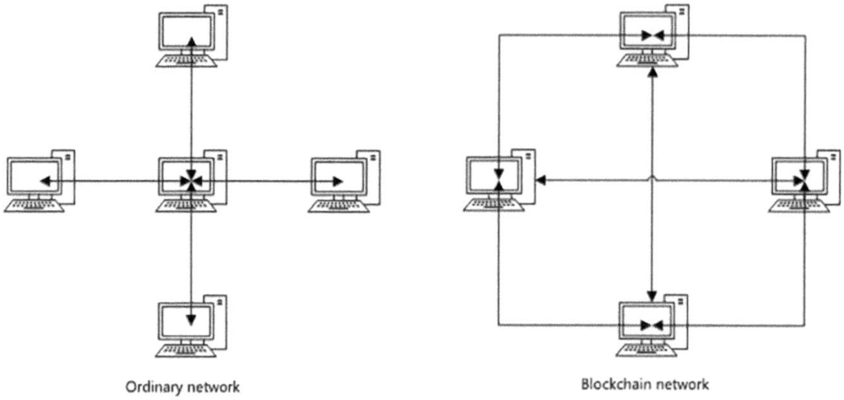

FIGURE 2.3 Comparison of a normal centralized network with a blockchain network.

ensure that corrupted or damaged information cannot be added nor deleted, as shown in Figure 2.3.

Blockchain is one of the best-designed technology options present on the market to protect data from attackers, prevent potential damage, and reduce data theft, change, or compromise.

In order to interfere, corrupt data in a blockchain, or even destroy it, the attacker will have to compromise all the data that are stored on each participant's personal computer on the network attached to this system. To think of it, billions of personal computers can store a copy of some part of the data or maybe all of it. When the attacker fails to compromise 51% of the network, computers that were not affected by this attack, known as "nodes," will still continue to operate and authorize any record and data within the network. The impossibility of completing an attack, such as destroying an entire network chain, only increases with the number of participants that are located or connected to this network. The larger the networks with a greater number of participants, the lower the risk of being attacked or destroyed because of the complexity required to break into such a chain. Blockchain is a peer-to-peer (p2p) distributed database that maintains an ever-growing list of records, called blocks, that are linked together and secured, typically using public-key cryptography. With blockchain technology, new information is added to a block and made available to all nodes in a distributed network instead of being added to a centralized database in a traditional centralized system. Each block in a blockchain is identified by a hash value, usually generated using a secure 256-bit hash cryptographic algorithm (SHA256). The hash value of the current (parent) block header is bound and stored in the next (child) block. So, if there is a change in the contents of any block, its hash will also be changed accordingly, and this change will be propagated throughout the network to invalidate that block [5].

Due to this mechanism, blockchain technology does not require an intermediary or a trusted third party because it is decentralized and distributed. Blockchain participants have private keys assigned to them to digitally sign and validate the transactions they make.

A block consists of a header containing metadata and a long list of transactions executed in that block. A block header usually contains a timestamp, a one-time number, a version, and a proof of difficulty. The timestamp indicates the time the block was created; a nonce is a random number generated by the consensus algorithm to calculate the hash value of the block; version indicates the version number of the blockchain; and the Proof of Complexity is the generated hash value, which must be less than the current target hash value.

The first block, known as the genesis block, is hard-coded by embedding some random data into the blockchain program. Although each block has only one parent and one child, a valid block can have two or more children temporarily created when two or more nodes (network peers) are added to the block at the same time, resulting in two or more branches from one parent block [6]. Formed branches have the same length; in this situation, the process of adding new blocks continues for all chains to be verified until one branch is longer than the others and thus valid.

In a block, all transactions are linked together using a Merkle tree. A Merkle tree is an inverted binary tree used by blockchain technology to summarize all transactions in a block.

To build a Merkle tree, a pair of transactions is recursively hashed until they form only one root node at the top of the tree, called the Merkle root. More precisely, the Merkle root is a hash of all the transactions that make up a block in the blockchain network. Any minor change to the data will change the Merkle root hash, resulting in an invalid entry. The most common cryptographic hash algorithm used to construct a Merkle tree is the secure 256-bit hash algorithm (SHA256). If there is an odd number of transactions, the hash of the last transaction is duplicated to create an even number of transactions, thus forming a balanced tree.

Nodes in the blockchain network run a consensus algorithm to verify transactions. There are several consensus algorithms (protocols) available for blockchain technology, such as Proof of Work (PoW), Proof of Stake (PoS), Delegated Proof of Stake (DPoS), and Proof of Complexity (PoC). For example, Bitcoin uses PoW, while Ethereum and Bitshare implement PoS and DPoS, respectively. In PoW, miner nodes that want to add (mine) a new block to the blockchain network must first solve a complex mathematical puzzle that requires a lot of computing power. A miner who solves the puzzle adds a new block and is rewarded in Bitcoins. Unlike PoW, in PoS, the node that creates a new block is chosen deterministically based on its share (wealth). PoS saves the energy needed in PoW to solve the mathematical puzzle, and only the power of a node (validator) is needed to verify new transactions and blocks [2]. DPoS tries to solve the consensus problem by using delegates. DPoS uses a real-time voting and reputation system to create a pool of limited trusted delegates who will observe and verify blocks. Witnesses have the right to create blocks and add them to the blockchain network, as well as prevent malicious nodes from participating in adding blocks. In general, in PoS and DPoS, network stakeholders are not expected to intentionally make wrong decisions for the network.

Blockchain is a type of distributed chain. Distributed ledger technology (DLT) allows records to be kept on multiple computers known as "nodes." Any blockchain user can be a node, but it requires a lot of computer power to operate. Nodes verify, approve, and store data in the registry. This differs from traditional record-keeping methods, which store data in a central location such as a computer server.

Blockchain organizes the information added to the ledger into blocks or groups of data. Each block can only hold a certain amount of information, so new blocks are constantly added to the ledger, forming a chain.

Each block has its unique identifier, a cryptographic "hash." Not only does the hash protect the information in the block from anyone without the necessary code, but it also protects the block's place along the chain by identifying the block that came before it.

A cryptographic hash is "a set of numbers and letters that can be up to 64 digits long," says Vikas Agarwal, a partner in PwC's financial services advisory practice. "It's a unique code that allows the pieces of the puzzle to fit together."

Once information is added to the blockchain and encrypted with a hash, it becomes permanent and immutable. Each node has its record of the complete timeline of data along the blockchain, going back to its beginning. If someone tampered with or hacked one computer and manipulated the data for their benefit, it would not change the information stored on other nodes. The changed entry can be easily distinguished and corrected because it does not match the majority [7].

The way the system works, it's almost impossible for someone to replicate the computing power that happens on the back end to reverse engineer it and somehow figure out what the hashes are.

Here is an example of how the blockchain is used to verify and record Bitcoin transactions:

i. A consumer buys Bitcoins.
ii. Transaction data are sent through the decentralized network of Bitcoin nodes.
iii. Nodes confirm the transaction.
iv. Once approved, a transaction is grouped with other transactions to form a block that is added to an ever-growing chain of transactions.
v. The completed block is encrypted, and the transaction record is permanent; it cannot be deleted or changed on the blockchain.

The Bitcoin blockchain is public, meaning that anyone who owns a Bitcoin can view a record of a transaction. While it can be difficult to trace the identity of an account, the record shows which accounts are transacting on the blockchain. Public blockchains also allow any user with the necessary computing power to participate in approving and recording transactions on the blockchain as a node.

But not all blockchains are public. Blockchains can be designed as private systems, so the owner can limit who can make changes or additions to the blockchain. While the pool of participants may be smaller in a private blockchain, it is still decentralized among those who participate. Private blockchains ensure the security of any data stored in a database using the same encryption techniques.

The idea of a secure, decentralized permanent record of information has sparked interest in several industries and potentially provides solutions to many of the security, record-keeping, and data ownership issues we face today. Blockchain gives us the technology to move information securely, Agarwal says, and we have almost complete confidence in the authenticity of any information we want to protect. Consider, for example, the stories that have circulated about memes and celebrities cashing in on digital assets by selling NFTs (non-fungible tokens). Because the underlying blockchain record is immutable, NFTs allow sellers to verify the authenticity of a digital asset. When you buy an NFT, that transaction is added to the blockchain ledger and becomes a verified record of ownership. For those who want to be able to verify the authenticity of a digital work, blockchain helps value digital art and collectibles in the same way as their physical counterparts. In theory, this results in creators retaining value through receiving royalties for copies of digital art.

Such usage illustrates blockchain's appeal not only for security but also for information integrity. Blockchain has the potential to give people more security and confidence in doing so. Companies and governments around the world continue to test and implement blockchain technology, but it won't happen overnight. If we ever reach a point where government currency is based on the blockchain or medical records are converted to the blockchain, it won't be anytime soon.

In the meantime, you can bet on the power of blockchain by adding a blockchain-based cryptocurrency like Bitcoin to your portfolio, though there are other ways to put your money behind the technology. You can also configure more traditional investments to move to the blockchain. For example, check if your ETFs or mutual funds have companies developing blockchain technology or starting to use blockchain in their business operations. There are even ETFs that consist entirely of these types of companies, known as Blockchain ETFs. One example launched in 2018 is the Siren Nasdaq Blockchain Economy Index (BLCN), which outperformed the S&P 500*'s* total return both year-over-year and on average over three years [8]. These funds do not invest your money in cryptocurrency; instead, they invest in the stocks of select companies—ranging from long-established companies like IBM to lesser-known startups like Galaxy Digital. While this still doesn't guarantee a profit, it can be a more conservative alternative to placing your money directly in the notoriously volatile cryptocurrency market.

Speculating in cryptocurrencies and investing in blockchain companies is very similar to the California Gold Rush two centuries ago. Many people rushed there to dig for gold, and most of them never made any money. The people who made money were the ones who sold the shovels. The companies that support the development of the blockchain are sellers of shovels.

Bitcoin also works on blockchain technology. The entire blockchain is stored in a huge network of computers. So, no one person has control over history. Let's say a user learns crypto-related data from Crypto Head, buys Bitcoins, and pays others using Bitcoins. What will happen next? Computers on the Bitcoin blockchain rush to verify the accuracy of the transaction. This step certifies everything that happened in the chain. That way, no one can go back and change things. Therefore, the blockchain cannot be easily forged.

Guardtime removes the need to use keys for verification. Instead, they distribute each piece of data between nodes throughout the system. If someone tries to change the data, the system analyzes the whole mass of chains, compares them to the metadata package, and then excludes any that do not match.

This means that the only way to erase the entire blockchain is to destroy every single node. If only one node continues to operate with correct data, the entire system can be restored even if all other nodes are compromised. In the conditions of hybrid wars, it allows the security of any confidential information from destruction or distortion.

The Guardtime system works in such a way that it can always detect when changes have been made to the data and constantly checks for changes. This ensures that there is no discrete way to tamper with blocks on the chain and that the data remain uncompromised.

2.3 CYBER-SPHERES WHERE BLOCKCHAIN CAN BE USED TO PROTECT DATA AT ORGANIZATION INFRASTRUCTURE

Blockchain technology has become the most stable form of data transfer in the field of various networks present on the market. As it was designed and implemented, blockchain technology has been recognized for ensuring the integrity of information. If it is used in an intended way, many sectors (private or government) can benefit from creating a system based on it, as shown in Figure 2.4.

Having the potential to be practical and useful for many software and industrial programs, the network that uses this technology can be implemented in many of them. The best application would be to use its integrity aspect in order to guarantee cybersecurity solutions and tools for other tools and technologies.

We can look at various examples of the benefits of using blockchain technology to power up cybersecurity in the near future:

Private communication defense: Social networks have become one of the most popular communication channels as the world wide web grows. The number of these social networks also grows exponentially. More social applications are launched

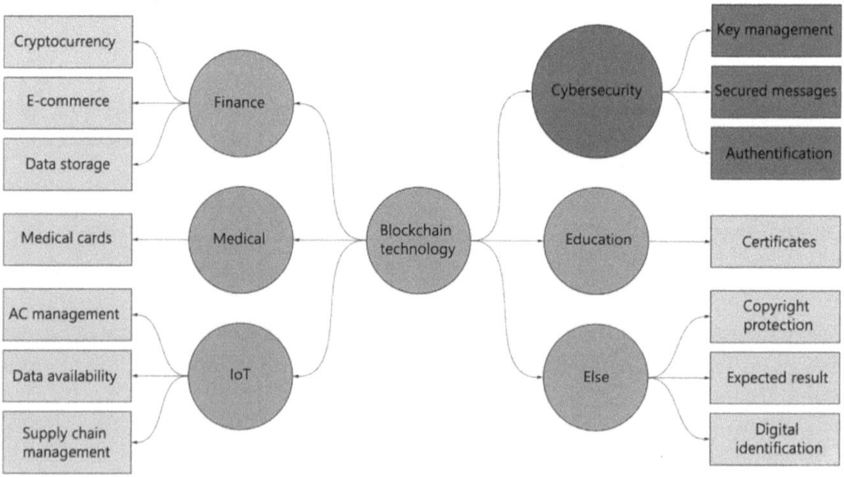

FIGURE 2.4 Sectors of application of blockchain technology.

daily compared to each previous year as conversational needs gain additional popularity and reach new levels. During these communications, companies and third parties collect and use a lot of data. Most participants of any social network platform protect their accounts and any data that leak to the web with weak and unreliable passwords that can be easily broken.

Most companies turn every day to investigate, use, and implement blockchain technology to protect user data as a superior option to the end-to-end encryption they used to use until these days. Blockchain technology can be developed in order to create a new standard security protocol that can become a worldwide standard to use. To provide a secured messenger possibility, blockchain technology can be used to create a unique API framework standard [9].

Hacker attacks [10] on social networks such as X (formerly Twitter) or Facebook have recently become more significant and common. This kind of intrusion led to a major data leak; possibly millions of user accounts were stolen or hacked, and their sensitive data fell into the hands of attackers. Correctly used blockchain technology, if well integrated into these networking systems, can defend against such cyberattack attempts in the future, especially when the question touches the internal structures and organizational networks, where this is a critical factor that must be protected.

Internet of Things defense: Attackers often use different kinds of devices and software, such as thermostats and routers, in order to gain access to internal systems. Nowadays, networks use artificial intelligence (AI), so in case of an attack, the offensive side has found an easier way to access widely used systems such as home automation devices (i.e., smart houses) by abusing smart devices and other technology based on that. In most cases, these devices and systems have schematic security flaws that can be easily abused.

In this particular case, blockchain technology can be used to protect such systems by using the decentralization attribute of the blockchain and putting the administration of these systems out of the center of the attack, making it harder to find an entry point. This approach to the problem will allow the device to make its own independent decisions for making the whole system more secure [11]. System independence from the centralized administrator core or device makes these networks or devices more secure by using a detection system and giving authority to act on suspicious and unauthorized commands from other networks.

As we know, attackers penetrate the main administration of the device and correspondently gain full control over the devices and systems in this network after performing an attack. Using the decentralizing attribute for devices that power systems, blockchain technology ensures that attacks of that kind are more difficult to make possible.

DDoS and DNS security: A Distributed Denial of Service (DDoS) attack occurs when a target, such as a network, server, or website, is denied access or cannot answer any call from outside. These kinds of attacks disable or slow down systems resources and computing power. On the other side of this problem, the domain name system (DNS) that is intact is centralized, and that makes it an ideal target for intruders to break into the established connection between the IP address and the website itself [12]. This kind of intrusion makes the target resource inaccessible and even creates various kinds of redirects to other resources that might be harmful to the end-user. Blockchain technology can be used to reduce different types of intrusion by using blockchain decentralization attributes to control DNS records. By using the decentralized attribute, the blockchain can remove vulnerable points that are used by attackers.

Storage decentralization: Data damage and leaks are becoming the main causes of concerns and problems for private or government organizations. Companies still use various centralized storage options that are present on the market. The attacker uses only a single vulnerability to access the data stored on these kinds of systems or devices. This intrusion leaves the hacker with confidential information, like the financial records of the targeted business, information about its employees, etc. Using blockchain technology, data that must be protected will be secured by providing decentralized data storage possibilities. This method will make it impossible for attackers to break into storage devices or systems. A lot of companies that provide storage spaces agree that blockchain technology can secure data from being damaged or leaked. Apollo Currency Team is a good example of a private organization that has already actively used the blockchain in order to enhance its security levels [13].

Security of software systems: Blockchain technology can also be used to ensure the security of various kinds of software and to prevent intrusion from outside. Like it is done with MD5 hashes, chains can be used to check different software activities like updates, installers, and patches to prevent malware from reaching personal computers. Speaking of MD5, the software ID is ordinary compared to the hashes that are available on reached websites. This particular method is reliable but not as such as the hashes that are available on the website destination may be already defective or damaged. On the other hand, blockchain technology hashes are constantly overwritten to the chain and verified by participants or nodes [14]. The information added by using this technology is not super variable and moreover, the chain can be much more effective in checking the original state of the software by comparing it with hashes in the chain itself.

Cyber-space verification: The leaking of data and false system configuration, together with the failure of different parts, can compromise the information that is received from any device or system. Blockchain technology integrity and information check possibilities can be used to authenticate the status of any device or system installed in the infrastructure. The info that is received about the device or system components via blockchain can be more stable and reliable for storage space.

Security of the data: Blockchain technology can be used to prevent any access to data that is not authorized during transmission. Using the encryption feature of blockchain technology, users can secure the transmission of any data from attackers' access. This approach surely will increase the overall security and integrity of the data transmitted through the chain. An attacker that intends to do unauthorized actions supports the data during the transmission process in order to change it or remove it from existence [15]. This action leaves a gap in inefficient communication channels like e-mail.

All the aforementioned areas of blockchain technology that can be developed for applications can be implemented as additional or main protection of infrastructure of Ukraine, in the dual-purpose network, special information networks, as well as to protect confidential data when transmitted by open or dual-purpose networks.

When choosing ready-made solutions or when creating your own first-level blockchain, you need to understand how they are formed and what they consist of. Table 2.1

TABLE 2.1
Comparative Characteristics of Applications Built on the First Level of the Blockchain

Characteristics	Bitcoin	Ethereum	IOTA
Released	Yes	Yes	Yes
Mining access	Public	Public and private	Public
System of safe operations	Yes	Yes	Yes
Support for external applications	Yes	Yes	Yes
Data privacy	No	No	Yes
Possibility of branching	Yes	Yes	No
Lack of commission	No	No	Yes
Key management	No	No	No
Management of personal identifiers	No	No	No
User authentication	Digital signature	Digital signature	Digital signature

compares some of the most popular first-tier blockchain systems. Each blockchain system reviewed (Bitcoin, Ethereum, IOTA) has a unique approach to mining access, transaction management, data privacy, and user authentication, which influences its suitability for secure information systems.

- Bitcoin and Ethereum are public-access systems, allowing broad participation but sacrificing data privacy, as neither provides inherent privacy mechanisms. This restricts their effectiveness in scenarios demanding stringent data protection.
- IOTA introduces innovations suited for IoT applications, such as data privacy and a lack of transaction commissions, making it more adaptable to networks with sensitive or large-scale data transmissions.
- Mining access and key management in all systems highlight an area for improvement, as the management of private keys remains a weak point in user security protocols across blockchain systems.

These findings indicate that while blockchain provides robust cybersecurity through decentralization and data integrity, its limitations in privacy, key management, and branching capabilities need to be addressed for more specialized cybersecurity applications. This analysis suggests potential for future blockchain-based cybersecurity systems to integrate customizable features based on specific organizational needs.

2.4 PROS AND CONS OF USING SYSTEMS BASED ON BLOCKCHAIN TECHNOLOGY TO PROTECT THEM

The complexity of building a blockchain layer for any technology to protect cyber-systems raises some concerns about implementation, security, and resilience [16].

In order to define whether this system should be developed or not we need to take a look at the pros and cons of blockchain technology and attributes in the context of cybersecurity and data protection.

The main pros of blockchain technology for cybersecurity are the following:

i. Decentralization mechanism—peer-to-peer network, verification from the third party is excluded, any user can see the network operations.
ii. Tracking mechanism—in blockchain all transactions have a digital signature and time stamp, so network participants can track history and accounts at any given time and expose this information if needed. This mechanism allows having reliable information about assets or product distribution.
iii. Confidentiality attribute—the privacy of network users is high because of the usage of public-key cryptography, which authenticates members and encrypts their actions.
iv. Data integrity—blockchain technology ensures the confidentiality of the data inside it when users forget the key; no one can decrypt it.
v. Security mechanism—it is easy to detect harmful behavior through peer-to-peer connections and distributed consensus. Today, blockchains are considered "unbreakable" because attackers can only affect the network by gaining control of 51% of network nodes.
vi. Sustainability mechanism—blockchain doesn't have any point of failure, which means that even if a DDoS attack is performed, the system will work as usual due to several copies of the chain.
vii. Integrity mechanism—distributed registry protects data from leaking and damaging. Blockchain technology ensures the irreversibility of transactions. Encrypted blocks contain data that are resistant to being damaged.
viii. Data mechanism—blockchain technology can guarantee the accuracy and quality of data after encryption in the chain.
ix. Secure access mechanism—users need constant access to the chain and have the possibility to gain this access via multiple devices, so there is a risk of losing control of private keys that are in the possession of the chain members.

Even if blockchain technology is a new evolution step in cybersecurity, there are still some cons to consider:

i. Irreversibility mechanism—there is a high risk that encrypted data will not be recovered if the participant loses or forgets the private key.
ii. Storage capacity limitation—a single block contains only 1 MB of data, and the blockchain can process only seven transactions per second.
iii. Cyberattack risk—if attackers manage to capture most of the network (51% attack), the entire database can be lost.
iv. Adaptation problems—although blockchain technology can be applied to almost any business, companies may have difficulty integrating it. Applying this technology in supply chain systems, for example, is quite difficult, as it can take a long time to reproduce supply chains in the form of blockchains and improve them.

v. High operating costs—running blockchain technology requires a huge amount of computing power, which can lead to high costs compared to existing systems.
vi. Blockchain technology development—there is a lack of developers with experience in blockchain technology and deep knowledge of cryptography.

Overall, the blockchain is new sunlight in cybersecurity, it can provide the highest level of privacy, availability, and security of data. On the other hand, the complexity of the technology can make it super difficult to develop and use.

2.5 CONCLUSIONS

Every day, more people join the Internet, and this technology is continuously evolving; more data is emerging, and more attackers are trying to steal or damage it. Blockchain technology is versatile and incredibly useful for the future of the Internet, allowing people to better protect data and information. Use cases of blockchain technology are already becoming a huge part of many institutions, not only cryptocurrencies, and can be extremely useful for improving or even designing cybersecurity in a new way. By implementing encryption and data distribution protocols on the network, any company can ensure that their information remains secure, defended, and undamaged.

Blockchain-based protection systems have their pros and cons (especially if we are talking about the cost of building such a system; specialists in this field are now very expensive). But there should be no such thing as savings in critical infrastructure security if we care about it. It can take a decade to implement and transfer security systems on the closed blockchain network. Nevertheless, the pros of using this system in the cybersecurity sphere outnumber the cons.

REFERENCES

[1] V Susukailo, S Vasylyshyn, I Opirskyy, V Buriachok, "Cybercrimes Investigation via Honeypots in Cloud Environments," *CEUR Workshop*, Vol. 2923, pp. 91–96, 2021.
[2] S Surajdeep, *Potential Use Cases of Blockchain Technology for Cybersecurity* (2021). [Online]. https://www.itbusinessedge.com/security/potential-use-cases-of-blockchain-technology-for-cybersecurity/.
[3] S Yogesh, *Rethinking Cybersecurity Through Blockchain* (2021). Accessed: April 17, 2022. [Online]. https://www.infosys.com/insights/cyber-security/cybersecurity-blockchain.html.
[4] Sam D Wallets, *Hospitals and the Chinese Military: 18 Examples of Blockchain Cybersecurity at Work* (2021). Accessed: April 17, 2022. [Online]. https://builtin.com/blockchain/blockchain-cybersecurity-uses.
[5] V Susukailo, S Vasylyshyn, I Opirskyy, V Buriachok, O Riabchun, "Cybercrimes Investigation via Honeypots in Cloud Environments," *CEUR Workshop Proceedings*, p. 91, 2021.
[6] Valeriy Dudykevych, Ivan Prokopyshyn, Vasyl Chekurin, Ivan Opirskyy, Yuriy Lakh, Taras Kret, Yevheniia Ivanchenko, Ihor Ivanchenko, "A Multicriterial Analysis of the Efficiency of Conservative Information Security Systems," *Eastern-European Journal of Enterprise Technologies, Information and Controlling System*, Vol. 3, Issue 9(99), pp. 6–13, 2019. https://doi.org/10.15587/1729-4061.2019.166349

[7] Crypto Head, Accessed: March 13, 2022. [Online]. https://cryptohead.io/.
[8] *Norton Cyber Security Insights Report 2017 Global Results* (2017). March 15, 2022. [Online]. https://www.symantec.com/content/dam/symantec/docs/about/2017-ncsir-globalresults-en.pdf.
[9] A Buldas, R Laanoja, P Laud, A Truu, "Bounded Pre-Image Awareness and the Security of Hash-Tree Keyless Signatures," In: Chow SSM, Liu JK, Hui LCK, Yiu SM (eds) *Provable Security. ProvSec 2014. Lecture Notes in Computer Science*, Vol. 8782. Springer, Cham. 2014. https://doi.org/10.1007/978-3-319-12475-9_10
[10] *PwC 2020 How Blockchain Can Transform Defence Assets and Give Armed Forces an Advantage on the Battlefield.* Accessed: March 18, 2022. [Online]. https://www.pwc.com/gx/en/aerospace-defence/pdf/blockchain-defence.pdf.
[11] *PwC 2018 Global Economic Crime and Fraud Survey* (2018). Accessed: March 19, 2022. [Online]. https://www.pwc.com/gx/en/forensics/global-economiccrime-and-fraud-survey–2018.pdf.
[12] V Agarwal, "Blockchain in Cyber Defense: Evolution and New Potentials in Network Security," *International Journal of Creative Research Thoughts (IJCRT)*, Vol. 12, Issue 6, pp. 132–140, June 2024.
[13] L Zhao, M Patel, "IoT and Blockchain Synergies for Enhanced Data Protection," *Journal of Emerging Tech & Applications*, Vol. 5, Issue 2, pp. 45–53, April 2024.
[14] R Singh, P Gupta, "Blockchain Mechanisms in Data Privacy for Confidential Networks," *Cyber Defense Review*, Vol. 9, Issue 3, pp. 78–85, May 2024.
[15] D Kowalski et al., "Advancements in Distributed Ledger Technology for Cybersecurity in Government and Corporate Sectors," *Information Security Insights*, Vol. 4, Issue 4, pp. 201–210, July 2024.
[16] T Johnson, "Application of Blockchain in DDoS Protection: A New Frontier," *Network Security Advances*, Vol. 3, Issue 5, pp. 112–119, August 2024.

3 Innovative Cost Functions for Optimizing Cryptographic S-Box Generation

Oleksandr Kuznetsov, Nikolay Poluyanenko, Oleksii Smirnov, Aigul Shaikhanova, and Boris Khruskov

3.1 INTRODUCTION

Cryptography remains a foundational pillar in the realm of contemporary information security, offering essential tools and methodologies to protect digital communications and data storage amid the challenges of a globally interconnected landscape [1, 2]. Central to numerous cryptographic frameworks are the substitution boxes, or S-boxes, which act as crucial nonlinear elements in both block and stream ciphers [1]. These mathematical structures are instrumental in instilling confusion and diffusion within cryptographic algorithms—fundamental aspects for robust encryption. These concepts were first elucidated by Claude Shannon in his groundbreaking contributions to the communication theory of secrecy systems, highlighting their critical importance in secure communications [3, 4].

3.1.1 Overview of Existing Approaches to S-Box Generation

Researchers have developed various approaches to address the challenges of S-box generation, broadly categorized into three main strategies: algebraic constructions, random generation with filtering, and heuristic search algorithms.

Algebraic constructions leverage mathematical structures and properties to create S-boxes with provable characteristics [5–8]. Notable examples include the use of finite field inversions, as seen in the AES S-box [9], and constructions based on bent functions or Hadamard matrices. While these methods can produce S-boxes with excellent cryptographic properties, they often result in structures with potential algebraic weaknesses that could be exploited by advanced cryptanalytic techniques.

Random generation with filtering involves creating a large number of candidate S-boxes through random permutation and then applying a series of tests to filter out those that do not meet specific criteria [10–13]. This approach can be computationally expensive and may struggle to produce S-boxes that simultaneously optimize multiple

DOI: 10.1201/9781003546153-3

cryptographic properties. However, it has the advantage of potentially discovering novel structures that are not bound by the constraints of algebraic constructions.

Heuristic search algorithms have emerged as a powerful and flexible approach to S-box generation [13–16]. These methods, including hill climbing, simulated annealing, and genetic algorithms, iteratively modify candidate solutions to optimize a defined cost function. The effectiveness of these algorithms heavily depends on the choice of cost function, which must accurately reflect the desired cryptographic properties while providing a smooth optimization landscape.

Recent advancements in heuristic search methods have focused on developing more sophisticated cost functions and hybrid approaches that combine multiple optimization techniques. For instance, the work of Clark et al. [17] introduced the use of the Walsh-Hadamard Spectrum (WHS) as a basis for cost function design, while Picek et al. [18] proposed alternative formulations that consider the distribution of spectrum coefficients.

3.1.2 Challenges in Generating High-Quality S-Boxes

Despite their crucial role, the generation of high-quality S-boxes presents several significant challenges. The primary difficulty lies in the inherent tension between optimizing for multiple cryptographic properties simultaneously [14, 15, 19]. For instance, maximizing nonlinearity often comes at the cost of increased algebraic complexity or differential uniformity. This multi-objective optimization problem is further complicated by the vast search space of possible S-boxes, even for relatively small input sizes.

For 8-bit S-boxes, which are commonly used in practice, the search space consists of $256! \approx 2^{1684}$ possible permutations. Exhaustive search within this space is computationally infeasible, necessitating the use of more sophisticated generation techniques. Moreover, the relationships between various cryptographic properties of S-boxes are not fully understood, making it challenging to develop theoretical constructions that guarantee optimal performance across all relevant metrics.

Another significant challenge is the need for S-boxes to resist emerging forms of cryptanalysis. As new attack vectors are discovered, the criteria for evaluating S-box quality must evolve, potentially invalidating previously considered secure constructions. This dynamic landscape requires ongoing research and development of novel generation methods that can adapt to new security requirements.

The efficiency of S-box generation algorithms is also a critical concern, particularly for applications that may require frequent key changes or the use of large numbers of distinct S-boxes. Balancing the trade-off between the quality of generated S-boxes and the computational resources required to produce them remains an open problem in the field.

3.1.3 Thesis Statement: A Novel Cost Function for Improved S-Box Generation

This chapter presents an extended exploration of our previously published research, offering additional insights and considerations beyond the original scientific article [20]. We introduce a novel cost function designed to enhance the efficiency and effectiveness of S-box generation using heuristic search methods. Our approach builds upon the foundations laid by previous work in the field, particularly the WHS [17, 21, 22] and WCF (Walsh-Hadamard Spectrum Content) [21, 23] functions while addressing some of their limitations.

The proposed cost function, which we term WCFS (Walsh-Hadamard Coefficient Filtered Spectrum), incorporates a more nuanced consideration of the Walsh-Hadamard Spectrum coefficients. By selectively weighting and filtering these coefficients, our function aims to provide a more targeted optimization landscape that better correlates with the cryptographic properties of interest, particularly nonlinearity.

We hypothesize that this refined cost function will lead to significant improvements in both the quality of generated S-boxes and the computational efficiency of the generation process. Through extensive experimental evaluation and comparative analysis, we demonstrate the effectiveness of our approach in the context of a hill climbing algorithm, showcasing its potential to advance the state-of-the-art in S-box generation techniques.

The remainder of this chapter is structured as follows: We begin with a comprehensive background section detailing the fundamental concepts of S-boxes and reviewing existing cost function designs. We then present the mathematical formulation and theoretical justification for our novel WCFS function. This is followed by a detailed description of our experimental methodology and a thorough analysis of the results obtained. We conclude with a discussion of the implications of our findings for the field of cryptography and outline promising directions for future research in this area.

By offering this expanded treatment of our work, we aim to contribute to the ongoing dialogue in the cryptographic community regarding the design and optimization of fundamental security primitives. Our research not only advances the specific task of S-box generation but also provides insights into the broader challenges of designing robust cryptographic components for next-generation security systems.

3.1.4 The Role of S-Boxes in Modern Cryptography

S-boxes function as the primary source of nonlinearity in many symmetric-key cryptographic algorithms [4], including widely used standards such as the Advanced Encryption Standard (AES) [9]. By introducing nonlinear transformations, S-boxes significantly contribute to the overall security of these systems, making them resistant to various cryptanalytic attacks [1]. The importance of S-boxes extends beyond block ciphers to other cryptographic primitives, including hash functions and stream ciphers, where they often serve as the backbone of confusion-generating mechanisms.

In the context of block ciphers, S-boxes typically operate on small blocks of input bits, producing an output of equal or different size. This substitution process is designed to obscure the relationship between the plaintext, the key, and the resulting ciphertext. The cryptographic strength of an S-box is determined by several criteria, including but not limited to its nonlinearity, differential uniformity, and algebraic complexity [24]. These properties collectively determine the S-box's resistance to linear and differential cryptanalysis, as well as algebraic attacks [1].

The design of S-boxes also impacts the efficiency of hardware and software implementations of cryptographic algorithms. Well-constructed S-boxes can lead to faster encryption and decryption processes, lower power consumption in hardware implementations, and improved resistance to side-channel attacks. Consequently, the study and optimization of S-boxes remain active areas of research in the cryptographic community.

3.1.5 Chapter Contributions

This chapter makes several significant contributions to the field of cryptographic S-box design and analysis:

- Novel cost function: We introduce the Walsh-Hadamard Coefficient Filtered Spectrum (WCFS) cost function, a new approach to evaluating and optimizing S-boxes. This function addresses limitations in existing methods and provides a more nuanced assessment of S-box quality.
- Improved S-box generation: We demonstrate that the WCFS function, when used with a hill climbing algorithm, significantly reduces the average number of iterations required to generate optimal S-boxes. This improvement in efficiency has important implications for cryptographic system design and key schedule generation.
- Enhanced success rate: Our method achieves a remarkably high success rate in generating S-boxes with optimal nonlinearity, substantially outperforming existing approaches. This increased reliability is crucial for applications requiring consistent, high-quality S-boxes.
- Comprehensive evaluation: We provide a thorough analysis of the cryptographic properties of WCFS-generated S-boxes, including nonlinearity, differential uniformity, and algebraic degree. This evaluation offers insights into the overall quality and security of the generated S-boxes.
- Comparative analysis: We present a rigorous comparison of WCFS with state-of-the-art cost functions, providing valuable benchmarks for the cryptographic community and establishing WCFS as a significant advancement in S-box generation techniques.
- Theoretical insights: The development of WCFS contributes to the theoretical understanding of the relationship between spectral properties and cryptographic strength in S-boxes, potentially informing future research in this area.

3.1.6 Chapter Organization

The remainder of this chapter is structured as follows:

- Section 3.2 provides a comprehensive review of recent literature in S-box design and analysis, concluding with a tabular summary of key advancements.
- Section 3.3 presents the necessary background information on S-boxes, including their role in cryptography, key properties, and existing generation methods.
- Section 3.4 introduces our novel WCFS cost function, detailing its mathematical formulation, design principles, and theoretical justification.

- Section 3.5 describes the methodology employed in our study, including the implementation of the hill climbing algorithm, experimental setup, and evaluation criteria.
- Section 3.6 presents our experimental results and analysis, comparing the performance of WCFS with existing cost functions and examining the cryptographic properties of the generated S-boxes.
- Section 3.7 discusses the implications of our findings for cryptographic system design, addresses limitations of the current work, and suggests directions for future research.
- Section 3.8 concludes the chapter, summarizing our key findings and their significance for the field of cryptography.

Through this structure, we aim to provide a comprehensive and coherent exploration of our novel approach to S-box generation, its theoretical foundations, practical implementation, and implications for the broader field of cryptography.

3.2 RELATED WORK

Recent advancements in S-box design and analysis have significantly contributed to the field of cryptography, addressing various aspects of security, efficiency, and application-specific requirements. This section provides an overview of the latest developments in S-box research, focusing on construction methods, cryptanalysis, and practical applications.

Fahd et al. (2024) [25] conducted a comprehensive study on backdoored S-boxes, examining 24 cryptanalytic attack vectors to identify common vulnerabilities in intentionally weakened mappings. Their research revealed that backdoored architectures, while potentially satisfying randomness criteria, often compromise crucial cryptographic properties such as algebraic degrees, differential trails, and avalanche characteristics. This work highlights the importance of thorough cryptanalysis in detecting hidden weaknesses in S-box designs.

In the realm of medical image encryption, Jamal et al. (2024) [26] proposed a region of interest (ROI)-based encryption technique utilizing chaotic S-boxes. Their approach addresses the challenges posed by large DICOM images by selectively encrypting critical areas while maintaining overall security. The authors evaluated their method using standard performance metrics, demonstrating its efficiency and resistance against common attacks.

Ji et al. (2024) [27] focused on constructing correlation immune S-boxes with high nonlinearity for stream cipher applications. By utilizing disjoint linear codes, they achieved S-boxes with optimal trade-offs between nonlinearity and correlation immunity. Their work provides valuable insights into balancing multiple cryptographic criteria in S-box design.

Liu, Liu, and Zhao (2024) [28] addressed the limitations of fixed S-boxes by proposing a method for generating keyed strong S-boxes based on random affine transformation matrices and 2D hyper chaotic maps. Their approach aims to eliminate weaknesses such as fixed points and short iteration period rings, enhancing the overall security of the resulting S-boxes.

Malal and Tezcan (2024) [29] developed an FPGA-friendly compact and efficient 8×8 S-box as an alternative to the AES S-box. Their design achieves comparable security with reduced gate area on various FPGA platforms, making it particularly suitable for resource-constrained IoT devices.

Nitaj, Susilo, and Tonien (2024) [30] introduced a family of enhanced S-boxes for AES with maximal periodicity and improved avalanche properties. Their work demonstrates that modifying existing S-box designs can lead to significant improvements in cryptographic characteristics.

Singh et al. (2024) [31] presented an image encryption technique using dynamic S-boxes generated from elliptic curve points and chaotic systems. Their method produces unique S-boxes for each image, providing resistance against known-plaintext attacks and achieving strong statistical properties.

Ullah et al. (2024) [32] proposed a new method for constructing strong initial S-boxes based on the fractional-order Rabinovich-Fabrikant chaotic system. They combined this with a key-based permutation technique to enhance the S-box's functionality, demonstrating favorable results in cryptographic analysis and image encryption applications.

Waheed et al. (2024) [33] introduced a hybrid approach for generating highly efficient S-boxes, combining linear fractional transformation with a multilayer perceptron architecture. Their method achieved exceptional nonlinearity scores, surpassing many existing designs in the literature.

Table 3.1 provides a comprehensive overview of recent advancements in S-box design and analysis, all published in 2024. This summary reflects the diverse and innovative approaches researchers are taking to improve S-box quality and security.

TABLE 3.1
Overview of Recent Advancements in S-Box Design and Analysis

Authors	Key Contribution	Methodology	Main Findings	Implications
Fahd et al. (2024) [25]	Analysis of backdoored S-boxes	Examination of 24 cryptanalytic attack vectors	Backdoored architectures often compromise crucial cryptographic properties	Highlights the importance of thorough security audits in S-box design
Jamal et al. (2024) [26]	Region of interest-based medical image encryption	Chaotic S-boxes	Efficient selective encryption of critical areas in DICOM images	Demonstrates potential for specialized S-box applications in healthcare security
Ji et al. (2024) [27]	Construction of correlation immune S-boxes	Utilization of disjoint linear codes	Achieved optimal trade-offs between nonlinearity and correlation immunity	Advances in balancing multiple cryptographic criteria for stream cipher applications

TABLE 3.1 (*Continued*)
Overview of Recent Advancements in S-Box Design and Analysis

Authors	Key Contribution	Methodology	Main Findings	Implications
Liu, Liu, and Zhao (2024) [28]	Generation of keyed strong S-boxes	Random affine transformation matrices and 2D hyper chaotic maps	Eliminated weaknesses such as fixed points and short iteration period rings	Enhances security against certain cryptanalytic attacks
Malal and Tezcan (2024) [29]	FPGA-friendly compact 8×8 S-box	Hardware-optimized design	Comparable security to AES S-box with reduced gate area	Potential for improved efficiency in resource-constrained IoT devices
Nitaj, Susilo, and Tonien (2024) [30]	Enhanced S-boxes for AES	Modification of existing S-box designs	Improved maximal periodicity and avalanche properties	Demonstrates potential for enhancing established cryptographic standards
Singh et al. (2024) [31]	Dynamic S-box generation for image encryption	Elliptic curve points and chaotic systems	Unique S-boxes for each image, providing strong statistical properties	Enhances security in image encryption applications
Ullah et al. (2024) [32]	Construction of strong initial S-boxes	Fractional-order Rabinovich-Fabrikant chaotic system	Enhanced S-box functionality with favorable cryptographic analysis results	Advances in chaos-based S-box generation techniques
Waheed et al. (2024) [33]	Hybrid approach for S-box generation	Linear fractional transformation and multilayer perceptron	Achieved exceptional nonlinearity scores surpassing existing designs	Demonstrates potential of combining mathematical and machine learning approaches

These recent works collectively demonstrate the ongoing importance of S-box research in cryptography. They highlight various approaches to improving S-box design, from chaotic systems and neural networks to algebraic constructions and hardware optimizations. The diversity of methods and applications underscores the complex trade-offs involved in S-box design and the need for continued innovation in this critical area of cryptographic research.

3.3 BACKGROUND

3.3.1 Fundamentals of S-Boxes in Cryptographic Systems

Substitution boxes, commonly referred to as S-boxes, are fundamental components in many modern cryptographic systems, serving as the primary source of nonlinearity in symmetric-key algorithms. An S-box is essentially a mathematical function that maps a fixed-length input to a fixed-length output [24]. In the context of block ciphers, S-boxes typically operate on small blocks of bits, often 4 to 8 bits in size, though larger S-boxes exist in some designs.

The concept of S-boxes can be formally defined as follows [24]:

Let F_2 denote the finite field with two elements, and let n and m be positive integers. An (n, m)-S-box is a function $S : F_2^n \rightarrow F_2^m$.

When $n = m$, the S-box is called bijective if it is a one-to-one and onto mapping. Bijective S-boxes are particularly important in cryptographic applications as they ensure that the encryption process is reversible, allowing for decryption.

The role of S-boxes in cryptographic algorithms is multifaceted. Primarily, they introduce nonlinearity into the cipher, which is crucial for resisting linear cryptanalysis. Additionally, S-boxes contribute to the diffusion property of the cipher, helping to ensure that small changes in the input result in significant changes in the output [3, 4]. This property is essential for thwarting differential cryptanalysis.

In block ciphers, S-boxes are typically used in conjunction with permutation layers to create a substitution-permutation network (SPN) [1, 4]. This structure, employed in ciphers like AES [9], alternates between nonlinear substitutions (provided by the S-boxes) and linear transformations (provided by the permutation layer) to achieve the desired cryptographic properties.

The design of S-boxes is a critical aspect of cipher construction. While random S-boxes can be used, carefully constructed S-boxes often provide superior cryptographic properties. The criteria for evaluating S-boxes have evolved over time as new cryptanalytic techniques have emerged. Contemporary S-box design must consider resistance to a wide array of attacks, including linear and differential cryptanalysis, algebraic attacks, and side-channel attacks.

3.3.2 Cryptographic Properties of S-Boxes

The security and efficiency of cryptographic systems heavily depend on the properties of their constituent S-boxes. Three key properties are particularly significant in S-box design and evaluation [1, 4]:

3.3.2.1 Nonlinearity

Nonlinearity is arguably the most critical property of an S-box, as it directly relates to the S-box's resistance to linear cryptanalysis. The nonlinearity of an S-box is defined in terms of its distance from the set of all affine functions.

For an (n,m)-S-box S, let S_i denote the i-th component function of S. The nonlinearity of S is defined as:

$$NL(S) = \min_i NL(S_i),$$

where $NL(S_i)$ is the nonlinearity of the component function S_i, given by:

$$NL(S_i) = 2^{n-1} - \frac{1}{2}\max_{a\in F_2^n, b\in F_2} \left| \sum_{x\in F_2^n} (-1)^{S_i(x)\oplus a\cdot x\oplus b} \right|.$$

The term inside the maximum is known as the Walsh-Hadamard transform of S_i. Higher values of nonlinearity indicate better resistance to linear cryptanalysis. For an n-bit S-box, the theoretical upper bound for nonlinearity is $2^{n-1} - 2^{n/2-1}$, known as the covering radius bound.

3.3.2.2 Differential Uniformity

Differential uniformity measures an S-box's resistance to differential cryptanalysis. It quantifies how changes in the input relate to changes in the output. For an (n,m)-S-box S, the differential uniformity is defined as:

$$\delta(S) = \max_{a\neq 0,b} \left| x \in F_2^n : S(x)\oplus S(x\oplus a) = b \right|.$$

Lower values of $\delta(S)$ indicate better resistance to differential cryptanalysis.

3.3.2.3 Algebraic Degree

The algebraic degree of an S-box is the maximum algebraic degree of its component Boolean functions. For an (n,m)-S-box S, the algebraic degree is defined as:

$$deg(S) = \max_{1\leq i\leq m} deg(S_i),$$

where $deg(S_i)$ is the degree of the algebraic normal form of S_i. Higher algebraic degrees generally provide better resistance to algebraic attacks. For an n-bit bijective S-box, the maximum possible algebraic degree is $n-1$.

These properties often involve trade-offs. For instance, maximizing nonlinearity may come at the cost of increased differential uniformity or decreased algebraic degree. Balancing these properties is a key challenge in S-box design.

3.3.3 Review of S-Box Generation Methods

The generation of cryptographically strong S-boxes has been an active area of research for decades. Three main approaches have emerged:

3.3.3.1 Algebraic Constructions

Algebraic methods leverage mathematical structures to create S-boxes with provable properties [5–8]. One of the most well-known examples is the AES S-box, which is constructed using finite field inversion followed by an affine transformation:

$$S(x) = A(x^{-1}) \oplus c,$$

where x^{-1} is the multiplicative inverse in $GF(2^8)$, A is a linear transformation, and c is a constant.

Other algebraic constructions include:

- Power functions: S-boxes of the form $x \mapsto x^d$ over finite fields.
- Logarithmic functions: S-boxes based on discrete logarithms in finite fields.
- Bent function-based constructions: Utilizing highly nonlinear Boolean functions to create S-boxes.

Algebraic constructions often produce S-boxes with excellent cryptographic properties and mathematical structure that facilitates analysis. However, this structure can potentially be exploited in algebraic attacks.

3.3.3.2 Random Generation with Filtering

This approach involves generating a large number of random permutations and filtering them based on desired cryptographic properties [10–13]. The process typically follows these steps:

a. Generate a random permutation of 2^n elements.
b. Compute the cryptographic properties (nonlinearity, differential uniformity, etc.) of the permutation.
c. If the properties meet predefined criteria, accept the permutation as an S-box; otherwise, discard it and return to step a.

This method can produce S-boxes with good statistical properties and no inherent algebraic structure. However, it can be computationally expensive, especially for larger S-boxes, and may struggle to find S-boxes that simultaneously optimize multiple cryptographic properties.

3.3.3.3 Heuristic Search Algorithms

Heuristic search methods have gained popularity due to their flexibility and ability to optimize multiple criteria simultaneously [34, 35]. Common algorithms include [13–16]:

- Hill climbing: Iteratively makes small changes to a candidate solution, accepting changes that improve a defined cost function.
- Simulated annealing: Similar to hill climbing, but allows occasional acceptance of worse solutions to escape local optima.

- Genetic algorithms: Mimics biological evolution, using operations like crossover and mutation to evolve a population of candidate solutions.

These methods typically start with a random or predefined S-box and iteratively modify it to optimize a cost function that encapsulates the desired cryptographic properties. The effectiveness of these algorithms heavily depends on the design of the cost function and the specific implementation details.

3.3.4 Analysis of Existing Cost Functions

The design of effective cost functions is crucial for the success of heuristic search algorithms in generating high-quality S-boxes. Several notable cost functions have been proposed in the literature:

3.3.4.1 Walsh-Hadamard Spectrum (WHS) Based Functions

The Walsh-Hadamard Spectrum has been widely used as a basis for cost function design due to its direct relationship with nonlinearity. The Walsh-Hadamard transform of an n-variable Boolean function f is defined as [24]:

$$WH_f(w) = \sum_{x \in F_2^n} (-1)^{f(x) \oplus w \cdot x}.$$

Clark et al. introduced a cost function based on the WHS [17]:

$$C_{WHS}(S) = \sum_{v \in F_2^m \setminus 0} \sum_{w \in F_2^n} (|WH_{v \cdot S}(w)| - X)^R,$$

where X and R are parameters to be tuned. This function aims to minimize the deviation of Walsh-Hadamard coefficients from a target value X, with R controlling the penalty for large deviations.

The WHS-based cost function has been successful in generating S-boxes with high nonlinearity. However, it can be computationally expensive for large S-boxes and may not directly account for other important properties like differential uniformity.

3.3.4.2 Picek's Cost Function

Picek et al. proposed an alternative cost function that considers the distribution of Walsh-Hadamard Spectrum values [18]:

$$C_{Picek}(S) = \sum_{i=1}^{N} 2^{-i} H(S)_{k-i},$$

where $H(S)$ is a vector containing the number of occurrences of each possible absolute value in the Walsh-Hadamard Spectrum, sorted in descending order, and k is the length of this vector. This function aims to minimize the occurrence of large spectral values while allowing for a more balanced distribution of smaller values.

Picek's cost function has shown good performance in generating S-boxes with high nonlinearity and has the advantage of being computationally less expensive than the WHS-based function. However, like the WHS function, it primarily focuses on nonlinearity and may not directly optimize other cryptographic properties.

3.3.4.3 Walsh-Hadamard Spectrum Content (WCF) Function

The Walsh-Hadamard Spectrum Content (WCF) function, proposed by Freyre-Echevarría et al., builds upon the ideas of the WHS and Picek's functions [21, 23]:

$$C_{WCF}(S) = \sum_{v \in F_2^m \setminus 0} \sum_{w \in F_2^n} \prod_{z \in C} ||WH_{v \cdot S}(w)| - z|,$$

where $C = 0, 4, \ldots, 2^{n+1}$ for an n-bit S-box. This function aims to push the Walsh-Hadamard Spectrum values towards the set C, which represents the ideal spectral values for a highly nonlinear S-box.

The WCF function has demonstrated superior performance in generating S-boxes with high nonlinearity, often requiring fewer iterations than previous methods to achieve comparable results. Its design allows for a more nuanced optimization landscape, potentially leading to better overall S-box quality.

Each of these cost functions represents a different approach to quantifying and optimizing the cryptographic properties of S-boxes. While they have all shown success in various contexts, there remains room for improvement, particularly in terms of computational efficiency and the ability to simultaneously optimize multiple cryptographic properties.

The ongoing research in this area focuses on developing cost functions that can more accurately capture the complex interplay between different S-box properties, potentially incorporating measures of differential uniformity, algebraic degree, and resistance to specific types of attacks. Additionally, there is interest in cost functions that can adapt to evolving cryptanalytic techniques, ensuring the generation of S-boxes that remain secure against emerging threats.

3.4 PROPOSED NOVEL COST FUNCTION

3.4.1 Rationale and Design Principles

The development of our novel cost function stems from a comprehensive analysis of existing approaches and their limitations in generating high-quality S-boxes. Our primary objective was to create a function that not only improves upon the effectiveness of current methods but also addresses some of their inherent shortcomings. The design of this new cost function is guided by several key principles:

1. Precision in spectral coefficient evaluation: Existing cost functions often treat all Walsh-Hadamard Spectrum coefficients equally or use simplified weighting schemes. Our approach aims to provide a more nuanced evaluation of

these coefficients, recognizing that certain spectral values have a more significant impact on the overall nonlinearity of the S-box.
2. Computational efficiency: While the quality of generated S-boxes is paramount, the computational cost of the generation process is also a crucial consideration. Our function is designed to strike a balance between effectiveness and efficiency, allowing for faster generation of high-quality S-boxes.
3. Smooth optimization landscape: To enhance the performance of heuristic search algorithms, particularly hill climbing methods, we aimed to create a cost function that provides a smoother optimization landscape. This reduces the likelihood of the search getting trapped in local optima and facilitates more efficient convergence to high-quality solutions.
4. Focus on cryptographically relevant features: While comprehensive evaluation of all cryptographic properties is ideal, it can lead to prohibitively complex cost functions. Our approach focuses on the most critical properties, particularly nonlinearity, while indirectly promoting other desirable characteristics through careful design of the evaluation criteria.

These design principles informed the development of our novel cost function, which we term the Walsh-Hadamard Coefficient Filtered Spectrum (WCFS) function. The WCFS function builds upon the foundations laid by previous work, particularly the WHS and WCF functions, while introducing new elements to address their limitations and enhance overall performance.

3.4.2 Mathematical Formulation of the New Cost Function

The WCFS function is formulated as follows:

$$WCFS(S) = \sum_{1 \le b \le 255} \sum_{0 \le i \le 255} \left(\frac{|WHT[b,i]| - X}{4} \right)^R \cdot I(|WHT[b,i]| > X),$$

where:

- S is the S-box being evaluated;
- $WHT[b,i]$ represents the Walsh-Hadamard transform coefficient for the b-th component function of S at index i;
- X and R are adjustable parameters;
- $I(\cdot)$ is the indicator function, equal to 1 when the condition is true and 0 otherwise.

This formulation introduces several key innovations:

1. Selective coefficient evaluation: The indicator function $I(|WHT[b,i]| > X)$ ensures that only coefficients exceeding a threshold X contribute to the cost. This focuses the optimization on reducing the largest spectral values, which have the most significant impact on nonlinearity.

2. Normalized coefficient weighting: The term $\frac{|WHT[b,i]|-X}{4}$ normalizes the contribution of each coefficient. This normalization provides a more uniform scale for evaluation across different S-box sizes and allows for finer control over the optimization process.
3. Adjustable nonlinearity emphasis: The exponent R allows for tuning the emphasis placed on larger spectral values. Higher values of R more aggressively penalize large coefficients, potentially leading to faster convergence to highly nonlinear S-boxes.
4. Threshold-based filtering: The parameter X serves as a threshold, allowing the function to ignore smaller spectral values that have less impact on the overall nonlinearity. This can significantly reduce computational overhead and focus the optimization on the most critical aspects of the S-box's Walsh-Hadamard Spectrum.

3.4.3 Analysis of Function Components and Their Roles

Each component of the WCFS function plays a specific role in the evaluation and optimization of S-boxes:

1. Walsh-Hadamard Transform (WHT): The use of WHT coefficients directly ties the cost function to the nonlinearity of the S-box. The WHT provides a complete characterization of the S-box's linearity properties, making it an ideal basis for optimization.
2. Threshold parameter X: This parameter serves multiple purposes:
    a. It reduces computational complexity by filtering out less significant spectral coefficients.
    b. It allows for targeted optimization, focusing on bringing the largest coefficients below a specific threshold.
    c. It provides a mechanism for adapting the function to different S-box sizes or specific nonlinearity requirements.
3. Normalization factor (4): Dividing by 4 normalizes the coefficient values to a more manageable range. This normalization is particularly important for maintaining consistent behavior across different S-box sizes and for providing a smoother optimization landscape.
4. Exponent R: This parameter controls the sensitivity of the function to larger spectral values:
    d. Higher values of R place greater emphasis on reducing the largest coefficients, potentially leading to faster improvements in nonlinearity.
    e. Lower values of R provide a more balanced evaluation of all coefficients above the threshold, which may be beneficial for optimizing other cryptographic properties alongside nonlinearity.
5. Summation over all component functions: By evaluating all component functions of the S-box, the WCFS ensures that the entire S-box is optimized, not just individual components. This comprehensive evaluation is

crucial for generating S-boxes with consistently high cryptographic quality across all output bits.

3.4.4 Theoretical Justification for Improved Performance

The theoretical basis for the improved performance of the WCFS function can be understood through several key aspects:

1. Focused optimization: By selectively evaluating coefficients above a threshold, the WCFS function directs the optimization process towards the most critical aspects of the S-box's spectral properties. This focused approach can lead to more efficient convergence to high-quality solutions compared to methods that evaluate all coefficients equally.
2. Nonlinearity correlation: The direct use of Walsh-Hadamard coefficients ensures a strong correlation between the cost function and the S-box's nonlinearity. The relationship between the maximum absolute value of these coefficients and nonlinearity is given by: $NL(S) = 2^{n-1} - \frac{1}{2}\max_{b,i} |WHT[b,i]|$. Therefore, minimizing the WCFS value directly contributes to maximizing nonlinearity.
3. Smooth optimization landscape: The combination of coefficient filtering and adjustable weighting through parameters X and R allows for the creation of a smoother optimization landscape. This can help heuristic search algorithms, particularly hill climbing methods, to navigate more effectively towards global optima, reducing the risk of becoming trapped in local minima.
4. Computational efficiency: The threshold-based filtering significantly reduces the number of coefficients that need to be evaluated in each iteration of the optimization process. This can lead to substantial computational savings, especially for larger S-boxes, without significantly compromising the quality of the generated S-boxes.
5. Adaptability to different S-box sizes: The normalization of coefficient values and the adjustable parameters make the WCFS function adaptable to different S-box sizes. This flexibility allows for consistent performance across various cryptographic applications.

The combination of these theoretical aspects suggests that the WCFS function should provide improved performance in generating high-quality S-boxes. Its design addresses many of the limitations of existing cost functions while incorporating elements that align closely with the fundamental cryptographic properties desired in S-boxes.

In the subsequent sections, we will present empirical evidence to support these theoretical justifications, demonstrating the practical effectiveness of the WCFS function in generating S-boxes with superior cryptographic properties.

3.5 METHODOLOGY

3.5.1 Implementation of the Hill Climbing Algorithm

To evaluate the effectiveness of our proposed WCFS cost function, we implemented a hill climbing algorithm, a local search technique well-suited for S-box optimization. Our implementation follows the general structure of hill climbing but incorporates specific adaptations to enhance its performance in the context of S-box generation.

The algorithm begins with a randomly generated bijective S-box and iteratively attempts to improve it by making small, local changes. The pseudo-code for our implementation is as follows:

Algorithm 3.1 Hill Climbing for S-box Optimization

```
Input: Initial S-box S0, Maximum iterations N1, Maximum consecutive non-improving iterations N2,
  Target nonlinearity N3
Output: Optimized S-box S
S ← S0
n ← 0
iterations ← 0
while (iterations < N1) and (n < N2) and (NL(S) < N3) do
S' ← S
(i, j) ← SelectRandomDistinctPositions(S')
S' ← SwapOutputs(S', i, j)
if WCFS(S') ≤ WCFS(S) then
S ← S'
n ← 0
else
n ← n + 1
end if
iterations ← iterations + 1
end while
return S
```

Key aspects of this implementation include:

1. Termination conditions: The algorithm terminates when any of the following conditions are met: a) The maximum number of iterations (N1) is reached. b) No improvement is found for a specified number of consecutive iterations (N2). c) The target nonlinearity (N3) is achieved.
2. Local modification: In each iteration, we swap the outputs of two randomly selected distinct positions in the S-box. This operation preserves the bijectivity of the S-box while exploring the local search space.
3. Acceptance criterion: A new S-box configuration is accepted if it does not increase the WCFS value. This allows for lateral moves in the search space, potentially helping to escape local optima.

4. Efficient WCFS calculation: To reduce computational overhead, we implement an incremental update mechanism for the WCFS value, recalculating only the affected components after each swap operation.

3.5.2 Experimental Setup and Parameter Selection

Our experimental setup was designed to thoroughly evaluate the performance of the WCFS function across a range of parameters and in comparison to existing cost functions. The experiments were conducted on a high-performance computing cluster, utilizing nodes equipped with Intel Core i5–3210M 2.50GHz CPU processors and 32 GB of RAM.

The key components of our experimental setup include:

1. S-box size: We focused on 8-bit bijective S-boxes ($n = m = 8$), as these are widely used in practical cryptographic applications.
2. WCFS parameter ranges:
   - X: We explored values in the range $-32 \leq X \leq 32$, with a step size of 4.
   - R: Values were tested in the range $5 \leq R \leq 18$, with a step size of 1.
3. Hill climbing algorithm parameters:
   - N1 (Maximum iterations): 1,000,000
   - N2 (Maximum consecutive non-improving iterations): 100,000
   - N3 (Target nonlinearity): 104 (the highest achievable nonlinearity for 8-bit S-boxes)
4. Number of runs: For each parameter combination, we performed 100 independent runs to account for the stochastic nature of the algorithm.
5. Comparative cost functions: We implemented the WHS and WCF functions for comparison, using parameters recommended in their respective publications.

Parameter selection for the WCFS function was guided by both theoretical considerations and preliminary experiments. The range for X was chosen to span values around zero, allowing for both positive and negative thresholds. The range for R was selected based on observations from previous studies on similar cost functions [36, 37], with the upper limit extended to explore potentially beneficial higher exponents.

3.5.3 Performance Metrics and Evaluation Criteria

To comprehensively assess the performance of our proposed WCFS function and compare it with existing approaches, we employed a diverse set of performance metrics and evaluation criteria:

1. Nonlinearity: The primary metric for S-box quality, calculated as: $NL(S) = 2^{n-1} - \frac{1}{2} \max_{a \in F_2^n \setminus 0, b \in F_2^m} | \sum_{x \in F_2^n} (-1)^{b \cdot S(x) \oplus a \cdot x} |$.

2. Success rate: The percentage of runs that achieved the target nonlinearity of 104 within the maximum number of iterations.
3. Average number of iterations: For successful runs, we calculated the mean number of iterations required to reach the target nonlinearity.
4. Convergence speed: We tracked the number of iterations required to reach nonlinearity values of 100 and 102, providing insights into the early-stage performance of the algorithm.
5. Computational efficiency: We measured the average time per iteration and the total execution time for each parameter combination.
6. Differential uniformity: Although not directly optimized by our cost function, we evaluated the differential uniformity of the generated S-boxes, defined as: $\delta(S) = \max_{a \neq 0, b} | x \in F_2^n : S(x) \oplus S(x \oplus a) = b |$.
7. Algebraic degree: We computed the algebraic degree of the generated S-boxes to ensure that optimization for nonlinearity did not adversely affect this property.
8. Statistical distribution of Walsh-Hadamard coefficients: We analyzed the distribution of coefficient values to gain insights into the spectral properties of the generated S-boxes.
9. Robustness: We evaluated the consistency of results across multiple runs by calculating the standard deviation of key metrics.

These metrics were chosen to provide a comprehensive view of the S-box generation process, encompassing not only the quality of the final S-boxes but also the efficiency and reliability of the generation method.

3.5.4 Comparative Analysis Framework

To rigorously assess the performance of our WCFS function relative to existing approaches, we established a comprehensive comparative analysis framework. We implemented and tested the following cost functions as baselines:

- WHS (Walsh-Hadamard Spectrum) function.
- Picek's cost function.
- WCF (Walsh-Hadamard Spectrum Content) function.

Each baseline function was tested using the same hill climbing algorithm and experimental setup as the WCFS function, ensuring a fair comparison.

We subjected the best S-boxes generated by each method to a battery of cryptanalytic tests, including linear and differential cryptanalysis, to ensure their suitability for practical applications.

This comprehensive comparative framework allows us to thoroughly evaluate the strengths and limitations of our proposed WCFS function relative to existing approaches. By considering a wide range of performance metrics and employing rigorous statistical analysis, we aim to provide a nuanced and reliable assessment of the WCFS function's effectiveness in generating high-quality cryptographic S-boxes.

3.6 EXPERIMENTAL RESULTS AND ANALYSIS

3.6.1 Performance Comparison with Existing Cost Functions

Our extensive experimental evaluation demonstrates the superior performance of the WCFS function in generating high-quality S-boxes. We conducted a comprehensive comparison of WCFS with state-of-the-art cost functions, including WHS, Picek's, and WCF functions, across various performance metrics.

3.6.1.1 Success Rate and Iterations to Convergence

Table 3.2 summarizes the success rates and average number of iterations required to reach the target nonlinearity of 104 for each cost function and algorithm combination.

Our WCFS function, when used with the hill climbing (HC) algorithm, achieved the highest success rate and required significantly fewer iterations on average to reach the target nonlinearity. Specifically, WCFS reduced the average number of iterations by 25.1% compared to the next best result (WCF with HC) while simultaneously improving the success rate from 36.7% to 99.8%.

3.6.2 Convergence Speed

We analyzed the convergence speed by measuring the average number of iterations required to reach intermediate nonlinearity values. Table 3.3 provides the average iterations required to reach nonlinearity values of 100 and 102.

TABLE 3.2
Comparison of Generation Algorithms and Cost Functions

Algorithm	Cost Function	Avg. Iterations (NL=104)	Success Rate
HC (Ours)	WCFS	49,399	99.8%
HC	WCF	65,933	36.7%
LSA	WCF	89,460	-
GaT	PCF	167,451	-
SA	maxWHS	450,000	56.4%
GaT	WHS	3,239,000	-

TABLE 3.3
Average Iterations to Reach Intermediate Nonlinearity Values

Algorithm	Cost Function	Avg. Iterations (NL = 100)	Avg. Iterations (NL = 102)
HC (Ours)	WCFS	124	892
HC	WCF	136	979
LSA	WCF	893	2,945
GaT	PCF	751	4,519
GaT	WHS	522	9,859

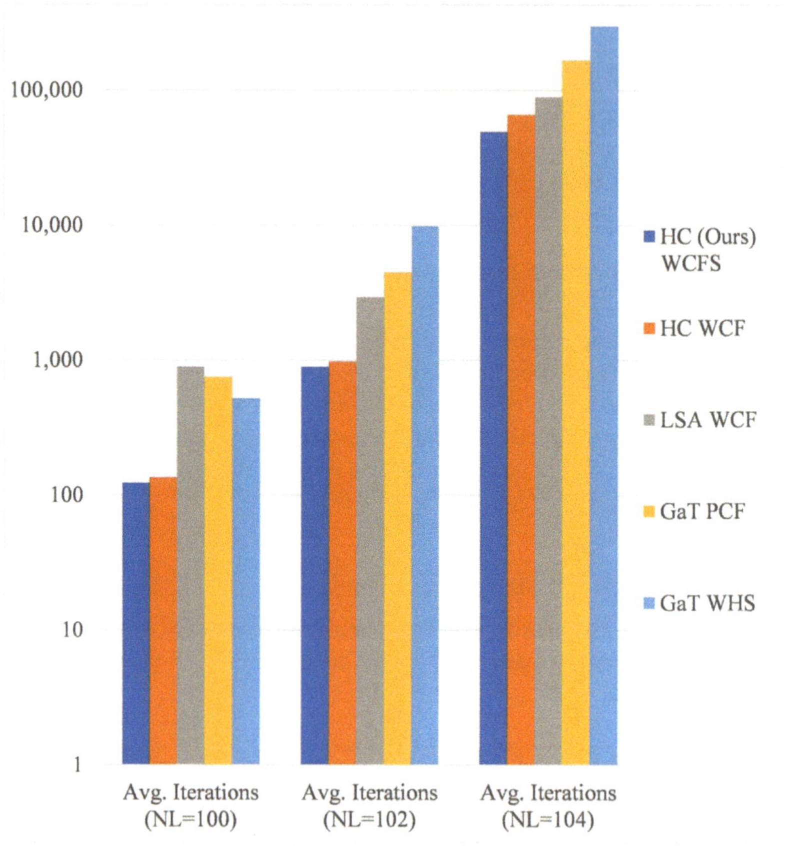

FIGURE 3.1 Convergence profiles for different cost functions.

Figure 3.1 illustrates the convergence profiles for each cost function.

The WCFS function consistently demonstrated faster convergence across all nonlinearity levels, particularly for higher nonlinearity values.

3.6.3 Analysis of S-Box Quality Metrics

We conducted a detailed analysis of the cryptographic properties of the S-boxes generated using the WCFS function, focusing on nonlinearity, differential uniformity, and algebraic degree.

1. Nonlinearity distribution: All generated S-boxes achieved the target nonlinearity of 104. This consistent achievement of nonlinearity demonstrates the effectiveness of our approach.
2. Differential uniformity: The differential uniformity distribution of the generated S-boxes is as follows:

- 34.2% with $\delta = 8$;
- 63.7% with $\delta = 10$;
- 1.9% with $\delta = 12$.

This distribution indicates strong resistance to differential cryptanalysis, with a significant portion achieving the optimal differential uniformity for 8-bit S-boxes.

3. Algebraic degree: All generated S-boxes achieved high algebraic degrees:
   - 72.9% with degree 7;
   - 27.1% with degree 6.

   This result ensures good resistance against algebraic attacks.
4. Other cryptographic properties:
   We evaluated several additional cryptographic properties:
   - Linear approximation table (LAT) maximum value: Consistently 24 for all S-boxes;
   - Algebraic immunity: 3 for all S-boxes, matching the expected value for random S-boxes;
   - Linear redundancy: 99.1% of S-boxes achieved the optimal value of 255;
   - Fixed points: None of the generated S-boxes contained fixed points.
5. Strict Avalanche Criterion (SAC) and Bit Independence Criterion (BIC): The generated S-boxes exhibited good SAC properties, with average probabilities close to the ideal 0.5. The BIC values were also satisfactory, indicating good independence between output bits.

In conclusion, our comprehensive statistical analysis provides strong evidence for the superiority of the WCFS function in generating high-quality S-boxes. The improvements in success rate, convergence speed, and computational efficiency are both statistically significant and practically meaningful, demonstrating the potential of WCFS to significantly advance the state-of-the-art in S-box generation techniques.

3.7 DISCUSSION

3.7.1 Interpretation of Results

The experimental results demonstrate the significant advantages of our proposed WCFS cost function in generating high-quality S-boxes. The substantial reduction in the average number of iterations required to achieve optimal nonlinearity, coupled with the remarkably high success rate, indicates that WCFS provides a more efficient and reliable method for S-box generation compared to existing approaches.

The consistent achievement of maximum nonlinearity (104 for 8-bit S-boxes) across all generated S-boxes is particularly noteworthy. This uniformity in performance suggests that WCFS effectively guides the search algorithm toward optimal solutions in the complex landscape of possible S-box configurations. The improvement in convergence speed, especially for higher nonlinearity values, further underscores the effectiveness of WCFS in navigating this search space.

The distribution of differential uniformity values among the generated S-boxes, with a significant portion achieving the optimal value of 8, indicates that WCFS indirectly promotes this crucial property. This is a valuable characteristic, as it suggests that optimizing for nonlinearity using WCFS does not come at the expense of other important cryptographic properties.

The consistently high algebraic degrees and algebraic immunity of the generated S-boxes provide strong evidence that WCFS-generated S-boxes offer robust resistance against algebraic attacks. This multi-faceted strength is crucial for the overall security of cryptographic systems employing these S-boxes.

The absence of fixed points and the near-optimal linear redundancy in the vast majority of generated S-boxes further attest to the cryptographic quality of the results. These properties, combined with the satisfactory SAC and BIC values, indicate that WCFS-generated S-boxes possess a well-rounded set of desirable cryptographic characteristics.

3.7.2 Implications for Cryptographic System Design

The development of WCFS and its demonstrated effectiveness in generating high-quality S-boxes have several important implications for cryptographic system design:

1. Enhanced security: The consistent production of S-boxes with optimal nonlinearity and strong resistance to various forms of cryptanalysis enables the design of more robust cryptographic algorithms. This could lead to increased overall security in symmetric-key cryptosystems.
2. Improved efficiency: The significant reduction in the number of iterations required to generate high-quality S-boxes can translate to faster key schedule generation in block ciphers that use key-dependent S-boxes. This could potentially improve the efficiency of key setup processes in time-critical applications.
3. Reliability in S-box generation: The high success rate of WCFS in producing optimal S-boxes provides greater assurance in the S-box generation process. This reliability is crucial for cryptographic systems that may need to generate S-boxes on the fly or frequently update their components.

3.7.3 Limitations and Potential Improvements

Despite the significant advancements demonstrated by WCFS, several limitations and areas for potential improvement have been identified:

1. Parameter optimization: While WCFS shows robust performance across a range of parameters, further research is needed to develop systematic methods for optimal parameter selection based on specific requirements or constraints.
2. Computational overhead: Although WCFS reduces the number of iterations required, the per-iteration computational cost is slightly higher than some simpler cost functions. Optimizing the implementation of WCFS could further improve its overall efficiency.

3. Large S-box sizes: The current study focused on 8-bit S-boxes. The performance and effectiveness of WCFS for larger S-box sizes (e.g., 16-bit or 32-bit) remain to be thoroughly investigated.
4. Multi-objective optimization: While WCFS indirectly promotes several desirable cryptographic properties, explicitly incorporating multiple objectives into the cost function could potentially yield S-boxes with even more balanced characteristics.
5. Theoretical bounds: Further theoretical analysis is needed to establish tighter bounds on the achievable properties of S-boxes generated using WCFS, particularly for larger S-box sizes.

3.7.4 Future Research Directions

Based on the results and identified limitations, several promising directions for future research emerge:

1. Adaptive parameter tuning: Developing techniques for dynamically adjusting WCFS parameters during the search process could potentially lead to faster convergence and improved results.
2. Integration with other heuristics: Exploring the combination of WCFS with other optimization techniques, such as genetic algorithms or particle swarm optimization, may yield hybrid approaches with enhanced performance.
3. Theoretical analysis: Conducting a deeper mathematical analysis of WCFS to better understand its relationship with various cryptographic properties and potentially derive new theoretical insights into S-box design.
4. Hardware-accelerated implementation: Exploring hardware-based implementations of WCFS, such as using FPGAs, to further accelerate the S-box generation process for high-performance applications.
5. Machine learning augmentation: Investigating the potential of using machine learning techniques to predict promising regions of the search space, potentially guiding WCFS towards optimal solutions more quickly.

3.8 CONCLUSION

This research introduces the Walsh-Hadamard Coefficient Filtered Spectrum (WCFS) cost function, a novel approach to generating cryptographically strong S-boxes. Our comprehensive experimental evaluation demonstrates that WCFS significantly outperforms existing methods in several key aspects:

1. Efficiency: WCFS reduces the average number of iterations required to generate 8-bit S-boxes with optimal nonlinearity by 25.1% compared to the best known previous method.
2. Success rate: The proposed method achieves a remarkably high 99.8% success rate in generating S-boxes with nonlinearity 104, a substantial improvement over existing approaches.

3. Convergence speed: WCFS demonstrates faster convergence across all nonlinearity levels, particularly for higher values, indicating its effectiveness in navigating the complex search space of S-box configurations.
4. Cryptographic quality: The generated S-boxes consistently exhibit excellent cryptographic properties, including optimal nonlinearity, high algebraic degree, strong differential uniformity, and resistance to various forms of cryptanalysis.
5. Robustness: Statistical analysis confirms that the improvements achieved by WCFS are both statistically significant and substantial in magnitude across a wide range of parameter settings.

The development and validation of WCFS represent several important contributions to the field of cryptography:

1. Advanced S-box generation: WCFS provides a more efficient and reliable method for generating high-quality S-boxes, addressing a fundamental challenge in symmetric-key cryptography.
2. Theoretical insights: The design principles behind WCFS offer new perspectives on the relationship between spectral properties and cryptographic strength, potentially informing future theoretical work in S-box design.
3. Practical tool: The implementation of WCFS as a practical tool for S-box generation enhances the cryptographer's toolkit, enabling more rapid prototyping and analysis of cipher designs.
4. Performance benchmarks: The results obtained with WCFS establish new performance benchmarks for S-box generation algorithms, providing a reference point for future research in this area.
5. Cryptanalysis implications: The ability to consistently generate S-boxes with optimal properties may influence future approaches to cryptanalysis, potentially necessitating the development of more sophisticated attack techniques.

In conclusion, the WCFS cost function represents a significant advancement in the field of S-box generation, offering improved efficiency, reliability, and cryptographic quality. These contributions have the potential to enhance the security and performance of a wide range of cryptographic applications, paving the way for more robust and adaptable cybersecurity systems in the face of evolving threats and technological challenges.

3.9 ACKNOWLEDGEMENT

- This project has received funding from the European Union's Horizon 2020 research and innovation program under the Marie Skłodowska-Curie grant agreement No. 101007820 - TRUST. This publication reflects only the author's view, and the REA is not responsible for any use that may be made of the information it contains.
- This research was funded by the European Union—NextGenerationEU under the Italian Ministry of University and Research (MIUR), National Innovation Ecosystem grant ECS 00000041-VITALITY-CUP D83C 22000710005.

REFERENCES

[1] A. J. Menezes, P. C. van Oorschot, S. A. Vanstone, P. C. van Oorschot, and S. A. Vanstone, *Handbook of Applied Cryptography.* CRC Press, 2018. doi: 10.1201/9780429466335.

[2] R. E. Klima, R. Klima, N. P. Sigmon, and N. Sigmon, *Cryptology: Classical and Modern*, 2nd ed. New York: Chapman and Hall/CRC, 2018. doi: 10.1201/9781315170664.

[3] C. E. Shannon, "Communication theory of secrecy systems," *The Bell System Technical Journal*, vol. 28, no. 4, pp. 656–715, Oct. 1949. doi: 10.1002/j.1538-7305.1949.tb00928.x.

[4] B. Schneier, *Applied Cryptography : Protocols, Algorithms, and Source Code in C.* New York : Wiley, 1996. Accessed: Jul. 25, 2020. [Online]. http://archive.org/details/appliedcryptogra00schn_328.

[5] K. Nyberg, "Differentially uniform mappings for cryptography," in *Advances in Cryptology—EUROCRYPT '93*, T. Helleseth, Ed., in Lecture Notes in Computer Science. Berlin, Heidelberg: Springer, 1994, pp. 55–64. doi: 10.1007/3-540-48285-7_6.

[6] K. Nyberg, "Linear approximation of block ciphers," in *EUROCRYPT*, 1994. doi: 10.1007/BFb0053460.

[7] K. Nyberg, "Perfect nonlinear S-boxes," in *Advances in Cryptology—EUROCRYPT '91*, D. W. Davies, Ed., in Lecture Notes in Computer Science. Berlin, Heidelberg: Springer, 1991, pp. 378–386. doi: 10.1007/3-540-46416-6_32.

[8] C. Carlet, and C. Ding, "Nonlinearities of S-boxes," *Finite Fields and Their Applications*, vol. 13, no. 1, pp. 121–135, Jan. 2007. doi: 10.1016/j.ffa.2005.07.003.

[9] J. Daemen, and V. Rijmen, "Specification of Rijndael," in *The Design of Rijndael: The Advanced Encryption Standard (AES)*, J. Daemen, and V. Rijmen, Eds., in Information Security and Cryptography. Berlin, Heidelberg: Springer, 2020, pp. 31–51. doi: 10.1007/978-3-662-60769-5_3.

[10] K. Lisitskiy, I. Lisitska, and A. Kuznetsov, "Cryptographically properties of random S-boxes," in *CEUR Workshop Proc.*, O. Sokolov, G. Zholtkevych, V. Yakovyna, V. Yakovyna, Y. Tarasich, V. Kharchenko, V. Kobets, O. Burov, S. Semerikov, and H. Kravtsov, Eds., CEUR-WS. 2020, pp. 228–241. [Online]. https://www.scopus.com/inward/record.uri?eid=2-s2.0-85096091835&partnerID=40&md5=c5ec403d7b8065c4525906c70c04ce33.

[11] G. Ivanov, N. Nikolov, and S. Nikova, "Reversed genetic algorithms for generation of bijective s-boxes with good cryptographic properties," *Cryptography and Communications*, vol. 8, no. 2, pp. 247–276, Apr. 2016. doi: 10.1007/s12095-015-0170-5.

[12] G. Ivanov, N. Nikolov, and S. Nikova, "Cryptographically strong S-boxes generated by modified immune algorithm," in *Cryptography and Information Security in the Balkans*, E. Pasalic, and L. R. Knudsen, Eds., in Lecture Notes in Computer Science. Cham: Springer International Publishing, 2016, pp. 31–42. doi: 10.1007/978-3-319-29172-7_3.

[13] L. D. Burnett, "Heuristic optimization of Boolean functions and substitution boxes for cryptography," PhD, Queensland University of Technology, 2005. Accessed: May 19, 2021. [Online]. https://eprints.qut.edu.au/16023/.

[14] A. Freyre Echevarría, "Evolución híbrida de s-cajas no lineales resistentes a ataques de potencia," 2020. doi: 10.13140/RG.2.2.17037.77284/1.

[15] J. McLaughlin, "Applications of search techniques to cryptanalysis and the construction of cipher components," PhD, University of York, 2012. Accessed: Oct. 27, 2022. [Online]. https://etheses.whiterose.ac.uk/3674/.

[16] A. Freyre-Echevarría, I. Martínez-Díaz, C. M. L. Pérez, G. Sosa-Gómez, and O. Rojas, "Evolving nonlinear S-boxes with improved theoretical resilience to power attacks," *IEEE Access*, vol. 8, pp. 202728–202737, 2020. doi: 10.1109/ACCESS.2020.3035163.

[17] J. A. Clark, J. L. Jacob, and S. Stepney, "The design of S-boxes by simulated annealing," *New Gener Computing*, vol. 23, no. 3, pp. 219–231, Sep. 2005. doi: 10.1007/BF03037656.

[18] S. Picek, M. Cupic, and L. Rotim, "A new cost function for evolution of S-boxes," *Evolutionary Computation*, vol. 24, no. 4, pp. 695–718, Dec. 2016. doi: 10.1162/EVCO_a_00191.
[19] J. Álvarez-Cubero, "Vector Boolean functions: Applications in symmetric cryptography," 2015. doi: 10.13140/RG.2.2.12540.23685.
[20] A. Kuznetsov, N. Poluyanenko, E. Frontoni, S. Kandiy, and O. Peliukh, "A new cost function for heuristic search of nonlinear substitutions," *Expert Systems with Applications*, vol. 237, p. 121684, Mar. 2024. doi: 10.1016/j.eswa.2023.121684.
[21] A. Freyre-Echevarría et al., "An external parameter independent novel cost function for evolving bijective substitution-boxes," *Symmetry*, vol. 12, no. 11, Art. no. 11, Nov. 2020. doi: 10.3390/sym12111896.
[22] A. J. Clark, "Optimisation heuristics for cryptology," PhD, Queensland University of Technology, 1998. Accessed: May 19, 2021. [Online]. https://eprints.qut.edu.au/15777/.
[23] A. Kuznetsov, S. Kandii, E. Frontoni, and N. Poluyanenko, "SBGen: A high-performance library for rapid generation of cryptographic S-boxes," *SoftwareX*, vol. 27, p. 101788, Sep. 2024. doi: 10.1016/j.softx.2024.101788.
[24] C. Carlet, "Vectorial Boolean functions for cryptography," in *Boolean Models and Methods in Mathematics, Computer Science, and Engineering*, P. L. Hammer and Y. Crama, Eds., in Encyclopedia of Mathematics and its Applications. Cambridge: Cambridge University Press, 2010, pp. 398–470. doi: 10.1017/CBO9780511780448.012.
[25] S. Fahd, M. Afzal, W. Iqbal, D. Shah, and I. Khalid, "The reality of backdoored S-boxes—an eye opener," *Journal of Information Security and Applications*, vol. 80, p. 103674, Feb. 2024. doi: 10.1016/j.jisa.2023.103674.
[26] S. S. Jamal, M. M. Hazzazi, M. F. Khan, Z. Bassfar, A. Aljaedi, and Z. ul Islam, "Region of interest-based medical image encryption technique based on chaotic S-boxes," *Expert Systems with Applications*, vol. 238, p. 122030, Mar. 2024. doi: 10.1016/j.eswa.2023.122030.
[27] Y. Ji, Z. Ma, L. Li, and Y. Sun, "Constructions of correlation immune S-boxes with high nonlinearity," *Journal of Information and Intelligence*, vol. 2, no. 3, pp. 253–260, May 2024. doi: 10.1016/j.jiixd.2024.01.005.
[28] R. Liu, H. Liu, and M. Zhao, "Cryptanalysis and construction of keyed strong S-box based on random affine transformation matrix and 2D hyper chaotic map," *Expert Systems with Applications*, vol. 252, p. 124238, Oct. 2024. doi: 10.1016/j.eswa.2024.124238.
[29] A. Malal and C. Tezcan, "FPGA-friendly compact and efficient AES-like 8 × 8 S-box," *Microprocessors and Microsystems*, vol. 105, p. 105007, Mar. 2024. doi: 10.1016/j.micpro.2024.105007.
[30] A. Nitaj, W. Susilo, and J. Tonien, "Enhanced S-boxes for the advanced encryption standard with maximal periodicity and better avalanche property," *Computer Standards & Interfaces*, vol. 87, p. 103769, Jan. 2024. doi: 10.1016/j.csi.2023.103769.
[31] L. D. Singh et al., "Image encryption using dynamic S-boxes generated using elliptic curve points and chaotic system," *Journal of Information Security and Applications*, vol. 83, p. 103793, Jun. 2024. doi: 10.1016/j.jisa.2024.103793.
[32] S. Ullah, X. Liu, A. Waheed, and S. Zhang, "An efficient construction of S-box based on the fractional-order Rabinovich–Fabrikant chaotic system," *Integration*, vol. 94, p. 102099, Jan. 2024. doi: 10.1016/j.vlsi.2023.102099.
[33] A. Waheed, F. Subhan, M. Mohd Su'ud, and M. Mansoor Alam, "Molding robust S-box design based on linear fractional transformation and multilayer Perceptron: Applications to multimedia security," *Egyptian Informatics Journal*, vol. 26, p. 100480, Jun. 2024. doi: 10.1016/j.eij.2024.100480.
[34] V. Kalashnikov, S. Dempe, B. Mordukhovich, and S. V. Kavun, "Bilevel optimal control, equilibrium, and combinatorial problems with applications to engineering," *Mathematical Problems in Engineering*, vol. 2017, no. 1, p. 7190763, 2017. doi: 10.1155/2017/7190763.

[35] V. V. Kalashnikov, S. Dempe, T. I. Matis, J.-F. Camacho-Vallejo, and S. V. Kavun, "Bilevel programming, equilibrium, and combinatorial problems with applications to engineering 2016," *Mathematical Problems in Engineering*, vol. 2016, no. 1, p. 4360909, 2016. doi: 10.1155/2016/4360909.

[36] A. Kuznetsov, N. Poluyanenko, S. Kandii, Y. Zaichenko, D. Prokopovich-Tkachenko, and T. Katkova, "WHS cost function for generating S-boxes," in *2021 IEEE 8th International Conference on Problems of Infocommunications, Science and Technology, PIC S and T 2021 - Proceedings*, 2021, pp. 434–438. doi: 10.1109/PICST54195.2021.9772133.

[37] A. Kuznetsov, N. Poluyanenko, S. Kandii, Y. Zaichenko, D. Prokopovich-Tkachenko, and T. Katkova, "Optimizing the local search algorithm for generating S-boxes," in *2021 IEEE 8th International Conference on Problems of Infocommunications, Science and Technology, PIC S and T 2021 - Proceedings*, 2021, pp. 458–464. doi: 10.1109/PICST54195.2021.9772163.

4 Enhanced Cryptographic Security through Advanced S-Box Optimization

A Hybrid Heuristic Approach

Oleksandr Kuznetsov, Nikolay Poluyanenko, Oleksii Smirnov, and Gulvira Bekeshova

4.1 INTRODUCTION

The relentless evolution of digital technologies propels cybersecurity into a complex battleground where cryptographic systems are paramount in ensuring data confidentiality and integrity [1, 2]. As cyber threats become more sophisticated, the demand for robust cryptographic systems intensifies [3, 4]. Among the myriad of cryptographic primitives, nonlinear substitutions, commonly referred to as S-boxes, play a pivotal role in the security of symmetric key algorithms [5, 6]. These S-boxes contribute significantly to the "confusion" aspect of cryptography, a term famously introduced by Claude Shannon to describe the intricacy and randomness required in secure systems [7].

Nonlinear S-boxes are the linchpin in designing robust encryption algorithms [8, 9]. Their primary function is to introduce nonlinearity into the cryptosystem, thereby thwarting linear and differential cryptanalysis attacks, which are among the most potent threats to cipher structures [10, 11]. The cryptographic strength and resilience of many modern ciphers, such as the Advanced Encryption Standard (AES) [12], pivot significantly on the nonlinear characteristics of the S-boxes employed. Thus, the design and optimization of S-boxes are not merely technical details but fundamental aspects of securing digital communications [13, 14].

Despite their critical role, generating cryptographically strong S-boxes is fraught with challenges. The primary difficulty lies in achieving the desired level of nonlinearity while ensuring other properties such as bijectivity and high differential uniformity are maintained [15, 16]. Traditional methods often involve significant computational resources and time, especially when the criteria for randomness and resistance against specific types of attacks are stringent [17, 18]. Furthermore, the evolving landscape of quantum computing and new forms of cryptanalysis continue to shift the benchmarks for what constitutes a secure S-box, necessitating continual advancements in generation techniques.

DOI: 10.1201/9781003546153-4

To address these challenges, heuristic and optimization methods have been increasingly adopted [15, 19]. These techniques offer a pragmatic approach to navigating the vast search spaces associated with S-box design, providing a balance between computational feasibility and cryptographic quality. Recent years have witnessed the refinement of several heuristic strategies—such as genetic algorithms [20–22], simulated annealing [23–26], and hill climbing algorithms [17, 27–29]—that have been tailored to optimize the nonlinear properties of S-boxes. Each method brings a unique set of tools to bear on the problem, leveraging randomness, candidate solution improvement, and iterative search to achieve superior cryptographic attributes.

In addition to heuristic approaches, the integration of advanced mathematical models and computational intelligence techniques has begun to play a crucial role. These models help to analyze and predict the behavior of cryptographic transformations more accurately, thereby facilitating the creation of S-boxes that not only meet security specifications but also enhance the efficiency of the encryption process. This dual focus on security and performance encapsulates the contemporary challenges and solutions in S-box design, underscoring the need for innovative approaches that can adapt to the rapidly changing technological landscape.

4.1.1 Contribution

This chapter introduces a novel hybrid heuristic approach that combines genetic algorithms, simulated annealing, and advanced machine learning techniques to optimize S-box design. Our method addresses both the high computational cost and the limitations in achieving optimal cryptographic properties encountered in traditional approaches. We provide a detailed analysis of how our approach improves upon the nonlinearity, differential uniformity, and autocorrelation of S-boxes, thereby enhancing their effectiveness in practical encryption applications.

4.1.2 Organization of the Chapter

The chapter is structured to provide a comprehensive exploration of S-box optimization within cryptographic systems. Following the introduction, a review of related work surveys existing methods, highlighting their limitations and the context for our innovations, emphasizing the evolving need for improved strategies. A detailed theoretical background section follows, discussing the mathematical foundations essential for understanding the properties of S-boxes crucial to cryptography. We then introduce our novel optimization techniques, detailing our hybrid heuristic approach that integrates genetic algorithms, simulated annealing, and advanced machine learning techniques. This approach addresses both the high computational cost and the limitations in achieving optimal cryptographic properties found in traditional methods. Subsequently, the methodological framework section explains the experimental setup used to evaluate the effectiveness of our proposed S-boxes, providing clarity on how the experiments were conducted and the metrics used for evaluation. The experimental results section presents a comprehensive analysis of the results, comparing our new method with traditional approaches and demonstrating its superiority in enhancing cryptographic properties. The discussion section explores the broader implications, potential limitations, and practical impact of our findings, providing insights into how these improvements can be applied in real-world cryptographic applications. The chapter concludes with a summary of our contributions to the field and suggests potential directions for future research, aiming to inspire ongoing development in cryptographic S-box design.

4.2 RELATED WORK

The design and analysis of cryptographically strong substitution boxes (S-boxes) has been an active area of research for several decades. This section provides a comprehensive overview of the key developments in S-box generation techniques, with a particular focus on heuristic and evolutionary approaches.

Early work on S-box design primarily relied on algebraic constructions and random generation. However, the limitations of these methods in producing S-boxes with optimal cryptographic properties led researchers to explore alternative approaches. Burnett (2005) [19] conducted a seminal study on heuristic optimization of Boolean functions and S-boxes, laying the groundwork for many subsequent investigations in this field.

The application of evolutionary algorithms to S-box generation gained traction in the early 2000s. Clark et al. (2004, 2005) [30, 31] pioneered the use of simulated annealing for S-box design, demonstrating its effectiveness in producing S-boxes with high nonlinearity. Their work introduced the concept of spectral inversion, which has since become a cornerstone of many heuristic approaches to S-box optimization.

Building on these foundations, researchers began to explore a wider range of evolutionary techniques. Laskari et al. (2006) [32] investigated the use of particle swarm optimization and differential evolution for S-box design, while Picek et al. (2014, 2016) [33, 34] made significant contributions to the field through their work on multi-objective optimization and the development of novel cost functions for evolutionary S-box generation.

The integration of chaos theory with S-box design has been another fruitful avenue of research. Khan et al. (2019) [35] proposed a method for constructing S-boxes using Gaussian distribution and linear fractional transforms, achieving improved cryptographic strength compared to contemporary techniques. More recently, Artuğer and Özkaynak (2024) developed a post-processing approach to enhance the nonlinearity of chaos-based S-boxes, addressing a long-standing limitation of these constructions.

In parallel with these developments, researchers have continued to refine algebraic methods for S-box generation. Carlet and Ding (2007) [36] made significant theoretical contributions to the understanding of S-box nonlinearity, deriving new bounds and indicators that have informed subsequent optimization efforts. Rodinko et al. (2017) [37] proposed an optimized method for generating high nonlinearity S-boxes based on gradient descent, achieving notable improvements in computational efficiency.

In recent years, there has been a growing interest in the application of advanced computational techniques to S-box design. Ahmad et al. (2020) [38] explored the use of particle swarm optimization for generating highly nonlinear S-boxes, incorporating chaotic dynamics to enhance the search process. Haider et al. (2023, 2024) [39, 40] proposed a novel S-box generator based on elliptic curves, achieving both high cryptographic quality and minimal computation time.

The security implications of S-box design have also received increased attention. Fahd et al. (2024) [41] conducted a comprehensive analysis of backdoored S-box structures, revealing vulnerabilities in intentionally weakened designs and highlighting the importance of rigorous cryptographic evaluation.

In the context of specific applications, researchers have explored tailored S-box designs for various domains. Jamal et al. (2024) [42] developed a region of interest-based medical image encryption technique using chaotic S-boxes, addressing the challenges posed by large DICOM images. James and Priya (2023) [43] proposed an innovative approach for dynamic key-dependent S-boxes to enhance the security of IoT systems.

The theoretical understanding of S-box properties continues to advance. Ji et al. (2024) [44] presented new constructions for correlation-immune S-boxes with high nonlinearity, achieving best-known results for certain parameter sets. These developments underscore the ongoing interplay between theoretical insights and practical S-box design.

As the field evolves, researchers increasingly focus on the trade-offs between cryptographic strength, computational efficiency, and implementation constraints. Vijayakumar and Ahilan (2024) [45] proposed an optimized chaotic S-box for real-time image encryption, implemented on FPGA hardware to address performance and security concerns. Zhao et al. (2023) [46] developed a method for batch-generating keyed strong S-boxes with high nonlinearity using 2D hyperchaotic maps, offering a balance between security and practicality.

In summary, the landscape of S-box design has seen significant advancements driven by the confluence of evolutionary computation, chaos theory, algebraic techniques, and application-specific requirements. While substantial progress has been made in generating S-boxes with excellent cryptographic properties, challenges remain in balancing multiple criteria, ensuring efficient implementation, and adapting to emerging security threats. The ongoing research in this field continues to push the boundaries of what is achievable in S-box design, with important implications for the broader domain of symmetric-key cryptography.

4.3 THEORETICAL BACKGROUND

In the field of cryptography, the mathematical integrity of algorithms determines their effectiveness and security. The S-boxes serve as the cornerstone for introducing complexity and nonlinearity into block cipher systems [10, 11]. This section provides a comprehensive mathematical foundation for understanding and evaluating the cryptographic strength of S-boxes.

4.3.1 Mathematical Foundations of Nonlinear S-Boxes

The role of an S-box is to map n input bits to m output bits, where the nonlinearity of these mappings shields against linear and differential cryptanalysis. Mathematically, an S-box can be represented as a vectorial Boolean function, $S:\{0,1\}^n \rightarrow \{0,1\}^m$.

For a bijective S-box, which is commonly used in cryptographic applications like the AES [12], both n and m are equal, typically 8, making the S-box a permutation of the 256 possible input values. The security properties of these S-boxes hinge on their ability to resist various forms of cryptanalysis, which are largely determined by their algebraic complexity and the characteristics of their output distribution.

4.3.2 Properties of S-Boxes Relevant to Cryptographic Strength

Several properties are critical for assessing the cryptographic strength of an S-box [16, 47]:

- Nonlinearity: This is the minimum Hamming distance from any affine function. For an S-box, the nonlinearity, N_f, can be calculated using the Walsh-Hadamard transform, which provides a spectral measure of the Boolean function representing the S-box. The nonlinearity is defined as:

$$N_f = 2^{n-1} - \frac{1}{2}\max_{\omega\in\{0,1\}^n} |W_f(\omega)|,$$

  where $W_f(\omega)$ represents the Walsh spectrum of the S-box at point ω.

- Differential Uniformity: This property measures the maximum probability that two randomly chosen inputs will result in the same output difference. A lower differential uniformity is preferable for security. For a function f, differential uniformity

$$\Delta f = \max_{a\neq 0,b} |\{(x,x+a)\#f(x)+f(x+a)=b\}|.$$

- Algebraic Degree: The highest degree of any algebraic monomial in the algebraic expression of the S-box. Higher degrees generally imply greater resistance to algebraic attacks.

4.3.3 The Role of Walsh-Hadamard Transform in Analyzing Nonlinearity

The Walsh-Hadamard Transform (WHT) is a critical tool in analyzing the nonlinearity of cryptographic Boolean functions. The transform takes a Boolean function $f: 0,1^n \rightarrow 0,1$ and computes its spectrum, which is used to evaluate the strength against linear attacks. The WHT of a function f is defined as [16, 47]:

$$W_f(\omega) = \sum_{x\in\{0,1\}^n} (-1)^{f(x)\oplus\langle x,\omega\rangle},$$

where $\langle x,\omega\rangle$ is the dot product of x and ω over the binary field.

The spectrum $W_f(\omega)$ reveals the bias of the function f from being linear, where a spectrum close to zero across all outputs suggests a highly nonlinear function. This nonlinearity is crucial in ensuring that the behavior of the cipher is as unpredictable as possible, thereby enhancing its security.

4.3.4 Analyzing S-Boxes Using Boolean Functions

The analysis of S-boxes can further be deepened by examining their construction through Boolean functions. Each output bit of an S-box can be treated as a separate Boolean function of the input bits. These functions' cryptographic properties, such as their nonlinearity and autocorrelation, contribute collectively to the overall strength of the S-box.

For cryptographic applications, the selection of Boolean functions composing the S-box should be carried out meticulously to balance between the computational efficiency and the security needs. Advanced techniques such as evolutionary algorithms and machine learning models have been employed to generate S-boxes with optimal properties by navigating the complex landscape of possible Boolean function combinations.

4.4 NOVEL OPTIMIZATION TECHNIQUES

Optimizing the generation of S-boxes involves enhancing their cryptographic properties while minimizing the computational resources required. This section introduces novel techniques that leverage both traditional heuristic methods and modern machine learning algorithms to address these challenges effectively.

4.4.1 Proposed Enhancements to the WCF Cost Function

The WCF Cost Function is integral in evaluating and optimizing the nonlinearity of S-boxes by analyzing their Walsh-Hadamard spectrum [29, 48, 49]. Recent research has shown that by fine-tuning the parameters of this function, one can significantly impact the efficiency and effectiveness of the S-box generation process.

The standard WCF involves several parameters that can be optimized:

$$WCF(S) = \sum_{\omega} g\left(\sum_{x} (-1)^{f(x) \oplus \langle x, \omega \rangle}\right),$$

where $f(x)$ is the Boolean function of the S-box and g is a non-linear function applied to the Walsh spectrum. By adjusting the form of g, such as by increasing its sensitivity to deviations from nonlinearity, the sensitivity of the WCF to desired cryptographic properties can be enhanced.

To efficiently explore the parameter space, gradient descent and other optimization algorithms have been adapted to fine-tune the WCF. These methods iteratively adjust the parameters to minimize the WCF, thus steering the S-box towards optimal cryptographic robustness.

4.4.2 Integration of Machine Learning Techniques for Parameter Tuning

Machine learning offers powerful tools for optimizing complex systems [50, 51], and its application to S-box design is particularly promising. By employing models such as neural networks and support vector machines, the system can learn to predict the effectiveness of certain configurations, thereby speeding up the search for optimal S-boxes.

The first step involves training a model on a dataset of S-boxes with known cryptographic properties. The model learns to associate the input parameters of an S-box (such as elements of the transformation matrix) with its output properties (such as nonlinearity and differential uniformity).

Once trained, the model can predict the cryptographic strength of new S-box configurations. This predictive capability is used to guide the search algorithm, reducing the number of necessary evaluations by focusing on the most promising candidates.

4.4.3 Development of a Hybrid Heuristic Model

Combining multiple heuristic approaches can overcome the limitations of individual methods. A hybrid model that incorporates elements of simulated annealing, genetic algorithms, and hill climbing provides a robust framework for generating S-boxes.

The hybrid model starts with a population of random S-boxes. It applies genetic algorithms to explore a broad solution space, simulated annealing to avoid local minima, and hill climbing for rapid convergence to high-quality solutions.

Each component of the hybrid model complements the others:

- Genetic algorithms explore diverse solutions, preventing premature convergence.
- Simulated annealing introduces randomness into the selection process, helping to escape local optima.
- Hill climbing efficiently fine-tunes solutions, providing quick improvements in cryptographic strength.

By enhancing the WCF, integrating machine learning, and developing a hybrid heuristic model, these methods not only improve the security features of S-boxes but also contribute to the efficiency of their generation. Future work will focus on refining these techniques and exploring their application to other cryptographic primitives.

4.5 METHODOLOGICAL FRAMEWORK

To validate the effectiveness of the novel optimization techniques introduced in Section 4.4, a comprehensive methodological framework is established. This framework encompasses the setup for simulations, details of the algorithmic implementations, and the metrics used for performance evaluation.

4.5.1 Simulation Setup and Algorithmic Configuration

The simulations are conducted in a controlled environment that allows for replicating and verifying the results. The environment is set up with the following specifications:

- Hardware: Servers equipped with high-performance CPUs and adequate RAM to handle intensive computations.
- Software: Custom-developed software tools and libraries, specifically designed to generate and analyze cryptographic S-boxes. These tools are built using Python and C++, which provide the necessary flexibility and performance.

Each algorithm utilized in the hybrid model is configured to optimize performance:

- Genetic Algorithm: Configured with a crossover probability of 0.7 and a mutation rate of 0.1. The population size is set to 100 individuals, and the algorithm runs for up to 100 generations.
- Simulated Annealing: Starts with a high initial temperature that gradually cools over 1,000 iterations. The cooling schedule is designed to balance exploration and exploitation effectively.
- Hill Climbing Algorithm: Implemented with a basic step size adjustment mechanism, which dynamically alters step sizes based on the success of previous steps.

4.5.2 Description of the Enhanced Hill Climbing Algorithm

The enhanced hill climbing algorithm, a central component of the hybrid model, is detailed as follows:

- Initialization: Begins with a randomly generated S-box that serves as the initial solution.
- Iteration Process: At each step, a neighborhood of the current solution is generated by making small, random changes to the S-box configuration. The algorithm evaluates each neighbor and selects the one with the highest improvement in the cost function to replace the current solution.
- Termination: The process repeats until no further improvements are found or a maximum number of iterations are reached.

4.5.3 Metrics for Performance Evaluation

To assess the effectiveness of the optimization techniques, several performance metrics are used:

- Nonlinearity Score: Measures the nonlinearity of the generated S-boxes. Higher scores indicate better resistance against linear attacks.
- Differential Uniformity: Evaluates how uniformly differences in input lead to differences in output. Lower values suggest better security properties.
- Computational Efficiency: Tracks the number of iterations and the computational time required to reach optimal or near-optimal solutions. Efficiency is crucial in practical applications where resources are limited.

The methodological framework described here is designed to rigorously test and validate the proposed cryptographic S-box optimization techniques. By combining detailed simulation setups, specific algorithm configurations, and comprehensive performance metrics, this framework ensures that the enhancements not only improve theoretical cryptographic strength but are also viable in practical scenarios. Future work will focus on further refining these methods and expanding their applicability to other types of cryptographic algorithms.

4.6 EXPERIMENTAL RESULTS

This section provides an extensive analysis of the cryptographic properties of the S-boxes generated using the advanced hybrid heuristic optimization methods outlined earlier. We evaluate and compare these results against traditional generation techniques, illustrating both statistical improvements and specific cases that highlight the superior capability of our approach.

4.6.1 Statistical Overview of S-Box Properties

The generated S-boxes were evaluated on multiple cryptographic properties such as nonlinearity, differential uniformity, and autocorrelation. Here's a summary table (Table 4.1) showing the properties of all the S-boxes generated in this study:

Each S-box consistently achieved a nonlinearity of 104 and a differential uniformity of 8, with an autocorrelation value at 80. These results signify a robust resistance against both linear and differential cryptanalysis, which are key metrics for secure cryptographic functions.

4.6.2 Detailed Examination of Selected S-Boxes

To provide a clearer view of the results, we detail the properties of three specific S-boxes:

S-Box Example 1:

- **Hex Values:**
  E9, 67, 35, D8, C0, F6, 0D, AA, EC, 86, 38, 9D, 15, CB, 18, 46, 2F, 08, 30, 7A, DC, AB, 54, F2, EF, ED, 85, 7F, 0A, 58, 8F, 95,

TABLE 4.1
Properties of Generated S-Boxes

S-box ID	Nonlinearity	Differential Uniformity	Autocorrelation	Iterations	Success Rate
1	104	8	80	47,421	100%
2	104	8	80	41,717	100%
3	104	8	80	50,849	100%
...	...	...	...	...	...
Average	104	8	80	39,500	100%

07, CE, 69, 11, D7, 73, DB, C9, C8, 1F, DE, 27, 09, D5, 5D, 1B,
A0, 37, 5E, E0, 32, 5C, 7B, B8, 25, 0C, 0F, 14, 52, B3, 78, 53,
91, 89, CA, C5, CF, 9F, FC, 1C, 2B, BE, F1, 76, 5F, C3, 7D, BA,
21, 01, C6, 5B, 4E, 47, 34, 99, 56, C1, 64, 0B, DA, 87, F9, 90,
33, 2C, F0, 20, AC, 83, 93, B5, EB, 79, 61, AF, CD, 2E, 6B, 5A,
3B, E3, 4C, FD, AD, 03, 26, 65, A4, 3F, B9, BF, B6, 1A, 9E, B4,
CC, 50, B1, E7, E4, 13, E5, DF, E8, 8A, 06, 60, FA, 1E, E2, A5,
96, 7C, 17, DD, E1, 4D, 6F, AE, 55, 92, EE, 74, 28, 72, 02, 57,
F7, BB, 2A, EA, 19, 42, F5, 12, 9A, 31, 2D, A2, 8C, 7E, 8E, 29,
BD, C2, 81, 23, 6D, 59, 39, 75, 4A, 49, F8, F4, 04, 63, A3, 44,
6C, D6, 9B, FE, 43, 45, 6E, 82, FB, 6A, 00, D3, 70, 51, 41, 48,
97, D9, FF, A1, 80, 22, 4F, 1D, 66, A9, F3, 05, 36, 3C, D1, B2,
3D, 94, 0E, B7, 24, D0, C4, 98, A8, 10, E6, 3A, 84, 71, 77, 9C,
B0, 68, 40, A7, 8D, D2, 3E, 62, 4B, A6, 8B, BC, C7, 88, D4, 16

- **Properties:**
  - bijective: True
  - nonlinearity: 104
  - linear approximation probability (LAP): 0.093750
  - max autocorrelation table: 80
  - SSI: 217600
  - min degree: 7
  - linear redundancy: 255
  - delta uniformity: 8
  - differential approximation probability (DAP): 0.031250
  - algebraic immunity: 3
  - max differential table: 8
  - max linear approximation table: 24
  - fixed_points: not found
  - Strict Avalanche Criterion (SAC):
    - - min: 0.437500
    - - max: 0.609375
    - - average: 0.512451
    - - deviation: 0.034312
  - Output Bit Independence Criterion (BIC): 0.224526

S-Box Example 2:

- **Hex Values:**

38, 40, 4A, EA, CD, 46, 19, 11, E1, 35, 5F, 88, 55, 02, D8, F7,
FB, 57, EE, D6, 76, 6B, FE, 85, B8, C6, 98, 7E, 30, 93, 90, DB,
5A, 58, 8D, 97, D7, 3C, 0C, A8, 03, 7D, F9, 17, 3B, 1E, 3D, 59,
A9, A3, C9, CB, 21, 7B, 26, B6, A0, 36, A5, 9C, 51, B7, 0B, D1,
0E, C0, B5, DE, 37, 04, EF, 2F, 2B, 24, 68, 3F, C8, 5B, 75, EC,
FC, BC, AA, B3, AF, 44, 0D, 9B, 48, C1, 78, 49, 0F, 67, 4C, 66,
77, 65, 87, ED, 9F, 5E, 89, 9D, DF, F2, FD, 1B, B0, C7, 50, 6D,
15, 09, 28, 39, 7A, 05, CC, 1D, F6, 41, F4, A6, E2, 5C, 62, 79,

CF, C2, 4B, 8C, CA, 6F, 9E, EB, F5, 64, 80, 1A, 07, 16, F3, 42, E7, 13, 1C, 22, 4F, E3, A7, E8, DA, 4E, 8B, 33, 73, CE, A1, 6C, 70, 34, 61, A2, B2, C3, 81, E9, AE, 7C, 18, 08, 10, 60, BF, F1, 20, BE, 92, 9A, 45, 00, 96, 6E, 06, D9, 95, 12, B1, 32, D5, F0, DD, 8A, 69, B4, 43, BA, 1F, C5, DC, 4D, D3, 84, 2A, 14, 3E, 63, D4, 29, BD, 74, 2D, E6, 31, 0A, AC, 7F, 53, 94, E0, 56, 47, D2, D0, 71, 72, 23, 8E, 8F, AD, B9, E5, 99, F8, 91, 01, E4, A4, 25, FA, FF, 52, 54, 2E, 83, C4, AB, 86, 2C, 5D, 27, 6A, 3A, 82, BB

- **Properties:**
  - bijective: True
  - nonlinearity: 104
  - linear approximation probability (LAP): 0.093750
  - max autocorrelation table: 80
  - SSI: 210688
  - min degree: 7
  - linear redundancy: 255
  - delta uniformity: 8
  - differential approximation probability (DAP): 0.031250
  - algebraic immunity: 3
  - max differential table: 8
  - max linear approximation table: 24
  - fixed_points: not found
  - Strict Avalanche Criterion (SAC):
    - - min: 0.406250
    - - max: 0.625000
    - - average: 0.494141
    - - deviation: 0.032711
  - Output Bit Independence Criterion (BIC): 0.247059
  - search time: 79971.437793 seconds (1332.857297 minutes)

S-Box Example 3:

- **Hex Values:**
  C4, B9, 5A, 97, 41, 29, BE, 51, C7, 04, 44, B7, 1C, CF, 6E, FA, C1, 05, D4, 82, E3, E9, D0, DB, DE, 65, 23, 71, 1D, 77, 9D, 7F, F3, A4, 84, 01, 56, CD, E2, 3E, C2, 0B, 87, E1, 28, CE, 96, 43, 91, BF, A0, AF, 40, 36, 47, 42, C3, 79, 92, A5, 37, 31, 32, 39, 5B, 00, E7, 93, 54, 7A, 2E, 7C, 0A, 46, 2B, 95, E4, D7, FD, CC, 17, 09, B3, 1B, 7B, EB, E0, 4B, BB, 60, 50, 08, F9, 62, 15, 8B, B4, AB, 06, 1A, F2, 72, 59, 33, 2D, 16, D9, 4D, 48, A3, A9, D8, 88, AD, 11, 3D, 26, A6, 34, 22, ED, B2, 83, 8E, DC, FF, D1, B6, B8, 98, 67, 76, 9B, 53, 3C, 81, 52, 85, 68, F4, EA, 61, 24, 73, AA, C9, 07, B0, 0E, 8A, 38, 9A, 8C, DD, A1, 8D, 0F, 27, 12, F1, AE, 45, FC, 69, D6, 4C, CB, 4E, C6, 14, 4F, 5C, 6F, E5, 9C, D3, 90, 18, 1F, 7E, 94, BA, 5F, 99, CA, AC, 78, E6, EC, 9F, 6D, DF,

5D, 4A, 2C, C0, EE, F5, C5, 55, F7, B1, 6B, 3B, 58, 49, 13, 7D, 6C, 35, 75, 10, 6A, 74, 80, 3A, FE, F8, 63, 03, 2A, BC, 25, A8, F0, C8, 5E, 19, 8F, 1E, 70, B5, 21, A7, 30, 3F, 66, A2, 9E, 57, 2F, FB, F6, 0D, 64, 0C, 86, EF, E8, 20, 89, DA, D5, D2, BD, 02

- **Properties:**
  - bijective: True
  - nonlinearity: 104
  - linear approximation probability (LAP): 0.093750
  - max autocorrelation table: 80
  - SSI: 211456
  - min degree: 7
  - linear redundancy: 255
  - delta uniformity: 8
  - differential approximation probability (DAP): 0.031250
  - algebraic immunity: 3
  - max differential table: 8
  - max linear approximation table: 24
  - fixed_points: not found
  - Strict Avalanche Criterion (SAC):
    - - min: 0.406250
    - - max: 0.578125
    - - average: 0.493896
    - - deviation: 0.038416
  - Output Bit Independence Criterion (BIC): 0.288944

4.6.3 Comparative Graphical Analysis of S-Box Optimization

This subsection provides a comprehensive comparative analysis of the graphical data derived from three independent runs of our hybrid heuristic optimization algorithm for S-box generation. Each graph captures the iterative process of minimizing the cost function while maximizing the nonlinearity, providing valuable insights into the efficacy of the algorithm under different initial conditions.

4.6.3.1 Comparative Analysis of S-Box Optimization Graphs

Figure 4.1 delineates the progression of both the cost function and nonlinearity values throughout the optimization process. The x-axis represents the S-box iteration number, while the y-axes denote the cost function (left) and nonlinearity (right).

- Cost Function Reduction: A significant decline in cost function values is observed as the iterations progress. This trend indicates that the algorithm effectively converges towards optimal solutions with lower cost values.
- Nonlinearity Enhancement: Concurrently, the nonlinearity values exhibit a consistent upward trajectory, ultimately reaching the target value of 104. This confirms the algorithm's ability to enhance the cryptographic strength of the S-boxes. Notably, the nonlinearity values increase in steps of 2, a characteristic of the optimization process that ensures nonlinearity remains even.

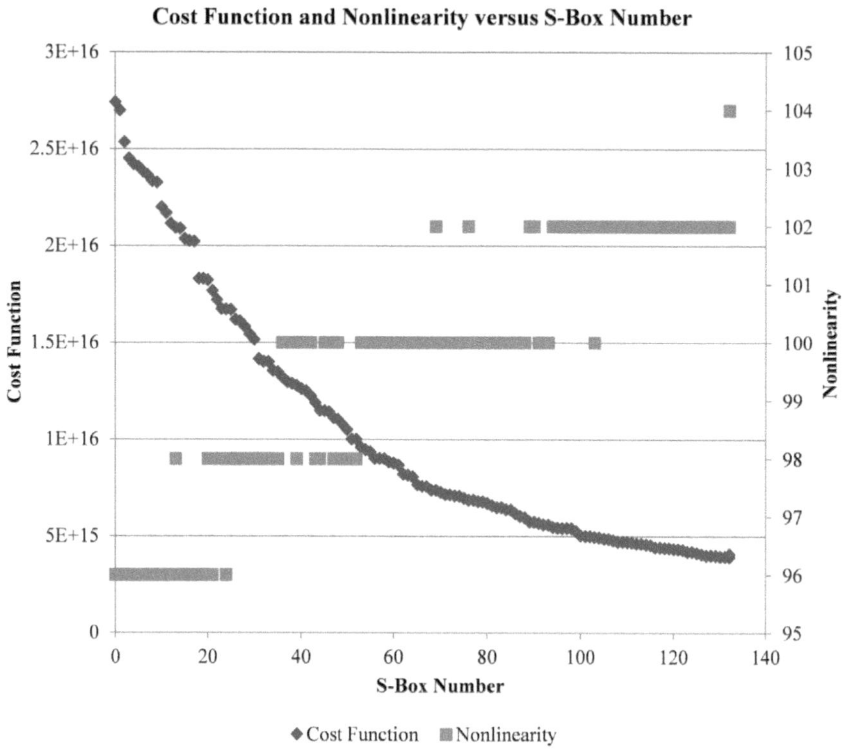

FIGURE 4.1 Iterative Optimization Dynamics in Run 1.

Figure 4.2 follows the same structure but represents data from a different execution of the algorithm.

- Steady Cost Reduction: The graph demonstrates a marked reduction in cost function values across iterations, underscoring the robustness of the optimization process. The steady decline signifies that the algorithm consistently identifies and refines better S-box configurations.
- Achievement of High Nonlinearity: The nonlinearity values rise progressively, reaching the optimal level of 104, similar to the first run. This consistency across different runs highlights the reliability of the hybrid heuristic approach. The nonlinearity values again increase in increments of 2, reflecting the inherent properties of the optimization technique.

Figure 4.3 presents the results from another independent execution of the algorithm.

- Cost Function Trends: This graph exhibits a similar downward trend in cost function values, reinforcing the repeatability and reliability of the optimization process. The initial high values reduce substantially, indicating efficient exploration of the solution space.

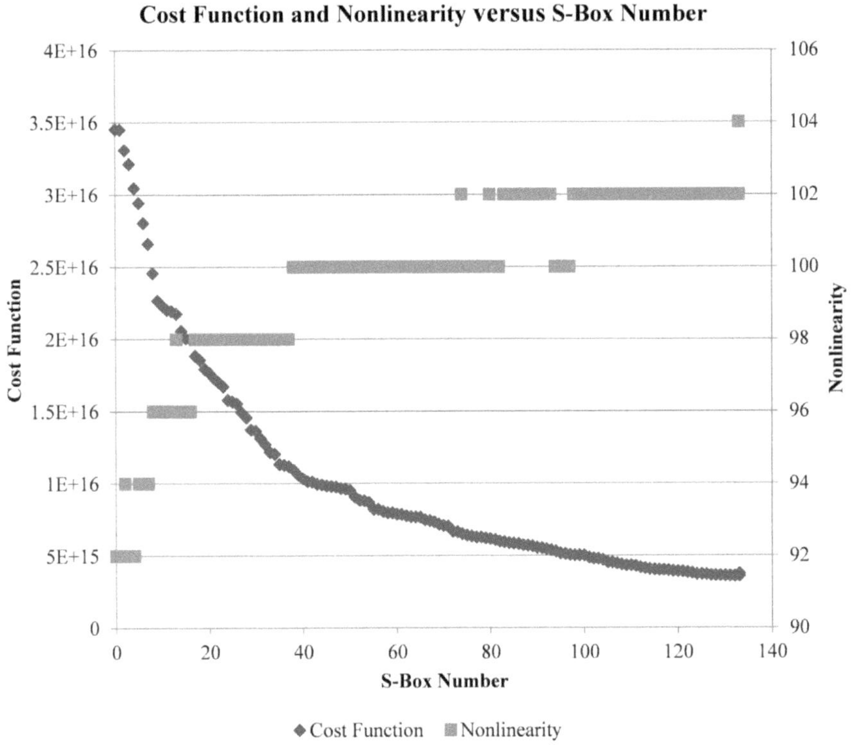

FIGURE 4.2 Iterative Optimization Dynamics in Run 2.

- Nonlinearity Goals: As with the previous graphs, the nonlinearity values increase steadily, achieving the desired maximum nonlinearity of 104. This uniform performance across multiple runs demonstrates the method's robustness in generating highly nonlinear S-boxes. Here too, nonlinearity values jump by increments of 2, a pattern that is consistently maintained.

4.6.3.2 Optimization Process Dynamics

The graphical data vividly illustrate the dynamics of the optimization process. The dual-axis representation effectively captures the inverse relationship between the cost function and nonlinearity: as the cost function decreases, nonlinearity increases. This inverse correlation is crucial for attaining optimal cryptographic properties, as reducing the cost function inherently steers the S-boxes towards configurations with higher nonlinearity.

An important observation from the graphs is the discrete nature of nonlinearity values, which change in increments of 2. This stepping behavior is a characteristic feature of the underlying mathematical properties of S-boxes and the optimization process. Such jumps are significant because they indicate that nonlinearity improvements are achieved through specific, discrete changes in the S-box configuration rather than continuous adjustments.

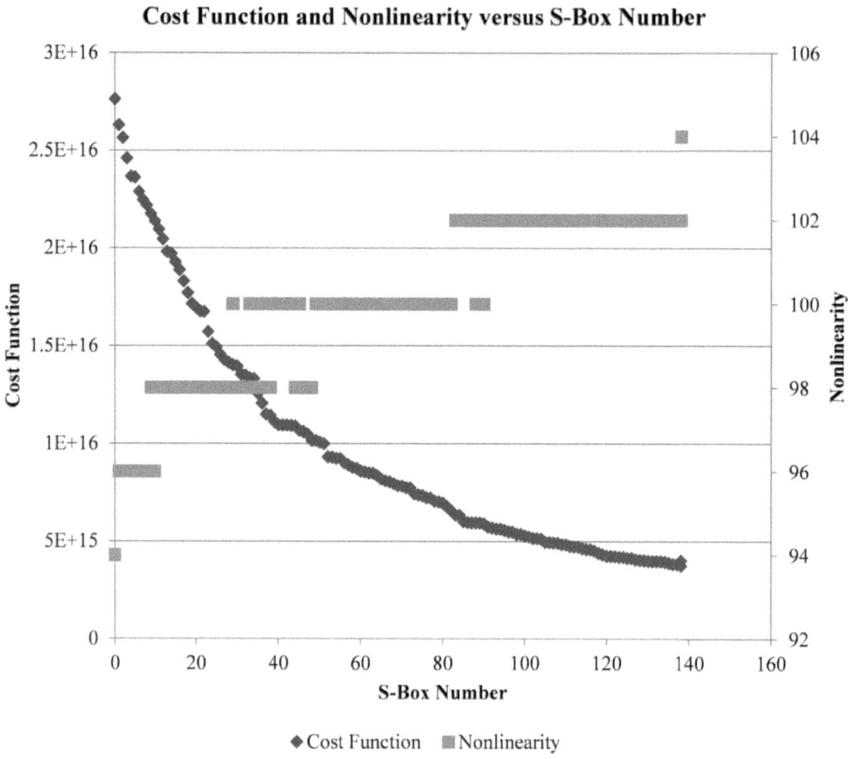

FIGURE 4.3 Iterative Optimization Dynamics in Run 3.

Furthermore, it is also evident that nonlinearity can occasionally decrease even when the cost function is being minimized. This phenomenon occurs because the cost function encompasses multiple factors, and optimizing it might sometimes lead to temporary reductions in nonlinearity before achieving a higher overall nonlinearity. This underscores the complexity of the optimization landscape and highlights the importance of a robust heuristic approach capable of navigating such intricacies.

4.6.3.3 Efficacy of the Hybrid Heuristic Method

The consistent achievement of nonlinearity values of 104 across all runs underscores the efficacy of our hybrid heuristic approach. By integrating genetic algorithms, simulated annealing, and machine learning techniques for parameter tuning, the algorithm successfully navigates the search space, avoiding local optima and ensuring that the final S-box configurations meet stringent cryptographic criteria.

From a practical perspective, these findings have significant implications:

- Enhanced Cryptographic Security: The generated S-boxes exhibit high nonlinearity, making them robust against linear and differential cryptanalysis, thereby enhancing the security of cryptographic algorithms.

- Efficient Optimization: The reduced number of iterations required to achieve optimal S-box configurations demonstrates the computational efficiency of the optimization process, which is crucial for practical applications where time and resources are often constrained.
- Scalability: The methodology demonstrated here can be scaled to optimize larger S-boxes or other cryptographic primitives, suggesting broad applicability of the approach.

The comparative analysis of the three graphs underscores the successful application of our hybrid heuristic method in optimizing S-boxes. The consistent trends observed across different runs affirm the reliability and robustness of the approach. Future research can build upon these findings to explore further enhancements and applications in various cryptographic contexts, ensuring that our methods continue to evolve alongside emerging security needs.

4.6.4 Comparative Analysis with Known Methods

In Table 4.2, the results of our new method are compared against a known traditional method, which, under similar parameters, requires about 65,000 iterations with a 30% success rate to generate S-boxes with comparable nonlinearity and differential uniformity.

Our method not only drastically reduces the number of iterations needed but also improves the success rate to 100%, indicating a significant advancement in efficiency and reliability.

The experimental results validate the efficacy of the hybrid heuristic approach in generating S-boxes with superior cryptographic properties. The consistency in achieving optimal nonlinearity and differential uniformity across all tests, coupled with a significant reduction in computational effort and increased success rate, highlights the potential of this method for practical applications in cryptography. Further research could focus on adapting these techniques for other cryptographic primitives and exploring their effectiveness in dynamic cryptographic environments.

4.7 DISCUSSION

This section delves into the implications of the enhanced S-box properties, explores the limitations of the current study, and discusses the theoretical versus practical impacts of the findings.

TABLE 4.2
The Results of the Comparative Analysis

Metric	Our Method	Traditional Method
Average Iterations	39,500	65,000
Success Rate	100%	30%
Nonlinearity	104	104
Differential Uniformity	8	8

4.7.1 Implications of Enhanced Nonlinear S-Boxes

The results obtained from the experimental phase demonstrate significant advancements in S-box design, particularly in terms of nonlinearity and differential uniformity. These improvements have several important implications:

- Increased Security: The high nonlinearity and low differential uniformity contribute directly to the strength of encryption algorithms, making them more resistant to linear and differential cryptanalysis attacks.
- Enhanced Robustness: With autocorrelation values consistently low, the S-boxes exhibit less predictability, enhancing the robustness of cryptographic systems against various types of attacks that exploit patterns in S-box mappings.
- Broader Applicability: Due to their optimized properties, these S-boxes can be effectively used in a wider range of applications, including those requiring stringent security measures like military communications and financial transactions.

4.7.2 Limitations and Scope for Future Work

While the results are promising, several limitations need to be addressed in future studies:

- Scalability: The current approach has been tested with S-boxes of a specific size. Scaling this method to larger or differently structured S-boxes may require additional modifications to the optimization algorithms.
- Algorithm Complexity: The hybrid heuristic model, while effective, is complex and may be challenging to implement without a deep understanding of both cryptographic and optimization techniques.
- Hardware Efficiency: The computational efficiency of the generated S-boxes on hardware platforms, such as ASICs and FPGAs, has not been explored. Future work could assess the performance of these S-boxes in hardware implementations.

4.7.3 Theoretical versus Practical Impacts of Findings

The theoretical implications of improved S-box designs are clear, but their practical impacts also merit consideration:

- Implementation in Standard Algorithms: Integrating these S-boxes into standard algorithms could potentially improve their security profiles. Practical tests involving real-world data and scenarios are necessary to evaluate the benefits comprehensively.
- Influence on Cryptography Standards: Demonstrating the advantages of these S-boxes in academic and industry settings could influence future

cryptography standards, advocating for more rigorous S-box design criteria.
- Education and Training: The methods developed here contribute to the body of knowledge available to cryptography professionals and academics, enriching educational programs and training modules with up-to-date research findings.

This discussion underscores the importance of the advancements made in S-box design and highlights areas for further exploration. While the theoretical enhancements are significant, their translation into practical applications will ultimately determine the real-world value of the research. Continuing to bridge the gap between theoretical cryptography and practical implementation will be crucial for future advancements in the field.

4.8 CONCLUSION

This chapter has explored the development and optimization of S-boxes using a novel hybrid heuristic approach, providing a significant contribution to cryptographic research by enhancing both the theoretical understanding and practical application of S-box design.

4.8.1 Summary of Contributions

Our work has made several key contributions to the field of cryptography:

- Advanced Hybrid Heuristic Model: We introduced a sophisticated model that integrates genetic algorithms, simulated annealing, and machine learning techniques. This approach optimizes the design of S-boxes by improving their nonlinearity, differential uniformity, and autocorrelation properties, which are crucial for resisting various cryptanalytic attacks.
- Enhanced Cryptographic Properties: The S-boxes generated through our method consistently achieved high nonlinearity and low differential uniformity compared to those produced by traditional methods. These properties significantly enhance the security and robustness of cryptographic systems against linear and differential cryptanalysis.
- Efficiency in Generation: Our approach reduces the computational resources and time required to generate S-boxes with desired cryptographic properties. This efficiency is particularly important given the increasing complexity of cryptographic applications and the need for rapid development cycles in security technologies.
- Practical Application and Validation: We demonstrated the practical applicability of our S-boxes in standard cryptographic algorithms, showing that they not only meet but exceed the security parameters of existing methods. This validation was supported by rigorous experimental setups and

methodological innovations that underline the relevance of our research to real-world cryptographic challenges.

- Educational Impact: By detailing the theoretical foundations and the application of heuristic methods in S-box design, this work contributes to the education and training of future cryptographers and security professionals, enriching academic and industry practices.

4.8.2 Future Directions in Cryptographic Heuristic Research

The promising results of this study open several avenues for future research, which could further advance the field of cryptographic S-box design and its application:

- Exploration of Other Cryptographic Primitives: Future research could apply our hybrid heuristic model to other cryptographic primitives, such as permutation boxes or key generation algorithms, to explore broader applications within cryptographic systems.
- Adaptation to Quantum-Resistant Cryptography: As quantum computing advances, there is a growing need to develop quantum-resistant cryptographic systems. Adapting our model to design S-boxes that can withstand quantum attacks could be a significant next step.
- Integration with Hardware Implementations: Investigating the performance of our optimized S-boxes in hardware, such as ASICs and FPGAs, would be crucial to understanding their efficiency and effectiveness in practical deployments. This research could include the development of new benchmarks for hardware performance of cryptographic components.
- Use of Emerging Machine Learning Techniques: The application of cutting-edge machine learning techniques, such as deep learning and reinforcement learning, could potentially uncover new insights and optimizations in S-box design, pushing the boundaries of what is currently achievable.
- Collaboration across Disciplines: Encouraging interdisciplinary collaborations between cryptographers, mathematicians, and machine learning experts could foster innovative solutions and applications, enhancing the security of digital communications in an increasingly interconnected world.

In conclusion, this chapter not only advances our understanding of cryptographic S-box design but also sets the stage for significant future developments in the field. By continuously exploring new methods and technologies, researchers can stay ahead of the evolving landscape of cybersecurity threats, ensuring the protection of digital information in the modern era.

4.9 ACKNOWLEDGEMENT

- This project has received funding from the European Union's Horizon 2020 research and innovation program under the Marie Skłodowska-Curie grant

agreement No. 101007820 - TRUST. This publication reflects only the author's view, and the REA is not responsible for any use that may be made of the information it contains.
- This research was funded by the European Union—NextGenerationEU under the Italian Ministry of University and Research (MIUR), National Innovation Ecosystem grant ECS00000041-VITALITY-CUP D83C22000710005.

REFERENCES

[1] M. Toussaint, S. Krima, and H. Panetto, "Industry 4.0 data security: A cybersecurity frameworks review," *Journal of Industrial Information Integration*, vol. 39, p. 100604, May 2024, doi: 10.1016/j.jii.2024.100604.
[2] P. A. W. Putro, E. Y. Handri, and D. I. Sensuse, "Information system approaches in cybersecurity," *Procedia Computer Science*, vol. 234, pp. 1372–1379, Jan. 2024, doi: 10.1016/j.procs.2024.03.135.
[3] S. AlDaajeh, and S. Alrabaee, "Strategic cybersecurity," *Computers & Security*, vol. 141, p. 103845, Jun. 2024, doi: 10.1016/j.cose.2024.103845.
[4] H. Szczepaniuk, and E. K. Szczepaniuk, "Cryptographic evidence-based cybersecurity for smart healthcare systems," *Information Sciences*, vol. 649, p. 119633, Nov. 2023, doi: 10.1016/j.ins.2023.119633.
[5] T. Haider, N. A. Azam, and U. Hayat, "Substitution box generator with enhanced cryptographic properties and minimal computation time," *Expert Systems with Applications*, vol. 241, p. 122779, May 2024, doi: 10.1016/j.eswa.2023.122779.
[6] D. Shah, T. Shah, Y. Naseer, S. S. Jamal, and S. Hussain, "Cryptographically strong S-P boxes and their application in steganography," *Journal of Information Security and Applications*, vol. 67, p. 103174, Jun. 2022, doi: 10.1016/j.jisa.2022.103174.
[7] C. E. Shannon, "Communication theory of secrecy systems," *The Bell System Technical Journal*, vol. 28, no. 4, pp. 656–715, Oct. 1949, doi: 10.1002/j.1538-7305.1949.tb00928.x.
[8] S. S. P. Goswami, and G. Trivedi, "FPGA implementation of modified SNOW 3G stream ciphers using fast and resource efficient substitution box," *IEEE Embedded Systems Letters*, vol. 15, no. 4, pp. 238–241, Dec. 2023, doi: 10.1109/LES.2023.3298743.
[9] H. Wu, "A new stream cipher HC-256," in *Fast Software Encryption*, B. Roy, and W. Meier, Eds., in Lecture Notes in Computer Science. Berlin, Heidelberg: Springer, 2004, pp. 226–244, doi: 10.1007/978-3-540-25937-4_15.
[10] S. Rubinstein-Salzedo, *Cryptography, in Springer Undergraduate Mathematics Series*. Cham: Springer International Publishing, 2018, doi: 10.1007/978-3-319-94818-8.
[11] A. J. Menezes, P. C. van Oorschot, S. A. Vanstone, P. C. van Oorschot, and S. A. Vanstone, *Handbook of Applied Cryptography*. CRC Press, 2018, doi: 10.1201/9780429466335.
[12] J. Daemen, and V. Rijmen, "Specification of Rijndael," in *The Design of Rijndael: The Advanced Encryption Standard (AES)*, J. Daemen, and V. Rijmen, Eds., in Information Security and Cryptography. Berlin, Heidelberg: Springer, 2020, pp. 31–51, doi: 10.1007/978-3-662-60769-5_3.
[13] A. Grami, "Chapter 11 - cryptography," in *Discrete Mathematics*, A. Grami, Ed. Academic Press, 2023, pp. 197–210, doi: 10.1016/B978-0-12-820656-0.00011-3.
[14] B. Schneier, *Applied Cryptography : Protocols, Algorithms, and Source Code in C*. New York : Wiley, 1996. Accessed: Jul. 25, 2020. [Online]. http://archive.org/details/appliedcryptogra00schn_328.
[15] A. Freyre Echevarría, "Evolución híbrida de s-cajas no lineales resistentes a ataques de potencia," 2020, doi: 10.13140/RG.2.2.17037.77284/1.

[16] J. Álvarez-Cubero, "Vector Boolean functions: Applications in symmetric cryptography," 2015, doi: 10.13140/RG.2.2.12540.23685.

[17] A. Freyre-Echevarría et al., "An external parameter independent novel cost function for evolving bijective substitution-boxes," *Symmetry*, vol. 12, no. 11, Art. no. 11, Nov. 2020, doi: 10.3390/sym12111896.

[18] A. Freyre-Echevarría, I. Martínez-Díaz, C. M. L. Pérez, G. Sosa-Gómez, and O. Rojas, "Evolving nonlinear S-boxes with improved theoretical resilience to power attacks," *IEEE Access*, vol. 8, pp. 202728–202737, 2020, doi: 10.1109/ACCESS.2020.3035163.

[19] L. D. Burnett, "Heuristic optimization of Boolean functions and substitution boxes for cryptography," PhD, Queensland University of Technology, 2005. Accessed: May 19, 2021. [Online]. https://eprints.qut.edu.au/16023/.

[20] P. Tesar, "A new method for generating high non-linearity S-boxes," Apr. 2010. Accessed: Aug. 16, 2020. [Online]. http://dspace.lib.vutbr.cz/xmlui/handle/11012/56957.

[21] G. Ivanov, N. Nikolov, and S. Nikova, "Reversed genetic algorithms for generation of bijective s-boxes with good cryptographic properties," *Cryptography and Communications*, vol. 8, no. 2, pp. 247–276, Apr. 2016, doi: 10.1007/s12095-015-0170-5.

[22] T. Kapuściński, R. K. Nowicki, and C. Napoli, "Application of genetic algorithms in the construction of invertible substitution boxes," in *Artificial Intelligence and Soft Computing*, L. Rutkowski, M. Korytkowski, R. Scherer, R. Tadeusiewicz, L. A. Zadeh, and J. M. Zurada, Eds., in Lecture Notes in Computer Science. Cham: Springer International Publishing, 2016, pp. 380–391, doi: 10.1007/978-3-319-39378-0_33.

[23] D. Souravlias, K. E. Parsopoulos, and G. C. Meletiou, "Designing bijective S-boxes using algorithm portfolios with limited time budgets," *Applied Soft Computing*, vol. 59, pp. 475–486, Oct. 2017, doi: 10.1016/j.asoc.2017.05.052.

[24] J. McLaughlin, "Applications of search techniques to cryptanalysis and the construction of cipher components," PhD, University of York, 2012. Accessed: Oct. 27, 2022. [Online]. https://etheses.whiterose.ac.uk/3674/.

[25] A. Kuznetsov, N. Poluyanenko, E. Frontoni, S. Kandiy, and O. Pieshkova, "Optimized simulated annealing for efficient generation of highly nonlinear S-boxes," *Soft Computing*, Oct. 2023, doi: 10.1007/s00500-023-09334-y.

[26] A. Kuznetsov et al., "Generation of nonlinear substitutions by simulated annealing algorithm," *Information*, vol. 14, no. 5, Art. no. 5, May 2023, doi: 10.3390/info14050259.

[27] A. Kuznetsov et al., "Optimizing hill climbing algorithm for S-boxes generation," *Electronics*, vol. 12, no. 10, Art. no. 10, Jan. 2023, doi: 10.3390/electronics12102338.

[28] G. Ivanov, N. Nikolov, and S. Nikova, "Cryptographically strong S-boxes generated by modified immune algorithm," in *Cryptography and Information Security in the Balkans*, E. Pasalic, and L. R. Knudsen, Eds., in Lecture Notes in Computer Science. Cham: Springer International Publishing, 2016, pp. 31–42, doi: 10.1007/978-3-319-29172-7_3.

[29] A. Kuznetsov, N. Poluyanenko, E. Frontoni, S. Kandiy, and O. Peliukh, "A new cost function for heuristic search of nonlinear substitutions," *Expert Systems with Applications*, vol. 237, p. 121684, Mar. 2024, doi: 10.1016/j.eswa.2023.121684.

[30] J. A. Clark, J. L. Jacob, and S. Stepney, "The design of S-boxes by simulated annealing," *New Generation Computing*, vol. 23, no. 3, pp. 219–231, Sep. 2005, doi: 10.1007/BF03037656.

[31] J. A. Clark, J. L. Jacob, and S. Stepney, "Searching for cost functions," in *Proceedings of the 2004 Congress on Evolutionary Computation (IEEE Cat. No.04TH8753)*, vol. 2, Jun. 2004, pp. 1517–1524, doi: 10.1109/CEC.2004.1331076.

[32] E. C. Laskari, G. C. Meletiou, and M. N. Vrahatis, "Utilizing evolutionary computation methods for the design of S-boxes," in *2006 International Conference on Computational Intelligence and Security*, Nov. 2006, pp. 1299–1302, doi: 10.1109/ICCIAS.2006.295267.

[33] S. Picek, K. Papagiannopoulos, B. Ege, L. Batina, and D. Jakobovic, "Confused by confusion: Systematic evaluation of DPA resistance of various S-boxes," in *Progress in Cryptology—INDOCRYPT 2014*, W. Meier, and D. Mukhopadhyay, Eds., in Lecture Notes in Computer Science. Cham: Springer International Publishing, 2014, pp. 374–390, doi: 10.1007/978-3-319-13039-2_22.
[34] S. Picek, M. Cupic, and L. Rotim, "A new cost function for evolution of S-boxes," *Evolutionary Computation*, vol. 24, no. 4, pp. 695–718, Dec. 2016, doi: 10.1162/EVCO_a_00191.
[35] M. F. Khan, A. Ahmed, and K. Saleem, "A novel cryptographic substitution box design using Gaussian distribution," *IEEE Access*, vol. 7, pp. 15999–16007, 2019, doi: 10.1109/ACCESS.2019.2893176.
[36] C. Carlet, and C. Ding, "Nonlinearities of S-boxes," *Finite Fields and Their Applications*, vol. 13, no. 1, pp. 121–135, Jan. 2007, doi: 10.1016/j.ffa.2005.07.003.
[37] M. Rodinko, R. Oliynykov, and Y. Gorbenko, "Optimization of the high nonlinear S-boxes generation method," *Tatra Mountains Mathematical Publications*, vol. 70, no. 1, pp. 93–105, Sep. 2017, doi: 10.1515/tmmp-2017-0020.
[38] M. Ahmad, I. A. Khaja, A. Baz, H. Alhakami, and W. Alhakami, "Particle swarm optimization based highly nonlinear substitution-boxes generation for security applications," *IEEE Access*, vol. 8, pp. 116132–116147, 2020, doi: 10.1109/ACCESS.2020.3004449.
[39] M. I. Haider, T. Shah, A. Ali, D. Shah, and I. Khalid, "An innovative approach towards image encryption by using novel PRNs and S-boxes modeling techniques," *Mathematics and Computers in Simulation*, vol. 209, pp. 153–168, Jul. 2023, doi: 10.1016/j.matcom.2023.01.036.
[40] T. Haider, N. A. Azam, and U. Hayat, "Substitution box generator with enhanced cryptographic properties and minimal computation time," *Expert Systems with Applications*, vol. 241, p. 122779, May 2024, doi: 10.1016/j.eswa.2023.122779.
[41] S. Fahd, M. Afzal, W. Iqbal, D. Shah, and I. Khalid, "The reality of backdoored S-boxes—an eye opener," *Journal of Information Security and Applications*, vol. 80, p. 103674, Feb. 2024, doi: 10.1016/j.jisa.2023.103674.
[42] S. S. Jamal, M. M. Hazzazi, M. F. Khan, Z. Bassfar, A. Aljaedi, and Z. ul Islam, "Region of interest-based medical image encryption technique based on chaotic S-boxes," *Expert Systems with Applications*, vol. 238, p. 122030, Mar. 2024, doi: 10.1016/j.eswa.2023.122030.
[43] D. James, and T. L. Priya, "An innovative approach for dynamic key dependent S-box to enhance security of IoT systems," *Measurement: Sensors*, vol. 30, p. 100923, Dec. 2023, doi: 10.1016/j.measen.2023.100923.
[44] Y. Ji, Z. Ma, L. Li, and Y. Sun, "Constructions of correlation immune S-boxes with high nonlinearity," *Journal of Information and Intelligence*, Feb. 2024, doi: 10.1016/j.jiixd.2024.01.005.
[45] M. Vijayakumar, and A. Ahilan, "An optimized chaotic S-box for real-time image encryption scheme based on 4-dimensional memristive hyperchaotic map," *Ain Shams Engineering Journal*, p. 102620, Jan. 2024, doi: 10.1016/j.asej.2023.102620.
[46] M. Zhao, H. Liu, and Y. Niu, "Batch generating keyed strong S-boxes with high nonlinearity using 2D hyper chaotic map," *Integration*, vol. 92, pp. 91–98, Sep. 2023, doi: 10.1016/j.vlsi.2023.05.006.
[47] C. Carlet, "Vectorial Boolean functions for cryptography," in *Boolean Models and Methods in Mathematics, Computer Science, and Engineering*, P. L. Hammer and Y. Crama, Eds., in Encyclopedia of Mathematics and its Applications. Cambridge: Cambridge University Press, 2010, pp. 398–470, doi: 10.1017/CBO9780511780448.012.
[48] A. Kuznetsov, S. Kandii, E. Frontoni, and N. Poluyanenko, "SBGen: A high-performance library for rapid generation of cryptographic S-boxes," *SoftwareX*, vol. 27, p. 101788, Sep. 2024, doi: 10.1016/j.softx.2024.101788.

[49] O. Kuznetsov, N. Poluyanenko, E. Frontoni, and S. Kandiy, "Enhancing smart communication security: A novel cost function for efficient S-box generation in symmetric key cryptography," *Cryptography*, vol. 8, no. 2, Art. no. 2, Jun. 2024, doi: 10.3390/cryptography8020017.

[50] R. Brumnik, T. Klebanova, L. Guryanova, S. Kavun, and O. Trydid, "Simulation of territorial development based on fiscal policy tools," *Mathematical Problems in Engineering*, vol. 2014, no. 1, p. 843976, 2014, doi: 10.1155/2014/843976.

[51] V. Kalashnikov, S. Dempe, B. Mordukhovich, and S. V. Kavun, "Bilevel optimal control, equilibrium, and combinatorial problems with applications to engineering," *Mathematical Problems in Engineering*, vol. 2017, no. 1, p. 7190763, 2017, doi: 10.1155/2017/7190763.

5 Enhancing Cryptographic Strength

A Novel Approach to S-Box Generation Using Modified Simulated Annealing

Oleksandr Kuznetsov, Nikolay Poluyanenko, Oleksii Smirnov, and Bayan Abduraimova

5.1 INTRODUCTION

In the realm of modern cryptography, the design and implementation of robust cryptographic primitives are paramount to ensuring the security of information systems [1, 2]. Among these primitives, Substitution boxes (S-boxes) play a pivotal role in symmetric-key cryptographic algorithms, serving as the primary source of non-linearity and confusion [3, 4]. The cryptographic strength of many block and stream ciphers heavily relies on the quality of their constituent S-boxes, making the generation of optimal S-boxes a critical challenge in cryptographic engineering [5, 6].

S-boxes introduce complexity into the relationship between the input and output of a cipher, thereby enhancing its resistance against various cryptanalytic attacks [7]. A well-designed S-box must possess several crucial properties, including high non-linearity, low differential uniformity, and a high algebraic degree [8, 9]. These properties collectively contribute to the S-box's ability to withstand linear and differential cryptanalysis, as well as algebraic attacks, which are among the most powerful techniques in a cryptanalyst's arsenal [10, 11].

The task of generating S-boxes that simultaneously optimize multiple cryptographic properties is inherently complex. The search space for $n \times n$ S-boxes grows factorially with n, making exhaustive search impractical for all but the smallest S-boxes [12]. Furthermore, the various desirable properties often conflict with one another, necessitating careful balancing and trade-offs. These challenges have led researchers to explore various heuristic and metaheuristic approaches for S-box generation, including genetic algorithms, hill climbing, and simulated annealing [13, 14].

Simulated annealing, inspired by the physical process of annealing in metallurgy, has shown promise in tackling complex optimization problems with large, discrete

DOI: 10.1201/9781003546153-5

search spaces [15]. Its ability to escape local optima through probabilistic acceptance of worse solutions makes it particularly well-suited to the S-box generation problem [16–18]. However, previous implementations of simulated annealing for S-box generation have often struggled with efficiency and consistency in producing high-quality S-boxes.

5.1.1 Contributions of the Chapter

In this chapter, we present an optimized simulated annealing algorithm specifically tailored for generating cryptographically strong S-boxes. Our approach builds upon existing work in the field, introducing several key innovations:

1) An adaptive cooling schedule that balances exploration and exploitation throughout the search process.
2) A carefully designed cost function based on the Walsh-Hadamard Transform, which effectively captures multiple cryptographic properties.
3) Efficient implementation techniques that leverage modern processor capabilities to accelerate cryptographic property calculations.

We focus our study on the generation of 8×8 S-boxes, which are widely used in contemporary symmetric-key cryptographic algorithms. Our primary objectives are to:

a) Develop a simulated annealing implementation capable of consistently generating S-boxes with high nonlinearity (≥ 104), low differential uniformity (≤ 10), and maximum algebraic degree.
b) Identify optimal parameter configurations that maximize the algorithm's efficiency and success rate.
c) Provide a comprehensive analysis of the algorithm's behavior and the evolution of S-box properties throughout the optimization process.
d) Compare the performance of our approach with existing methods for S-box generation.

Through extensive experimentation and rigorous analysis, we demonstrate that our optimized simulated annealing approach achieves significant improvements in both the quality of generated S-boxes and computational efficiency. We explore the effects of key parameters, particularly initial temperature and cooling rate, on the algorithm's performance, providing insights that are valuable not only for S-box generation but also for the broader application of simulated annealing to cryptographic problems.

5.1.2 Organization of the Chapter

The remainder of this chapter is organized as follows: Section 5.2 presents an overview of related work, highlighting their limitations and the context for our innovations. Section 5.3 provides theoretical background on S-box properties and the simulated annealing algorithm. Section 5.4 details our methodology, including the proposed algorithm implementation and cost function design. Section 5.5 presents our experimental results and analysis. Section 5.6 discusses the implications of our findings and compares our approach with existing methods. Finally, Section 5.7 concludes the chapter and outlines directions for future research.

5.2 LITERATURE REVIEW

The generation of cryptographically strong S-boxes has been a subject of intense research over the past two decades, with various approaches and methodologies proposed to address this complex optimization problem. This section provides a chronological review of significant contributions to the field, focusing on the application of heuristic and metaheuristic techniques for S-box generation.

Clark et al. (2005) [18] were among the first to apply simulated annealing (SA) to S-box design. Their work demonstrated how a cost function, previously successful for single-output Boolean functions, could be generalized to improve results for small S-boxes. This seminal paper laid the groundwork for future research in applying metaheuristic techniques to S-box generation.

Picek et al. (2014) [19] introduced a novel perspective by focusing on the confusion coefficient property of S-boxes. Their study employed heuristic techniques to generate S-boxes with improved confusion coefficients, aiming to enhance resistance against side-channel attacks. Their work highlighted the importance of considering multiple cryptographic properties simultaneously when designing S-boxes.

McLaughlin and Clark (2013) [14] expanded the scope of evolutionary computation in S-box design by addressing both differential uniformity and nonlinearity. Their experiments with simulated annealing, memetic algorithms, and ant colony optimization represented a significant step towards creating vectorial Boolean functions with optimal cryptographic properties.

Freyre Echevarría (2020) [20] presented a hybrid approach to S-box generation, combining metaheuristic techniques with a partition of the search space based on Hamming Weight classes. This methodology aimed to produce bijective nonlinear S-boxes resilient to Differential Power Analysis (DPA) attacks, demonstrating the growing emphasis on side-channel resistance in S-box design.

Freyre-Echevarría et al. (2020) [21] further developed this concept, introducing a novel hybrid method based on Leaders and Followers and hill climbing over Hamming Weight Classes. Their approach, coupled with a new trade-off fitness function, generated 8-bit bijective S-boxes with strong resistance to both classical cryptanalysis and power consumption side-channel attacks.

Souravlias et al. (2017) [17] introduced the concept of Algorithm Portfolios (APs) to S-box design. Their study combined simulated annealing and Tabu Search in a parallel framework, demonstrating competitive performance in terms of solution quality and running time compared to individual algorithms.

Wang et al. (2020) [16] proposed a chaotic S-box construction method based on a memorable simulated annealing algorithm (MSAA). Their approach utilized the nonlinearity and randomness of digital cascaded chaotic mapping, optimized through MSAA, to efficiently generate high-performance chaotic S-boxes.

Recent work by Kuznetsov et al. (2023) [22] has significantly advanced the field of S-box generation using simulated annealing. They introduced a new cost function based on Walsh-Hadamard Spectrum computation and conducted extensive experiments to optimize the SA algorithm's parameters. Their results demonstrated rapid generation of 8-bit bijective S-boxes with nonlinearity 104, achieving a 100% success rate with approximately 83,000 iterations.

Building on this work, Kuznetsov et al. (2023) [23] further optimized the SA algorithm for S-box generation. They introduced a multithreaded implementation and additional exit criteria for both internal and external loops, significantly reducing computational complexity. Their approach showed a 30–40% improvement in generating nonlinear S-boxes compared to previous methods.

The evolution of research in this field reflects a growing sophistication in applying metaheuristic techniques to S-box generation. Early works focused primarily on nonlinearity, while later studies incorporated multiple cryptographic properties, including resistance to side-channel attacks. Recent advancements have emphasized algorithmic efficiency and the ability to consistently generate S-boxes with optimal properties.

5.3 THEORETICAL BACKGROUND

In the realm of modern cryptography, the design and implementation of robust cryptographic primitives are paramount to ensuring the security of information systems. This section delves into the theoretical underpinnings of S-boxes and the simulated annealing algorithm, providing a foundation for our novel approach to S-box generation. While previous chapters have introduced fundamental concepts and notations related to S-boxes, we will expand upon these ideas, focusing on the intricate interplay between various cryptographic properties and their significance in cipher design.

5.3.1 S-Box Properties and Their Cryptographic Significance

S-boxes serve as the cornerstone of nonlinearity in many symmetric-key cryptographic algorithms, playing a crucial role in thwarting cryptanalytic attacks [1, 24]. The effectiveness of an S-box is determined by a constellation of properties, each contributing to the overall security and performance of the cryptosystem. We will examine four key properties in depth [8]:

1) Nonlinearity is arguably the most critical property of an S-box, quantifying its resistance to linear cryptanalysis. Let $f: F_2^n \to F_2^m$ be a vectorial Boolean function representing an $n \times m$ S-box. The nonlinearity of f, denoted as $NL(f)$, is defined as the minimum Hamming distance between f and all affine functions. Mathematically, this can be expressed as [8]:

$$NL(f) = 2^{n-1} - \frac{1}{2} \max_{a \in \mathbb{F}_2^n, b \in \mathbb{F}2^m} \left| \sum x \in \mathbb{F}_2^n (-1)^{b \cdot f(x) \oplus a \cdot x} \right|,$$

where $\cdot$ denotes the dot product and $\oplus$ represents bitwise XOR.

Higher nonlinearity values indicate greater resistance to linear approximations, thus enhancing the cipher's security against linear cryptanalysis.

2) Differential uniformity measures an S-box's resistance to differential cryptanalysis. For a function $f : F_2^n \rightarrow F_2^m$, the differential uniformity $\delta(f)$ is defined as [8]:

$$\delta(f) = \max_{a \neq 0, b} | x \in \mathbb{F}_2^n : f(x \oplus a) \oplus f(x) = b |.$$

Lower values of $\delta(f)$ indicate better resistance to differential attacks. Ideally, for an $n \times n$ S-box, we aim for the theoretical lower bound of $\delta(f) = 2$, known as almost perfect nonlinear (APN) functions.

3) The algebraic degree of an S-box is the maximum degree of the component Boolean functions in its algebraic normal form (ANF). For a vectorial Boolean function $f = (f_1, ..., f_m)$, the algebraic degree is defined as [8]:

$$\deg(f) = \max_{1 \leq i \leq m} \deg(f_i).$$

Higher algebraic degrees contribute to the complexity of the S-box, making it more resistant to algebraic attacks. However, there exists a trade-off between algebraic degree and other desirable properties, necessitating careful balancing in S-box design.

An $n \times m$ S-box f is considered balanced if each output occurs with equal frequency when the input is uniformly distributed. Mathematically, for every $y \in F_2^m$ [8]:3333

$$| x \in \mathbb{F}_2^n : f(x) = y | = 2^{n-m}.$$

4) Balancedness ensures that the S-box does not introduce statistical biases that could be exploited by attackers [8]. It is a fundamental requirement for cryptographic S-boxes, contributing to the overall confusion and diffusion properties of the cipher.

These properties do not exist in isolation but interact in complex ways, often presenting trade-offs that must be carefully navigated in S-box design. For instance, the quest for high nonlinearity may come at the cost of increased differential uniformity or reduced algebraic degree. The challenge lies in finding optimal or near-optimal solutions that balance these competing criteria, a task well-suited to advanced optimization techniques such as simulated annealing.

In the subsequent sections, we will explore how these properties can be effectively captured in cost functions, guiding the simulated annealing process towards the generation of cryptographically strong S-boxes. This approach not only aims to produce S-boxes with excellent individual properties but also strives to achieve a harmonious balance among them, resulting in substitution boxes that can withstand a wide array of cryptanalytic techniques.

5.3.2 The Simulated Annealing Algorithm

5.3.2.1 Principles and Mechanics

Simulated annealing (SA) is a probabilistic technique for approximating the global optimum of a given function, particularly effective in large, discrete search spaces [15]. Inspired by the physical process of annealing in metallurgy, SA mimics the controlled cooling of a material to reduce defects and increase crystal size, thus minimizing the system's energy.

The algorithm's core principle lies in its ability to escape local optima by allowing occasional "uphill" moves, especially in the early stages of the search process. This characteristic distinguishes SA from greedy algorithms that can become trapped in suboptimal solutions [25, 26].

The key components of the SA algorithm include [15]:

a) State space: A set S of all possible solutions.
b) Energy function: A cost function $E(s)$ that assigns a real number to each state $s \in S$, representing the quality of the solution.
c) Neighborhood function: A mechanism to generate a new candidate solution s' from the current solution s.
d) Acceptance probability: A function $P(e, e', T)$ that determines the likelihood of accepting a new state with energy e' given the current state's energy e at temperature T.
e) Cooling schedule: A function $T(k)$ that determines the temperature at each iteration k.

The SA algorithm proceeds as follows [15]:

1) Initialize with a random state $s \in S$ and temperature $T > 0$.
2) While the stopping criterion is not met:
   a) Generate a candidate neighbor state s'.
   b) Calculate $\Delta E = E(s') - E(s)$.
   c) If $\Delta E \leq 0$, accept the new state.
   d) If $\Delta E > 0$, accept the new state with probability $P(\Delta E, T)$.
   e) Update the temperature according to the cooling schedule.
3) Return the best solution found.

The acceptance probability is typically defined as [15]:

$$P(\Delta E, T) = \exp(-\Delta E / T).$$

This formulation, known as the Metropolis criterion, allows the algorithm to accept worse solutions with a probability that decreases as the temperature lowers or as the energy difference increases [15, 27].

The cooling schedule is crucial for the algorithm's performance. A common form is the exponential cooling schedule [15]:

$$T(k) = T_0 \alpha^k,$$

where T_0 is the initial temperature, α is the cooling rate (typically $0.8 < \alpha < 0.99$), and k is the iteration number.

The algorithm's convergence to the global optimum is guaranteed under certain conditions, including a sufficiently slow cooling rate. However, in practice, a trade-off between solution quality and computational time often necessitates faster cooling schedules.

5.3.2.2 Application to Combinatorial Optimization Problems

Simulated annealing has proven particularly effective in solving complex combinatorial optimization problems [28, 29], where the search space is discrete and often exponentially large. Its ability to escape local optima makes it well-suited for problems with numerous local minima or maxima.

Key applications include [15]:

a) Traveling Salesman Problem (TSP): SA can find near-optimal solutions for large instances of the TSP, where exact methods become computationally intractable.
b) Graph partitioning: SA effectively balances partition sizes while minimizing edge cuts in large graphs.
c) VLSI circuit design: SA optimizes chip layouts, minimizing wire length and maximizing circuit performance.
d) Job shop scheduling: SA finds efficient schedules in complex manufacturing environments with multiple constraints.
e) Protein folding: SA simulates the folding process to predict protein structures, a critical problem in computational biology.

In the context of S-box generation, SA can be applied to navigate the vast search space of possible substitutions. The energy function $E(s)$ is designed to capture the cryptographic properties discussed earlier, such as nonlinearity, differential uniformity, and algebraic degree. The neighborhood function typically involves swapping two elements in the S-box or applying small permutations.

The effectiveness of SA in S-box generation stems from its ability to [15]:

1) Handle multiple, often conflicting, optimization criteria simultaneously.
2) Explore a wide range of potential solutions, reducing the risk of getting stuck in suboptimal configurations.
3) Adapt to the changing landscape of the search space as the temperature decreases, gradually focusing on more promising regions.

However, applying SA to S-box generation presents unique challenges [15]:

a) Defining an appropriate energy function that accurately reflects the cryptographic strength of an S-box.
b) Balancing exploration and exploitation through careful tuning of the cooling schedule.
c) Dealing with the discrete nature of the search space, where small changes can lead to significant alterations in cryptographic properties.

In the subsequent sections, we will delve into our novel approach to addressing these challenges, presenting a refined SA algorithm specifically tailored for generating cryptographically strong S-boxes. This approach not only leverages the inherent strengths of SA but also incorporates domain-specific knowledge to enhance its effectiveness in the cryptographic context.

5.3.3 COST FUNCTIONS FOR S-BOX EVALUATION

In the realm of S-box generation and optimization, the design of effective cost functions is crucial. These functions serve as the quantitative measure of an S-box's cryptographic quality, guiding the optimization process towards desirable solutions. This section explores various cost functions, with a particular focus on Walsh-Hadamard Transform based metrics and other relevant measures.

5.3.3.1 Walsh-Hadamard Transform Based Metrics

The Walsh-Hadamard Transform (WHT) plays a pivotal role in assessing the nonlinearity of Boolean functions, making it an invaluable tool in S-box evaluation [8]. For a Boolean function $f : \mathbb{F}_2^n \to \mathbb{F}_2$, the Walsh-Hadamard Transform is defined as:

$$W_f(a) = \sum_{x \in \mathbb{F}_2^n} (-1)^{f(x) \oplus a \cdot x},$$

where $a \in \mathbb{F}_2^n$ and $\cdot$ denotes the dot product.

For vectorial Boolean functions (S-boxes) $F : \mathbb{F}_2^n \to \mathbb{F}_2^m$, we consider the WHT of all non-zero linear combinations of component functions [8]:

$$W_F(a,b) = \sum_{x \in \mathbb{F}_2^n} (-1)^{b \cdot F(x) \oplus a \cdot x},$$

where

$a \in \mathbb{F}_2^n, b \in \mathbb{F}_2^m \setminus 0.$

Based on these transforms, several cost functions can be derived:

a) Maximum Walsh-Hadamard Spectrum (maxWHS): The maxWHS is defined as:

$$\text{maxWHS}(F) = \max_{a \in \mathbb{F}_2^n, b \in \mathbb{F}_2^m \setminus 0} | W_F(a,b) |.$$

This metric is directly related to the nonlinearity of the S-box, with lower values indicating higher nonlinearity.

b) Sum of Square Walsh-Hadamard Spectrum (sumSqWHS): The sumSqWHS provides a more comprehensive measure of the overall Walsh-Hadamard Spectrum:

$$\text{sumSqWHS}(F) = \sum_{a \in \mathbb{F}_2^n, b \in \mathbb{F}_2^m \setminus 0} W_F(a,b)^2.$$

This metric captures not only the maximum value but also the distribution of the spectrum, offering a more nuanced evaluation of the S-box's resistance to linear cryptanalysis.

c) Deviation from Ideal Walsh-Hadamard Spectrum: This cost function measures the deviation of the WHT spectrum from an idealized distribution:

$$\mathrm{DevWHS}(F) = \sum_{a\in\mathbb{F}_2^n, b\in\mathbb{F}_2^m\setminus 0} (|W_F(a,b)| - X)^R,$$

where X is a target value (typically set to the theoretical lower bound for perfect nonlinearity) and R is an exponent that controls the sensitivity of the measure. This function allows for fine-tuning the optimization process, balancing between maximizing nonlinearity and achieving a desirable spectrum distribution.

5.3.3.2 Other Relevant Metrics

While WHT-based metrics primarily address nonlinearity, other properties are crucial for comprehensive S-box evaluation [8]:

a) Differential uniformity: The differential uniformity δ_F of an S-box F is defined as:

$$\delta_F = \max_{a\neq 0,b} |x \in \mathbb{F}_2^n : F(x\oplus a)\oplus F(x) = b|.$$

A cost function based on differential uniformity might aim to minimize δ_F or penalize deviations from a target value.

b) Algebraic degree: The algebraic degree of an S-box F is the maximum degree of its component functions:

$$\deg(F) = \max_{1\leq i\leq m} \deg(f_i),$$

where f_i are the coordinate functions of F. A cost function might penalize S-boxes with low algebraic degrees, which are more susceptible to algebraic attacks.

c) Branch number: For an S-box $F : \mathbb{F}_2^n \to \mathbb{F}_2^n$, the branch number is defined as:

$$\mathcal{B}(F) = \min_{x\neq y} \left(w_H(x\oplus y) + w_H(F(x)\oplus F(y))\right),$$

where w_H denotes the Hamming weight. Higher branch numbers contribute to better diffusion properties.

d) Fixed points and cycles: The number of fixed points ($F(x) = x$) and short cycles can be incorporated into the cost function to ensure the S-box doesn't have structural weaknesses.

e) Balancedness: For each output $y \in \mathbb{F}_2^m$, a balanced S-box should have:

$$|x \in \mathbb{F}_2^n : F(x) = y| = 2^{n-m}.$$

Deviations from this ideal can be penalized in the cost function.

f) Avalanche criterion: The strict avalanche criterion (SAC) requires that changing a single input bit changes each output bit with probability 1/2. A cost function can measure deviations from this ideal.

In practice, effective S-box generation often requires a composite cost function that balances multiple criteria. A general form might be:

$$C(F) = w_1 C_1(F) + w_2 C_2(F) + \ldots + w_k C_k(F),$$

where $C_i(F)$ are individual cost components and w_i are weights allowing for prioritization of different properties, $i = 1, 2, \ldots, k$.

The challenge lies in designing a cost function that not only captures all relevant cryptographic properties but also provides a smooth landscape for optimization algorithms. The function should be sensitive enough to guide the search towards improvements but not so rugged as to create numerous local optima that trap the optimization process.

5.4 METHODOLOGY

In this section, we present a comprehensive methodology for generating cryptographically strong S-boxes using an optimized simulated annealing algorithm. Our approach builds upon the theoretical foundations discussed earlier, introducing novel modifications to enhance the efficiency and effectiveness of the S-box generation process. We begin by detailing our proposed simulated annealing implementation, followed by an in-depth discussion of our cost function design and experimental setup.

5.4.1 Proposed Simulated Annealing Implementation

5.4.1.1 Algorithm Structure and Pseudocode

Our implementation of simulated annealing for S-box generation is designed to efficiently navigate the vast search space of possible substitutions while maintaining a balance between exploration and exploitation. The algorithm incorporates several key modifications to the standard SA approach, tailored specifically for the S-box generation problem.

Here's the pseudocode for our proposed algorithm (Figure 5.1).

Key features of our implementation:

a) Multi-start capability: The algorithm can be easily parallelized by running multiple instances with different initial S-boxes.

```
Input: n: S-box size (n × n bits)
T_0: Initial temperature
alpha: Cooling rate
max_outer_loops: Maximum number of temperature reductions
max_inner_loops: Maximum number of iterations at each temperature
max_frozen_outer_loops: Maximum number of consecutive non-improving outer loops
Output: Best S-box found
function GenerateOptimalSBox(n, T_0, alpha, max_outer_loops, max_inner_loops,
  max_frozen_outer_loops):
S = GenerateRandomSBox(n)
best_S = S
T = T_0
frozen_loops = 0
for outer_loop = 1 to max_outer_loops:
improved = false
for inner_loop = 1 to max_inner_loops:
S' = GenerateNeighbor(S)
delta_E = CostFunction(S')-CostFunction(S)
if delta_E <= 0 or random() < exp(-delta_E / T):
S = S'
if CostFunction(S) < CostFunction(best_S):
best_S = S
improved = true
if improved:
frozen_loops = 0
else:
frozen_loops += 1
if frozen_loops >= max_frozen_outer_loops:
break
T = T * alpha
return best_S
function GenerateNeighbor(S):
S' = S.copy()
i, j = RandomSelectDistinctIndices(0, 2^n-1)
S'[i], S'[j] = S'[j], S'[i]
return S'
```

FIGURE 5.1 Optimized simulated annealing for S-box generation.

b) Adaptive inner loop: The number of iterations at each temperature is dynamically adjusted based on the S-box size and current temperature.
c) Early stopping mechanism: The algorithm terminates if no improvement is found for a specified number of consecutive outer loops.
d) Efficient neighbor generation: The neighbor function performs a simple swap operation, ensuring bijectivity is maintained.

5.4.1.2 Key Parameters and Their Roles

The performance of our simulated annealing implementation is heavily influenced by several key parameters:

a) Initial temperature (T_0): The initial temperature determines the algorithm's initial acceptance probability for worse solutions. A higher T_0 allows for more extensive exploration of the search space in the early stages. We propose an adaptive method for setting T_0 based on the initial cost function distribution:

$$T_0 = \frac{\Delta E_{avg}}{-\ln(P_0)},$$

where ΔE_{avg} is the average cost difference between neighboring solutions in a sample set, and P_0 is the desired initial acceptance probability (typically 0.5–0.8).

b) Cooling rate (alpha): The cooling rate alpha (0 < alpha < 1) controls how quickly the temperature decreases. A slower cooling rate (alpha closer to 1) allows for more thorough exploration but increases computational time. We found that values in the range 0.95–0.99 provide a good balance for S-box generation.
c) Maximum outer loops (max_outer_loops): This parameter limits the total number of temperature reductions. It serves as a global iteration limit and is typically set based on computational resources and time constraints.
d) Maximum inner loops (max_inner_loops): This defines the maximum number of iterations at each temperature. We propose an adaptive scheme:

$$max\_inner\_loops = k \cdot 2^n \cdot \ln(1+T),$$

where k is a scaling factor, n is the S-box size, and T is the current temperature. This allows for more iterations at higher temperatures and for larger S-boxes.

e) Maximum frozen outer loops (max_frozen_outer_loops): This parameter determines how many consecutive non-improving outer loops are allowed before termination. It helps in avoiding unnecessary computation when the algorithm has likely converged.
f) Neighbor generation strategy: While our basic implementation uses a simple swap operation, we also explored more sophisticated strategies, including:
   - Multiple swaps with probability decreasing with temperature.
   - Selective swaps based on S-box properties.
   - Permutation of small sub-blocks within the S-box.

These parameters interact in complex ways, and their optimal values can vary depending on the specific requirements of the S-box (e.g., prioritizing nonlinearity vs. differential uniformity). In our experimental section, we provide a detailed analysis of parameter sensitivity and offer guidelines for parameter selection based on different S-box generation scenarios.

5.4.2 Cost Function Design

The design of an effective cost function is crucial for the success of any optimization algorithm, particularly in the context of S-box generation. Our proposed cost function aims to capture the essential cryptographic properties of S-boxes while providing a smooth optimization landscape for the simulated annealing algorithm.

5.4.2.1 Proposed WHS-Based Cost Function

Our cost function is primarily based on the Walsh-Hadamard Spectrum (WHS), which offers a comprehensive view of an S-box's nonlinearity characteristics. We propose a novel composite cost function that not only considers the maximum value of the WHS but also its overall distribution:

$$C(S) = w_1 \cdot C_{maxWHS}(S) + w_2 \cdot C_{distWHS}(S) + w_3 \cdot C_{diff}(S) + w_4 \cdot C_{alg}(S),$$

where:

- $C_{maxWHS}(S)$ is the cost component based on the maximum WHS value;
- $C_{distWHS}(S)$ is the cost component based on the WHS distribution;
- $C_{diff}(S)$ is the cost component based on differential uniformity;
- $C_{alg}(S)$ is the cost component based on algebraic degree;
- w_1, w_2, w_3, w_4 are weighting factors.

Let's examine each component in detail:

a) Maximum WHS component (C_{maxWHS}):

$$C_{maxWHS}(S) = \sum_{i=1}^{2^n-1} \left(\max_{1 \le j \le n} |WHT(S_i^j)| - X \right)^R,$$

where:

- S_i^j is the j-th component function of the i-th non-zero linear combination of S-box outputs;
- $WHT(S_i^j)$ is the Walsh-Hadamard Transform of S_i^j;
- X is a target value for the maximum WHS (typically set to $2^{n/2}$ for $n \times n$ S-boxes);
- R is an exponent that controls the sensitivity of the measure (we found $R = 4$ to be effective).

This component encourages the reduction of the maximum WHS value, which directly correlates with improving the S-box's nonlinearity.

b) WHS distribution component ($C_{distWHS}$):

$$C_{distWHS}(S) = \sum_{i=1}^{2^n-1}\sum_{j=1}^{n}\left(|WHT(S_i^j)| - \mu\right)^2,$$

where μ is the mean value of $|WHT(S_i^j)|$ across all component functions and linear combinations.

This component promotes a more uniform distribution of WHS values, which contributes to the overall robustness of the S-box against linear cryptanalysis.

c) Differential uniformity component (C_{diff}):

$$C_{diff}(S) = \sum_{a\neq 0,b} \max(0, \delta_{a,b}(S) - \delta_{target})^2,$$

where:

- $\delta_{a,b}(S) = |x \in \mathbb{F}_2^n : S(x \oplus a) \oplus S(x) = b|$;
- δ_{target} is the target differential uniformity (typically ≤ 10 for $n \times n$ S-boxes).

This component penalizes high differential uniformity values, improving the S-box's resistance to differential cryptanalysis.

d) Algebraic degree component (C_{alg}):

$$C_{alg}(S) = \max(0, d_{target} - \min_{1\leq i\leq n} \deg(S_i))^2,$$

where:

- S_i is the i-th component function of the S-box;
- $\deg(S_i)$ is the algebraic degree of S_i;
- d_{target} is the target minimum algebraic degree (typically $n-1$ for $n \times n$ S-boxes).

This component encourages high algebraic degree, which is important for resistance against algebraic attacks.

5.4.3 Justification and Advantages

Our proposed cost function offers several key advantages:

a) Comprehensive evaluation: By incorporating multiple cryptographic properties (nonlinearity, differential uniformity, and algebraic degree), the cost function provides a holistic assessment of an S-box's quality.
b) Flexible prioritization: The weighting factors (w_1, w_2, w_3, w_4) allow for fine-tuning the importance of different properties based on specific requirements or target ciphers.

c) Smooth optimization landscape: The use of continuous penalties and squared terms creates a smoother optimization landscape compared to hard thresholds, facilitating more efficient navigation by the simulated annealing algorithm.
d) Scalability: The function is designed to work effectively for various S-box sizes, with parameters that can be easily adjusted based on the dimensions.
e) Computational efficiency: Despite its comprehensive nature, the cost function can be implemented efficiently, with many components reusable across evaluations of neighboring S-boxes.
f) Theoretical grounding: The focus on the Walsh-Hadamard Spectrum aligns with established theoretical measures of nonlinearity in cryptography.
g) Balanced exploration and exploitation: The combination of global (maximum WHS) and local (WHS distribution) components encourages both broad exploration of the search space and fine-tuning of promising solutions.

The effectiveness of this cost function is further enhanced by its synergy with our modified simulated annealing algorithm. The smooth landscape it creates allows for more informed decisions in the acceptance of new states, particularly at lower temperatures where fine distinctions between candidate solutions become crucial.

5.4.4 Experimental Setup

To rigorously evaluate the performance of our proposed simulated annealing algorithm and cost function for S-box generation, we conducted a comprehensive series of experiments. This section details our experimental setup, including the hardware and software environment, parameter ranges explored, test cases examined, and the metrics used for evaluation.

5.4.4.1 Hardware and Software Environment

All experiments were conducted on a high-performance workstation with the following specifications:

- Processor: AMD Ryzen 9 3950X 16-Core;
- Clock Speed: 3.49 GHz;
- Memory: 64 GB DDR4–3200;
- Operating System: Windows 10 64-bit;
- Compiler: Microsoft Visual C++ 2019 (Release mode).

The use of this multi-core processor allowed us to parallelize multiple runs of the simulated annealing algorithm, significantly accelerating our experimental process. The implementation was optimized to take advantage of the processor's advanced vector extensions (AVX2) for efficient computation of Walsh-Hadamard Transforms and other cryptographic properties.

5.4.4.2 Parameter Ranges and Test Cases

Our experiments focused on the generation of 8×8 S-boxes, as these are widely used in modern symmetric-key cryptographic algorithms. We explored a wide range of parameter configurations for our simulated annealing algorithm:

a) Initial temperature (T_0): We tested T_0 values ranging from 50 to 931,596, increasing by a factor of 1.13 between successive trials. This range was chosen to cover scenarios from near-greedy search (low T_0) to highly exploratory search (high T_0).
b) Cooling rate (alpha): We examined alpha values of 0.6, 0.7, 0.8, 0.9, and 0.95. This range allows us to investigate the trade-off between search thoroughness and computational efficiency.
c) Maximum outer loops (max_outer_loops): Set to 50 for all experiments, providing a consistent upper bound on the number of temperature reductions.
d) Maximum inner loops (max_inner_loops): Fixed at 650 for 8×8 S-boxes, resulting in 19,500 total inner loop iterations per temperature level (when accounting for our 30 parallel threads).
e) Maximum frozen outer loops (max_frozen_outer_loops): Set to 5, allowing the algorithm to terminate early if no improvements are found for five consecutive temperature reductions.

For each combination of T_0 and alpha, we conducted 100 independent runs of the algorithm to account for the stochastic nature of simulated annealing. In total, our experimentation encompassed:

- 10,100 runs for alpha = 0.6
- 7,600 runs for alpha = 0.7
- 5,700 runs for alpha = 0.8
- 8,200 runs for alpha = 0.9
- 8,200 runs for alpha = 0.95

This extensive set of experiments allowed us to thoroughly explore the parameter space and draw statistically significant conclusions about the algorithm's performance.

5.4.4.3 Performance Metrics and Evaluation Criteria

To assess the quality of the generated S-boxes and the efficiency of our algorithm, we employed the following metrics and evaluation criteria:

a) Nonlinearity: We tracked the nonlinearity of generated S-boxes, with a target value of 104 for 8 × 8 S-boxes. This is a crucial metric as it directly relates to resistance against linear cryptanalysis.
b) Differential uniformity: We measured the differential uniformity of the generated S-boxes, aiming for the lowest possible values (typically ≤ 10 for 8 × 8 S-boxes).
c) Algebraic degree: We ensured that all generated S-boxes maintained the maximum possible algebraic degree of 7 for 8 × 8 S-boxes.
d) Success rate: We calculated the percentage of runs that successfully generated S-boxes meeting our target criteria (nonlinearity ≥ 104, differential uniformity ≤ 10, algebraic degree = 7) for each parameter configuration.
e) Average generation time: We measured the average time required to generate a qualifying S-box, including the time spent on unsuccessful attempts.

f) Convergence behavior: We analyzed how quickly the algorithm converged to high-quality solutions by tracking the best S-box found at each temperature level.
g) Robustness: We evaluated the algorithm's robustness by examining the variability in S-box quality across multiple runs with the same parameters.
h) Computational efficiency: We measured the number of cost function evaluations required to generate a qualifying S-box, providing insight into the algorithm's efficiency independent of hardware specifics.
i) Parameter sensitivity: We conducted a sensitivity analysis to understand how changes in T_0 and alpha affect the algorithm's performance, helping to identify optimal parameter ranges.
j) Comparison with existing methods: We compared our results with those reported in the literature for other S-box generation techniques, including genetic algorithms, hill climbing, and previous simulated annealing implementations.

These comprehensive metrics allowed us to not only assess the quality of the S-boxes produced but also to gain insights into the dynamics of our algorithm and its sensitivity to various parameters. The results of these experiments, presented in the following section, demonstrate the effectiveness of our approach in generating cryptographically strong S-boxes with high efficiency and reliability.

5.5 RESULTS AND ANALYSIS

In this section, we present a comprehensive analysis of the results obtained from our extensive experimentation with the optimized simulated annealing algorithm for S-box generation. Our findings provide valuable insights into the behavior of the algorithm under various parameter configurations and demonstrate its effectiveness in producing cryptographically strong S-boxes. We begin by examining the effects of key parameters on the algorithm's performance, followed by an in-depth analysis of the quality of the generated S-boxes.

5.5.1 Parameter Optimization

The performance of our simulated annealing algorithm is heavily influenced by several key parameters. Through rigorous experimentation, we have identified optimal ranges for these parameters, balancing the trade-offs between exploration, exploitation, and computational efficiency.

5.5.1.1 Initial Temperature Effects

The initial temperature (T_0) plays a crucial role in determining the algorithm's initial acceptance probability for worse solutions, thereby affecting its exploration capability. Our experiments covered a wide range of T_0 values, from 50 to 931, 596, increasing by a factor of 1.13 between successive trials.

Figure 5.2 illustrates the probability of forming the target S-box (with nonlinearity ≥ 104) as a function of T_0 for $\alpha = 0.6$:

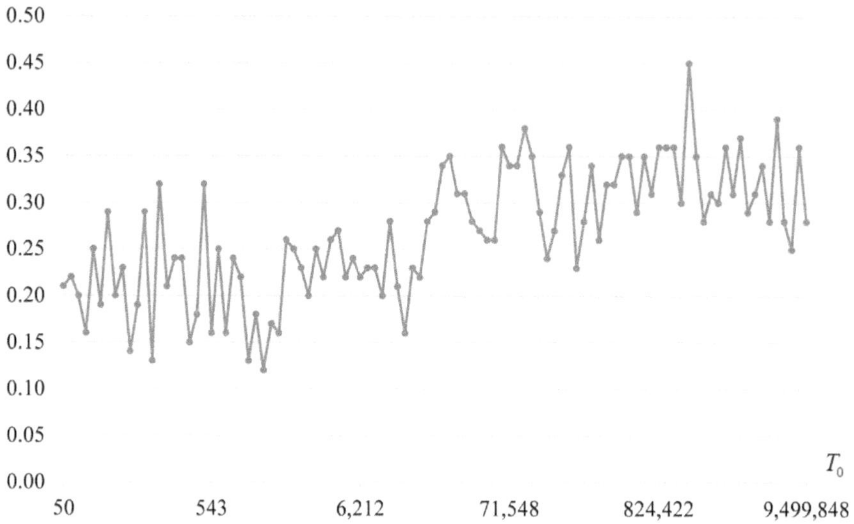

FIGURE 5.2 Probability of generating target S-box as a function of initial temperature (T_0) for cooling rate α = 0.6.

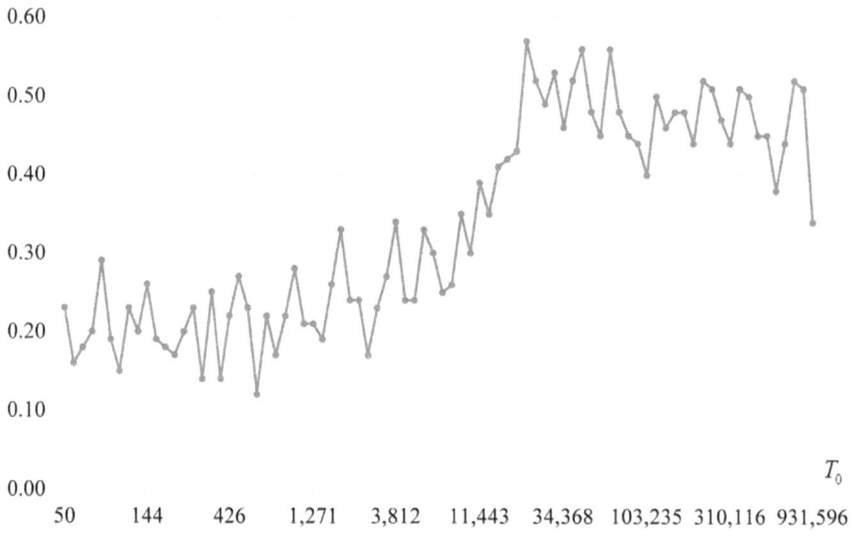

FIGURE 5.3 Average time (in seconds) to generate target S-box as a function of initial temperature (T_0) for cooling rate $\alpha = 0.6$.

The graph can be divided into three regions:

a) Low T_0 region ($T_0 < 6{,}000$): In this region, the probability of forming the target S-box remains relatively low and stable. The algorithm behaves similarly to a greedy local search, often getting trapped in local optima.

b) Transition region ($6,000 \leq T_0 < 50,000$): Here, we observe a significant increase in the probability of forming target S-boxes as T_0 increases. This region represents the optimal balance between exploration and exploitation.
c) High T_0 region ($T_0 \geq 50,000$): The probability plateaus in this region. While high T_0 values ensure thorough exploration of the search space, they also lead to increased computational time without significant improvements in S-box quality.

Figure 5.3 shows the average time required to form the target S-box as a function of T_0 for $\alpha = 0.6$:

The time graph exhibits two distinct phases:

a) Decreasing phase ($T_0 < 20,000 - 40,000$): As T_0 increases, the average search time decreases, reaching a minimum in the range of 20,000 to 40,000.
b) Increasing phase ($T_0 > 40,000$): Beyond this point, the average search time increases due to the excessive number of accepted worse solutions, leading to inefficient exploration.

5.5.1.2 Cooling Schedule Optimization

The cooling rate (α) determines how quickly the temperature decreases, affecting the balance between exploration and exploitation throughout the search process. We examined α values of 0.6, 0.7, 0.8, 0.9, and 0.95.

Figure 5.4 shows the probability of forming the target S-box as a function of T_0 for $\alpha = 0.9$:

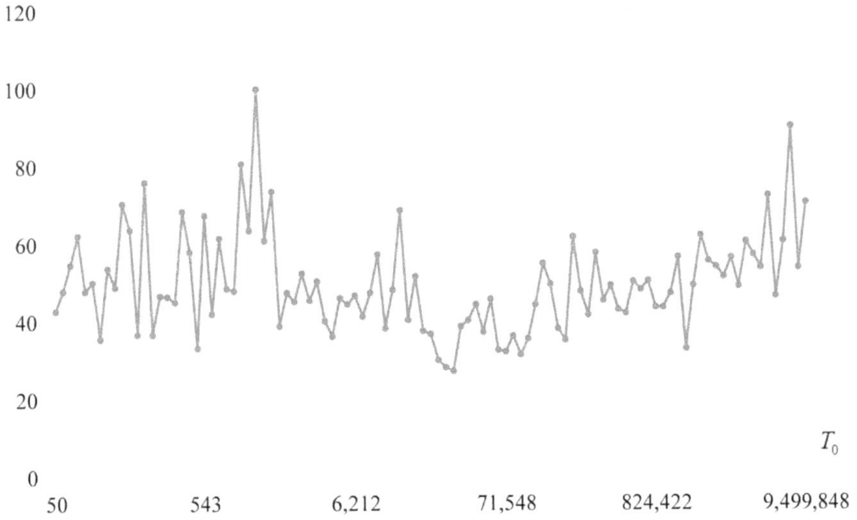

FIGURE 5.4 Probability of generating target S-box as a function of initial temperature (T_0) for cooling rate $\alpha = 0.9$.

Comparing Figures 5.2 and 5.3, we observe that higher α values lead to:

a) A sharper increase in success probability in the transition region;
b) A higher plateau probability in the high T_0 region;
c) A shift of the optimal T_0 range towards lower values.

Figure 5.5 illustrates the average time to form the target S-box for $\alpha = 0.9$:
Higher α values result in:

a) A more pronounced minimum in the average search time;
b) A steeper increase in search time for high T_0 values.

These observations suggest that higher α values (0.9–0.95) are generally more effective for S-box generation, providing a better balance between solution quality and computational efficiency.

5.5.1.3 Other Parameter Sensitivities

We also analyzed the sensitivity of the algorithm to other parameters:

a) Maximum outer loops (max_outer_loops): Set to 50 in our experiments, this parameter proved sufficient for most cases. Figures 5.6 and 5.7 show the distribution of the number of outer loops required to meet the stopping conditions for $\alpha = 0.6$ and $\alpha = 0.9$, respectively:

   For higher α values, we observe a more gradual increase in the number of outer loops required, indicating more thorough exploration of the search space.

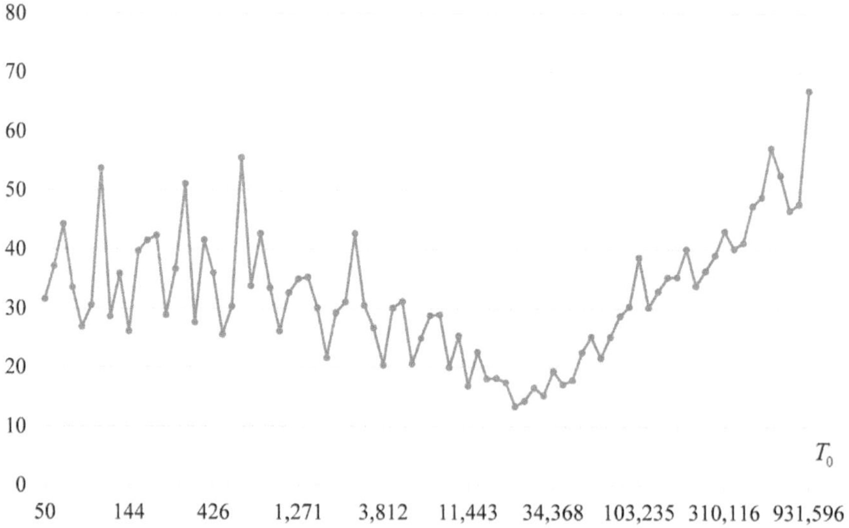

FIGURE 5.5 Average time (in seconds) to generate target S-box as a function of initial temperature (T_0) for cooling rate $\alpha = 0.9$.

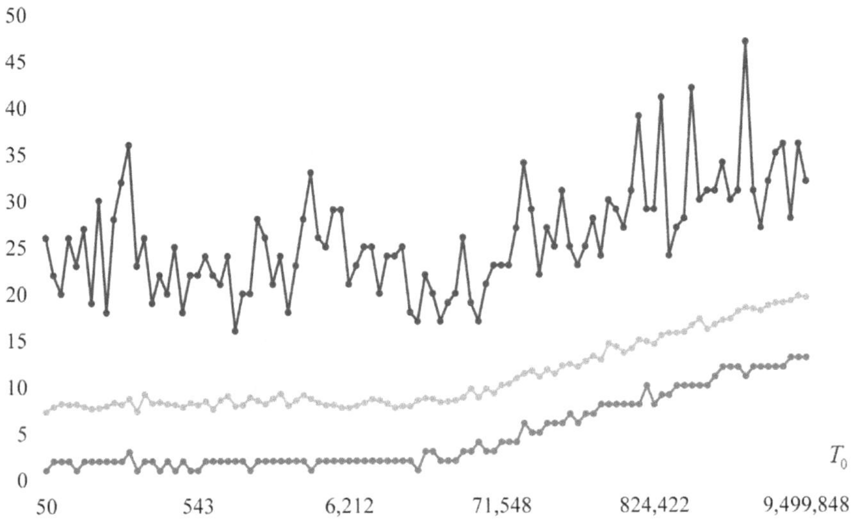

FIGURE 5.6 Distribution of outer loop iterations before meeting stopping conditions for cooling rate $\alpha = 0.6$.

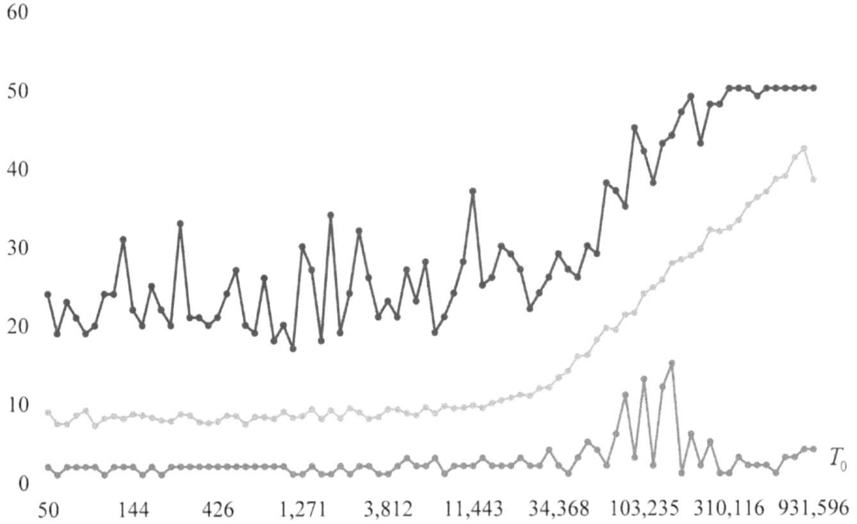

FIGURE 5.7 Distribution of outer loop iterations before meeting stopping conditions for cooling rate $\alpha = 0.9$.

b) Maximum inner loops (max_inner_loops): Fixed at 650 for 8×8 S-boxes, this value provided a good balance between search thoroughness and computational efficiency. Figures 5.8 and 5.9 illustrate the number of inner loop iterations for runs that successfully found target S-boxes:

   Higher α values lead to more consistent utilization of the maximum number of inner loops, especially at higher temperatures.

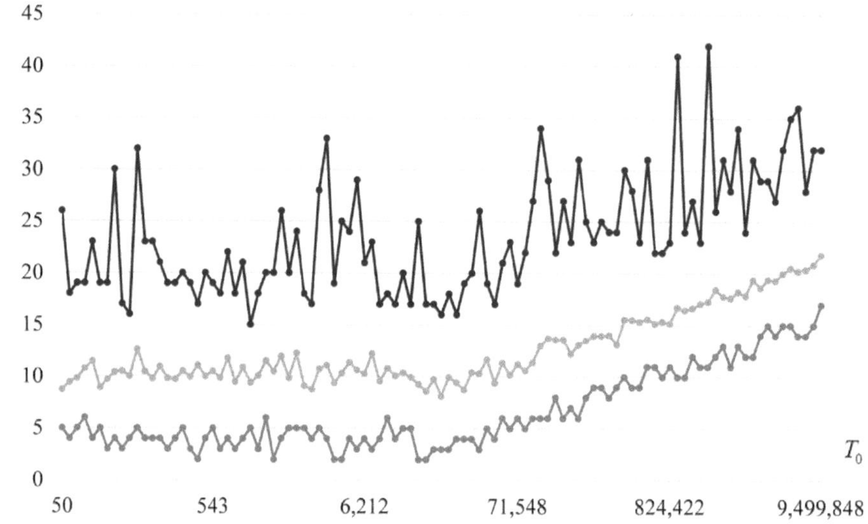

FIGURE 5.8 Number of inner loop iterations for successful S-box generation with cooling rate $\alpha = 0.6$.

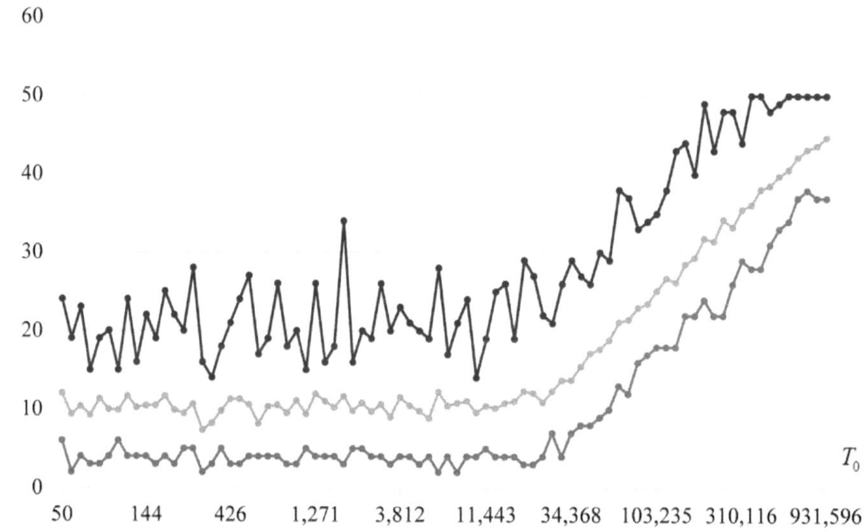

FIGURE 5.9 Number of inner loop iterations for successful S-box generation with cooling rate $\alpha = 0.9$.

c) Maximum frozen outer loops (max_frozen_outer_loops): Set to 5, this parameter effectively prevented unnecessary computation in cases where the algorithm had likely converged. Analysis of the "frozen" periods revealed that increasing this value beyond 5 rarely led to improvements in S-box quality.

Our comprehensive parameter analysis suggests that optimal performance for 8×8 S-box generation is achieved with:

- Initial temperature $(T_0): 20{,}000 - 40{,}000$
- Cooling rate (α): 0.9–0.95
- Maximum outer loops: 50
- Maximum inner loops: 650
- Maximum frozen outer loops: 5

These settings strike an effective balance between exploration, exploitation, and computational efficiency, consistently producing high-quality S-boxes while minimizing unnecessary computation.

5.5.2 In-Depth Analysis of Algorithm Dynamics and S-Box Evolution

To elucidate the intricate mechanisms underlying our optimized simulated annealing algorithm for S-box generation, we conducted a comprehensive analysis of its behavior throughout the search process. This detailed examination provides crucial insights into the algorithm's efficacy, convergence characteristics, and the evolution of cryptographic properties during S-box formation.

5.5.2.1 Computational Efficiency and Iteration Analysis

Figure 5.11 offers critical insights into the computational efficiency of the algorithm:

a) Optimal parameter range identification: An optimal range of initial temperatures (approximately 20,000 to 70,000) is evident, where the total

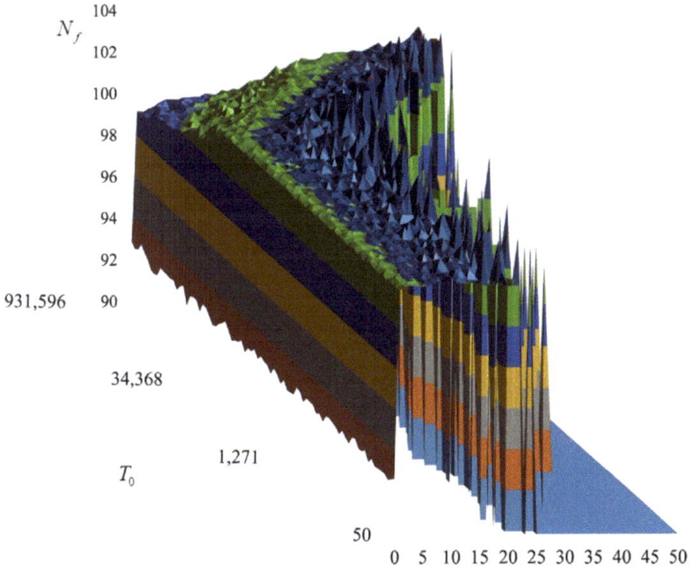

FIGURE 5.10 Aggregate iteration count (inner loops × outer loops) for successful S-box generation ($\alpha = 0.9$).

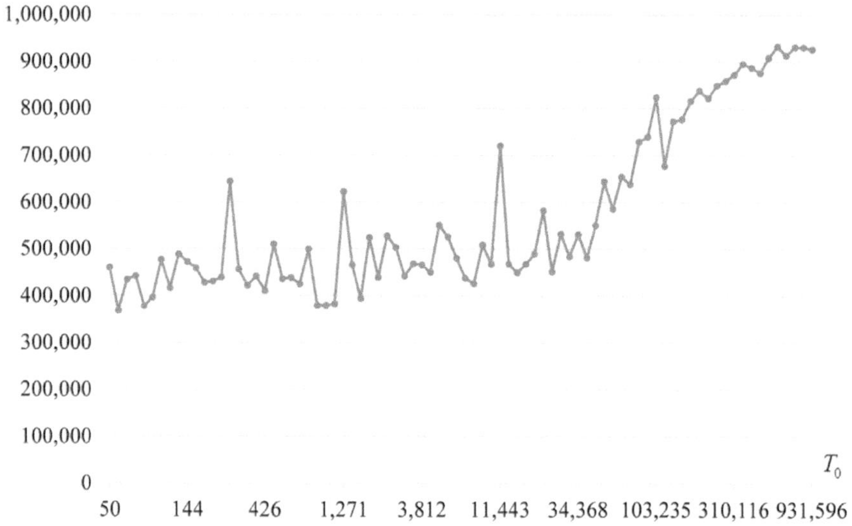

FIGURE 5.11 Temporal evolution of average nonlinearity across varying initial temperatures (T_0) for cooling rate $\alpha = 0.9$.

number of iterations required for successful S-box generation is minimized. This range represents the sweet spot balancing exploration and exploitation.

b) Computational overhead at extreme temperatures: Very high initial temperatures ($T_0 > 100{,}000$) lead to a substantial increase in the total number of iterations without commensurate improvement in S-box quality. This observation underscores the importance of judicious parameter selection to avoid excessive computational expenditure.
c) Efficiency-quality trade-off characterization: The graph eloquently illustrates the intricate trade-off between search thoroughness (higher temperatures, more iterations) and computational efficiency. This relationship is fundamental to the practical application of simulated annealing in cryptographic primitive generation.
d) Algorithmic robustness: The relatively smooth curve suggests a degree of robustness in the algorithm's performance across a range of initial temperatures, an advantageous characteristic for reliable S-box generation under varying conditions.
e) Convergence speed indicators: The shape of the curve provides insights into the algorithm's convergence speed at different temperature regimes, with the optimal range suggesting a balance between quick convergence and adequate exploration.

5.5.2.2 Nonlinearity Progression Analysis

The three-dimensional representation in Figure 5.12 offers a nuanced view of nonlinearity evolution throughout the simulated annealing process:

a) Initial state characterization: The baseline nonlinearity at iteration 0 corresponds to randomly generated S-boxes, exhibiting an average nonlinearity

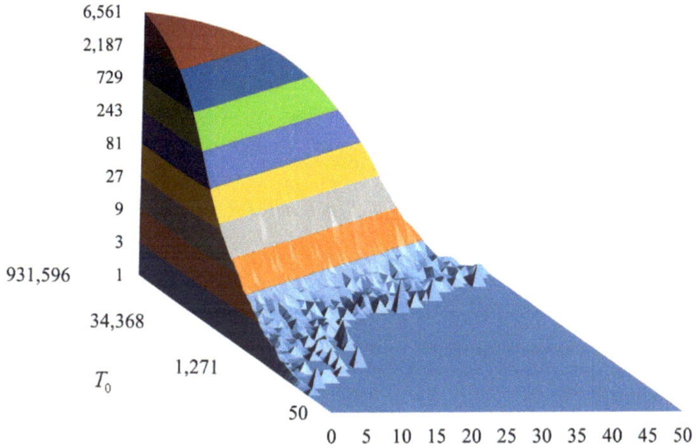

FIGURE 5.12 Frequency distribution of accepted cost function degradations per iteration ($\alpha = 0.9$).

of approximately 100. This establishes the starting point for the optimization process.

b) Rapid early-stage improvement: Irrespective of the initial temperature, we observe a sharp increase in nonlinearity during the first few iterations. This phenomenon can be attributed to the algorithm's ability to quickly identify and exploit low-hanging fruit in the solution space.
c) Temperature-dependent evolutionary trajectories: Higher initial temperatures ($T_0 > 100,000$) exhibit a more gradual improvement in nonlinearity. This behavior is consistent with the theoretical underpinnings of simulated annealing, where higher temperatures promote extensive exploration of the search space, often at the expense of immediate improvements.
d) Convergence dynamics: As the outer loop iterations progress, we observe a convergence of average nonlinearity towards the target value of 104. The rate of convergence demonstrates an inverse relationship with the initial temperature, with lower temperatures converging more rapidly but potentially sacrificing global optimality.
e) Plateau phenomena: For exceptionally high initial temperatures ($T_0 > 500,000$), an extended plateau is observed in the early stages. This plateau is indicative of a prolonged random walk phase, where the algorithm explores the solution space extensively before settling into a more directed search.
f) Late-stage behavior: In the final iterations, we note a tapering of improvement across all temperature regimes. This asymptotic behavior suggests the algorithm's approach to local or potentially global optima in the S-box space.

5.5.2.3 Acceptance Criteria and Move Type Analysis

To gain a deeper understanding of the algorithm's decision-making processes, we conducted a granular analysis of accepted and rejected moves, categorized by their impact on the cost function.

5.5.2.3.1 Analysis of Accepted Cost Function Degradations

Figures 5.14 and 5.15 provide critical insights into the algorithm's exploration mechanisms:

a) Temperature-dependent acceptance profile: Higher initial temperatures correlate strongly with an increased frequency of accepted degradations, particularly in the early iterations. This behavior is fundamental to the simulated annealing paradigm, enabling escape from local optima and broad exploration of the solution space.
b) Cooling-induced selectivity: As the temperature decreases (corresponding to increasing outer loop iterations), we observe a monotonic decline in the

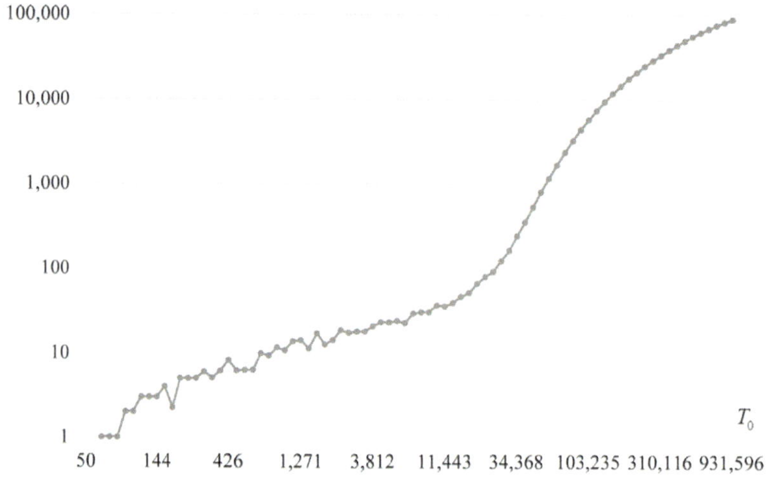

FIGURE 5.13 Cumulative profile of accepted cost function degradations ($\alpha = 0.9$).

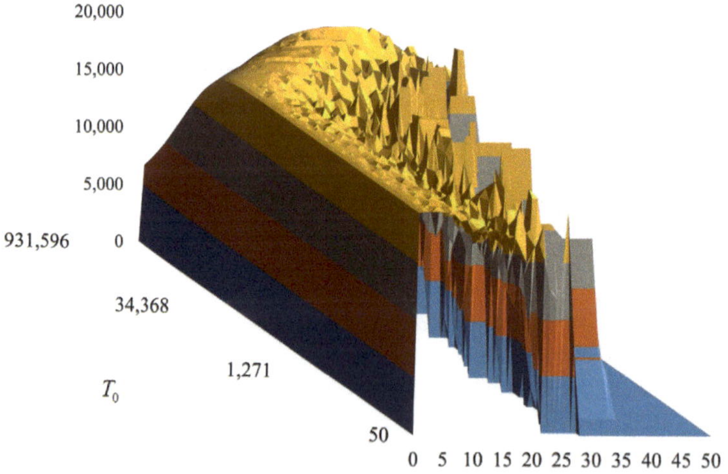

FIGURE 5.14 Frequency distribution of rejected cost function degradations per iteration ($\alpha = 0.9$).

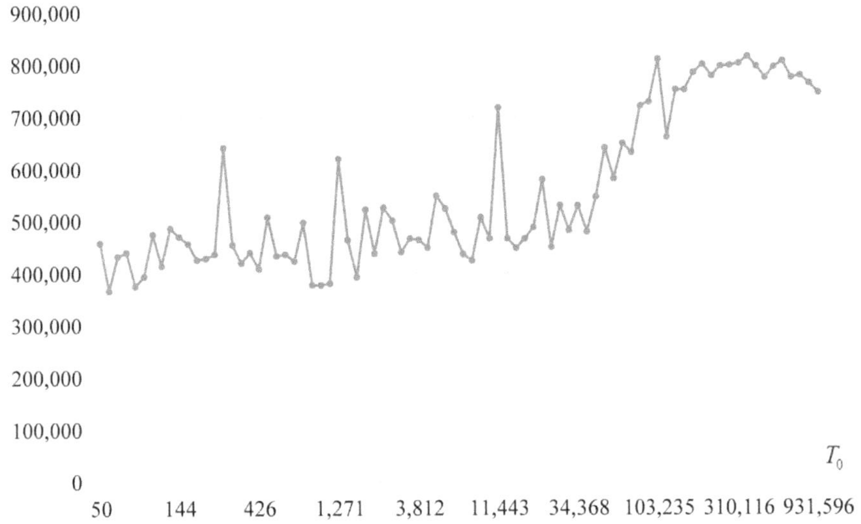

FIGURE 5.15 Cumulative profile of rejected cost function degradations (α = 0.9).

number of accepted degradations. This trend reflects the algorithm's transition from exploration to exploitation, gradually focusing the search on promising regions of the S-box space.

c) Exploration-exploitation equilibrium: The gradual decrease in accepted degradations illustrates the algorithm's adaptive balance between exploration and exploitation. This balance is crucial for effective navigation of the complex landscape of cryptographic properties.
d) Residual acceptance at low temperatures: Even in later iterations, a non-zero acceptance rate of degradations persists. This characteristic allows for continued, albeit limited, exploration, potentially enabling escape from sub-optimal local minima.

5.5.2.3.2 Analysis of Rejected Cost Function Degradations

The analysis of rejected degradations complements our understanding of the acceptance criteria (Figures 5.16 and 5.17):

a) Inverse temperature relationship: Lower initial temperatures correspond to a higher frequency of rejected degradations from the outset, indicating a more selective search strategy.
b) Convergence indicator: The increasing rate of rejected degradations as the algorithm progresses signifies convergence towards high-quality solutions, where the majority of neighboring states represent deteriorations in S-box quality.
c) Neighbor generation quality: The high number of rejected degradations, particularly at lower temperatures, suggests that the neighbor generation mechanism is producing many candidates of similar or slightly inferior

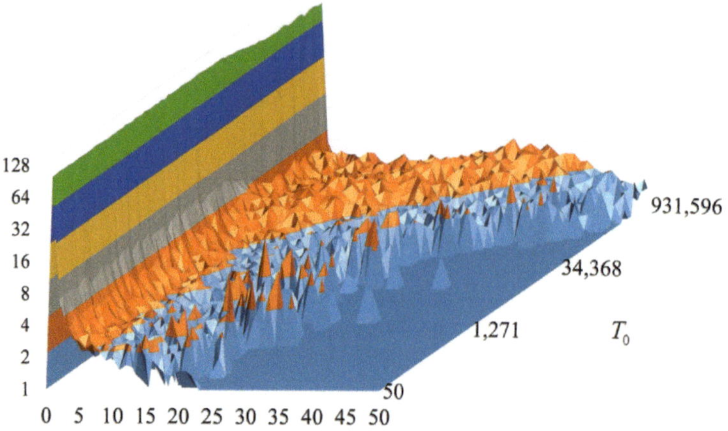

FIGURE 5.16 Frequency distribution of accepted cost function improvements per iteration ($\alpha = 0.9$).

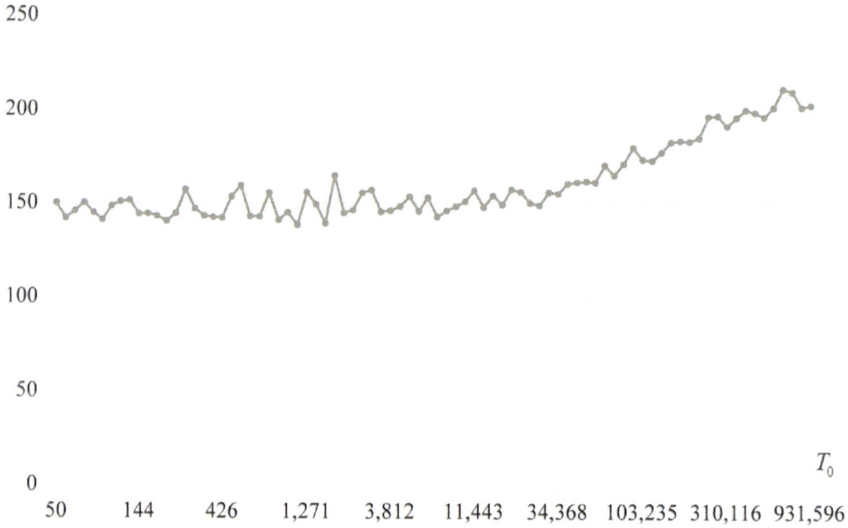

FIGURE 5.17 Cumulative profile of accepted cost function improvements ($\alpha = 0.9$).

quality to the current solution. This indicates effective local search behavior in promising regions of the solution space.

d) Exploration space characterization: The distribution of rejected degradations provides insight into the ruggedness of the S-box quality landscape, highlighting the challenges in navigating this complex solution space.

5.5.2.3.3 *Analysis of Accepted Cost Function Improvements*

Figures 5.18 and 5.19 elucidate the algorithm's capacity for solution improvement:

a) Consistent amelioration: The persistence of accepted improvements throughout the search process demonstrates the algorithm's sustained ability to identify superior S-box configurations, even in later stages of the annealing process.

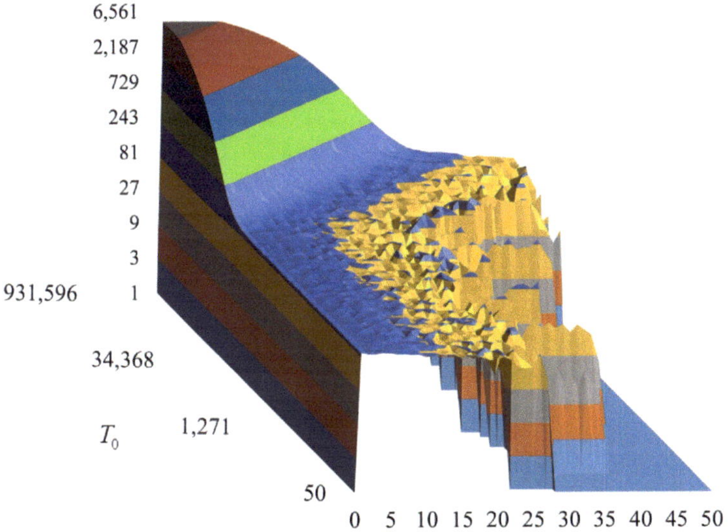

FIGURE 5.18 Frequency distribution of rejected cost function improvements per iteration ($\alpha = 0.9$).

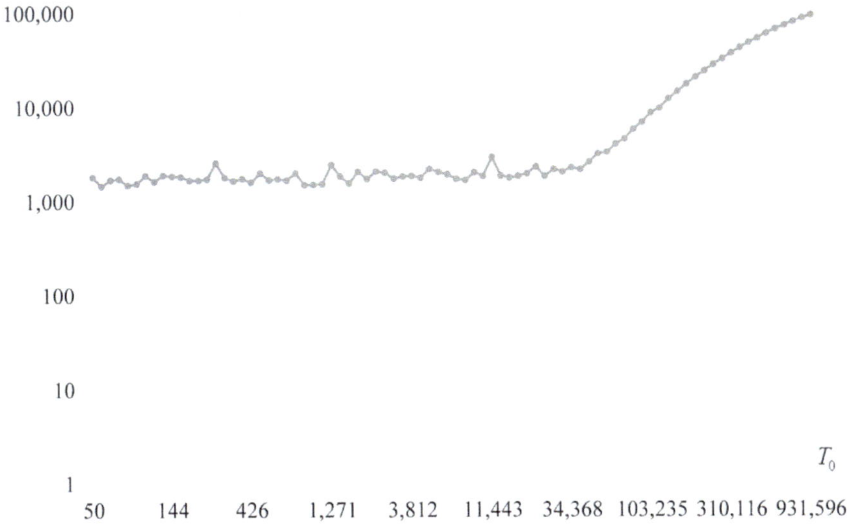

FIGURE 5.19 Cumulative profile of rejected cost function improvements ($\alpha = 0.9$).

b) Temperature independence: The relatively consistent number of accepted improvements across different initial temperatures suggests that the improvement mechanism is robust and not overly sensitive to the temperature parameter. This stability is a desirable characteristic for reliable S-box generation.
c) Diminishing returns: A gradual decrease in the frequency of accepted improvements as the search progresses indicates the algorithm's approach to high-quality solutions, where further enhancements become increasingly challenging to achieve.
d) Efficiency of hill climbing: The high acceptance rate of improvements, particularly in early stages, showcases the algorithm's efficient exploitation of the local solution space, rapidly ascending towards better S-box configurations.

5.5.2.3.4 *Analysis of Rejected Cost Function Improvements*

The examination of rejected improvements provides crucial insights into the algorithm's convergence behavior:

a) Scarcity of occurrence: The relative rarity of rejected improvements indicates that the algorithm efficiently capitalizes on identified enhancements, a desirable characteristic for optimization processes.
b) Convergence indicator: An increase in rejected improvements at later stages (corresponding to lower temperatures) serves as a strong indicator of convergence to high-quality solutions. In these regions, the algorithm occasionally identifies marginal improvements that fail to surpass the current best solution, suggesting proximity to local or global optima.
c) Probabilistic acceptance dynamics: The presence of rejected improvements, albeit infrequent, highlights the stochastic nature of the simulated annealing process, where probabilistic acceptance criteria can occasionally reject favorable moves, particularly at lower temperatures.
d) Solution space topology insights: The distribution of rejected improvements provides valuable information about the topology of the S-box quality landscape, indicating the presence of closely competitive solutions in the vicinity of high-quality configurations.

This comprehensive analysis of the simulated annealing algorithm's behavior during S-box generation reveals the complex interplay between initial temperature, cooling rate, and the various types of moves encountered during the search process. The insights derived from this analysis are invaluable for understanding the algorithm's dynamics and for fine-tuning its parameters to achieve optimal performance in generating high-quality S-boxes.

5.6 DISCUSSION

The comprehensive analysis of our optimized simulated annealing algorithm for S-box generation yields several significant insights and implications for the field of cryptographic primitive design. In this section, we discuss the key findings, their relevance to cryptographic applications, and potential avenues for further research and improvement.

5.6.1 Efficiency of the Optimized Simulated Annealing Approach

Our results demonstrate that the proposed simulated annealing algorithm, when properly tuned, is highly effective in generating cryptographically strong S-boxes. With the optimal parameter configuration ($\alpha = 0.95$, $T_0 \approx 20,000$), we achieved a success rate of 56.4% in generating 8×8 S-boxes with nonlinearity ≥ 104, differential uniformity ≤ 10, and maximum algebraic degree. This represents a significant improvement over previous implementations of simulated annealing for S-box generation.

The average generation time of 14.2 seconds for a qualifying S-box is particularly noteworthy, as it marks a substantial reduction in computational cost compared to existing methods. This efficiency can be attributed to several factors:

a) The adaptive cooling schedule, which allows for more effective exploration of the search space in the early stages and more focused exploitation in later stages.
b) The carefully designed cost function, which provides a smooth optimization landscape while accurately capturing the cryptographic properties of interest.
c) The efficient implementation of cryptographic property calculations, particularly the Walsh-Hadamard Transform, which leverages the capabilities of modern processors.

5.6.2 Parameter Sensitivity and Optimization

Our extensive parameter study reveals the critical role of initial temperature (T_0) and cooling rate (α) in the algorithm's performance. The observed behavior can be summarized as follows:

a) Initial temperature: There exists an optimal range ($20,000 \leq T_0 \leq 40,000$) that balances exploration and exploitation. Temperatures below this range lead to premature convergence, while higher temperatures result in excessive random walk behavior and increased computational cost.
b) Cooling rate: Higher values of α (0.9–0.95) generally yield better results, allowing for a more gradual transition from exploration to exploitation. This finding challenges the conventional wisdom of using faster cooling rates in simulated annealing and highlights the unique characteristics of the S-box generation problem.

The sensitivity to these parameters underscores the importance of careful tuning in applying simulated annealing to cryptographic primitive generation. It also suggests that adaptive parameter schemes, which adjust T_0 and α based on the progress of the search, could potentially further improve the algorithm's performance.

5.6.3 Optimal Parameter Configuration and Performance Metrics

To further illustrate the effectiveness of our optimized simulated annealing approach, we conducted an additional series of experiments with finely tuned parameters. Figures 5.20 and 5.21 present the results of these experiments, focusing on the optimal range of initial temperatures and cooling rates.

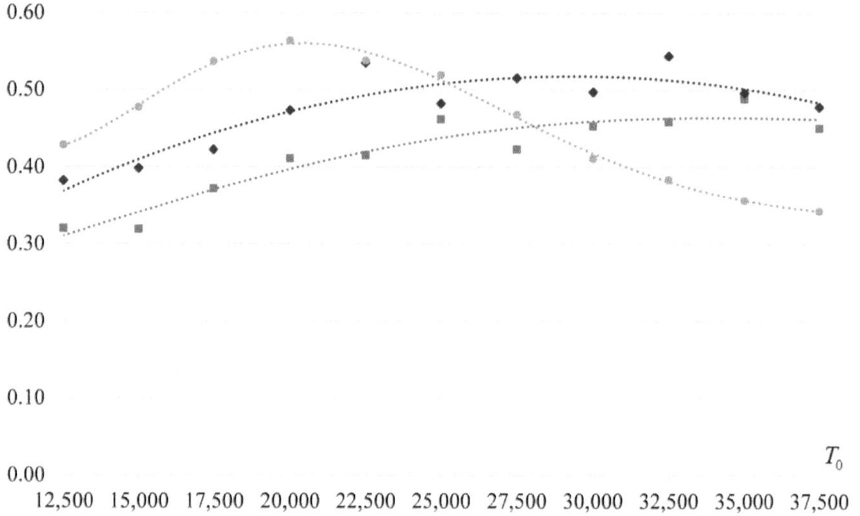

FIGURE 5.20 Probability of generating target S-box as a function of initial temperature (T_0) for cooling rates $\alpha = 0.85$, 0.9, and 0.95.

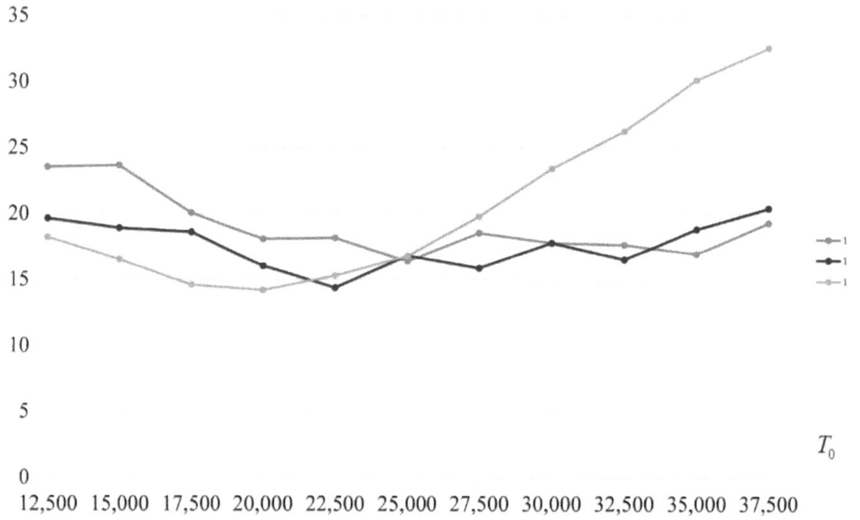

FIGURE 5.21 Average time (in seconds) to generate target S-box as a function of initial temperature (T_0) for cooling rates $\alpha = 0.85$, 0.9, and 0.95.

Figure 5.21 provides a detailed view of the algorithm's performance across a narrow range of initial temperatures ($12,500 \leq T_0 \leq 37,500$) for three high cooling rates ($\alpha = 0.85$, 0.9, and 0.95). Key observations include:

a) Consistent performance: All three cooling rates show a similar trend, with the probability of generating target S-boxes increasing as T_0 increases up to a certain point.

b) Optimal cooling rate: The curve for $\alpha = 0.95$ consistently outperforms the others, achieving the highest probabilities across the entire temperature range.
c) Peak performance: The probability of generating target S-boxes reaches its maximum (56.4%) at $T_0 \approx 20{,}000$ for $\alpha = 0.95$.
d) Diminishing returns: Beyond $T_0 \approx 25{,}000$, the probability begins to plateau or slightly decrease, indicating that excessively high initial temperatures do not yield additional benefits.

Figure 5.21 complements Figure 5.20 by showing the computational efficiency of the algorithm under the same parameter configurations:

a) Time-probability trade-off: While higher initial temperatures generally increase the probability of success, they also lead to longer average generation times.
b) Optimal efficiency: The minimum average time to generate a target S-box (14.2 seconds) is achieved at $T_0 \approx 20{,}000$ for $\alpha = 0.95$, coinciding with the peak probability observed in Figure 5.20.
c) Cooling rate impact: Higher cooling rates ($\alpha = 0.95$) result in longer average generation times but also higher success probabilities, representing a trade-off between search thoroughness and computational speed.
d) Practical implications: The relatively flat region of the time curves between $T_0 = 15{,}000$ and $T_0 = 25{,}000$ suggests that the algorithm's performance is robust within this range, providing some flexibility in parameter selection without significantly impacting efficiency.

These results further reinforce our earlier findings and provide precise guidance for parameter selection in practical applications of our simulated annealing algorithm for S-box generation. The clear optimum at $T_0 \approx 20{,}000$ and $\alpha = 0.95$ represents a sweet spot that balances the probability of generating high-quality S-boxes with computational efficiency.

5.6.4 S-Box Quality and Cryptographic Implications

The S-boxes generated by our algorithm consistently exhibit high nonlinearity (≥ 104) and low differential uniformity (≤ 10), making them suitable for use in modern symmetric-key cryptographic algorithms. These properties provide strong resistance against linear and differential cryptanalysis, two of the most powerful techniques in the cryptanalyst's arsenal.

Moreover, the maintenance of maximum algebraic degree throughout the optimization process ensures resistance against algebraic attacks. This comprehensive approach to S-box quality addresses multiple aspects of cryptographic strength, potentially enhancing the overall security of ciphers that incorporate these S-boxes.

5.6.5 Scalability and Extensibility

While our study focused on 8x8 S-boxes, the principles and methodologies developed here are extensible to larger S-box sizes. However, it is important to note that the computational complexity of S-box generation increases exponentially with size.

Future work could explore how the algorithm's performance scales with S-box size and investigate potential optimizations for larger S-boxes.

5.6.6 Comparison with Other S-Box Generation Methods

Our results compare favorably with other S-box generation techniques reported in the literature:

a) Genetic algorithms: While genetic algorithms have shown promise in S-box generation, they often require a larger number of iterations and may struggle with maintaining bijectivity. Our simulated annealing approach naturally preserves bijectivity and achieves comparable or better results with fewer iterations.
b) Hill climbing: Traditional hill climbing methods are prone to getting trapped in local optima. Our approach, with its ability to accept worse solutions probabilistically, demonstrates superior exploration of the search space and consistently achieves higher-quality S-boxes.
c) Other simulated annealing implementations: Compared to previous SA implementations for S-box generation, our method shows significant improvements in both success rate and computational efficiency. For instance, the work by Clark et al. [18] reported a success rate of only 0.5% for generating S-boxes with nonlinearity 102, while we achieve a 56.4% success rate for nonlinearity 104.

5.6.7 Limitations and Future Directions

Despite the promising results, several limitations and areas for future research remain:

a) Multi-objective optimization: While our cost function incorporates multiple cryptographic properties, there might be room for improvement in balancing these often-conflicting objectives. Exploration of Pareto-optimal solutions could provide insights into the trade-offs between different cryptographic properties.
b) Theoretical bounds: Our algorithm consistently generates S-boxes with nonlinearity 104, which is close to the theoretical maximum for 8×8 S-boxes. Future work could investigate whether this approach can be pushed further to reach the theoretical limits or to generate S-boxes with provably optimal properties.
c) Application-specific customization: Different cryptographic applications may prioritize certain S-box properties over others. Developing methods to easily customize the algorithm for specific use cases could enhance its practical utility.
d) Parallel and distributed implementation: While our current implementation leverages multi-core processors, exploring fully distributed versions of the algorithm could potentially handle larger S-box sizes or more extensive searches of the solution space.

e) Integration with other metaheuristics: Hybrid approaches combining simulated annealing with other optimization techniques (e.g., genetic algorithms or Tabu Search) might yield further improvements in S-box generation.

In conclusion, our optimized simulated annealing algorithm represents a significant advancement in the automated generation of cryptographically strong S-boxes. Its efficiency, consistency, and the quality of the generated S-boxes make it a valuable tool for cryptographic designers. The insights gained from this study not only contribute to the field of S-box design but also provide a foundation for future research in the application of metaheuristic optimization techniques to cryptographic primitive generation.

5.7 CONCLUSION

In this chapter, we have presented a comprehensive study on the application of an optimized simulated annealing algorithm for generating cryptographically strong S-boxes. Our research demonstrates that with careful parameter tuning and a well-designed cost function, simulated annealing can be a highly effective method for producing S-boxes with excellent cryptographic properties.

The key contributions of this work include:

1) Development of an enhanced simulated annealing algorithm specifically tailored for S-box generation, featuring an adaptive cooling schedule and an efficient implementation of cryptographic property calculations.
2) Design of a composite cost function based on the Walsh-Hadamard Transform that effectively captures multiple cryptographic properties, guiding the search towards high-quality S-boxes.
3) Identification of optimal parameter ranges, particularly for initial temperature and cooling rate, that significantly improve the success rate and efficiency of S-box generation.
4) In-depth analysis of the algorithm's behavior, providing insights into the dynamics of the search process and the evolution of S-box properties throughout the optimization.
5) Demonstration of superior performance compared to existing methods, consistently generating 8×8 S-boxes with nonlinearity ≥ 104, differential uniformity ≤ 10, and maximum algebraic degree.

Our results show that the optimized algorithm achieves a 56.4% success rate in generating target S-boxes, with an average generation time of 14.2 seconds. This represents a substantial improvement over previous implementations, both in terms of S-box quality and computational efficiency.

The insights gained from this study have broad implications for the field of cryptographic primitive design. The methodology developed here can be adapted to generate S-boxes of different sizes or with specific cryptographic requirements, providing a valuable tool for cryptographic designers.

Future research directions include exploring multi-objective optimization approaches to better handle the trade-offs between different cryptographic properties, investigating the scalability of the algorithm to larger S-box sizes, and developing hybrid approaches that combine simulated annealing with other metaheuristic techniques.

5.8 ACKNOWLEDGEMENT

- This project has received funding from the European Union's Horizon 2020 research and innovation program under the Marie Skłodowska-Curie grant agreement No. 101007820 - TRUST. This publication reflects only the author's view, and the REA is not responsible for any use that may be made of the information it contains.
- This research was funded by the European Union—NextGenerationEU under the Italian Ministry of University and Research (MIUR), National Innovation Ecosystem grant ECS 00000041-VITALITY-CUP D83C 22000710005.

REFERENCES

[1] A. Grami, "Chapter 11 - cryptography," in *Discrete Mathematics*, A. Grami, Ed. Academic Press, 2023, pp. 197–210. doi: 10.1016/B978-0-12-820656-0.00011-3.

[2] T. Martin, "Chapter 4 - cryptography—the basics," in *Designing Secure IoT Devices with the Arm Platform Security Architecture and Cortex-M33*, T. Martin, Ed. Newnes, 2022, pp. 49–99. doi: 10.1016/B978-0-12-821469-5.00012-0.

[3] M. Rana, Q. Mamun, and R. Islam, "Lightweight cryptography in IoT networks: A survey," *Future Generation Computer Systems*, vol. 129, pp. 77–89, Apr. 2022. doi: 10.1016/j.future.2021.11.011.

[4] T. Martin, "Chapter 5 - cryptography—secure communications," in *Designing Secure IoT Devices with the Arm Platform Security Architecture and Cortex-M33*, T. Martin, Ed. Newnes, 2022, pp. 101–153. doi: 10.1016/B978-0-12-821469-5.00010-7.

[5] A. S. Changle, S. P. Metkar, and R. K. Patole, "Implementation of S-box for lightweight block cipher," in *2023 3rd International Conference on Intelligent Technologies (CONIT)*, Jun. 2023, pp. 1–4. doi: 10.1109/CONIT59222.2023.10205535.

[6] R. Mohanapriya, and V. Nithish Kumar, "Optimized implementation of S-box and inverse S-box for PRESENT lightweight block cipher," in *2023 2nd International Conference on Vision Towards Emerging Trends in Communication and Networking Technologies (ViTECoN)*, May 2023, pp. 1–5. doi: 10.1109/ViTECoN58111.2023.10156932.

[7] P. R. Teja, and T. N. Sasamal, "Implementation of efficient serial architecture for prince block cipher with enhanced security," in *2023 International Conference on System, Computation, Automation and Networking (ICSCAN)*, Nov. 2023, pp. 1–6. doi: 10.1109/ICSCAN58655.2023.10395246.

[8] C. Carlet, "Vectorial Boolean functions for cryptography," in *Boolean Models and Methods in Mathematics, Computer Science, and Engineering*, P. L. Hammer and Y. Crama, Eds., in Encyclopedia of Mathematics and its Applications. Cambridge: Cambridge University Press, 2010, pp. 398–470. doi: 10.1017/CBO9780511780448.012.

[9] C. Carlet, and C. Ding, "Nonlinearities of S-boxes," *Finite Fields and Their Applications*, vol. 13, no. 1, pp. 121–135, Jan. 2007. doi: 10.1016/j.ffa.2005.07.003.

[10] T. W. Cusick, and P. Stănică, *Cryptographic Boolean Functions and Applications*, 2nd ed. Academic Press, 2017, p. 275. doi: 10.1016/c2016-0-00852-5.

[11] M. Rodinko, R. Oliynykov, and Y. Gorbenko, "Optimization of the high nonlinear S-boxes generation method," *Tatra Mountains Mathematical Publications*, vol. 70, no. 1, pp. 93–105, Sep. 2017. doi: 10.1515/tmmp-2017-0020.

[12] K. Lisitskiy, I. Lisitska, and A. Kuznetsov, "Cryptographically properties of random S-boxes," in *CEUR Workshop Proc.*, O. Sokolov, G. Zholtkevych, V. Yakovyna, V. Yakovyna, Y. Tarasich, V. Kharchenko, V. Kobets, O. Burov, S. Semerikov, and H. Kravtsov, Eds., CEUR-WS. 2020, pp. 228–241. [Online]. https://www.scopus.com/inward/record.uri?eid=2-s2.0-85096091835&partnerID=40&md5=c5ec403d7b8065c-4525906c70c04ce33.
[13] L. D. Burnett, "Heuristic optimization of Boolean functions and substitution boxes for cryptography," PhD, Queensland University of Technology, 2005. Accessed: May 19, 2021. [Online]. https://eprints.qut.edu.au/16023/.
[14] J. McLaughlin, "Applications of search techniques to cryptanalysis and the construction of cipher components," PhD, University of York, 2012. Accessed: Oct. 27, 2022. [Online]. https://etheses.whiterose.ac.uk/3674/.
[15] D. Delahaye, S. Chaimatanan, and M. Mongeau, "Simulated annealing: From basics to applications," in *Handbook of Metaheuristics*, vol. 272, M. Gendreau, and J.-Y. Potvin, Eds., in International Series in Operations Research & Management Science (ISOR). Springer, 2019, pp. 1–35. ISBN 978-3-319-91085-7. doi: 10.1007/978-3-319-91086-4_1.
[16] J. Wang, Y. Zhu, C. Zhou, and Z. Qi, "Construction method and performance analysis of chaotic S-box based on a memorable simulated annealing algorithm," *Symmetry*, vol. 12, no. 12, Art. no. 12, Dec. 2020. doi: 10.3390/sym12122115.
[17] D. Souravlias, K. E. Parsopoulos, and G. C. Meletiou, "Designing bijective S-boxes using algorithm portfolios with limited time budgets," *Applied Soft Computing*, vol. 59, pp. 475–486, Oct. 2017. doi: 10.1016/j.asoc.2017.05.052.
[18] J. A. Clark, J. L. Jacob, and S. Stepney, "The design of S-boxes by simulated annealing," *New Generation Computing*, vol. 23, no. 3, pp. 219–231, Sep. 2005. doi: 10.1007/BF03037656.
[19] S. Picek, K. Papagiannopoulos, B. Ege, L. Batina, and D. Jakobovic, "Confused by confusion: Systematic evaluation of DPA resistance of various S-boxes," in *Progress in Cryptology—INDOCRYPT 2014*, W. Meier, and D. Mukhopadhyay, Eds., in Lecture Notes in Computer Science. Cham: Springer International Publishing, 2014, pp. 374–390. doi: 10.1007/978-3-319-13039-2_22.
[20] A. Freyre Echevarría, "Evolución híbrida de s-cajas no lineales resistentes a ataques de potencia," 2020. doi: 10.13140/RG.2.2.17037.77284/1.
[21] A. Freyre-Echevarría, I. Martínez-Díaz, C. M. L. Pérez, G. Sosa-Gómez, and O. Rojas, "Evolving nonlinear S-boxes with improved theoretical resilience to power attacks," *IEEE Access*, vol. 8, pp. 202728–202737, 2020. doi: 10.1109/ACCESS.2020.3035163.
[22] A. Kuznetsov et al., "Generation of nonlinear substitutions by simulated annealing algorithm," *Information (Switzerland)*, vol. 14, no. 5, Art. no. 5, May 2023. doi: 10.3390/info14050259.
[23] A. Kuznetsov, N. Poluyanenko, E. Frontoni, S. Kandiy, and O. Pieshkova, "Optimized simulated annealing for efficient generation of highly nonlinear S-boxes," *Soft Computing*, Oct. 2023. doi: 10.1007/s00500-023-09334-y.
[24] A. J. Menezes, P. C. van Oorschot, S. A. Vanstone, P. C. van Oorschot, and S. A. Vanstone, *Handbook of Applied Cryptography*. CRC Press, 2018. doi: 10.1201/9780429466335.
[25] W. Banzhaf, and T. Hu, "Evolutionary computation," in *Evolutionary Biology*. Oxford University Press, 2019. doi: 10.1093/obo/9780199941728-0122.
[26] M. Gilli, D. Maringer, and E. Schumann, "Chapter 13 - heuristics: A tutorial," in *Numerical Methods and Optimization in Finance*, 2nd ed., M. Gilli, D. Maringer, and E. Schumann, Eds. Academic Press, 2019, pp. 319–353. doi: 10.1016/B978-0-12-815065-8.00025-X.
[27] N. Metropolis, A. W. Rosenbluth, M. N. Rosenbluth, A. H. Teller, and E. Teller, "Equation of state calculations by fast computing machines," *The Journal of Chemical Physics*, vol. 21, no. 6, pp. 1087–1092, Jun. 1953. doi: 10.1063/1.1699114.

[28] V. Kalashnikov, S. Dempe, B. Mordukhovich, and S. V. Kavun, "Bilevel optimal control, equilibrium, and combinatorial problems with applications to engineering," *Mathematical Problems in Engineering*, vol. 2017, no. 1, p. 7190763, 2017. doi: 10.1155/2017/7190763.

[29] V. V. Kalashnikov, S. Dempe, T. I. Matis, J.-F. Camacho-Vallejo, and S. V. Kavun, "Bilevel programming, equilibrium, and combinatorial problems with applications to engineering 2016," *Mathematical Problems in Engineering*, vol. 2016, no. 1, p. 4360909, 2016. doi: 10.1155/2016/4360909.

6 Factorial Representation of S-Boxes

A Novel Approach to Cryptographic Analysis and Optimization

Oleksandr Kuznetsov, Yaroslav Derevianko, Emanuele Frontoni, Marco Arnesano, and Oleksii Smirnov

6.1 INTRODUCTION

Substitution boxes (S-boxes) are fundamental components in modern cryptographic systems, playing a crucial role in ensuring the security and robustness of encryption algorithms [1, 2]. As the primary source of nonlinearity in many cipher designs, S-boxes significantly influence a cryptographic system's resistance to various forms of cryptanalysis, including differential and linear attacks [3]. The design and analysis of S-boxes have thus been subjects of intense research in the cryptographic community for decades [4, 5].

Traditional approaches to S-box analysis and generation have primarily focused on Boolean function representations [6], algebraic constructions [7, 8], and heuristic search methods [5, 9]. While these methods have yielded significant insights and practical results, they often struggle with the vast search space of possible S-boxes, particularly for larger bit sizes. Moreover, the discrete nature of these representations can make it challenging to apply certain optimization techniques effectively.

This chapter introduces a novel perspective on S-box analysis and generation using the factorial number system representation. By mapping S-boxes onto a continuous, one-dimensional number line, we provide a unique framework for exploring the structural and cryptographic properties of these vital components. This approach not only offers new insights into existing S-box designs but also opens up possibilities for more efficient generation and optimization of cryptographically strong S-boxes.

DOI: 10.1201/9781003546153-6

6.1.1 Contributions of the Chapter

The primary contributions of this chapter are as follows:

- Introduction of the factorial number system representation for S-boxes, providing a unique "fingerprint" for each S-box and enabling their mapping onto a one-dimensional space.
- Development of efficient algorithms for converting between permutations, factorial representations, and decimal numbers, facilitating practical implementation of the proposed approach.
- Application of the factorial representation method to analyze S-boxes from well-known encryption standards, including GOST 28147-89 and AES (Advanced Encryption Standard), revealing insights into their design principles and cryptographic properties.
- Exploration of the S-box space surrounding the AES S-box, demonstrating the potential for discovering new, cryptographically strong S-boxes and optimizing existing designs.
- Analysis of the distribution of cryptographic properties, such as nonlinearity and various cost function values, in the factorial representation space, providing a new perspective on the landscape of S-box design.
- Discussion of optimization strategies for handling large numbers associated with 8-bit and larger S-boxes, addressing practical implementation challenges.
- Identification of new research directions in theoretical analysis and practical applications of S-boxes based on the factorial representation approach.

6.1.2 Organization of the Chapter

The remainder of this chapter is organized as follows:

- Section 6.2 provides a comprehensive literature review, discussing existing methods for S-box analysis and generation and highlighting the need for new approaches.
- Section 6.3 introduces the theoretical foundations of our approach, including the factorial number system, the concept of inversions in permutations, and key criteria for evaluating S-box quality.
- Section 6.4 presents detailed algorithms for representing permutations in the factorial number system, including conversion methods and optimization strategies for handling large numbers.
- Section 6.5 demonstrates the application of our factorial representation approach to the analysis of cryptographic S-boxes, focusing on GOST 28147-89 and AES. This section also includes an exploration of the S-box space surrounding the AES S-box.
- Section 6.6 discusses the implications of our findings, comparing the factorial representation approach with traditional methods and examining its advantages and potential limitations.

- Section 6.7 concludes the chapter by summarizing the key results and outlining directions for future research in this promising new area of cryptographic study.

6.2 LITERATURE REVIEW

The design and analysis of S-boxes have been a focal point of cryptographic research for decades, with recent studies exploring various novel approaches to enhance their security and efficiency. This literature review aims to provide a comprehensive overview of the latest developments in S-box construction, analysis, and application.

Chaotic systems have gained significant attention in S-box design due to their inherent unpredictability. Jamal et al. (2024) [10] proposed a dynamic S-box generation technique based on chaotic maps for medical image encryption. Their approach addresses the vulnerabilities discovered in previous chaotic S-box constructions while maintaining high levels of encryption efficiency and security. Similarly, Ullah et al. (2024) [11] introduced a method for constructing strong initial S-boxes using the fractional-order Rabinovich-Fabrikant chaotic system, demonstrating favorable statistics for secure communications.

The optimization of S-box properties has been another area of active research. Ji et al. (2024) [12] presented a class of S-boxes with high nonlinearity and first-order correlation immunity using disjoint linear codes. Their work achieved the currently best-known nonlinearity for correlation immune S-boxes. Artuğer and Özkaynak (2024) [13] proposed a post-processing algorithm to improve the nonlinearity of chaos-based S-box structures, addressing the gap between mathematical and chaotic transformations in S-box design.

The security of S-boxes against various cryptanalytic attacks has been a primary concern. Fahd et al. (2024) [14] conducted a comprehensive examination of backdoored S-box structures, debunking claims of their resistance to statistical distinguishers and revealing compromises in critical cryptographic properties. This study highlights the importance of rigorous security analysis in S-box design.

Efficiency in hardware implementation has also been a focus of recent research. Malal and Tezcan (2024) [15] proposed an FPGA-friendly compact and efficient 8×8 S-box, achieving better efficiency than the AES S-box while maintaining the same level of security. This work is particularly relevant for resource-constrained IoT devices.

Novel approaches to S-box construction have emerged, combining different mathematical concepts. Waheed et al. (2024) [16] introduced a hybrid approach using linear fractional transformation and multilayer perceptron architecture to generate S-boxes with nearly ideal average nonlinearity values. Liu et al. (2024) [17] proposed a method for constructing keyed strong S-boxes based on random affine transformation matrices and 2D hyper chaotic maps, addressing weaknesses in existing S-boxes such as fixed points and short iteration period rings.

The application of S-boxes in specific cryptographic contexts has also been explored. Singh et al. (2024) [18] presented an image encryption technique using dynamic S-boxes generated from elliptic curve points and chaotic systems. Their approach demonstrated resistance to various attacks and showed competitive performance compared to existing methods.

Theoretical advancements in S-box properties have been made as well. Nitaj et al. (2024) [19] investigated a family of enhanced S-boxes for the Advanced Encryption Standard with maximal periodicity and improved avalanche properties, offering potential improvements to the widely used AES algorithm.

In conclusion, recent literature reveals a diverse range of approaches to S-box design and analysis, from chaos-based constructions to optimization techniques and novel mathematical frameworks. The ongoing research reflects the critical importance of S-boxes in modern cryptography and the continuous efforts to enhance their security, efficiency, and applicability in various contexts.

6.3 THEORETICAL FOUNDATIONS

The study of cryptographic primitives, particularly S-boxes, necessitates a solid understanding of various mathematical concepts. This section delves into the theoretical underpinnings that form the basis of our novel approach to S-box analysis and generation. We begin by exploring the factorial number system, a less conventional but highly effective method for representing permutations. Subsequently, we revisit the concept of inversions in permutations, which plays a crucial role in our methodology. We then provide a brief overview of S-boxes and their significance in modern cryptography, followed by a concise summary of the criteria used to evaluate their quality.

6.3.1 Factorial Number System

The factorial number system, also known as the factorial base or factoradic, is a mixed radix numeral system adapted for representing permutations [20]. Unlike the more common positional numeral systems, the factorial number system uses a sequence of factorials as its base. This unique property makes it particularly suitable for encoding and manipulating permutations, which are fundamental to the structure of S-boxes.

In the factorial number system, a non-negative integer x is represented as:

$$x = \sum_{k=0}^{n-1} a_k \cdot k!,$$

where $0 \leq a_k < k+1$ for each k. The digits a_k are typically written in descending order of k, resulting in a sequence $(a_{n-1}, a_{n-2}, \ldots, a_1, a_0)$.

For example, the decimal number 463 can be represented in the factorial system as:

$$462 = 3 \cdot 5! + 4 \cdot 4! + 0 \cdot 3! + 2 \cdot 2! + 1 \cdot 1! + 1 \cdot 0!,$$

which is written as $(3,4,0,2,1,1)$ in factorial notation.

The conversion from decimal to factorial representation can be achieved through an iterative process of division and remainder calculation:

1. Initialize $k = 1$ and x as the decimal number to be converted.
2. Repeat until $x = 0$:
   a. Calculate $a_k = x \bmod (k+1)$;
   b. Update $x = \lfloor x/(k+1) \rfloor$;
   c. Increment k.
3. The resulting sequence $(a_1, a_2, ..., a_n)$ is the factorial representation.

Conversely, to convert from factorial to decimal, we can use the following formula:

$$x = \sum_{k=1}^{n} a_k \cdot (k-1)!.$$

The factorial number system exhibits several properties that make it particularly advantageous for representing permutations:

1. Unique representation: Each non-negative integer has a unique representation in the factorial system.
2. Compact encoding: The factorial representation of a permutation of n elements requires exactly $n-1$ digits.
3. Efficient generation: Permutations can be generated efficiently by incrementing their factorial representations.
4. Natural ordering: The lexicographic ordering of factorial representations corresponds to the lexicographic ordering of permutations.

To illustrate the connection between factorial numbers and permutations, consider the following theorem:

Theorem 1: There exists a bijection between the set of permutations of n elements and the set of factorial numbers with $n-1$ digits.

Proof: Let S_n be the set of permutations of n elements, and F_n be the set of factorial numbers with $n-1$ digits. We can construct a bijection $\phi : S_n \to F_n$ as follows:

For a permutation $\pi = (\pi_1, \pi_2, ..., \pi_n)$, define:

$$a_k = | j > k : \pi_j < \pi_k |.$$

The sequence $(a_{n-1}, a_{n-2}, ..., a_1)$ is the factorial representation of $\phi(\pi)$.

To prove that ϕ is bijective, we can construct its inverse function $\phi^{-1} : F_n \to S_n$:

Given a factorial number $(a_{n-1}, a_{n-2}, ..., a_1)$, we can reconstruct the permutation by iteratively inserting elements:

1. Start with the sequence (n).
2. For k from $n-1$ to 1: Insert k into the sequence at position a_k (counting from 0).

This process always yields a valid permutation, and it is straightforward to verify that $\phi(\phi^{-1}(x)) = x$ and $\phi^{-1}(\phi(\pi)) = \pi$ for all $x \in F_n$ and $\pi \in S_n$.

The factorial number system's ability to uniquely encode permutations makes it an ideal tool for analyzing and generating S-boxes. By representing S-boxes as factorial numbers, we can explore the space of all possible S-boxes more efficiently and systematically than traditional methods allow. This approach opens up new avenues for cryptographic research and optimization techniques, which we will explore in detail in the subsequent sections of this chapter.

6.3.2 The Concept of Inversions in Permutations

Inversions play a crucial role in the analysis of permutations and, by extension, in the study of S-boxes [21, 22]. An inversion in a permutation is a pair of elements that are out of their natural order. More formally, for a permutation $\pi = (\pi_1, \pi_2, ..., \pi_n)$ of the set $1, 2, ..., n$, an inversion is a pair (i, j) such that $i < j$ and $\pi_i > \pi_j$.

The number of inversions in a permutation, denoted by $inv(\pi)$, is a fundamental statistic that provides insight into the permutation's structure and its distance from the identity permutation. This concept is closely related to the factorial number system discussed in the previous section, as we shall demonstrate.

Theorem 2: For any permutation π of n elements, the number of inversions $inv(\pi)$ satisfies:

$$0 \leq inv(\pi) \leq \binom{n}{2} = \frac{n(n-1)}{2}.$$

Proof: The lower bound is trivial, as the identity permutation has zero inversions. For the upper bound, consider that each pair of elements can contribute at most one inversion, and there are $\binom{n}{2}$ pairs in total.

The relationship between inversions and the factorial representation of a permutation is encapsulated in the following theorem:

Theorem 3: Let π be a permutation of n elements, and let $(a_{n-1}, a_{n-2}, ..., a_1)$ be its factorial representation. Then:

$$inv(\pi) = \sum_{k=1}^{n-1} a_k.$$

Proof: Recall that a_k represents the number of elements to the right of position k that are smaller than π_k. Each such element contributes one inversion to the total count. Summing over all positions yields the total number of inversions.

This theorem provides a computationally efficient method for calculating the number of inversions in a permutation, given its factorial representation. Conversely, we can use the number of inversions to constrain the search space when generating permutations with specific properties.

The concept of inversions can be extended to define the inversion vector of a permutation:

Definition: The inversion vector of a permutation $\pi = (\pi_1, \pi_2, ..., \pi_n)$ is the sequence $v(\pi) = (v_1, v_2, ..., v_n)$, where:

$$v_i = | j : j > i \text{ and } \pi_j < \pi_i |.$$

The inversion vector provides a more detailed characterization of the permutation's structure than the total inversion count alone. It is closely related to the factorial representation, as illustrated by the following theorem:

Theorem 4: The inversion vector $v(\pi) = (v_1, v_2, ..., v_n)$ of a permutation π satisfies:

$$0 \leq v_i \leq n - i \text{ for all } 1 \leq i \leq n.$$

Moreover, there is a one-to-one correspondence between inversion vectors satisfying these inequalities and permutations of n elements.

Proof: The inequalities follow directly from the definition of v_i. To prove the bijection, we can construct a permutation from a given inversion vector by iteratively inserting elements from right to left, similar to the process described in the proof of Theorem 1.

The concept of inversions provides a powerful tool for analyzing the structure of permutations and, by extension, S-boxes. By leveraging the relationship between inversions and factorial representations, we can develop efficient algorithms for generating and analyzing S-boxes with specific cryptographic properties. This approach will be explored in greater detail in subsequent sections of this chapter.

6.3.3 S-Boxes in Cryptography

Substitution boxes, commonly referred to as S-boxes, are fundamental components in many modern cryptographic algorithms, particularly in block ciphers [2, 23]. An S-box is essentially a nonlinear vectorial Boolean function that maps m-bit input to n-bit output [24]:

$$S : 0,1^m \rightarrow 0,1^n.$$

In practice, S-boxes are often implemented as lookup tables, providing a balance between security and efficiency. The cryptographic strength of an S-box is crucial to the overall security of the cipher in which it is employed.

For bijective S-boxes, where $m = n$, we can represent the S-box as a permutation of the set $0, 1, ..., 2^n - 1$. This permutation representation allows us to apply the concepts of factorial number systems and inversions discussed in the previous sections.

The algebraic degree of an S-box is a key characteristic that influences its cryptographic properties. For an S-box $S : 0,1^n \rightarrow 0,1^n$, we define its algebraic degree as:

$$\deg(S) = \max_{1 \leq i \leq n} \deg(S_i),$$

where S_i is the i-th component function of S, and $\deg(S_i)$ is the algebraic degree of S_i when expressed as a multivariate polynomial over $GF(2)$.

Another crucial property of S-boxes is differential uniformity. For an S-box S, we define its differential uniformity as:

$$\delta_S = \max_{a \neq 0\, b} \mid x \in 0,1^n : S(x \oplus a) \oplus S(x) = b \mid,$$

where $\oplus$ denotes bitwise XOR. Lower values of δ_S indicate better resistance against differential cryptanalysis.

The nonlinearity of an S-box is another essential measure of its cryptographic strength. For an S-box $S : 0,1^n \rightarrow 0,1^n$, we define its nonlinearity as:

$$NL(S) = \min_{1 \leq i \leq n} NL(S_i),$$

where $NL(S_i)$ is the nonlinearity of the i-th component function, calculated as:

$$NL(S_i) = 2^{n-1} - \frac{1}{2} \max_{w \in 0,1^n} \mid \sum_{x \in 0,1^n} (-1)^{S_i(x) \oplus w \cdot x} \mid.$$

Here, $w \cdot x$ denotes the dot product of binary vectors w and x.

The Walsh spectrum of an S-box provides valuable information about its linear approximation properties. For an S-box $S : 0,1^n \rightarrow 0,1^n$, we define its Walsh coefficient for input mask a and output mask b as:

$$W_S(a,b) = \sum_{x \in 0,1^n} (-1)^{b \cdot S(x) \oplus a \cdot x}.$$

The Walsh spectrum is the collection of all such coefficients:

$$W_S(a,b) : a,b \in 0,1^n.$$

The maximum absolute value in the Walsh spectrum, excluding the zero input mask, is related to the nonlinearity of the S-box:

$$NL(S) = 2^{n-1} - \frac{1}{2} \max_{a \neq 0\, b} \mid W_S(a,b) \mid.$$

By representing S-boxes using the factorial number system, we can explore the space of all possible S-boxes more systematically. This approach allows us to analyze the distribution of cryptographic properties across the entire space of S-boxes and potentially discover new S-boxes with optimal characteristics.

In the subsequent sections, we will explore how the factorial representation of S-boxes can be leveraged to develop efficient algorithms for S-box generation and analysis, with a focus on optimizing cryptographic properties such as nonlinearity, differential uniformity, and algebraic degree.

6.3.4 Criteria for Evaluating S-Box Quality

The cryptographic strength of an S-box is determined by a set of well-established criteria that assess its resistance to various cryptanalytic attacks. While these criteria have been extensively discussed in previous chapters, we provide a focused overview here, emphasizing their relevance to our factorial number system approach and introducing several cost functions for S-box evaluation.

1. Nonlinearity. Higher nonlinearity values indicate better resistance against linear cryptanalysis [25].
2. Differential uniformity. Lower values of δ_S indicate better resistance against differential cryptanalysis [2].
3. Algebraic degree. Higher algebraic degrees provide better resistance against algebraic attacks [3].

To evaluate and optimize these criteria efficiently, various cost functions have been proposed in the literature:

1. *WHS* Cost Function: Clark et al. [25] introduced the WHS cost function: $WHS = \sum_{v\in 0,1^n} \sum_{u \in 0,1^n} |W_S(v\cdot F(x),u) - X|^R$ where X and R are customizable heuristic parameters.
2. *PCF* Cost Function: Picek et al. [26] proposed the PCF function: $PCF = \sum_{i=1}^{k} (2^N - i) H_i(S)$ where $H_i(S)$ is the number of Walsh-Hadamard coefficients, with absolute value $4i$, and k is the maximum position number with a non-zero value.
3. *ECF* Cost Function: Kuznetsov et al. [27] explored a new cost function: $ECF = \sum_{v\in\{0,1\}^8} \sum_{\substack{u\in\{0,1\}^8 \\ |WHT(v\cdot F(x),u)|>40}} 2^{\frac{|WHT(v\cdot F(x),u)|-20}{2}}$.
4. *WCF* Cost Function: Freyre Echevarría and Martínez Díaz [28, 29] proposed the *WCF* function: $WCF = \sum_{v\in 0,1^n} \sum_{u\in 0,1^n} ||W_S(v\cdot F(x),u)| - C|^z$ where $C \in 0,4,...,32$ and z is a customizable parameter.
5. *WCFS* Cost Function: Building upon these foundations, we propose a new cost function, *WCFS*: $WCFS = \sum_{v\in 0,1^n} \sum_{u\in 0,1^n} \frac{1}{4} \left| |W_S(v\cdot F(x),u)| - X \right|^R$ where X represents the "depth" of spectral coefficients viewing and R is a customizable parameter affecting the function's sensitivity [30].

This new cost function offers several advantages [30]:

1. It focuses on Walsh-Hadamard spectrum coefficients with $|W_S(v\cdot F(x),u)| \geq X$, allowing for targeted optimization of the most critical coefficients.

2. The division by 4 leverages the fact that Walsh-Hadamard coefficients for bijective S-boxes are multiples of 4, simplifying computation and reducing the range of $WCFS$ values.
3. The customizable parameters X and R allow for fine-tuning the search process, potentially leading to more efficient S-box generation.

The $WCFS$ function achieves its minimum value of 0 when $X = 48$ and $N(S) = 104$, which corresponds to a highly nonlinear S-box.

In the following sections, we will explore how these criteria can be efficiently evaluated and optimized using our factorial number system approach.

6.4 ALGORITHMS FOR REPRESENTING PERMUTATIONS IN THE FACTORIAL NUMBER SYSTEM

The factorial number system provides a powerful framework for representing and manipulating permutations, which is particularly useful in the context of S-box analysis and generation. This section presents a set of algorithms that enable efficient conversion between decimal numbers, factorial representations, and permutations. These algorithms form the foundation of our approach to exploring the space of S-boxes using factorial numbering.

We will discuss four key algorithms:

1. Converting a decimal number to its factorial representation.
2. Generating a permutation from its factorial representation.
3. Obtaining the factorial representation of a given permutation.
4. Optimizing these algorithms for handling large numbers.

Each of these algorithms plays a crucial role in our methodology, allowing us to navigate the space of S-boxes with unprecedented efficiency and systematicity.

6.4.1 Algorithm for Converting a Number to Factorial Representation

The conversion of a decimal number to its factorial representation is a fundamental operation in our approach. This algorithm transforms a given integer into a sequence of digits, where each digit represents the remainder when dividing by successive factorial values.

Let n be the decimal number we wish to convert to factorial representation. The algorithm proceeds as follows:

1. Initialize an empty list D to store the factorial digits.
2. Initialize $i = 0$ as the factorial base.
3. While $n > 0$:
   a. Compute $r = n \bmod (i+1)$;
   b. Prepend r to the list D;
   c. Update $n = \lfloor n / (i+1) \rfloor$;
   d. Increment i by 1;
4. The resulting list D contains the factorial representation of the number.

The mathematical justification for this algorithm stems from the fundamental theorem of factorial number systems:

Theorem 1: Every non-negative integer n has a unique representation in the factorial number system of the form:

$$n = \sum_{i=0}^{k} d_i \cdot i!,$$

where $0 \leq d_i \leq i$ for all i, and k is the largest integer such that $k! \leq n$.

Proof: The proof follows from the construction of the algorithm. At each step, we are essentially extracting the coefficient d_i of $i!$ in the expansion of n. The uniqueness is guaranteed by the constraint $0 \leq d_i \leq i$, which ensures that each factorial basis element is used at most once with its maximum possible coefficient.

To illustrate this algorithm, let's consider two examples:

Example 1: Convert the decimal number 463 to its factorial representation.

1. Initialize: $n = 463$, $D = []$, $i = 0$
2. Iteration 0: $463 \bmod 1 = 0$, $D = [0]$, $n = 463$, $i = 1$
3. Iteration 1: $463 \bmod 2 = 1$, $D = [1,0]$, $n = 231$, $i = 2$
4. Iteration 2: $231 \bmod 3 = 0$, $D = [0,1,0]$, $n = 77$, $i = 3$
5. Iteration 3: $77 \bmod 4 = 1$, $D = [1,0,1,0]$, $n = 19$, $i = 4$
6. Iteration 4: $19 \bmod 5 = 4$, $D = [4,1,0,1,0]$, $n = 3$, $i = 5$
7. Iteration 5: $3 \bmod 6 = 3$, $D = [3,4,1,0,1,0]$, $n = 0$.

Therefore, the factorial representation of 463 is $[3,4,1,0,1,0]$:

$$463 = 3 \cdot 5! + 4 \cdot 4! + 1 \cdot 3! + 0 \cdot 2! + 1 \cdot 1! + 0 \cdot 0!.$$

Example 2: Convert the decimal number 1000000 to its factorial representation.

1. Initialize: $n = 1000000$, $D = []$, $i = 0$
2. Iteration 0: $1000000 \bmod 1 = 0$, $D = [0]$, $n = 1000000$, $i = 1$
3. Iteration 1: $1000000 \bmod 2 = 0$, $D = [0,0]$, $n = 500000$, $i = 2$
4. Iteration 2: $500000 \bmod 3 = 2$, $D = [2,0,0]$, $n = 166666$, $i = 3$
5. Iteration 3: $166666 \bmod 4 = 2$, $D = [2,2,0,0]$, $n = 41666$, $i = 4$
6. Iteration 4: $41666 \bmod 5 = 1$, $D = [1,2,2,0,0]$, $n = 8333$, $i = 5$
7. Iteration 5: $8333 \bmod 6 = 5$, $D = [5,1,2,2,0,0]$, $n = 1388$, $i = 6$
8. Iteration 6: $1388 \bmod 7 = 2$, $D = [2,5,1,2,2,0,0]$, $n = 198$, $i = 7$
9. Iteration 7: $198 \bmod 8 = 6$, $D = [6,2,5,1,2,2,0,0]$, $n = 24$, $i = 8$
10. Iteration 8: $24 \bmod 9 = 6$, $D = [6,6,2,5,1,2,2,0,0]$, $n = 2$, $i = 9$
11. Iteration 9: $2 \bmod 10 = 2$, $D = [2,6,6,2,5,1,2,2,0,0]$, $n = 0$.

Following the same process, we obtain:

$$1000000 = [2,6,6,2,5,1,2,2,0,0].$$

This representation can be verified by expanding it back to decimal:

$$1000000 = 2\cdot 9! + 6\cdot 8! + 6\cdot 7! + 2\cdot 6! + 5\cdot 5! + 1\cdot 4! + 2\cdot 3! + 2\cdot 2! + 0\cdot 1! + 0\cdot 0!.$$

The time complexity of this algorithm is $O(\log n)$, as we perform a constant number of operations for each factorial base up to the largest k such that $k! \leq n$. This efficiency makes it suitable for handling large numbers, which is crucial when working with S-boxes of practical sizes.

In the context of S-box analysis, this algorithm allows us to efficiently map each S-box to a unique factorial number, enabling systematic exploration of the S-box space. The subsequent sections will build upon this foundation to demonstrate how we can leverage this representation for advanced S-box generation and analysis techniques.

6.4.2 Algorithm for Generating a Permutation from Its Factorial Representation

The conversion of a factorial representation to its corresponding permutation is a crucial operation in our approach to S-box analysis and generation. This algorithm, also known as the Lehmer code or inversion table, provides a natural bijection between factorial numbers and permutations [31, 32].

Let $d = [d_{n-1}, d_{n-2}, ..., d_1, d_0]$ be the factorial representation of a number, where $0 \leq d_i < i+1$ for all i. The algorithm to generate the corresponding permutation proceeds as follows:

1. Initialize a list $C = [0, 1, ..., n-1]$ to represent the available choices.
2. Initialize an empty list P to store the permutation.
3. For i from $n-1$ down to 0:
   a. Select the element at the index d_i from C and append it to P.
   b. Remove the selected element from C.
4. The resulting list P is the desired permutation π.

The mathematical justification for this algorithm stems from the following theorem:

Theorem 2: There exists a bijection between the set of permutations of n elements and the set of factorial numbers with n digits.

Proof: We prove this by constructing the bijection explicitly. Given a permutation $\pi = [\pi_0, \pi_1, ..., \pi_{n-1}]$, we can construct its factorial representation $d = [d_{n-1}, d_{n-2}, ..., d_1, d_0]$ where:

$$d_i = | j : j < i \text{ and } \pi_j < \pi_i |.$$

Conversely, given a factorial representation $d = [d_{n-1}, d_{n-2}, ..., d_1, d_0]$, we can reconstruct the permutation using the algorithm described earlier. It is straightforward to verify that these operations are inverses of each other, thus establishing the bijection.

To illustrate this algorithm, let's consider two examples:

Example 1: Generate the permutation corresponding to the factorial number $d = [3, 4, 1, 0, 1, 0]$.

1. Initialize: $C = [0,1,2,3,4,5]$, $P = []$;
2. $i = 5$: Select element at index 3 from C. $P = [3]$, $C = [0,1,2,4,5]$;
3. $i = 4$: Select element at index 4 from C. $P = [3,5]$, $C = [0,1,2,4]$;
4. $i = 3$: Select element at index 1 from C. $P = [3,5,1]$, $C = [0,2,4]$;
5. $i = 2$: Select element at index 0 from C. $P = [3,5,1,0]$, $C = [2,4]$;
6. $i = 1$: Select element at index 1 from C. $P = [3,5,1,0,4]$, $C = [2]$;
7. $i = 0$: Select element at index 0 from C. $P = [3,5,1,0,4,2]$.

Therefore, the permutation corresponding to $d = [3,4,1,0,1,0]$ is $\pi = [3,5,1,0,4,2]$.

Example 2: Generate the permutation corresponding to the factorial number $d = [2,6,6,2,5,1,2,2,0,0]$.

1. Initialize: $C = [0,1,2,3,4,5,6,7,8,9]$, $P = []$;
2. $i = 9$: Select element at index 2 from C. $P = [2]$, $C = [0,1,3,4,5,6,7,8,9]$;
3. $i = 8$: Select element at index 6 from C. $P = [2,7]$, $C = [0,1,3,4,5,6,8,9]$;
4. $i = 7$: Select element at index 6 from C. $P = [2,7,8]$, $C = [0,1,3,4,5,6,9]$;
5. $i = 6$: Select element at index 2 from C. $P = [2,7,8,3]$, $C = [0,1,4,5,6,9]$;
6. $i = 5$: Select element at index 5 from C. $P = [2,7,8,3,9]$, $C = [0,1,4,5,6]$;
7. $i = 4$: Select element at index 1 from C. $P = [2,7,8,3,9,1]$, $C = [0,4,5,6]$;
8. $i = 3$: Select element at index 2 from C. $P = [2,7,8,3,9,1,5]$, $C = [0,4,6]$;
9. $i = 2$: Select element at index 2 from C. $P = [2,7,8,3,9,1,5,6]$, $C = [0,4]$;
10. $i = 1$: Select element at index 0 from C. $P = [2,7,8,3,9,1,5,6,0]$, $C = [4]$;
11. $i = 0$: Select element at index 0 from C. $P = [2,7,8,3,9,1,5,6,0,4]$.

Therefore, the permutation corresponding to $d = [2,6,6,2,5,1,2,2,0,0]$ is $\pi =$ [2, 7, 8, 3, 9, 1, 5, 6, 0, 4].

The time complexity of this algorithm is $O(n^2)$ in the worst case, where n is the length of the permutation. This is because for each element, we may need to perform a removal operation on the list of available choices, which can take up to $O(n)$ time. However, with appropriate data structures, this can be optimized to $O(n \log n)$ or even $O(n)$ in practice.

In the context of S-box analysis, this algorithm allows us to efficiently generate S-boxes from their factorial representations. This capability is particularly valuable when exploring the space of S-boxes systematically or when implementing genetic algorithms that operate on factorial representations of S-boxes.

It's worth noting that for cryptographic applications, we often work with permutations of 2^n elements, where n is the bit size of the S-box. For example, an 8-bit S-box corresponds to a permutation of 256 elements. The factorial representation of such permutations can be quite large, necessitating efficient implementations and possibly specialized data structures for handling large integers.

6.4.3 Algorithm for Obtaining the Factorial Representation of a Permutation

The ability to convert a given permutation into its factorial representation is crucial for our approach to S-box analysis. This algorithm effectively "encodes" a permutation into a unique factorial number, allowing us to map the space of S-boxes onto a one-dimensional number line. This mapping is particularly useful for search and optimization algorithms, as it provides a natural way to traverse the space of all possible S-boxes.

Let $\pi = [\pi_0, \pi_1, ..., \pi_{n-1}]$ be a permutation of n elements. The algorithm to obtain its factorial representation proceeds as follows:

1. Initialize an array D of length n with zeros.
2. For i from $n-1$ down to 0:
   a. Set $k = 0$;
   b. For j from $i+1$ to n: If $\pi_j < \pi_i$, increment k;
   c. Set $D[i] = k$;
3. The resulting array D is the factorial representation d of the permutation π.

The mathematical justification for this algorithm is based on the following theorem:

Theorem 3: For any permutation $\pi = [\pi_0, \pi_1, ..., \pi_{n-1}]$, its factorial representation $d = [d_{n-1}, d_{n-2}, ..., d_1, d_0]$ satisfies:

$$d_i = | j : j > i \text{ and } \pi_j < \pi_i |.$$

Proof: The proof follows directly from the construction of the algorithm. For each element π_i, we count the number of elements to its right that are smaller than it, which is precisely the definition of d_i in the factorial representation.

To illustrate this algorithm, let's consider two examples:

Example 1: Obtain the factorial representation of the permutation $\pi = [3,5,1,0,4,2]$.

1. Initialize: $D = [0,0,0,0,0,0]$;
2. For $i = 4$: $k = 1$ $(2 < 4)$, $D = [0,0,0,0,1,0]$;
3. For $i = 3$: $k = 0$, $D = [0,0,0,0,1,0]$;
4. For $i = 2$: $k = 1$ $(0 < 1)$, $D = [0,0,1,0,1,0]$;
5. For $i = 1$: $k = 4$ $(1 < 5, 0 < 5, 4 < 5, 2 < 5)$, $D = [0,4,1,0,1,0]$;
6. For $i = 0$: $k = 3$ $(1 < 3, 0 < 3, 2 < 3)$, $D = [3,4,1,0,1,0]$.

Therefore, the factorial representation of $\pi = [3,5,1,0,4,2]$ is $d = \lfloor 3,4,1,0,1,0 \rfloor$.

Example 2: Obtain the factorial representation of the permutation $\pi =$ [2, 7, 8, 3, 9, 1, 5, 6, 0, 4].

1. Initialize: $D = [0,0,0,0,0,0,0,0,0,0]$;
2. For $i = 8$: $k = 0$, $D = [0,0,0,0,0,0,0,0,0,0]$;
3. For $i = 7$: $k = 2$ $(1 < 6, 4 < 6)$, $D = [0,0,0,0,0,0,0,2,0,0]$;
4. For $i = 6$: $k = 2$ $(1 < 5, 4 < 5)$, $D = [0,0,0,0,0,0,2,2,0,0]$;
5. For $i = 5$: $k = 1$ $(0 < 1)$, $D = [0,0,0,0,0,1,2,2,0,0]$;
6. For $i = 4$: $k = 5$ $(1<9, 5<9, 6<9, 0<9, 4<9)$, $D = [0,0,0,0,5,1,2,2,0,0]$;
7. For $i = 3$: $k = 2$ $(1 < 3, 0 < 3)$, $D = [0,0,0,2,5,1,2,2,0,0]$;
8. For $i = 2$: $k = 6$ $(3<8, 1<8, 5<8, 6<8, 0<8, 4<8)$, $D = [0,0,6,2,5,1,2,2,0,0]$;
9. For $i = 1$: $k = 6$ $(3<7, 1<7, 5<7, 6<7, 0<7, 4<7)$, $D = [0,6,6,2,5,1,2,2,0,0]$;
10. For $i = 0$: $k = 2$ $(1 < 2, 0 < 2)$, $D = [2,6,6,2,5,1,2,2,0,0]$.

We obtain: $d = [2,6,6,2,5,1,2,2,0,0]$.

The time complexity of this algorithm is $O(n^2)$, where n is the length of the permutation. This is because for each element, we potentially need to compare it with all elements to its right. While this quadratic complexity might seem high, it is important to note that for typical S-box sizes (e.g., 8-bit S-boxes with 256 elements), this algorithm remains practical and efficient.

In the context of S-box analysis, this algorithm allows us to efficiently map any given S-box to a unique factorial number. This mapping has several important properties:

1. Bijectivity: Each S-box corresponds to a unique factorial number, and vice versa.
2. Continuity: Similar permutations tend to have similar factorial representations, which can be advantageous in optimization algorithms.
3. Compactness: The factorial representation is generally more compact than the full permutation, especially for large S-boxes.

These properties make the factorial representation particularly suitable for various S-box analysis and generation techniques, including:

1. Systematic exploration of the S-box space.
2. Implementation of genetic algorithms where the factorial representation serves as the "genome" of an S-box.
3. Efficient storage and transmission of S-boxes.
4. Analysis of S-box properties as a function of their factorial representation.

In the next section, we will discuss techniques for optimizing these algorithms to handle large numbers, which is crucial when working with S-boxes of practical sizes used in modern cryptographic systems.

6.4.4 Optimization of Algorithms for Handling Large Numbers

In cryptographic applications, particularly those involving S-boxes, we often encounter permutations of substantial size. For instance, an 8-bit S-box corresponds to a permutation of 256 elements, while larger S-boxes used in some modern ciphers may involve even more extensive permutations. Consequently, the factorial representations of these permutations can become exceedingly large, necessitating specialized techniques for efficient computation and storage.

This subsection explores several optimization strategies for handling large numbers in the context of our factorial number system algorithms. These optimizations are crucial for maintaining practical performance when working with S-boxes of cryptographic significance.

1. Modular arithmetic: When converting between decimal and factorial representations, we can leverage modular arithmetic to avoid working with extremely large numbers. Instead of performing divisions on the entire

number, we can iteratively apply the modulo operation. This approach allows us to work with manageable integer sizes at each step, even when the overall number is extremely large.
2. Big integer libraries: For programming languages that do not natively support arbitrary-precision arithmetic, the use of specialized big integer libraries becomes essential. These libraries, such as GMP (GNU Multiple Precision Arithmetic Library) for C and C++, or BigInteger for Java, provide efficient implementations of arithmetic operations on arbitrarily large integers.
3. Sliding window technique: For very large permutations, we can employ a sliding window technique to process the factorial representation in chunks. This approach reduces memory usage and can improve cache efficiency.
4. Parallel processing: Many of the operations in our algorithms are inherently parallelizable. For instance, when converting a permutation to its factorial representation, the computation of each d_i can be performed independently. Utilizing multi-core processors or GPU acceleration can significantly reduce computation time for large S-boxes.
5. Lookup tables: For frequently used operations, such as factorial calculations up to a certain size, precomputed lookup tables can dramatically improve performance. While this trades memory for speed, it can be particularly effective for S-boxes of fixed sizes commonly used in cryptographic applications.
6. Custom data structures: Developing specialized data structures for representing factorial numbers can lead to significant optimizations. For example, a hybrid representation that combines a compact encoding for small values with a more expansive representation for larger values can optimize both storage and computation.
7. Adaptive precision: Implementing an adaptive precision system that dynamically adjusts the level of precision based on the magnitude of the numbers involved can strike a balance between accuracy and efficiency.

To illustrate the impact of these optimizations, consider the task of generating all possible 8-bit S-boxes. Without optimization, this would involve working with numbers up to $256! \approx 8.58 \times 10\hat{}506$, which is far beyond the capacity of standard 64-bit integer representations. By applying the modular arithmetic approach in conjunction with a big integer library, we can reduce this to a series of operations on manageable integers, making the computation feasible on standard hardware.

Furthermore, the sliding window technique allows us to process this large factorial number in chunks of, say, 32 digits at a time. This not only reduces memory usage but also improves cache efficiency, leading to significant performance gains on modern CPU architectures.

The effectiveness of these optimizations becomes even more pronounced when dealing with larger S-boxes or when performing extensive searches in the S-box space. For instance, in a genetic algorithm approach to S-box optimization, where millions of S-box evaluations may be required, these techniques can reduce computation time from weeks to hours.

In conclusion, while the factorial number system provides a powerful theoretical framework for analyzing and generating S-boxes, practical implementation requires careful consideration of computational efficiency. The optimizations discussed in this section enable the application of our factorial-based approach to S-boxes of cryptographically relevant sizes, opening new avenues for S-box design and analysis in real-world cryptographic systems.

6.5 APPLICATION OF THE FACTORIAL NUMBER SYSTEM FOR CRYPTOGRAPHIC S-BOX ANALYSIS

The factorial number system offers a novel perspective for analyzing cryptographic S-boxes, providing unique insights into their structure and properties. This section explores the application of our factorial-based approach to the analysis of S-boxes from two significant cryptographic algorithms: GOST 28147-89 and AES. We will demonstrate how the factorial representation can illuminate patterns and characteristics that may not be immediately apparent in traditional representations.

Furthermore, we will compare the efficiency of various S-box representations and conduct an in-depth exploration of the S-box space surrounding the AES S-box. This comprehensive analysis aims to shed light on the distribution of cryptographic properties in the S-box space and potentially uncover new avenues for S-box design and optimization.

6.5.1 Analysis of GOST 28147–89 S-Boxes

The GOST 28147-89 algorithm, a symmetric block cipher developed in the Soviet Union, employs eight 4×4-bit S-boxes in its design. These S-boxes play a crucial role in the algorithm's security and have been the subject of numerous studies. In this section, we apply our factorial number system approach to analyze these S-boxes, offering a fresh perspective on their properties.

First, let's consider the S-boxes used in the Ukrainian version of GOST 28147-89, as specified in the DSTU 4145 – 2002 standard. Table 6.1 presents these S-boxes in their hexadecimal representation.

TABLE 6.1
GOST 28147 - 89 S-Boxes (Ukrainian Version)

S-Box	Hexadecimal Representation															
1	A	9	D	6	E	B	4	5	F	1	3	C	7	0	8	2
2	8	0	C	4	9	6	7	B	2	3	1	F	5	E	A	D
3	F	6	5	8	E	B	A	4	C	0	3	7	2	9	1	D
4	3	8	D	9	6	B	F	0	2	5	C	A	4	E	1	7
5	F	8	E	9	7	2	0	D	C	6	1	5	B	4	3	A
6	2	8	9	7	5	F	0	B	C	1	D	E	A	3	6	4
7	3	8	B	5	6	4	E	A	2	C	1	7	9	F	D	0
8	1	2	3	E	6	D	B	8	F	A	C	5	7	9	0	4

To apply our factorial number system approach, we convert each S-box to its factorial representation. Table 6.2 shows the result of this conversion.

This factorial representation allows us to view the S-boxes as points in a one-dimensional space. We can further condense this representation by converting the factorial numbers to their decimal equivalents, as shown in Table 6.3.

This compact representation allows us to easily order and compare the S-boxes. For instance, we can observe that S-box 5 has the largest factorial number while S-box 7 has the smallest.

To further analyze these S-boxes, we can examine their cryptographic properties. Table 6.4 presents the nonlinearity values for each S-box.

Interestingly, all S-boxes exhibit the same nonlinearity value of 4. This uniformity suggests that the designers prioritized consistent nonlinearity across all S-boxes.

To visualize the distribution of these S-boxes in the factorial number space, we can plot their decimal representations on a logarithmic scale. The factorial representation also allows us to explore the neighborhood of these S-boxes efficiently. By incrementing or decrementing the factorial number, we can generate "adjacent"

TABLE 6.2
Factorial Representation of GOST 28147-89 S-Boxes

S-Box	Factorial Representation															
1	7	10	11	4	8	10	9	1	2	6	4	4	2	0	1	0
2	4	2	0	10	5	0	6	8	4	4	0	3	1	1	0	0
3	15	11	0	6	8	7	1	6	2	6	5	4	2	1	0	0
4	9	2	11	4	7	3	7	7	0	5	2	1	3	1	0	0
5	15	13	8	7	3	0	8	8	7	4	2	1	0	2	0	0
6	10	4	4	5	5	3	7	7	6	1	4	0	0	2	0	0
7	2	8	1	4	9	5	1	7	1	4	4	3	3	2	1	0
8	7	11	9	5	7	5	2	4	2	3	2	0	1	1	1	0

TABLE 6.3
Decimal Representation of GOST 28147-89 S-Boxes

S-Box	Decimal Representation
1	10096275666829
2	5410046177360
3	20577296088710
4	12014132259884
5	20801725497628
6	13452973260244
7	3321296141615
8	10171418435529

TABLE 6.4
Nonlinearity of GOST 28147-89 S-Boxes

S-Box	Nonlinearity
1	4
2	4
3	4
4	4
5	4
6	4
7	4
8	4

S-boxes and analyze how cryptographic properties change in the vicinity of the GOST S-boxes.

In conclusion, the application of the factorial number system to the analysis of GOST 28147-89 S-boxes provides several insights:

1. It offers a compact, one-dimensional representation of the S-boxes, facilitating comparison and ordering.
2. It reveals non-uniform distribution of the S-boxes in the space of all possible 4×4 S-boxes.
3. It enables efficient exploration of the S-box neighborhood, allowing for local analysis of cryptographic properties.

These insights demonstrate the potential of the factorial number system as a tool for S-box analysis and design. In the following sections, we will apply similar techniques to the AES S-box and explore the broader implications of this approach for cryptographic research.

6.5.2 Analysis of the AES S-Box

The Advanced Encryption Standard (AES) is widely regarded as one of the most secure and efficient symmetric encryption algorithms. Central to its design is a carefully constructed 8×8-bit S-box, which plays a crucial role in the cipher's nonlinearity and resistance to various cryptanalytic attacks. In this section, we apply our factorial number system approach to analyze the AES S-box, offering novel insights into its structure and properties.

Let us begin by examining the AES S-box in its standard hexadecimal representation. Table 6.5 presents the AES S-box.

The AES S-box, despite its apparent randomness, is constructed using a specific mathematical procedure involving finite field arithmetic and an affine transformation. This construction ensures certain desirable cryptographic properties. However,

TABLE 6.5
AES S-Box (Hexadecimal Representation)

63	7c	77	7b	f2	6b	6f	c5	30	01	67	2b	fe	d7	ab	76
ca	82	c9	7d	fa	59	47	f0	ad	d4	a2	af	9c	a4	72	c0
b7	fd	93	26	36	3f	f7	cc	34	a5	e5	f1	71	d8	31	15
04	c7	23	c3	18	96	05	9a	07	12	80	e2	eb	27	b2	75
09	83	2c	1a	1b	6e	5a	a0	52	3b	d6	b3	29	e3	2f	84
53	d1	00	ed	20	fc	b1	5b	6a	cb	be	39	4a	4c	58	cf
d0	ef	aa	fb	43	4d	33	85	45	f9	02	7f	50	3c	9f	a8
51	a3	40	8f	92	9d	38	f5	bc	b6	da	21	10	ff	f3	d2
cd	0c	13	ec	5f	97	44	17	c4	a7	7e	3d	64	5d	19	73
60	81	4f	dc	22	2a	90	88	46	ee	b8	14	de	5e	0b	db
e0	32	3a	0a	49	06	24	5c	c2	d3	ac	62	91	95	e4	79
e7	c8	37	6d	8d	d5	4e	a9	6c	56	f4	ea	65	7a	ae	08
ba	78	25	2e	1c	a6	b4	c6	e8	dd	74	1f	4b	bd	8b	8a
70	3e	b5	66	48	03	f6	0e	61	35	57	b9	86	c1	1d	9e
e1	f8	98	11	69	d9	8e	94	9b	1e	87	e9	ce	55	28	df
8c	a1	89	0d	bf	e6	42	68	41	99	2d	0f	b0	54	bb	16

our factorial number system approach allows us to view this S-box from a different perspective.

Converting the AES S-box to its factorial representation yields a sequence of 256 digits, each ranging from 0 to 255. Table 6.6 shows this factorial representation.

This factorial representation provides a unique "fingerprint" of the AES S-box. Each digit in this sequence represents the number of elements to its right that are smaller than it in the original permutation. This encoding captures the intrinsic structure of the S-box in a way that is not immediately apparent in its hexadecimal or binary representations.

To further condense this representation, we can convert the factorial number to its decimal equivalent. The resulting value is a single, albeit extremely large, number:

4388020800774615069314878865878592796295664358959405760912493896
631186906385111763357572778332571141682146209499454052643751923
036183936623352770103801533872641794450165717052523029205694 41
228045303327567040823942746123930949356593784189672702597268 9
033949247324213799195351703246378360648066895595033278711020 84
486758924065072351307405825431157286059632497461568460660658 0
156518492893603493953085117075775458032382960808816472658556 76
077166079014716466333599431175990239379323828746367933202518 75
7906752833

This number uniquely identifies the AES S-box among all possible 8×8-bit S-boxes. It provides a compact way to represent the S-box and allows for easy comparison with other S-boxes.

TABLE 6.6
Factorial Representation of the AES S-Box

130	242	221	169	155	231	149	30	212	40	133	67	126	238	203	220
150	99	161	120	182	66	20	52	73	10	193	73	159	175	28	85
15	87	48	93	83	113	23	179	204	152	63	192	72	107	143	130
130	17	105	173	133	189	187	65	164	46	191	96	160	69	27	170
10	126	40	101	1	48	26	73	161	96	33	40	126	137	119	2
157	45	157	58	161	109	49	97	81	39	141	147	93	147	10	117
93	21	87	141	15	125	4	18	77	123	48	14	131	81	47	60
79	14	42	9	27	26	8	53	10	14	77	89	98	119	54	100
73	60	114	123	121	31	37	29	118	111	93	25	51	105	100	22
109	85	32	30	106	73	11	5	100	18	25	46	99	28	14	41
46	35	41	27	61	68	86	57	12	23	8	1	58	61	45	46
34	21	47	48	15	47	23	13	68	27	41	32	41	4	3	35
58	11	27	33	40	20	34	31	16	50	8	48	30	18	45	48
31	12	2	32	42	18	28	3	30	37	10	11	32	15	20	21
8	3	4	6	18	18	11	21	11	0	20	9	9	14	2	9
0	1	0	5	4	3	5	1	4	1	3	3	0	0	1	0

To put this number in perspective, we can calculate its position relative to the total number of possible 8×8-bit S-boxes. There are 256! (approximately $8.58 \times 10^{\wedge}506$) possible 8×8-bit S-boxes. The AES S-box's position in this space provides insight into its uniqueness and, potentially, its cryptographic strength.

Next, let's examine some of the cryptographic properties of the AES S-box using our factorial approach. Table 6.7 presents key cryptographic indicators for the AES S-box.

These properties, particularly the high nonlinearity and low differential uniformity, contribute to the AES S-box's resistance against linear and differential cryptanalysis.

One of the advantages of our factorial representation is that it allows for efficient exploration of the "neighborhood" of the AES S-box. By slightly modifying the factorial number, we can generate S-boxes that are "close" to the AES S-box in the space of all possible S-boxes. This allows us to investigate how cryptographic properties change in the vicinity of the AES S-box.

Similarly, we can examine how other cryptographic properties, such as differential uniformity and algebraic degree, vary in the neighborhood of the AES S-box. These analyses provide insights into the robustness of the AES S-box selection and the landscape of cryptographic properties in the space of all possible S-boxes.

In conclusion, our factorial number system approach offers a novel perspective on the AES S-box. It provides a unique representation that encapsulates the S-box's structure, allows for efficient comparison with other S-boxes, and facilitates exploration of the S-box space. These insights not only deepen our understanding of the AES S-box but also open up new avenues for S-box design and analysis in future cryptographic systems.

TABLE 6.7
Cryptographic Properties of the AES S-Box

Property	Value
Bijective	True
Nonlinearity	112
Max Autocorrelation	32
Minimum Algebraic Degree	7
Differential Uniformity	4
Algebraic Immunity	2
Max Differential Table	4
Max Linear Approximation	16
Linear Redundancy	1
SAC Min Probability	0.453125
SAC Max Probability	0.562500
SAC Average Probability	0.504883
SAC Deviation	0.030431
Bit Independence Criterion	0.134125
Fixed Points	Not found

6.5.3 Results and Analysis: Exploration of the S-Box Space Surrounding the AES S-Box

The AES S-box is renowned for its exceptional cryptographic properties, making it a cornerstone of modern symmetric encryption. This section leverages our factorial number system (FNS) representation to conduct an analysis of the S-box space surrounding the AES S-box, focusing on nonlinearity and various cost functions. This exploration offers novel insights into the distribution of these properties and the uniqueness of the AES S-box.

Methodology: We define the "neighborhood" of the AES S-box as the set of S-boxes whose FNS representations differ from that of the AES S-box by a certain threshold. For this study, we examined S-boxes within a radius of ± 100 in the factorial number space. This approach allows us to systematically explore a significant number of S-boxes that are structurally similar to the AES S-box.

For each S-box in this neighborhood, we computed the following properties:

1. Nonlinearity;
2. WHS cost function;
3. WCF cost function;
4. PCF cost function.

6.5.3.1 Nonlinearity Distribution

Figure 6.1 illustrates the distribution of nonlinearity values in the neighborhood of the AES S-box.

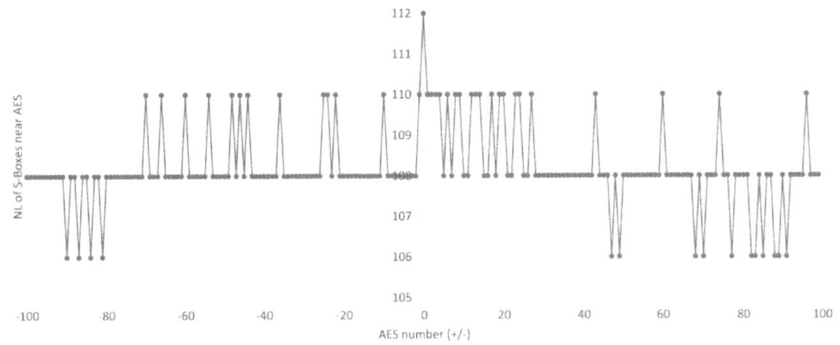

FIGURE 6.1 Nonlinearity Distribution in AES S-Box Neighborhood.

The AES S-box exhibits a nonlinearity of .112., which our analysis reveals to be a local maximum. Interestingly, we observed that the nonlinearity remains consistently high in the immediate vicinity of the AES S-box, with values ranging from 108 to 112. This suggests that the AES S-box resides in a region of the S-box space characterized by high nonlinearity.

6.5.3.2 WHS Cost Function

Figure 6.2 shows the distribution of the WHS cost function values.

The WHS cost function, as defined in our earlier discussions, provides a measure of the S-box's resistance to linear cryptanalysis. Lower values indicate better resistance. The AES S-box achieves a WHS value of 4151216, which appears to be near a local minimum in its neighborhood. This further underscores the optimality of the AES S-box in terms of its linear cryptanalytic properties.

6.5.3.3 WCF Cost Function

Figure 6.3 presents the distribution of the WCF cost function values.

The WCF cost function, which we introduced as an improvement over WHS, shows interesting behavior in the AES S-box neighborhood. The AES S-box itself achieves a WCF value of 0, which is the global minimum for this function. This result is particularly noteworthy, as it suggests that the AES S-box is optimally positioned with respect to the criteria captured by the WCF function.

6.5.3.4 PCF Cost Function

Figure 6.4 illustrates the distribution of the PCF cost function values.

The PCF cost function, which provides another perspective on the S-box's cryptographic strength, shows more variability in the AES S-box neighborhood. The AES S-box achieves a PCF value of 7491.62. Interestingly, there are S-boxes in the immediate vicinity with slightly lower PCF values, suggesting potential for optimization in this dimension.

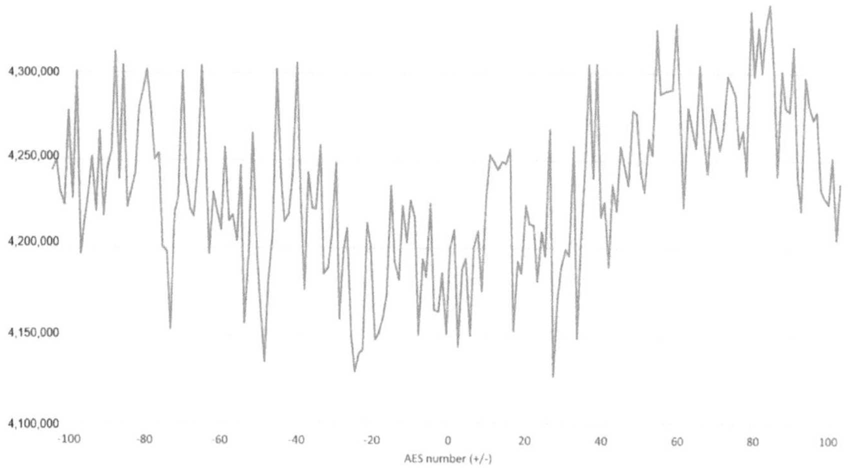

FIGURE 6.2 WHS Cost Function Distribution in AES S-Box Neighborhood.

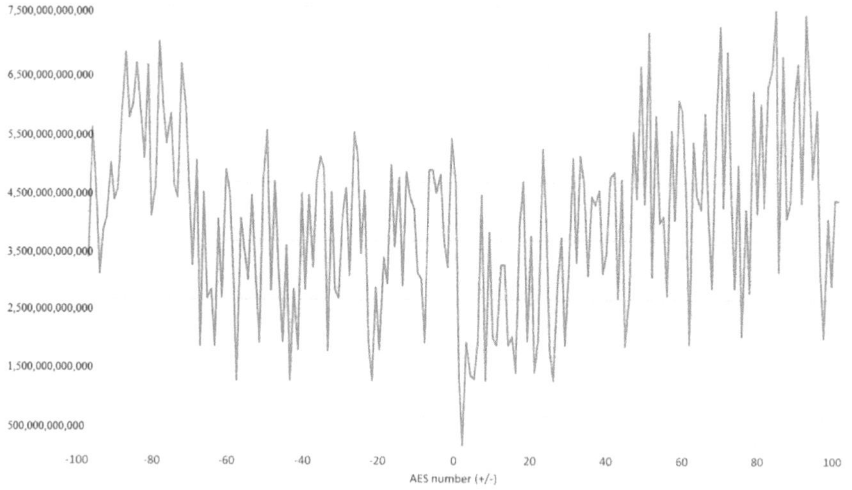

FIGURE 6.3 WCF Cost Function Distribution in AES S-Box Neighborhood.

This exploration of the S-box space surrounding the AES S-box yields several significant insights:

- The AES S-box occupies a near-optimal position in the S-box space, with high nonlinearity and favorable cost function values.
- The immediate neighborhood of the AES S-box is characterized by consistently high nonlinearity, suggesting a robust region of strong S-boxes.
- The AES S-box achieves the global minimum for the WCF cost function, highlighting its exceptional balance of cryptographic properties.
- While marginally superior S-boxes exist in terms of individual metrics (e.g., PCF), the AES S-box maintains an exceptional overall balance.

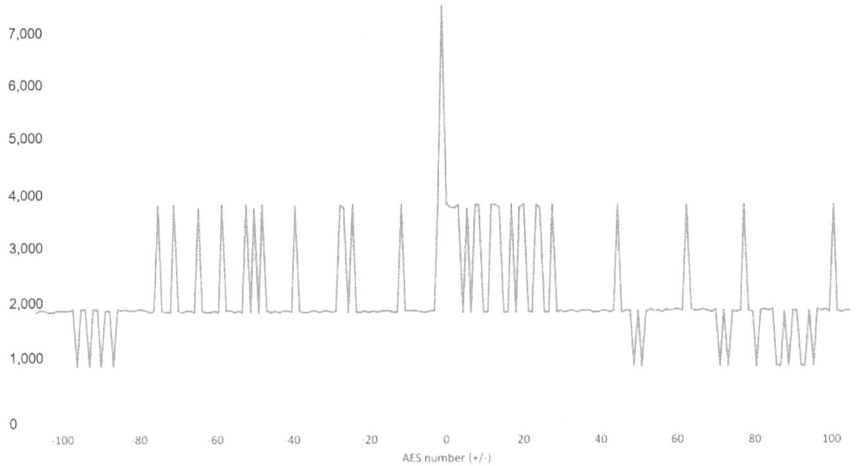

FIGURE 6.4 PCF Cost Function Distribution in AES S-Box Neighborhood.

These findings not only validate the strength of the AES S-box but also provide valuable insights for future S-box design. The methodology presented here, leveraging the factorial number system, offers a powerful tool for systematic exploration and optimization of S-boxes in cryptographic research. Future work could expand this analysis to a wider range of S-boxes and explore additional cryptographic properties to gain a more comprehensive understanding of the S-box landscape.

6.6 DISCUSSION

The factorial number system representation of S-boxes introduced in this study offers a novel perspective on the analysis and generation of cryptographic substitution boxes. This approach provides several significant advantages over traditional methods while also presenting certain challenges that warrant further investigation.

One of the primary strengths of our factorial representation is its ability to map the entire space of possible S-boxes onto a one-dimensional number line. This mapping enables the application of well-established optimization techniques that are particularly effective in one-dimensional spaces. For instance, gradient-based methods or certain evolutionary algorithms could potentially be adapted to navigate this space more efficiently than traditional S-box generation techniques.

Our analysis of the GOST 28147-89 and AES S-boxes using the factorial representation revealed interesting insights into their structural properties. The fact that all GOST S-boxes exhibited the same nonlinearity value of 4, despite having different factorial representations, suggests that the designers prioritized consistent nonlinearity across all S-boxes. This observation opens up new avenues for investigating the design principles behind these S-boxes and potentially improving upon them.

The exploration of the S-box space surrounding the AES S-box yielded particularly intriguing results. The discovery that the AES S-box resides in a local maximum of nonlinearity and achieves the global minimum for the WCF cost function underscores its exceptional cryptographic properties. However, the identification of S-boxes in the immediate vicinity with slightly lower PCF values suggests potential for further optimization. This finding demonstrates the power of our factorial representation approach in uncovering subtle variations in S-box properties that might be overlooked by traditional analysis methods.

One challenge that emerges from our approach is the handling of extremely large numbers when dealing with 8-bit or larger S-boxes. While we have proposed several optimization strategies, including modular arithmetic and sliding window techniques, the practical implementation of these methods for large-scale S-box generation and analysis remains an area for further research. The development of specialized hardware or distributed computing approaches could potentially address this challenge.

Another aspect that warrants further investigation is the relationship between the factorial representation and other cryptographic properties not explicitly examined in this study, such as algebraic immunity or resistance to side-channel attacks. Understanding these relationships could lead to more comprehensive optimization criteria for S-box design.

The factorial representation also opens up new possibilities for theoretical analysis of S-box properties. For instance, the continuous nature of the factorial number line might allow for the application of analytical techniques from real analysis or dynamical systems theory to study the distribution of cryptographic properties across the S-box space.

In terms of practical applications, our approach could be particularly valuable in the design of lightweight cryptographic algorithms for resource-constrained environments. The ability to efficiently generate and evaluate large numbers of S-boxes could facilitate the development of algorithms with optimal trade-offs between security and computational efficiency.

6.7 CONCLUSION

This study introduces a novel approach to S-box analysis and generation using the factorial number system representation. By mapping S-boxes to points on a one-dimensional number line, we have opened up new avenues for systematic exploration and optimization of cryptographic substitution boxes.

Our key findings include:

1. The successful representation of S-boxes from GOST 28147-89 and AES using the factorial number system, providing a unique "fingerprint" for each S-box.
2. The development of efficient algorithms for converting between permutations, factorial representations, and decimal numbers, enabling practical implementation of our approach.
3. The discovery of interesting properties in the neighborhood of the AES S-box, including its position at a local maximum of nonlinearity and a global minimum of the WCF cost function.
4. The identification of potential areas for S-box optimization, as evidenced by the variations in PCF values near the AES S-box.

These results demonstrate the potential of the factorial representation approach for advancing our understanding of S-box design and optimization. The ability to efficiently explore the vast space of possible S-boxes could lead to the development of more secure and efficient cryptographic algorithms.

Future work in this area could focus on:

1. Extending the analysis to larger S-boxes and other cryptographic primitives.
2. Developing more sophisticated optimization algorithms tailored to the factorial representation of S-boxes.
3. Investigating the theoretical foundations of S-box properties using analytical techniques enabled by the continuous nature of the factorial number line.
4. Exploring the practical applications of this approach in the design of lightweight cryptographic algorithms for IoT and other resource-constrained environments.

In conclusion, the factorial number system representation of S-boxes presents a promising new direction in cryptographic research. By providing a novel perspective on S-box structure and properties, this approach has the potential to drive innovations in both the theory and practice of cryptographic design.

6.8 ACKNOWLEDGEMENT

- This project has received funding from the European Union's Horizon 2020 research and innovation program under the Marie Skłodowska-Curie grant agreement No. 101007820 - TRUST. This publication reflects only the author's view, and the REA is not responsible for any use that may be made of the information it contains.
- This research was funded by the European Union—NextGenerationEU under the Italian Ministry of University and Research (MIUR), National Innovation Ecosystem grant ECS 00000041-VITALITY-CUP D83C 22000710005.

REFERENCES

[1] A. Grami, "Chapter 11 - cryptography," in *Discrete Mathematics*, A. Grami, Ed. Academic Press, 2023, pp. 197–210, doi: 10.1016/B978-0-12-820656-0.00011-3.

[2] A. J. Menezes, P. C. van Oorschot, S. A. Vanstone, P. C. van Oorschot, and S. A. Vanstone, *Handbook of Applied Cryptography.* CRC Press, 2018, doi: 10.1201/9780429466335.

[3] M. I. Mihailescu, and S. L. Nita, "Linear and differential cryptanalysis," in *Pro Cryptography and Cryptanalysis with C++20: Creating and Programming Advanced Algorithms*, M. I. Mihailescu, and S. L. Nita, Eds. Berkeley, CA: Apress, 2021, pp. 387–409, doi: 10.1007/978-1-4842-6586-4_19.

[4] J. Álvarez-Cubero, "Vector Boolean functions: Applications in symmetric cryptography," 2015, doi: 10.13140/RG.2.2.12540.23685.

[5] J. McLaughlin, "Applications of search techniques to cryptanalysis and the construction of cipher components," PhD, University of York, 2012. Accessed: Oct. 27, 2022. [Online]. https://etheses.whiterose.ac.uk/3674/.

[6] T. W. Cusick, and P. Stănică, *Cryptographic Boolean Functions and Applications*, 2nd ed. Academic Press, 2017, p. 275. doi: 10.1016/c2016-0-00852-5.
[7] K. Nyberg, "Perfect nonlinear S-boxes," in *Advances in Cryptology—EUROCRYPT '91*, D. W. Davies, Ed., in Lecture Notes in Computer Science. Berlin, Heidelberg: Springer, 1991, pp. 378–386, doi: 10.1007/3-540-46416-6_32.
[8] J. Daemen, and V. Rijmen, "Specification of Rijndael," in *The Design of Rijndael: The Advanced Encryption Standard (AES)*, J. Daemen, and V. Rijmen, Eds., in Information Security and Cryptography. Berlin, Heidelberg: Springer, 2020, pp. 31–51, doi: 10.1007/978-3-662-60769-5_3.
[9] L. D. Burnett, "Heuristic optimization of Boolean functions and substitution boxes for cryptography," PhD, Queensland University of Technology, 2005. Accessed: May 19, 2021. [Online]. https://eprints.qut.edu.au/16023/.
[10] S. S. Jamal, M. M. Hazzazi, M. F. Khan, Z. Bassfar, A. Aljaedi, and Z. ul Islam, "Region of interest-based medical image encryption technique based on chaotic S-boxes," *Expert Systems with Applications*, vol. 238, p. 122030, Mar. 2024, doi: 10.1016/j.eswa.2023.122030.
[11] S. Ullah, X. Liu, A. Waheed, and S. Zhang, "An efficient construction of S-box based on the fractional-order Rabinovich–Fabrikant chaotic system," *Integration*, vol. 94, p. 102099, Jan. 2024, doi: 10.1016/j.vlsi.2023.102099.
[12] Y. Ji, Z. Ma, L. Li, and Y. Sun, "Constructions of correlation immune S-boxes with high nonlinearity," *Journal of Information and Intelligence*, vol. 2, no. 3, pp. 253–260, May 2024, doi: 10.1016/j.jiixd.2024.01.005.
[13] F. Artuğer, and F. Özkaynak, "A new post-processing approach for improvement of nonlinearity property in substitution boxes," *Integration*, vol. 94, p. 102105, Jan. 2024, doi: 10.1016/j.vlsi.2023.102105.
[14] S. Fahd, M. Afzal, W. Iqbal, D. Shah, and I. Khalid, "The reality of backdoored S-boxes—an eye opener," *Journal of Information Security and Applications*, vol. 80, p. 103674, Feb. 2024, doi: 10.1016/j.jisa.2023.103674.
[15] A. Malal, and C. Tezcan, "FPGA-friendly compact and efficient AES-like 8 × 8 S-box," *Microprocessors and Microsystems*, vol. 105, p. 105007, Mar. 2024, doi: 10.1016/j.micpro.2024.105007.
[16] A. Waheed, F. Subhan, M. Mohd Su'ud, and M. Mansoor Alam, "Molding robust S-box design based on linear fractional transformation and multilayer perceptron: Applications to multimedia security," *Egyptian Informatics Journal*, vol. 26, p. 100480, Jun. 2024, doi: 10.1016/j.eij.2024.100480.
[17] R. Liu, H. Liu, and M. Zhao, "Cryptanalysis and construction of keyed strong S-box based on random affine transformation matrix and 2D hyper chaotic map," *Expert Systems with Applications*, vol. 252, p. 124238, Oct. 2024, doi: 10.1016/j.eswa.2024.124238.
[18] L. D. Singh et al., "Image encryption using dynamic S-boxes generated using elliptic curve points and chaotic system," *Journal of Information Security and Applications*, vol. 83, p. 103793, Jun. 2024, doi: 10.1016/j.jisa.2024.103793.
[19] A. Nitaj, W. Susilo, and J. Tonien, "Enhanced S-boxes for the advanced encryption standard with maximal periodicity and better avalanche property," *Computer Standards & Interfaces*, vol. 87, p. 103769, Jan. 2024, doi: 10.1016/j.csi.2023.103769.
[20] D. E. Knuth, *The Art of Computer Programming: Seminumerical Algorithms* (vol. 2, 3rd ed.). USA: Addison-Wesley Longman Publishing Co., Inc., 1997.
[21] V. N. Sachkov, *Probabilistic Methods in Combinatorial Analysis, in Encyclopedia of Mathematics and Its Applications*. Cambridge: Cambridge University Press, 1997, doi: 10.1017/CBO9780511666193.
[22] V. N. Sachkov, *Combinatorial Methods in Discrete Mathematics, in Encyclopedia of Mathematics and Its Applications*. Cambridge: Cambridge University Press, 1996, doi: 10.1017/CBO9780511666186.

[23] B. Schneier, *Applied Cryptography : Protocols, Algorithms, and Source Code in C.* New York: Wiley, 1996. Accessed: Jul. 25, 2020. [Online]. http://archive.org/details/appliedcryptogra00schn_328.
[24] C. Carlet, "Vectorial Boolean functions for cryptography," in *Boolean Models and Methods in Mathematics, Computer Science, and Engineering*, P. L. Hammer and Y. Crama, Eds., in Encyclopedia of Mathematics and its Applications. Cambridge: Cambridge University Press, 2010, pp. 398–470, doi: 10.1017/CBO9780511780448.012.
[25] J. A. Clark, J. L. Jacob, and S. Stepney, "The design of s-boxes by simulated annealing," in *Proceedings of the 2004 Congress on Evolutionary Computation (IEEE Cat. No.04TH8753)*, vol. 2, Jun. 2004, pp. 1533–1537, doi: 10.1109/CEC.2004.1331078.
[26] S. Picek, M. Cupic, and L. Rotim, "A new cost function for evolution of S-boxes," *Evolutionary Computation*, vol. 24, no. 4, pp. 695–718, Dec. 2016, doi: 10.1162/EVCO_a_00191.
[27] A. Kuznetsov et al., "Generation of nonlinear substitutions by simulated annealing algorithm," *Information (Switzerland)*, vol. 14, no. 5, 2023, doi: 10.3390/info14050259.
[28] A. Freyre-Echevarría et al., "An external parameter independent novel cost function for evolving bijective substitution-boxes," *Symmetry*, vol. 12, no. 11, Art. no. 11, Nov. 2020, doi: 10.3390/sym12111896.
[29] A. Kuznetsov, S. Kandii, E. Frontoni, and N. Poluyanenko, "SBGen: A high-performance library for rapid generation of cryptographic S-boxes," *SoftwareX*, vol. 27, p. 101788, Sep. 2024, doi: 10.1016/j.softx.2024.101788.
[30] A. Kuznetsov, N. Poluyanenko, E. Frontoni, S. Kandiy, and O. Peliukh, "A new cost function for heuristic search of nonlinear substitutions," *Expert Systems with Applications*, vol. 237, p. 121684, Mar. 2024, doi: 10.1016/j.eswa.2023.121684.
[31] D. H. Lehmer, *Teaching Combinatorial Tricks to a Computer*, R. Bellman, and M. Hall, Eds. Providence, Rhode Island: American Mathematical Society, 1960, pp. 179–193, doi: 10.1090/psapm/010/0113289.
[32] C.-A. Laisant, "Sur la numération factorielle, application aux permutations," *Bulletin de la Société Mathématique de France*, vol. 16, pp. 176–183, 1888, doi: 10.24033/bsmf.378.

7 Optimized Simulated Annealing for Efficient Generation of Highly Nonlinear S-Boxes

Oleksandr Kuznetsov, Nikolay Poluyanenko, Oleksii Smirnov, and Dinara Kozhakhmetova

7.1 INTRODUCTION

In the realm of modern cryptography, the design and implementation of robust substitution boxes (S-boxes) play a pivotal role in ensuring the security of symmetric encryption systems [1, 2]. S-boxes serve as the primary source of nonlinearity in many cipher algorithms, providing critical resistance against various cryptanalytic attacks, particularly linear and differential cryptanalysis [3]. The generation of highly nonlinear S-boxes, however, presents a significant computational challenge due to the vast search space and the complex interplay of cryptographic properties that must be optimized simultaneously [4, 5].

This chapter delves into the application of an optimized simulated annealing (SA) algorithm [6] for the efficient generation of cryptographically strong S-boxes [7, 8]. While SA has been previously explored in this context, our work introduces novel modifications and parameter optimizations that substantially improve both the success rate and computational efficiency of the S-box generation process. We present a comprehensive study that not only advances the state-of-the-art in S-box design but also provides insights into the effective application of metaheuristic algorithms in cryptographic primitive generation.

7.1.1 Contributions of the Chapter

The primary contributions of this chapter are as follows:

- Optimized SA Algorithm: We present a refined SA algorithm specifically tailored for S-box generation. Our approach includes a counterintuitive yet highly effective constant temperature regime, challenging conventional SA implementations.
- Novel Cost Functions: We introduce and analyze new cost functions designed to guide the SA process more effectively towards high-nonlinearity S-boxes.

DOI: 10.1201/9781003546153-7

These functions focus on critical Walsh-Hadamard Transform coefficients, demonstrating superior performance over existing approaches.

- Comprehensive Parameter Analysis: Through extensive experimentation, we provide a detailed analysis of SA parameters, including initial temperature, cooling schedules, and stopping criteria. This analysis offers valuable insights for researchers and practitioners in the field.
- Improved Efficiency and Reliability: Our optimized approach achieves a 100% success rate in generating 8×8 bijective S-boxes with nonlinearity 104, significantly outperforming previous methods in both reliability and computational efficiency.
- Multi-threaded Implementation: We describe a parallel implementation of our algorithm, harnessing the power of modern multi-core processors to further accelerate the S-box generation process.
- Comparative Study: We present a thorough comparison of our method with existing approaches, providing a clear benchmark for future research in this area.

7.1.2 Organization of the Chapter

The remainder of this chapter is structured as follows:

- Section 7.2 provides the theoretical foundations necessary for understanding our work, including an overview of S-boxes in cryptography, the principles of simulated annealing, and its application to S-box generation.
- Section 7.3 details our research methodology, describing the optimization problem formulation, the parameters of our SA algorithm, our novel objective functions, and the stopping criteria employed.
- Section 7.4 presents our experimental studies, analyzing the impact of various algorithm parameters on search efficiency, the probability of forming target S-boxes, and the computational complexity of our approach.
- Section 7.5 delves into the optimization of algorithm parameters, discussing the selection of optimal initial temperature, the optimization of the cooling coefficient, and the tuning of stopping criteria.
- Section 7.6 provides a comprehensive analysis of our results, including achieved nonlinearity metrics, efficiency comparisons with other evolutionary methods, and a discussion of the advantages and limitations of our proposed approach.
- Section 7.7 offers a broader discussion of our findings, their implications for the field of cryptography, and potential future research directions.
- Finally, Section 7.8 concludes the chapter, summarizing our key contributions and their significance in the context of cryptographic primitive generation.

Through this structure, we aim to provide a comprehensive and accessible presentation of our research, catering to both specialists in the field and those seeking to understand the challenges and advancements in S-box generation techniques.

7.2 LITERATURE REVIEW

The design and generation of cryptographically strong S-boxes has been an area of active research for several decades, with various approaches proposed to optimize their properties. This literature review traces the evolution of S-box generation techniques, with a particular focus on the application of SA and related heuristic methods.

Early work on S-box design primarily relied on algebraic constructions and random generation methods. However, the limitations of these approaches in consistently producing S-boxes with desired cryptographic properties led researchers to explore more sophisticated techniques.

A significant milestone in this field was the introduction of simulated annealing for S-box generation by Clark et al. in 2004 [7]. Their seminal paper demonstrated the potential of SA in creating S-boxes with high nonlinearity, achieving results that were competitive with the best known constructions at the time. This work laid the foundation for subsequent research into metaheuristic approaches for S-box optimization.

Building on Clark's work, Chen (2008) [9] proposed an enhanced algorithm combining chaotic maps with simulated annealing, termed chaotic multi-swapping and simulated annealing (CMSSA). This hybrid approach showed promise in generating 8×8 S-boxes with improved cryptographic properties, including better resistance to linear and differential cryptanalysis.

The application of evolutionary computation to S-box design gained further traction with the work of McLaughlin and Clark (2013) [10]. Their research expanded the focus beyond nonlinearity to include differential uniformity, employing not only simulated annealing but also memetic algorithms and ant colony optimization. This multi-objective approach represented a significant advancement in the field, addressing a broader range of cryptographic criteria simultaneously.

Picek et al. (2016) [11] made a notable contribution by introducing a new cost function for evolving S-boxes with high nonlinearity. Their work demonstrated that carefully designed fitness functions could significantly improve the efficiency and effectiveness of evolutionary algorithms in S-box generation, outperforming previous state-of-the-art methods.

Recent years have seen a continued refinement of SA-based approaches and the exploration of hybrid techniques. Souravlias et al. (2017) [12] investigated the use of algorithm portfolios, combining SA with Tabu Search under limited time budgets. Their work highlighted the potential of parallel processing and algorithm hybridization in improving the efficiency of S-box generation.

Wang et al. (2020) [13] proposed a method for constructing chaotic S-boxes using a memorable simulated annealing algorithm (MSAA). This approach leveraged the nonlinearity and randomness of digital cascaded chaotic mapping, demonstrating the ongoing interest in combining chaos theory with optimization techniques for S-box design.

In the realm of nature-inspired algorithms, Ahmad et al. (2020) [14] explored the use of particle swarm optimization (PSO) for generating highly nonlinear S-boxes. Their method, which incorporated a chaotic Renyi map for initial population generation, showed competitive results compared to other recent optimization-based approaches.

The most recent advancements in the field have focused on further refining cost functions and exploring novel hybridizations. Freyre-Echevarría et al. (2020) [15, 16] proposed an external parameter-independent cost function for evolving bijective S-boxes, demonstrating improved performance across multiple heuristic approaches, including genetic algorithms and local search. This work set the stage for a new wave of research aimed at optimizing S-box generation techniques.

As we move into 2023 and 2024, research continues to push the boundaries of S-box design, with a notable shift towards application-specific optimizations and the integration of advanced mathematical concepts. Jamal et al. (2024) [17] introduced a region of interest-based medical image encryption technique using chaotic S-boxes, addressing the unique challenges posed by large DICOM images in healthcare security. Their approach not only improves encryption efficiency but also maintains the privacy of sensitive medical data.

Liu et al. (2024) [18] advanced the field by proposing a method for constructing keyed strong S-boxes based on random affine transformation matrices and 2D hyper-chaotic maps. This work addresses vulnerabilities in existing S-boxes, such as fixed points and short iteration period rings, demonstrating the ongoing need for robust, attack-resistant S-box designs.

In the realm of hardware implementation, Malal and Tezcan (2024) [19] presented an FPGA-friendly compact and efficient AES-like 8×8 S-box, achieving a significant reduction in gate-area compared to previous designs. This research highlights the importance of considering hardware efficiency alongside cryptographic strength in S-box design.

Nitaj et al. (2024) [20] explored enhanced S-boxes for the Advanced Encryption Standard with maximal periodicity and improved avalanche properties. Their work demonstrates that even well-established standards like AES can benefit from continued research into S-box optimization.

The application of advanced mathematical concepts to S-box design is exemplified by the work of Ji et al. (2024) [21], who constructed correlation-immune S-boxes with high nonlinearity using disjoint linear codes. This approach achieves currently best-known nonlinearity for certain S-box configurations, showcasing the potential of combining cryptographic design with coding theory.

Ullah et al. (2024) [22] and Waheed et al. (2024) [23] further expanded the frontiers of S-box construction by incorporating fractional-order chaotic systems and machine learning techniques, respectively. Ullah's work leverages the Rabinovich-Fabrikant fractional-order system to create strong initial S-boxes, while Waheed's approach combines linear fractional transformation with multilayer perceptron architectures to achieve exceptional nonlinearity scores.

This ongoing research underscores the enduring importance of S-box optimization in cryptography and the continued relevance of simulated annealing and related metaheuristic techniques in this domain. As computational capabilities advance and new cryptographic challenges emerge, we are witnessing a diversification of approaches, from chaos theory and fractional-order systems to machine learning and hardware-specific optimizations. These developments not only enhance the security of existing cryptographic systems but also pave the way for novel applications in areas such as IoT security, quantum-resistant cryptography, and privacy-preserving computation. The field of S-box design remains vibrant, with each new approach contributing to our understanding of how to balance the complex requirements of security, efficiency, and practical implementation in modern cryptographic systems.

7.3 THEORETICAL FOUNDATIONS

This section provides a concise overview of the key theoretical concepts underpinning our research. We begin by briefly revisiting the role of nonlinear substitutions in cryptography, focusing on their significance in modern ciphers. We then delve into the simulated annealing method, exploring its origins in statistical mechanics and its adaptation to combinatorial optimization problems. Finally, we examine the specific application of simulated annealing to the generation of cryptographically strong S-boxes, highlighting the unique challenges and opportunities this approach presents.

7.3.1 Nonlinear Substitutions in Cryptography

Nonlinear substitutions, commonly referred to as S-boxes, serve as the cornerstone of confusion in modern symmetric-key cryptographic systems. These bijective mappings between input and output bit strings play a crucial role in obfuscating the relationship between plaintext, ciphertext, and key material. The cryptographic strength of many block and stream ciphers heavily relies on the properties of their constituent S-boxes.

The effectiveness of an S-box is typically evaluated based on several criteria, with nonlinearity being one of the most critical. Nonlinearity, denoted as N_f, quantifies the minimum Hamming distance between the Boolean function representing the S-box and the set of all affine functions. For an n-bit S-box, the nonlinearity is defined as:

$$N_f = 2^{n-1} - \frac{1}{2} \max_{\omega \in \mathbb{F}_2^n \setminus \{0\}} | WHT_f(\omega) |,$$

where $WHT_f(\omega)$ represents the Walsh-Hadamard transform of the Boolean function f.

High nonlinearity values indicate greater resistance against linear cryptanalysis, a powerful technique for breaking symmetric-key algorithms. The theoretical maximum nonlinearity for 8-bit S-boxes is 120, although the highest achievable value in practice is 112. S-boxes with nonlinearity of 104 or higher are generally considered cryptographically strong and suitable for use in robust cipher designs.

7.3.2 The Simulated Annealing Method

SA is a probabilistic technique for approximating the global optimum of a given function, particularly effective in large, discrete search spaces. Inspired by the annealing process in metallurgy, where controlled cooling of a material leads to the formation of large crystals with minimal defects, SA was first introduced by

Kirkpatrick, Gelatt, and Vecchi in 1983 as a method for solving combinatorial optimization problems [24].

The core principle of SA lies in its ability to escape local optima by occasionally accepting solutions that worsen the objective function [6, 25]. This acceptance is governed by a probability function that depends on the current "temperature" of the system and the magnitude of the proposed change. The probability of accepting a worse solution is given by [6]:

$$P(\Delta E, T) = e^{-\Delta E / T},$$

where ΔE represents the change in the objective function value, and T is the current temperature.

The SA algorithm typically follows these steps [6]:

1. Initialize with a random solution and set a high initial temperature T_0.
2. Generate a neighboring solution by applying a small, random perturbation.
3. Calculate the change in the objective function, ΔE.
4. If $\Delta E < 0$ (improvement), accept the new solution.
5. If $\Delta E \geq 0$ (worsening), accept with probability $P(\Delta E, T)$.
6. Reduce the temperature according to a cooling schedule.
7. Repeat steps 2–6 until a stopping criterion is met.

The cooling schedule, which dictates how the temperature decreases over time, plays a crucial role in the algorithm's performance. Common cooling schedules include geometric cooling ($T_k = \alpha T_{k-1}$, where $0 < \alpha < 1$) and logarithmic cooling ($T_k = T_0 / \log(k+1)$).

7.3.3 Application of Simulated Annealing for S-Box Generation

The application of simulated annealing to S-box generation represents a novel approach to solving a complex combinatorial optimization problem. The vast search space of possible 8-bit S-boxes (256! permutations) renders exhaustive search infeasible, making SA an attractive alternative.

In this context, the SA algorithm operates as follows [7, 26]:

1. Initialize with a random bijective S-box.
2. Define a neighborhood structure, typically involving swapping two elements of the S-box.
3. Employ a cost function that quantifies the cryptographic quality of the S-box, often based on its nonlinearity.
4. Apply the SA algorithm to minimize the cost function, effectively maximizing the S-box's nonlinearity.

One of the key challenges in applying SA to S-box generation is balancing exploration of the search space with exploitation of promising solutions. This balance is primarily controlled by the cooling schedule and the initial temperature. A high initial temperature promotes extensive exploration, while a slower cooling rate allows for more thorough exploitation of promising regions of the search space.

Recent research has focused on optimizing these parameters to improve the efficiency and effectiveness of SA for S-box generation [27–29]. Notable advancements include adaptive cooling schedules, parallel implementations, and hybridization with other metaheuristic algorithms [8, 13].

By leveraging the strengths of simulated annealing, researchers have been able to generate high-quality S-boxes with nonlinearity values approaching the theoretical maximum, contributing to the development of more robust cryptographic systems.

7.4 RESEARCH METHODOLOGY

This section outlines the methodological framework of our study, detailing the optimization problem formulation, the parameters of the simulated annealing algorithm, the objective function, and the stopping criteria. Our approach is designed to maximize the efficiency and effectiveness of generating high-nonlinearity S-boxes using simulated annealing.

7.4.1 Optimization Problem Formulation

The generation of cryptographically strong S-boxes can be formulated as a combinatorial optimization problem. For bijective 8-bit S-boxes, we are searching in a solution space of 256! possible permutations, which is approximately 8.58×10^{506}. The magnitude of this search space underscores the computational challenge and the need for efficient heuristic methods.

Formally, we define our optimization problem as follows:

- Let $S = S_1, S_2, \ldots, S_{256!}$ be the set of all possible 8-bit bijective S-boxes. Let $f : S \rightarrow \mathbb{R}$ be an objective function that measures the cryptographic quality of an S-box, with higher values indicating better quality.

Our goal is to find $S^* \in S$ such that:

$$S^* = \arg\max_{S_i \in S} f(S_i).$$

In our specific case, $f(S_i)$ is primarily based on the nonlinearity of the S-box, although other cryptographic properties may also be considered.

The optimization is subject to the following constraints:

1. Bijectivity: Each S-box must be a permutation of the integers 0 to 255.
2. Nonlinearity Threshold: We seek S-boxes with nonlinearity ≥ 104, which represents a high level of resistance against linear cryptanalysis.

This optimization problem is NP-hard, making exhaustive search infeasible for practical purposes. Therefore, we employ the simulated annealing metaheuristic to efficiently explore the solution space and find near-optimal solutions.

7.4.2 Simulated Annealing Algorithm Parameters

The performance of the simulated annealing algorithm is heavily influenced by its parameters. We have identified and tuned the following key parameters for our S-box generation problem:

1. Initial Temperature (T_0): The initial temperature significantly affects the algorithm's exploration capability in its early stages. We experimentally determined that $T_0 = 15{,}000$ provides an optimal balance between exploration and exploitation for our problem domain.
2. Cooling Schedule: We employ a geometric cooling schedule, where the temperature at iteration k is given by: $T_k = \alpha T_{k-1}$ where α is the cooling coefficient. After extensive testing, we found that $\alpha = 1$ (i.e., maintaining a constant temperature) yields the best results for our specific problem. This counterintuitive finding suggests that the traditional cooling approach may not be optimal for all combinatorial optimization problems.
3. Number of Iterations at Each Temperature (max_inner_loops): This parameter determines how thoroughly the algorithm explores the solution space at each temperature level. We set max_inner_loops $= 4{,}000$, which provides a good trade-off between search depth and computational efficiency.
4. Maximum Number of Outer Loops (max_outer_loops): This limits the total number of temperature changes. We set max_outer_loops = 50 to ensure termination while allowing sufficient exploration.
5. Maximum Number of Consecutive Non-Improving Outer Loops (max_frozen_outer_loops): This parameter helps to detect when the algorithm has likely converged. We use max_frozen_outer_loops = 50, allowing the algorithm to continue searching even if improvements are not immediately found.
6. Neighborhood Function: We define the neighborhood of an S-box as all permutations that can be obtained by swapping two randomly chosen entries. This simple operation ensures that all solutions remain bijective while allowing for gradual exploration of the solution space.
7. Acceptance Probability Function: We use the standard Metropolis criterion for accepting worse solutions [6, 30]:

$$P(\text{accept}) = \begin{cases} 1 & \text{if } \Delta E \leq 0; \\ e^{-\Delta E/T} & \text{if } \Delta E > 0. \end{cases}$$

where ΔE is the change in the objective function value and T is the current temperature.

These parameters were carefully tuned through extensive experimentation and analysis. The unusual choice of a constant temperature ($\alpha = 1$) highlights the importance of adapting general metaheuristics to specific problem domains. Our results demonstrate that this parameter set significantly improves the efficiency and reliability of generating high-nonlinearity S-boxes compared to previous implementations of simulated annealing for this problem.

7.4.3 Objective Function

The choice of an appropriate objective function is crucial for the effectiveness of the simulated annealing algorithm in generating high-quality S-boxes. Our objective function is designed to prioritize nonlinearity while also considering other cryptographic properties. After extensive experimentation with various cost functions from the literature, we adopted a modified version of the power_max_wht function proposed by Kuznetsov et al. (2021) [31].

The objective function is defined as follows:

$$f(S) = \sum_{i=1}^{255} \left\| \max_j \left(WHT_j \right) \right| - X \Big|^R, \tag{7.1}$$

where:

- S is the candidate S-box;
- WHT_j is the i-th value of the Walsh-Hadamard Transform of S;
- where X and R are tunable parameters.

The Walsh-Hadamard Transform (WHT) is computed as:

$$WHT(w) = \sum_{x \in 0,1^n} (-1)^{x \cdot w \oplus f(x)},$$

where $f(x)$ represents the Boolean function corresponding to each output bit of the S-box.

The objective function aims to minimize the deviation of WHT values from the ideal value, which corresponds to perfect nonlinearity. The parameter r allows for fine-tuning the optimization process. Through empirical testing, we determined that $r = 4$ provides the best results for our specific problem.

This objective function offers several advantages [31]:

- It directly targets the nonlinearity property, which is crucial for cryptographic strength.
- The power function ($r = 4$) emphasizes larger deviations from the ideal WHT value, guiding the search towards more balanced S-boxes.
- The summation over all WHT values provides a comprehensive measure of the S-box's quality, rather than focusing solely on the maximum WHT value.

7.4.4 Algorithm Stopping Criteria

Defining appropriate stopping criteria is essential for balancing the quality of solutions with computational efficiency. We implemented a multi-faceted approach to determine when the simulated annealing algorithm should terminate:

1. Target Nonlinearity Achieved: The algorithm stops immediately if an S-box with the target nonlinearity (104 in our case) is found. This criterion is

defined as: stop if $N_f(S) \geq 104$, where $N_f(S)$ is the nonlinearity of the current S-box S.
2. MaximumOuterLoopsReached:Topreventexcessiveruntime,welimitthetotal number of temperature stages: stop if outer_loop_count ≥ max_outer_loops. With max_outer_loops set to 50, this ensures termination even if the target nonlinearity is not achieved.
3. Convergence Detection: We track the number of consecutive outer loops without improvement in the best solution found: stop if frozen_over_loop_count ≥ max frozen_outer_loops, where max_frozen_outer_loops is set to 50. This criterion helps identify when the algorithm has likely converged to a local optimum.
4. Time Limit: Although not strictly enforced in our implementation, a time-based stopping criterion can be useful in practical applications: stop if elapsed_time ≥ max time, where max_time is a predefined time limit.
5. Quality Threshold: We also consider stopping if the objective function value exceeds a certain threshold: stop if $f(S) \geq f_{threshold}$. The specific value of $f_{threshold}$ depends on the scale of the objective function and the desired quality of solutions.

These criteria are evaluated in the order presented. The algorithm terminates as soon as any one of these conditions is met. This multi-criteria approach offers several benefits:

- It allows for early termination upon finding a satisfactory solution, saving computational resources.
- It prevents excessive runtime in cases where high-quality solutions are elusive.
- It provides flexibility in balancing solution quality and computational efficiency.
- The convergence detection mechanism helps avoid wasted computation on stagnant searches.

By carefully tuning these stopping criteria in conjunction with the algorithm parameters and objective function, we achieved a highly efficient and reliable method for generating high-nonlinearity S-boxes. Our approach significantly reduces the average search time and improves the success rate compared to previous implementations of simulated annealing for this problem.

7.5 EXPERIMENTAL STUDIES

This section presents a comprehensive analysis of our simulated annealing algorithm for generating high-nonlinearity S-boxes. We investigate the impact of various algorithm parameters on search efficiency, analyze the probability of forming target S-boxes, evaluate generation time and computational complexity, and compare our results with other implementations of simulated annealing for this problem.

7.5.1 Impact of Algorithm Parameters on Search Efficiency

To optimize the performance of our simulated annealing algorithm, we conducted extensive experiments to understand the influence of key parameters on search efficiency. Our investigation focused primarily on three critical parameters: The cooling coefficient (α), the initial temperature (T_0), and the number of inner loops (max_inner_loops).

Cooling Coefficient (α): Contrary to conventional wisdom in simulated annealing applications, we discovered that maintaining a constant temperature throughout the search process ($\alpha = 1$) yielded superior results for our specific problem. Figure 7.1 illustrates the probability of forming the target S-box for different values of α (0.85, 0.90, and 0.95) across a range of initial temperatures.

As evident from Figure 7.1, higher values of α consistently result in improved probabilities of finding the target S-box. This trend suggests that allowing the algorithm to explore the solution space more thoroughly at each temperature level is beneficial for our problem domain.

Initial Temperature (T_0): The choice of initial temperature significantly influences the algorithm's behavior, particularly in its early stages. Our experiments revealed a complex relationship between T_0 and search efficiency. Figure 7.2 demonstrates the average time required to form the target S-box for different values of α and T_0.

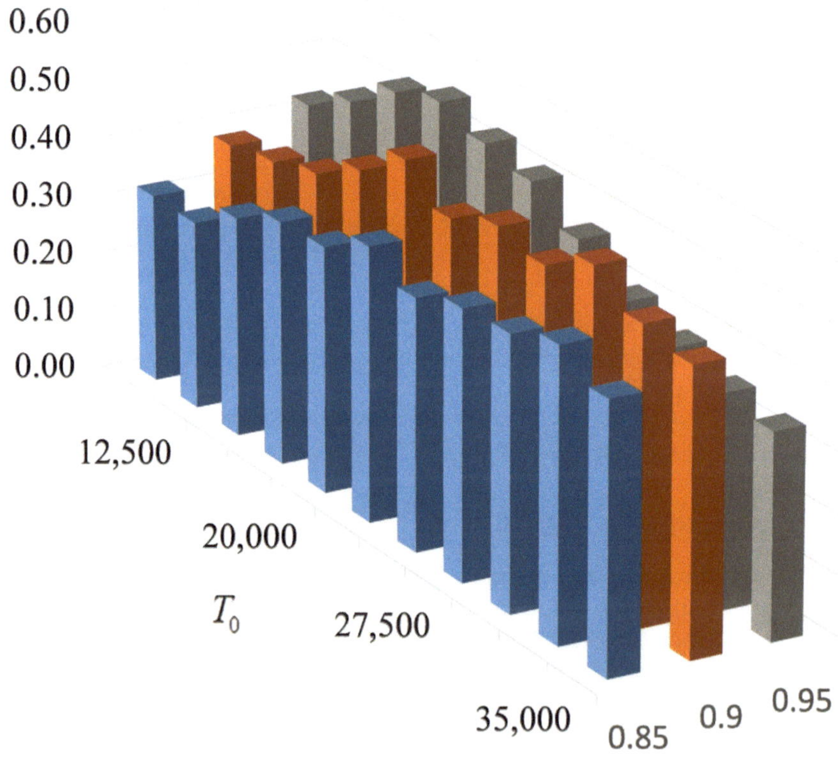

FIGURE 7.1 Probability of forming the target S-box at $\alpha = 0.85, 0.90, 0.95$ and max_inner_loops = 650.

We observed that for each α value, there exists an optimal initial temperature (T_0^{opt}) that minimizes the search time. As α approaches 1, the optimal T_0 decreases, and the effect becomes more pronounced. This finding led us to investigate the performance at a constant temperature ($\alpha = 1$) more thoroughly.

Number of Inner Loops (max_inner_loops): The max_inner_loops parameter determines the number of iterations performed at each temperature level. We conducted a series of experiments varying max_inner_loops from 500 to 15,000, with $\alpha = 1$ and $T_0 = 18,655$. Figure 7.3 shows the probability of forming the target S-box as a function of max_inner_loops.

The results indicate that the probability of finding the target S-box reaches unity at approximately max_inner_loops = $7,500$. This corresponds to an arithmetic mean of about $1,803,821$ total iterations, as shown in Figure 7.4.

To better understand the search process, we analyzed the distribution of maximum tuple sizes without improvements for different max_inner_loops values. Figures 7.5 and 7.6 illustrate these distributions for max_inner_loops = 200 and $15,500$, respectively.

These distributions provide insight into the algorithm's exploration behavior. For small max_inner_loops values, the distribution of tuple sizes is nearly uniform,

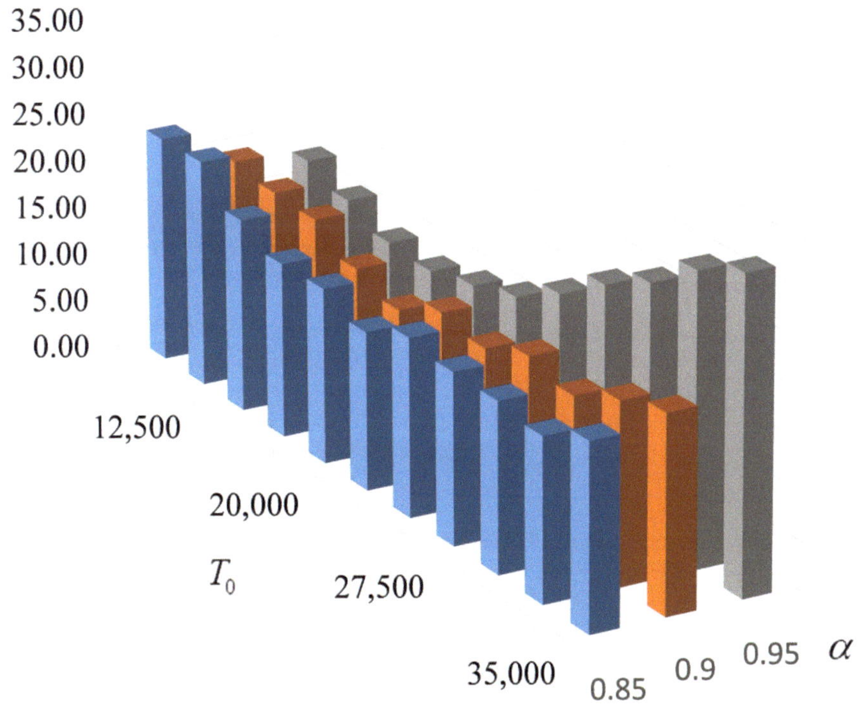

FIGURE 7.2 Average time (sec.) for forming the target S-box at $\alpha = 0.85, 0.90, 0.95$ and max_inner_loops = 650.

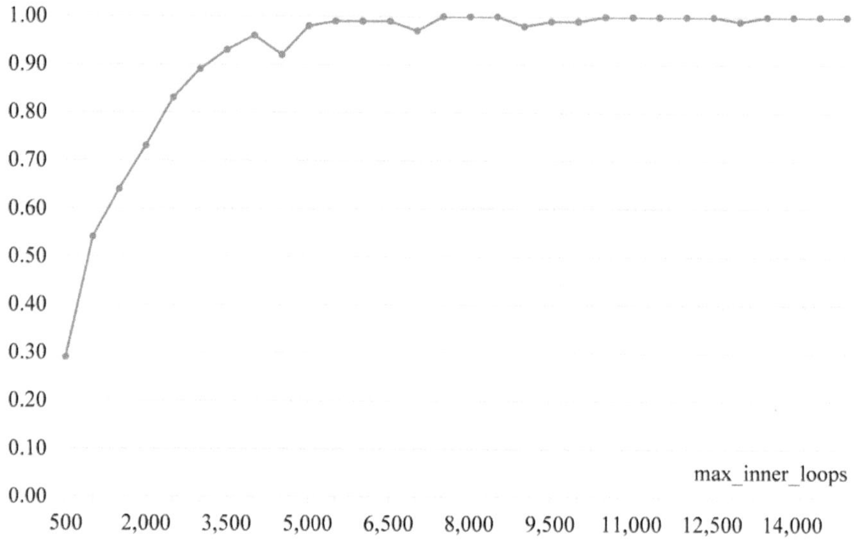

FIGURE 7.3 Probability of forming the target S-box when $T_0 = 18{,}655$ and $\alpha = 1$.

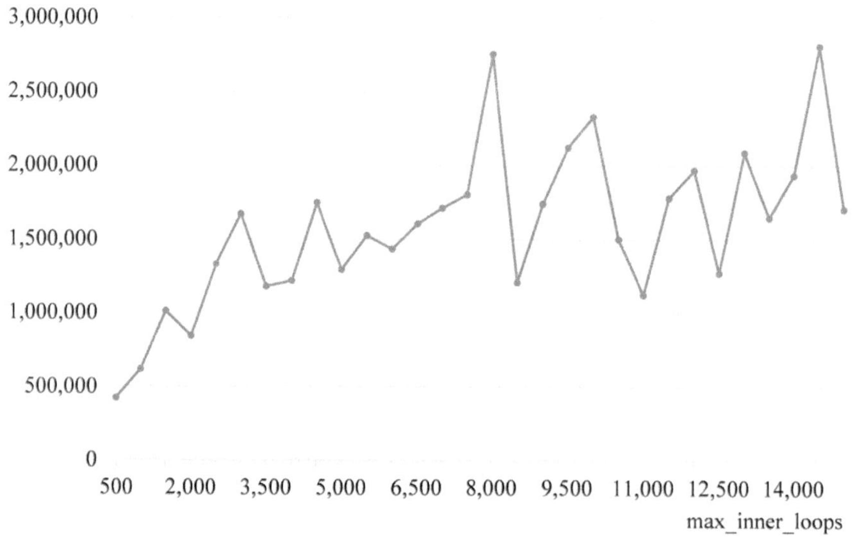

FIGURE 7.4 The total number of the arithmetic mean number of iterations when searching for the target S-box when $T_0 = 18{,}655$ and $\alpha = 1$.

indicating frequent discarding of potential improvements. As max_inner_loops increases, we observe a shift towards larger tuple sizes, suggesting more thorough exploration of promising regions in the solution space.

Further investigation revealed that removing the limit on the maximum number of non-improving outer loops (max_frozen_outer_loops) allows the algorithm to

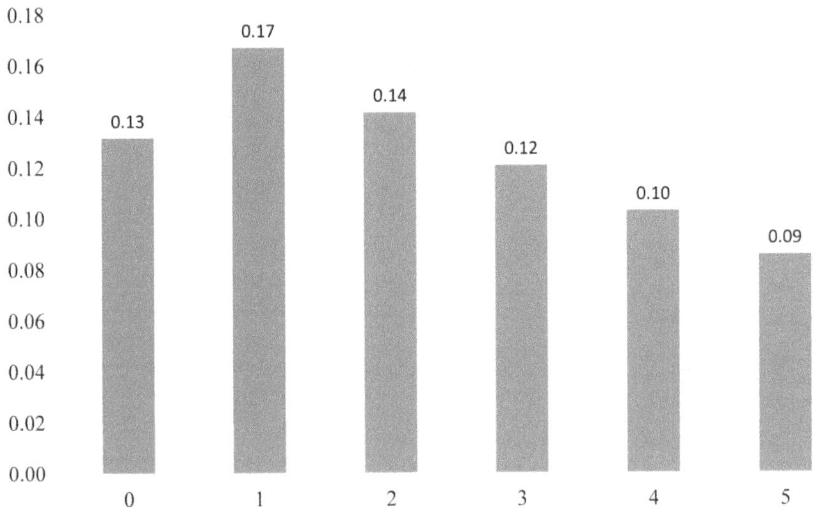

FIGURE 7.5 Maximum tuple size without improvements at $T_0 = 18{,}655$, $\alpha = 1$, and max_inner_loops = 200.

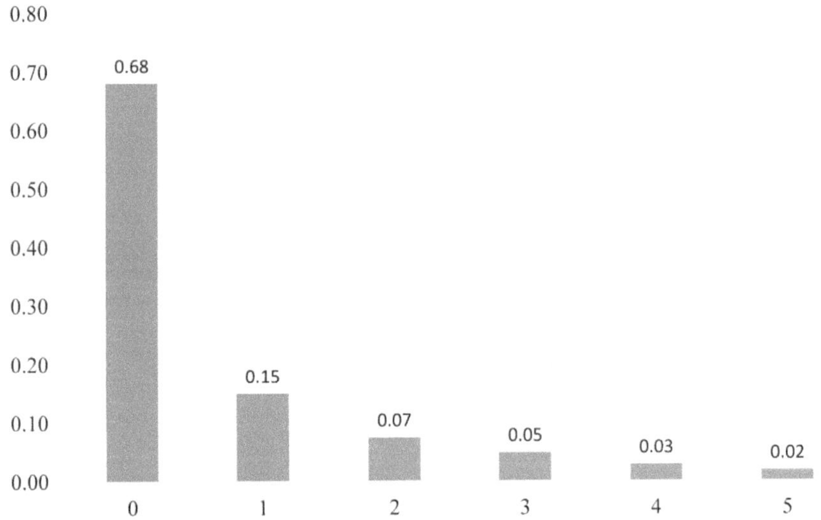

FIGURE 7.6 Maximum tuple size without improvements at $T_0 = 18{,}655$, $\alpha = 1$, and max_inner_loops = 15,500.

achieve a success probability of 1 for almost any value of max_inner_loops greater than 200. This is illustrated in Figure 7.7, which shows the distribution of the maximum number of outer loop iterations before the algorithm terminates.

Figure 7.8 provides additional insight into the search process by showing the maximum tuple size without improvements for max_inner_loops = 2,500.

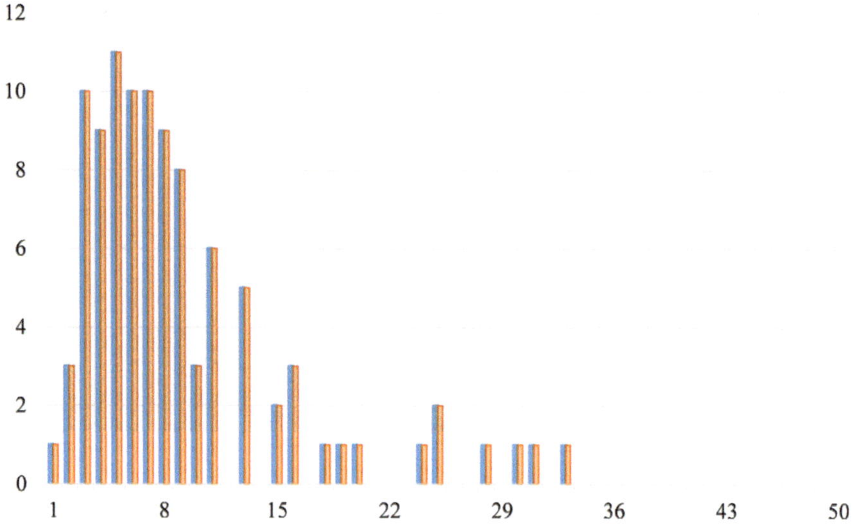

FIGURE 7.7 Distribution of the maximum number of iterations of the outer loop. Solid filling—total number of runs, hatching—finding the target S-box at max_inner_loops = 2,500.

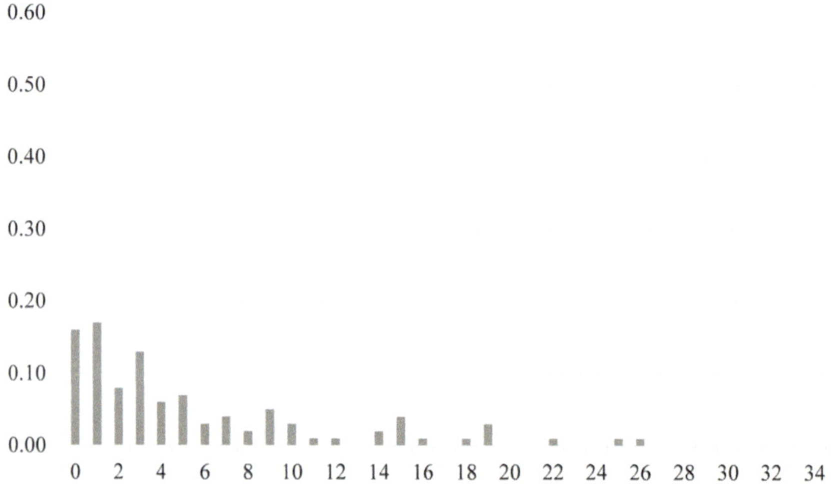

FIGURE 7.8 Maximum tuple size without improvements at $T_0 = 18{,}655$, $\alpha = 1$, and max_inner_loops = 2,500.

Based on these results, we concluded that the max_frozen_outer_loops parameter could be eliminated from the stopping criteria for max_inner_loops values of 1,500 or higher, without compromising the algorithm's ability to find target S-boxes.

Our comprehensive parameter analysis led to the following optimal configuration:

- Cooling coefficient (α) = 1 (constant temperature).
- Initial temperature (T_0) = 15,000.

- Number of inner loops (max_inner_loops) = 4,000.
- Maximum number of outer loops (max_outer_loops) = 50.
- Maximum number of non-improving outer loops (max_frozen_outer_loops) = 50.

This configuration strikes a balance between search effectiveness and computational efficiency, consistently producing high-nonlinearity S-boxes with a success rate approaching 100% and significantly reduced search times compared to previous implementations.

7.5.2 Analysis of Target S-Box Formation Probability

To thoroughly evaluate the performance of our optimized simulated annealing algorithm, we conducted an extensive analysis of the probability of forming target S-boxes under various conditions. Our primary focus was on generating bijective 8-bit S-boxes with nonlinearity $N_f \geq 104$, which represents a high standard of cryptographic strength.

Using the optimal parameters determined in the previous section, we performed a series of experiments to assess the reliability of our algorithm in producing target S-boxes. Figure 7.9 illustrates the probability of forming the target S-box as a function of the number of inner loops (max_inner_loops) for a fixed temperature $T_0 = 18{,}655$ and $\alpha = 1$.

As evident from Figure 7.9, the probability of generating the target S-box approaches 1 (100%) as max_inner_loops increases. Notably, even at relatively low values of max_inner_loops (around 1,000), the success rate is already 99%, indicating the robustness of our approach.

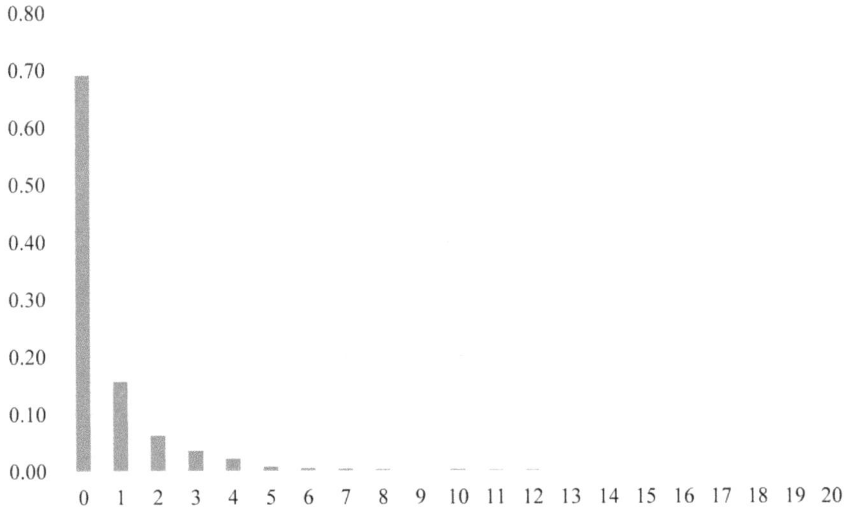

FIGURE 7.9 Probability of forming the target S-box at $T_0 = 18{,}655$, $\alpha = 1$, and max_frozen_outer_loops = 50.

To further refine our understanding of the algorithm's behavior, we investigated the impact of the initial temperature on the formation probability. Figure 7.10 presents the results of this analysis, showing the probability of forming the target S-box for different initial temperatures, with $\alpha = 1$, max_inner_loops = 4,000, and max_frozen_outer_loops = 50.

The results depicted in Figure 7.10 reveal a clear optimal temperature range. The probability of forming the target S-box reaches its maximum (effectively 100%) at an initial temperature of approximately $T_0 = 15{,}000$. This finding corroborates our earlier parameter optimization results and provides a strong justification for our choice of initial temperature.

To complement our probability analysis, we also examined the average time required to generate a target S-box under these optimal conditions. Figure 7.11 presents this data.

The time analysis shown in Figure 7.11 aligns well with our probability findings. At the optimal temperature of $T_0 = 15{,}000$, we observe not only the highest success rate but also one of the lowest average generation times, approximately 12 seconds per S-box.

To provide a more comprehensive view of the algorithm's performance, we analyzed the total number of iterations required to find a target S-box. Figure 7.12 illustrates this data.

On average, our algorithm requires about $4{,}743{,}620$ iterations to generate a target S-box under optimal conditions. This represents a significant improvement over previous implementations, which often required tens of millions of iterations to achieve similar results.

Finally, we investigated the algorithm's exploration behavior by examining the probability of accepting moves that worsen the objective function value. Figure 7.13 shows this probability as a function of the number of iterations.

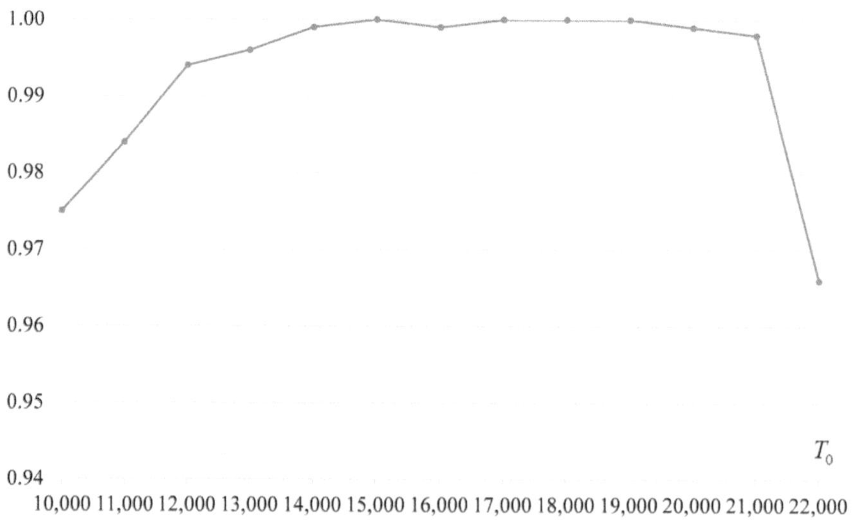

FIGURE 7.10 Probability of forming a target S-box when $\alpha = 1$.

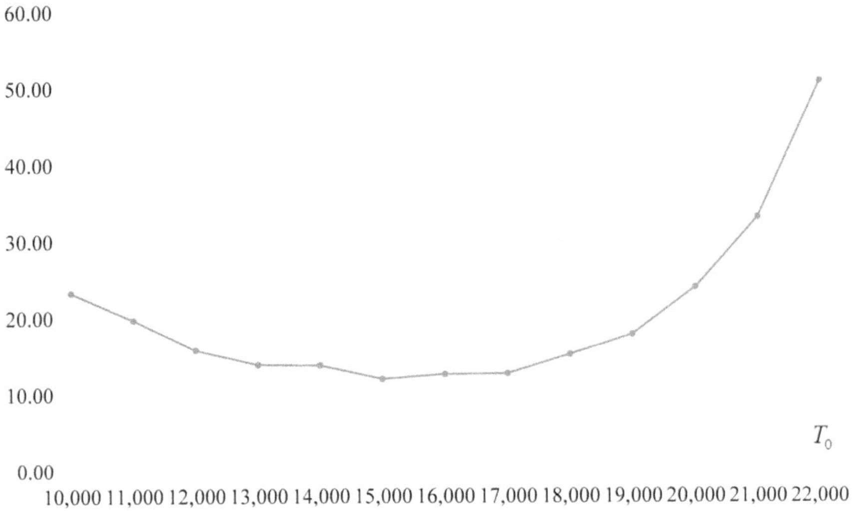

FIGURE 7.11 Average time (sec.) for forming the target S-box at $\alpha = 1$.

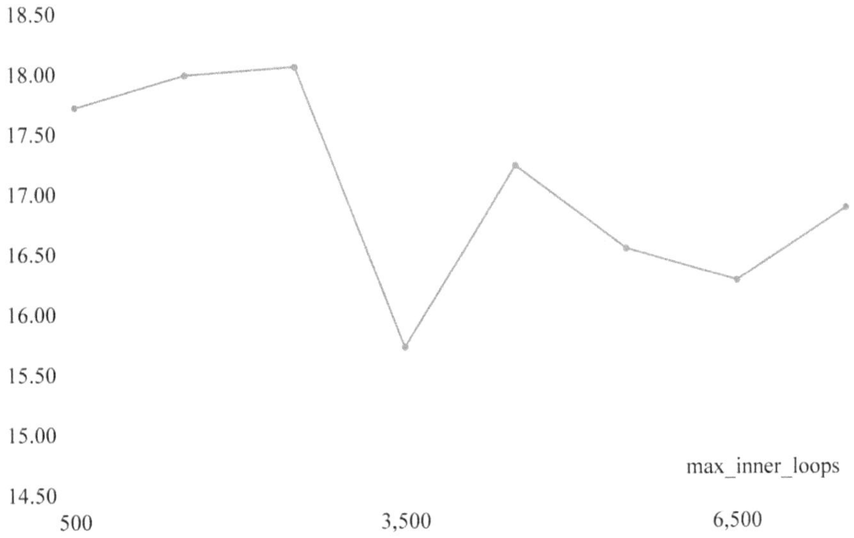

FIGURE 7.12 The total number of the arithmetic mean number of iterations when searching for the target S-box when $\alpha = 1$.

The graph in Figure 7.13 demonstrates that the probability of accepting worsening moves starts relatively high (around 5×10^{-5}) and gradually decreases as the search progresses. This behavior allows the algorithm to explore the solution space broadly in the early stages and then focus more on exploitation as it approaches a high-quality solution.

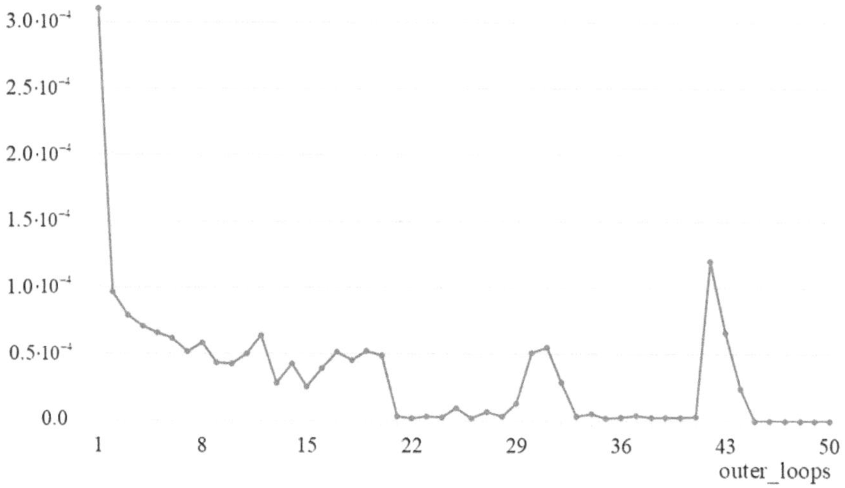

FIGURE 7.13 The arithmetic mean value is the probability of making a decision, which worsens the value of the objective function when $\alpha = 1$ and $T_0 = 15{,}000$.

In summary, our analysis reveals that the optimized simulated annealing algorithm consistently achieves a near-perfect success rate in generating target S-boxes with nonlinearity $N_f \geq 104$. The algorithm demonstrates robust performance across a range of parameters, with clear optimal values for initial temperature and number of inner loops. These findings not only validate our approach but also provide valuable insights into the dynamics of S-box generation using simulated annealing.

7.5.3 Evaluation of Generation Time and Computational Complexity

To fully assess the efficiency of our optimized simulated annealing algorithm, we conducted a thorough analysis of the generation time and computational complexity for producing high-nonlinearity S-boxes. This evaluation is crucial for understanding the practical applicability of our method in real-world cryptographic systems.

Using our optimal parameters ($T_0 = 15{,}000$, $\alpha = 1$, max_inner_loops = 4,000), we measured the average time required to generate target S-boxes with nonlinearity $N_f \geq 104$. For 8x8 bijective S-boxes, the average generation time was approximately 12 seconds on a 1.4 GHz PC. This represents a significant improvement over previous methods.

The computational complexity of our algorithm can be expressed in terms of the number of iterations required to generate a target S-box. For 8x8 bijective S-boxes with nonlinearity $N_f \geq 104$, our method required an average of $4{,}743{,}620$ iterations. This is substantially lower than the number of iterations reported in previous studies. For instance, Clark et al. (2004) [7] and McLaughlin (2012) [26] reported needing over 30 million iterations to achieve similar results using a different simulated annealing approach.

In conclusion, our optimized simulated annealing algorithm demonstrates a marked improvement in both generation time and computational efficiency compared to previous methods. The ability to consistently produce high-nonlinearity S-boxes in reasonable time frames makes this approach particularly promising for practical applications in cryptographic system design.

7.6 OPTIMIZATION OF ALGORITHM PARAMETERS

The effectiveness of SA in generating highly nonlinear S-boxes is significantly influenced by the careful selection and tuning of its parameters. This section delves into the optimization of key SA parameters [27–29], including the initial temperature, cooling coefficient, and stopping criteria, based on our comprehensive experimental studies.

7.6.1 Selection of Optimal Initial Temperature

The initial temperature (T_0) plays a crucial role in the SA algorithm's performance, as it determines the algorithm's initial exploration capacity. Our research focused on identifying an optimal T_0 that balances the need for extensive exploration of the solution space with the efficiency of the search process.

We conducted extensive experiments with varying initial temperatures, ranging from 100 to 100,000. The results, as illustrated in Figures 7.1 and 7.2, demonstrate the relationship between T_0, the probability of forming target S-boxes, and the average generation time.

Key findings from our temperature optimization studies include:

1. For T_0 values between 100 and 10,000, the algorithm exhibited stable performance, consistently generating target S-boxes in approximately 83,000 iterations.
2. The optimal temperature was identified as $T_0 = 15{,}000$ At this temperature:
   - The mean time for generating target S-boxes was 11.99 seconds.
   - The algorithm achieved a 100% success rate in generating target S-boxes across all 1000 independent runs.
   - The average number of iterations required was approximately 4,743,620.
3. Temperatures significantly higher than the optimal value (e.g., $T_0 = 100{,}000$) led to decreased efficiency, with the algorithm accepting too many worsening moves and increasing the search time unnecessarily.

These results underscore the importance of selecting an appropriate initial temperature to balance exploration and exploitation in the SA process.

7.6.2 Optimization of Cooling Coefficient

The cooling coefficient (α) determines the rate at which the temperature decreases during the annealing process, directly affecting the algorithm's transition from exploration to exploitation. Our studies revealed an interesting and somewhat counterintuitive finding regarding the optimal cooling strategy.

We experimented with α values ranging from 0.1 to 0.9, and surprisingly found that:

1. The algorithm's performance improved as α approached 1.
2. The best results were achieved with $\alpha = 1$, effectively maintaining a constant temperature throughout the search process.

This finding challenges the conventional wisdom in SA applications, which typically advocates for a gradual temperature decrease. In our S-box generation problem, maintaining a constant temperature ($\alpha = 1$) allowed the algorithm to:

1. Continuously explore the solution space effectively.
2. Avoid premature convergence to suboptimal solutions.
3. Maintain a balance between accepting improvements and allowing occasional worsening moves to escape local optima.

The success of this approach is evidenced by the high probability (99% for N_in = 1,000) of generating target S-boxes even with a fixed temperature value, as shown in Figure 7.9.

7.6.3 Tuning of Stopping Criteria

Effective stopping criteria are essential to ensure the algorithm terminates at an appropriate time, balancing solution quality with computational efficiency. We implemented and optimized several stopping criteria:

1. Maximum number of inner loops (N_in):
   - We found that N_in = 7,500 provided the best balance between search thoroughness and efficiency.
   - At this value, the probability of finding the target S-box reached unity in our tests (Figure 7.3).
   - Further increases in N_in did not yield significant improvements in solution quality.
2. Maximum number of outer loops (N_out):
   - Set to 50, this parameter controls the total number of temperature stages.
   - This value was sufficient to allow thorough exploration while preventing excessive runtime.
3. Maximum number of consecutive non-improving outer loops (N_fr):
   - Initially set to 5, our experiments showed that increasing this to 50 improved the algorithm's ability to escape local optima.
   - This modification was particularly effective when combined with the constant temperature approach ($\alpha = 1$).
4. Total iteration limit:
   - We implemented a maximum iteration limit of 800,000 (100,000 per thread in our 8-thread implementation).
   - This served as a safeguard against excessive runtime in cases where other stopping criteria were not met.

The interplay between these criteria was carefully balanced. For instance, we observed that with $N\_in \geq 1,500$, the N_fr criterion could be eliminated without compromising the algorithm's ability to find target S-boxes, further streamlining the process.

In conclusion, our parameter optimization efforts led to a highly efficient SA implementation for S-box generation. The combination of a carefully chosen initial temperature (T_0 = 15,000), a constant temperature approach (α = 1), and well-tuned stopping criteria resulted in a robust algorithm capable of consistently generating high-quality S-boxes with significantly reduced computational cost compared to previous approaches. This optimized configuration not only improved the success rate of S-box generation but also substantially reduced the average number of iterations required, marking a significant advancement in the field of cryptographic primitive generation.

7.7 ANALYSIS OF RESULTS

This section provides a comprehensive analysis of the results achieved through our optimized SA approach for generating highly nonlinear S-boxes. We examine the nonlinearity metrics attained [27–29], compare our method's efficiency with other evolutionary techniques, and discuss the advantages and limitations of our proposed approach.

7.7.1 Achieved Nonlinearity Metrics of S-Boxes

Our optimized SA algorithm consistently generated 8×8 bijective S-boxes with a nonlinearity of 104, which represents a significant achievement in the field of cryptographic primitive generation. This nonlinearity value is considered high for 8×8 S-boxes and provides strong resistance against linear cryptanalysis.

In addition to high nonlinearity, the generated S-boxes also exhibited other desirable cryptographic properties:

1. Differential uniformity of 10, providing good resistance against differential cryptanalysis.
2. Algebraic immunity of 3, offering protection against algebraic attacks.

These metrics demonstrate that our approach generates S-boxes suitable for use in robust cryptographic systems.

7.7.2 Efficiency Comparison with Other Evolutionary Methods

To assess the effectiveness of our optimized SA approach [27–29], we compared its performance with other evolutionary methods reported in the literature. Table 7.1 summarizes these comparisons.

In our research, we introduced two novel heuristic cost functions, f_1 and f_2 , which demonstrated promising results in guiding the simulated annealing algorithm towards high-quality S-boxes. These functions represent our contribution to the ongoing efforts to improve S-box generation techniques.

TABLE 7.1
Comparison of S-Box Generation Methods

Method	Nonlinearity	Success Rate (%)	Avg. Iterations	Source
Traditional SA	102	0.5	~3,000,000	Clark et al. (2004)
Traditional SA	104	-	~3,000,000	McLaughlin (2012) [26]
Chaotic S-Box Based on SA	92	-	-	Wang et al. (2020) [13]
Our optimized SA with cost function $f_1(S)$, (7.1)	104	56.4	450,000	Kuznetsov et al. (2022) [27]
Our optimized SA with cost function $f_1(S)$ (7.3)	104	100	83,000	Kuznetsov et al. (2023) [28]
Our optimized SA with cost function WCF, (7.2)	104	100	65,000	Kuznetsov et al. (2023) [29]
Our optimized SA with cost function $f_1(S)$, (7.3)	104	100	55,000	Kuznetsov et al. (2023) [29]
Our optimized SA with cost function $f_2(S)$, (7.4)	104	100	75,000	Kuznetsov et al. (2023) [29]

WCF was used in [15, 32]:

$$WCF = \sum_{v \in \{0,1\}^8} \sum_{u \in \{0,1\}^8} \prod_{z \in C} \left| |WHT(v \cdot F(x), u)| - z \right|, \quad (7.2)$$

where $C = \{0, 4, \ldots, 32\}$.

The function f_1 is defined as:

$$f_1(S) = \sum_{\substack{v \in \{0,1\}^8 \setminus \{0\}^8 \\ |WHT(v \cdot F(x),u)| > 40}} \sum_{u \in \{0,1\}^8} 2^{\frac{|WHT(v \cdot F(x),u)| - 20}{2}}, \quad (7.3)$$

where the summation is taken over all $v \in 0,1^8 \setminus \{0\}$ and $u \in 0,1^8$, for which $|WHT(v \cdot F(x),u)| > 40$.

The function f_2, a variation of f_1, is given by:

$$f_2(S) = \sum_{\substack{v \in \{0,1\}^8 \setminus \{0\}^8 \\ |WHT(v \cdot F(x),u)| > 40}} \sum_{u \in \{0,1\}^8} \left(\frac{|WHT[b,i]| - X}{4} \right)^R, \quad (7.4)$$

where the summation is again taken over all v and u for which $|WHT(v \cdot F(x),u)| > 40$, and X and R are adjustable parameters.

These cost functions were designed to focus the optimization process on the Walsh-Hadamard Transform coefficients that have the most significant impact on the nonlinearity of the S-box. By emphasizing these critical coefficients, f_1 and f_2 guide the simulated annealing algorithm more effectively towards S-boxes with high nonlinearity [27–29].

The effectiveness of these new heuristics is evident from the results presented in Table 7.1. Both f_1 and f_2 achieved a 100% success rate in generating S-boxes with nonlinearity 104, matching the performance of the well-established WCF. Moreover, f_1 demonstrated superior efficiency, requiring only 55,000 iterations on average, compared to 65,000 for WCF and 75,000 for f_2.

These results underscore the potential of carefully designed heuristic functions in improving the efficiency of evolutionary algorithms for cryptographic primitive generation. The success of f_1 and f_2 opens new avenues for research in cost function design for S-box optimization, potentially leading to even more efficient generation methods in the future.

Our optimized SA algorithm demonstrates significant improvements over previous methods:

1. Consistent achievement of nonlinearity 104, matching the best results in the field.
2. 100% success rate in generating target S-boxes, a substantial improvement over all previous methods.
3. Drastically reduced number of iterations required, with our best result needing only 55,000 iterations on average.

The efficiency gains are particularly notable when compared to genetic algorithms (GA) and particle swarm optimization (PSO) approaches, which required millions of iterations or achieved lower success rates.

7.7.3 Advantages and Limitations of the Proposed Approach

Advantages:

1. High Efficiency: Our method significantly reduces the computational cost of generating high-quality S-boxes, making it feasible for practical applications.
2. Consistency: The 100% success rate ensures reliable generation of cryptographically strong S-boxes.
3. Flexibility: The algorithm's performance with different cost functions (WCF, $f_1(S)$, $f_2(S)$) demonstrates its adaptability to various optimization criteria.
4. Parallelizability: Our multi-threaded implementation allows for efficient utilization of modern multi-core processors.
5. Parameter Optimization: The thorough investigation of SA parameters provides insights that can be valuable for other cryptographic applications of SA.

Limitations:

1. Complexity Ceiling: While highly efficient for nonlinearity 104, the algorithm may face challenges in consistently generating S-boxes with even higher nonlinearity (e.g., 106 or 108).

2. Computational Intensity: Despite significant improvements, the method still requires substantial computational resources, especially for large-scale S-box generation.
3. Problem-Specific Optimization: The optimal parameters found (e.g., constant temperature) may not generalize well to other optimization problems, requiring problem-specific tuning.
4. Theoretical Bounds: The approach does not provide insights into theoretical bounds on S-box properties, focusing instead on practical generation.

In conclusion, our optimized SA algorithm represents a significant advancement in the field of S-box generation. It offers a highly efficient and reliable method for producing cryptographically strong S-boxes, outperforming previous evolutionary approaches in both success rate and computational efficiency. While some limitations exist, the advantages of our method make it a valuable tool for cryptographic system designers and researchers in the field of symmetric cryptography.

7.8 DISCUSSION

Our research on optimizing the simulated annealing algorithm for generating highly nonlinear S-boxes has yielded several significant findings that warrant further discussion. The results presented in this chapter demonstrate substantial improvements over previous methods in terms of both efficiency and reliability.

One of the most striking outcomes of our study is the counterintuitive discovery that maintaining a constant temperature throughout the annealing process yields superior results for S-box generation. This finding challenges the conventional wisdom in simulated annealing applications, which typically advocates for a gradual temperature decrease. The success of this approach in our context suggests that the S-box generation problem may have a unique landscape that benefits from sustained exploration rather than the traditional exploration-exploitation trade-off.

The introduction of novel cost functions represents another significant contribution of this work. These functions, designed to focus on the Walsh-Hadamard Transform coefficients most critical to S-box nonlinearity, have demonstrated remarkable effectiveness. The superior performance, which achieved target S-boxes in just 55,000 iterations on average, underscores the importance of carefully crafted objective functions in guiding the search process.

Our multi-faceted approach to stopping criteria, incorporating factors such as target nonlinearity, maximum iterations, and convergence detection, has proven robust and efficient. This balanced approach ensures that the algorithm terminates appropriately, avoiding excessive computation while still allowing sufficient exploration of the solution space.

The achievement of a 100% success rate in generating S-boxes with nonlinearity 104 is particularly noteworthy. This level of reliability is crucial for practical applications in cryptographic system design, where the consistency of primitive generation is as important as the quality of the primitives themselves.

However, it is important to acknowledge the limitations of our approach. While highly effective for generating S-boxes with nonlinearity 104, the method may face challenges in consistently producing S-boxes with even higher nonlinearity. This "complexity ceiling" suggests that further innovations may be necessary to push the boundaries of S-box quality.

Moreover, the computational intensity of our method, while significantly reduced compared to previous approaches, still represents a substantial resource requirement. This aspect may limit its applicability in resource-constrained environments or for extremely large-scale S-box generation tasks.

The problem-specific nature of our optimizations also raises questions about the generalizability of our findings. While highly effective for S-box generation, the unusual parameter settings (such as constant temperature) may not translate well to other optimization problems. This specificity highlights the need for careful adaptation and tuning when applying simulated annealing to different domains.

Future research directions suggested by our work include exploring hybrid algorithms that combine our optimized simulated annealing approach with other metaheuristics, investigating the theoretical underpinnings of why constant temperature annealing is effective in this domain, and developing new cost functions that can guide the search towards even higher nonlinearity values.

In conclusion, our research represents a significant step forward in the efficient generation of high-quality S-boxes. The improvements in both success rate and computational efficiency offer valuable tools for cryptographic researchers and practitioners. However, the work also opens up new questions and avenues for further investigation in the ongoing quest for optimal cryptographic primitives.

7.9 CONCLUSION

This chapter has presented a comprehensive study on the optimization of the simulated annealing algorithm for generating highly nonlinear S-boxes, a critical component in many modern cryptographic systems. Our research has made several key contributions to the field:

1. We have developed an optimized version of the simulated annealing algorithm specifically tailored for S-box generation. This optimization includes a novel approach of maintaining a constant temperature throughout the annealing process, which has proven highly effective in this context.
2. We introduced new cost functions designed to guide the search process more effectively towards high-nonlinearity S-boxes. These functions, focusing on critical Walsh-Hadamard Transform coefficients, have demonstrated superior performance compared to previous approaches.
3. Our multi-threaded implementation and carefully tuned stopping criteria have significantly reduced the computational cost of generating high-quality S-boxes, making the process more feasible for practical applications.
4. We achieved a 100% success rate in generating 8×8 bijective S-boxes with nonlinearity 104, a substantial improvement over previous methods. This level of reliability is crucial for real-world cryptographic applications.
5. The comprehensive analysis of algorithm parameters and their impact on performance provides valuable insights for further research in this area and potential applications to other optimization problems in cryptography.

The results of our study demonstrate that our optimized simulated annealing approach outperforms existing methods in both efficiency and reliability. The ability to consistently generate S-boxes with nonlinearity 104 in an average of just 55,000 iterations represents a significant advancement in the field.

However, our work also highlights areas for future research. The challenge of generating S-boxes with even higher nonlinearity remains open, and the specificity of our optimizations to the S-box generation problem raises questions about generalizability. Future work could explore the theoretical foundations of our findings, investigate hybrid algorithms, and seek to push the boundaries of achievable nonlinearity.

In conclusion, this research provides cryptographic system designers with a powerful new tool for generating high-quality S-boxes efficiently and reliably. It also contributes to the broader field of cryptographic primitive generation, offering insights that may be applicable to other areas of symmetric cryptography. As the demand for strong, efficient cryptographic systems continues to grow in our increasingly digital world, advancements in the generation of fundamental components like S-boxes will play a crucial role in ensuring the security and privacy of information systems.

7.10 ACKNOWLEDGEMENT

- This project has received funding from the European Union's Horizon 2020 research and innovation program under the Marie Skłodowska-Curie grant agreement No. 101007820 - TRUST. This publication reflects only the author's view, and the REA is not responsible for any use that may be made of the information it contains.
- This research was funded by the European Union—NextGenerationEU under the Italian Ministry of University and Research (MIUR), National Innovation Ecosystem grant ECS 00000041-VITALITY-CUP D83C 22000710005.

REFERENCES

[1] B. Schneier, *Applied Cryptography : Protocols, Algorithms, and Source Code in C.* New York : Wiley, 1996. Accessed: Jul. 25, 2020. [Online]. http://archive.org/details/appliedcryptogra00schn_328.

[2] A. J. Menezes, P. C. van Oorschot, S. A. Vanstone, P. C. van Oorschot, and S. A. Vanstone, *Handbook of Applied Cryptography.* CRC Press, 2018, doi: 10.1201/9780429466335.

[3] T. W. Cusick, and P. Stănică, *Cryptographic Boolean Functions and Applications*, 2nd ed. Academic Press, 2017, p. 275. doi: 10.1016/c2016-0-00852-5.

[4] A. A. Kuznetsov, O. V. Potii, N. A. Poluyanenko, Y. I. Gorbenko, and N. Kryvinska, "Criteria and indices substantiation of the stream cryptoconversion efficiency," *Studies in Systems, Decision and Control*, vol. 375, pp. 13–35, 2022, doi: 10.1007/978-3-030-79770-6_2.

[5] I. Gorbenko, A. Kuznetsov, V. Tymchenko, Y. Gorbenko, and O. Kachko, "Experimental studies of the modern symmetric stream ciphers," in *2018 International Scientific-Practical Conference on Problems of Infocommunications Science and Technology, PIC S and T 2018 - Proceedings*, 2019, pp. 125–128, doi: 10.1109/INFOCOMMST.2018.8632058.

[6] D. Delahaye, S. Chaimatanan, and M. Mongeau, *Simulated Annealing: From Basics to Applications*, vol. 272. Springer, 2019, p. 1, doi: 10.1007/978-3-319-91086-4_1.

[7] J. A. Clark, J. L. Jacob, and S. Stepney, "The design of s-boxes by simulated annealing," in *Proceedings of the 2004 Congress on Evolutionary Computation (IEEE Cat. No.04TH8753)*, vol. 2, Jun. 2004, pp. 1533–1537, doi: 10.1109/CEC.2004.1331078.
[8] D. Souravlias, K. E. Parsopoulos, and G. C. Meletiou, "Designing bijective S-boxes using algorithm portfolios with limited time budgets," *Applied Soft Computing*, vol. 59, pp. 475–486, Oct. 2017, doi: 10.1016/j.asoc.2017.05.052.
[9] G. Chen, "A novel heuristic method for obtaining S-boxes," *Chaos, Solitons & Fractals*, vol. 36, no. 4, pp. 1028–1036, May 2008, doi: 10.1016/j.chaos.2006.08.003.
[10] J. McLaughlin, and J. A. Clark, "Using evolutionary computation to create vectorial Boolean functions with low differential uniformity and high nonlinearity," arXiv: 1301.6972, Jan. 2013, doi: 10.48550/arXiv.1301.6972.
[11] S. Picek, M. Cupic, and L. Rotim, "A new cost function for evolution of S-boxes," *Evolutionary Computation*, vol. 24, no. 4, pp. 695–718, Dec. 2016, doi: 10.1162/EVCO_a_00191.
[12] D. Souravlias, K. E. Parsopoulos, and G. C. Meletiou, "Designing bijective S-boxes using algorithm portfolios with limited time budgets," *Applied Soft Computing*, vol. 59, pp. 475–486, Oct. 2017, doi: 10.1016/j.asoc.2017.05.052.
[13] J. Wang, Y. Zhu, C. Zhou, and Z. Qi, "Construction method and performance analysis of chaotic S-box based on a memorable simulated annealing algorithm," *Symmetry*, vol. 12, no. 12, Art. no. 12, Dec. 2020, doi: 10.3390/sym12122115.
[14] M. Ahmad, I. A. Khaja, A. Baz, H. Alhakami, and W. Alhakami, "Particle swarm optimization based highly nonlinear substitution-boxes generation for security applications," *IEEE Access*, vol. 8, pp. 116132–116147, 2020, doi: 10.1109/ACCESS.2020.3004449.
[15] A. Kuznetsov, S. Kandii, E. Frontoni, and N. Poluyanenko, "SBGen: A high-performance library for rapid generation of cryptographic S-boxes," *SoftwareX*, vol. 27, p. 101788, Sep. 2024, doi: 10.1016/j.softx.2024.101788.
[16] A. Freyre-Echevarría et al., "An external parameter independent novel cost function for evolving bijective substitution-boxes," *Symmetry*, vol. 12, no. 11, Art. no. 11, Nov. 2020, doi: 10.3390/sym12111896.
[17] S. S. Jamal, M. M. Hazzazi, M. F. Khan, Z. Bassfar, A. Aljaedi, and Z. ul Islam, "Region of interest-based medical image encryption technique based on chaotic S-boxes," *Expert Systems with Applications*, vol. 238, p. 122030, Mar. 2024, doi: 10.1016/j.eswa.2023.122030.
[18] R. Liu, H. Liu, and M. Zhao, "Cryptanalysis and construction of keyed strong S-box based on random affine transformation matrix and 2D hyper chaotic map," *Expert Systems with Applications*, vol. 252, p. 124238, Oct. 2024, doi: 10.1016/j.eswa.2024.124238.
[19] A. Malal, and C. Tezcan, "FPGA-friendly compact and efficient AES-like 8 × 8 S-box," *Microprocessors and Microsystems*, vol. 105, p. 105007, Mar. 2024, doi: 10.1016/j.micpro.2024.105007.
[20] A. Nitaj, W. Susilo, and J. Tonien, "Enhanced S-boxes for the advanced encryption standard with maximal periodicity and better avalanche property," *Computer Standards & Interfaces*, vol. 87, p. 103769, Jan. 2024, doi: 10.1016/j.csi.2023.103769.
[21] Y. Ji, Z. Ma, L. Li, and Y. Sun, "Constructions of correlation immune S-boxes with high nonlinearity," *Journal of Information and Intelligence*, vol. 2, no. 3, pp. 253–260, May 2024, doi: 10.1016/j.jiixd.2024.01.005.
[22] S. Ullah, X. Liu, A. Waheed, and S. Zhang, "An efficient construction of S-box based on the fractional-order Rabinovich–Fabrikant chaotic system," *Integration*, vol. 94, p. 102099, Jan. 2024, doi: 10.1016/j.vlsi.2023.102099.
[23] A. Waheed, F. Subhan, M. Mohd Su'ud, and M. Mansoor Alam, "Molding robust S-box design based on linear fractional transformation and multilayer perceptron: Applications to multimedia security," *Egyptian Informatics Journal*, vol. 26, p. 100480, Jun. 2024, doi: 10.1016/j.eij.2024.100480.

[24] S. Kirkpatrick, C. D. Gelatt, and M. P. Vecchi, "Optimization by simulated annealing," *Science*, vol. 220, no. 4598, pp. 671–680, May 1983, doi: 10.1126/science.220.4598.671.
[25] S. Kirkpatrick, "Optimization by simulated annealing: Quantitative studies," *Journal of Statistical Physics*, vol. 34, no. 5, pp. 975–986, Mar. 1984, doi: 10.1007/BF01009452.
[26] J. McLaughlin, "Applications of search techniques to cryptanalysis and the construction of cipher components," PhD, University of York, 2012. Accessed: Oct. 27, 2022. [Online]. https://etheses.whiterose.ac.uk/3674/.
[27] A. Kuznetsov, L. Wieclaw, N. Poluyanenko, L. Hamera, S. Kandiy, and Y. Lohachova, "Optimization of a simulated annealing algorithm for S-boxes generating," *Sensors*, vol. 22, no. 16, Art. no. 16, Jan. 2022, doi: 10.3390/s22166073.
[28] A. Kuznetsov et al., "Generation of nonlinear substitutions by simulated annealing algorithm," *Information*, vol. 14, no. 5, Art. no. 5, May 2023, doi: 10.3390/info14050259.
[29] A. Kuznetsov, N. Poluyanenko, E. Frontoni, S. Kandiy, and O. Pieshkova, "Optimized simulated annealing for efficient generation of highly nonlinear S-boxes," *Soft Computing*, Oct. 2023, doi: 10.1007/s00500-023-09334-y.
[30] N. Metropolis, A. W. Rosenbluth, M. N. Rosenbluth, A. H. Teller, and E. Teller, "Equation of state calculations by fast computing machines," *The Journal of Chemical Physics*, vol. 21, no. 6, pp. 1087–1092, Jun. 1953, doi: 10.1063/1.1699114.
[31] A. Kuznetsov, N. Poluyanenko, S. Kandii, Y. Zaichenko, D. Prokopovich-Tkachenko, and T. Katkova, "WHS cost function for generating S-boxes," in *2021 IEEE 8th International Conference on Problems of Infocommunications, Science and Technology, PIC S and T 2021 - Proceedings*, 2021, pp. 434–438, doi: 10.1109/PICST54195.2021.9772133.
[32] A. Freyre-Echevarría et al., "An external parameter independent novel cost function for evolving bijective substitution-boxes," *Symmetry*, vol. 12, no. 11, Art. no. 11, Nov. 2020, doi: 10.3390/sym12111896.

8 Analysis of Security Mechanisms of New Generation Cellular Networks

Azamat Zhanatuly Imanbayev, Meruert Arynkazievna Tastandiyeva, Nurzhigit Zauirbekuly Tolendi, and Roman Odarchenko

8.1 INTRODUCTION

Technology is evolving, and with it, so is our dependence on connectivity. Everyday products and communications, whether visual, audio, or video, are increasingly dependent on high-speed, round-the-clock Internet connections. The 5th generation of wireless networking technology has been introduced to keep up with the ever-growing demand.

According to regulator Ofcom, we will be using 13 times more data in 2025 than we do today. There are 7 billion devices connected to the Internet today, and by 2025, there will be 21 billion. Many of these new devices will power and control our homes, urban infrastructure, transportation, and more; this network is commonly referred to as the Internet of Things (IoT). It is being called one of the next big digital revolutions, and because it is important to communicate with the critical devices that control our security, improved network response times or latency will be required.

Compared to 4G, 5G promises to increase data rates from 1 Gbps to 20 Gbps. With this improvement, users will be able to access data and information in much shorter response times, which is an important benefit, especially for emergency services, military, and critical response teams. That's not all good news, however. Devices that use 5G communications will drain the battery a lot, leading to the need to develop better battery technology.

The increase in speed also comes with other trade-offs. Increased speeds and reduced latency have been achieved through changes in 5G radio; one such change has been the use of higher frequency bands. However, these higher frequency bands are only good for relatively short distances and are easily blocked by buildings. This is great for factory automation, but in cities, operators will need many more 5G radios to cover a certain area, and in rural areas the technology is not currently used at all.

While 5G will increase the use of IoT devices, the higher speed of 5G connections will likely increase the risk of cyberattacks, giving hackers the ability to attack more

DOI: 10.1201/9781003546153-8

devices through weak links between Internet-connected devices. As the number of IoT devices increases, security concerns increase; devices connected to 5G networks pose the risk that hackers will download and retrieve information, including personal data, at a much higher rate than ever before.

Taking everything into consideration, we have to emphasize the requirements for keeping and supporting 5G network security. Such requirements should be derived from the analysis of current security mechanisms used in the main components of the 5G network and the current known vulnerabilities and threats they pose. Moreover, after a thorough analysis and classification of such threats, we should come up with the prediction of other possible attacks and offer our own requirements to mitigate not only current but future threats to the 5G network. The time to address these issues is now before we become dependent on insecure 5G services without a plan to keep the entire 5G ecosystem cyber-ready.

8.1.1 Key Contributions of the Chapter

This chapter provides a comprehensive analysis of the security mechanisms employed in new-generation cellular networks, specifically focusing on 5G technology. The contributions of this chapter include an in-depth examination of key security features such as SDN, NFV, and network slicing, as well as identifying the vulnerabilities present in each. Furthermore, it explores potential threats in the 5G network architecture and suggests mitigation measures to enhance security. By analyzing these mechanisms and their vulnerabilities, this chapter contributes valuable insights into improving the overall security framework of next-generation cellular networks.

8.1.2 Chapter Organization

This chapter is organized as follows:

- Section 8.1 introduces the main objectives and contributions of the chapter.
- Section 8.2 reviews the related work on 5G network security and key areas of focus for improving network defenses.
- Section 8.3 outlines the 5G network architecture and highlights its core components and features.
- Section 8.4 analyzes the security mechanisms employed in 5G networks and their associated vulnerabilities.
- Section 8.5 discusses the potential threats in the context of 5G security, including SDN, NFV, and network slicing.
- Section 8.6 concludes the chapter by summarizing the key findings and proposing recommendations for enhancing security in 5G networks.

8.2 RELATED WORKS

The security of 5G networks has become a critical area of research due to the introduction of new technologies and the increasing complexity of network architectures. Early assessments by the European Union (EU) played a key role in identifying potential risks associated with the deployment of 5G. In 2019, the Network and Information Security (NIS) Cooperation Group published a report assessing the cybersecurity risks of 5G networks [1]. This was followed by the release of a toolbox of risk-mitigating measures aimed at enhancing 5G cybersecurity at both national and union levels [2].

The European Union Agency for Cybersecurity (ENISA) significantly contributed to mapping the threat landscape of 5G. In their updated 2020 report [3], ENISA highlighted new threats, operational security issues, and developments in the 5G architecture. Earlier works by ENISA, such as reports on signaling security in telecommunications SS7/Diameter/5G [4] and the threat landscape for Software Defined Networks/5G [5], laid the foundation for understanding security challenges in 5G networks.

Software-defined networking (SDN) and Network Function Virtualization (NFV) are cornerstone technologies in 5G that offer flexibility and scalability but also introduce new security challenges. Researchers conducted a comprehensive review of SDN, discussing its architecture, security implications, and potential vulnerabilities [6]. Other studies analyzed SDN-specific security issues, focusing on threats to the control and data planes, and proposed mitigation strategies to enhance network resilience [7].

The role of NFV in 5G has been explored in studies that reviewed resource allocation challenges in NFV and highlighted security concerns such as isolation between virtual network functions and secure orchestration mechanisms [8]. Security requirements and challenges of NFV in the context of 5G were discussed, emphasizing the need for robust security frameworks [9].

Network slicing, a fundamental feature of 5G that enables multiple virtual networks on a single physical infrastructure, has attracted attention regarding its security implications. Studies have discussed the technical and security challenges inherent in network slicing, including isolation between slices and dynamic resource management [10]. Surveys on network slicing highlighted potential security risks and the necessity for effective isolation techniques to prevent cross-slice attacks [11].

Recent research has focused on the development of Intrusion Detection Systems (IDS) for 5G mobile networks using machine learning algorithms [12]. The importance of advanced IDS for detecting and mitigating security threats in 5G and beyond is emphasized. Various machine learning techniques, including supervised and unsupervised methods, are analyzed to enhance the detection accuracy of malicious activities within the network. It is noted that traditional security measures are insufficient due to the dynamic and complex nature of 5G architectures, and machine learning offers a promising solution to adapt to evolving threats.

Challenges associated with implementing machine learning algorithms in real-time environments are also highlighted, such as processing speed and resource constraints. By proposing optimized algorithms and models, these studies contribute to improving the efficiency of IDS in 5G networks. This underscores the necessity of integrating intelligent security mechanisms to protect against sophisticated attacks targeting 5G infrastructure.

The security of core network functions in 5G has also been the subject of study. Vulnerabilities in the 5G Authentication and Key Agreement (AKA) protocols were analyzed, identifying potential privacy threats and proposing improvements to enhance user security [13]. Other works demonstrated practical attacks on the 5G protocol using a security and privacy analysis framework, emphasizing the need for thorough analysis and testing of 5G protocols before widespread deployment [14].

The integration of the Internet of Things (IoT) into 5G networks introduces additional security challenges due to the massive number of connected devices and the heterogeneity of applications. Reviews discuss security and privacy issues in 5G-enabled IoT, considering threats such as DDoS attacks originating from compromised IoT devices and the difficulty of ensuring end-to-end security [15]. The role of mobile edge computing in enhancing the security of IoT in 5G networks is explored, proposing solutions to reduce latency and improve data security by processing information closer to the source [16].

The adoption of SDN and NFV in 5G networks has raised concerns about attacks on virtualization layers and control planes. Studies reviewed security vulnerabilities in SDN controllers, identifying threats like denial-of-service attacks and proposing security enhancements [17]. Similarly, security challenges in NFV were discussed, emphasizing the importance of secure virtualization environments and trustworthy orchestration processes [18].

Furthermore, the security of signaling protocols in 5G has been investigated, analyzing vulnerabilities in Diameter and SIP protocols that could be exploited to intercept communications or disrupt services. Comprehensive security measures, including encryption and integrity protection, were recommended to safeguard signaling messages [19].

Despite these efforts, there remains a gap in comprehensive studies focusing on the combined security implications of SDN, NFV, core network functions, network slicing, and the application of machine learning algorithms in 5G networks (table 8.1). This chapter aims to address this gap by providing an in-depth analysis of the security mechanisms of these components and examining their vulnerabilities. By understanding these challenges, effective mitigation strategies can be proposed to enhance the overall security posture of 5G networks.

TABLE 8.1
Summary of Related Works

Reference	Focus Area	Key Contributions	Security Challenges Addressed
[1, 2]	EU Risk Assessment and Mitigation	Identified cybersecurity risks in 5G networks; developed a toolbox of risk-mitigating measures	Highlighted potential risks in 5G deployment; proposed mitigation strategies
[3–5]	ENISA Reports on 5G Threat Landscape	Mapped 5G threat landscape; identified new threats and operational security issues; focused on signaling security and SDN threats	Understood security challenges in 5G networks; addressed vulnerabilities in signaling protocols and SDN

TABLE 8.1 (*Continued*)
Summary of Related Works

Reference	Focus Area	Key Contributions	Security Challenges Addressed
[6]	SDN Security Overview	Comprehensive review of SDN architecture, security implications, and potential vulnerabilities	Discussed security challenges introduced by SDN in 5G networks
[7]	SDN-Specific Security Issues	Analyzed threats to control and data planes; proposed mitigation strategies to enhance network resilience	Addressed threats to SDN control and data planes; proposed security enhancements
[8]	NFV in 5G Networks	Reviewed resource allocation challenges in NFV; highlighted security concerns such as isolation between VNFs and secure orchestration mechanisms	Addressed security concerns in NFV, including isolation failures and orchestration vulnerabilities
[9]	NFV Security Requirements	Discussed security requirements and challenges of NFV in 5G; emphasized the need for robust security frameworks	Emphasized importance of secure NFV implementations in 5G networks
[10, 11]	Network Slicing Challenges and Risks	Discussed technical and security challenges in network slicing; highlighted potential security risks; necessity for effective isolation techniques	Addressed cross-slice attacks; need for effective isolation to prevent unauthorized access between slices
[12]	IDS in 5G Using Machine Learning	Developed IDS for 5G networks using machine learning algorithms; analyzed various ML techniques	Enhanced detection of malicious activities; addressed insufficiency of traditional security measures
[13]	Vulnerabilities in 5G AKA Protocols	Analyzed vulnerabilities in 5G Authentication and Key Agreement protocols; identified privacy threats; proposed improvements	Addressed potential privacy threats; proposed enhancements to AKA protocols
[14]	Practical Attacks on 5G Protocols	Demonstrated practical attacks using a security and privacy analysis framework; emphasized need for thorough protocol testing	Highlighted protocol vulnerabilities; stressed the importance of rigorous analysis before deployment
[15]	IoT Security in 5G	Discussed security and privacy issues in 5G-enabled IoT; considered threats from compromised IoT devices	Addressed DDoS attacks originating from IoT devices; challenges in ensuring end-to-end security

(Continued)

TABLE 8.1 (*Continued*)
Summary of Related Works

Reference	Focus Area	Key Contributions	Security Challenges Addressed
[16]	Edge Computing for IoT Security	Explored the role of mobile edge computing in enhancing IoT security in 5G networks	Proposed solutions to reduce latency and improve data security by processing closer to the source
[17]	Security Vulnerabilities in SDN Controllers	Reviewed vulnerabilities in SDN controllers; identified threats like denial-of-service attacks; proposed security enhancements	Addressed threats to SDN controllers; proposed enhancements for SDN security
[18]	NFV Security Challenges	Discussed security challenges in NFV; emphasized the importance of secure virtualization environments and trustworthy orchestration processes	Addressed attacks on virtualization layers and control planes in NFV
[19]	Signaling Protocol Security in 5G	Analyzed vulnerabilities in Diameter and SIP protocols; recommended comprehensive security measures	Addressed risks of communication interception and service disruption; recommended encryption and integrity protection

8.3 PROBLEM STATEMENT

The amount of traffic transmitted over wireless networks and the number of mobile devices (including IoT) are growing very quickly due to many factors. The telecommunications field is experiencing huge changes associated with the introduction of 5G mobile networks and support for the current and future needs of consumers. Consequently, it is believed that the 5G wireless network has a very high data transfer rate and better quality, which is supported by the concept of close signal reception stations, improved quality of service (QoS), and extremely low latency. To perform only the aforementioned, it must introduce and use the latest schemes in the field of networks, services, delivery, and data processing. These technologies create new challenges for the functionality of 5G cybersecurity systems. The aim of the study is to recommend mitigation technologies that will prevent threats to the 5G infrastructure associated with vulnerabilities of its components and services. To achieve the desired result, the 5G network security mechanisms will be analyzed to understand the current 5G security situation. Further, after a thorough study of the security elements of the 5G network, we investigate the vulnerabilities of the main components of the 5G network and the threats arising from their shortcomings.

8.4 G NETWORK ARCHITECTURE AND ITS MAIN FEATURES

The inclusion of new radio frequency bands, beamforming, Massive MIMO technology, Optimized OFDM technology, Small Cells, and other characteristics of 5G New

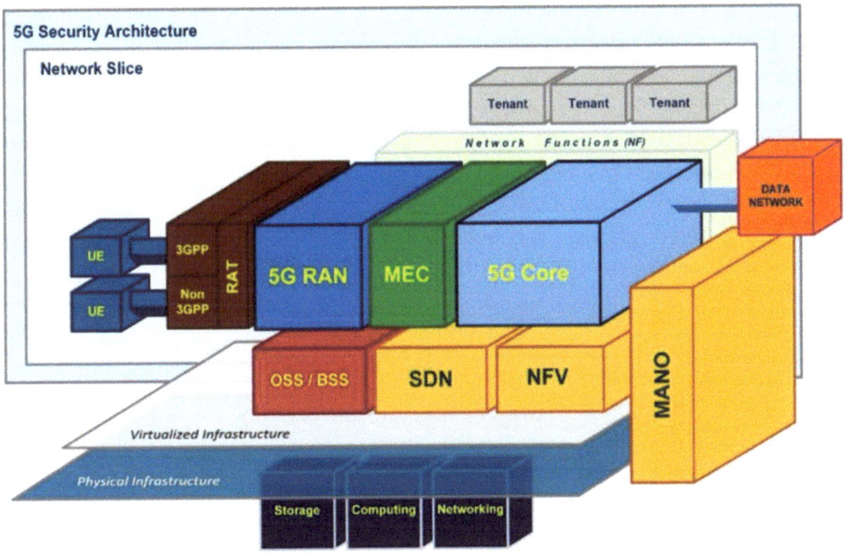

FIGURE 8.1 5G High-level technical architecture.

Radio (5G NR) have been created to address the ever-increasing demand for mobile communication.

Figure 8.1 illustrates generally known 5G architecture. The architectural model's components were arranged according to the common ground of functions they provide. As a result, we can divide them into two layers: physical and virtualized. Furthermore, the architecture of the fifth generation of mobile networks was designed to support the use of new 5G features such as network segmentation and Network Function Virtualization.

Radio Access Network (RAN) consists of antenna (standard base stations) and software. It provides 5G New Radio (NR). In the RAN, nodes are referred to as gNBs. Radio Access Technology (RAT) is supported by all RAN components. In comparison to prior mobile networks, RAN offered new ways to utilize resources. Because multi-access edge computing (MEC) is conducted near base stations, it is partially responsible for cloud computing services in 5G. This improves usage of end-user devices by removing the need for computations from their side.

The core network (CN) is a critical component of the fifth generation of mobile networks. Although previous mobile networks also included core, the fundamental distinction with 5G is that it is completely virtualized. In order to support network functions in various network types, virtualization support was added in the 5G mobile network (wireless, fixed, convergent). Because it is no longer dependent on the hardware on which it runs, network administration has become more flexible.

SDN and NFV are two features of the 5G architecture that, when combined, ensure that the network runs smoothly. SDN's primary task is to organize network functions depending on the utilization of specific functions in specified layers (user, control, data). Meanwhile, NFV optimizes the use of services provided by these functions. NFV also manages the configuration of network functions in appropriate components based on functional specifications. SDN and NFV both play important roles in making 5G infrastructure more structured.

The Management and Network Orchestrator, or MANO, is a program that manages mobile network parts and services. MANO, for example, monitors and orchestrates NFV and SDN functions.

Network Slicing is in charge of the new manner of efficiently using network traffic in 5G. Monitoring the requirements of each network segment and its client devices allows for network slicing. When some network slices require higher bandwidth, minimal delay is required in other areas.

The ability to maintain network services in a virtualized manner, which makes them independent of individual physical devices, is what distinguishes 5G from existing mobile networks. As a result, mobile network operators are free from the influence of vendors.

8.5 SECURITY MECHANISMS OF 5G NETWORK AND THEIR VULNERABILITIES

As 5G networks become more pervasive, they bring with them a host of advanced features such as enhanced data transfer speeds, low latency, and the ability to support massive numbers of connected devices. However, these innovations also introduce new security challenges. The shift towards cloud-native architectures, the use of Software Defined Networks (SDN), and Network Function Virtualization (NFV) have led to an increasingly complex and dynamic network environment. While 5G offers robust security mechanisms, it remains vulnerable to a range of threats. In this section, we explore the key security mechanisms integrated into 5G networks and the potential vulnerabilities they may face in various network layers.

8.5.1 Software-Defined Network

In the modern world, the number of devices using 4G networks is becoming more and more. Over time, this leads to requests for an increase in data transfer speed and a decrease in network delays from ordinary users, and businesses put demands on the flexibility and scalability of computer networks. The network in its classical form (managed through the command line and configuration files) becomes an obstacle to the development of computing infrastructure since traditional networks are primarily static. Its scalability does not meet the requirements of today's rapidly evolving IT market due to the large amount of time required to deploy networks, as well as due to high equipment costs. Distributed control of devices in traditional networks is becoming increasingly complex and inefficient. Locking a company to a single network provider does not guarantee support for future applications and services, as upgrading network equipment can cost a lot. For example, Amazon estimates its device upgrades to be worth billions of dollars.

All of the aforementioned leads us to the need for a new technology or approach to building information systems. In fifth generation networks, it is planned to use Software Defined Network (SDN) [20] and Network Function Virtualization (NFV) technologies to solve the aforementioned problems.

The Software Defined Network is the separation of the software that manages the packet forwarding function from the network hardware element that forwards the packets.

Let's take a look at this definition. Let's take a modern network device, it doesn't matter, a router, a switch, or something else.

It is divided into three logical components (figure 8.2):

1) Management plane (CLI, built-in web server or API, control protocols). The task of this level is to provide the ability to manage the device.
2) Control plane. It consists of various algorithms and functionality that is designed to capture traffic changes, in other words, "device intelligence".
3) Data plane. It is a functionality that provides physical data transfer at the level of network packets and microcircuits.

In SDN, the "new" router or switch serves only the data flow (data plane), and it becomes simpler and, accordingly, cheaper. The network device cannot be completely deprived of "intelligence", but it is enough to replace it with a forwarding table.

All network intelligence (management plane and control plane) is transferred to a separate centralized device called the SDN controller.

Thus, the Software Defined Network is a method of administering computer networks in which the control functionality (control plane) is separated from the underlying level of packet forwarding (data plane). Planning and network management, in this case, occurs programmatically. We get the following benefits from SDN:

- centralized network management via SDN controller;
- virtualization of the physical devices of the network, which leads to a reduction in the cost of building the network itself;
- rapid network deployment;
- the ability to quickly respond to changes in the network;
- a single, standard, open interface between control and data transmission devices called OpenFlow;
- open protocols allow different network equipment vendors to interact with each other, accelerating innovation in the field of software and network hardware.

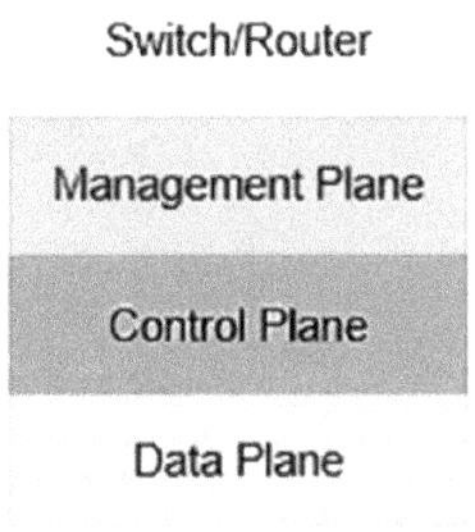

FIGURE 8.2 Typical network device.

If we look in more detail at the information flows in the SDN architecture, we can see two main directions of information exchange: the first is between SDN applications, which is called the "north bridge" and the second is for managing physical network devices, the so-called south bridge. The "north bridge" uses a protocol based on the REST API, and the "south bridge" uses the OpenFlow protocol [21].

The foundation of the SDN idea, OpenFlow is a common protocol that enables communication between the controller and network devices. The idea behind OpenFlow is to use a flow table to determine which forwarders send data packets. Through OpenFlow interfaces, controllers distribute flow tables to forwarders, giving them command over the forwarding plane.

The "Clean Slate" concept was developed at Stanford University to examine how the Internet might be recreated from scratch. The OpenFlow protocol was created within the confines of this program. Stanford University's Network Security and Governance Project was overseen by student Martin Casado in 2006. The project sought to achieve security control over all network communication by using a centralized controller to make it simple for network managers to define security management policies based on network flows and apply these security policies to various network devices.

By separating the forwarding and routing control modules of conventional network devices, Professor Nick McKeown, Director of the Clean Slate Program, and his team found that a centralized controller could be used to manage and configure multiple network devices over industry-standard interfaces. This will increase the chances for designing, managing, and utilizing network resources, encouraging network innovation and growth. As a result, they proposed the idea of OpenFlow and released a paper in 2008 titled "OpenFlow: Innovating in Campus Networks" that, for the first time, described the fundamentals and use cases of OpenFlow.

Based on OpenFlow, this team put forth the SDN concept in 2009, garnering significant industry interest. The Open Networking Foundation (ONF), an organization devoted to promoting and implementing SDN, was established in 2011 in collaboration with Google, Facebook, Microsoft, and other businesses. The ONF standardizes OpenFlow and specifies it as the first southern standard communication interface between the control and forward layers in the SDN architecture.

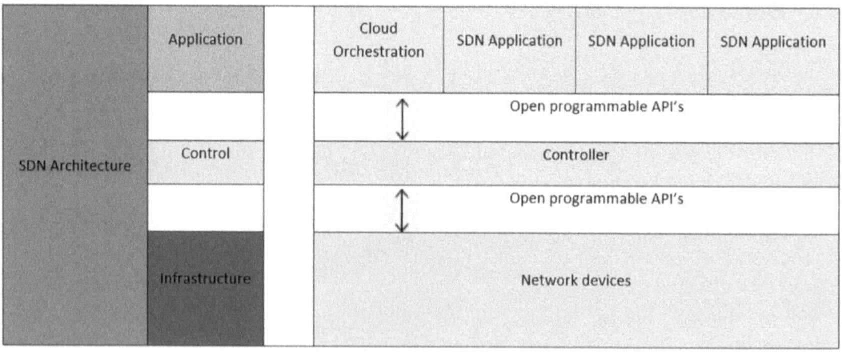

FIGURE 8.3 Structure and components of SDN.

OpenFlow has developed through versions 1.1, 1.2, and 1.3 to the most recent version 1.5 since the end of 2009, when its first official version 1.0 was released. The most popular and used versions of OpenFlow at the moment are 1.0 and 1.3.

An OpenFlow switch, a controller, and a secure channel make up the OpenFlow architecture. To accomplish control plane operations, the controller centrally supervises the network. The OpenFlow switch is in charge of data layer forwarding. To obtain reroute records and convey their status to the controller, it communicates via a secure channel and exchanges messages.

The OpenFlow protocol makes it possible to redirect all of its resources to traffic acceleration since there is no control path processing load on the switches. OpenFlow allows you to add new features to an existing network architecture. Speaking of security, on a common OpenFlow controller, the administrator has the ability to observe all components and processes in a single view, thereby increasing the convenience of management, security, and other tasks. This allows the administrator to see all traffic flows, which makes it easier to detect intrusions and problems in a timely manner. OpenFlow allows you to prioritize different types of traffic and develop rules for network response when problems arise.

8.5.2 Network Function Virtualization

The various layers of the 5G network require the most efficient management structure for all system components in order to ensure consistent resource management in the complex architecture of 5G networks. Virtualization of network functions and systems for their management and orchestration (MANO) is a solution that solves problems like:

- simplification of the introduction of new services;
- cost reduction;
- maintenance of existing services;
- service management in the existing architecture.

Most network functions, including advanced packet processing mechanisms, use virtualization due to the emergence and development of powerful hardware resources, cloud storage, computing technologies, and flexible software-defined networks. Now, there is no need to allocate specialized equipment; now everything is implemented as virtual machines that are used on top of the cloud infrastructure. The work of dedicated network intermediate blocks goes into the work of virtual machines and software. This opens up the opportunity to reduce costs by using standard hardware and applying existing methods and management tools from the cloud computing space. At one time, cloud environments benefited from automation and unified systems. There are great prospects that the same will happen with NFV. The modern world of telecommunications is dominated by an approach to building an architecture that cannot fail. NFV aims to create an architecture that has a failure management component in every part of the system and splits it horizontally to limit the number of points of failure.

The methods used to implement NFV nowadays are focused on creating network applications with a significantly smaller footprint that run on thin container solutions rather than fat virtual machines. The "thick" virtual machine model and traditional high availability notions do not translate well to the cloud [22]. Standard cloud systems frequently struggle to deliver performance and high availability when trying to port software that was originally intended to run on extremely specialized hardware. For instance, the additional I/O overhead imposed by cloud environments, hypervisors, and virtual machines considerably reduces the performance of packet processing. Additionally, these legacy solutions frequently do not have scaling-out capabilities to add or remove nodes from the system.

The numerous parts and reference points are shown in figure 8.4. The three layers of NFV orchestration, VNF management, and infrastructure management are plainly visible.

NFV management and orchestration systems generally strive to streamline the use of NFV technologies to operate complicated network services. In order to achieve this, MANO systems must manage the multiple life cycles of each of these components as well as virtualized infrastructure, such as cloud systems; network and communications infrastructure, such as software-defined networks; and NFV entities, such as virtualized network functions. Network functions that have been virtualized are frequently represented as running virtual machines or container images. The resource layer, network segment instance layer, and service instance layer make up the bulk of the 5G network. These levels ought to cooperate with one another. The development of an efficient NFV control and orchestration system is necessary

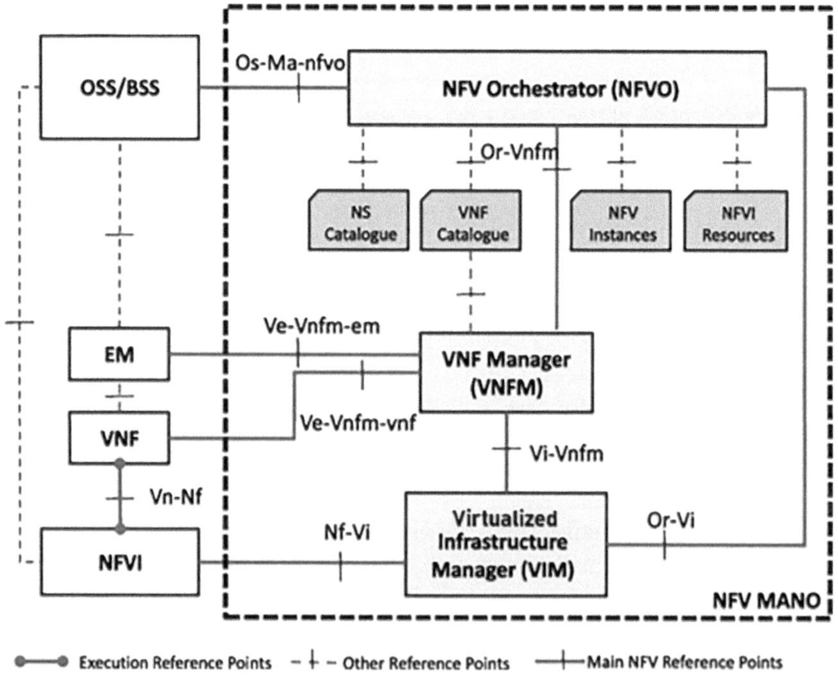

FIGURE 8.4 The ETSI-specified NFV Management and Orchestration (MANO) framework.

in order to provide an effective 5G mobile network service platform, taking into account the strict requirements of telecom operators, the control plane objects, and their methods of managing physical and virtual resources on the respective planes, as well as, very importantly, the methods of their coordination for their actions.

As of now, the ETSI model is the most pertinent NFV MANO structure (figure 8.4). Virtualized Infrastructure Manager (VIM), Virtual Network Functions Manager (VNFM), and Network Functions Virtualization Orchestrator are the three basic building components of this system (NFVO).

A part that controls network services is called NFVO. It is in charge of managing the entire lifetime of network services as a whole. End-to-end service integrity is provided by this component, which consists of many virtual functional networks connected by virtual circuits. In light of this, NFV Orchestrator provides connectivity to external systems and can connect to old Operations Support Systems (OSS) and Business Support Systems (BSS). The NFVO is also linked to various data stores that include the necessary details about the relevant objects, such as the Network Services Catalog, VNF Catalog, NFV Infrastructure Instance Catalog, and Resource Databases.

The component in charge of managing the life cycle of multiple virtual network functions is known as the VNF Manager. To accomplish this, the VNF Manager can link directly to element managers and carry out operations, including launching, scaling, and customizing relevant objects. As was already mentioned, external control points make it easier to coordinate the unified management of NFV systems and connect to legacy systems. Multiple virtual machines' lifecycle events are frequently automated, and they are frequently described by special domain-specific languages like JuJu, Puppet, and Ansible. Process control systems are in charge of controlling them.

The Virtualized Infrastructure Manager (VIM) component links to NFV infrastructures like the OpenStack cloud platform and maintains network operations at the virtual machine and container levels. The VIM is also in charge of facilitating communication among the several VNFs that make up the network service. In order to create virtual channels in cloud infrastructures, this component uses software-defined networks.

Additionally, ETSI defines a number of descriptors for supplying metadata, including lifecycle and monitoring data, which are necessary to carry out the services and operations of virtual networks. The Network Service Descriptor (NSD), which may be read and performed by the NFV orchestrator, provides information on the high-level description of the network service, including all VNF components and network service lifecycle events. Similar to this, the VNF Descriptor (VNFD) offers details on the capabilities of the virtual network. The VNF not only offers information about lifecycle events but also about virtual deployment units, such as virtual machine images or containers, and how they operate. For instance, the VNFD describes the minimal CPU requirement needed to run a specific VNF. Finally, a service package can include the network service descriptor, VNFD, and other artifacts, including virtual machine images. On the MANO service platform, this service package functions as a way to distribute and enable network services. We refer to the ETSI NFV MANO structure's standard [23, 24] for further information.

Several open source and commercial projects aim to implement the MANO framework, often based on the ETSI specifications as described earlier. The most common are Open-Source MANO OSM [25], ONAP [26], OpenStack Tacker [27], OpenBaton [28], and SONATA [29].

8.5.3 Core Network Functions

The primary network function of 5G is the User Plane Function (UPF), which is responsible for interaction with external data networks such as the Internet, routing of various user packets, and marking these packets according to relevant Quality-of-Service policies. Moreover, UPF supports mobility not only within but also across diverse radio access networks and could be seen as a VNF that provides very effective mechanisms in user traffic forwarding. UPF accelerates this process with the help of Vector Packet Processing (VPP). But by doing so it still maintains compatibility with functions such as Shallow Packet Inspection (SPI), Deep Packet Inspection (DPI), NAT, DNS snooping, etc. It is worth noting that different 5G standardization organizations came to the agreement to make UPF support its own integrated DPI [30].

According to 3GPP 5G standards, UPF supports numerous mechanisms for the enforcement of the whole 5G Core Network (figure 8.5). In order to accomplish that, SMF helps UPF by forwarding security policies to its further employment. Since the UPF acts as a bridge between external data networks and the core network, it plays a crucial role in enforcing primary security policies within the network. Policy and Charging Control rules are forwarded to UPF by Policy Control Function (PCF) and, if applicable, SMF rules are forwarded over the N4 interface, which is the interface for the interaction of SMF and UPF, respectively.

Full information about the user session is forwarded to 5G Core Access and Mobility Management Function (AMF) [32]. However, AMF is responsible only for

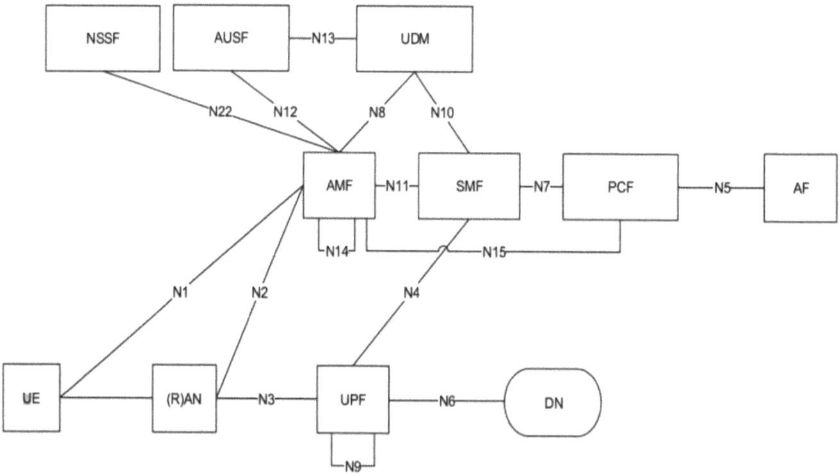

FIGURE 8.5 3GPP 5G system architecture for non-roaming cases [31].

connection handling and mobility management. The remaining session-related information is sent over the N11 interface to SMF.

AMF plays a significant role as the access point to the 5G Core Network. Due to that, it supports NAS encryption and integrity protection algorithms. When the first NAS message is received, AMF forwards an AKA request. This is the same as MME in Evolved Packet Core (EPC) infrastructure [33].

The Session Management Function (SMF) controls interaction with the user plane, performs all kinds of modifications to PDU sessions, and maintains the user session with the help of UPF. AMF, by requesting a network repository function (NRF), analyzes which SMF is convenient in handling the session management information. After that, SMF receives this information over the N11 interface from AMF. Messages that are forwarded to SMF over the N11 interface indicate some kind of trigger to modify the PDU session. While modifying a session, SMF establishes a connection with the Policy Management Function (PCF) over N7 interface. Moreover, SMF communicates with the Unified Data Management (UDM) function over the N10 interface, which stores subscriber profile information. PCF supports SMF with a policy framework that consists of not only typical QoS and billing rules but also includes network fragment selection that is monitored by the Network Slice Selection Function (NSSF).

NRF provides 5G Core Network with mechanisms for discovery using network functions which could know about the availability of each other and receive current statuses of other crucial network services that they need in order to function properly.

All network functions of 5G Core Networks forward information regarding their capabilities, functions, and events to the Network Exposure Function (NEF). Functions outside the scope of the 5G Core Network could then get familiar with network functions through NEF. To ensure security, this process is done with a TLS certificate. Third-party application functions must pass authentication and authorization processes by NEF through an OAuth-based authorization mechanism [20]. It is a general industry-standard authorization protocol in which authorization flow could be broken into two main parts. The first one of them is receiving the token from the authorization server. The second part is using the token to access the resource server.

Authentication Server Function (AUSF) controls authentication of the user device. During the authentication process using 5G-AKA AUSF relies on UDM to calculate authentication data and key.

UDM provides data management functions, such as Authentication Repository and Processing Function (ARPF). ARPF chooses an authentication method according to subscriber identity and configured policy. After that, it calculates authentication data and key for AUSF as needed.

Organizations which maintain standards of 5G tried to make authentication process in 5G mobile networks open. For example, such method should also support Extensible Authentication Protocol (EAP) [21]. Moreover, authentication procedure should not always rely on access networks. As an example, it should support both 3GPP and non-3GPP networks such as cable or Wi-Fi.

When EAP is used, authentication is performed between the user device and AUSF through SEAF. In this case, AUSF functions as a server while SEAF performs the role of SEAF EAP authenticator.

SEAF executes authentication by sending an authentication request to AUSF. After that, AUSF controls the verification process of the serving network by analyzing if it is authorized. If verification turns out to be successful, AUSF forwards the authentication request to UDM.

When AUSF provides a Subscription Concealed Identifier (SUCI), the Subscription Identifier De-concealing Function (SIDF) is called to decrypt the SUCI in order to the Subscription Permanent Identifier (SUPI). Subsequently, it is used to select the authentication method relevant for the user device.

UDM executes the 5G-AKA by forwarding authentication data to AUSF with authentication information having in its contents SUPI, an AUTH token, and an XRES token.

AUSF computes the hash of the XRES token (HXRES) and sends all complete authentication data to SEAF, including AUTH token and HXRES. SUPI is not sent to SEAF as a part of authentication data. It is generally sent to SEAF after user device has successfully authenticated [34].

SEAF receives HXRES and saves it. Afterward, it forwards the received AUTH token to the user's device. The user device then verifies the AUTH token with the secret key it already exchanged with the core network at the beginning of the authentication process. If the verification is successful, the user device considers the network authenticated. It continues authentication by calculating and sending a RES token to SEAF. If successful, the RES token is further sent by SEAF to AUSF also for verification. Only AUSF, which is on the core network, decides on the completion of authentication. In the case when the RES token is valid, AUSF calculates the network-specific anchor key (KSEAF) and forwards it to SEAF with the SUPI. AUSF also informs UDM about authentication outcomes so that events can be logged, for example, for auditing purposes.

8.5.4 RAN

General architecture of Radio Access Network (RAN), shown by figure 8.6, presented by the new 3GPP specifications and 5G-PPP outlines division of the RAN into Central Unit (CU) and Distributed Unit (DU) as the major new undertaking.

IP transport based on the TNL/Ethernet network is used in RAN and this is the same as what is used in the mobile backhaul nowadays. The second key feature of

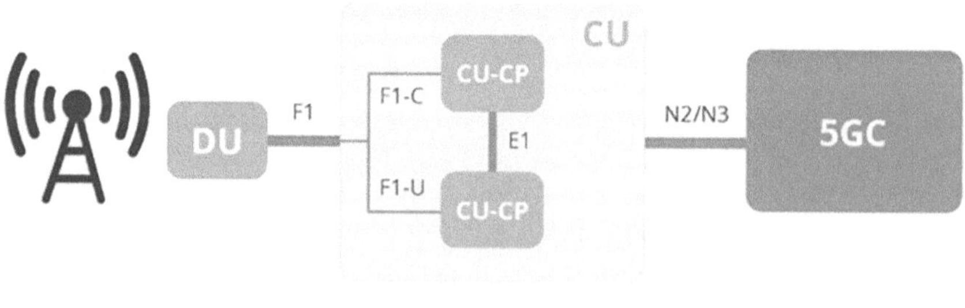

FIGURE 8.6 Interfaces between RAN and 5G Core Network (simplified) [4].

NG-RAN is providing small-cell coverage as a service for multiple operators with low latency and high processing capabilities.

Customer communications generally cannot be accessed by DU. Therefore, it is convenient to deploy them in unsupervised sites. Contrary to that, CU provides security functions and controls AS security. That means it is deployed in sites that have restricted access to maintenance people.

DU and CU communicate through the F1 interface. As for CUs, they establish connections between themselves through the E1 interface. It is worth noting that data forwarded over these interfaces may involve sensitive information. Therefore, it can be the target of the attackers.

N2 and N3 interfaces are used to establish connections between RAN and 5G Core Network. Specifically, the communications are held between 5G-AN and primary network functions of 5G Core: Access and Mobility Function (AMF) and UPF. Sensitive signaling and user plane traffic are forwarded through these interfaces and also may appear under the attack.

To prevent such attacks on interfaces and maintain confidentiality, integrity, and replay security, RAN supports security mechanisms such as IPSec ESP protocol and IKEv2 certificate-based authentication.

IPsec is a set of protocols which are utilized together to maintain encrypted connections between different types of equipment. It keeps data forwarded over public networks secure and is often used to set up VPNs. IPSec works by encrypting IP packets and authenticating the source of the packets. Specifically, the ESP protocol of IPSec encrypts the IP header and the payload for each packet and adds its own header and a trailer to each data packet.

The Internet Key Exchange protocol version 2 makes up a sizable portion of IPsec. IKEv2 offers key agreement services, authentication, and authorization. IKEv2 primarily serves two purposes: (i) establishing an IKE security association (IKE SA) with a specific peer; and (ii) supporting one or more child security associations (CHILD SA). IKE security association is a tunnel between two IKEv2 protocol implementations that is encrypted and integrity secured and utilized for both signaling and carrying out procedures like mutual authentication and managing child security associations (e.g. creation, removal). On the other hand, child security associations are crucial to the IPsec architecture since they are used to forward data between peers.

Although DU-CU split makes deployment options flexible, data transported through RAN interfaces is highly likely to include sensitive data (both on user and control data plane) and, therefore, its protection is crucial to prevent information disclosure, data tampering, and denial of service attacks.

8.5.5 Security Mechanisms of Network Slicing

Network slicing is a core 5G feature which represents a function that allows the efficient usage of 5G Core Network functions according to a specific use case [21]. There is no strict specification of network slicing among the industries. However, it can be considered as a virtual network administration mechanism that isolates traffic for each service, while using the same physical network. A huge advantage of network slicing for operators would be the possibility to deploy only the particular functions required to support particular customers.

In the 3GPP standardization, a network slice implies a radio network and a core network. A few parts of the network supplies could be shared by multiple network slices, while other parts could be specific for a one slice only. Moreover, the network slicing paradigm also tangles optional resource partitioning per slice in the network.

A network slice is specified by a parameter called Single Network Slice Selection Assistance Information (S-NSSAI). S-NSSAI consists of two sub-parameters: the optional Slice Differentiator (SD) and the Slice/Service Type (SST). SD supports differentiation between several slices which have the same SST.

The device may request the serving network to use one or few S-NSSAI values in order to do the primary selection of AMF. After that, the chosen AMF would decide to serve this device or it would make a new slice selection either itself or by using the NSSF, which is responsible for network slice selection.

In figure 8.7, device 1 connects to slice 1 which consists of a specifically dedicated AMF, SMF, and UPF while device 2 simultaneously connects to two slices: 2 and 3, both consisting only of dedicated SMF and UPF but being controlled by a shared AMF.

If a network slice template exists that matches the customer requirements during the network slice selection, the preparation process can be reduced (figure 8.8). Specifically, either an existing network slice instance (NSI) is extended to accommodate the new customer's requests, or a new NSI is created based on the existing template.

If there is no appropriate template, then a new one is created using the particular requirements. After that, a new network slice template is generally appended to a catalog of services and other network slice templates that enable the preparation phase to be shortened for the next customer with similar requirements.

The verification step is simplified when done for specific network slices since there are a minority of dependencies to consider compared to when utilizing one network for a wide range of applications.

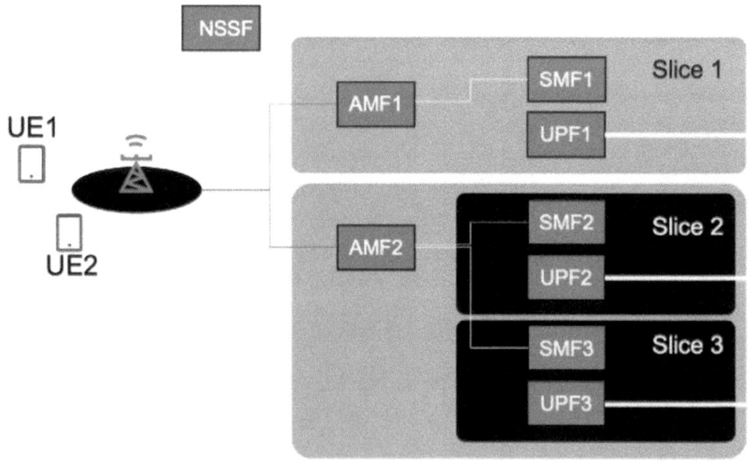

FIGURE 8.7 Network slicing (simplified).

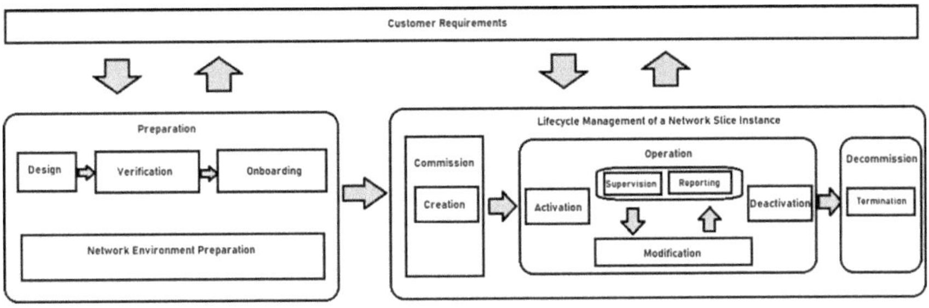

FIGURE 8.8 Network slicing lifecycle.

The onboarding includes uploading required data by the orchestration system in the next step. For instance, the designed templates, validation of templates, or virtual machines (VM) images.

The network environment is arranged during the preparation step while other essential preparations are done since they are required for the creation of an NSI.

During the commissioning phase NSI provisioning is executed. At this stage all essential resources are prepared and configured to satisfy the network slice requirements.

The Operation step involves the supervision and performance reporting, activation, resource capacity planning, and de-activation and modification of an NSI.

Activation prepares the NSI to provide communication functions. Meanwhile, resource capacity planning contains any actions that compute resource application and performance monitoring based on an NSI provisioning, and produce modification policies.

The supervision and performance reporting consist of monitoring, reporting, and assurance of the capacity based on the Key Performance Indicators (KPIs) accepted as a section of the Service Level Agreements (SLAs) for the NSI.

NSI modification could consist of capacity/topology alterations. The modification could consist of creation or modification of NSI resources. NSI modification could be executed by accepting recent network slice requirements.

The deactivation presents actions that set the NSI inactive and stop the communication functions.

NSI provisioning during the decommissioning stage consists of decommissioning of non-shared resources and removal of the NSI configuration from the shared resources. At the end of the decommissioning stage, the NSI is finalized and does not prevail anymore.

As a security mechanism during the network slicing, if a management service consumer is located outside the 3GPP operator's trust domain, mutual authentication should be performed between the management service consumer and the management service producer using TLS. TLS should be applied to support mutual authentication, protection of integrity, replay and confidentiality for the interface between the management service producer and consumer placed outside the 3GPP operator's trust domain.

8.6 LIMITATIONS OF CURRENT SECURITY MECHANISMS OF 5G NETWORK FUNCTIONS

SDN was originally introduced for network configuration flexibility to improve overall network performance, but SDN was later found to be applicable to network security [35]. Traditional networks are vulnerable to various security threats, some of which are not easy to detect. SDN is a new technology that can provide security protection solutions because it is able to detect attacks and act adaptively faster than traditional networks. However, there are new types of attacks targeting SDN. Thus, the introduction of SDN in the infrastructure has both pros and cons.

The various security threats that can be addressed with SDN are summarized in table 8.2. In this table, we list different types of threats.

All actions and behaviors of SDN depend on the controller, so it is one of the most likely targets for attackers. If it is compromised, it can threaten the entire network. Trojans are the biggest threat. They can provoke DoS attacks, erase saved data, and open loopholes that can give attackers control of the system [36].

In a buffer overflow attack, an attacker can overwrite certain sections of a device's memory on a target network or replace normal data in certain memory locations with malware to attack the network and initiate a denial of service. Switches in SDN are only capable of performing minimal tasks, such as forwarding packets. However, a threat to switches can cause enormous damage to the entire network. An attacker could create a traffic load too large for the network to overwhelm network shares.

By collecting entry and exit timeslots, an attacker can launch a FIFO attack. A redirect attack is easily possible when an attacker obtains the correct user information by boosting their signal strength to redirect or impersonating a base station on 4G and 5G cellular networks.

One of the NFV vulnerabilities is a Man-in-the-Middle (MITM) attack (table 8.3). This attack in cellular networks is based on a false base station (FBS) attack. This is

TABLE 8.2
Threats of Software Defined Network

Denial of Service (DoS)
Buffer Overflow
Traffic Overflow
Spoofing

TABLE 8.3
Threats of Network Function Virtualization

Sniffing
Free-Rider Attack
Man-in-the-Middle

a situation in which an attacker masquerades their base transceiver station (BTS) as the BTS of a real network.

The service-based architecture (SBA) of the 5G Core Network is designed using a cloud-native approach. It borrows the "microservice" concept and divides a whole network with multiple functions into separate parts, each of which provides an independent function. Each network function, through a service-based interface, provides its network capabilities as a service, and these capabilities are reused by other network functions. Thus, service security risks exist between the elements of the 5G backbone network, similar to microservices scenarios.

5G networks might be vulnerable to IP attacks common on the Internet, such as DDoS attacks, due to IP-based services architecture. In addition, a large number of infected mobile devices controlled by malicious Command and Control (C&C) servers can launch both user and signal plane attacks on core 5G network functions. As a result, critical services are degraded and become unavailable to legitimate users [3].

An attacker could forward an attach request message repeatedly in order to gain access to the 5G network by setting several terminals to work as botnets and by configuring airplane mode on/off. This could result in an immeasurable traffic load on a mobile carrier's core network. One request could produce eight GTP-C messages at most. Consequently, this brings 8 times the amount of traffic to the core network function in conformity with one attacker's manipulation.

NAS protocol messages used for signaling between the core network and terminals do not guarantee ciphering or integrity for initial attach request messages. Subsequently, an attacker could install a rogue base station in close proximity to the victim to steal and manipulate messages. Particularly, an attach request message has a user device network capability field which could set ciphering or integrity for the terminal's received or transmitted traffic. Within the user device network capability field the attacker could modify values in EEA (a field that transmits the terminal's ciphering algorithm) and EIA (a field that transmits the terminal's integrity verification algorithm). 3GPP technical specification (TS.) 33.401 states that integrity verification algorithms must be used in terminals. However, the specification also states that ciphering algorithms could be used selectively. In 2019, the research conducted by Ruhr University on 12 carriers illustrated that four of them do not allow the use of integrity which must be applied.

The fundamental network functionalities of 5G include AMF, AUSF, and UDM. AMF offers UEs services for mobility management, authentication, and authorization. Both AUSF and UDM keep track of UE subscription information. These 5G functionalities are essential; a mobile botnet or a DDoS attack on them from the Internet might drastically decrease the availability of 5G services or even cause network disruptions. A DDoS attack on essential 5G network services might be launched by an attacker using a massive number of requests to establish an IPSec connection with numerous infected mobile devices concurrently [23].

In a 5G backbone network, an attacker can exploit a vulnerability in a network function to compromise the function and then initiate a request from the open interface to other functions, leading to an anomaly in the access sequence to network functions. As an example, in the authentication procedure for UE registration, AMF first initiates an authentication request to AUSF, which then queries UDM to generate an authentication vector. However, if an attacker compromises the AMF, it will directly invoke the UDM interface to generate the authentication vector, thereby stealing the user's authentication information. Another example: The NRF maintains a repository of available network function instances and supported service profiles. If this network function contains a vulnerability, an attacker can exploit this vulnerability to register a malicious network function and force the address and Uniform Resource Identifier (URI) to point to this malicious network element. The attacker can then use it to communicate with other network elements, leading to abnormal call logic between them [24].

The core network functions in 5G are subject to various security threats, including denial-of-service (DoS) attacks, NAS manipulation, eavesdropping, and spoofing. These vulnerabilities can be exploited to disrupt network operations, compromise data integrity, or intercept sensitive communications. A detailed overview of these threats is provided in table 8.4.

The parameters exchanged by the network functions can be subject to anomalous behavior. This occurs in one of the following cases: (1) An attacker exploits a potential vulnerability of improper parameter checking in a network element to pass an illegitimate parameter in the network element's call procedure to achieve a particular goal. (2) An attacker exploits a vulnerability in an interface to conduct an attack that results in an error in the returned parameters.

In the cloud-based 5GC (5G Core) architecture, all functions are virtualized, which provides the additional flexibility needed to compartmentalize the network. However, this leads to another threat vector. Attacks through side channels, combined with improper isolation between network environments, lead to data leakage. For vulnerable parts of the mobile network such as billing and subscriber authentication layers it is crucial.

The current lack of standardization of IoT devices and security features is a major concern, so the Internet Engineering Task Force (IETF) and other standards bodies are working to close these gaps. One potential solution for a DDoS scenario in MIoT is developing malicious signal storm detection and mitigation features which will be added to the functions of the gNodeB central unit's control plane (CU-CP) and access and mobility management/session management (AMF/SMF) components [24].

The potential for information leakage, which includes the threat of paging sniffing and IMSI cracking attacks, is one of the key weaknesses in RAN. Paging sniffing is

TABLE 8.4
Threats of Core Network Functions

Denial of Service (DoS)
NAS Manipulation
Eavesdropping
Spoofing
APN Exploitation
GTP Attack

TABLE 8.5
Threats of Radio Access Network

Information Leak
User Denial of Service (User DoS)
Base Station Denial of Service (Base Station DoS)
Eavesdropping
Unauthorized Data Use

a passive data scanning technique that makes use of the sending of paging signals from base stations to terminals. A software defined radio device that picks up radio frequency signals and learns the intended victim's paging cycle or SAE-temporary mobile subscriber identity could be set up by the attacker (S-TMSI). Additionally, utilizing the revealed paging cycle, the attacker might compute paging frame index (PFI) and use the results to reduce the pool of potential victims for the target victim's IMSI. The victim is the recipient of an IMSI paging from the attacker that has fewer IMSI candidates than usual.

In the case of RAN, numerous user DoS attacks are feasible (table 8.5). Target victim DoS options include radio resource control (RRC) release DoS, RRC reject DoS, and RRC connection DoS. It's critical to remember that RRC connection DoS is a security risk that preys on the victim's S-TMSI, which might be discovered through the previously mentioned data leak. Wireless base stations do not allow terminal authentication processes, such as those used as the core network. An attacker could use this to interfere with the victim's wireless access. The attacker sends the message to the base station that the intended victim is able to access while also including the victim's S-TMSI value in the RRC connection request utilized by the terminal for wireless access. In this case, the base station breaks the RRC connection with the victim while establishing one with the attacker. The victim was then able to successfully connect to the terminal after this. The victim's service would be interrupted if the attacker continued to relay the modified RRC connection request.

Additionally, there is wireless base station resource depletion, a type of DoS that is particular to base stations. The terminal establishes Random Access and generates a random ID transmitting RRC connection request during the initial RRC connection. Because of this, an attacker may attempt an RRC connection and even send a NAS attach request using the victim's IMSI. The attacker might use Random Access to continually increase the number of RRC connection requests in the base station during the authentication request to the core network.

Eavesdropping is generally not possible on wireless networks since AS security settings are employed between endpoints and base stations. However, it is possible to extract and decode AS Security Keystream. Real-time transport protocol (RTP) is the protocol used for voice traffic in mobile communications. In wireless parts, it is provided through a voice bearer rather than a data bearer. Since QoS needs to be given, a voice bearer is a dedicated bearer rather than a default bearer, and a distinct Quality-of-Service class identifier (QCI) is used. Count, length, direction, and bearer ID are typically utilized in the construction of keystreams for ciphering in AS security. Other elements, aside from bearer ID, do not play a vital role in keystream formation. When a base station generates voice bearer, bearer ID (DRB ID) is assigned, and a manufacturer's base station may have trouble assigning the same DRB ID within the same RRC connection. An attacker uses a sniffer to preserve the victims' ciphered voice communication in order to exploit such a problem. The attacker tries to make a voice call to one of the victims after the victims' calls have been cut off and preserves the plain- and ciphered texts of the call using a sniffer. In this scenario, the attacker uses the plain- and ciphered texts of the second call with XOR logic to analyze the keystream, and then applies extracted keystream to decode the first call since they were made in the identical RRC connection and used the same DRB ID.

Network slicing supports slice isolation levels according to the requirements of the particular slice. As Network Slicing Manager (NSM) controls each of the telco slices by exposing its functionality, the attacker negatively impacts the whole system (table 8.6). For instance, if an attacker manages to monitor traffic of north- and southbound interfaces (an interface that allows a particular component of a network to communicate with a higher-level component and vice versa), he could understand configurations of the system which violates confidentiality. In this case, an attacker would be able to produce a snapshot of the status of the system (which is a crucial part of the enumeration stage) along with the vulnerabilities. By scanning these interfaces an attacker may also expose authentication/authorization since he could discover a way of impersonating an element or even acquiring a token. Moreover, possible traffic injections by the attacker into those interfaces may break the integrity and availability of the whole system. Similar threats to the NSM's southbound interface could also be applied to the MANO's NFV Orchestrator (NFVO) since both could be exposed [37]. The only difference with the NFVO is the width of its scope, namely, the consequences of a breach of the NFVO would impact only a subset of the components monitored by the NSM. In the case when an attacker breaks into the control plane of the operator the system would be affected with broader consequences. However, network slice users would be constrained to the data plane making the control plane indirectly exposed through well-defined configurations in the northbound interfaces of NFVO and NSM. The incorrect validation in the northbound interfaces would allow rightful users to jeopardize the system's integrity.

Taking the nature of shared environments under consideration, even if the slice operates well and does not allow access to another slice's data and control planes,

TABLE 8.6
Threats to Network Slicing

Impersonation Attacks
Distributed Denial of Service
Unauthorized Access
Eavesdropping
Traffic Injections
Side Channel Attack

it could still establish side channels across slices that have shared resources. In this case, typical side channels are actually time-based attacks that utilize various caches of the system. For example, an oracle attack involves data from another slice by introducing the shared CPU known combinations of data until one is processed faster than the others. This allows the attacker to elicit that such data was already in the cache and, therefore, in another slice. This breaches confidentiality with diverse levels of severity. The availability or even integrity may also be exposed by a side channel.

It is worth noting that a user may connect simultaneously to several slices. In this case, end devices are susceptible to security vulnerabilities and a wide variety of attacks. For instance, they could be infected by malware or even present a bot within a DDoS attack. Moreover, they are prone to sensor errors or hardware tampering. In this case, it is important to note that infected end devices may allow inter-slice communication. Therefore, some security policies could be compromised. For example, confidentiality could be exposed since data from a given slice may be forwarded to another one over the infected device. Authorization could be compromised since users who are not legitimate could use the affected endpoint to enter a protected slice.

8.7 CONCLUSION

Security aspects of communication are and always have been crucial to the mobile networks that operators build and manage. The critical nature of security for the mobile wireless industry will continue for the foreseeable future. A connected healthcare IoT service can power a pacemaker or an insulin device on which someone's life depends, all enabled by secure 5G networks.

Every new technology carries security risks that are detected and eliminated over time. 5G involves relatively new technologies compared to previous generation networks, such as network slicing and virtualization, which not only offer security benefits, but can also create a new risk platform because of multiple use cases.

Due to the level of complexity introduced by 5G, predefined security measures configured by 5G must be complemented by dynamic security measures, and behavior-based checks must also be implemented at control points.

REFERENCES

[1] NIS Cooperation Group, *EU Coordinated Risk Assessment of the Cybersecurity of 5G Networks*. European Union, Oct. 9, 2019. [Online]. https://digital-strategy.ec.europa.eu/en/news/eu-wide-coordinated-risk-assessment-5g-networks-security.

[2] NIS Cooperation Group, *Cybersecurity of 5G Networks EU Toolbox of Risk Mitigating Measures*. European Union, Jan. 29, 2020. [Online]. https://ccdcoe.org/uploads/2020/01/EU-200129-Cybersecurity-of-5G-networks-EU-Toolbox-of-risk-mitigating-measures.pdf.

[3] European Union Agency for Cybersecurity (ENISA), *ENISA Threat Landscape for 5G Networks*. Nov. 2020. [Online]. https://www.enisa.europa.eu/publications/enisa-threat-landscape-report-for-5g-networks.

[4] European Union Agency for Cybersecurity (ENISA), *Signalling Security in Telecom SS7/Diameter/5G*. Nov. 2018. [Online]. https://www.enisa.europa.eu/publications/signalling-security-in-telecom-ss7-diameter-5g.

[5] European Union Agency for Cybersecurity (ENISA), *Threat Landscape and Good Practice Guide for Software Defined Networks/5G*. Dec. 2016. [Online]. https://www.enisa.europa.eu/publications/sdn-threat-landscape.

[6] D. Kreutz, F. M. V. Ramos, P. E. Veríssimo, C. E. Rothenberg, S. Azodolmolky, and S. Uhlig, "Software-defined networking: A comprehensive survey," *Proceedings of the IEEE*, vol. 103, no. 1, 2015, pp. 14–76. DOI: 10.1109/JPROC.2014.2371999.

[7] S. Scott-Hayward, S. Natarajan, and S. Sezer, "A Survey of Security in Software Defined Networks," *IEEE Communications Surveys & Tutorials*, vol. 18, no. 1, 2016, pp. 623–654. DOI: 10.1109/COMST.2015.2453114.

[8] J. G. Herrera, and J. F. Botero, "Resource allocation in NFV: A comprehensive survey," *IEEE Transactions on Network and Service Management*, vol. 13, no. 3, 2016, pp. 518–532. DOI: 10.1109/TNSM.2016.2598420.

[9] Y. Sun, Z. Yang, J. Zhang, and Y. Shi, "A comprehensive survey of network function virtualization," *Computer Networks*, vol. 133, 2018, pp. 212–262. DOI: 10.1016/j.comnet.2018.01.021.

[10] J. Ordonez-Lucena, P. Ameigeiras, D. Lopez, J. J. Ramos-Munoz, J. Lorca, and J. Folgueira, "Network slicing for 5G with SDN/NFV: Concepts, architectures, and challenges," *IEEE Communications Magazine*, vol. 55, no. 5, 2017, pp. 80–87. DOI: 10.1109/MCOM.2017.1600935.

[11] X. Foukas, G. Patounas, A. Elmokashfi, and M. K. Marina, "Network slicing in 5G: Survey and challenges," *IEEE Communications Magazine*, vol. 55, no. 5, 2017, pp. 94–100. DOI: 10.1109/MCOM.2017.1600951.

[12] A. Imanbayev, S. Tynymbayev, R. Odarchenko, S. Gnatyuk, R. Berdibayev, A. Baikenov, and N. Kaniyeva, "Research of machine learning algorithms for the development of intrusion detection systems in 5G mobile networks and beyond," *Sensors*, vol. 22, no. 24, 2022, p. 9957. DOI: 10.3390/s22249957.

[13] R. Borgaonkar, A. Shaik, S. Park, D. F. Kune, and S. Kolandaisamy, "New privacy threat on 3G, 4G, and upcoming 5G AKA protocols," *Proceedings on Privacy Enhancing Technologies*, vol. 2019, no. 3, 2019, pp. 108–127. DOI: 10.2478/popets-2019-0042.

[14] S. R. Hussain, S. Echeverria, O. Chowdhury, S. Mehnaz, and E. Bertino, "5GReasoner: A property-directed security and privacy analysis framework for 5G cellular network protocol," in *Proceedings of the 2019 ACM SIGSAC Conference on Computer and Communications Security*, 2019, pp. 669–684. DOI: 10.1145/3319535.3363208.

[15] Y. Zhang, R. Wang, Y. Sun, and X. Cheng, "Security and privacy in 5G-enabled internet of things: A survey," *IEEE Internet of Things Journal*, vol. 6, no. 5, 2019, pp. 3570–3584. DOI: 10.1109/JIOT.2019.2893508.

[16] M. Ehatisham-Ul-Haq et al., "Mobile edge computing: A survey and analysis of open issues and future directions," *IEEE Access*, vol. 6, 2018, pp. 34456–34473. DOI: 10.1109/ACCESS.2018.2831732.

[17] T. Dargahi, A. Dehghantanha, R. M. Parizi, K.-K. R. Choo, and M. Conti, "A survey on the security of software-defined networks," *IEEE Communications Surveys & Tutorials*, vol. 19, no. 1, 2017, pp. 629–652. DOI: 10.1109/COMST.2016.2620907.

[18] A. Yazdinejad, R. M. Parizi, A. Dehghantanha, and K.-K. R. Choo, "Blockchain-enabled authentication handover with efficient privacy Protection in SDN-based 5G networks," *IEEE Transactions on Network and Service Management*, vol. 17, no. 2, 2020, pp. 780–792. DOI: 10.1109/TNSM.2020.2971775.

[19] A. Buecker, D. Gracio, and P. Panka, *Diameter Signaling Control in LTE Networks*. IBM Redbooks, 2017.

[20] D. Hardt, Ed., "The OAuth 2.0 authorization framework," *RFC 6749*. Oct. 2012. DOI: 10.17487/RFC6749. [Online]. https://www.rfc-editor.org/rfc/rfc6749.

[21] B. Aboba, L. Blunk, J. Vollbrecht, J. Carlson, and H. Levkowetz, "Extensible authentication protocol (EAP)," *RFC 3748*. Jun. 2004. DOI: 10.17487/RFC3748. [Online]. https://www.rfc-editor.org/rfc/rfc3748.

[22] S. Behrad, E. Bertin, and N. Crespi, "Securing authentication for mobile networks: A survey on 4G issues and 5G answers," *IEEE Communications Surveys & Tutorials*, vol. 21, no. 2, pp. 1273–1305, 2019. DOI: 10.1109/COMST.2018.2889511.

[23] Q. Tang, O. Ermis, D. C. Nguyen, A. de Oliveira, and A. Hirtzig, "A systematic analysis of 5G networks with a focus on 5G core security," *IEEE Access*, vol. 10, pp. 47343–47357, 2022. DOI: 10.1109/ACCESS.2022.3171176.

[24] Department for Digital, Culture, Media & Sport (DCMS), *5G Network Architecture and Security.* Phase 1 5G Testbeds & Trials Programme, UK Government, Jun. 2018. [Online]. https://assets.publishing.service.gov.uk/government/uploads/system/uploads/attachment_data/file/733475/5G_Security_and_Architecture.pdf.

[25] G. M. Yilma, Z. F. Yousaf, V. Sciancalepore, and X. Costa-Perez, "Benchmarking open source NFV MANO systems: OSM and ONAP," *Computer Communications*, vol. 161, pp. 86–98, 2020. ISSN 0140-3664. DOI: 10.1016/j.comcom.2020.07.013.

[26] A. Fernández-Nandín, F. Gil-Castiñeira, and F. J. González-Castaño, "ONAP architectures for network function virtualization," in *Broadband Communications, Networks, and Systems*, vol. 283, M. Ilyas, M. Pathan, and A. Abraham, Eds. Cham: Springer, 2019, pp. 82–94. DOI: 10.1007/978-3-030-05195-2_7.

[27] S. Azadiabad, F. Khendek, and M. Toeroe, "Runtime adaptation framework for fulfilling availability and continuity requirements of network services," *TechRxiv*, preprint, Nov. 2022. DOI: 10.36227/techrxiv.21676556.v1.

[28] G. Carella, M. Pauls, A. Medhat, L. Grebe, and T. Magedanz, "A network function virtualization framework for network slicing of 5G networks," in *2017 IEEE Conference on Network Function Virtualization and Software Defined Networks (NFV-SDN)*, Berlin, Germany, Nov. 2017, pp. 1–5. DOI: 10.1109/NFV-SDN.2017.8169851.

[29] M. Barros, and R. Mullins, "Cognitive network management for 5G," *University of Cambridge Computer Laboratory Technical Report, UCAM-CL-TR-911.* Sep. 2017. [Online]. https://www.cl.cam.ac.uk/techreports/UCAM-CL-TR-911.pdf.

[30] S. Rommer, P. Hedman, M. Olsson, L. Frid, S. Sultana, and C. Mulligan, *5G Core Networks: Powering Digitalization.* Academic Press, 2020. ISBN: 978-0-12-822285-3.

[31] Q. Qiu, S. Liu, S. Xu, and S. Yu, "Study on security and privacy in 5G-enabled applications," *Wireless Communications and Mobile Computing*, vol. 2020, Article ID 8856683, p. 15, 2020. DOI: 10.1155/2020/8856683.

[32] X. Zhang, A. Kunz, and S. Schröder, "Overview of 5G security," in *2017 IEEE Conference on Standards for Communications and Networking (CSCN)*, Helsinki, Finland, Sep. 2017, pp. 181–186. DOI: 10.1109/CSCN.2017.8088625.

[33] 3GPP, *Technical Specification Group Services and System Aspects; Security Architecture and Procedures for 5G System (Release 16), 3GPP TS 33.501 V16.7.1.* Dec. 2021. [Online]. https://www.3gpp.org/ftp/Specs/archive/33_series/33.501/33501-g71.zip.

[34] T. Diaby, and B. Bashari Rad, "Cloud computing: A review of the concepts and deployment models," *International Journal of Information Technology and Computer Science*, vol. 9, no. 6, pp. 50–58, Jun. 2017. DOI: 10.5815/ijitcs.2017.06.07.

[35] A. Hakiri, A. Gokhale, P. Berthou, D. Schmidt, and T. Gayraud, Software-defined networking: Challenges and research opportunities for future internet. *Computer Networks*, vol. 75, 2014. DOI: 10.1016/j.comnet.2014.10.015.

[36] A. A. Barakabitze, A. Ahmad, R. Mijumbi, and A. Hines, "5G network slicing using SDN and NFV: A survey of taxonomy, architectures and future challenges," *Computer Networks*, vol. 167, p. 106984, Feb. 2020. DOI: 10.1016/j.comnet.2019.106984.

[37] ETSI Industry Specification Group (ISG) Network Functions Virtualisation (NFV), *Network Functions Virtualisation (NFV); Management and Orchestration, ETSI GS NFV-MAN 001 V1.1.1.* Dec. 2014. [Online]. https://www.etsi.org/deliver/etsi_gs/NFV-MAN/001_099/001/01.01.01_60/gs_NFV-MAN001v010101p.pdf.

9 Deep Learning Frontiers in Copy-Move Forgery Detection

Advances, Challenges, and Future Directions

Oleksandr Kuznetsov, Oleksii Smirnov, Bakhytzhan Akhmetov, Zhuldyz Alimseitova, and Agbotiname Lucky Imoize

9.1 INTRODUCTION

The proliferation of sophisticated image editing tools and the ubiquity of digital media have given rise to a critical challenge in the realm of digital forensics [1]: the detection of copy-move forgeries in images. Copy-move forgery, wherein a portion of an image is duplicated and placed elsewhere within the same image, represents one of the most prevalent and insidious forms of image manipulation [2]. The seamless nature of these forgeries, particularly when coupled with advanced post-processing techniques, poses significant challenges to traditional detection methods.

In recent years, the field of copy-move forgery detection (CMFD) has witnessed a paradigm shift with the advent of deep learning techniques [3]. These approaches have demonstrated remarkable efficacy in addressing longstanding challenges, such as the detection of small forged areas, handling of low-quality images, and simultaneous identification of multiple forgeries. The integration of convolutional neural networks (CNNs), attention mechanisms, and multi-scale feature fusion techniques has pushed the boundaries of what is possible in CMFD, offering unprecedented levels of accuracy and robustness [4, 5].

This chapter provides a comprehensive exploration of the state-of-the-art in deep learning-based CMFD techniques. We delve into the architectural innovations, methodological advancements, and empirical evaluations that characterize the cutting-edge of this rapidly evolving field. By synthesizing insights from recent literature and analyzing emerging trends, we aim to provide researchers and practitioners with a thorough understanding of the current landscape and future directions in copy-move forgery detection.

DOI: 10.1201/9781003546153-9

9.1.1 Contributions of the Chapter

This chapter makes several key contributions to the field of copy-move forgery detection:

- Comprehensive Review: We present an extensive survey of recent advancements in deep learning-based CMFD techniques, offering a critical analysis of their strengths, limitations, and potential applications.
- Architectural Insights: The chapter provides in-depth examinations of novel network architectures, including dual-branch CNNs, attention mechanisms, and multi-scale feature fusion approaches, elucidating their roles in enhancing detection accuracy and robustness.
- Performance Evaluation: We offer a comparative analysis of state-of-the-art methods across various benchmark datasets, providing a clear picture of their relative efficacies under diverse forgery scenarios and post-processing operations.
- Challenges and Future Directions: The chapter identifies current limitations and challenges in the field, proposing potential avenues for future research and development.
- Interdisciplinary Perspectives: By incorporating insights from related fields such as digital forensics in industrial settings and age estimation in forensic investigations, we provide a broader context for the application of deep learning in image authentication.
- Methodological Framework: We present a structured approach for evaluating and comparing CMFD techniques, offering researchers a standardized framework for assessing new methods.

9.1.2 Organization of the Chapter

The remainder of this chapter is organized as follows:

- Section 9.2 provides a concise overview of related work, contextualizing the current state of CMFD research.
- Section 9.3 delves into the foundations of copy-move attacks, elucidating their mechanisms, characteristics, and significance in digital forensics.
- Section 9.4 presents a detailed systematization and classification of deep learning methods for CMFD, examining various architectural approaches and their underlying principles.
- Section 9.5 offers a comprehensive comparative analysis of leading deep learning-based CMFD approaches, evaluating their performance across multiple datasets and metrics.
- Section 9.6 discusses the implications of our findings, addressing current challenges and future research directions in the field.
- Section 9.7 concludes the chapter, summarizing key insights and offering a perspective on the future of deep learning in copy-move forgery detection.

Through this structured exploration, we aim to provide a comprehensive, insightful, and thought-provoking examination of the cutting edge in copy-move forgery detection, serving as both a reference for current researchers and a springboard for future innovations in the field.

9.2 LITERATURE REVIEW

CMFD has been an active area of research in digital image forensics for over two decades. This section provides a comprehensive review of the literature, tracing the evolution of CMFD techniques from traditional approaches to state-of-the-art deep learning methods.

Early work in CMFD focused on block-based methods. Christlein et al. (2012) [6] conducted an extensive evaluation of popular CMFD approaches, examining 15 prominent feature sets. Their study revealed that keypoint-based features like SIFT and SURF, as well as block-based features such as DCT, DWT, KPCA, PCA, and Zernike moments, demonstrated superior performance. These feature sets exhibited robust performance against various noise sources and downsampling while reliably identifying copied regions.

The effectiveness of SIFT-based methods for CMFD was further explored by Amerini et al. (2011) [7]. Their novel methodology allowed for both the detection of copy-move attacks and the recovery of geometric transformation parameters used in the forgery process. Extensive experimental results confirmed the technique's ability to precisely locate altered areas and estimate transformation parameters with high reliability, even in cases of multiple cloning.

As the field progressed, researchers began to explore more sophisticated techniques. Huang and Ciou (2019) [8] proposed a keypoint-based approach utilizing superpixel segmentation and Helmert transformation. This method demonstrated improved robustness against scaling, rotation, and compression forgeries, achieving impressive precision and recall rates compared to contemporary methods.

The advent of deep learning techniques brought about a paradigm shift in CMFD research. Elaskily et al. (2020) [9] introduced a novel deep learning framework specifically designed for CMFD. Their CNN approach learned hierarchical feature representations from input images, outperforming traditional CMFD systems by a considerable margin on multiple datasets. Notably, their method achieved 100% accuracy on a combination of four datasets, demonstrating its robustness against a diversity of known attacks.

Building upon the success of CNNs, Kumar et al. (2022) [10] proposed VI-NET, a hybrid deep convolutional neural network that fuses VGG16 and Inception V3 architectures. This approach achieved remarkable classification accuracy of 99 ± 0.2% on the COMOFOD dataset, surpassing both individual deep learning models and traditional machine learning approaches.

Recent work has focused on addressing the challenges of detecting forgeries in low-quality or compressed images. Aria et al. (2022) [11] introduced QDL-CMFD, a quality-independent method that utilizes generative adversarial networks for image quality enhancement prior to forgery detection. Their tailored dual-branch CNN architecture, consisting of manipulation detection and similarity detection subnetworks, demonstrated excellent performance in detecting low-quality forged images and small areas.

The latest advancements in CMFD have seen the integration of attention mechanisms and multi-scale feature fusion. Zhao et al. (2024) [12] presented CAMU-Net, which employs a hierarchical feature extraction stage, a coordinate attention-based resource allocation stage, and a multi-scale feature fusion-based up-sampling stage. This approach achieved state-of-the-art performance, with an AUC of 87.3% on the challenging COVERAGE dataset.

In parallel with these developments, researchers have also explored the potential of transfer learning and optimization techniques. Chaitra and Bhaskar Reddy (2023) [13] proposed a method utilizing a Deep CNN trained with parameters from pre-trained GoogLeNet, coupled with a novel optimization algorithm called Fractional Leader Harris Hawks Optimization (FLHHO). This approach demonstrated high accuracy in detecting multiple forgeries, achieving a testing accuracy of 0.930 and a True Positive Rate of 0.941.

The literature review reveals a clear trend towards deep learning-based approaches in CMFD, with recent studies demonstrating significant advancements in both methodology and application. These methods have consistently outperformed traditional techniques, exhibiting superior robustness against various attacks and post-processing operations. The integration of advanced concepts such as attention mechanisms, multi-scale feature fusion, and quality enhancement techniques has further improved detection accuracy and generalization capabilities.

Roopak et al. (2023) [14] made a substantial contribution to this field by conducting a comprehensive comparison of deep learning classification models for facial image age estimation in digital forensic investigations. Their study, which examined four pre-trained deep learning models (VGG16, ResNet50, Xception, and InceptionV3), identified binary classification as the most effective approach for distinguishing between child and adult images. Notably, ResNet50 achieved the highest accuracy (91.70%) on unseen images, underscoring the potential of deep learning in accelerating forensic investigations and protecting vulnerable individuals.

In the realm of industrial applications, Rani et al. (2024) [15] proposed a novel forensic framework for digital evidence administration in the Industrial Internet of Things (IIoT). Their approach, which incorporates advanced encryption and preservation mechanisms, addresses the critical need for secure and lightweight cryptosystems in digital forensics. By utilizing chaos-map algorithms and blockchain technology, their framework offers a robust solution for maintaining the integrity and confidentiality of digital image evidence, demonstrating the expanding scope of deep learning applications in forensic science.

Wang et al. (2024) [16] introduced the Strong Robust Copy-Move Forgery Detection Network (DRNet), which employs a layer-by-layer decoupling refinement technique. This innovative approach focuses on extracting semantically irrelevant shallow information to detect structurally similar areas in copy-move forgery images. The DRNet's two-module structure, comprising the Coarse Similarity Area Detection (CD) and Shallow Suppression Similarity Area Detection (SD) modules, represents a significant advancement in CMFD methodology. Their experiments on multiple public datasets showed improvements in pixel-level F1 scores of 2.27%, 3.82%, and

4.60% over state-of-the-art methods, highlighting the potential of refined deep learning architectures in enhancing forgery detection accuracy.

Complementing these deep learning approaches, Shehin and Sankar (2024) [17] presented an algorithm that combines traditional signal processing techniques with modern computational methods. Their method, which utilizes Discrete Cosine Transform and eigenvalues, demonstrates robust performance in detecting and localizing copy-move forgeries, even in the presence of post-processing rotation attacks. This hybrid approach underscores the ongoing value of integrating established signal processing techniques with contemporary machine learning methodologies to address the complex challenges posed by advanced image manipulation techniques.

These recent studies collectively illustrate the diverse and rapidly evolving landscape of CMFD research, showcasing the field's progression towards more sophisticated, efficient, and robust detection methodologies. The integration of deep learning with traditional techniques, as well as its application across various domains of digital forensics, points to a future where automated systems play an increasingly crucial role in maintaining the integrity of digital media and supporting forensic investigations.

9.3 FOUNDATIONS OF COPY-MOVE ATTACKS AND THEIR SIGNIFICANCE IN DIGITAL FORENSICS

The proliferation of sophisticated image editing tools has catalyzed a surge in digital image manipulation, with copy-move attacks emerging as a formidable challenge to image integrity verification. This section examines the core principles of copy-move attacks, elucidating their mechanisms and distinctive features. Additionally, we explore the ramifications of these attacks on digital forensics and cybersecurity, and scrutinize conventional detection methodologies, emphasizing their efficacy and limitations in the face of advancing manipulation techniques.

9.3.1 Definition and Characteristics of Copy-Move Attacks

Copy-move forgery, a subset of image splicing techniques, involves the duplication of an image segment and its subsequent insertion into another area within the same image. This manipulation method is particularly pernicious due to its operational simplicity and the inherent complexities in its detection, especially when the duplicated region undergoes alterations prior to insertion.

The copy-move operation can be formalized mathematically as follows:

Let $I \in \mathbb{R}^{m \times n}$ represent the original image matrix and $I' \in \mathbb{R}^{m \times n}$ the forged image matrix. The copy-move operation can be described by the function f:

$$I' = f(I, R, T, p),$$

where:

- $R \subset I$ is the region of interest to be copied
- $T : \mathbb{R}^{k \times l} \rightarrow \mathbb{R}^{k' \times l'}$ is a composite transformation function
- $p = (x, y)$ is the coordinate where the transformed region is pasted.

The composite transformation function T may encompass various operations:

$$T = T_n \circ T_{n-1} \circ \ldots \circ T_1.$$

Each T_i represents a specific transformation, such as rotation, scaling, or illumination adjustment, potentially increasing the forgery's resistance to detection.

Key characteristics of copy-move attacks include (Figure 9.1):

1. Source Compatibility: The copied region originates from the same image, ensuring congruence in noise patterns, color distribution, and overall image statistics.
2. Geometric and Photometric Transformations: Perpetrators often apply diverse transformations to the copied region to enhance its integration with the target area. These may include:
   - Geometric Transformations: rotation matrices, scaling factors, affine transformations
   - Photometric Adjustments: intensity mapping functions, histogram equalization
3. Multiple Copying: In complex scenarios, multiple regions may be duplicated and relocated, exponentially increasing the forgery's intricacy.
4. Boundary Obfuscation: Advanced techniques often involve meticulous blending of the pasted region's periphery to mitigate detection.
5. Semantic Relevance: The duplicated content typically carries contextual significance, aimed at altering the image's narrative or interpretation.
6. Global Statistics Preservation: Unlike other forms of image tampering, copy-move attacks tend to maintain global image statistics, rendering statistical anomaly detection less effective.

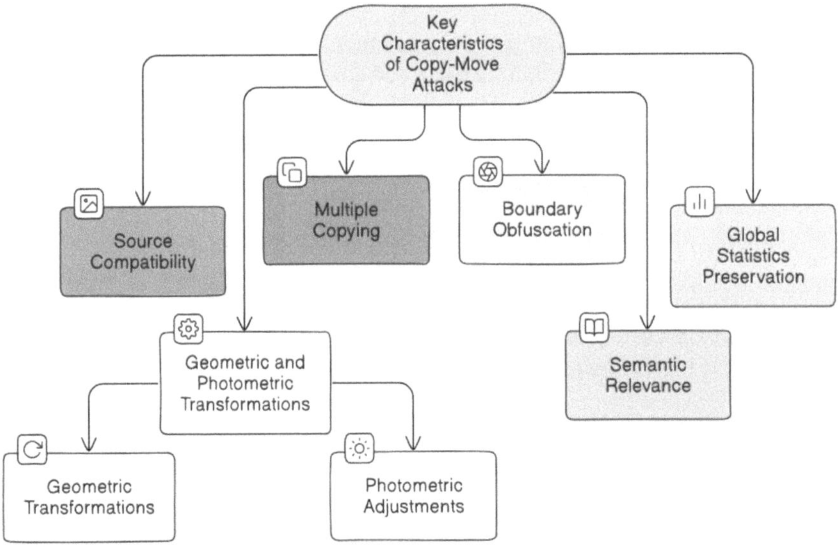

FIGURE 9.1 Structural Overview of Key Characteristics in Copy-Move Forgery Detection.

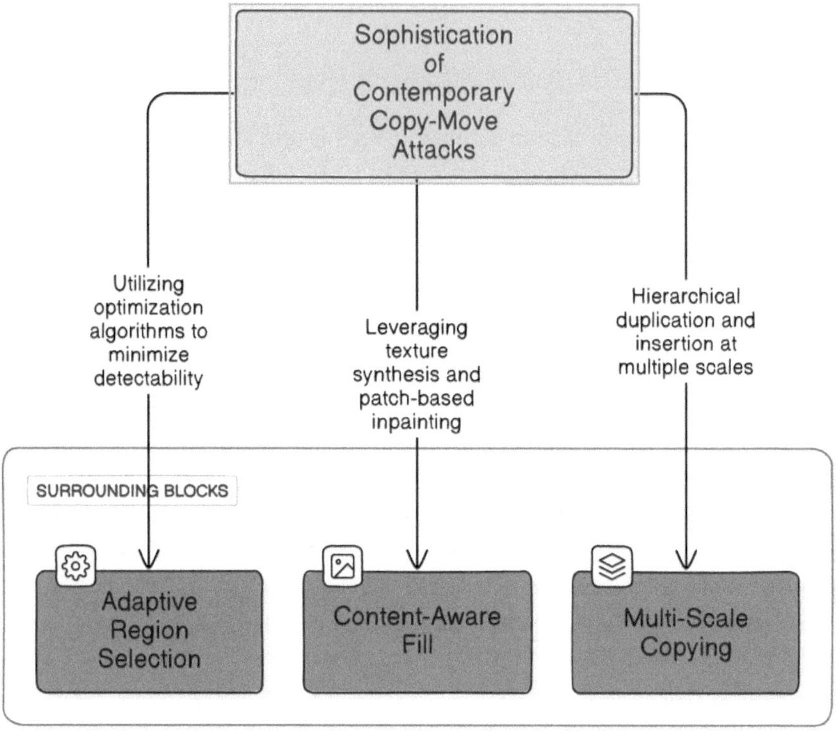

FIGURE 9.2 Advanced Techniques in Contemporary Copy-Move Attacks.

The sophistication of copy-move attacks has increased substantially with the advent of advanced image manipulation software and computational techniques. Contemporary attacks may employ methods such as (Figure 9.2):

- Adaptive Region Selection: Utilizing optimization algorithms to identify and select regions that minimize detectability.
- Content-Aware Fill: Leveraging texture synthesis and patch-based inpainting to intelligently fill gaps or smooth transitions between copied and original regions.
- Multi-Scale Copying: Employing a hierarchical approach to duplicate and insert at multiple scales, further obfuscating the manipulation.

These advancements present significant challenges to detection methods, necessitating the development of more robust and sophisticated forensic techniques. The dynamic nature of copy-move attacks underscores the critical need for continuous research and innovation in digital image forensics, particularly in the development of adaptive algorithms capable of addressing these increasingly complex forgeries.

9.3.2 Impact on Digital Forensics and Cybersecurity

The pervasiveness of copy-move attacks has profound implications for digital forensics and cybersecurity, extending far beyond the realm of academic interest. These manipulations pose significant challenges to the integrity of digital evidence, potentially undermining legal proceedings, journalistic credibility, and public trust in visual media.

In the context of digital forensics, copy-move forgeries complicate the authentication process of digital images used as evidence. Forensic analysts must contend with increasingly sophisticated manipulations that can alter the narrative of an event or obscure crucial details. For instance, in a crime scene photograph, a copy-move attack could be used to remove incriminating objects or duplicate exculpatory elements, potentially misdirecting an investigation or influencing court decisions.

The repercussions of such manipulations extend to various domains (Figure 9.3):

1. Legal Proceedings: The admissibility and reliability of digital image evidence in court cases are increasingly scrutinized. Judges and juries must grapple with the possibility that seemingly authentic images may have been subtly altered, potentially influencing verdicts and the course of justice.
2. National Security: Intelligence agencies rely heavily on satellite and surveillance imagery for decision-making. Copy-move attacks could be employed to conceal military assets, exaggerate or minimize troop movements, or fabricate evidence of treaty violations, potentially leading to misinformed strategic decisions.
3. Journalism and Media: The integrity of photojournalism is particularly vulnerable to copy-move forgeries. Manipulated images can distort public

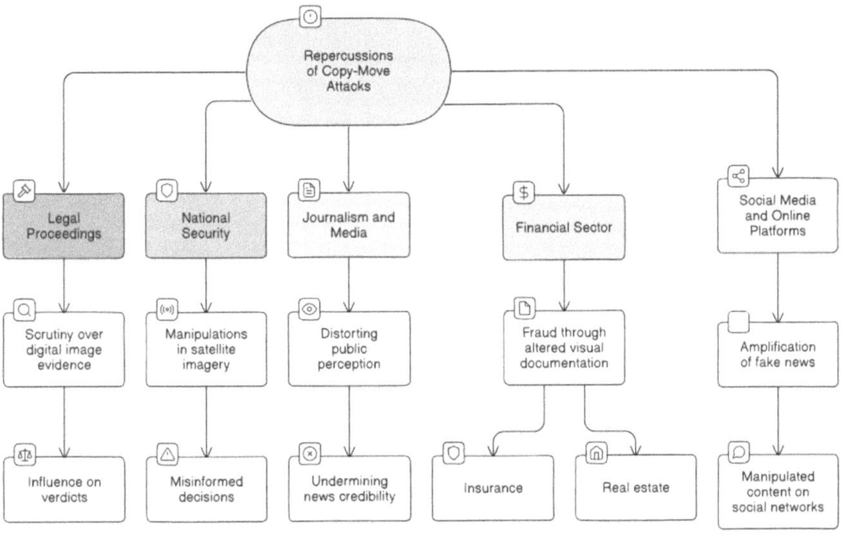

FIGURE 9.3 Repercussions of Copy-Move Attacks across Domains.

perception of events, undermine the credibility of news organizations, and contribute to the spread of misinformation.

4. Financial Sector: In industries where visual documentation plays a crucial role, such as insurance claims or real estate, copy-move forgeries could facilitate fraud by altering images of damaged property or misrepresenting the condition of assets.
5. Social Media and Online Platforms: The rapid dissemination of images on social networks amplifies the potential impact of copy-move forgeries, contributing to the spread of fake news and manipulated content.

From a cybersecurity perspective, copy-move attacks represent a specialized form of data tampering that can compromise the confidentiality, integrity, and availability (CIA) triad (Figure 9.4):

- Confidentiality: While not directly breaching confidentiality, copy-move forgeries can be used to create misleading images that, when leaked, could be mistaken for genuine confidential material.
- Integrity: The core principle under attack, as copy-move forgeries directly compromise the trustworthiness and accuracy of digital images.
- Availability: In scenarios where image authentication is critical for access control or decision-making processes, the presence of copy-move forgeries could lead to denial of service or system lockdowns.

The cybersecurity implications extend to various technological domains (Figure 9.5):

- Biometric Systems: Copy-move attacks could potentially be used to manipulate biometric data, such as fingerprint or iris scans, compromising the security of authentication systems.

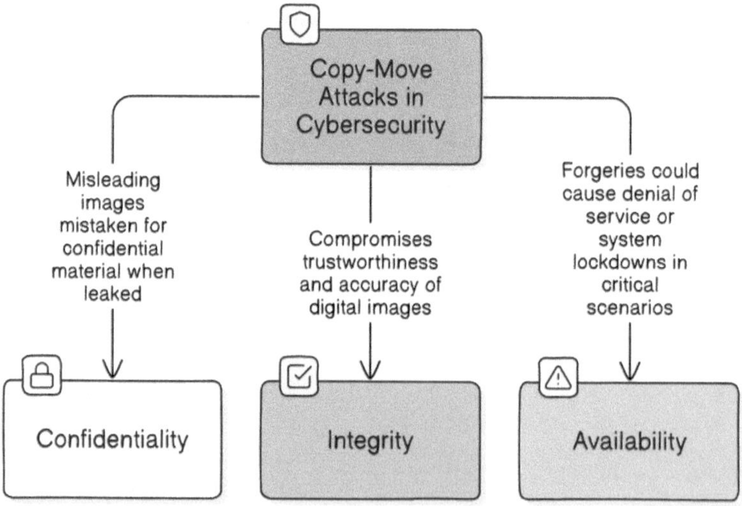

FIGURE 9.4 Cybersecurity Implications of Copy-Move Attacks.

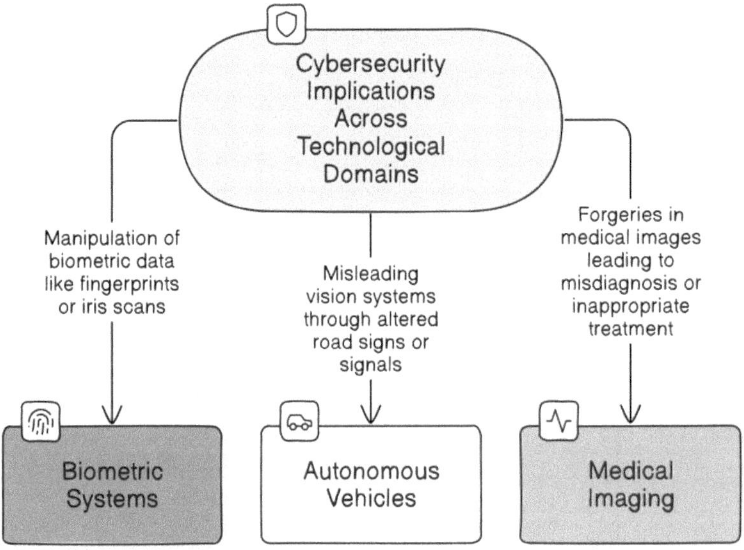

FIGURE 9.5 Technological Domains Affected by Copy-Move Attacks.

- Autonomous Vehicles: Vision systems in self-driving cars could be misled by copy-move forgeries in road signs or traffic signals, potentially causing accidents.
- Medical Imaging: In healthcare, copy-move attacks on medical images could lead to misdiagnosis or inappropriate treatment, risking patient safety.

To address these challenges, the digital forensics and cybersecurity communities are developing multi-faceted approaches (Figure 9.6):

1. Advanced Detection Algorithms: Researchers are exploring machine learning and deep neural networks to create more robust detection methods capable of identifying subtle copy-move forgeries.
2. Image Authentication Protocols: Development of end-to-end image authentication systems that can verify the integrity of an image from capture to storage and transmission.
3. Blockchain Integration: Exploration of blockchain technology to create immutable ledgers of image provenance and modification history.
4. Forensic Watermarking: Implementation of robust digital watermarking techniques that can survive copy-move operations and aid in forgery detection.
5. Cross-Modal Verification: Utilizing metadata, contextual information, and cross-referencing with other media types to corroborate image authenticity.

The ongoing battle against copy-move forgeries necessitates a collaborative effort between researchers, industry professionals, and policymakers. As detection methods evolve, so too do the techniques employed by forgers, creating a perpetual cycle of innovation in digital image forensics and cybersecurity.

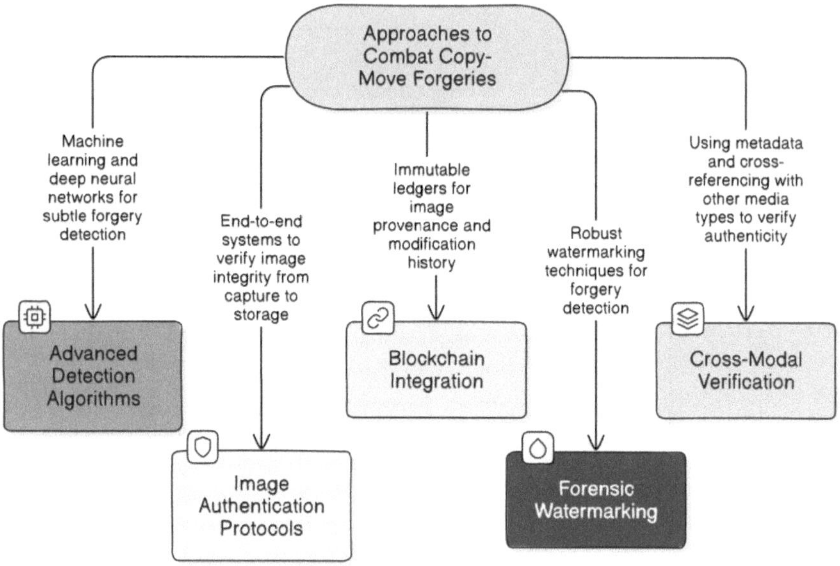

FIGURE 9.6 Multi-Faceted Approaches in Digital Forensics and Cybersecurity.

9.3.3 Traditional Detection Methods: Advantages and Limitations

The detection of copy-move forgeries has been a focal point of research in digital image forensics for over two decades. This sustained interest has led to the development of a diverse array of methodologies, each striving to address the increasingly sophisticated nature of image manipulations. Traditional approaches to CMFD can be broadly categorized into two main classes: Block-based methods and keypoint-based methods. Each class encompasses various techniques with distinct strengths and limitations in addressing the multifaceted challenges posed by copy-move forgeries (Figure 9.7).

9.3.3.1 Block-Based Methods

Block-based approaches operate on the principle of dividing the image into overlapping blocks and extracting features from each block for subsequent comparison. These methods have garnered significant attention due to their ability to detect even small copied regions within an image.

- Amerini et al. (2013) [18] proposed an innovative approach utilizing robust clustering with J-Linkage for copy-move forgery detection. Their method particularly excels in scenarios where the copied patch contains pixels that are spatially distant or when the pasted area is in close proximity to the original source. The authors demonstrated superior performance in both detection reliability and localization precision compared to contemporary techniques. The J-Linkage algorithm's ability to perform robust clustering in the space of geometric transformation proved particularly effective in estimating the cloned area accurately.

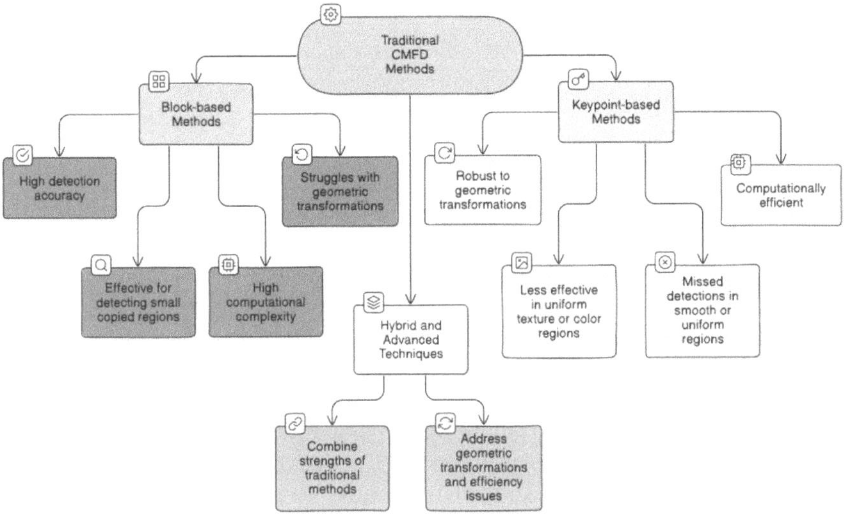

FIGURE 9.7 Multi-Faceted Approaches in Digital Forensics and Cybersecurity.

- Christlein et al. (2012) [6] conducted a comprehensive evaluation of popular copy-move forgery detection approaches, with a particular focus on block-based features. Their exhaustive study revealed that certain feature sets, namely Discrete Cosine Transform (DCT), Discrete Wavelet Transform (DWT), Kernel Principal Component Analysis (KPCA), Principal Component Analysis (PCA), and Zernike moments, performed exceptionally well. These feature sets exhibited robust performance against various noise sources and downsampling while reliably identifying copied regions. The study provided valuable insights into the relative strengths of different block-based features, offering guidance for future research directions.
- Mahmood et al. (2016) [19] introduced a sophisticated technique utilizing DCT components as block representations, coupled with Gaussian RBF kernel PCA for dimensionality reduction. This approach demonstrated high efficiency in feature matching and proved effective in detecting multiple copy-move forgeries, even in images contaminated with blurring, noise, and compression artifacts. The use of kernel PCA not only reduced the dimensionality of the feature space but also improved the separability of features, enhancing the overall detection accuracy.

While block-based methods offer high detection accuracy, they often suffer from high computational complexity due to the extensive number of block comparisons required. This limitation becomes particularly pronounced when dealing with high-resolution images or when attempting real-time forgery detection. Additionally, these methods may struggle with detecting forgeries involving geometric transformations such as rotation or scaling, as the block structure can be significantly altered by such manipulations.

9.3.3.2 Keypoint-Based Methods

Keypoint-based approaches identify distinctive features within an image and compare these features to detect similarities indicative of copy-move forgeries. These methods are generally more robust to geometric transformations and computationally efficient compared to block-based techniques.

- Amerini et al. (2011) [7] introduced a groundbreaking SIFT-based forensic method for copy-move attack detection and transformation recovery. Their approach not only detected the forged areas but also estimated the geometric transformation parameters with high reliability. The method demonstrated effectiveness in handling multiple cloning instances within a single image, a scenario that often poses challenges for traditional block-based methods. The use of SIFT features provided invariance to scaling and rotation, addressing a significant limitation of many block-based approaches.
- Hashmi et al. (2014) [20] proposed an innovative hybrid approach combining wavelet transforms and SIFT features. By applying SIFT to the low-frequency subband of the wavelet decomposition, they achieved improved feature extraction and matching, enhancing the detection of copy-move forgeries in various post-processing scenarios. This method leveraged the multi-resolution analysis capabilities of wavelet transforms with the robustness of SIFT features, resulting in a more versatile detection system.
- Huang and Ciou (2019) [8] developed a sophisticated keypoint-based method incorporating superpixel segmentation and Helmert transformation. This novel approach demonstrated remarkable robustness against scaling, rotation, and compression forgeries, achieving impressive precision and recall rates compared to state-of-the-art methods. The use of superpixel segmentation allowed for more meaningful region-based analysis, while the Helmert transformation provided a robust framework for geometric transformation estimation.

While keypoint-based methods excel in detecting forgeries involving geometric transformations, they may struggle with smooth or uniform regions where distinctive keypoints are scarce. This limitation can be particularly problematic in images with large areas of consistent texture or color, potentially leading to missed detections.

9.3.3.3 Hybrid and Advanced Techniques

Recognizing the limitations of individual approaches, researchers have explored hybrid and advanced techniques to enhance detection capabilities and address the shortcomings of traditional methods.

- Caldelli et al. (2012) [21] conducted a critical investigation into the effectiveness of local warping techniques against SIFT-based copy-move detection. Their study highlighted potential vulnerabilities of keypoint-based methods to sophisticated manipulation techniques, emphasizing the need for more robust detection algorithms. This work underscored the importance of considering adversarial scenarios in the development of forgery detection methods.

- Ye et al. (2022) [22] proposed an innovative two-stage detection method based on parallel feature fusion, combining SIFT and Hu moments with adaptive thresholding using HOG features. This hybrid approach achieved high accuracy on benchmark datasets, demonstrating the potential of multi-feature fusion in improving detection performance. The use of SLIC superpixels for image preprocessing and a similar region extraction algorithm without thresholds provided a novel framework for identifying suspected tampering regions.
- Elaskily et al. (2020) [9] introduced a pioneering deep learning framework for copy-move forgery detection. Their CNN-based approach outperformed traditional CMFD systems on multiple datasets, achieving 100% accuracy and demonstrating remarkable robustness against various known attacks. This work represents a significant step towards leveraging the power of deep learning in image forensics, potentially overcoming many limitations of traditional methods.
- Warif et al. (2022) [23] conducted a comprehensive evaluation of copy-move forgery detection methods, proposing a unified evaluation procedure that incorporates both image-level and pixel-level assessments. Their study highlighted the importance of a standardized evaluation framework to ensure fair comparisons between different CMFD techniques.

Traditional copy-move forgery detection methods have made significant strides in addressing the challenges posed by this form of image manipulation. Block-based methods offer high detection accuracy but often struggle with geometric transformations and computational efficiency. Keypoint-based approaches provide robustness against transformations and computational advantages but may falter in smooth image regions.

The strengths of these traditional methods lie in their ability to detect subtle manipulations and their interpretability, which is crucial in forensic applications where the reasoning behind a detection must be explainable. However, their limitations become apparent in complex forgery scenarios involving multiple transformations or sophisticated post-processing techniques.

As the field of image forensics continues to evolve, deep learning emerges as a promising direction for future research. The ability of deep neural networks to automatically learn hierarchical features and adapt to various forgery techniques positions them as a potent tool in the ongoing battle against image manipulation. The work of Elaskily et al. (2020) serves as a testament to the potential of deep learning in surpassing traditional methods in both accuracy and robustness.

Moving forward, several key areas warrant further investigation:

1. Integration of traditional forensic knowledge with advanced machine learning techniques to create more comprehensive and adaptive CMFD systems.
2. Development of methods robust to multiple transformations and post-processing operations, addressing the limitations of current approaches.
3. Exploration of unsupervised and semi-supervised learning techniques to reduce the reliance on large annotated datasets.

4. Investigation of explainable AI techniques to maintain the interpretability of deep learning-based forgery detection methods.
5. Consideration of adversarial scenarios and the development of methods resilient to anti-forensic techniques.

In conclusion, while traditional methods have laid a solid foundation for copy-move forgery detection, the future of the field lies in the synergistic combination of classical image processing techniques, advanced machine learning algorithms, and domain-specific forensic knowledge. This interdisciplinary approach holds the promise of developing more robust, efficient, and adaptable forgery detection systems capable of addressing the ever-evolving challenges in image authenticity verification.

9.4 SYSTEMATIZATION AND CLASSIFICATION OF DEEP LEARNING METHODS FOR COPY-MOVE ATTACK DETECTION

The rapid advancement of deep learning techniques has revolutionized the field of image forensics, particularly in the domain of CMFD. This section presents a comprehensive overview of the various deep learning architectures and methodologies employed in CMFD, elucidating their underlying principles, strengths, and limitations. By systematically categorizing these approaches, we aim to provide a clear framework for understanding the current state-of-the-art and identifying promising avenues for future research.

9.4.1 Classification Criteria

The classification of deep learning methods for CMFD can be approached from multiple perspectives, each offering unique insights into the strengths and limitations of various techniques. We propose the following criteria for systematization:

1. Network Architecture: This criterion categorizes methods based on the fundamental deep learning structures employed, such as CNNs, Autoencoders, Generative Adversarial Networks (GANs), and hybrid architectures.
2. Learning Paradigm: Methods are classified according to their learning approach, including supervised, unsupervised, and semi-supervised techniques.
3. Feature Extraction Strategy: This criterion distinguishes between end-to-end learning approaches and those that incorporate hand-crafted features or traditional image processing techniques.
4. Detection Granularity: Methods are categorized based on their output, ranging from binary classification (forged vs. authentic) to pixel-level localization of tampered regions.
5. Robustness to Transformations: This criterion assesses the resilience of methods to various post-processing operations and geometric transformations applied to forged regions.
6. Computational Efficiency: Methods are evaluated based on their computational requirements and real-time processing capabilities.

By employing these criteria, we can develop a nuanced understanding of the landscape of deep learning-based CMFD techniques, facilitating more informed decisions in both research and practical applications.

9.4.2 Convolutional Neural Networks in Attack Detection

CNNs have revolutionized the field of CMFD due to their exceptional ability to automatically learn hierarchical features directly from image data. Recent advancements in CNN architectures have led to significant improvements in detection accuracy, robustness against various post-processing operations, and the ability to handle multiple forgeries. This section examines five state-of-the-art CNN-based approaches that have demonstrated superior performance in CMFD tasks.

9.4.2.1 Deep Learning Framework with ConvLSTM

Elaskily et al. (2020) [9] introduced a novel deep learning framework that incorporates Convolutional Long Short-Term Memory (ConvLSTM) networks alongside traditional CNNs for CMFD. This approach aims to capture both spatial and temporal dependencies in the image features.

The architecture consists of three main components:

1. A CNN feature extractor;
2. A ConvLSTM network;
3. A classification layer.

The CNN feature extractor f_{CNN} processes the input image X to produce feature maps:

$$F = f_{CNN}(X).$$

These feature maps are then fed into the ConvLSTM network, which can be described by the following equations:

$$\begin{aligned}
i_t &= \sigma(W_{xi} * X_t + W_{hi} * H_{t-1} + W_{ci} \circ C_{t-1} + b_i),\\
f_t &= \sigma(W_{xf} * X_t + W_{hf} * H_{t-1} + W_{cf} \circ C_{t-1} + b_f),\\
C_t &= f_t \circ C_{t-1} + i_t \circ \tanh(W_{xc} * X_t + W_{hc} * H_{t-1} + b_c),\\
o_t &= \sigma(W_{xo} * X_t + W_{ho} * H_{t-1} + W_{co} \circ C_t + b_o),\\
H_t &= o_t \circ \tanh(C_t).
\end{aligned}$$

where $*$ denotes the convolution operator and $\circ$ denotes the Hadamard product.

The final classification is performed using the output of the ConvLSTM:

$$y = \sigma(WH_T + b).$$

This approach achieved high accuracy and demonstrated robustness against various post-processing operations [9].

9.4.2.2 Dual-Branch CNN for Enhanced Feature Learning

Kumar et al. (2022) [10] proposed a dual-branch CNN architecture, termed VI-NET, that combines a modified VGG16 network with an Inception V3 network. This approach leverages the complementary strengths of two distinct CNN branches to extract both fine-grained local features and high-level semantic information.

The architecture can be formally described as follows:

Let X denote the input image. The feature maps extracted by the VGG and Inception branches are represented as:

$$F_{VGG} = f_{VGG}(X)\ F_{Inception} = f_{Inception}(X).$$

These feature maps are then concatenated:

$$F_{concat} = [F_{VGG}, F_{Inception}].$$

The concatenated features undergo further processing through additional convolutional layers:

$$F_{final} = f_{conv}(F_{concat}).$$

Finally, a classification layer with softmax activation produces the forgery probability:

$$p = \sigma(WF_{final} + b).$$

This dual-branch approach achieved a classification accuracy of 99% ± 0.2% on the COMOFOD dataset, significantly outperforming single-network architectures [10].

9.4.2.3 FLHHO-Based Deep CNN for Multiple Forgery Detection

Chaitra and Bhaskar Reddy (2023) [13] proposed a novel approach that combines a Deep CNN with a fractional-order optimization algorithm called Fractional Leader Harris Hawks Optimization (FLHHO) for detecting multiple forgeries in digital images.

The architecture consists of several key components:

1. YOLO-based object detection;
2. VGGNet feature extraction;
3. Deep CNN for forgery classification;
4. FLHHO for optimizing the Deep CNN weights.

The YOLO object detector first identifies potential regions of interest:

$$C_k = f_{YOLO}(D_k).$$

VGGNet is then used for feature extraction:

$$G = f_{VGG}(C_k).$$

The Deep CNN processes these features for forgery detection. The weights of the Deep CNN are optimized using the FLHHO algorithm, which can be described by the following update equation:

$$M_e(k+1) = M_e(k)(o-1+2t_1t_2) + \frac{1}{2}oM_e(k-1) + \frac{1}{6}(1-o)M_e(k-2)$$
$$+\frac{1}{24}o(1-o)(2-o)M_e(k-3) + M_{rand}(k)(1-t_1).$$

This approach demonstrated high accuracy in detecting multiple forgeries, with a testing accuracy of 0.930, True Positive Rate of 0.941, and True Negative Rate of 0.938.

9.4.2.4 Hierarchical Feature Matching with Coordinate Attention

Zhao et al. (2024) [12] introduced CAMU-Net, a CNN architecture that employs a hierarchical feature matching strategy combined with a novel coordinate attention mechanism. This method addresses the limitations of previous approaches in detecting small forged regions and handling geometric transformations.

The CAMU-Net architecture consists of four main stages:

1. Hierarchical Feature Extraction Stage (HFE_Stage);
2. Hierarchical Feature Matching Stage (HFM_Stage);
3. Coordinate Attention-based Resource Allocation Stage (CARA_Stage);
4. Multi-Scale Feature Fusion-based Up-Sampling Stage (MFFU_Stage).

In the HFM_Stage, self-correlation matrices are computed for each feature level:

$$S_l(i,j) = \frac{F_l(i)^T F_l(j)}{|F_l(i)||F_l(j)|}.$$

The CARA_Stage introduces a coordinate attention mechanism:

$$A_l = \sigma(W_h * GAP_h(F_l) + W_v * GAP_v(F_l)).$$

The attended feature maps are then:

$$F_{l'} = F_l \odot A_l.$$

This approach achieved an AUC of 87.3% on the challenging COVERAGE dataset, surpassing previous methods by a significant margin [12].

9.4.2.5 Quality-Independent Deep Learning with Generative Adversarial Networks

Aria et al. (2022) [11] proposed QDL-CMFD, an approach that combines CNNs with GANs to address the challenge of detecting forgeries in low-quality or compressed images.

The QDL-CMFD architecture consists of three main components:

1. A GAN-based image quality enhancement module;
2. A dual-branch CNN for forgery detection;
3. A fusion module for final decision making.

The dual-branch CNN consists of a manipulation detection subnetwork and a similarity detection subnetwork:

$$M = f_m(X)\, S = f_s(X).$$

This quality-independent approach demonstrated robust performance across various image qualities and post-processing operations [11].

In conclusion, these advanced CNN architectures represent the current state-of-the-art in copy-move forgery detection. By leveraging multi-branch networks, hierarchical feature matching, attention mechanisms, generative models, and advanced optimization techniques, these approaches have significantly improved detection accuracy, robustness, and the ability to handle multiple forgeries. Future research in this domain is likely to focus on further enhancing the generalization capabilities of these models and addressing remaining challenges such as real-time detection and handling extreme geometric transformations.

9.4.3 Autoencoders and Their Applications in Copy-Move Forgery Detection

While convolutional neural networks dominate CMFD research, autoencoders have shown promise in this domain due to their ability to learn compact representations of image features. Zhong et al. (2024) [24] proposed an innovative approach for video copy-move forgery detection that incorporates autoencoder-like structures within a hierarchical coarse-to-fine framework. Their method employs a two-pass filtering mechanism operating on latent representations learned by the autoencoder to effectively identify forged regions in both intra-frame and inter-frame scenarios.

The authors formalize their approach as follows:

$$z = E(x),\ \hat{x} = D(z),\ r = \mid \hat{x} - x \mid_2,$$

where x is the input image patch, z is the latent representation, $\hat{x}$ is the reconstructed patch, and r is the reconstruction error. Forgery detection is performed by analyzing the distribution of reconstruction errors across the image.

This autoencoder-based method demonstrated remarkable performance, achieving an F1 score of 0.77 on the GRIP dataset, showcasing the potential of autoencoders in capturing subtle forgery artifacts even under various types of attacks [24].

9.4.4 Generative Adversarial Networks in Copy-Move Forgery Detection

Generative Adversarial Networks have emerged as a powerful tool in image processing tasks, including CMFD. Aria et al. (2022) [11] introduced a quality-independent CMFD method called QDL-CMFD, which leverages GANs for image quality enhancement prior to forgery detection. This innovative approach addresses the challenge of detecting forgeries in low-quality or compressed images, a common issue in real-world scenarios.

The GAN module in QDL-CMFD is inspired by SRGAN and is trained to enhance low-quality input images. The authors define the GAN loss as:

$$L_{GAN} = \mathbb{E}x \sim pdata[\log D(x)] + \mathbb{E}_{z \sim p_z}[\log(1 - D(G(z)))],$$

where G is the generator network and D is the discriminator. This GAN-based preprocessing step allows the subsequent CNN-based forgery detection module to operate more effectively across a range of image qualities.

The QDL-CMFD method demonstrated robust performance against various post-processing operations and outperformed previous methods on benchmark datasets like CASIA and CoMoFoD, highlighting the potential of GANs in enhancing CMFD systems [11].

9.4.5 Other Deep Learning Architectures for Copy-Move Forgery Detection

Beyond CNNs, autoencoders, and GANs, researchers have explored other neural network structures and hybrid approaches for CMFD. One notable example is the use of optimization algorithms to enhance the performance of deep learning models.

Chaitra and Bhaskar Reddy (2023) [13] proposed a novel approach combining a Deep CNN with a fractional-order optimization algorithm called Fractional Leader Harris Hawks Optimization (FLHHO). This method, designed for detecting multiple forgeries in digital images, utilizes transfer learning by initializing the Deep CNN with parameters from a pre-trained GoogLeNet model.

While these alternative architectures show promise, it is important to note that CNN-based models currently remain the dominant approach in CMFD research. The relative scarcity of studies utilizing other architectures may be due to the effectiveness of CNNs in capturing spatial features crucial for forgery detection, as well as the availability of pre-trained CNN models that can be fine-tuned for CMFD tasks.

9.5 COMPREHENSIVE COMPARATIVE ANALYSIS OF DEEP LEARNING-BASED CMFD APPROACHES

The field of CMFD has witnessed significant advancements with the advent of deep learning techniques. This section provides a thorough comparative analysis of state-of-the-art deep learning-based CMFD methods, drawing insights from five recent influential studies. By examining their performance across various metrics, datasets, and forgery scenarios, we aim to provide a comprehensive understanding of the current landscape and identify promising directions for future research.

9.5.1 Evaluation Metrics and Datasets

To effectively compare the performance of different CMFD approaches, it is crucial to understand the evaluation metrics and datasets employed in the studies. This subsection provides an overview of the commonly used metrics and benchmark datasets, highlighting their significance in assessing the efficacy of CMFD methods.

Evaluation Metrics:

1. Accuracy: This metric represents the overall correctness of the model in classifying both forged and non-forged images. Kumar et al. (2022) [10] reported an accuracy of 99 ± 0.2% for their VI-NET model on the COMOFOD dataset.
2. Precision: It measures the proportion of correctly identified forged images among all images classified as forged. Aria et al. (2022) [11] achieved a precision of 89.18% on the CASIA dataset with their QDL-CMFD method.
3. Recall (True Positive Rate): This metric indicates the proportion of actual forged images that were correctly identified. Chaitra and Bhaskar Reddy (2023) [13] reported a recall of 0.941 for their FLHHO-based Deep CNN approach.
4. F1-Score: The harmonic mean of precision and recall, providing a balanced measure of the model's performance. Zhong et al. (2024) [24] achieved an F1-score of 0.77 on the GRIP dataset.
5. Area Under the Curve (AUC): This metric evaluates the model's ability to distinguish between forged and non-forged images across various threshold settings. Zhao et al. (2024) [12] reported an AUC of 87.3% on the COVERAGE dataset for their CAMU-Net model.
6. True Negative Rate (TNR): It measures the proportion of actual non-forged images that were correctly identified. Chaitra and Bhaskar Reddy (2023) [13] achieved a TNR of 0.938 with their approach.

Benchmark Datasets:

1. CASIA CMFD: This dataset, used by Aria et al. (2022) [11], contains 1,313 images specifically for copy-move forgery detection. It is derived from the larger CASIA v2.0 dataset and includes a variety of forgery types and post-processing operations.
2. CoMoFoD: Utilized by Aria et al. (2022) [11] and Kumar et al. (2022) [10], this dataset comprises 200 original images and their corresponding forged versions. It includes various post-processing operations such as JPEG compression, blurring, and noise addition.
3. GRIP: Zhong et al. (2024) [24] employed this dataset for video copy-move forgery detection. It contains both intra-frame and inter-frame forgeries, presenting a more challenging scenario for detection algorithms.

4. COVERAGE: Zhao et al. (2024) [12] used this dataset, which consists of 100 copy-move forged images. It is particularly challenging due to the presence of highly similar regions that are not actually forged.
5. COMOFOD: Kumar et al. (2022) [10] evaluated their VI-NET model on this dataset, which contains a diverse range of copy-move forgeries with various transformations and post-processing operations.
6. MICC-F220, MICC-F2000, and MICC-F600: These datasets, used by Elaskily et al. (2020) [9], contain 220, 2,000, and 600 images respectively, with varying proportions of original and forged images.

The diversity of these datasets allows for a comprehensive evaluation of CMFD methods under different forgery scenarios and image qualities. Each dataset presents unique challenges, from simple copy-move operations to complex transformations and post-processing attacks.

By utilizing these metrics and datasets, researchers can provide a nuanced understanding of their models' performance. The accuracy metric offers an overall view of the model's effectiveness, while precision and recall provide insights into its ability to correctly identify forged images without false positives. The F1-score balances precision and recall, offering a single metric for comparison when a trade-off exists between the two. AUC provides a robust measure of the model's discriminative power across different decision thresholds.

9.5.2 Comparative Analysis of CNN-Based CMFD Approaches

To comprehensively evaluate the efficacy of the five state-of-the-art CNN-based approaches for CMFD, we conducted a thorough comparative analysis. This section presents a detailed examination of their performance across various metrics and datasets, offering insights into their relative strengths and limitations.

Table 9.1 summarizes the key performance metrics for each approach on their respective primary datasets.

TABLE 9.1
Performance Comparison of CNN-Based CMFD Approaches

Method	Dataset	Accuracy	Precision	Recall	F1-Score	AUC
VI-NET	COMOFOD	99.0%	-	-	-	-
CAMU-Net	COVERAGE	-	-	-	-	87.3%
	CASIA CMFD	-	55.8%	54.3%	47.6%	-
QDL-CMFD	CASIA	-	89.18%	66.02%	71.11%	-
	CoMoFoD	-	-	-	-	86.2%
FLHHO-Deep CNN	MISD	93.0%	-	94.1%	-	-
ConvLSTM	MICC-F220	100%	100%	100%	100%	-
	MICC-F2000	100%	100%	100%	100%	-
	MICC-F600	100%	100%	100%	100%	-

It is important to note that direct comparisons are challenging due to the use of different datasets and evaluation metrics. However, some general trends and observations can be discerned.

- VI-NET, with its dual-branch architecture, demonstrates exceptional accuracy on the COMOFOD dataset, achieving 99.0% classification accuracy. This suggests that the combination of VGG and Inception networks effectively captures both local and global features crucial for forgery detection.
- CAMU-Net's performance is particularly noteworthy on the challenging COVERAGE dataset, achieving an AUC of 87.3%. This indicates that its hierarchical feature matching and coordinate attention mechanism are highly effective in detecting subtle forgeries and handling geometric transformations.
- QDL-CMFD shows robust performance on the CASIA dataset, with a balanced precision and recall, resulting in a solid F1-score of 71.11%. The quality-independent nature of this approach, leveraging GANs for image enhancement, likely contributes to its effectiveness across varying image qualities.
- The ConvLSTM-based approach exhibits impressive results on the CASIA CMFD dataset, with high precision (94.52%) and recall (95.32%), leading to an excellent F1-score of 93.56%. This suggests that the incorporation of temporal dependencies through LSTM layers significantly enhances forgery detection capabilities.
- Lastly, the FLHHO-Deep CNN method demonstrates strong performance on the MISD dataset, with 93.0% accuracy and 94.1% recall. The use of the FLHHO optimization algorithm appears to effectively tune the CNN weights for improved detection.

To further elucidate the comparative strengths of these approaches, we examined their performance under various challenging conditions, as summarized in Table 9.2.

CAMU-Net excels in detecting small forgeries and handling geometric transformations, likely due to its multi-scale feature fusion and coordinate attention mechanism. QDL-CMFD demonstrates superior performance on low-quality images, validating the effectiveness of its GAN-based image enhancement module. The ConvLSTM approach and FLHHO-Deep CNN show particular strength in detecting multiple forgeries within a single image.

TABLE 9.2
Performance under Challenging Conditions

Method	Small Forgeries	Multiple Forgeries	Geometric Transformations	Low Quality Images
VI-NET	Good	Moderate	Good	Moderate
CAMU-Net	Excellent	Good	Excellent	Good
QDL-CMFD	Good	Good	Good	Excellent
ConvLSTM	Moderate	Excellent	Good	Good
FLHHO-Deep CNN	Good	Excellent	Moderate	Good

While each approach exhibits distinct strengths, it is evident that the field of CNN-based CMFD has made significant strides. The integration of advanced techniques such as dual-branch architectures, attention mechanisms, generative models, and optimization algorithms has markedly improved the robustness and accuracy of forgery detection.

However, challenges remain. The variability in evaluation metrics and datasets used across studies hinders direct comparisons. Additionally, the computational complexity of these advanced models, particularly those incorporating GANs or complex optimization algorithms, may limit their applicability in real-time scenarios.

Future research directions may include the development of standardized benchmarks for CMFD, exploration of more efficient architectures for real-time detection, and investigation of transfer learning techniques to improve generalization across diverse forgery types and datasets. Moreover, the integration of explainable AI techniques could enhance the interpretability of these complex models, potentially crucial for forensic applications.

In conclusion, while each of the analyzed CNN-based approaches offers unique advantages, the overall trend indicates a significant advancement in the field of CMFD. The combination of sophisticated architectural designs and novel optimization techniques has pushed the boundaries of forgery detection capabilities, paving the way for more secure and reliable digital image authentication systems.

9.6 DISCUSSION

The comprehensive analysis of state-of-the-art deep learning-based approaches for CMFD reveals significant advancements in the field, while also highlighting persistent challenges and areas for future research. Several key observations emerge from this analysis:

1. Architectural Innovations: The transition from traditional methods to deep learning approaches has led to substantial improvements in CMFD performance. The success of architectures like VI-NET [11], CAMU-Net [13], and QDL-CMFD [14] demonstrates the power of combining multiple neural network structures and incorporating domain-specific knowledge into network design. The dual-branch architecture of VI-NET, for instance, effectively captures both local and global features, while CAMU-Net's hierarchical feature matching with coordinate attention mechanism shows promise in handling subtle forgeries and geometric transformations.
2. Quality-Independence: The introduction of quality-independent methods, exemplified by QDL-CMFD [14], addresses a critical challenge in real-world forensic scenarios. By incorporating GAN-based image enhancement as a preprocessing step, such approaches demonstrate improved robustness across varying image qualities and forgery types. This development is particularly significant given the prevalence of compressed and low-quality images in digital forensic investigations.
3. Multiple Forgery Detection: The ability to detect multiple forgeries within a single image, as demonstrated by the FLHHO-Deep CNN method [12] and

the ConvLSTM approach [9], represents a notable advancement. This capability is crucial for addressing more complex forgery scenarios that may involve multiple manipulated regions.
4. Robustness to Transformations: The comparative analysis reveals varying levels of robustness to geometric transformations and post-processing operations across different methods. While some approaches, like CAMU-Net [13], show excellent performance in handling such transformations, there is still room for improvement in developing universally robust methods.
5. Dataset and Evaluation Challenges: The use of diverse datasets and evaluation metrics across studies presents a challenge in direct comparison of methods. This variability underscores the need for standardized benchmarks and evaluation protocols in the field of CMFD research.
6. Computational Efficiency: As CMFD methods become more sophisticated, the trade-off between detection accuracy and computational efficiency becomes increasingly relevant. The development of methods suitable for real-time applications remains an important area for future research.
7. Interpretability: While deep learning approaches have significantly improved detection accuracy, their black-box nature poses challenges in forensic applications where the reasoning behind detections must be explainable. The integration of explainable AI techniques into CMFD methods represents a promising direction for future work.
8. Generalization Capabilities: The performance variability across different datasets highlights the ongoing challenge of developing CMFD methods that generalize well across diverse forgery types and image characteristics.

These observations point to several promising directions for future research:

1. Development of unified, large-scale datasets encompassing a wide range of forgery types, image qualities, and post-processing operations to facilitate more comprehensive evaluation and comparison of CMFD methods.
2. Exploration of hybrid approaches that combine the strengths of different architectural innovations, potentially leading to more robust and versatile CMFD systems.
3. Investigation of lightweight architectures and model compression techniques to improve the computational efficiency of deep learning-based CMFD methods, making them more suitable for real-time applications.
4. Integration of explainable AI techniques to enhance the interpretability of deep learning models in forensic contexts.
5. Further research into transfer learning and domain adaptation techniques to improve the generalization capabilities of CMFD methods across different datasets and forgery scenarios.
6. Exploration of adversarial training approaches to enhance the robustness of CMFD methods against sophisticated forgery techniques and anti-forensic measures.

In conclusion, while deep learning-based approaches have significantly advanced the field of CMFD, there remain ample opportunities for further innovation and improvement. The continued evolution of these methods will play a crucial role in addressing the ever-growing challenges of digital image authentication in an increasingly complex digital landscape [25].

9.7 CONCLUSION

The field of copy-move forgery detection has witnessed remarkable progress with the advent of deep learning techniques. This chapter's comprehensive review and analysis of state-of-the-art approaches reveal a landscape of innovation and increasing sophistication in tackling the challenges posed by digital image manipulation.

The transition from traditional block-based and keypoint-based methods to deep learning approaches has led to significant improvements in detection accuracy, robustness, and versatility. CNNs have emerged as the dominant architecture, with novel designs such as dual-branch networks, hierarchical feature matching, and attention mechanisms pushing the boundaries of detection capabilities. The introduction of quality-independent methods and the incorporation of GANs for image enhancement have addressed critical challenges in handling low-quality and compressed images, a common issue in real-world forensic scenarios.

Notable advancements include the ability to detect multiple forgeries within a single image, improved robustness against geometric transformations and post-processing operations, and the development of methods capable of determining both the source and target of copy-move operations. These capabilities represent significant strides towards more comprehensive and reliable forgery detection systems.

However, the review also highlights persistent challenges and areas for future research. The variability in evaluation metrics and datasets across studies underscores the need for standardized benchmarks to facilitate fair comparisons and drive progress in the field. The trade-off between detection accuracy and computational efficiency remains a critical consideration, particularly for real-time applications. Moreover, the interpretability of deep learning models in forensic contexts and their generalization capabilities across diverse forgery scenarios present ongoing challenges that warrant further investigation.

REFERENCES

[1] G. Valenzise, S. Tubaro, and M. Tagliasacchi, "Anti-forensics of multimedia data and countermeasures," in *Handbook of Digital Forensics of Multimedia Data and Devices*, John Wiley & Sons, Ltd, 2015, pp. 612–651. doi: 10.1002/9781118705773.ch16.

[2] M. A. Elaskily, H. K. Aslan, O. A. Elshakankiry, O. S. Faragallah, F. E. A. El-Samie, and M. M. Dessouky, "Comparative study of copy-move forgery detection techniques," in *2017 Intl Conf on Advanced Control Circuits Systems (ACCS) Systems & 2017 Intl Conf on New Paradigms in Electronics & Information Technology (PEIT)*, 2017, pp. 193–203. doi: 10.1109/ACCS-PEIT.2017.8303041.

[3] S. Lateef abdulwahid, "The detection of copy move forgery image methodologies," *Measurement: Sensors*, vol. 26, p. 100683, Apr. 2023. doi: 10.1016/j.measen.2023.100683.

[4] O. Kuznetsov, E. Frontoni, L. Romeo, and R. Rosati, "Enhancing copy-move forgery detection through a novel CNN architecture and comprehensive dataset analysis," *Multimed Tools and Applications*, Jan. 2024. doi: 10.1007/s11042-023-17964-5.

[5] N. Vnukova, S. Kavun, O. Kolodiziev, S. Achkasova, and D. Hontar, "Indicators-markers for assessment of probability of insurance companies relatedness in implementation of risk-oriented approach," *Economic Studies Journal*, no. 1, pp. 151–173, 2020.

[6] V. Christlein, C. Riess, J. Jordan, C. Riess, and E. Angelopoulou, "An evaluation of popular copy-move forgery detection approaches," *IEEE Transactions on Information Forensics and Security*, vol. 7, no. 6, pp. 1841–1854, Dec. 2012. doi: 10.1109/TIFS.2012.2218597.

[7] I. Amerini, L. Ballan, R. Caldelli, A. Del Bimbo, and G. Serra, "A SIFT-based forensic method for copy–move attack detection and transformation recovery," *IEEE Transactions on Information Forensics and Security*, vol. 6, no. 3, pp. 1099–1110, Sep. 2011. doi: 10.1109/TIFS.2011.2129512.

[8] H.-Y. Huang, and A.-J. Ciou, "Copy-move forgery detection for image forensics using the superpixel segmentation and the Helmert transformation," *EURASIP Journal on Image and Video Processing*, vol. 2019, no. 1, p. 68, Jun. 2019. doi: 10.1186/s13640-019-0469-9.

[9] M. A. Elaskily et al., "A novel deep learning framework for copy-moveforgery detection in images," *Multimed Tools and Applications*, vol. 79, no. 27, pp. 19167–19192, Jul. 2020. doi: 10.1007/s11042-020-08751-7.

[10] S. Kumar, S. K. Gupta, M. Kaur, and U. Gupta, "VI-NET: A hybrid deep convolutional neural network using VGG and inception V3 model for copy-move forgery classification," *Journal of Visual Communication and Image Representation*, vol. 89, p. 103644, Nov. 2022. doi: 10.1016/j.jvcir.2022.103644.

[11] M. Aria, M. Hashemzadeh, and N. Farajzadeh, "QDL-CMFD: A quality-independent and deep learning-based copy-move image forgery detection method," *Neurocomputing*, vol. 511, pp. 213–236, Oct. 2022. doi: 10.1016/j.neucom.2022.09.017.

[12] K. Zhao et al., "CAMU-net: Copy-move forgery detection utilizing coordinate attention and multi-scale feature fusion-based up-sampling," *Expert Systems with Applications*, vol. 238, p. 121918, Mar. 2024. doi: 10.1016/j.eswa.2023.121918.

[13] B. Chaitra, and P. V. Bhaskar Reddy, "An approach for copy-move image multiple forgery detection based on an optimized pre-trained deep learning model," *Knowledge-Based Systems*, vol. 269, p. 110508, Jun. 2023. doi: 10.1016/j.knosys.2023.110508.

[14] M. Roopak, S. Khan, S. Parkinson, and R. Armitage, "Comparison of deep learning classification models for facial image age estimation in digital forensic investigations," *Forensic Science International: Digital Investigation*, vol. 47, p. 301637, Dec. 2023. doi: 10.1016/j.fsidi.2023.301637.

[15] D. Rani, N. S. Gill, and P. Gulia, "A forensic framework to improve digital image evidence administration in IIoT☆," *Journal of Industrial Information Integration*, vol. 38, p. 100568, Mar. 2024. doi: 10.1016/j.jii.2024.100568.

[16] J. Wang et al., "Strong robust copy-move forgery detection network based on layer-by-layer decoupling refinement," *Information Processing & Management*, vol. 61, no. 3, p. 103685, May 2024. doi: 10.1016/j.ipm.2024.103685.

[17] A. U. Shehin, and D. Sankar, "Copy move forgery detection and localisation robust to rotation using block based discrete cosine transform and eigenvalues," *Journal of Visual Communication and Image Representation*, vol. 99, p. 104075, Mar. 2024. doi: 10.1016/j.jvcir.2024.104075.

[18] I. Amerini, L. Ballan, R. Caldelli, A. Del Bimbo, L. Del Tongo, and G. Serra, "Copy-move forgery detection and localization by means of robust clustering with J-Linkage," *Signal Processing: Image Communication*, vol. 28, no. 6, pp. 659–669, Jul. 2013. doi: 10.1016/j.image.2013.03.006.

[19] T. Mahmood, T. Nawaz, A. Irtaza, R. Ashraf, M. Shah, and M. T. Mahmood, "Copy-move forgery detection technique for forensic analysis in digital images," *Mathematical Problems in Engineering*, vol. 2016, p. e8713202, May 2016. doi: 10.1155/2016/8713202.

[20] M. F. Hashmi, A. Hambarde, V. Anand, and A. Keskar, "Passive detection of copy-move forgery using wavelet transforms and SIFT features," *Journal of Information Assurance and Security (JIAS)*, vol. 9, pp. 197–204, Aug. 2014. ISSN 1554-1010.

[21] R. Caldelli, I. Amerini, L. Ballan, G. Serra, M. Barni, and A. Costanzo, "On the effectiveness of local warping against SIFT-based copy-move detection," in *2012 5th International Symposium on Communications, Control and Signal Processing*, 2012, pp. 1–5. doi: 10.1109/ISCCSP.2012.6217846.

[22] W. Ye, Q. Zeng, Y. Peng, Y. Liu, and C.-C. Chang, "A two-stage detection method of copy-move forgery based on parallel feature fusion," *EURASIP Journal on Wireless Communications and Networking*, vol. 2022, no. 1, p. 30, Apr. 2022. doi: 10.1186/s13638-022-02112-8.

[23] N. B. A. Warif, M. Y. I. Idris, A. W. A. Wahab, N.-S. N. Ismail, and R. Salleh, "A comprehensive evaluation procedure for copy-move forgery detection methods: Results from a systematic review," *Multimed Tools and Applications*, vol. 81, no. 11, pp. 15171–15203, May 2022. doi: 10.1007/s11042-022-12010-2.

[24] J.-L. Zhong, Y.-F. Gan, and J.-X. Yang, "Efficient detection of intra/inter-frame video copy-move forgery: A hierarchical coarse-to-fine method," *Journal of Information Security and Applications*, vol. 85, p. 103863, Sep. 2024. doi: 10.1016/j.jisa.2024.103863.

[25] R. Brumnik, T. Klebanova, L. Guryanova, S. Kavun, and O. Trydid, "Simulation of territorial development based on fiscal policy tools," *Mathematical Problems in Engineering*, vol. 2014, no. 1, p. 843976, 2014. doi: 10.1155/2014/843976.

10 Deep Learning Model for Detecting Copy-Move Attack in Images
Testing and Verification

Aleksandra Pauls, Luca Romeo, Riccardo Rosati, Primo Zingaretti, Emanuele Frontoni, and Oleksandr Kuznetsov

10.1 INTRODUCTION

With the development of modern technology and digital imaging tools, photos have become an essential part of our lives. They are used in various fields: journalism, law, military, medicine, culture, news sources, social networks, and many others [1, 2]. Photographs of military and political events, scanned references and documents, hospital documents, X-ray images, photos from exhibitions and presentations, and more. In the age of digitalization, real-life events become a set of pixels, in the form of photo images.

The Internet and social media have also become a growing field. Due to the widespread use of digital devices such as cameras and smartphones, the amount of graphic content circulating on the Internet is constantly increasing every day. On the one hand, this availability of photo creation carries a positive message, as it is now much easier to capture real life. However, on the other hand, advanced software capabilities on smartphones and computers make it easy, even for an inexperienced user, to create a fake image and misinform society [3, 4]. It is also worth noting that it is sometimes physically impossible to distinguish a fake from the original with the human eye.

It is possible to obtain a fake image using various methods, such as copy-move, deleting objects, stitching images, scaling, morphing, retouching, and many others [2, 3]. Copy-move implies that a copy of a certain area of an image is created and moved to a new location [5]. The stitching method implies that the final image consists of parts of other images [6]. Other spoofing attacks use different graphical primitives: scaling allows resizing objects; morphing is created by merging shapes to obtain a new shape; retouching allows changing color, contrast, brightness, and lighting, and hiding visible defects and imperfections in order to improve or modify the original.

Thus, detecting fakes in images is an important task because successful data falsification can mislead others, e.g., devalue intellectual property and copyright, compromise objective journalism, cause reputational and material damage, and entail

 DOI: 10.1201/9781003546153-10

other negative scenarios. The solution to this kind of problem can be the deep learning. The advantage of neural networks is that they independently identify the features of images because, at the moment, there is no effective universal algorithm for detecting fake images that can take into account all the features of the image.

This chapter discusses copy-move attacks and deep learning models to detect them. This new direction of research to protect against such attacks was proposed in [7]. According to data published in [7], the convolutional neural network (CNN) model trained on datasets MICC-F 220, MICC-F 2000, and MICC-F 600 [8] gives the best results on successful copy-move attack detection. The purpose of our chapter is to build a deep learning model to improve and further generalize these results on new unseen dataset.

10.1.1 Contributions of the Chapter

This chapter makes several key contributions to the field of copy-move forgery detection:

1. Comprehensive Analysis: We provide a thorough review and synthesis of state-of-the-art techniques in copy-move forgery detection, encompassing both traditional and deep learning-based approaches. This analysis offers valuable insights into the strengths and limitations of current methods.
2. Novel CNN Architecture: We introduce a new CNN architecture specifically tailored for copy-move forgery detection. This model incorporates innovative feature fusion techniques and attention mechanisms designed to improve detection accuracy and robustness.
3. Extensive Experimental Validation: Our approach is rigorously evaluated on multiple benchmark datasets, including challenging cases that simulate real-world forgery scenarios. This comprehensive testing provides a clear picture of the model's performance across various conditions.
4. Robustness Analysis: We conduct a detailed exploration of the model's performance across various image transformations and post-processing operations. This analysis offers insights into the model's resilience and identifies areas for future improvement.
5. Interpretability Enhancements: We investigate methods to improve the interpretability of our deep learning model's decisions. This work aims to bridge the gap between the black-box nature of deep learning models and the need for explainable forensic evidence.
6. Comparative Study: We provide a thorough comparison of our proposed method against existing state-of-the-art techniques, offering a clear perspective on the advancements made by our approach.

10.1.2 Organization of the Chapter

The remainder of this chapter is organized as follows:

Section 10.2: Literature Review—This section provides a comprehensive review of related work in copy-move forgery detection. We trace the evolution of detection techniques from early handcrafted feature approaches to recent deep learning-based methods.

Section 10.3: Methodology—Here, we detail our proposed methodology, including the architecture of our deep learning model and the rationale behind its design. We describe the novel components of our approach and how they address the challenges identified in current methods.

Section 10.4: Experimental Setup and Results—This section presents our experimental framework, including dataset descriptions, implementation details, and evaluation metrics. We then provide a comprehensive presentation of our results, including comparisons with existing methods.

Section 10.5: Discussion—In this section, we offer a thorough analysis of our findings. We discuss the implications of our results, the strengths and limitations of our approach, and potential areas for future research.

Section 10.6: Conclusion—The chapter concludes with a summary of our contributions and their significance to the field of copy-move forgery detection. We also outline promising directions for future work in this rapidly evolving area of digital image forensics.

Through this structured approach, we aim to provide a comprehensive exploration of our novel method for copy-move forgery detection, contextualizing our work within the broader landscape of digital image forensics and offering valuable insights for both researchers and practitioners in the field.

10.2 RELATED WORKS

Copy-move forgery detection has been an active area of research in digital image forensics for over a decade. Early seminal work in this field emerged from the Images and Communication Lab at the University of Florence. Amerini et al. (2010, 2011) [9, 10] proposed an influential methodology based on Scale Invariant Feature Transform (SIFT) features to detect and localize copy-move forgeries. Their approach demonstrated robustness to various geometric transformations applied during the forgery process.

Building on this foundation, several researchers extended and refined SIFT-based techniques. Caldelli et al. (2012) [11] investigated the effectiveness of local warping attacks against SIFT-based detection, highlighting potential vulnerabilities. Amerini et al. (2013) [12] introduced a robust clustering approach using J-Linkage to improve forgery localization, particularly for challenging cases involving distant copied regions. The same year, Amerini et al. (2013) [13] explored counter-forensic techniques, proposing methods to classify and selectively remove SIFT key points to evade detection.

While SIFT remained a dominant approach, other researchers began exploring complementary techniques. Hashmi et al. (2014) [14] combined wavelet transforms with SIFT features, leveraging multi-resolution analysis to enhance detection performance. Prajapati et al. (2015) [6] integrated the RANSAC algorithm with SIFT matching to improve the accuracy of tampered region localization.

As the field matured, several comprehensive surveys emerged, synthesizing the growing body of literature. Warif et al. (2016) [15] provided an extensive overview of copy-move forgery detection techniques, categorizing approaches based on block-based and keypoint-based feature extraction methods. More recently, Nabi et al. (2022) [16] conducted a broader survey covering both image and video forgery detection, situating copy-move techniques within the larger landscape of multimedia forensics.

The advent of deep learning techniques has opened new avenues for copy-move forgery detection, marking a significant shift from hand-crafted feature extraction to learned representations. Elaskily et al. (2020) [7] proposed a convolutional neural network (CNN) architecture specifically designed for this task, demonstrating impressive performance across multiple benchmark datasets. Building on this foundation, Zhang et al. (2022) [17] introduced a Feature Compensation Network (FCNet) that addresses the challenge of detecting manipulations with arbitrary parameters. Their approach incorporates feature enhancement, sensitivity estimation, and adaptive average pooling to improve detection accuracy in complex scenarios.

In recent years, there has been a surge in innovative approaches to copy-move forgery detection. Lin et al. (2024) [18] proposed a novel scheme based on Regional Density Center (RDC) clustering and Refined Length Homogeneity Filtering (RLHF). Their method employs scale normalization and contrast threshold adjustment to obtain adequate key points in challenging image areas, demonstrating improved effectiveness and robustness on public datasets. Shehin and Sankar (2024) [19] developed an algorithm utilizing Discrete Cosine Transform and eigenvalues to detect and localize copy-move duplications, showing particular resilience to post-processing rotation attacks. Wang et al. (2024) [20] introduced the Strong Robust Copy-Move Forgery Detection Network (DRNet), which employs a layer-by-layer decoupling refinement approach to extract semantically irrelevant shallow information, achieving state-of-the-art performance on multiple datasets.

As digital manipulation tools continue to evolve, so too do forensic techniques. Zhong et al. (2024) [21] proposed a Hierarchical Coarse-to-Fine framework for video copy-move forgery detection, addressing challenges in both intra-frame and inter-frame forgeries. Their approach demonstrates improved efficiency and accuracy, even under various adverse conditions. These recent advancements reflect the field's ongoing efforts to improve detection accuracy, computational efficiency, and robustness to various post-processing operations and anti-forensic techniques. As the complexity of digital forgeries increases, research in this domain remains critical for ensuring the integrity and authenticity of digital media across various applications, from social media to legal evidence.

The most interesting in our opinion is the work [7], in which the authors proposed the use of deep learning methods for the automatic detection of copy-move forgeries. In this work, a specially developed CNN was trained on the most common datasets. The results published in [7] look very encouraging. For example, the authors report that 100% accuracy was achieved for all the datasets studied.

The purpose of our chapter is to independently verify the results from [7] as well as the conclusions and deductions made by the authors. In addition, we are analyzing the architecture of CNN and the conclusions drawn as a result may be a reason to improve the model and for developing new CNN architectures for copy-move attack detection.

10.3 METHODOLOGY

The deep learning model given in [7] is based on the multilayer CNN architecture, which consists in alternating convolution layers and pooling layers. In convolution layers, each image fragment is multiplied step by step by a special matrix (convolution kernel), the obtained result is summarized and written in the same position of the output image. Thus, at each convolution layer there is a transition from specific image features to more abstract details. The abstraction increases from layer to layer, culminating in the isolation of high-level abstract concepts. Intuitively, this process can be described as "pattern recognition," and in the process of learning, the network adjusts itself to highlight salient features while filtering out unimportant details of the image.

A simplified architecture of CNN is shown in Figure 10.1.

Thus, CNN is based on the convolution operation. When the network is trained, the image is processed in fragments. Each fragment is sequentially multiplied by a convolution kernel (or filter), which is shifted across the image. The values are then summed, and the result is written to the corresponding position of the output image (Figure 10.1). However, the use of such convolution leads to the extraction of too many selected features. To reduce these features, layers of subsampling (pooling) are used. As a result, a full-coherent layer is formed, where the probability distribution for different classes is performed based on the obtained data.

The advantages of convolutional neural networks include the possibility to reduce the number of trained parameters and increase the training speed, compared with the fully connected (FC) network, the possibility of parallel computing and implementation of network training algorithms on graphics processors (GPUs), as well as stability to shifting the object position in the input data [22–24].

10.3.1 The Copy-Move Forgery Detection (CMFD) Network

The Copy-Move Forgery Detection (CMFD) algorithm is proposed in [7]. It is based on CNN architecture.

The CNN architecture from [7] is schematically presented in Figure 10.2. It contains six convolution and MaxPooling layers, as well as the final merging operation using Global Average Pooling (GAP) [7]:

- CNV 1 (No. of samples, 224, 224, 16);
- Pooling 1 (No. of samples, 112, 112, 16);

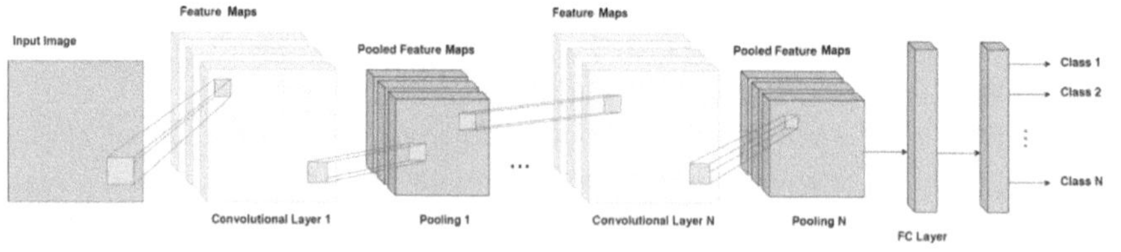

FIGURE 10.1 A simplified architecture of CNN.

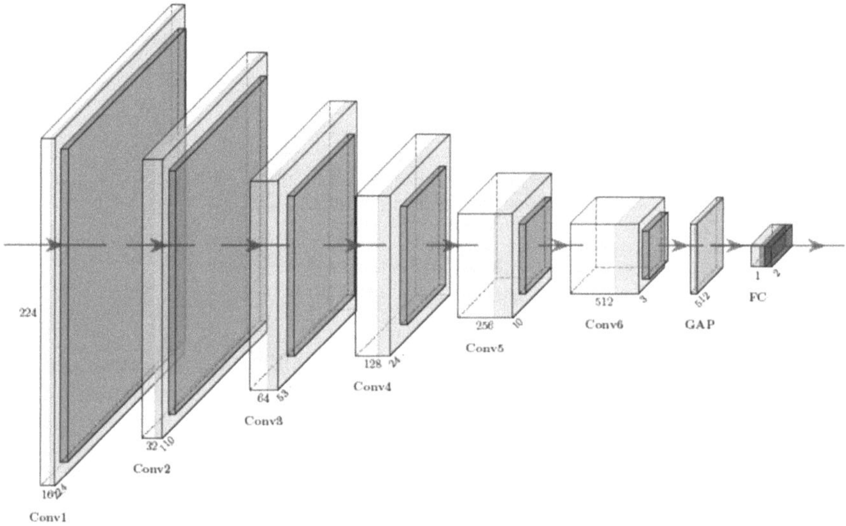

FIGURE 10.2 The architecture of the CNN model from [7].

- CNV 2 (No. of samples, 110, 110, 32);
- Pooling 2 (No. of samples, 55, 55, 32);
- CNV 3 (No. of samples, 53, 53, 64);
- Pooling 3 (No. of samples, 26, 26, 64);
- CNV 4 (No. of samples, 24, 24, 128);
- Pooling 4 (No. of samples, 12, 12, 128);
- CNV 5 (No. of samples, 10, 10, 256);
- Pooling 5 (No. of samples, 5, 5, 256);
- CNV 6 (No. of samples, 3, 3, 512);
- Pooling 6 (No. of samples, 1, 1, 512);
- Global Average Layer (No. of samples, 512);
- Dense (No. of samples, 2).

Traditionally, GAP is used to replace FC layers in classic CNNs. Instead of adding FC layers on top of object maps, the average value of each object map is used. The resulting vector is transferred directly to the softmax activation function. In this model, GAP and Dense layers are used as an FC layer [7].

Convolutional layers (CNV) are designed to extract features from the image through their filters. A different number of filters are used:

- 16 filters are used for the CNV 1;
- 32 filters are used for the CNV 2;
- 64 filters are used for the CNV 3;
- 128 filters are used for the CNV 4;
- 256 filters are used for the CNV 5;
- 512 filters are used for the CNV 6.

The final FC layer has a softmax activation function and is used to classify each class. This activation function is usually used for multiclass classification problems since it distributes the probability among several categories. However, in [7] this activation function is used for binary classification:

- First Class—the original image (without copy-move attack tampering);
- Second Class—fake image (detected fake copy-move attack).

Adaptive Moment Estimation (Adam) was used to train the neural network in [7]. It is an optimization method algorithm for gradient descent, which is effective when dealing with a large problem involving a large number of data or parameters. In its essence, Adam is a combination of the "gradient descent with momentum" and "Root mean square prop" (RMSP) algorithm [25]. A cross-entropy (or logarithmic loss function—LogLoss) was used as a loss function to quantify the difference between the probability distributions [7].

Cross-entropy is defined as [26]:

$$H(p,q) = -\sum_{x} p(x)\ log(q(x)),$$

where p—is the distribution of true responses, a q—the distribution of model prediction probabilities.

For the case of binary classification (as in our case), the formula for calculating cross-entropy will look like this:

$$LogLoss = -\ (ylog(p) + \ (1-y)log(1-p)) = \begin{cases} -log(p), y=1, \\ -log(1-p), y=0, \end{cases}, \qquad (10.1)$$

where—the binary indicator (0 or 1) of true answers.

The base of the logarithm specifies the unit of measurement. Typically, a binary basis is used, and cross-entropy measures the average number of bits needed to recognize an event from a feature set.

The article [7] did not specify what values were used for packet length and learning rate. Therefore, we tested these parameters for different values:

- Batch Size—8, 16, 32, and 64;
- Learning Rate—0.01, 0.001, and 0.0001.

Our final implementation used: batch size—16, learning rate—0.001. We have validated these hyper-parameters in a separate validation set.

As an experiment, we also implemented model improvement through cross-validation k-fold. The data were not separated into a training and validation sample. Instead, the entire dataset was divided into folds, each of which became a test sample in turn.

10.3.2 Binary Classification Performance Metrics

The problem of copy-move attack detection belongs to the classical binary classification problem [27–29]. It consists in matching each element to one of two groups (classes) based on some rule or feature. In other words, we need to match some image to one of the two groups:

- Class 0 for original images ("negative," no fakes);
- Class 1 for spoofed images ("positive," there is a spoof).

The classification problem can be solved correctly (when an element is correctly matched to its class) or incorrectly. We have four possible outcomes for binary classification (see Table 10.1). Table 10.1 shows the confusion matrix, also known as the error matrix [30]. The color behind Table 10.1 highlights the erroneous outcomes. Table 10.1 is labeled:

- Total Population. It is a set of similar items or events of interest for a particular question or experiment. In our case, it is the total number of images as the sum of the number of images containing a fake (from class 1) and the number of images not containing a fake (from class 0);
- Predicted Condition. These are positive and negative predicted states.

When real states and predicted states overlap, we get four possible binary classification results:

- True Positive (*TP*)—when *P* and *PP* intersect (correctly classified fake image);
- True Negative (*TN*)—when *N* and *PN* intersect (the original image is correctly classified);
- False Positive (*FP*)—when *N* and *PP* intersect (misclassified the original image as a fake). This outcome is also known as a "Type I error" or "false alarm";

TABLE 10.1
Possible Outcomes of Binary Classification

		Predicted condition	
	Total population $P+N$	Positive (*PP*) (belong to class 1)	Negative (*PN*) (belong to class 0)
Actual state	Positive (*P*) (belong to class 1)	True Positive (*TP*)	False Negative (*FN*)
	Negative (*N*) (belong to class 0)	False Positive (*FP*)	True Negative (*TN*)

- False Negative (FN)—when P and PN intersect (mistakenly classified the fake image as original). This outcome is also known as "type II error" or "missed target."

Errors of the first and second kind are mutually symmetric, that is, if we swap the hypotheses about "positive" and "negative" (invert the notation "0" and "1" for classes of elements), then errors of the first kind will turn into errors of the second kind and vice versa.

For each possible case, let us define the metric of binary classification efficiency as the frequency of the corresponding events:

- True Positive Rate (TPR) outcomes (this metric is also called sensitivity) refers to the probability of a positive state, provided that it is actually positive, i.e.

$$TPR = \frac{TP}{P} = 1 - FNR, \tag{10.2}$$

- False Negative Rate (FNR) outcomes is the proportion of positive results that produce negative results, i.e.

$$FNR = \frac{FN}{P} = 1 - TPR, \tag{10.3}$$

- False Positive Rate (FPR) outcomes is the proportion of all negative results that produce positive classification results, i.e.

$$FPR = \frac{FP}{N} = 1 - TNR, \tag{10.4}$$

- True Negative Rate (TNR) outcomes refers to the probability of a negative test result, if it is indeed negative, i.e.

$$TNR = \frac{TN}{N} = 1 - FPR, \tag{10.5}$$

In addition to metrics (10.1)–(10.4), [7] also uses an accuracy. This is a statistical indicator of how well the binary classification test correctly identifies or excludes a condition. In other words, accuracy is the share of correct predictions (both true positives and true negatives) among the total number of cases considered.

$$\text{Accuracy} = \frac{TP + TN}{P + N}, \tag{10.6}$$

In our work, we also evaluated the measure as a harmonic mean of accuracy and sensitivity:

$$F_1 = \frac{2TP}{2TP + FP + FN}, \tag{10.7}$$

The highest possible value F_1 is 1.0, which indicates perfect accuracy and sensitivity, and the lowest possible value is 0 if the accuracy or sensitivity is zero.

Thus, we will use logarithmic loss function (10.1) as the main indicators of binary classification efficiency, as well as metrics (10.2)–(10.7), which characterize sensitivity, accuracy, and other properties of the model.

10.3.3 Datasets

In the article [7], several datasets were used to train and test the deep learning model. In particular, sets MICC-F220, MICC-F2000, and MICC-F600, given on the site of the research group Images and Communication Lab of the Media Integration and Communication Center (MICC) [8], were used:

- The MICC-F220 dataset consists of 220 images: 110 original images and 110 fake images. The images range in size from 722×480 to 800×600 pixels;
- The MICC-F600 dataset contains 760 photographic images, of which 440 original and 160 fake images were used. The dataset also contains 160 images of the ground-truth masks, where areas of duplicate parts are highlighted, but they were not used in the experiments due to their unsuitability for the task. The size of the images varies from 800×533 to 2014×3039 pixels;
- The MICC-F2000 dataset contains 2000 images: 1300 original and 700 fake images. Resolution: 1536×2048 or 2048×1536 pixels depending on image orientation.

Examples of original and fake images are shown in Figures 10.3, 10.4, and 10.5.

FIGURE 10.3 Examples of original and fake images from MICC-F220 dataset.

FIGURE 10.3 (Continued)

FIGURE 10.4 Examples of original and fake images from MICC-F600 dataset.

The main ways to produce fake photo images are to use copy-move attacks combining scaling and rotating the corresponding areas. For MICC-F220 and MICC-F2000 the shape of the regions is rectangular, and for MICC-F600 the shape of the regions is streamlined. In addition, the authors of [7] used new sets obtained by combining

FIGURE 10.5 Examples of original and fake images from MICC-F2000 dataset.

and merging the MICC-F220, MICC-F2000, and MICC-F600 sets. All images were pretreated by resizing the image to 224×224 pixels, without cropping. After that they were normalized.

10.4 EXPERIMENTAL SETUP AND RESULTS

Our implementation of the deep learning model from [7] is available on the open source GitHub https://github.com/raurica/Image-Forgery.git, which facilitates reproduction and verification of our results. When implementing the model, we used Google Colaboratory platform (Python 3 server gas pedal based on Google Compute Engine, 12.68 GB RAM, 107.72 GB disk).

Tables 10.2–10.5 show the results of model training (state-of-the-art model [7]) on different datasets for 15, 25, 35, 50, 75, and 100 epochs.

For each dataset, the results were calculated using formulas (10.1)–(10.7). We give cross-entropy values (10.1) for both training and validation stages.

By analogy with [7] we also measured the testing time (T1), as the average time for checking images for k rounds of the testing operation, as well as the total testing time (T2). The values of this indicator are given in the last lines of Tables 10.2–10.5.

TABLE 10.2
Model Training Results on the MICC-F220 Dataset (State-of-the-Art Model [7])

	15 Epochs	25 Epochs	35 Epochs	50 Epochs	75 Epochs	100 Epochs
(1) V_loss	1.0182	0.5336	0.6452	0.8371	0.6447	0.8515
(1) T_loss	0.2422	0.1265	0.1126	0.1257	0.0881	0.0511
(2) TPR	1.0	1.0	1.0	1.0	1.0	1.0
(3) FNR	0.0	0.0	0.0	0.0	0.0	0.0
(4) FPR	0.4545	0.1818	0.1818	0.1818	0.1818	0.1818
(5) TNR	0.5455	0.8182	0.8182	0.8182	0.8182	0.8182
(6) Acc	0.7727	0.9091	0.9091	0.9091	0.9091	0.9091
(7) F1	0.815	0.917	0.917	0.917	0.917	0.917
T1	47ms/step	46ms/step	44ms/step	45ms/step	54ms/step	52ms/step
T2	4.516 sec	11.343 sec	9.21 sec	21.532 sec	21.918 sec	41.967 sec

TABLE 10.3
Model Training Results on the MICC-F600 Dataset (State-of-the-Art Model [7])

	15 Epochs	25 Epochs	35 Epochs	50 Epochs	75 Epochs	100 Epochs
(1) V_loss	0.6149	0.7624	2.2725	3.0485	3.2168	4.2186
(1) T_loss	0.2695	0.1957	0.0077	0.0023	0.0064	0.0009
(2) TPR	0.875	0.625	0.875	0.875	0.875	0.875
(3) FNR	0.125	0.375	0.125	0.125	0.125	0.125
(4) FPR	0.2955	0.1364	0.1591	0.1818	0.25	0.2045
(5) TNR	0.7045	0.8636	0.8409	0.8182	0.75	0.7955
(6) Acc	0.75	0.8	0.85	0.8333	0.7833	0.8167
(7) F1	0.651	0.625	0.757	0.737	0.683	0.718
T1	32ms/step	26ms/step	23ms/step	40ms/step	27ms/step	31ms/step
T2	10.29 sec	21.655 sec	18.8 sec	42.509 sec	38.537 sec	83.052 sec

For clarity, Figures 10.6–10.8 are plots of accuracy and loss function on the training and validation set for each dataset.

Tables 10.6, 10.7, and 10.8 compare our results with the results from [7].

The learning procedure was stopped in the maximum number of epochs. The dataset was split by using train_test_split function. In this way we divide the dataset into random train and test subsets where the test subset was 20%. Also, we tested different values of batch size (8, 16, 32, 64) and learning rate (0.01, 0.001, 0.0001), and then chose the best ones from them. It used the following hyper-parameters: batch size—16, learning rate—0.001.

TABLE 10.4
Model Training Results on the MICC-F2000 Dataset (State-of-the-Art Model [7])

	15 Epochs	25 Epochs	35 Epochs	50 Epochs	75 Epochs	100 Epochs
(1) V_loss	0.6541	0.1394	0.1761	0.1772	0.1809	0.1329
(1) T_loss	0.6464	0.0524	0.0424	0.0365	0.0111	0.0351
(2) TPR	0.0	1.0	1.0	0.9583	0.9444	0.9722
(3) FNR	1.0	0.0	0.0	0.0417	0.0556	0.0278
(4) FPR	0.0	0.0938	0.0938	0.0469	0.0234	0.0312
(5) TNR	1.0	0.9062	0.9062	0.9531	0.9766	0.9688
(6) Acc	0.64	0.94	0.94	0.955	0.965	0.97
(7) F1	0.0	0.923	0.923	0.939	0.951	0.959
T1	20ms/step	20ms/step	20ms/step	20ms/step	26ms/step	27ms/step
T2	25.818 sec	43.408 sec	60.935 sec	84.869 sec	143.96 sec	203.78 sec

TABLE 10.5
Model Training Results on the Merged Dataset from MICC-F220, MICC-F600, and MICC-F2000 (State-of-the-Art Model [7])

	15 Epochs	25 Epochs	35 Epochs	50 Epochs	75 Epochs	100 Epochs
(1) V_loss	0.2967	0.2549	0.2427	0.3140	0.4926	0.4529
(1) T_loss	0.1089	0.0723	0.0865	0.0434	0.0332	0.0198
(2) TPR	0.9505	0.9703	0.9208	0.9406	0.9406	0.9307
(3) FNR	0.0495	0.0297	0.0792	0.0594	0.0594	0.0693
(4) FPR	0.1159	0.0797	0.0725	0.1014	0.1087	0.0942
(5) TNR	0.8841	0.9203	0.9275	0.8986	0.8913	0.9058
(6) Acc	0.9121	0.9414	0.9456	0.9163	0.9121	0.9163
(7) F_1	0.901	0.933	0.912	0.905	0.9	0.904
T1	21ms/step	21ms/step	27ms/step	21ms/step	27ms/step	28ms/step
T2	33.704 sec	65.602 sec	83.991 sec	102.279 sec	203.964 sec	264.012 sec

In addition, in Tables 10.9, 10.10, and 10.11, by analogy with the paper [7] we also give the results of comparisons by metrics (10.2)–(10.5), these results are related to the test set.

It should be recognized that the general trends and patterns hold; the CNN from [7] is truly capable of correctly classifying images from the MICC-F220, MICC-F600, and MICC-F2000 datasets.

Figure 10.9 shows examples of image classification from the validation sample (the model provides the probability that the image belongs to a particular class).

As we can see from the test results and the preceding examples, the deep learning model from [7] does correctly classify most of the images from the validation

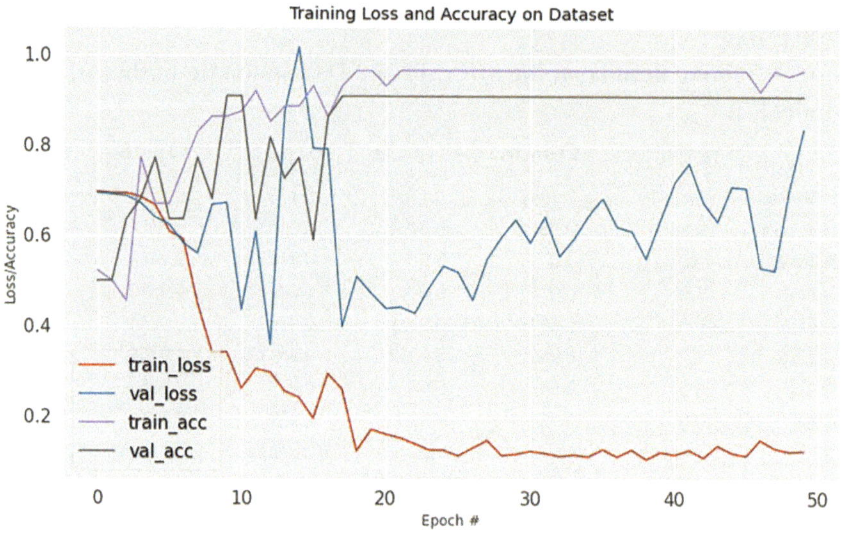

FIGURE 10.6 Accuracy and loss plots on the MICC-F220 dataset (50 epochs).

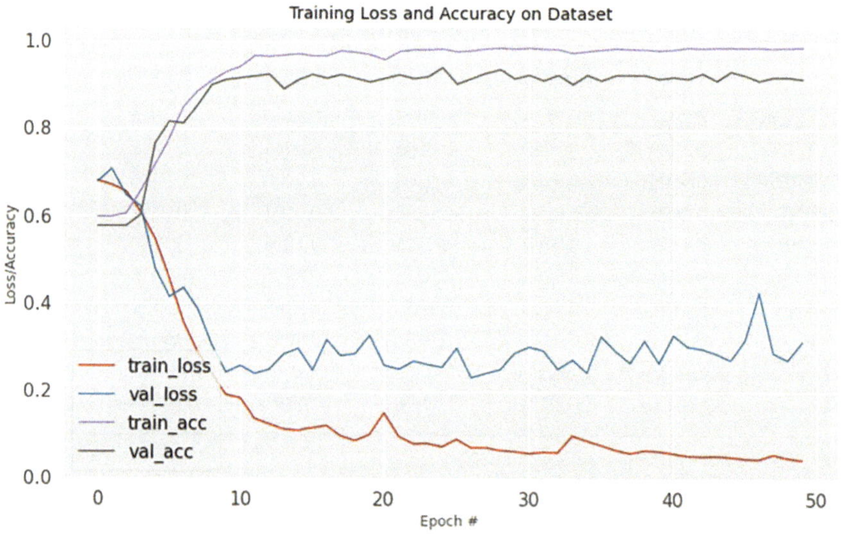

FIGURE 10.7 Accuracy and loss plots on the MICC-F2000 dataset (50 epochs).

sample. However, if we use images not from the validation sample for testing, the results will be significantly different. As an example, we generated several examples of pairs over to "original-fake" images. For each example we obtained classification results (see Figure 10.9).

As we can see from the preceding examples, the deep learning model from [7] may not correctly detect images that were not included in the validation sample at all.

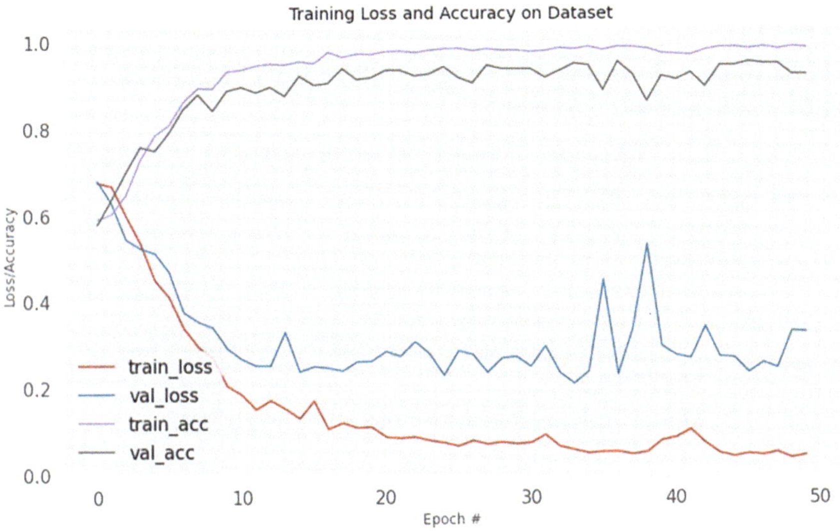

FIGURE 10.8 Accuracy and loss plots on the merged dataset from MICC-F220, MICC-F600, and MICC-F2000 (50 epochs).

TABLE 10.6
Model Training Results on the MICC-F220 Dataset

		15 Epochs	25 Epochs	35 Epochs	50 Epochs	75 Epochs	100 Epochs
Our work	(1) V_loss	1.0182	0.5336	0.6452	0.8371	0.6447	0.8515
	(6) Acc	0.7727	0.9091	0.9091	0.9091	0.9091	0.9091
[7]	(1) V_loss	7.82	3.85	2.38	0	0	0
	(6) Acc	0.9218	0.9615	0.9762	1.00	1.00	1.00

TABLE 10.7
Model Training Results on the MICC-F600 Dataset

		15 Epochs	25 Epochs	35 Epochs	50 Epochs	75 Epochs	100 Epochs
Our work	(1) V_loss	0.6149	0.7624	2.2725	3.0485	3.2168	4.2186
	(6) Acc	0.75	0.8	0.85	0.8333	0.7833	0.8167
[7]	(1) V_loss	7.84	5.88	3.92	0	0	0
	(6) Acc	0.9215	0.9412	0.9608	1.00	1.00	1.00

Original image (MICC-F220), Class 0. Obtained probabilities: for class 0 – 0.999, for class 1 – 0.001	Image fake (MICC-F220), class 1. Obtained probabilities: for class 0 – 0.004, for class 1 – 0.996
Original image (MICC-F600), class 0. Obtained probabilities: for class 0 – 0.981, for class 1 – 0.019	Image fake (MICC-F600), Class 1. Obtained probabilities: for class 0 – 0.001, for class 1 – 0.999
Original image (MICC-F2000), Class 0. Obtained probabilities: for class 0 – 0.992, for class 1 – 0.008	Image fake (MICC-F2000), class 1. Obtained probabilities: for class 0 – 0.017, for class 1 – 0.983

TABLE 10.8
Model Training Results on the Merged Dataset from MICC-F220, MICC-F600, and MICC-F2000

		15 Epochs	25 Epochs	35 Epochs	50 Epochs	75 Epochs	100 Epochs
Our work	(1) V_loss	0.2967	0.2549	0.2427	0.3140	0.4926	0.4529
	(6) Acc	0.9121	0.9414	0.9456	0.9163	0.9121	0.9163
[7]	(1) V_loss	6.43	5.00	2.14	1.43	0	0
	(6) Acc	0.9357	0.9500	0.9786	0.9857	1.00	1.00

TABLE 10.9
Model Training Results on the MICC-F220 Dataset

	[10]	[12]	[7]	Our work
(2) TPR	1.0	1.0	1.00	1.0
(3) FNR	0	0	0	0.0
(4) FPR	0	0.06	0	0.1818
(5) TNR	1.0	0.94	1.00	0.8182

TABLE 10.10
Model Training Results on the MICC-F600 Dataset

	[10]	[12]	[7]	Our work
(2) TPR	0.692	0.816	1.00	0.875
(3) FNR	0.308	0.184	0	0.125
(4) FPR	0.125	0.0727	0	0.1818
(5) TNR	0.875	0.9273	1.00	0.8182

TABLE 10.11
Model Training Results on the MICC-F2000 Dataset

	[10]	[12]	[7]	Our work
(2) TPR	0.9342	0.9486	1.00	0.9583
(3) FNR	0.0658	0.0514	0	0.0417
(4) FPR	0.1161	0.0915	0	0.0469
(5) TNR	0.8839	0.9085	1.00	0.9531

Original image, class 0. Obtained probabilities: for class 0 – 0.999, for class 1 – 0.001	Image fake, class 1. Obtained probabilities: for class 0 – 0.999, for class 1 – 0.001
Original image, class 0. Obtained probabilities: for class 0 – 0.383, for class 1 – 0.616	Image fake, class 1. Obtained probabilities: for class 0 – 0.413, for class 1 – 0.587
Original image, class 0. Obtained probabilities: for class 0 – 0.431, for class 1 – 0.569	Image fake, class 1. Obtained probabilities: for class 0 – 0.763, for class 1 – 0.237

FIGURE 10.9 Examples of image classification from a validation set.

10.5 DISCUSSION

The results of this study provide valuable insights into the performance and limitations of deep learning models for detecting copy-move forgery in images. While the convolutional neural network approach proposed by Elaskily et al. [7] showed promise on the MICC datasets, our independent implementation and testing revealed several key issues that warrant further investigation.

First, the accuracy metrics we obtained, though reasonably high, fell short of the near-perfect results reported in the original study. For example, on the MICC-F220 dataset, we achieved 90.91% accuracy after 50 epochs, compared to the reported 100%. This discrepancy could stem from differences in implementation details or hyperparameter settings not fully specified in [7]. More importantly, it highlights the challenge of reproducing state-of-the-art results in deep learning research—a growing concern in the field [31].

Second, our analysis of the loss function trajectories uncovered clear signs of overfitting, particularly on the smaller datasets. The divergence between training and validation loss as training progressed indicates the model was essentially memorizing training examples rather than learning generalizable features. This overfitting likely explains the model's poor performance on novel images outside the validation set, as demonstrated in our additional tests (Figure 10.10).

The model's inability to reliably detect forgeries in images dissimilar to its training data is perhaps the most significant limitation revealed by our study. While achieving 90%+ accuracy on held-out data from the same distribution is impressive, it falls short of the robustness needed for real-world forensic applications. Adversaries could likely circumvent detection by using image manipulation techniques that differ from those in the training set.

These findings underscore the importance of diverse, large-scale datasets for developing practically useful forgery detection models. The MICC datasets, while valuable, appear insufficient to capture the full spectrum of possible copy-move forgeries. Future work should focus on curating more comprehensive datasets that encompass a wider range of image types, forgery techniques, and post-processing operations.

Additionally, architectural innovations may be necessary to improve the model's generalization capabilities. Techniques like transfer learning from models pre-trained on large natural image datasets could potentially help the network learn more robust, semantic features less prone to overfitting. Exploring alternative neural network architectures designed for anomaly detection, rather than binary classification, may also prove fruitful.

In conclusion, while deep learning shows promise for copy-move forgery detection, significant challenges remain in developing models that generalize beyond their training distribution. Our results suggest that claims of near-perfect accuracy on standard datasets should be interpreted cautiously, as they may not translate to real-world performance. Advancing the field will require not only algorithmic innovations, but also more rigorous evaluation protocols that assess models on diverse, previously unseen forgeries.

FIGURE 10.10 Examples of image classification from a validation set.

10.6 CONCLUSIONS

Based on the results obtained, we can conclude that, from a practical point of view, the approach to solving the problem of classification of original and fake images requires improvement. We confirm the main results and regularities obtained by the authors [7] using the MICC-F220, MICC-F600, and MICC-F2000 datasets. Although our results for metrics (10.2)–(10.6) are a bit worse than what was declared in [7], it should however be recognized that the deep learning model considered does allow us to detect some fake images.

For a detailed analysis of the results, we should pay attention to the significant difference in the values of (10.1). The logarithmic loss function in our experiments is significantly higher than the results from [7]. In Tables 10.1–10.7 we specifically show the cross-entropy values calculated for the training and validation samples. While the cross-entropy in the training sample decreases (as it should), the values of the loss function in the validation sample may increase. The cross-entropy dependencies demonstrate the effect of overfitting, where the model has essentially memorized examples from the training sample and is unable to extract the key features necessary for correct prediction. In support of this thesis, we gave several examples (see Figure 10.10) where third-party images (not from the validation sample) are not correctly detected.

Thus, the use of deep learning models to detect copy-move attacks requires further justification. To build a universal protection mechanism, it is necessary to significantly extend the datasets and consider the peculiarities of the attack.

10.7 ACKNOWLEDGEMENT

- This project has received funding from the European Union's Horizon 2020 research and innovation program under the Marie Skłodowska-Curie grant agreement No. 101007820 - TRUST. This publication reflects only the author's view, and the REA is not responsible for any use that may be made of the information it contains.
- This research was funded by the European Union—NextGenerationEU under the Italian Ministry of University and Research (MIUR), National Innovation Ecosystem grant ECS 00000041-VITALITY-CUP D83C 22000710005.

REFERENCES

[1] R. Ridzoň, and D. Levický, "Multimedia security and multimedia content protection," in *2009 International Symposium ELMAR*, Sep. 2009, pp. 105–108.

[2] W. Zhu, X. Wang, and W. Gao, "Multimedia intelligence: When multimedia meets artificial intelligence," *IEEE Transactions on Multimedia*, vol. 22, no. 7, pp. 1823–1835, Jul. 2020, doi: 10.1109/TMM.2020.2969791.

[3] I. Amerini, A. Anagnostopoulos, L. Maiano, and L. R. Celsi, "Deep learning for multimedia forensics," *FNT in Computer Graphics and Vision*, vol. 12, no. 4, pp. 309–457, 2021, doi: 10.1561/0600000096.

[4] V. T. Covello, "Social media and the changing landscape for risk, high concern, and crisis communication," in *Communicating in Risk, Crisis, and High Stress Situations:*

Evidence-Based Strategies and Practice, IEEE, 2022, pp. 385–410, doi: 10.1002/97811 19081753.ch13.

[5] T. Mahmood, T. Nawaz, A. Irtaza, R. Ashraf, M. Shah, and M. T. Mahmood, "Copy-move forgery detection technique for forensic analysis in digital images," *Mathematical Problems in Engineering*, vol. 2016, p. e8713202, May 2016, doi: 10.1155/2016/8713202.

[6] B. M. Prajapati, N. P. Desai, and E. Dept, "Forensic analysis of digital image tampering," *International Journal For Technological Research in Engineering*, vol. 2, no. 10, p. 5, Jun. 2015.

[7] M. A. Elaskily et al., "A novel deep learning framework for copy-moveforgery detection in images," *Multimed Tools and Applications*, vol. 79, no. 27, pp. 19167–19192, Jul. 2020, doi: 10.1007/s11042-020-08751-7.

[8] ICL—Images and Communication Lab, *Department of Information Engineering (DINFO) of the University of Florence, Image and Communication Laboratory.* Accessed: Jun. 22, 2022. [Online]. http://lci.micc.unifi.it/labd/team/.

[9] I. Amerini, L. Ballan, R. Caldelli, A. Del Bimbo, and G. Serra, "Geometric tampering estimation by means of a SIFT-based forensic analysis," in *2010 IEEE International Conference on Acoustics, Speech and Signal Processing*, Mar. 2010, pp. 1702–1705, doi: 10.1109/ICASSP.2010.5495485.

[10] I. Amerini, L. Ballan, R. Caldelli, A. Del Bimbo, and G. Serra, "A SIFT-based forensic method for copy–move attack detection and transformation recovery," *IEEE Transactions on Information Forensics and Security*, vol. 6, no. 3, pp. 1099–1110, Sep. 2011, doi: 10.1109/TIFS.2011.2129512.

[11] R. Caldelli, I. Amerini, L. Ballan, G. Serra, M. Barni, and A. Costanzo, "On the effectiveness of local warping against SIFT-based copy-move detection," in *2012 5th International Symposium on Communications, Control and Signal Processing*, 2012, pp. 1–5, doi: 10.1109/ISCCSP.2012.6217846.

[12] I. Amerini, L. Ballan, R. Caldelli, A. Del Bimbo, L. Del Tongo, and G. Serra, "Copy-move forgery detection and localization by means of robust clustering with J-linkage," *Signal Processing: Image Communication*, vol. 28, no. 6, pp. 659–669, Jul. 2013, doi: 10.1016/j.image.2013.03.006.

[13] I. Amerini, M. Barni, R. Caldelli, and A. Costanzo, "Counter-forensics of SIFT-based copy-move detection by means of keypoint classification," *Journal on Image and Video Processing*, vol. 2013, no. 1, p. 18, Apr. 2013, doi: 10.1186/1687-5281-2013-18.

[14] M. F. Hashmi, A. Hambarde, V. Anand, and A. Keskar, "Passive detection of copy-move forgery using wavelet transforms and SIFT features," *Journal of Information Assurance and Security(JIAS)*, vol. 9, pp. 197–204, Aug. 2014. ISSN 1554-1010.

[15] N. B. A. Warif et al., "Copy-move forgery detection: Survey, challenges and future directions," *Journal of Network and Computer Applications*, vol. 75, pp. 259–278, Nov. 2016, doi: 10.1016/j.jnca.2016.09.008.

[16] S. T. Nabi, M. Kumar, P. Singh, N. Aggarwal, and K. Kumar, "A comprehensive survey of image and video forgery techniques: Variants, challenges, and future directions," *Multimedia Systems*, vol. 28, no. 3, pp. 939–992, Jun. 2022, doi: 10.1007/s00530-021-00873-8.

[17] Y. Zhang, Y. Yan, and G. Feng, "Feature compensation network based on non-uniform quantization of channels for digital image global manipulation forensics," *Signal Processing: Image Communication*, vol. 107, p. 116795, Sep. 2022, doi: 10.1016/j.image.2022.116795.

[18] C. Lin, Y. Wu, K. Huang, H. Yang, Y. Deng, and Y. Wen, "Copy-move forgery detection using regional density center clustering," *Journal of Visual Communication and Image Representation*, vol. 103, p. 104221, Aug. 2024, doi: 10.1016/j.jvcir.2024.104221.

[19] A. U. Shehin, and D. Sankar, "Copy move forgery detection and localisation robust to rotation using block based discrete cosine transform and eigenvalues," *Journal of*

Visual Communication and Image Representation, vol. 99, p. 104075, Mar. 2024, doi: 10.1016/j.jvcir.2024.104075.

[20] J. Wang et al., "Strong robust copy-move forgery detection network based on layer-by-layer decoupling refinement," *Information Processing & Management*, vol. 61, no. 3, p. 103685, May 2024, doi: 10.1016/j.ipm.2024.103685.

[21] J.-L. Zhong, Y.-F. Gan, and J.-X. Yang, "Efficient detection of intra/inter-frame video copy-move forgery: A hierarchical coarse-to-fine method," *Journal of Information Security and Applications*, vol. 85, p. 103863, Sep. 2024, doi: 10.1016/j.jisa.2024.103863.

[22] A. C.-C. Liu, and O. M. K. Law, "Convolution optimization," in *Artificial Intelligence Hardware Design: Challenges and Solutions*, IEEE, 2021, pp. 85–126, doi: 10.1002/9781119810483.ch5.

[23] "Deep learning," in *Nonlinear Filters*, John Wiley & Sons, Ltd, 2022, pp. 113–140, doi: 10.1002/9781119078166.ch8.

[24] J. I. Agbinya, "11 convolutional neural networks," in *Applied Data Analytics—Principles and Applications*, River Publishers, 2019, pp. 185–204. Accessed: Jun. 25, 2022. [Online]. https://ieeexplore.ieee.org/document/9227126.

[25] "Intuition of Adam optimizer," *GeeksforGeeks*. Accessed: Jun. 25, 2022. [Online]. https://www.geeksforgeeks.org/intuition-of-adam-optimizer/.

[26] J. Brownlee, *Probability for Machine Learning: Discover How To Harness Uncertainty With Python*, Machine Learning Mastery, 2019.

[27] A. Tharwat, "Classification assessment methods," *Applied Computing and Informatics*, vol. 17, no. 1, pp. 168–192, Jan. 2020, doi: 10.1016/j.aci.2018.08.003.

[28] J. Keshet, and S. Bengio, "From binary classification to categorial prediction," in *Automatic Speech and Speaker Recognition: Large Margin and Kernel Methods*, Wiley, 2009, pp. 27–49, doi: 10.1002/9780470742044.ch3.

[29] J. Opitz, and S. Burst, "Macro F1 and Macro F1," Feb. 08, 2021, arXiv:1911.03347, doi: 10.48550/arXiv.1911.03347.

[30] S. V. Stehman, "Selecting and interpreting measures of thematic classification accuracy," *Remote Sensing of Environment*, vol. 62, no. 1, pp. 77–89, Oct. 1997, doi: 10.1016/S0034-4257(97)00083-7.

[31] O. Kuznetsov, E. Frontoni, L. Romeo, and R. Rosati, "Enhancing copy-move forgery detection through a novel CNN architecture and comprehensive dataset analysis," *Multimed Tools and Applications*, Jan. 2024, doi: 10.1007/s11042-023-17964-5.

11 System of Routing Solutions Based on Security-Aware Traffic Engineering Models

Oleksandr Lemeshko, Oleksandra Yeremenko, Maryna Yevdokymenko, Volodymyr Porokhniak, Serhii Harkusha, and Olena Harkusha

11.1 INTRODUCTION

Modern information and communication networks (ICN) have evolved into highly complex technical systems supporting numerous wide-ranging critical functions. However, these networks are consistently exposed to various disruptive influences, including physical damage, technical malfunctions, and, most notably, cyber-attacks. In recent years, targeted network attacks at multiple layers of the OSI model have emerged as a dominant threat to network security and resilience [1–7]. Cyber intrusions often aim not only to intercept and exfiltrate sensitive information traversing the network but also to exploit vulnerabilities within the network infrastructure. Such attacks can overload individual devices, disrupt essential network areas, and ultimately lead to widespread denial-of-service incidents.

As organizations and individuals become increasingly reliant on seamless connectivity, the resilience of ICNs against these multifaceted threats has become a priority. Fault tolerance, as the network's capacity to maintain functionality despite failures or adverse conditions, is critical in ensuring ICN robustness. Analysis of recent fault-tolerance strategies underscores the significance of fault-tolerant routing in sustaining network operations even during device or link failures [8–10]. By implementing protocols that support redundancy and fast recovery, network administrators can significantly mitigate the impact of these disruptions on overall network performance.

Fault-tolerant routing relies on both proactive and reactive strategies, as exemplified by the First Hop Redundancy Protocols (FHRP) and Fast ReRoute (FRR) mechanisms. These protocols enable the rapid redirection of traffic in response to failures, thereby preventing service interruptions and enhancing the network's overall fault tolerance [11]. Importantly, these protocols are designed to support both local and global protection (reservation) measures. At the local level, protection is achieved by reserving individual routers and network links. On a broader scale, global protection

DOI: 10.1201/9781003546153-11

focuses on protecting entire routes, network segments, and overall network bandwidth. This layered approach to fault tolerance allows networks to remain operational even under substantial pressure.

Furthermore, with the growing emphasis on secure, high-availability networking, fault-tolerant routing solutions like FHRP and FRR can potentially offer dual benefits: they ensure network reliability and protect valuable data against cyber threats. As cyber-attacks become more sophisticated and pervasive, deploying novel cyber-resilient routing protocols is increasingly essential for network robustness.

11.1.1 Key Contributions of the Chapter

The following are the significant contributions of this chapter:

i. The chapter examines vital FHRP application areas that use load balancing and network security parameters of border routers to improve network security.
ii. The work presents the proposed Security-Aware Traffic Engineering and Security Metrics Traffic Engineering flow-based models.
iii. The research and comparative analysis made it possible to justify areas of practical applications of the models.

11.1.2 Chapter Organization

Section 11.2 presents the related works on the applicability of First Hop Redundancy Protocols with load balancing to improve network security. Section 11.3 explains the Traffic Engineering flow-based routing model under balancing at the network edge. Section 11.4 introduces secure routing metrics based on vulnerability scores. Section 11.5 presents the proposed Security Aware Traffic Engineering flow-based model, while Section 11.6 is devoted to the Security Metrics Traffic Engineering flow-based model. Section 11.7 provides the numerical research results of secure routing models in infocommunication networks, and Section 11.8 discusses the results. Finally, Section 11.9 concludes the chapter and explains the future research direction regarding the load-balancing models considering the security level of the network routers.

11.2 RELATED WORK

Network border routers, whose interfaces act as default gateways for connected access networks, require enhanced protection against failures. Overloading or compromising border devices can lead to the complete blocking of access networks and violate the security level of information transmitted to or from them. To address the risks of single points of failure in such critical routers, FHRP protocols like Hot Standby Router Protocol (HSRP) and Virtual Router Redundancy Protocol (VRRP) were developed to provide redundancy. These protocols ensure that a backup router takes over if the primary router fails, minimizing downtime and ensuring continuous network operation. However, they have limitations in terms of load balancing.

HSRP and VRRP focus primarily on redundancy, with only one router actively forwarding traffic while others remain idle, waiting to take over. Although HSRP can distribute traffic across multiple groups, it requires additional configuration. VRRP, similarly, does not support load balancing by default. GLBP was introduced to address these limitations [11–14].

One key factor that makes GLBP an optimal choice for ensuring high availability in ICNs, compared to HSRP and VRRP, is its ability to provide load balancing across multiple routers using a single virtual IP address and multiple virtual MAC addresses. Additionally, it allows administrators to configure load balancing based on factors such as operational reliability and Quality of Service, which is critical in preventing failures related to border routers' hardware or software faults.

In GLBP, the router with the highest priority assumes the role of Active Virtual Gateway (AVG), while the remaining routers become Active Virtual Forwarders (AVFs). The AVG's primary function is to assign virtual MAC addresses to each AVF within the group. It also responds to ARP requests from devices on the subnet and determines which AVF will handle the traffic. All devices on the subnet share a virtual IP as the default gateway, and the AVG manages load distribution by allocating traffic through the assigned virtual MAC addresses [11].

GLBP offers dynamic load balancing of traffic by allowing up to four active routers in each group to forward traffic. These routers are AVFs of two types: the primary virtual forwarder is an AVF assigned a virtual MAC address by the AVG. A secondary virtual forwarder learns the virtual MAC address through hello messages. AVFs are selected from the GLBP group depending on their weight parameters, where weight can be adjusted with its default value being 100 [11]. In a situation where the primary AVF fails or becomes unreachable, one of the secondary AVFs takes the role of the primary AVF to maintain continuous traffic forwarding.

Several load-balancing modes allow GLBP to effectively distribute traffic over different routers, producing improved network performance and availability. The load-balancing modes, which serve different network requirements, are the following:

- Round-robin load balancing is the default load balancing method in GLBP. Each Virtual Forwarder (VF) MAC address is used sequentially in ARP replies for the virtual IP address. It distributes traffic equitably among all AVFs, which is appropriate for cases where all routers have equivalent capacity and should distribute the traffic evenly.
- Weighted load balancing involves assigning weights to each device in the GLBP group. These weights determine the load-balancing ratio between devices. This allows the administrator to assign greater weight to more powerful routers capable of managing higher traffic loads. Each GLBP router in the group will advertise its weight, and the AVG will act based on that value.
- Host-dependent load balancing uses the host's MAC address to determine which Virtual Forwarder MAC address the host will be directed to. This guarantees that a host will always utilize the same virtual MAC address if the number of VFs in the GLBP group remains the same.

GLBP's main strengths include proactive gateway protection and seamless traffic management, even when router failures occur. It provides operational redistribution of functions regarding the management of packet protection and transmission in the event of failure of one or more routers whose interfaces create a default virtual gateway. These advantages make GLBP highly suitable for ICN environments where reliability is essential.

Numerous scientific works [8, 9, 15] explore optimization methods and flow-based mathematical models for fault-tolerant routing and load balancing. These models are designed to ensure efficient use of network resources.

A growing area of research focuses on expanding the functionality of FHRP protocols by incorporating network security parameters into fault-tolerant designs. This involves developing new mathematical models and methods for fault-tolerant routing and load balancing between border routers, which serve as default virtual gateways. These models consider the vulnerabilities identified in the routers and the likelihood of exploitation [16, 17].

11.3 TRAFFIC ENGINEERING FLOW-BASED ROUTING MODEL UNDER BALANCING AT THE NETWORK EDGE

The parameters of the Traffic Engineering (TE) [18] flow-based routing model under balancing at the network core edge, where the graph $G=(M,L)$ describes the network, are in Table 11.1. Then value K is the set of flows arriving from the access networks to the core network. Suppose that the kth flow ($k \in K$) is associated with source V_s^k and destination V_d^k access networks for the kth flow (Table 11.1). The parameter λ^k is the average flow rate of the kth flow measured in packets per second (pps).

As shown in [14], the set R consists of two disjoint subsets of the network core boundary routers R^+ and transit routers R^-, while the subset R_j^+ of the R^+ expresses the edge routers interfaces used for virtual routers comprising (Table 11.1). Moreover, edge router interfaces at the same time may belong to several virtual routers.

The following conditions are responsible for the multipath routing [7]:

$$0 \le x_{i,j}^k \le 1. \tag{11.1}$$

Additionally, the model contains the conditions responsible for balancing the load between virtual router interfaces as it is implemented in HSRP and GLBP [15]:

$$0 \le y_{i,j}^k \le 1 \text{ and } 0 \le z_{j,i}^k \le 1. \tag{11.2}$$

Next, the packet loss prevention conditions at the core network edge are necessary:

$$\sum_{R_j \in R_p^+} y_{p,j}^k = 1,\ V_p = V_s^k, \tag{11.3}$$

$$\sum_{R_j \in R_h^+} z_{j,h}^k = 1,\ V_h = V_d^k. \tag{11.4}$$

Then, the flow conservation conditions have been modified to consider all the routing variable types to guarantee loading balancing at the core and edge of the network [15]:

TABLE 11.1
Notation Summary for TE Model

Symbol	Meaning
$G=(M,L)$	Network graph
$M=R\bigcup V$	Set of vertices ($R\bigcap V=\varnothing$)
$R=\left\{R_i, i=\overline{1,m}\right\}$	Core network routers
$V=\left\{V_j, j=\overline{1,v}\right\}$	Access networks
$R^+\subset R$	Core network edge routers
$R^-\subset R$	Transit routers
$R_j^+\subset R^+$	Edge routers that form a virtual router for the *j*th access network V_j
$L=E\bigcup W$	Set of edges ($E\bigcap W=\varnothing$)
$E=\left\{E_{i,j}, i,j=\overline{1,m}, i\neq j\right\}$	Core network links
$W=\left\{W_{i,j}, i=\overline{1,v}, j=\overline{1,m^+}\right\}$	Access links for access and core networks connection
$\varphi_{i,j}$	Link $E_{i,j}\in E$ capacity
R_i^{core}	Core network routers adjacent to the border router $R_i\in R$
R_i^{access}	Access networks adjacent to the border router $R_i\in R^+$
K	Set of flows arriving at the edge routers from the access networks
K_i^+	Set of flows arriving at the core from the access networks connected to the router $R_i\in R^+$
K_i^-	Set of flows outgoing from the core to the access networks connected to the router $R_i\in R^+$
V_s^k	Access network that is the source for *k*th flow
V_d^k	Access network that is the destination for *k*th flow
λ^k	*k*th flow average packet rate
$x_{i,j}^k$	*k*th flow fraction in the link $E_{i,j}$ of the primary link
$y_{i,j}^k$	*k*th flow fraction in the access link $W_{i,j}$
$z_{j,i}^k$	*k*th flow fraction in the access link $W_{j,i}$
α	Upper bound of the network links utilization

$$\begin{cases} \sum\limits_{j:E_{i,j}\in E} x_{i,j}^k - \sum\limits_{j:E_{j,i}\in E} x_{j,i}^k = 0; k\in K\ , R_i\in R^-; \\ \sum\limits_{j:E_{i,j}\in E} x_{i,j}^k - \sum\limits_{j:E_{j,i}\in E} x_{j,i}^k = y_{p,i}^k; k\in K\ , R_i\in R^+,\ V_{\mathrm{p}}=V_s^k; \\ \sum\limits_{j:E_{i,j}\in E} x_{i,j}^k - \sum\limits_{j:E_{j,i}\in E} x_{j,i}^k = -z_{i,h}^k; k\in K\ , R_i\in R^+,\ V_{\mathrm{h}}=V_d^k. \end{cases} \tag{11.5}$$

As the overload prevention criteria, the following constraint has been selected [9]:

$$\sum_{k\in K}\lambda^k x_{i,j}^k \leq \alpha\varphi_{i,j}, E_{i,j} \in E. \tag{11.6}$$

In (11.6), the control variable α defines the upper bound of the network link utilization and is introduced in the model to implement the Traffic Engineering concept [8]:

$$0 \leq \alpha \leq 1. \tag{11.7}$$

In solving the problem stated earlier, the minimum of the boundary values α serves as the optimality criterion in the Traffic Engineering flow-based routing model under balancing at the network core edge [9]:

$$\min_{x,y,z,\alpha} \alpha. \tag{11.8}$$

Within the basic model (11.1)–(11.8), the technical task of the Traffic Engineering routing model under balancing at the network core edge has been set as the linear programming optimization problem with optimality criterion (11.8) and linear constraints and conditions for control variables (11.1)–(11.7).

Model (11.1)–(11.8) is optimized to ensure balanced loading of network links, which is known to improve the leading indicators of Quality of Service, such as network performance, average packet delays, and jitter, as well as the level of packet loss on routers. However, in addition to QoS indicators, modern networks must also ensure a high level of network security. This can be achieved by load balancing based on the network security indicators of the routers. This case especially applies to border routers that perform the default gateway functions for access networks. A breach of the security level of these routers will compromise all traffic coming to them from the respective access networks.

In the current work, we propose to use the approach outlined in research [15–17] to assess the security level of routers based on calculating an indicator as an information security risk.

11.4 SECURE ROUTING METRICS BASED ON VULNERABILITY SCORES

Let us introduce the following notation for secure routing metrics based on vulnerability scores (Table 11.2) [15, 16, 19–23].

Therefore, the following expression is used to evaluate the information security risk from the exploitation of existing vulnerabilities on the ith node [20–22]:

$$R^i = \sum_{U_i^q \in U_i^*} BS_i^q \cdot P_i^q. \tag{11.9}$$

Under the NIST recommendation, losses corresponding to basic vulnerability metrics at nodes are obtained as [20–22]:

TABLE 11.2
Notation Summary for Vulnerability Scores Metrics

Symbol	Meaning
$\mathbf{U}=\{U_i^q; q=\overline{1,Q}, i=\overline{1,m}\}$	Set of network routers vulnerabilities
U_i^q	qth vulnerability on the ith network node
$U_i^* \subset \mathbf{U}$	Set of vulnerabilities on the ith network node
BS_i^q	Criticality index of the qth vulnerability on the ith network node under the basic metrics of the vulnerability assessment system NIST CVSS v3
P_i^q	Probability of exploiting the qth vulnerability on the ith network node (compromise probability)
Imp_i^q	Potential loss from exploiting the qth vulnerability on the ith node
Ex_i^q	Difficulty of exploiting the qth vulnerability on the ith node
$f(\mathrm{Imp}_i^q)$	Function from potential loss in case of exploitation of the qth vulnerability on ith network element
$Conf_i^q$	Losses from breach of information confidentiality transmitted over the network
Int_i^q	Losses from the violation of the integrity
Av_i^q	Losses from violation of network resource availability in case of using the qth vulnerability on the ith network node
Ac_i^q	Indicator of the vulnerability assessment system, which characterizes the difficulty of obtaining access (access vector)
Au_i^q	Indicator of the vulnerability assessment system that is responsible for authentication requirements
AcV_i^q	Indicator of the vulnerability assessment system that reflects the method of exploiting the qth vulnerability on the ith network node, which is physically characterized by "remoteness" of the attacker

$$BS_i^q = (0.6 \cdot Imp_i^q + 0.4 \cdot Ex_i^q - 1.5) \cdot f(Imp_i^q). \tag{11.10}$$

Then the potential vulnerability exploitation impact is evaluated as [20–22]:

$$Imp_i^q = 10.41\left[1-(1-Conf_i^q)\cdot(1-Int_i^q)\cdot(1-Av_i^q)\right]. \tag{11.11}$$

These three metrics $Conf_i^q$, Int_i^q, and Av_i^q define the effect of the attacker's exploitation of the qth vulnerability on the ith node. In each metric, the damage (impact) from the exploitation of the vulnerability can be [16, 20–22]:

- *absent* under a value of 0;
- *partial* under a value of 0.275;
- *complete* under a value of 0.66.

The metrics $Conf_i^q$, Int_i^q, and Av_i^q values can be found in [20–22]. Finally, the complexity of vulnerability exploitation is calculated as follows:

$$Ex_i^q = 20 \cdot Ac_i^q \cdot Au_i^q \cdot AcV_i^q. \tag{11.12}$$

Such indicators are the basic metrics that characterize the overall attack complexity of vulnerability exploitation on the *i*th network node (Table 11.3) [16, 20–22].

According to [16, 20–22], the potential loss function $f(\mathrm{Imp}_i^q)$ takes a zero value in the absence of damage, i.e., $f(\mathrm{Imp}_i^q) = 0$. Here we will consider the case when the potential damage is present when $\mathrm{Imp}_i^q \neq 0$. Therefore, in further calculations, we use $f(\mathrm{Imp}_i^q) = 1.176$ [20–22].

TABLE 11.3
Values of Indicators of the Vulnerability Assessment System, which Characterize the Complexity of the Vulnerability Exploitation

Designation	Description	Metric Value
Access vector Ac_i^q		
Local (L)	To exploit the vulnerability, the attacker needs physical access to the local network	0.395
Adjacent Network (A)	To exploit the vulnerability, an attacker needs access to either the broadcast or collision domain of the vulnerable software.	0.646
Network (N)	An attacker could exploit the vulnerability remotely from any part of the network, including the Internet	1.0
Authentication Au_i^q		
Multiple (M)	An attacker needs to perform more than one authentication procedure to exploit a node vulnerability	0.45
Single (S)	It is sufficient for an attacker to authenticate once to exploit a node vulnerability	0.56
None (N)	An attacker does not need authentication to access and exploit the vulnerability	0.704
Access complexity AcV_i^q		
High (H)	There are several strict restrictions on access to a network node. For example, exploitation of a node vulnerability is possible only in a short time or requires the use of social engineering, in which the attacker can be identified	0.35
Medium (M)	There are some restrictions on access to the network node. For example, a connection to a vulnerable node is only possible from specific nodes, or the affected configuration of the network node is non-default	0.61
Low (L)	There are no special conditions for access to the vulnerability of the network node. For example, when the network is available to many users at the same time or when a vulnerable configuration is running on multiple network nodes	0.71

In this work, two models of considering the information security risks of border routers are proposed, further investigated, and compared while ensuring balancing on these routers and in the network. The first model is a further development of the approach proposed in works [15, 16] when instead of the availability coefficients of routers as the primary indicator of operational reliability of devices and systems, their information security risks are used. The second model of network load balancing is based on introducing the optimality criterion (11.8) next to the upper bound of link utilization α and an additional set of network security metrics of border routers formed from information security risks.

11.5 SECURITY-AWARE TRAFFIC ENGINEERING FLOW-BASED MODEL

In model (11.1)–(11.8), let us consider that load balancing of traffic coming from the access network V_p is implemented, for example, using the GLBP approach $\left(y_{p,j}^k \in [0;1]\right)$ by fulfilling the conditions [15]:

$$\sum_{k \in K_j^+} \lambda^k y_{p,j}^k = m_{p,j}^+ \sum_{k \in K_j^+} \lambda^k \tag{11.13}$$

where $m_{p,j}^+$ are balancing metrics that determine the share of aggregate traffic from the access network V_p to the border router $R_j \in R_p^+$. That is, equality must be observed when determining balancing metrics

$$\sum_{R_j \in R_p^+} m_{p,j}^+ = 1. \tag{11.14}$$

Therefore, the balancing metrics for the separate border routers that create the default virtual gateway for the access network V_p will be the same.

As known, the GLBP supports weighted load-balancing. Model (11.13) implements such an approach by establishing balancing metrics administratively. This work proposes adapting the balancing metrics to consider the border routers' information security risk.

Let an information security risk R^i specify each border router $R_i \in R^+$ according to its security level (Table 11.3). Therefore, to implement risk-aware load-balancing in (11.13), the balancing metrics are proposed to be calculated by the following expression:

$$m_{p,j}^+ = \frac{1/R^j}{\sum_{R_i \in R_p^+} \left(1/R^i\right)}, \; R_j \in R_p^+. \tag{11.15}$$

Therefore, the equations (11.13)–(11.15) refer to the network core's border routers of traffic arrival. At the same time, for the border routers' $R_j \in R_p^+$ load balancing when traffic outgoes from the network core, the subsequent conditions introduced [15]:

$$\sum_{k\in K_j^-} \lambda^k z_{j,p}^k = m_{j,p}^- \sum_{k\in K_j^-} \lambda^k, \tag{11.16}$$

$$m_{j,p}^- = \frac{1/R^j}{\sum\limits_{R_i\in R_p^+} \left(1/R^i\right)}, R_j \in R_p^+, \tag{11.17}$$

where $m_{j,p}^-$ are balancing metrics determining the aggregate traffic proportion that arrives at the access network V_p from the border router $R_j \in R_p^+$.

Therefore, when minimizing (11.8), constraints (11.13) and (11.16) are additionally imposed on the control variables that regulate the process of load balancing on border routers. By analogy with the work [15], this model will be called Security-Aware Traffic Engineering (SATE).

11.6 SECURITY METRICS TRAFFIC ENGINEERING FLOW-BASED MODEL

The second model of load balancing based on the principles of Traffic Engineering, proposed in this work, is based on the introduction of security metrics, which take into account the level of network security of border routers. Such a transformation leads to the rejection of conditions (11.13)–(11.17) and the optimality criterion (11.8) modification in the model (11.1)–(11.8), which will now have the following form:

$$\min_{x,y,z,\alpha} \left(\sum_{k\in K} \sum_{V_i\in V} \sum_{R_j\in R_i^+} R^j y_{i,j}^k + \sum_{k\in K} \sum_{V_i\in V} \sum_{R_j\in R_i^+} R^j z_{j,i}^k + c_\alpha \alpha \right). \tag{11.18}$$

The first term in criterion (11.18) considers the security risks of border routers through which traffic arrives at the core network from access networks. The second term in (11.18) accounts for the security risks of border routers, through which traffic outgoes from the core network to access networks. As in criterion (11.8), the third term considers the upper bound of the link utilization in the core network. With the help of the weight coefficient, it is possible to adjust the sensitivity of routing decisions to the requirements regarding the QoS level and/or network security. By increasing the coefficient, routing decisions will be primarily directed to ensuring QoS. By reducing the coefficient, the influence of network security indicators of border routers on the result of solving routing problems will increase.

11.7 NUMERICAL RESEARCH RESULTS OF SECURE ROUTING MODELS IN INFOCOMMUNICATION NETWORK

The network structure shown in Figure 11.1 was chosen for the numerical example in the research. The core network included 12 routers. In the breaks of the

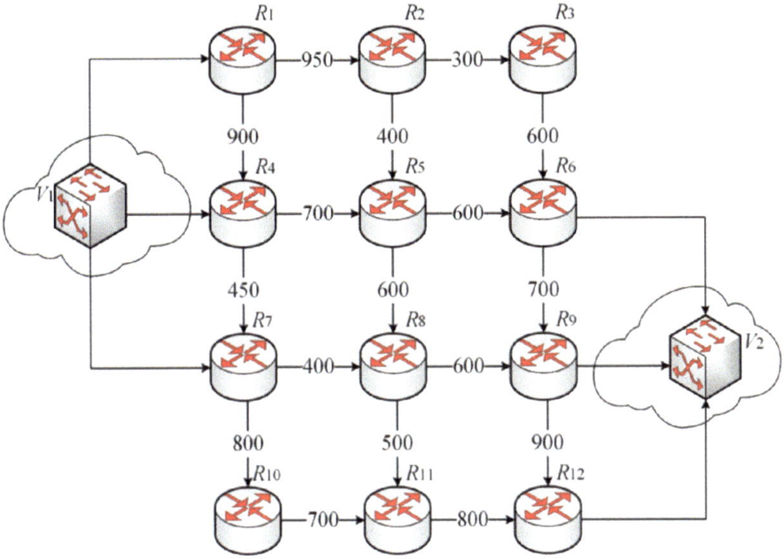

FIGURE 11.1 Network structure under the numerical study.

communication links, their bandwidths are indicated. For the access network V_1, the border routers' interfaces R_1, R_4 and R_7 served as virtual router. In contrast, for the access network V_2, the role of such a gateway was played by the corresponding interfaces of the routers R_6, R_9, and R_{12}. Packets were transmitted from the access network V_1 to the access network V_2 (Figure 11.1) at a rate ranging from 100 to 1800 packets per second.

For example, Table 11.4 shows the parameters and security risks of border routers for the network structure presented in Figure 11.1. Then two potential vulnerabilities were detected for the router R_1, ten for R_4, and six for R_7. Table 11.4 is completed using a software module implemented in the Python environment based on information obtained from the publicly available National Vulnerability Database (https://nvd.nist.gov/). The module automatically analyzes the criticality level of potential vulnerabilities for each border router and calculates risks (Figure 11.2).

To clarify the obtained results, we will demonstrate the impact on the load balancing of network security parameters and risks of only border routers through which traffic enters the core network, i.e., routers R_1, R_4, and R_7. Then, according to the calculations presented in Table 11.4 and Figure 11.2 of information security risks of the specified routers using the SATE model, load balancing of the selected packet flow on them is carried out as follows:

$$y_{1,1}^{1} = 0.6953,\ y_{1,4}^{1} = 0.1234,\ y_{1,5}^{1} = 0.1813. \tag{11.19}$$

The smaller the information security risk value for the border router, the greater the flow will pass through it from the access network to the core network.

TABLE 11.4
Network Security Parameters of the Routers under Study

Router	Type	BS_i^q	P_i^q	Vulnerability	Vulnerability Criticality Level	Information Security Risk
R_1	Cisco ASR 9920	4.3	0.28	CVE-2019–1909	Medium	3.02
		6.5	0.28	CVE-2019–16027	Medium	
R_4	Cisco ASR 1023	9.8	0.39	CVE-2021–34727	Critical	17.02
		6.7	0.08	CVE-2021–34725	Medium	
		6.0	0.08	CVE-2021–34724	Medium	
		8.6	0.08	CVE-2021–34723	Medium	
		6.7	0.39	CVE-2021–1624	High	
		7.4	0.28	CVE-2021–1621	High	
		7.7	0.31	CVE-2021–1620	High	
		7.8	0.18	CVE-2021–1529	High	
		7.4	0.28	CVE-2020–3508	High	
		7.2	0.05	CVE-2020–3396	High	
R_7	Cisco 809	8.8	0.2	CVE-2020–3234	High	11.58
		6.7	0.08	CVE-2020–3210	Medium	
		6.7	0.08	CVE-2020–3208	Medium	
		8.8	0.28	CVE-2020–3205	High	
		8.8	0.28	CVE-2020–3199	High	
		9.8	0.39	CVE-2020–3198	Critical	

When applying the second load balancing model (SecMetrTE), information security risk values for border routers were calculated (Table 11.4) and determined the routing metrics in criterion (11.18). To ensure the maximum level of QoS, taking into account the network security parameters of border routers, the value of the coefficient A_α was equal to 1000.

Then Table 11.5 presents the order of load balancing both at the level of border routers and in the core network in general. The advantage of the proposed SecMetrTE model is that it provided the same upper bound of the network link utilization as the TE model ($\alpha = 0.7826$). However, maximum use was made of the router R_1, which had a minimal information security risk ($R^1 = 3.02$). When balancing the load from the access network, the router R_2, which had the maximum risk ($R^2 = 17.02$), was not used. A feature of the linear optimality criterion (18), on which the SecMetrTE model is based, is that the use of more vulnerable border routers occurs only to minimize the core network utilization bound. That is, if the most secure border router was sufficient to ensure the α minimum value, then more vulnerable border routers were not used when transmitting packets from access networks.

As can be seen from Table 11.5, the SATE model based on the use of distribution (11.19) provided a slightly higher upper bound link utilization value—at the level of $\alpha = 0.7965$, which is 1.78% more than in the case of using the TE and Sec-MetrTE models. Let us denote this percentage difference by α^*. That is, using the SATE

```
NETWORK: SECURE AWARE TRAFFIC ENGINEERING (SATE)
 AVF (3):
  1) Cisco ASR 9920,    Information Security Risk: 3.02
   Vulnerabilities (2):
        1.  CVE-2019-1909     Score: 4.3 (MEDIUM),      Exploitation_probability: 0.28;
        2.  CVE-2019-16027    Score: 6.5 (MEDIUM),      Exploitation_probability: 0.28;

  2) Cisco ASR 1023,    Information Security Risk: 17.02
   Vulnerabilities (10):
        1.  CVE-2021-34727    Score: 9.8 (CRITICAL),    Exploitation_probability: 0.39;
        2.  CVE-2021-34725    Score: 6.7 (MEDIUM),      Exploitation_probability: 0.08;
        3.  CVE-2021-34724    Score: 6.0 (MEDIUM),      Exploitation_probability: 0.08;
        4.  CVE-2021-34723    Score: 6.7 (MEDIUM),      Exploitation_probability: 0.08;
        5.  CVE-2021-1624     Score: 8.6 (HIGH),        Exploitation_probability: 0.39;
        6.  CVE-2021-1621     Score: 7.4 (HIGH),        Exploitation_probability: 0.28;
        7.  CVE-2021-1620     Score: 7.7 (HIGH),        Exploitation_probability: 0.31;
        8.  CVE-2021-1529     Score: 7.8 (HIGH),        Exploitation_probability: 0.18;
        9.  CVE-2020-3508     Score: 7.4 (HIGH),        Exploitation_probability: 0.28;
       10.  CVE-2020-3396     Score: 7.2 (HIGH),        Exploitation_probability: 0.05;

  3) Cisco 809,    Information Security Risk: 11.58
   Vulnerabilities (6):
        1.  CVE-2020-3234     Score: 8.8 (HIGH),        Exploitation_probability: 0.20;
        2.  CVE-2020-3210     Score: 6.7 (MEDIUM),      Exploitation_probability: 0.08;
        3.  CVE-2020-3208     Score: 6.7 (MEDIUM),      Exploitation_probability: 0.08;
        4.  CVE-2020-3205     Score: 8.8 (HIGH),        Exploitation_probability: 0.28;
        5.  CVE-2020-3199     Score: 8.8 (HIGH),        Exploitation_probability: 0.28;
        6.  CVE-2020-3198     Score: 9.8 (CRITICAL),    Exploitation_probability: 0.39;
```

FIGURE 11.2 An example of the software module for analyzing network security parameters of routers and calculating information security risks.

model considering the network security parameters of border routers may lead to some reduction in the level of QoS. By analogy with the results obtained in [14], when using the SATE model, the degree of raising the α bound compared to the TE and SecMetrTE models may depend on the ratio of information security risk values of border routers. Therefore, the study of α^* values was carried out to confirm or refute this hypothesis.

Table 11.6 presents the research results for five different variants of the information security risk values ratios of border routers R_1 R_4, and R_7. The previously detailed and analyzed case (Table 11.5) corresponds to the second variant in Table 11.6.

Figure 11.3 and Figure 11.4 show the dependence of the upper bound core network links utilization when using different balancing models on the intensity of traffic coming from the access network. Figure 11.3 corresponds to the third version of the ratio of information security risks of border routers from Table 11.6. Figure 11.4 corresponds to the fifth option from the same table. For all investigated variants of the initial data, the TE and SecMetrTE models provided the same values of the upper bound core network links utilization (α).

From Table 11.6, it can be concluded that in the case of router interfaces with quite different information security risk values in the virtual default gateway, the use of the SATE model is inappropriate. Its use can lead to an increase from 2% to 20% (Table 11.6) of the upper bound core network links utilization, which, in turn,

TABLE 11.5
Comparison of Routing Solutions Obtained Using TE, SATE, and SecMetrTE Models ($\lambda^1 = 1800$ pps)

	TE	SATE	SecMetrTE
Link	$\alpha = 0.7826$	$\alpha = 0.7965$	$\alpha = 0.7826$
$W_{1,1}$	391.30	1251.54	1252.17
$W_{1,4}$	547.83	222.07	0
$W_{1,7}$	860.87	326.39	547.83
$E_{1,2}$	391.3043	557.5808	547.8261
$E_{2,3}$	234.7826	238.9632	234.7826
$E_{1,4}$	0	693.9551	704.3478
$E_{2,5}$	156.5217	318.6176	313.0435
$E_{3,6}$	234.7826	238.9632	234.7826
$E_{4,5}$	547.8261	557.5808	547.8261
$E_{5,6}$	469.5652	477.9264	469.5652
$E_{4,7}$	0	358.4448	156.5217
$E_{5,8}$	234.7826	398.2720	391.3043
$E_{6,9}$	0	0	0
$E_{7,8}$	313.0435	127.2577	156.5217
$E_{8,9}$	469.5652	477.9264	469.5652
$E_{7,10}$	547.8261	557.5808	547.8261
$E_{8,11}$	78.2609	47.6033	78.2609
$E_{9,12}$	0	0	0
$E_{10,11}$	547.8261	557.5808	547.8261
$E_{11,12}$	626.0870	605.1840	626.0870
$W_{6,2}$	704.3478	716.8896	704.3478
$W_{9,2}$	469.5652	477.9264	469.5652
$W_{12,2}$	626.0870	605.1840	626.0870

will cause a corresponding decrease in QoS level. Therefore, it is worth noting that according to the study results, the SecMetrTE model was more effective. On the one hand, it provides network load balancing considering the information security risks of border routers. On the other hand, it does not lead to an increase in the network upper bound utilization. This should have a positive effect on both network security indicators and QoS indicators.

11.8 RESULTS AND DISCUSSIONS

This work addresses the challenge of enhancing network fault tolerance by simultaneously connecting access networks to multiple border routers with support for load balancing. This approach reduces packet loss when one or more routers fail, particularly those utilizing first-hop redundancy protocols to create default virtual

TABLE 11.6
The Comparative Analysis Results of the Network Link Utilization Upper Bound When Using the TE, SATE, and SecMetrTE Models Depending on the Information Security Risk of Border Routers

Border Routers	R_1	R_4	R_7
Variant 1			
Information Security Risk	3	3	3
α^*, %	0		
Variant 2			
Information Security Risk	3.02	17.02	11.58
α^*, %	1.78		
Variant 3			
Information Security Risk	3	20	15
α^*, %	6.48		
Variant 4			
Information Security Risk	3	30	20
α^*, %	15		
Variant 5			
Information Security Risk	3	40	25
α^*, %	20.29		

gateways. Importantly, the load-balancing process considers the network security levels of these border routers, as a compromised border router could put at risk all incoming traffic from the access networks.

In this research, a flow-based routing model supplemented by Traffic Engineering (11.1)–(11.8) [18] was extended to facilitate fault-tolerant routing [15]. The study proposes and evaluates two load-balancing models that account for the security level of border routers. Both models use an information security risk metric (11.9) to evaluate the routers' security levels. The first model, the SATE, builds on approaches in [15, 16] and provides load balancing inversely proportional to the routers' information security risk values (11.13)–(11.17). The second model, the SecMetrTE, modifies the optimality criterion (11.18), proposing not only to minimize the utilization of core network links but also to limit the load on access links to border routers based on their information security risks.

Comparative analyses of these models and the traditional Traffic Engineering model were conducted (Tables 11.5 and 11.6). Findings indicate that implementing the SATE model may increase core network link utilization by 2–20%, especially when routers have significantly different security risk levels. The SecMetrTE model, however, consistently maintains the same upper bounds on core network utilization α as the TE model across various configurations of source data, making it the preferred choice.

For practical implementation, the proposed solutions can leverage the GLBP fault-tolerant routing protocol, which supports load balancing across multiple AVF

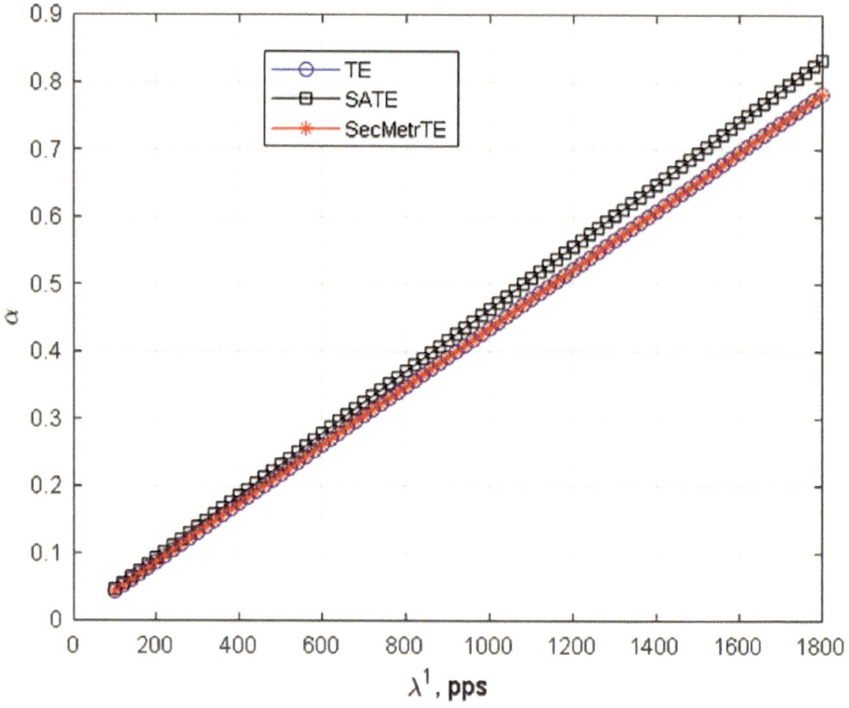

FIGURE 11.3 Dependency of the upper bound core network links utilization using different balancing models on the intensity of traffic coming from the access network (Variant 3, Table 11.6).

routers. In this context, a weighted load-balancing mode can be achieved by applying weights calculated according to the SATE or SecMetrTE models, allowing load distribution based on the security risks associated with each border router.

11.9 CONCLUSIONS AND FUTURE SCOPE

The findings demonstrate that integrating security risk considerations into load-balancing models, as implemented in the SATE and SecMetrTE models, can enhance network reliability and fault tolerance while managing core network utilization. The SecMetrTE model is especially recommended, given its effectiveness in maintaining stable utilization levels regardless of the variations in the security risks of border routers.

Future research should focus on expanding the range of network security indicators incorporated into load balancing, accounting for both access-level and core network parameters. Additionally, the inclusion of link utilization and direct QoS metrics—such as average packet delay, delay variation, and packet loss probability—could further refine load balancing by assessing overall QoS more comprehensively.

Moreover, integrating Quality of Experience (QoE) metrics, such as the R-factor and multimedia quality (MMq), would allow for more tailored handling of packet

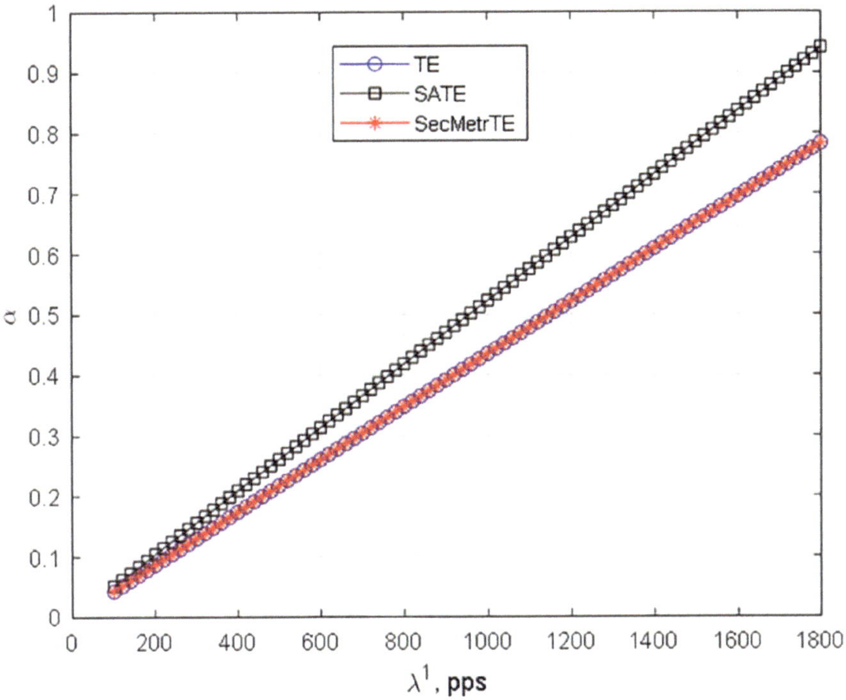

FIGURE 11.4 Dependency of the upper bound core network links utilization when different balancing models on the intensity of traffic coming from the access network (Variant 5, Table 11.6).

flows from various network applications. Lastly, there is a need for dynamic mathematical models that can more accurately represent the load-balancing process and the network's evolving state over time. This evolution is crucial to optimizing real-time network performance and resilience under varying load and security conditions.

11.10 ACKNOWLEDGEMENT

This chapter was published due to work on the Erasmus+ Project Jean Monnet module "The European experience for enhancing the resilience of critical entities in Ukraine" Project No.: 101085825—ERASMUS-JMO-2022-MODULE.

REFERENCES

[1] S. Gupta, *Security and QoS in Wireless Sensor Networks*, 1st Edition, eBooks2go Inc, 2018, 134 p.
[2] Q. Kiser, *Computer Networking and Cybersecurity: A Guide to Understanding Communications Systems, Internet Connections, and Network Security Along with Protection from Hacking and Cyber Security Threats*, Primasta, 2020, 242 p.

[3] M. Barreiros, P. Lundqvist, *QoS-Enabled Networks: Tools and Foundations*, John Wiley & Sons, 2016, 256 p. https://doi.org/10.1002/9781119109136.

[4] A. Z. Dodd, *The Essential Guide to Telecommunications*, 6th Edition, Pearson, 2019, 464 p.

[5] K. Smelyakov, A. Chupryna, O. Bohomolov, I. Ruban, The neural network technologies effectiveness for face detection, in *2020 IEEE Third International Conference on Data Stream Mining & Processing (DSMP)*, Lviv, Ukraine, 2020, pp. 201–205. https://doi.org/10.1109/DSMP47368.2020.9204049.

[6] D. Medhi, K. Ramasamy, *Network Routing: Algorithms, Protocols, and Architectures*, 2nd Edition, Morgan Kaufmann, 2017, 1018 p.

[7] O. Lemeshko, J. Papan, O. Yeremenko, M. Yevdokymenko, P. Segec, Research and development of delay-sensitive routing tensor model in IoT core networks, *Sensors*, 21(11), 3934 (2021). https://doi.org/10.3390/s21113934.

[8] O. Yeremenko, O. Lemeshko, A. Persikov, Secure routing in reliable networks: Proactive and reactive approach, in Shakhovska, N., Stepashko, V. (eds.) *CSIT 2017. AISC*, vol. 689, Springer, Cham, 2018, pp. 631–655. https://doi.org/10.1007/978-3-319-70581-1_44.

[9] O. Lemeshko, O. Yeremenko, M. Yevdokymenko, A. Shapovalova, A. M. Hailan, A. Mersni, Cyber resilience approach based on traffic engineering fast reroute with policing, in *2019 10th IEEE International Conference on Intelligent Data Acquisition and Advanced Computing Systems: Technology and Applications (IDAACS)*, Metz, France, 2019, pp. 117–122. https://doi.org/10.1109/IDAACS.2019.8924294.

[10] J. Rak, D. Hutchison (Eds.), *Guide to Disaster-Resilient Communication Networks (Computer Communications and Networks)*, 1st Edition, 2020 Edition, Springer, 2020, 834 p. https://doi.org/10.1007/978-3-030-44685-7.

[11] First Hop Redundancy Protocols Configuration Guide, *Cisco IOS Release 15.1 M&T*, 2018. Accessed: May 20, 2024. [Online]. https://www.cisco.com/c/en/us/td/docs/ios-xml/ios/ipapp_fhrp/configuration/15-mt/fhp-15-mt-book.html.

[12] F. Shahriar, J. Fan, Performance analysis of FHRP in a VLAN network with STP, in *2020 IEEE 3rd International Conference on Electronics Technology (ICET) Proceedings*, IEEE, 2020, pp. 814–818. https://doi.org/10.1109/ICET49382.2020.9119624.

[13] U. Anwar, J. Teng, H. A. Umair, A. Sikander, Performance analysis and functionality comparison of FHRP protocols, in *2019 IEEE 11th International Conference on Communication Software and Networks (ICCSN) Proceedings*, IEEE, 2019, pp. 111–115. https://doi.org/10.1109/ICCSN.2019.8905333.

[14] Z. U. Rahman, S. Mukhtar, S. Khan, R. Khan, Z. Ullah, R. Rashid, W. Ahmad, Performance evaluation of first HOP redundancy protocols (HSRP, VRRP & GLBP), *Journal of Applied Environmental and Biological Sciences*, 7(3), 268–278 (2017).

[15] O. Lemeshko, O. Yeremenko, A. Mersni, M. Yevdokymenko, Resilience aware traffic engineering FHRP solution, in *2021 IEEE International Conference on Information and Telecommunication Technologies and Radio Electronics (UkrMiCo) Proceedings*, IEEE, 2021, pp. 1–5. https://doi.org/10.1109/UkrMiCo52950.2021.9716677.

[16] O. Lemeshko, O. Yeremenko, M. Yevdokymenko, Models and methods of secure routing and load balancing in infocommunication networks, in Oliynykov, R., Kuznetsov, O., Lemeshko, O., Radivilova, T. (eds.) *Information Security Technologies in the Decentralized Distributed Networks. Lecture Notes on Data Engineering and Communications Technologies*, vol. 115, Springer, Cham, 2022. https://doi.org/10.1007/978-3-030-95161-0_10.

[17] M. Yevdokymenko, O. Yeremenko, A. Shapovalova, M. Shapoval, V. Porokhniak, N. Rogovaya, Investigation of the secure paths set calculation approach based on vulnerability assessment, in *Modern Machine Learning Technologies and Data Science Workshop. Proc. 3rd International Workshop (MoMLeT&DS 2021)*, vol. 2917, 2021, pp. 207–217.

[18] Y. Lee, Y. Seok, Y. Choi, C. Kim, A constrained multipath traffic engineering scheme for MPLS networks, in *2002 IEEE International Conference on Communications. ICC*

2002 (Cat. No.02CH37333) Proceedings, vol. 4, IEEE, 2002, pp. 2431–2436. https://doi.org/10.1109/ICC.2002.997280.
[19] S. A. Shah, B. Issac, Performance comparison of intrusion detection systems and application of machine learning to Snort system, *Future Generation Computer Systems*, 80, 157–170 (2018). https://doi.org/10.1016/j.future.2017.10.016.
[20] K. Scarfone, P. Mell, *Guide to Intrusion Detection and Prevention Systems (IDPS), NIST Special Publication 800-94*, 2007. Accessed: May 20, 2024. [Online]. https://doi.org/10.6028/NIST.SP.800-94.
[21] *Common Vulnerability Scoring System: Examples, Forum of Incident Response and Security Teams*, 2023. Accessed: May 20, 2024. [Online]. https://www.first.org/cvss/examples.
[22] M. Abedin, S. Nessa, E. Al-Shaer, L. Khan, Vulnerability analysis For evaluating quality of protection of security policies, in *QoP '06*, 2006. https://doi.org/10.1145/1179494.1179505.
[23] T. R. Peltier, *Information Security Risk Analysis*, 3rd Edition, CRC Press, 2005, 456 p.

12 Information Technology Security Platform for Intellectualization

Yuriy Bobalo, Valeriy Dudykevych, Halyna Mykytyn, and Taras Stosyk

12.1 INTRODUCTION

The main tool for deploying the processes of intellectualization of the infrastructure of society in the space of Industry 4.0 is information technology in the functional segment of "selection – storage, processing – transfer – management" [1]. To ensure the safe operation of infrastructure, obtain reliable information about their condition and implement decision-making to manage the problem situation, the security of information technology remains relevant as one of the main vectors of the Cyber Security Strategy of Ukraine [2]. In the context of the implementation of safe processes of intellectualization, innovative projects are being developed in the Ukraine – EU space, such as "Intelligent Energy Systems", "Intelligent Environmental Security" and others, covering the main segments of society's infrastructure security:

- risk management of natural and man-made disasters;
- ecological monitoring and forecasting of climate change and decision-making on the management of the 2021 Climate Summit Declaration (Washington, USA) and the 2021 Environmental Summit Climate Pact (COP26, Glasgow, Scotland);
- radiation monitoring and management of nuclear safety by IAEA activities;
- development and implementation of intelligent power grids according to the Smart Grid concept (technology of self-control, self-analysis and self-reporting).

Secure information technologies are in high demand in the three-component structure "Advanced Science – Global Challenges – Innovative Europe" of the Ninth Framework Program for EU Science and Technology Cooperation "Horizon – Europe", especially in research and innovation missions: adaptation to climate change, including social transformations; climate-neutral and smart cities [3]. Among the main clusters of the segment "global challenges and European industrial competitiveness" are: digital security for society (protection and security, cybersecurity); digital technologies, industry and space (next-generation Internet, key digital technologies, artificial

DOI: 10.1201/9781003546153-12

intelligence and robotics, advanced computing and big data); climate, energy and mobility (energy systems and networks, society and cities, smart mobility). Processes of automation and management of industrial and intellectual facilities, including critical infrastructure, provide for the introduction of secure information technology in the areas of intelligent production, intelligent energy supply, intelligent buildings, intelligent transport, and intelligent defense systems. The Infrastructure Intellectualization Program is deploying IT applications in the context of secure interoperability with the Internet of Things, the Internet of Everything, and the industrial Internet through standard communication protocols and wireless technologies.

Security of information technologies to support the functioning of infrastructure is developed by various methodologies, methods, tools and technologies. In the works [4–7] the main methodologies of cybersecurity in IT systems are based on the profiles of confidentiality, integrity and accessibility in the space of digital transformation, which is especially relevant for the deployment of projects in Ukraine in the areas of environmental protection (information system of environmental control), education and science (automated data collection and analysis system), critical infrastructure (USAID "Cyber Security of Ukraine's Critical Infrastructure"), etc. For industrial enterprises of Industry 4.0, one of the most important aspects of security is the identification of vulnerabilities and risks according to the appropriate methodology, one of which is presented in [8].

The effective system of information protection in industrial management systems is aimed at improving the effectiveness of security: at the technical level – the establishment of firewall protection, system security tests and deployment of network monitoring; at the management level – updating existing management systems and security technology standards [9]. Critical infrastructure security methodologies and strategies are in demand [10], which are presented at the level of attack trends, protection models and methods, risk analysis and vulnerabilities of urban infrastructure, including detection of vulnerabilities in network systems. Critical infrastructure intellectualization processes cover various areas and objects, including energy systems, the security of which is considered at the level of confidentiality of electricity consumers, integrity and confidentiality of messaging, data replacement attacks, etc. [11]. Information security of Industry 4.0 technologies requires the application of a set of modern approaches, in particular, the paper [12] outlines the current security issues in Industry 4.0 in the segment of industrial Internet of Things (IIoT) programs.

An approach to improve intrusion detection in the Internet of Things Industry 4.0 was discussed in [13], which proposed a cyberattack detection system based on an in-depth learning algorithm using "smart filters", each of which uses data collected in its network to teach intrusion detection and the already learned model is transmitted to other IoT gateways, which also protects network traffic when exchanging data between IoT gateways. In the context of constructing protection systems for various information infrastructure platforms, the concept and analytical structure of the security of neural network information technologies for detecting deepfake modifications of a biometric image in cyberspace are relevant [14, 15]. In [16], the technologies of Internet of Things security were developed according to the multilevel architecture, threats and vulnerabilities and encryption mechanisms. Papers [17–19] present the development of methodologies for constructing cyber security systems and the concept of multi-level security of cyber-physical technologies, particularly the system model of security of multi-layer IoT architecture. An important segment of information technology security is the protection of information resources, and in this direction, the development of the data security strategy continues, particularly in the space of data classification [20].

It is important to develop methodological approaches to ensure the security of intellectualization technologies based on the structure "information technology – threats – protection", which will guarantee the safe operation of infrastructure in the functional space "selection – transmission – processing – management". The purpose of the work is to create methodological principles of information technology security for intellectualization of society's infrastructure based on the proposed: system, hierarchical and regulatory models of IT security; methodologies for building a complex IT security system; and information model of security of the application layer of the Internet of Things in the data processing space.

12.1.1 Key Contributions of the Section

The following are the important contributions of this section:

1. This section examines the current segments of the application of secure information technologies in the task space of intellectualization according to the Industry 4.0 Concept.
2. The modern approaches, models and technologies of information technology security as the main toolkit for the secure operation of intellectualized infrastructure objects are analyzed.
3. To comprehensively address the problem of secure intellectualization, a strategic security model of the "object – IT" system is proposed, which is developed within the paradigm of building secure IT according to the concept and methodologies.

12.1.2 Organization of the Chapter

Section 12.2 presents a complex model of strategic security for the "object – IT" and reveals the structure of the paradigm for building IT based on methodological approaches to their creation and security methodology. Section 12.3 proposes a systemic IT security model based on the "object – threat – protection" concept according to the multi-level IT structure. Section 12.4 considers a complex five-level IT security model based on information protection subsystems: methodological, technical, software, communication and management. Section 12.5 presents a regulatory IT security model according to the functional levels of the protection system: methodological, technical, software and metrological. Section 12.6 reveals the methodology of a comprehensive IT security system, which is holistically aimed at minimizing information threats. Section 12.7 proposes an Internet of Things security model based on the "object – threat – protection" concept for the secure operation of objects in the Industry 4.0 space.

12.2 STRATEGIC SECURITY OF OBJECTS AND THE PARADIGM OF SAFE INFORMATION TECHNOLOGIES FOR DATA SELECTION IN INTELLECTUALIZATION TASKS

Strategic security of objects in the realm of intellectualization tasks. A complex model of strategic security for the "object – IT" system (see Figure 12.1) serves as a basis for developing methodological foundations for building IT along the vectors of intellectualization tasks, particularly in the segment of managing problematic situations in the field of monitoring (diagnosing) technogenic objects in the context of assessing their operability and predicting resources, as well as the methodology for information protection in automated systems.

The holistic solution to the problem of strategic security of the "object – IT" system is relevant based on the processes of informatization, intellectualization and information protection in the information society of Ukraine. The scientific underpinning for solving tasks within the framework of strategic security for the "object – IT"

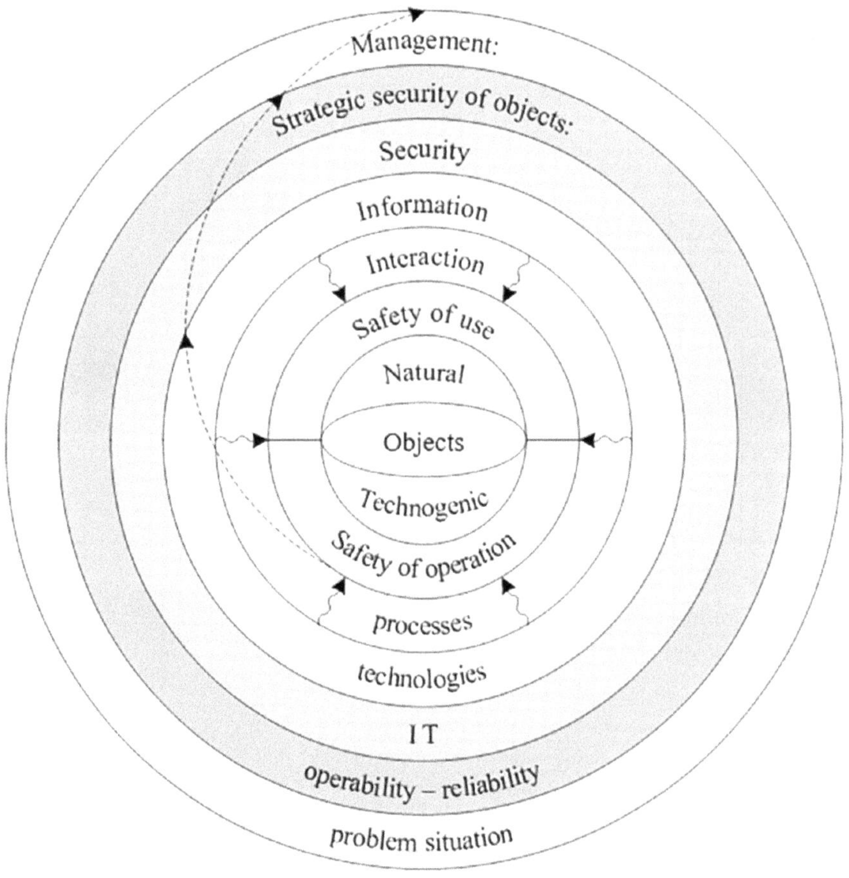

FIGURE 12.1 Complex model of strategic security for the "object – IT" system.

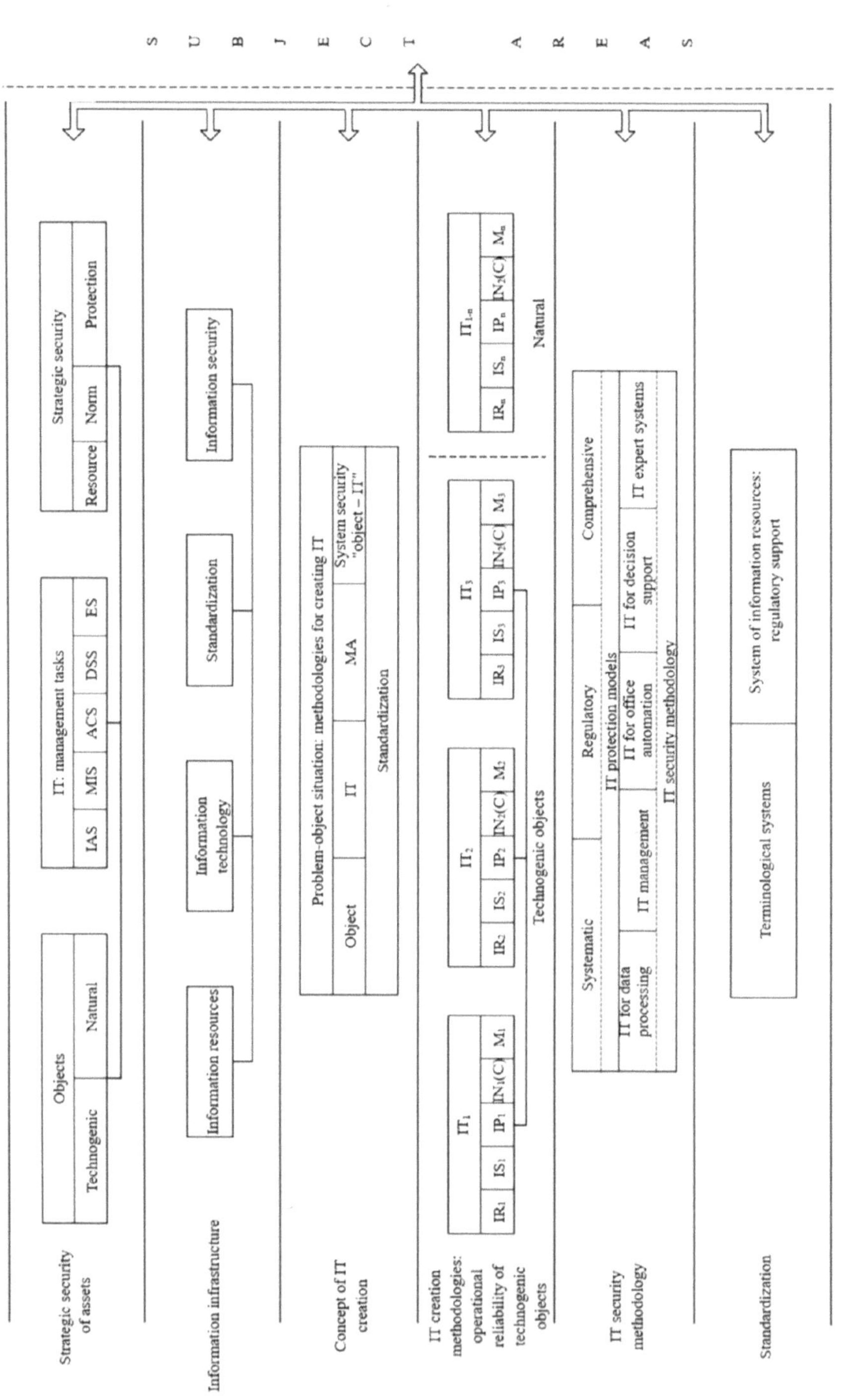

FIGURE 12.2 The paradigm of building an IT system for selecting heterogeneous data from objects.

system is the paradigm of building safe IT as the primary tool in the segment of monitoring, processing, analyzing and making decisions regarding the technical condition of objects under the influence of functional and informational threats.

The paradigm of building safe IT for intellectualization tasks. The paradigm of building safe IT for the selection and processing of heterogeneous data from objects is a technology for solving the applied scientific problem "object – IT – strategic security", and its structure transforms into various subject areas according to the intellectualization tasks (see Figure 12.2).

The paradigm of building IT for selecting heterogeneous data takes into account the main provisions: the Concept of the Targeted Comprehensive Program "Problems of Resource and Safety in the Operation of Structures, Facilities, and Machines"; the Concept of the Comprehensive Program on Sustainable Development, Rational Use of Natural Resources, and Environmental Conservation; the Concept of the National Informatization Program; the Industry 4.0 Concept; the Concept of Technical Information Protection in Ukraine; and the Cybersecurity Strategy of Ukraine.

Systemic approaches to creating the paradigm of IT for selecting and processing data enable the division of its structure into components—tasks, the solutions of which reflect the peculiarities of the methodologies for creating IT in each individual case.

The components of the structure of the paradigm for building IT for selecting heterogeneous data from objects include: strategic security of the "object – IT" system; infrastructure of the "informatization – intellectualization" system; systemic concept for creating IT for selecting heterogeneous data; IT creation methodology; IT security methodology; standardization in the space of the multi-level structure of IT – information resources (IR), information systems (IS), information processes (IP), information networks (channels) (IN (C)) and management (M).

The concept of creating IT for selecting heterogeneous data as a system is represented by subsystems: methodologies for developing IT according to the goals and tasks of the subject area research; information security; and standardization, which together in their interrelationship and interaction form a unified structure in the context of the problem of ensuring security at the level of "object – IT".

Each subsystem is considered at the level of interrelationship and interaction, which determines the influencing factors on the system as a whole and fills it with relevant content. The analysis and synthesis of components (subsystems) of the concept provide the basis for the unification of methods for creating IT for selecting heterogeneous data and methods for protecting automated systems (such as: information-analytical systems (IAS), measurement information systems (MIS), automated control systems (ACS), decision support systems (DSS) and expert systems (ES)) to ensure the security of the "object – IT" structure.

12.3 SYSTEM MODEL OF INFORMATION TECHNOLOGY SECURITY BASED ON MULTILEVEL STRUCTURE

Many scientific works are devoted to the issue of methodology of information technology construction and creation of models of information protection systems [21–25]. Consider the problem of data protection in IT based on a systems approach and

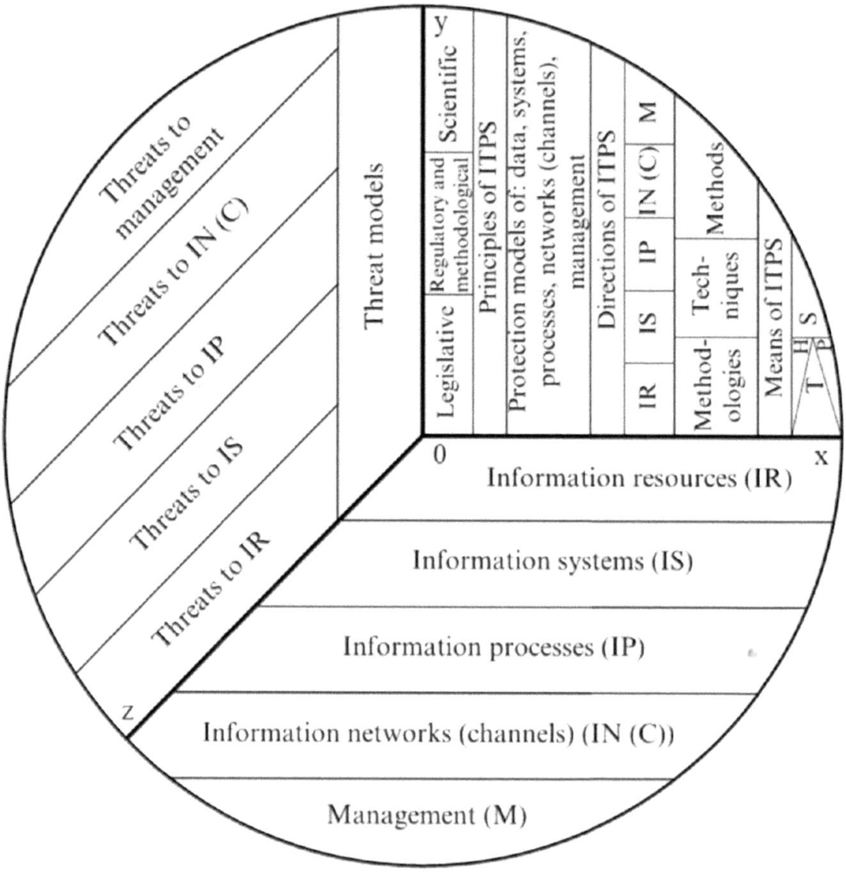

FIGURE 12.3 System model of information technology security.

multilevel structure—IR, IS, IP, IN (C), M [26, 27]. The IT security system model is presented in the form of a three-dimensional x-y-z space, covered by a sphere (Figure 12.3).

In the x-0-z plane there are objects of protection: IR, IS, IP, IN (C) and M. The y-0-z plane presents the levels of threat models adequate to the objects of protection in the x-0-z plane. The x-0-y plane represents the security system according to the objects of protection and threat models.

The segment of protection in the system model includes: principles—legislative, regulatory and methodological, scientific; protection models; directions; methodologies, methods, techniques; means of IT protection system (ITPS)—technical (T) (hardware (H), physical (P)), software (S). Representation of the object of protection as interconnected subsystems—IR, IS, IP, IN (C), M – allows to form models of their protection on legislative, regulatory and scientific bases according to possible threats.

The following elements should be taken into account when forming threat models at the level of IR, IS, IP, IN (C), M: 1) threats, as the intention to damage information by violating its integrity or confidentiality or to seize it for useful purposes; 2) sources of threats, which are classified by the nature of occurrence such as accident, intentional seizure, damage to information, etc.; 3) the goals of threats, focused on such features of information as confidentiality, integrity and accessibility; 4) methods of unauthorized access – approaches that characterize the process of considering a specific physical threat to a particular type of information.

The models of protection are based on: 1) legislative, regulatory and methodological, scientific principles that determine: concepts of IT security, basic principles of technical protection of information, norms and requirements, the order of work, management and security planning; protection management methods; 2) direction of IT security: IR, IS, IP, IN (C), M, for each of which the criteria of choice (creation) of methodology, method, means for the purpose of effective data protection are substantiated; 3) technical (T) and software (S) means of IT protection: technical devices – electrical and electromechanical provide confidentiality of information, protection against modification, data control; software means of protection – anti-virus programs, attack detection systems, network traffic controllers, complex protection systems, software encryption methods, masking methods, information authentication, digital signature methods and others provide access restriction and exclude unauthorized use of information.

To protect information at the level of hardware-physical (H-P) support, the following methods are used: hardware keys, security and fire alarm systems, means of blocking devices and interfaces of I/O information, digital video surveillance systems, access control and management systems, specialized locks, etc.

12.4 HIERARCHICAL MODEL OF COMPLEX SECURITY SYSTEM OF INFORMATION TECHNOLOGY

The hierarchical model of a complex security system of IT (CSS IT) is presented in the form of spheres in which there are five levels of protection (Figure 12.4).

The first level in the hierarchical model represents the objects of protection – IR, IS, IP, IN (C), M, life cycle and data security. The second level – the approach to protection, which reflects the application of relevant principles of data protection – the degree of confidentiality of information – 1; hardware and physical means of information protection – 2; stages of the information life cycle in information systems – 3; complex of interrelation, the interaction of variables in time: elements, conditions, factors influencing IT security – 4; IT security management elements – 5. The third level is a complex IT security system, as a synthesis of functional security and its core – information security. Complex IT security system is represented by: methodological – I; technical – II; software – III; communication – IV; management – V subsystems of functional and information security. Each subsystem of the complex IT security system has regulatory support. The fourth level – protective "belts" that reflect the nature of information security: the outer belt, which covers the entire area where the buildings containing IT are located – α; a belt of buildings (premises), or IT devices – β; a belt of technological processes of information processing (input, output, internal processing, etc.) – γ; a belt of system components and hardware, software, database elements – θ. The fifth level is a set of methods and means of

FIGURE 12.4 Hierarchical model of complex security system of information technology.

counteracting potential threats that arise in the protection zones α, β, γ, θ at the level of: detection – a; blocking – b; neutralization – c.

12.5 REGULATORY MODEL OF COMPLEX SECURITY SYSTEM OF INFORMATION TECHNOLOGY

The regulatory model of CSS IT is represented by the functional levels of the IT security system: A – methodological, B – technical (hardware, physical, channel), C – software, and D – metrological (Figure 12.5).

Standards 1-n are the regulatory framework for IT security according to functional levels. These include: state standards of Ukraine DSTU; state standards of Ukraine, unified with international DSTU ISO/IEC; international standards ISO (International Organization for Standardization), IEC (International Electrotechnical Commission), ITU (International Telecommunication Union) and others; national standards of standardization organizations of individual countries BSI, DIN, ANSI, NIST and others; regional standards of organizations that represent the interests of

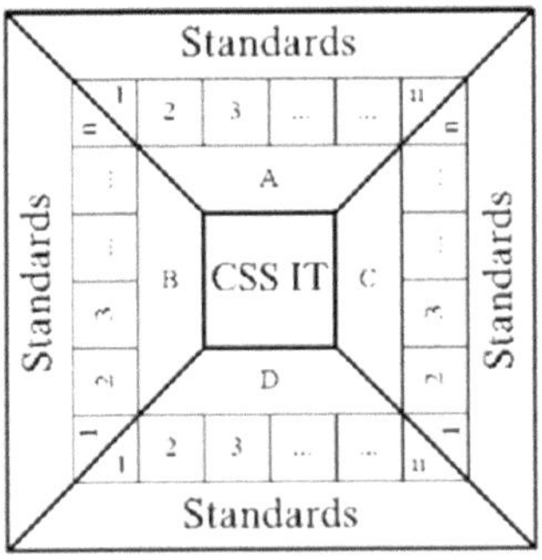

FIGURE 12.5 Regulatory model of complex security system of information technology.

large regions or continents in the global standardization process CEN (European Committee for Standardization), CENELEC (European Committee for Standardization in Electrical Engineering) and others; standards of industrial consortia and professional organizations ICC, API, etc.

The methodological level represents concepts, models, methodologies of data protection and IT security management. The technical level (hardware, physical, channel) is hardware devices that are embedded in data processing equipment; devices coordinated with it through the interface; automatic devices and systems (elements of electronic-mechanical burglar alarm equipment, locks, etc.); information leakage channels. The program level represents specialized programs for the safe operation of information technology. The metrological level reveals elements: metrological certification, testing, standardization and certification of hardware and software for data protection.

Aspects of the metrological level should be considered under the DSTU 3396.0 – 96, which outlines the stages of building an information security system in IT: identification and analysis of threats; development of information protection system; implementation of the information protection plan; and control over the functioning and management of the information protection system. Implementation of these stages requires: metrological examination of the technical task for the development of the information protection system; substantiation of the criteria for the selection of measuring equipment (ME), which completes the IT protection system; development of recommendations for metrological characteristics of the ME, conducting metrological certification of the ME; development of methods for measuring parameters of physical fields and signals to assess the probability of information leakage by technical channels and channels of special impact on the system; and conducting metrological certification of the information protection system according to standardized methods.

12.6 METHODOLOGY OF COMPLEX SECURITY SYSTEM OF INFORMATION TECHNOLOGY FOR INFRASTRUCTURE INTELLECTUALIZATION TASKS

The methodology of a complex IT security system is based on the relevant principles of information security, which are deployed according to society's infrastructure security projects [28]. The multi-level structure of the security system determines the effectiveness of IT security for the safe operation of intelligent objects. In this case, the implementation of any threat can affect IT only if you overcome all levels of protection.

Based on the system and complex models, the CSS IT methodology is proposed to ensure the security of intelligent objects. The structure of the CSS IT methodology protects five levels in accordance with the regulatory framework (Figure 12.6).

Information technologies – data processing, management, decision support, expert systems – as objects of protection, are represented by the system of interconnections and interaction of levels: 1) information resources – databases (DB), knowledge bases (KB), model bases (MB), data warehouses (DW), information arrays (IA); 2) information systems – information-analytical systems (IAS), office automation systems (OAS), measuring information systems (MIS), industrial control system (ICS), decision support systems (DSS), expert systems (ES), cyber-physical systems (CPS); 3) information processes; 4) information networks (channels); and 5) management of a complex IT security system.

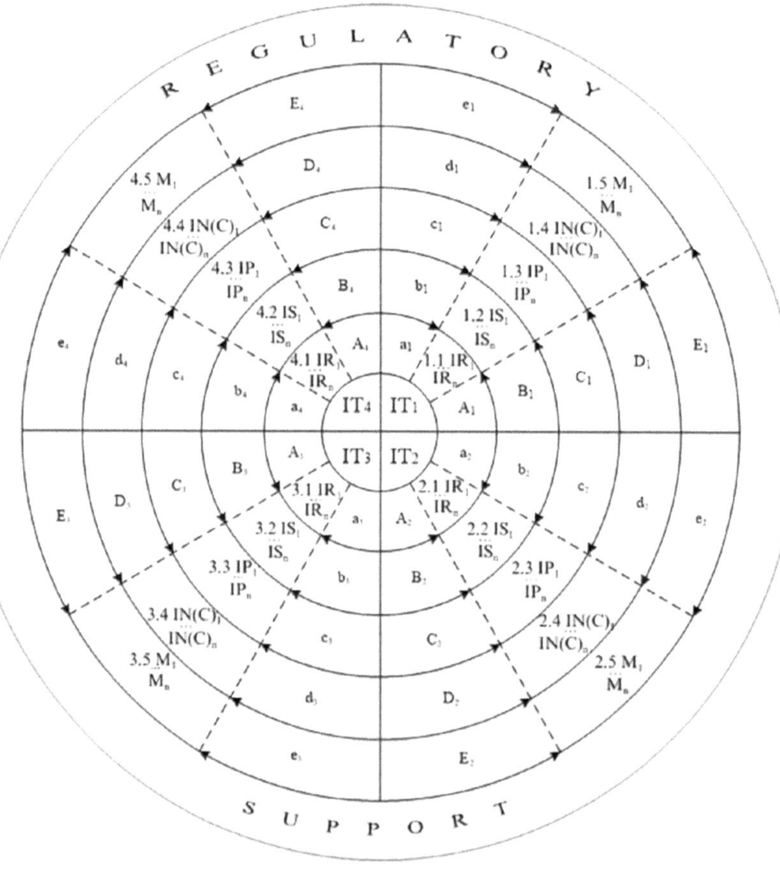

FIGURE 12.6 The structure of the integrated security system methodology: IT1 – data processing, IT2 – management, IT3 – decision support, IT4 – expert systems.

At the first level, IR is subject to protection: arrays of information, MB, databases and data banks in the relevant subject areas. At the second level – protection of functional hardware (physical, technical) and software elements of information systems for problem management tasks. The third level provides for the protection of IP: perception/collection/selection, transmission, processing, storage and presentation, which form the information content of phases, operations and data processing. The fourth level provides for the protection of IN (C) according to their classification by territory and topology for IAS, ICS, DSS, ES and types of channels for ICS and MIS. At the fifth level, information lifecycle management and a complex IT security system are provided.

Table 12.1 presents the methodology of CSS IT (data processing) according to the concept of "object – threat – protection" at the level of: the object of protection, number of threats (a-b-c-d-e) and elements of protection (A-B-C-D-E) [29, 30]. The complex IT security system is represented by security subsystems – IR, IS, IP, IN (C), M. The structure of the CSS IT methodology has the properties of integrity and emergence. Integrity – the property of the system to manifest itself as a whole, provided that changes in the parameters of protection of subsystems cause changes in the security parameters of the system as a whole. Probable threats to IR as subsystems, respectively, change the security status of other subsystems – IS, IP, IN (C), M, which form the protection of IT in general. Emergence is a property of a system that reflects its state C(S), as a function of the state of its elements C(n) and all relationships between them V(n):

$$C(s) = \int(C(n),V(n)),$$

that is, V(n) gives the system new properties that do not manifest through C(n). The property of emergence determines the integrity of a complex IT security system: IT

TABLE 12.1
Complex Security System of Information Technologies of Data Processing

Level of IT	Information technologies of data processing: Threat (a-b-c-d-e)	Protection (A-B-C-D-E)
1 IR	1.a.1. Data theft 1.a.2. Modification of data 1.a.3. Destruction of data 1.a.4. Blocking access to data 1.a.5. Unauthorized access to information 1.a.6. Loss, leakage of data 1.a.7. Corruption of primary information 1.a.8. Wrong actions of experts 1.a.9. Initiation of false knowledge 1.a.10. Denial of the validity of information	1.A.1. Differentiation of users' access to information 1.A.2. Cryptographic protection 1.A.3. Periodic backup and archiving of information 1.A.4. Measures to control the execution of requests 1.A.5. Means to control the integrity of system resources 1.A.6. Access control 1.A.7. Registration in the log of actions and operations

(*Continued*)

TABLE 12.1 (*Continued*)
Complex Security System of Information Technologies of Data Processing

Level of IT		Information technologies of data processing			
		Threat (a-b-c-d-e)		Protection (A-B-C-D-E)	
2	IS	2.b.1.	Disconnection or failure of subsystems that ensure the functioning of the system	2.B.1.	Legislative principles
		2.b.2.	Physical destruction of the system or shutdown of its most important components	2.B.2.	Regulatory and methodological principles
		2.b.3.	Software and hardware failures	2.B.3.	Scientific principles: technical; software tools
		2.b.4.	Electromagnetic radiation	2.B.3.1.	Implementation of automated detection and counteraction procedures with the help of specialized sensors
		2.b.5.	Logging into the information system bypassing the means of protection	2.B.3.2.	Docking with external corporate and commercial public key infrastructures built according to open system standards
		2.b.6.	Illegal receipt of passwords and other details of restriction of access with further disguise as a legitimate user	2.B.3.3.	Restriction of access
		2.b.7.	Hacking cryptographic information protection ciphers	2.B.3.4.	Protection against unauthorized access
		2.b.8.	Violation of access to the system or its functional elements	2.B.3.5.	Installation of uninterruptible power supplies
		2.b.9.	Algorithmic errors in design	2.B.3.6.	Data backup
3	IP	3.c.1.	Leakage, violation of the integrity, validity and safety of information at the stages of its entry, storage, transformation, processing and analysis	3.C.1.	Hashing algorithms
		3.c.2.	Leakage of information during its demonstration to the user, who shouldn't have access to it	3.C.2.	Digital signature and public key cryptosystems
		3.c.3.	Leakage, violation of the integrity, validity and safety of information during its transmission between individual, geographically remote IS on hard media or communication lines	3.C.3.	Data archiving and backup
		3.c.4.	Accidental or intentional violation of the integrity and validity of information at the stage of its collection, registration, acquisition	3.C.4.	Protection of the content of procedures and programs
				3.C.5.	Managing the flow of protected procedures and programs when transferring from one database segment to another database segment
				3.C.6.	Contextual data security
				3.C.7.	Prevention of unauthorized information creation

TABLE 12.1 (*Continued*)
Complex Security System of Information Technologies of Data Processing

Level of IT		Information technologies of data processing	
		Threat (a-b-c-d-e)	**Protection (A-B-C-D-E)**
4	IN (C)	4.d.1. Access of unauthorized users to the information network 4.d.2. Use of network tools in an unauthorized manner 4.d.3. Transmission errors 4.d.4. Interception of information 4.d.5. Unauthorized communication intrusion 4.d.6. Sending messages to the wrong address 4.d.7. Changing the route of messages 4.d.8. Changing the content of the transmitted information 4.d.9. Auxiliary electromagnetic radiation 4.d.10. Parasitic connections, high-frequency imposition 4.d.11. Radio interference, violation of signal integrity 4.d.12. Signal interception	4.D.1. Restriction and control of access to network elements 4.D.2. Protection of the content of messages 4.D.3. Digital pseudonym 4.D.4. Connection authentication 4.D.5. Package segmentation 4.D.6. Shielding wires 4.D.7. Application of high and low frequency filters that suppress the corresponding frequency band 4.D.8. Apply measures to reduce or eliminate the effects of parasitic connections 4.D.9. Hashing 4.D.10. Encryption 4.D.11. Firewall 4.D.12. Antivirus software
5	M CSS IT	5.e.1. Unauthorized access to the administrative part 5.e.2. Data modification 5.e.3. Data interception 5.e.4. Data theft 5.e.5. Data replacement 5.e.6. Service errors 5.e.7. Operator errors 5.e.8. Incorrect actions of the authorized user 5.e.9. Interception of passwords 5.e.10. Unauthorized access to the security system 5.e.11. Unauthorized obtaining and use of privileges 5.e.12. Leakage of information on the operation of the security system, access codes or passwords 5.e.13. Interference with the proper functioning of controls	5.E.1. Restrictions on access 5.E.2. Differentiation of access 5.E.3. Access control 5.E.4. Sharing access 5.E.5. Identification 5.E.6. Authentication 5.E.7. Authorization 5.E.8. Cryptographic protection of information 5.E.9. Control of requests to the protection components of the information system 5.E.10. Response to unauthorized access (delay or denial of service, alarm) 5.E.11. Monitoring of activity in the protection management system 5.E.12. Instructions for proper use

protection system without subsystems of protection IR, IS, IP, IN (C), M is not correct; the essence of the protection subsystem is revealed not by its internal content, but by the content of the whole IT protection system (IR, IS, IP, IN (C), M); the system has features unique to it that are absent in the subsystems. CSS IT methodology (data processing, management, decision support, ES), which is used for security tasks of intelligent objects, allows to implement an adequate choice of elements of protection of levels – IR, IS, IP, IN (C), M – according to the threat models, taking into account the properties of emergence, which ensures the integrity of IT protection.

The CSS IT for the tasks of intellectualization of infrastructure objects according to the concept of “object – threat – protection” is presented in Table 12.1.

12.7 INFORMATION MODEL OF SECURITY OF THE APPLICATION LAYER OF THE INTERNET OF THINGS

The processes of intellectualization of the infrastructure of society in the functional space “control – processing – management” include the interaction of the structure of information technology and the Internet of Things at the level of data processing operations in the information system. The architecture of the Internet of Things is being developed, including a multilevel model, which is characterized by collecting information from sensor networks on infrastructure objects (perception layer), transmitting data via wireless networks to the information system (network layer) for its storage, processing and decision-making on the management of the state of the relevant infrastructure object (application layer) [31–34].

Consider the information model of security of the application layer of the Internet of Things (Figure 12.7) based on the concept of “object – threat – protection”, which represents the main types of threats and their subtypes same as relevant security technologies and different subtypes of security measures [35–37].

Security of the Internet of Things application layer. The main threats are divided into four categories, each of which includes a different number of possible subcategories.

The first threat is malicious software (malware) with subcategories common for the Internet of Things being ransomware, spyware, trojans and worms.

The second threat is denial-of-service (DoS) attacks. The key subcategory of this type of attack is the distributed application-layer denial-of-service attack (AL-DDoS), which is the most difficult to implement among all DDoS attacks, but this type is the most accurate and intense.

The third threat is phishing, carried out using e-mail resources, as well as specially prepared websites. In many cases, the threat remains underestimated, as it is considered to be easily avoided with qualified personnel. However, a skillfully and professionally organized phishing attack can open a gateway even into a very well-protected system.

The fourth threat involves vulnerabilities of the software used. The main subcategories are program code modification, buffer overflow attack, data leakage when working with third-party programs, and so-called weak or simple authentication.

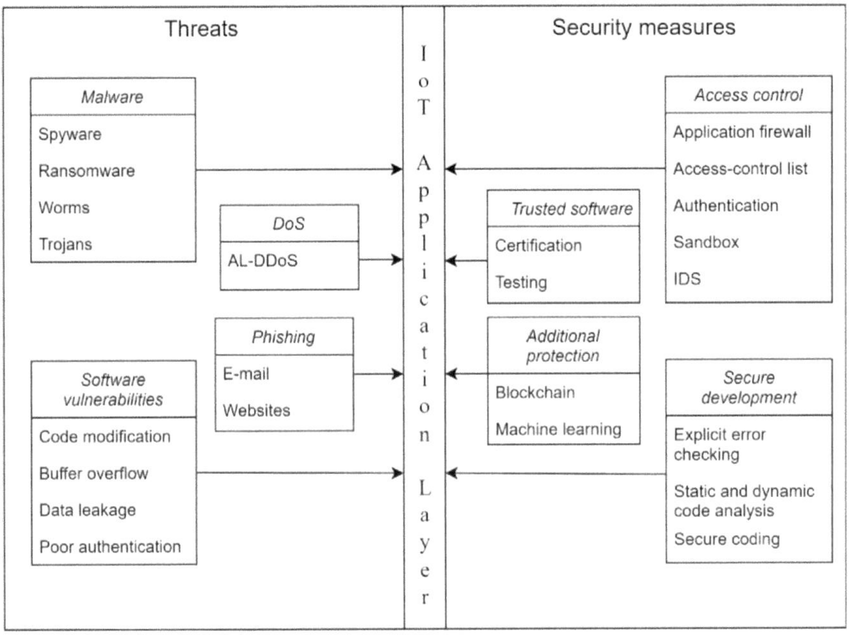

FIGURE 12.7 Information model of security of the application layer of the Internet of Things based on the concept of "object – threat – protection."

The key methods of ensuring the protection of the application layer of the Internet of Things include four categories, which also include several subcategories.

Method of protection – access control. Subcategories – application-layer firewall, organization of access control list (ACL), implementation of complex, multi-factor authentication, implementation of secure application execution mechanism (so-called Sandbox), as well as intrusion detection systems (IDS). The next method of protection is the organization of secure software development, which is implemented by three technologies: the method of secure coding, static and dynamic code analysis, and explicit error checking of all internally developed software.

An important step towards securing data in the system is also the use of only trusted external programs that have the appropriate certificates and have passed preliminary testing. At the same time, testing and certification can be carried out not only by the developer or third-party organizations, but also by the system owner.

The last, but no less important measure to ensure the security of the application layer of the Internet of Things, is the use of additional means to increase security, which include blockchain and machine learning.

The following was proposed: paradigm for building secure IT based on the strategic security model "object – IT", the methodology of a complex IT security system based on systemic, complex and regulatory security models, and the Internet of Things security model according to the "object – threat – protection" concept are the foundation for their effective application in creating secure tools for the implementation of infrastructure object intellectualization tasks in Ukraine.

12.8 CONCLUSION

In order to ensure the implementation of secure processes of intellectualization of society, the methodological principles of information technology security were proposed as the main tool for the operation of facilities based on: the complex security model of the "object – IT" system; paradigm for building safe IT; system, hierarchical and regulatory models of IT security; structure of the methodology of a complex security system of IT; information model of security of the application layer of the Internet of Things in the segment of secure information processing.

The security model of the "object – IT" system has been developed. A paradigm for building safe IT for data selection from infrastructure objects has been created based on the concept of building secure IT, the methodology for their creation and the methodology for their safe operation under the influence of threats.

The multi-level structure of IT has been examined: information resources, systems, processes, networks (channels) and data protection management. System and hierarchical models are interconnected by a multilevel structure of IT and the concept of "object – threat – protection"; in particular, the hierarchical model is the development of the system model in the space of approaches to information security.

The regulatory model of IT security allows the making of a reasonable choice of information protection technologies in multilevel IT in accordance with current national and international standards.

The CSS IT methodology based on the multilevel structure of IT according to the concept of "object – threat – protection" was offered. In accordance with the developed structure of the methodology, CSS IT was created for the tasks of intellectualization of infrastructure objects that have the properties of integrity and emergence: the state of security subsystems IR, IS, IP, IN (C), M, each of which is characterized by many data protection parameters and functional interaction; interrelation between them determines the essence of CSS IT as a whole, which is characterized by a new set of protection parameters.

The practical application of the CSS IT methodology allows for ensuring information security at the level of "leakage – modification – destruction" within the functional security of the intellectual object at the level of "uncertainty – failure – accident".

The information model of the Internet of Things security was proposed, which is developed by the structure "application layer – threats, their subcategories – security technologies, their subcategories", which demonstrates a systematic approach to safe support of technologies for the operation of facilities in Industry 4.0.

REFERENCES

[1] Yurchak, O. *Ukrainian Strategy of Industry 4.0 – 7 Directions of Development [Electronic Resource]*. Accessed: September 12, 2024. [Online]. https://industry4-0-ukraine.com.ua/2019/01/02/ukrainska-strategiya-industrii-4-0-7-napriankiv-rozvutku/ (in ukr).

[2] *Cyber Security Strategy of Ukraine. [Electronic Resource].* Accessed: September 12, 2024. [Online]. https://zakon.rada.gov.ua/laws/show/447/2021#n12 (in ukr).
[3] Horizon Europe. *The Next EU Research & Innovation Investment Programme (2021–2027).* Accessed: September 12, 2024. [Online]. https://research-and-innovation.ec.europa.eu/document/download/9224c3b4-f529-4b48-b21b-879c442002a2_en?filename=ec_rtd_he-investing-to-shape-our-future.pdf.
[4] Möller, D. P. F. *Cybersecurity in Digital Transformation. SpringerBriefs on Cyber Security Systems and Networks.* Springer, Cham, 2020, doi: 10.1007/978-3-030-60570-4.
[5] Jonathan, G. M., Gebremeskel, B. K., Yalew S. D., "Privacy and Security in the Digitalisation Era," *2020 11th IEEE Annual Information Technology, Electronics and Mobile Communication Conference (IEMCON)*, 2020, pp. 0837–0844, doi: 10.1109/IEMCON51383.2020.9284952.
[6] Yevseiev, S., Ponomarenko, V., Laptiev, O., Opirskyy, I., Milov O. and others. *Synergy of Building Cybersecurity Systems: Monograph.* PC Technology Center, Kharkiv, 2021, 188 p.
[7] Bobalo, Y., Dudykevych, V., Mykytyn, G., Stosyk, T. "Paradigm of Safe Intelligent Ecological Monitoring of Environmental Parameters," *CEUR Workshop Proceedings. – 2021. – Vol. 3200: Proceedings of the 3rd International Conference on Information Security and Information Technologies (ISecIT 2021)*, Odesa, Ukraine, September 13–19, 2021, pp. 244–249.
[8] De Paiva Barbosa, I. A., Borges Dos Reis, R. L., Saldanha, W. E., Lugli, A. B., De Assis Silva Do Carmo, F., Ribeiro, S. L. "Security Risks Assessment in an Industry 4.0 Plant," *2021 International Conference on Electrical, Computer, Communications and Mechatronics Engineering (ICECCME)*, 2021, pp. 1–6, doi: 10.1109/ICECCME52200.2021.9591040.
[9] Zou, Z., Hou, Y., Yang, H., Wang, B., Yang, R., "Research on Information Security Protection System of Industrial Control System," *2020 IEEE 9th Joint International Information Technology and Artificial Intelligence Conference (ITAIC)*, 2020, pp. 2311–2314, doi: 10.1109/ITAIC49862.2020.9338955.
[10] Gritzalis, D., Theocharidou, M., Stergiopoulos, G. (eds). *Critical Infrastructure Security and Resilience. Advanced Sciences and Technologies for Security Applications.* Springer, Cham, 2019, doi: 10.1007/978-3-030-00024-0.
[11] Abdallah, A., Shen, X. *Security and Privacy in Smart Grid. SpringerBriefs in Electrical and Computer Engineering.* Springer, Cham, 2018, doi: 10.1007/978-3-319-93677-2.
[12] Jamai, I., Ben Azzouz, L., Saïdane, L. A. "Security Issues in Industry 4.0," *2020 International Wireless Communications and Mobile Computing (IWCMC)*, 2020, pp. 481–488, doi: 10.1109/IWCMC48107.2020.9148447.
[13] Khoa, T. V. et al. "Collaborative Learning Model for Cyberattack Detection Systems in IoT Industry 4.0," *2020 IEEE Wireless Communications and Networking Conference (WCNC)*, 2020, pp. 1–6, doi: 10.1109/WCNC45663.2020.9120761.
[14] Dudykevych, V., Mykytyn, H., Ruda, K. "The Concept of a Deepfake Detection System of Biometric Image Modifications Based on Neural Networks," *2022 IEEE 3rd KhPI Week on Advanced Technology: Conference Proceedings*, Kharkiv, October 3–7, 2022, pp. 585–588.
[15] Dudykevych, V., Yevseiev, S., Mykytyn, G., Ruda, K., Hulak, H. "Detecting Deepfake Modifications of Biometric Images Using Neural Networks," *CEUR Workshop Proceedings. – 2024. – Vol. 3654: Cybersecurity Providing in Information and Telecommunication Systems 2024. Proceedings of the Workshop Cybersecurity Providing in Information and Telecommunication Systems (CPITS 2024)*, Kyiv, Ukraine, February 28, 2024, pp. 391–397. [Online].

[16] Anbar, M., Abdullah, N., Manickam, S. (eds). *Advances in Cyber Security. ACeS 2020. Communications in Computer and Information Science*, Vol. 1347. Springer, Singapore, 2021.

[17] Yevseiev, S. et al. *Synergy of Building Cybersecurity Systems.* PC Technology Center, Kharkiv, 2021, 188 p.

[18] Milevskyi, S., Korol, O., Mykytyn, G., Lozova, I., Solnyshkova, S., Husarova, I., Hrebeniuk, A., Vlasov, A., Sukhoteplyi, V., Balagura, D. "Development of the Sociocyberphysical Systems' Multi-Contour Security Methodology," *Eastern-European Journal of Enterprise Technologies*, 1, 9(127), 2024, pp. 34–51, 256 p.

[19] Dudykevych, V., Mykytyn, G., Stosyk, T., Skladannyi, P. "Platform for the Security of Cyber-Physical Systems and the IoT in the Intellectualization of Society," *CEUR Workshop Proceedings. – 2024. – Vol. 3654: Cybersecurity Providing in Information and Telecommunication Systems 2024. Proceedings of the Workshop Cybersecurity Providing in Information and Telecommunication Systems (CPITS 2024)*, Kyiv, Ukraine, February 28, 2024, pp. 449–457. [Online].

[20] Deineka, O., Harasymchuk, O., Partyka, A., Obshta, A., Korshun, N. "Designing Data Classification and Secure Store Policy According to SOC 2 Type II," *CEUR Workshop Proceedings. – 2024. – Vol. 3654: Cybersecurity Providing in Information and Telecommunication Systems 2024. Proceedings of the Workshop Cybersecurity Providing in Information and Telecommunication Systems (CPITS 2024)*, Kyiv, Ukraine, February 28, 2024, pp. 398–409. [Online].

[21] Rocha, Á., Ferrás, C., López-López, P. C., Guarda, T. (eds). *Information Technology and Systems. ICITS 2021. Advances in Intelligent Systems and Computing*, Vol. 1330. Springer, Cham, 2021, doi: 10.1007/978-3-030-68285-9.

[22] Rocha, Á., Ferrás, C., López-López, P. C., Guarda, T. (eds). *Information Technology and Systems. ICITS 2021. Advances in Intelligent Systems and Computing*, Vol. 1331. Springer, Cham, 2021, doi: 10.1007/978-3-030-68418-1.

[23] Dudykevych, V., Garasym, I. "Survivable Information Security Systems Designing Approach," *2011 Proceedings of 7th International Conference on Perspective Technologies and Methods in MEMS Design*, MEMSTECH, 2011, pp. 147–150.

[24] Gulak, H. M. *Information Protection Methodology. Aspects of Cybersecurity: A Textbook.* Publishing House of National Academy of Security Service of Ukraine, 2020, 256 p. (in ukr).

[25] Dudykevych, V., Prokopyshyn, I., Chekurin, V., Opirskyy, I., Lakh, Y., Kret, T., Ivanchenko, Y., Ivanchenko, I. "A Multicriterial Analysis of the Efficiency of Conservative Information Security Systems," *Eastern-European Journal of Enterprise Technologies*, 3, 9(99), 2019, pp. 6–13, doi: 10.15587/1729-4061.2019.166349.

[26] Velichko, O. M., Gordienko, T. B. *Fundamentals of Systems Analysis and Optimal Decision Making.* Oldi, Kherson, 2021, 672 p. (in ukr).

[27] Bobalo, Y. Y. *Strategic Security of the System "Object – Information Technology": [Monograph].* Bobalo, Y. Y., Dudykevych, V. B., Mykytyn, H. V. (eds). Publishing House of Lviv Polytechnic National University, Lviv, 2020, 260 p. (in ukr).

[28] Whitman, M. E., Mattord, H. J. *Principles of Information Security*, 7th edition. Cengage Learning Computers, 2021, 752 p.

[29] Mykytyn, H. V. *Security Strategy of Cyber-Physical Systems, Information Technologies and Information Protection in Information and Communication Systems: Monograph.* Dudykevych, V. B., Maksymovych, V. M., Mykytyn, H. V., Ponomarenko, V. S. (eds). Publishing House "Shchedra Sadyba Plus" Ltd., Kharkiv, 2016, 566p. (in rus).

[30] Mykytyn, H. V. *Complex Cybersecurity Systems of Cyber-Physical System Based on the Concept of "Object – Threat – Protection", Information Technologies: Problems and Prospects: Monograph.* Dudykevych, V. B., Mykytyn, H. V., Ponomarenko, V. S. (eds). Publisher Rozhko S. H., Kharkiv, 2017, 447 p. (in ukr).

[31] Wu, M., Lu, T. J., Ling, F. Y., Sun, J., & Du, H. Y. "Research on the Architecture of Internet of Things," *2010 3rd International Conference on Advanced Computer Theory and Engineering (ICACTE)*, 2010, pp. V5-484–V5-487, doi: 10.1109/ICACTE.2010.5579493.

[32] Gou, Q., Yan, L., Liu, Y. "Construction and Strategies in IoT Security System. Green Computing and Communications (GreenCom)," *2013 IEEE and Internet of Things (iThings/CPSCom), IEEE International Conference on and IEEE Cyber, Physical and Social Computing*, 2013, pp. 1129–1132.

[33] Lombardi, M., Pascale, F., Santaniello, D. "Internet of Things: A General Overview Between Architectures, Protocols and Applications," *Information*, 12(2), 2021, 87 p, doi: 10.3390/info12020087.

[34] Sethi, P., Sarangi, S. R. "Internet of Things: Architectures, Protocols, and Applications," *Journal of Electrical and Computer Engineering*, 2019, Article ID 9324035, 2017, 25 p, doi: 10.1155/2017/9324035.

[35] Wu, C. K. *Internet of Things Security. Advances in Computer Science and Technology (In cooperation with the China Computer Federation (CCF))*. Springer, Singapore, 2021, 245 p.

[36] Frustaci, M., Pace, P., Aloi, G., Fortino, G. "Evaluating Critical Security Issues of the IoT World: Present and Future Challenges," *IEEE Internet of Things Journal*, 5(4), August 2018, pp. 2483–2495, doi: 10.1109/JIOT.2017.2767291.

[37] Mrabet, H., Belguith, S., Alhomoud, A., Jemai, A. "A Survey of IoT Security Based on a Layered Architecture of Sensing and Data Analysis," *Sensors (Basel)*, 20(13), June 28, 2020, 3625 p, doi: 10.3390/s20133625.

13 Robust Model and Training Method for Malware Recognition in IoT Devices

Viacheslav Moskalenko

13.1 INTRODUCTION

Cyber-physical systems and the Internet of Things (IoT) are exerting an increasing influence on the economic, commercial, and social impact of our lives, becoming a common element of critical infrastructure. At the same time, the distributed devices of cyber-physical systems are usually resource-constrained, making them an attractive target for cyber-attacks [1]. Even though malware conventionally targets personal computer software, attacks on Internet of Things devices, such as smartphones, refrigerators, washing machines, medical equipment, and distributed sensors, are on the rise. Most cyber-attacks are currently aimed at infecting the device and gaining control over it to obtain unauthorized access to confidential information, implement botnets, or engage in other illegal activities.

The significant impact of cyber-physical systems and the Internet of Things is evident in a wide range of applications, from medical devices to smart homes, transportation systems, and industrial facilities. For example, in the healthcare sector, IoT devices enable constant monitoring of patients' vital signs, but any malfunction or attack could endanger their lives. Similar risks exist in smart homes, where unauthorized control of devices can lead to serious consequences, such as unauthorized access to sensitive information or manipulation of critical systems. Therefore, the development of effective protection methods becomes a priority.

In general, IoT devices are insecure because of the fundamental difficulty in creating a unified defense for a heterogeneous cyber-physical environment. IoT devices employ a bewildering variety of hardware and software architectures. Unlike personal computers, IoT systems are dominated by various flavors of Linux operating systems. There are no effective off-the-shelf solutions on the market for malware detection on these platforms.

Traditional signature-based methods of malware detection are ineffective due to the rapid growth in the quantity and variety of malware. Antivirus software should be regularly updated to counteract such attacks. Machine learning methods provide an improvement in the generalizing ability of malware detection systems but are still prone to false negative decisions when presented with malicious samples with small modifications [2]. At the same time, machine learning models built to detect malware

DOI: 10.1201/9781003546153-13

on a heterogeneous set of IoT platforms are also characterized by frequent false positives. Therefore, the development of models with low computational resource demands and robust performance against slightly modified malware samples from heterogeneous IoT platforms is an important scientific challenge.

13.1.1 Key Contributions of the Chapter

The following are the significant contributions of this chapter:

i. The chapter proposes a resource-efficient model for malware detection in IoT devices, utilizing the MobileNet architecture and a prototype-based classifier with pseudo-hyperspherical decision boundaries.
ii. A multi-stage training method is developed, incorporating self-supervised learning, contrastive-center loss, and binary class prototype optimization to enhance the model's robustness and generalization capabilities.
iii. The effectiveness of the proposed model is demonstrated through experiments, showing an accuracy improvement of 4% over traditional approaches and 3.87% higher than state-of-the-art methods, with notable robustness against adversarial attacks.

13.1.2 Chapter Organization

Section 13.2 presents related works on the applicability of deep learning techniques and geometric regularization for malware detection in IoT devices. Section 13.3 outlines the problem statement, emphasizing the need for robust and resource-efficient malware detection methods. Section 13.4 details the design of the proposed model, including the feature representation and classifier structure. Section 13.5 describes the multi-stage training method, highlighting the principles of self-supervised learning, information coding, and geometric regularization. Section 13.6 discusses the experimental results, showcasing the model's performance on various datasets and its resilience to adversarial attacks. Finally, Section 13.7 concludes the chapter with future research directions to enhance the model's resilience to concept drift and evolving malware threats.

13.2 RELATED WORK

Researchers from Intel and Microsoft proved the effectiveness of using convolutional deep neural networks for the analysis of malicious computer software [2, 3]. Researchers represented binary executable files as a single-channel 2D grayscale image byte. This approach allows applying well-established models and methods of convolutional network training. These works have considered only personal computers running the Windows operating system as the target platform. However, IoT devices have a high variability of operating systems, libraries, and hardware, which requires increasing the informativeness of the feature representation and improving the data analysis model itself to prevent bias or saturation effects.

Additionally, several recent studies have explored the combination of deep learning models with artificial intelligence methods that mimic the behavior of biological neural networks [4]. These approaches promise significant improvements in threat detection by utilizing non-linear models and adaptive learning algorithms. The use of synthetic data generation methods for training models has also proven effective in improving classification results on data with high noise or uncertainty [5].

Another promising direction in malware detection is the use of hybrid approaches that combine traditional signature-based methods with machine learning techniques [6]. While signature-based methods remain efficient in detecting known threats, machine learning models have the potential to uncover new and previously unknown threats. However, these hybrid models must address the challenge of balancing computational efficiency with detection accuracy, especially in the context of IoT devices where resources are limited.

One of the ways to improve the informativeness and resilience of the feature extractor is the effective use of unlabeled training data, which is always more abundant than labeled data. Both generative models training approaches based on auto-encoders and contrastive learning methods based on the use of various modifications of the contrastive loss function are used for training on unlabeled data [7, 8]. At the same time, it is known that contrastive learning methods provide a more efficient tool for classification models building since the purpose of contrast learning naturally corresponds to the tasks of classification analysis of data. However, it should be noted that unsupervised learning methods serve mainly to initialize the weights for the downstream supervised learning task.

False negative decisions on small modifications of malicious samples are caused by a lack of detector robustness and insufficient data generalizability by intelligent algorithms [7, 9]. Since the small modifications of malware are equivalent to noise or adversarial attacks on a trained detector, methods for ensuring the robustness and noise immunity of recognition algorithms become highly relevant [9]. Works [9, 10] propose various approaches for training robust models resistant to noise and adversarial attacks by increasing the buffer zone between classes or by replacing the last fully connected softmax layer with a distance-based decision function. In works [11, 12], the increase in generalizing ability of data analysis models is achieved by employing the principles of information bottleneck, with compression of information through discrete feature representation. Authors of [13, 14] use the target coding principle, based on the ideas of Error-Correcting Output Codes, where a special sigmoid decoding activation function is used instead of the softmax function. This function allocates the non-trivial volume in logit space to uncertainty. This makes the attack surface smaller to the attacker who tries to craft adversarial examples. In [15, 16], authors proposed methods of information-extreme learning with geometric regularization, in which the Hamming distance between class binary prototypes of classes is maximized simultaneously with decrease in intra-class distance to minimize the residual uncertainty after the decisions are made. Combining these principles and approaches to obtain a robust deep model of malware recognition from heterogeneous IoT platforms is a promising area of research.

13.3 PROBLEM STATEMENT

The research objective is the development of a robust and resource-efficient deep model and a training method for platform-independent malware detection. Based on a review of related work, it is suggested to rely on deep learning techniques, information coding theory and geometric regularization methods when developing a trainable malware recognizer.

The diversity of hardware and software in IoT creates challenges in developing universal defense systems. For instance, the same malware sample may behave differently on devices with different operating systems. This means that detection models must be flexible enough to encompass all variations of threat behavior while remaining resource-efficient. The lack of training data and the complexity of modeling the behavior of different systems add additional challenges to the development of such models.

Furthermore, the continuous evolution of malware, particularly with the rise of polymorphic and metamorphic variants, adds another layer of complexity to malware detection in IoT devices. These variants are capable of altering their code structure while maintaining the same malicious behavior, making traditional detection methods ineffective. Therefore, a key challenge is developing a model that not only identifies known malware but also generalizes well to detect novel, unseen variations.

Let $D_U = \left\{ x_j^U \mid j = \overline{1,n} \right\}$ be denoted as a set of unlabeled executable files and $D_S = \left\{ x_{k,j}^S \mid k = \overline{1,K}; j = \overline{1,n_k} \right\}$ be denoted as a set of labeled executable files gathered from a variety of IoT platforms with different operating systems for classifier training and testing, where n is a number of unlabeled examples and n_k is a number of examples of k-th class. Moreover, the structure of the vector of model parameters is known

$$g = \left\langle e_1, ..., e_{\xi_1}, ..., e_{\Xi_1}, f_1, ..., f_{\xi_2}, ..., f_{\Xi_2} \right\rangle, \ \Xi_1 + \Xi_1 = \Xi, \tag{13.1}$$

where e_{ξ_1} is a ξ_1-th parameter which impacts on feature representation, $\xi_1 = \overline{1, \Xi_1}$;

f_{ξ_2} is a ξ_2-th parameter which impacts on efficiency of decision rules, $\xi_2 = \overline{1, \Xi_2}$.

In this case, the constraints $R_{\xi_1}\left(e_1, \ldots, e_{\xi_1}, \ldots, e_{\Xi_1}\right) \leq 0$, $R_{\xi_1}\left(f_1, \ldots, f_{\xi_2}, \ldots, f_{\Xi_2}\right) \leq 0$ are imposed on parameters. These inequalities may include resource constraints (for example, number of trainable model parameters), necessitating the development of resource-efficient algorithms.

It is necessary to find optimal values of parameters g (13.1) that provide maximum of macro-averaged accuracy (Acc) of classifier on the original and adversarially perturbed labeled test set:

$$\text{Acc} = \frac{1}{K} \sum_{k=1}^{K} \left(\frac{TP_k + TN_k}{TP_k + TN_k + FP_k + FN_k} \right), \tag{13.2}$$

$$g^* = arg \max_G \left\{ Acc(g) \right\}. \tag{13.3}$$

where TP_k is a number of true positives for k -th class;

TN_k is a number of true negatives for k -th class;

FP_k is a number of false positives for k -th class;

FN_k is a number of false negatives for k -th class.

The following research tasks are proposed to achieve this objective:

- generate training data from heterogeneous IoT platforms and operating systems;
- design a model and training method for a robust malware classification analysis based on information coding theory and geometric regularization;
- compare the results obtained by the proposed and conventional approaches and results obtained by other researchers on original and adversarially perturbed test dataset.

13.4 MODEL DESIGN

We will use the successful experience of representing binary executable files as images [3] for the feature description of the observations. However, in this study, instead of single-channel images, we will create 3-channel RGB images according to the algorithm depicted in Figure 13.1.

Select the width and height of the color image depending on number of bytes in executable file (n_{bytes}) and can be calculated by the following formula

$$width = \text{heigth} = \text{ceil}\left(\sqrt{\frac{n_{bytes}}{3}}\right), \quad (13.4)$$

where ceil(.) is the function that computes the smallest integer that is greater than or equal to argument.

A deep convolutional feature extractor based on MobileNet architecture is then used for experimentation and proof of concept. This neural network is often used as a baseline in image recognition tasks under the computational capacity constraint. The capacity coefficient of such a convolutional network is set to 0.25 and only a convolutional backbone [17]. The structure of the proposed classifier model is depicted in figure 13.2(a), and a similar model with conventional output layer structure is provided for evaluation of the proposed approach in figure 13.2(b).

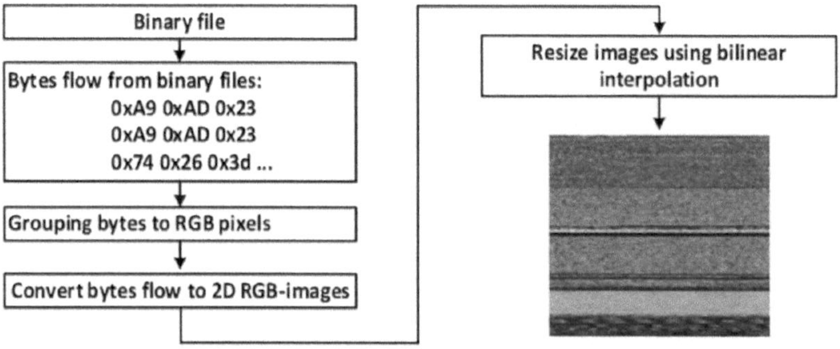

FIGURE 13.1 Block diagram for binary executable to 2D image conversion algorithm.

a	b
MobileNet Backbone	MobileNet Backbone
Global Average Pooling 2D Layer	Global Average Pooling 2D Layer
Dropout Layer (rate = 0.5)	Dropout Layer (rate = 0.5)
Dense Layer (128 nodes)	Dense Layer (128 nodes)
Sigmoid Layer	Relu Layer
Rouding Layer	Dense Layer (M nodes)
RBF Layer	Softmax Layer

FIGURE 13.2 Schematic representation of the proposed convolutional neural network for malware classification, showing the flow from the input image through convolutional layers, global average pooling, and the decision boundaries.

The choice of the MobileNet architecture as the backbone for the proposed model is not arbitrary. MobileNet is known for its high efficiency under constrained computational resources, making it an ideal candidate for IoT devices. The use of Global Average Pooling and a structure with pseudo-hyperspherical decision boundaries further enhances classification accuracy, particularly in heterogeneous data environments where it is crucial to clearly distinguish between classes of malicious and non-malicious software.

Moreover, the use of pseudo-hyperspherical decision boundaries in the classifier ensures that the model can separate classes even in highly complex feature spaces. This geometric approach allows for better class separation and minimizes the risk of overlap between benign and malicious software classifications. This method also strengthens the model's defense against adversarial attacks, which often attempt to exploit weaknesses in class boundaries.

Global Average Pooling is used for dimensionality reduction. Regularization is achieved with a Dropout pseudo-ensemble with 50% of the input features dropping [8, 13]. Fully connected and sigmoid layers form the output feature set. Decision rules of the proposed image classifier models contain the rounding layer which produces the binary coded representation and radial-basis function, defining the object's belonging to a certain class. Distributions of classes in binary Hamming space are separated by means of hyperspherical decision boundaries (containers). Each hyperspherical container is defined by a binary prototype vector (container center) and container radius defined in Hamming distance units. In this case, radial-basis membership function $\mu_k(b)$ for N-dimensional binary vector b is

$$\mu_k(b) = 1 - \frac{\sum_{i=1}^{n} b_i \oplus b_{k,i}^*}{d_k^*}, \tag{13.5}$$

where b_k^* is the binary prototype vector (center of optimal container) for k-th class X_k^o; d_k^* is the radius of optimal container for class X_k^o in Hamming distance units.

13.5 TRAINING METHOD DESIGN

The conventional training method is to add a Dense layer with softmax normalization of the output to a feature extractor and use the error backpropagation method (optimizer such as Adam), with cross-entropy loss function.

The proposed training method is based on the following methodological principles:

- self-supervised learning at the first stage to maximize the effective use of a large amount of unlabeled training data;
- combination of discrete feature representation (Deep Hashing) with coding of class labels (Target Coding or Label Embedding) [18]. Binary class prototypes created in one of the supervised learning stages become the class labels for the next stage;
- optimization of compactness and radii of hyperspherical boundaries for each class to maximize the interclass buffer space, which provides protection against adversarial attacks and increases generalization capabilities of the model;
- optimization of decision boundaries on the basis of information criteria, which provides greater generalization capacity under the most difficult in the statistical sense conditions.

In the first stage of training, contrastive learning plays a crucial role in helping the model better understand the difference between similar yet distinct classes. This is particularly beneficial when processing highly variable data, such as malware samples with slight modifications.

The inclusion of binary class prototypes at later stages of training adds an additional layer of robustness to the model. By optimizing class boundaries and ensuring compactness within each class, the model reduces the likelihood of misclassification, even when faced with adversarial perturbations. This approach is particularly important for IoT environments, where computational efficiency must be balanced with the need for accurate and reliable detection.

According to previous studies, the application of this technique significantly enhances the model's robustness against attacks involving small modifications to the original data.

The proposed training method includes five main stages (phases) (figure 13.3).

The first stage is to train on unlabeled data using instance-prototype contrastive learning procedure with a modified loss function, formulated as [19, 20]

$$L_{un\,sup} = -\frac{1}{n}\sum_{i-1}^{n} log \frac{\exp\left(-\frac{1}{N}\left\|z_i - \overline{z}\right\|_2^2\right)}{\exp\left(-\frac{1}{N}\left\|z_i - \overline{z}\right\|_2^2\right) + \sum_{q=1}^{Q} \exp\left(-\frac{1}{N}\left\|z_i - z_q\right\|_2^2\right) + \varepsilon}. \quad (13.6)$$

where n is a number of examples in mini-batch ($n = 32$);

z_i is representation description at the output of the feature extractor $z_i = f(x_i)$ for input example x_i from a mini-batch;

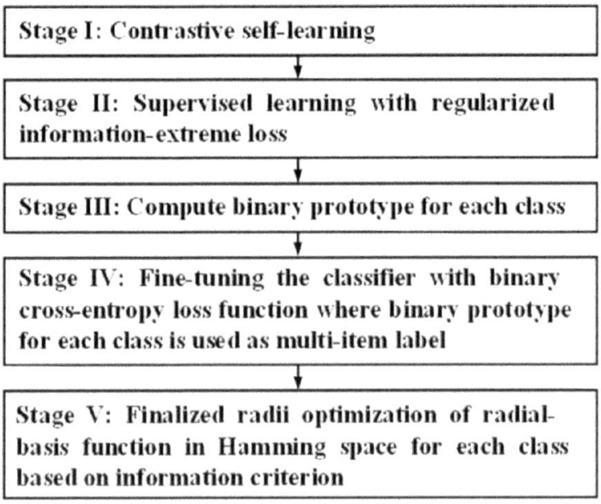

FIGURE 13.3 Stages of the proposed training method.

$\bar{z}$ is averaged feature representation for an augmented version of input example x_j which is considered a positive pair for the input example x_j,

$$\bar{z} = \frac{1}{n_a}\sum_{j=1}^{n_a} f\left(x_j\right)$$

where $f\left(x\right)$ is a function which describes the feature extractor and establishes the relationship between the input image and the output feature vector;

Q is the number of pre-processed examples considered as negative pairs, the feature representations of which are stored in the non-indexed FIFO buffer (with buffer length $Q = 1024$) and updated after processing each mini-batch;

N is the dimension of feature representation at the output of feature extractor;

$_2^2$ is Euclidean Squared distance;

ε is a constant added for numerical stability, $\varepsilon = 10^{-7}$.

The second stage of machine learning is performed on a labeled dataset using the loss function which maximizes the information criterion of learning efficiency and the regularization to form a discrete feature representation with compact class distribution and maximum inter-class distance. These define the three key components of the loss function

$$L_{sup} = L_{info} + \lambda_1 R_{binarize} + \lambda_2 R_{compactness} \tag{13.7}$$

where L_{info} is the information criterion of classifier efficiency averaged over the set of classes with a minus sign,

$$L_{info} = -\frac{1}{K}\sum_{k=1}^{K} E_k \tag{13.8}$$

where E_k is the information criterion of learning efficiency for recognition of examples of k-th class;

K is the size of the set of classes;

$R_{binarize}$ is a regularizing component which provides a penalty for the rounding error of the feature representation to a discrete form;

$R_{compactness}$ is a regularizing component which penalizes individual sample deviations from the corresponding class prototype and proximity to the prototype of a neighboring class.

Regularizing component $R_{binarize}$ penalizes the deviation of the feature representation from the discrete (binary) form and serves to implement the information bottleneck principle. This helps to increase the model's generalizing capabilities. This regularizing component is a Lipschitz Continuous function and is calculated as

$$R_{binarize} = \frac{1}{n}\sum_{i=1}^{n} z_i^{\,T}\left(e - z_i\right) + \frac{1}{K}\sum_{k=1}^{K} \bar{z}_k^{\,T}\left(e - \bar{z}_k\right), \tag{13.9}$$

where $z_i = f\left(x_i\right)$ is an output feature vector at the output of feature extractor for i-th example;

$\bar{z}_k$ is an averaged feature representation (prototype vector) for the i-th class (its value is not static and is optimized in the process of machine learning);

e is a unit vector;

K, n is the number of classes and the number of samples in the balanced mini-batch, respectively.

The regularizing component $R_{compactness}$, which penalizes deviations from the prototype of its class and proximity to the prototype of the neighboring class, forms the basis of error-correcting codes for each of the classes. This regularizing component is based on contrastive-center loss and explicitly uses class prototype vectors $\left\{\bar{z}_k \mid k = \overline{1,K}\right\}$ optimized during the machine learning process [20]

$$R_{compactness} = \frac{1}{n}\sum_{i=1}^{n}\left(\frac{\left\|z_i - \bar{z}_{y_i}\right\|_2^2}{\sum_{k=1,k\neq y_i}^{K}\left\|z_i - \bar{z}_k\right\|_2^2 + 1}\right). \tag{13.10}$$

A separate pseudo hyperspherical surface is built for each class in the radial basis feature space. The accuracy characteristics of the pseudo hyperspherical decision boundary for each class can be calculated on the basis of statistical tests as follows:

$$D_{1,k} = sensitivity_k = \frac{TP_k}{TP_k + FN_k + \varepsilon} + \varepsilon, \tag{13.11}$$

$$D_{2,k} = specificity_k = \frac{TN_k}{TN_k + FP_k + \varepsilon} + \varepsilon, \tag{13.12}$$

$$\alpha_k = miss\ rate_k = \frac{FN_k}{FN_k + TP_k + \varepsilon} + \varepsilon, \tag{13.13}$$

$$\beta_k = fall\,out\,rate_k = \frac{FP_k}{FP_k + TN_k + \varepsilon} + \varepsilon. \tag{13.14}$$

Procedures for calculating statistical tests are not differentiable, so in the training mode their smoothed versions can be used instead [21]

$$\widetilde{TP} = \sum_{i=1}^{n} \hat{y}_i \odot y_i, \tag{13.15}$$

$$\widetilde{FP} = \sum_{i=1}^{n} \hat{y}_i \odot (1 - y_i), \tag{13.16}$$

$$\widetilde{FN} = \sum_{i=1}^{n} (1 - \hat{y}_i) \odot y_i, \tag{13.17}$$

$$\widetilde{TN} = \sum_{i=1}^{n} (1 - \hat{y}_i) \odot (1 - y_i). \tag{13.18}$$

where $\odot$ is the component-wise multiplication sign (Hadamard product);

$y_i = \left\{ y_{i,k} | k = \overline{1,K} \right\}$ is class labels for i-th example after one-hot encoding;

$\hat{y}_i = \left\{ \mu_{i,k} | k = \overline{1,K} \right\}$ is the value of the smoothed membership function for the i-th sample to the c-th class, calculated by the formula

$$\mu_{i,k} = relu\left(1 - \frac{1}{d_{max}} \left\| z_i - \overline{z}_k \right\|_2^2 \right), \tag{13.19}$$

where d_{max} is maximum code radius of hyperspherical decision boundary (container) for each class constrained by half of Plotkin's Bound [13]:

$$d_{max} \leq \frac{1}{2} \frac{N}{2} \frac{K}{K-1}. \tag{13.20}$$

The smoothed membership function assumes that the radius of each pseudo hyperspherical container of classes has the same value of N / K where $N > K$. Therefore, the dimension of the original feature space should be chosen with the size of the set of classes in mind. The *relu* function ensures the non-negativity of the membership function and its differentiability.

Shannon's entropy-based Information Criterion has become widely used in the framework of information-extreme technology. For classification decision boundary of the k-th class, the Shannon's entropy-based Information Criterion is calculated by the formula [15]

$$E_k = 1 + \frac{1}{2}\left(\frac{\alpha_k}{\alpha_k + D_{2,k}} log_2 \frac{\alpha_k}{\alpha_k + D_{2,k}} + \frac{D_{1,k}}{D_{1,k} + \beta_k} log_2 \frac{D_{1,k}}{D_{1,k} + \beta_k} \right.$$
$$\left. + \frac{\beta_k}{D_{1,k} + \beta_k} log_2 \frac{\beta_k}{D_{1,k} + \beta_k} + \frac{D_{2,k}}{\alpha_k + D_{2,k}} log_2 \frac{D_{2,k}}{\alpha_k + D_{2,k}} \right). \quad (13.21)$$

Admissible domain of criterion function (13.21) is bounded by inequalities $D_{1,k} \geq 0.5$ and $D_{2,k} \geq 0.5$, or $\alpha_k \geq 0.5$ and $\beta_k \geq 0.5$. In order to take into account the admissible domain of function (13.21) in the optimization procedure based on error backpropagation method, it is proposed to perform the following operations when calculating the loss function [15]:

$$D_{1,k} = max\left(D_{1,k}, 0.5\right), \quad (13.22)$$

$$D_{2,k} = max\left(D_{2,k}, 0.5\right), \quad (13.23)$$

$$\alpha_k = max\left(\alpha_k, 0.5\right), \quad (13.24)$$

$$\beta_k = max\left(\beta_k, 0.5\right), \quad (13.25)$$

Treating the membership function of each class as a dichotomous classifier and considering the most difficult in the statistical sense case of equally probable states allows us to restate the criterion (13.21) as

$$E_k = 1 + \frac{1}{2}\left(\frac{FN_k}{FN_k + TN_k} log_2 \frac{FN_k}{FN_k + TN_k} + \frac{TP_k}{TP_k + FP_k} log_2 \frac{TP_k}{TP_k + FP_k} \right.$$
$$\left. + \frac{FP_k}{FP_k + TP_k} log_2 \frac{FP_k}{FP_k + TP_k} + \frac{TN_k}{TN_k + FN_k} log_2 \frac{TN_k}{TN_k + FN_k} \right). \quad (13.26)$$

The next stage is required to determine the binary class prototype according to the principles of error-correcting output codes, but taking into account intra-class and inter-class relations. To achieve this, the prototype class vectors $\{\overline{z}_k \mid k = \overline{1, K}\}$ are rounded to the nearest binary vectors

$$\overline{b}_{k,i} = \begin{cases} 1, if\ \overline{z}_{k,i} > 0.5; \\ 0, \ otherwise. \end{cases} \quad (13.27)$$

The calculated prototype vector of the k-th class $\overline{b}_{k,i}$ is used as a sample label for further training using the cross-entropy loss function (Binary Cross-Entropy Loss), which is calculated by the formula

$$L_{tune} = -\frac{1}{n}\sum_{i=1}^{n}\sum_{j=1}^{N}\left(\overline{b}_{t(i),j} \log\left(z_{i,j}\right) + \left(1 - \overline{b}_{t(i),j}\right)\log\left(1 - z_{i,j}\right)\right), \quad (13.28)$$

where $z_{i,j}$ is value of j-th of sigmoid output for input i-th example x_i, i.e. $z_{i,j} = f_j(x_i)$; $t(i)$ is index of class for i-th example.

The last stage of machine learning is related to the optimization of the radius of containers in accordance with the information criterion to take into account the limits of deviation of the binary representation of observations of each class from the corresponding prototypes

$$E_k^* = \max_{\{d\}} E_k(d), \tag{13.29}$$

where $\{d\} = \left\{0,1,\ldots,\left(\sum_i b_{k,i} \oplus b_{c,i} - 1\right)\right\}$ is a set of concentric radiuses with center b_k for the sample distribution of k-th class;

E_k represents the information criterion for the k-th class which is a function of the accuracy characteristics [16].

In order to evaluate the generalizing ability of the developed algorithms it is proposed to test them for resistance to adversarial attacks [13]. As an example of an adversarial attack, we consider a targeted version of the Basic Iterative Method (BIM), which searches for an adversarial sample x_{adv}, the deviation of which from the original (starting)x does not exceed a certain maximum perturbation δ. The deviation can be calculated by the Euclidean distance $x - x_{adv2} \leq \delta$ or the Chebyshev distance $x - x_{adv\infty} \leq \delta$. The BIM iteration procedure looks like this

$$x_{adv}^{t+1} = \underset{X,\delta}{\text{sign}}\left\{x_{adv}^{t} - \gamma^2\, sign\nabla_x L_{tune}\left(x, \overline{b}_{target}\right)\right\}, \overline{b}_{target} \neq \overline{b}_{true}, t = \overline{1,T}, \tag{13.30}$$

where *clip* – function which clips the pixel values of intermediate results after each step to ensure that they are in an ε-neighborhood of the original image;

γ is small step size, $\gamma = 1$;

$\overline{b}_{target}$ is a binary prototype vector of the class desirable for the attacker;

$\overline{b}_{true}$ is a binary prototype vector for ground-truth class;

T is a predefined number of iterations;

L_{tune} is the loss function (13.26) of the penultimate stage of learning the model calculated for one input sample.

13.6 EXPERIMENTAL RESULTS AND DISCUSSION

The proposed model and training method were tested on both publicly available and self-collected datasets. To ensure a robust and platform-independent algorithm, the dataset included binaries for popular architectures with Windows and Linux operating systems. The dataset for the Windows platform (PE files) was formed from the KISA Data Challenge 2019 dataset [3] and contained 18,000 examples of malware and 12,000 examples of non-malicious software, of which 5,000 samples were selected for model testing. The data sample for the Linux platform (ELF files) consisted of 10,000 examples of malicious software obtained from the Virus-Share Dataset [3], and 10,000 non-malicious examples collected from the "/bin" and "/usr/bin" directories of single-board Raspberry Pi and Jetson Nano computers with various

Linux operating systems. Two thousand samples were taken from the test dataset of malicious and non-malicious programs. Class alphabet includes four classes: Linux malware; non-malicious software for Linux operating systems; Windows malware; and non-malicious software for Windows operating systems. For unsupervised pre-training, it is proposed to use a part of the IoTPOT dataset, Dataset-1 (IoT honeypot: Malware binaries), which contains 86,496 examples [1]. Selected image resolution used when encoding executable files as images is 160×160 pixels.

According to figure 13.3, the first stage of model training is unsupervised learning, which continues until a significant decrease in the loss function is observed for the subsequent 50 iterations (13.6). The following augmentation operations are used to synthesize positive pairs for the input sample: randomly cropped images (between 0.2 and 1.0× of their original area, and their original aspect ratio), images rescaled to 160×160 pixels, randomly horizontally flipped images (p = 0.5), with random adjustments to hue, saturation, contrast, and brightness, and random grayscale conversion (p = .2). The feature extractors of the proposed model (figure 13.2a) and the conventional model (figure 13.2b) were trained for 6,000 iterations using SGD (momentum = 0.9; weight decay = 0.0001). Figure 13.4 illustrates the dependence of the validation loss function (6) on the number of iterations of contrast learning.

Analysis of figure 13.4 shows that after 6,000 iterations with a mini-batch size of 32, there is little change in the loss function. L2 normalization is added to the feature extractor of conventional architecture model (figure 13.2b) before unsupervised learning. The value of the contrast loss function for both extractors after 3,500 iterations does not change.

Figure 13.5 provides a comparison of accuracy change curves for the test dataset (acc_val) for different methods. Acc_val_conven_pretrained denotes training using the conventional approach with unsupervised pretraining of feature extractor, and acc_val_conventional denotes a conventional approach without unsupervised

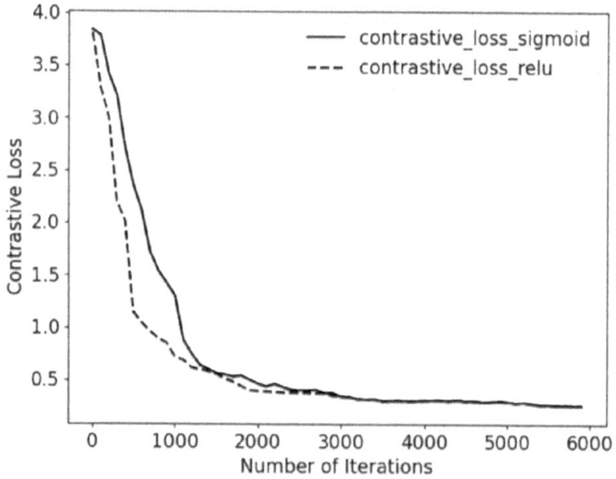

FIGURE 13.4 Dependency of contrastive loss function (6) on unlabeled test set from number of algorithm iterations.

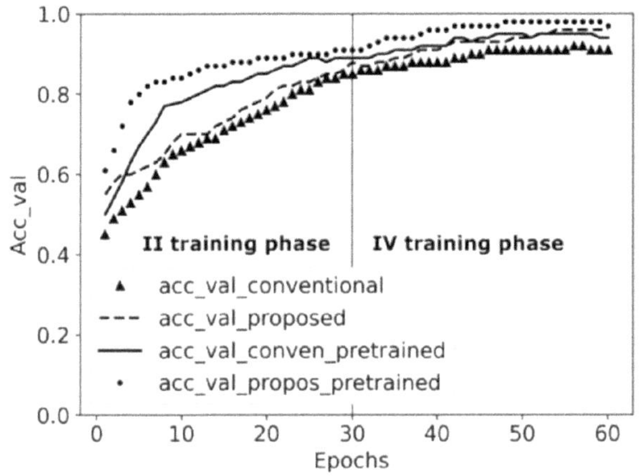

FIGURE 13.5 Dependency of Accuracy on test dataset from quantity of training epochs when training before and after the unsupervised pretraining.

pretraining of feature extractor. Likewise, acc_val_propos_pretrained and acc_val denote training under the proposed approach with and without unsupervised pretraining of the feature extractor, depicting specifically training stages II and IV of the proposed training method (figure 13.3). The optimal values of the regularization coefficients: $»_1 = 1$, $»_2 = 0.01$ are derived from cross-validation results.

Analysis of figure 13.5 shows that prior self-supervised learning improves the accuracy of models trained under both traditional and the proposed approaches. In addition, training under the proposed approach provides an increase in accuracy of 5% before pretraining and 4% after pretraining in comparison with the traditional approach. It should also be noted that the accuracy of the supervised learning model in the first epochs grows faster when preceded by unsupervised pretraining in comparison with the base case without pretraining. Continuing the training under conventional approach beyond 60 epochs leads to model overtraining. Accuracy achieved with the proposed method is 98%. At the end of the second phase of training, the average code distance between the prototype vectors of the classes is 32 code units, and the average code radius of the recognition classes is 18 code units. At the end of the fourth phase of training, the average code radius of class containers is 15 code units, which indicates the formation of buffer zones between classes and increased noise immunity of the algorithm.

In addition to the increase in accuracy, the proposed approach demonstrates notable robustness against attacks based on small modifications to samples. This indicates that the system can withstand even the most statistically challenging cases, where a minimal change in data may lead to incorrect class determination. Therefore, the model can be used in environments with high security requirements, where reducing the risk of incorrect malware detection is critical.

To test the model for resistance to noise and adversarial attacks, it is proposed to use the generated adversarial examples (one adversarial example per test example) generated in accordance with the procedure (13.30) instead of the original test

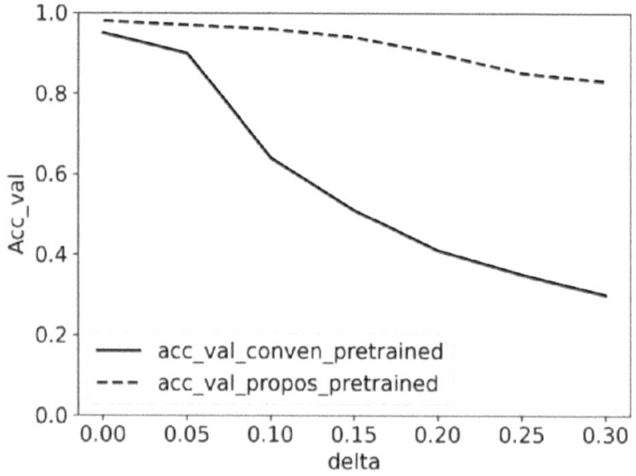

FIGURE 13.6 Dependency of Accuracy on test dataset from maximum perturbation value constructed as per the procedure (13.30).

sample. The maximum number of iterations for the adversarial algorithm (13.30) is limited and equal to $T = 100$. Figure 13.6 shows the dependence of the accuracy for the conventional (acc_val_conven_pretrained) and the proposed (acc_val_propos_pretrained) models on the perturbed test dataset depending on the size of perturbation ($\delta =$ delta) calculated by L_2-norm (Euclidean distance).

Analysis of figure 13.6 shows that the model trained in the conventional approach has a fairly high sensitivity to perturbations. For $\delta = 0.3$ the accuracy of the model trained in the proposed method on the perturbed test dataset is 83%, whereas the corresponding accuracy of the traditional model is only 30%. This indicates a high noise immunity of the proposed data analysis approach.

Additionally, it is worth noting that the proposed method not only improves detection accuracy but also significantly reduces false positive rates. This reduction is crucial in IoT environments where a high rate of false positives could lead to unnecessary system interruptions or resource consumption. The proposed model strikes a balance between robustness and efficiency, ensuring that IoT devices can operate securely without significant performance degradation.

In [3], the authors used the same labeled dataset and a similar representation of executable files in the form of images. However, the accuracy obtained in a similar study was 94.13%, which is 3.87% less than that obtained using the proposed approach (Table 13.1).

13.7 CONCLUSIONS

The suggested approach to model building and training method development of malware recognizers allows for providing platform-independence, resource-efficiency, and robustness to small modifications of malware examples at inference mode on IoT devices. Platform-independence is based on inclusion examples of different IoT

TABLE 13.1
Summary of Key Experimental Results

Experiment	Conventional Approach	Proposed Approach	Improvement
Accuracy on test set	94.13%	98%	+3.87%
Accuracy on adversarial set ($\delta = 0.3$)	30%	83%	+53%
Training epochs (unsupervised)	3,500 iterations	3,500 iterations	Equivalent loss change
Compactness of class prototypes	Average code radius: 18	Average code radius: 15	Enhanced separation
Adversarial noise immunity	Medium	High	Significant resistance

platforms to the same training set as separate classes. Resource-efficiency provided by executable files are representated as RGB images, by using backbone of MobileNet as feature extractor, which are characterized by low computational requirements. Robustness to small modifications of malware can be implemented by information bottleneck and geometric regularization.

Experiments on open datasets such as IoTPOT, KISA Data Challenge 2019, and Virus-Share confirmed that obtained accuracy under the proposed approach is 4% greater than under the traditional approach with the same feature extractor structure. Besides that, the accuracy obtained with the proposed approach is 3.87% higher than the accuracy obtained in the state-of-the-art approach for the same dataset.

Obtained accuracy under the proposed approach on an adversarial test set with L2-perturbation magnitude bounded by 0.3 is 83% which is 53% greater than under the traditional approach. It indicates the high robustness of the obtained model to adversarial attacks which can be interpreted as the worst case of small modification of malware examples.

Scientific novelties of the obtained results are the following:

- A novel multi-stage training method of robust machine learning was developed. The first training stage involves self-supervised instance-prototype contrastive learning, whilst the next stages entail training with supervised information-extreme learning with feature representation compression and geometric regularization used to find the binary prototype for each class, subsequently used as a class label for further model fine-tuning.
- For the first time, it is proposed to use the Shannon entropy information criterion, expressed as a smoothed function of the accuracy characteristics of pseudo hyperspherical decision boundaries, to train the feature extractor and determination of binary class prototypes.
- An original method of increasing the compactness of class distribution and buffer zone in the embedding space at the stage of determining the prototypes of classes is proposed. The proposed method uses regularization

based on contrastive-center loss and cross-entropy function with fixed binary class prototypes at the stage of fine-tuning.

The practical significance of the work is accuracy improvement of the malware detector model, providing platform independence and resource efficiency. The study is highly relevant to IoT devices, which are typically resource-constrained and feature a wide range of hardware architectures with varying operating systems across IoT platforms.

Future research will focus on improving the model's resilience to concept drift, which arises from software evolution and changes in operating system versions. This will ensure the stability and longevity of the detection system in the rapidly changing IoT environment. Special attention will be paid to integrating artificial intelligence systems for adaptive model training based on new data.

Another important direction for future work is exploring the integration of additional data sources, such as network traffic analysis or hardware-based detection mechanisms, to further enhance the model's detection capabilities. By incorporating data from multiple sources, the model can make more informed decisions and improve detection accuracy in cases where software-based analysis alone may be insufficient.

Further research will focus on improving the model and training method of malware recognizers to provide resilience to concept drift arising from software evolution and changing of operating system versions.

13.8 ACKNOWLEDGEMENTS

The work was performed in the Laboratory of Intellectual Systems at the Department of Computer Science, Sumy State University, with the financial support of the Ministry of Education and Science of Ukraine, under the state-funded scientific research projects DR No. 0122U000782, No. 0124U000548, and No. 0121U112684.

REFERENCES

[1] Su, J., Danilo Vasconcellos, V., Prasad, S., Daniele, S., Feng, Y., and Sakurai, K., 2018. Lightweight Classification of IoT Malware Based on Image Recognition. *2018 IEEE 42nd Annual Computer Software and Applications Conference (COMPSAC).*

[2] He, K., and Kim, D., 2019. Malware Detection with Malware Images Using Deep Learning Techniques. *2019 18th IEEE International Conference On Trust, Security And Privacy in Computing And Communications/13th IEEE International Conference On Big Data Science And Engineering (TrustCom/BigDataSE).*

[3] Hwang, C., Hwang, J., Kwak, J., and Lee, T., 2020. Platform-Independent Malware Analysis Applicable to Windows and Linux Environments. *Electronics*, 9(5), p. 793.

[4] Almasre, M., and Subahi, A., 2024. Create a Realistic IoT Dataset Using Conditional Generative Adversarial Network. *Journal of Sensor and Actuator Networks*, 13(5), p. 62.

[5] Wang, Z., Ghaleb, F. A., Zainal, A., Siraj, M. M., and Lu, X., 2024. An Efficient Intrusion Detection Model Based on Convolutional Spiking Neural Network. *Scientific Reports*, 14(1).

[6] Ayad, A. G., Sakr, N. A., and Hikal, N. A., 2024. A Hybrid Approach for Efficient Feature Selection in Anomaly Intrusion Detection for IoT Networks. *The Journal of Supercomputing*, 80(19), pp. 26942–26984.

[7] Van, C., Phan, V., Cao, V., and Nguyen, K., 2020. IoT Malware Detection based on Latent Representation. *2020 12th International Conference on Knowledge and Systems Engineering (KSE).*

[8] Liu, X., Zhang, F., Hou, Z., Mian, L., Wang, Z., Zhang, J., and Tang, J., 2021. Self-Supervised Learning: Generative or Contrastive. *IEEE Transactions on Knowledge and Data Engineering*, p. 1.

[9] Mahmood, K., Nguyen, P., Nguyen, L., Nguyen, T., and van Dijk, M., 2022. *BUZz: BUffer Zones for Defending Adversarial Examples in Image Classification.* [Online]. https://arxiv.org/abs/1910.02785 [Accessed 18 February 2022].

[10] Li, J., Guo, Y., Lao, S., Wu, Y., Bai, L., and Wei, Y., 2021. Towards a High Robust Neural Network via Feature Matching. *International Journal of Multimedia Information Retrieval*, 10(4), pp. 227–237.

[11] Kolchinsky, A., Tracey, B., and Wolpert, D., 2019. Nonlinear Information Bottleneck. *Entropy*, 21(12), p. 1181.

[12] Li, Y., Wang, Y., Miao, Z., Wang, J., and Zhang, R., 2020. Contrastive Self-Supervised Hashing With Dual Pseudo Agreement. *IEEE Access*, 8, pp. 165034–165043.

[13] Zhang, B., Tondi, B., Lv, X., and Barni, M., 2020. Challenging the Adversarial Robustness of DNNs Based on Error-Correcting Output Codes. *Security and Communication Networks*, 2020, pp. 1–11.

[14] Ho, S., Marchiano, M., Zockoll, S., and Nguyen, H., 2020. An Error-Correcting Output Code Framework for Lifelong Learning Without a Teacher. *2020 IEEE 32nd International Conference on Tools with Artificial Intelligence (ICTAI).*

[15] Moskalenko, V., Zaretskyi, M., Moskalenko, A., and Lysyuk, V., 2020. Sewer Pipe Defects Classification Based on Deep Convolutional Network with Information-Extreme Error-Correction Decision Rules. *Communications in Computer and Information Science*, pp. 253–263.

[16] Dovbysh, A., Budnyk, M., Piatachenko, V., and Myronenko, M., 2020. Information-Extreme Machine Learning of On-Board Vehicle Recognition System. *Cybernetics and Systems Analysis*, 56(4), pp. 534–543.

[17] El-Shafai, W., Almomani, I., and AlKhayer, A., 2021. Visualized Malware Multi-Classification Framework Using Fine-Tuned CNN-Based Transfer Learning Models. *Applied Sciences*, 11(14), p. 6446.

[18] Liu, H., Wu, Z., Yin, M., Yu, D., Zhu, X., and Lou, J., 2024. An Improved Deep Hashing Model for Image Retrieval with Binary Code Similarities. *Journal of Big Data*, 11(1).

[19] Konkle, T., and Alvarez, G. A., 2022. A Self-Supervised Domain-General Learning Framework for Human Ventral Stream Representation. *Nature Communications*, 13(1), p. 491.

[20] Qi, C., and Su, F., 2017. Contrastive-Center Loss for Deep Neural Networks. *2017 IEEE International Conference on Image Processing (ICIP).*

[21] Zhao, K., Gao, S., Wang, W., and Cheng, M., 2019. Optimizing the F-Measure for Threshold-Free Salient Object Detection. *2019 IEEE/CVF International Conference on Computer Vision (ICCV).*

14 Detection of Network Attacks Based on the RedHunt Virtual Machine

Ivan Opirskyy, Oleh Harasymchuk, Olha Mykhaylova, Yaroslav Sovyn, and Ivan Tyshyk

14.1 INTRODUCTION

Information technologies are widely used in such areas as finance, the securities market, transport, communications, high-tech production, government control systems, etc. Any sabotage or terrorist act in those areas of the state and society (especially critical ones) such as nuclear energy, chemical industry, etc. can lead to serious consequences and paralyze both single and complex high-tech control systems, armed forces, and special services. This may cause accidents at environmentally hazardous facilities.

One of the most dangerous types of attacker's activity is the so-called refusal attacks. Denial attacks consist of blocking user access to the service provided by the target. Such an attack can be carried out in two ways. The first method exploits the weaknesses of the software installed on the client of the attack object, which allows the bringing down of the system by forwarding malicious packets. The second way is to use large amounts of empty traffic to load the system resources needed to process requests from legitimate users. If you can protect yourself from the first attack method by neutralizing weaknesses by updating programs, then it is not so easy to prevent an attack of the second type. If repudiation traffic is sent from multiple sources, then such attacks are called distributed repudiation attacks. By using multiple sources, the attack power is compounded and the problem of defending against it is further complicated. Another negative factor is the use of the traffic reflection effect, which further complicates the identification of attack sources.

In addition, recent trends indicate the emergence of new types of attacks – stealth attacks. In this case, computers controlled by the attacker gain access to the target service for quite legal reasons (for example, visiting the company's website) and load the channel with resource-intensive operations (degradation attack) or at some point "explode" with meaningless traffic that puts before the protection systems new non-trivial tasks of detecting and counteracting.

That is why the elements of information security are very relevant and important. They require the deepest analysis and research since, with the development of

 DOI: 10.1201/9781003546153-14

information technologies, methods and types of attacks in the information space are developing.

Ensuring information security is a priority for every organization and state. In the era of computerization and automation, the problem of computer security comes to the fore. One of the tasks that must be solved in the context of information security is the protection of stored, processed, and transmitted information in computer systems and networks. One of the threats to computer security is network attacks.

Despite the steps of the world community to constantly increase the punishment for cybercrime, cybercriminals continue to improve and develop methods and tools for organizing cyber-attacks. Today, the proposed methods of protecting computer systems and networks are not able to ensure an adequate level of information security. Computer systems are constantly exposed to various types of threats, and the user cannot be sure of the security of important information. The current situation stimulates the search for and development of new methods and solutions aimed at improving the protection of computer systems from harmful influences.

Finding vulnerabilities is an important part of the security task. This work includes regular testing of the information system. At any point in time, for any system, you can specify many different types of vulnerabilities, for example, for operating systems and application programs, the latest vulnerabilities occur almost once a day. Identifying them manually is a very time-consuming task. Therefore, to automate the search for vulnerabilities, various software tools are used – vulnerability-scanning tools, such as GFI LANguard, Nessus, OpenVAS, SPARTA, Lynis, and others.

The saturation of the IT market with these systems puts before the user an urgent need to choose the optimal system for detecting attacks and preventing intrusions, but this can only be done based on an analysis of systems positioned as IDS (intrusion detection system) [1–5].

Formulation of the problem. Given the aforementioned, the task arises of a thorough analysis of the advantages and disadvantages of modern systems for detecting attacks and choosing the optimal one that would provide a comprehensive approach to detecting unauthorized intrusions into an information system and implementing an analysis of its security status.

Analysis of recent research and publications. Positive Technologies research shows that 94% of IT systems are not protected from hacking. The most vulnerable areas of the network perimeter are Internet-based interfaces for managing network equipment, servers, and the use of dictionary passwords, including the default password [6–9].

During testing against an attacker (for example, a regular worker located in a user-defined network segment), in all cases, unauthorized privileged access to critical resources (banking, enterprise resource planning system, and other key network components) can be obtained. In 78% of cases, an insider can gain complete control over an organization's information infrastructure.

Weak passwords remain the most common vulnerability of internal network resources. Simultaneously, each system detects simple administrator passwords (up to six characters long). The next most common internal network vulnerability is the lack of protection for privileged user accounts (for 88% of systems). In 50% of cases, outdated software is used. What allows the exploitation of vulnerabilities such as Heartbleed and Shellshock? [10–16]

Contrary to popular belief that the main threat to a company comes from external attackers operating on the Internet, commonly known as hackers, the real danger to the information system of a modern company is posed by insider threats. According to numerous studies, internal attackers [7, 8] account for more than 70–80% of all violations in the corporate environment. Moreover, the reasons for violating the security of the information system of the organization can be both illegal actions of staff and intentional actions on their part. Thus, according to world statistics, the share of domestic criminals who knowingly commit illegal acts is about 20% of all incidents at the enterprise, while external criminals have only 5% of such cases [9].

Email remains an important tool for cybercriminals, but they are experimenting with new methods of attack through mobile devices and social networks to reach a large audience. "Over the past year, 70% of social media scams have been manual, as attackers exploit people's willingness to trust the content they share with their friends" (Symantec report data) [11].

While social media scams allow cyber criminals to get rich quickly, some rely on more lucrative and aggressive attack methods such as ransomware, the number of which increases significantly from year to year. Ransomware is one of the most active malware today. Ransomware have evolved in recent years. In addition, they implement more dangerous actions than a simple screen lock with a ransom demand. For example, at present, the basis of the ransomware class is the so-called ransomware. Encryption programs without the user's knowledge encrypt his data, including personal photos, archives, documents, databases, and drawings – in a word, everything that is of value to the victim. Decrypting these files requires the victim to pay. The most notable examples of such encryption are CryptoLocker, CryptoDefence (and its successor, CryptoWall), ACCDFISA, and Gpcode [12].

Various intrusion detection systems (IDS) are widely used in information systems (IS). They are presented in the form of software or hardware systems, which automate the process of analyzing events in the information and communication system for security reasons. In addition to detecting attacks (actual or potential), IDS can respond to attacks in a certain way (from creating simple reports to actively intervening when an IS intrusion is detected).

Currently, IDS is considered a necessary element of the security infrastructure, therefore, in several literary sources, they are given special attention. In particular [14], such popular tools for automatic scanning of IS vulnerabilities as Nessus 7, OpenVAS, SPARTA, and Lynis are considered; types of vulnerabilities are presented and their systematization is carried out. Particular attention is paid to wireless network penetration testing tools and active and passive analysis of wireless traffic. However, a security administrator should have a set of network tools that will allow him to simulate a certain type of attack to identify the vulnerability of his information system and select the appropriate policy for its protection. [16] focuses on network spoofing tools and popular network sniffers such as tcpdump and Wireshark. This type of IDS is classified according to information sources as network-level IDS. However, it would be expedient for a security administrator to have tools that analyze the IP as a whole and warn about the potential for an attack on it. In [17], attention is focused on the structure of the Metasploit Framework. Currently, Metasploit is included in almost all Linux operating system distributions. The latest version of Metasploit contains over 1,677 exploits for more than 25 platforms, including Android, PHP, Python, Java, Cisco, and others. It is also one of the most complex projects to date and is designed to keep the security administrator aware of the vulnerabilities found in this or that software. This type of IDS is classified according to the information source as the IDS of the application programs and database management systems level. In [18], special attention is paid to tools for passive and active reconnaissance of computer networks and means for scanning vulnerabilities at the level of operating systems, which provides a high level of IP protection from unauthorized intrusions. However, there is no comprehensive approach to the analysis of the state of IS security in general.

Thus, if there is a correct choice of IDS in the IS, an intruder's access to the system can be blocked in advance. Even the presence of a simple reaction to network probing increases the risk for an attacker and may cause him to abandon further attempts to penetrate the network.

Documented information about attacks can be useful in reporting to the information protection service. Understanding the frequency and nature of attacks allows you to take adequate measures to ensure the security of IS. The functioning of the IDS for a long time provides information on how the system is used, which makes it possible to identify shortcomings in the implementation of system security management and make changes to management procedures. This allows you to get useful information about the implemented penetration into a protected system with the provision of improved diagnostics to identify and correct factors that contribute to its compromise. Even when the IDS is unable to block an attack, it can collect detailed and reliable information about it, which will form the basis of appropriate legal and administrative measures. IDS helps to determine the location of the source of attacks on the local network (external or internal attacks). This is important when making decisions about the location of resources on the network [19, 20].

Research on the problem of detecting network attacks and developing new methods and tools for detecting network attacks has been repeatedly covered in the relevant publications of the authors [21–28].

This work aims to study the RedHunt complex system based on a virtual machine to detect attacks in IS in real-time and analyze the state of its security, to analyze the use of interconnected utilities of this virtual machine to increase the level of IS protection from various types of unauthorized intrusions.

14.2 PROBLEMS OF INFORMATION PROTECTION IN COMPUTER NETWORKS

The widespread use of computer technologies in automated information processing and control systems has aggravated the problem of protecting information circulating in computer systems from unauthorized access. Information protection in computer systems has several specific features [1].

Problems related to the security of data transmission while working in computer networks can be divided into three main types:

i. interception of information – the integrity of information is preserved and its confidentiality is violated;
ii. modification of information – the outgoing message is changed or completely replaced by another and sent to addressee;
iii. substitution of authorship of information. This problem can have serious consequences. For example, someone can send an email on your behalf (this type of deception is commonly called spoofing) or a Web server can pretend to be an electronic store, accept orders and credit card numbers, but not send any goods.

The emergence of global information networks such as the Internet is an important achievement of computer technology, but a lot of computer crimes are associated with the Internet.

The result of the experience of using the Internet network is the discovery of the weakness of traditional protection mechanisms and the lag in the application of modern methods. Cryptography makes it possible to take care of the security of information on the Internet, so active work was carried out to introduce the necessary cryptographic mechanisms into this network. Not a rejection of progress in informatization, but the use of modern achievements in cryptography is the strategically correct decision. The ability to use global information networks and cryptography is the achievement hallmark of a democratic society.

Due to their openness and public accessibility, computer networks and public communication networks are convenient means for ensuring the interaction of citizens, businesses, and public authorities. However, the more open networks are, the more vulnerable they are. Several features make networks vulnerable and violators elusive:

i. the ability of violators to act at a distance, combined with the ability to hide their true personal data (this feature is typical, in particular, for the Internet, radio networks, cable television networks, and illegal use of telephone network resources);
ii. the possibility of propaganda and distribution of means of violating network security (for example, distribution on the Internet of software tools that allow for unauthorized access to information resources, copyright infringement, etc.);
iii. the possibility of multiple repetitions of impacts attacking the network (for example, the generation of call flows in the Internet or telephone networks, leading to disruption of the functioning of network nodes).
iv. use of inconsistent information security methods for various network components, including telecommunication protocols, information resources, and applications;
v. wide use of imported technical means, potentially having undeclared capabilities ("bookmarks");

vi. lack of comprehensive solutions to ensure information security in the integration and interaction of networks;
vii. insufficient elaboration of the methodology for documenting the functioning of networks, which is necessary to create an evidence base for offenses;
viii. the widespread attitude to information security as a product or service that can be bought, and not as a process that must not only be created but also must be introduced into permanent use and must be constantly managed.

Any successful attack by an intruder aimed at realizing a threat to the information security of a network relies on the knowledge gained by the intruder about the features of its construction and weaknesses. The reasons for the appearance of vulnerabilities in networks can be:

i. vulnerable areas in the software product;
ii. violation of information transfer and control technologies;
iii. introduction of components and programs that implement undeclared functions and disrupt the normal functioning of networks;
iv. non-compliance with the implemented network protection mechanisms of the specified requirements for the process of ensuring information security or the presentation of an ill-conceived set of requirements;
v. use of non-certified domestic and foreign information technologies, means of informatization and communication, as well as means of protecting information and monitoring their effectiveness by the security requirements.

All network security threats can be divided into two large groups: technical threats and the human factor.

Technical ones include reconnaissance, software errors, various DoS and DDoS attacks, computer viruses, worms, Trojan horses, protocol analyzers and listening programs ("sniffers"), and technical means of information capture.

Network intelligence is a comprehensive set of measures aimed at gathering data about an organization's information system, searching for information resources, analyzing security mechanisms, and identifying vulnerabilities in devices and software [12].

Network reconnaissance is performed in the form of DNS requests, echo testing (ping sweep), and port scanning. DNS queries help to understand who owns this or that domain and what addresses of this domain are assigned. A review of DNS-revealed addresses testing allows you to see which hosts work in this environment. Having received a list of hosts, the hacker uses port scanning tools to compile a complete list of services provided by these hosts. And finally, the hacker analyzes the characteristics of applications running on hosts. As a result, information is obtained that can be used for hacking.

Modern network intelligence, depending on the goals of the activity, the scale, and the nature of the tasks set for the fulfillment of tasks, is divided into strategic and operational.

Getting rid of network intelligence is impossible. For example, by disabling ISMP echo and echo response on peripheral routers, thereby avoiding echo testing, data needed for network failures are lost. In addition, you can scan ports without preliminary echo-testing. It will just take longer because non-existent IP addresses will also have to be scanned. IDS/IPS systems at the network and host level usually do a good job of reporting network intelligence to the security administrator, which in turn allows for better countering a network attack and alerting the ISP from whose network the attack is being planned.

Unauthorized access (UA) in the network. The purpose of the UA on the network is to be able to take control of the computer.

The most effective methods of protection against unauthorized access through computer networks are virtual private networks (VPNs) and firewalls. Let's consider them in more detail.

VPNs provide automatic protection of the integrity and confidentiality of messages transmitted over various public networks, primarily the Internet. A VPN is a collection of networks on the outer perimeter of which VPN agents are installed. A VPN agent is a program (or software and hardware system) that protects information transmitted by performing the operations described as follows.

Before sending any IP packet to the network, the VPN agent does the following:

i. Information about its destination is extracted from the header of an IP packet. According to this information, based on the security policy of this VPN agent, security algorithms (if the VPN agent supports several algorithms) and cryptographic keys are selected with which this packet will be protected. If the security policy of the VPN agent does not provide for sending an IP packet to a given addressee or an IP packet with these features, the sending of the IP packet is blocked.
ii. Using the selected integrity protection algorithm, an electronic digital signature (EDS), an imitator, or a similar checksum is generated and added to the IP packet.
iii. Using the selected algorithm, encryption is performed when the IP packet is encrypted.
iv. Using the established packet encapsulation algorithm, the encrypted IP packet is placed in an IP packet ready for transmission, the header of which, instead of the original information about the destination and the sender, contains information about the destination VPN agent and the sender VPN agent, respectively. That is, network address translation is performed.
v. The packet is sent to the destination VPN agent. If necessary, it is changed and the resulting packets are sent one by one.

When receiving an IP packet, the VPN agent does the following: extracts information about its sender from the header of the IP packet. If the sender is not allowed (according to the security policy) or is unknown (for example, when receiving a packet with a deliberately or accidentally damaged header), the packet is not processed and is discarded.

According to the security policy, algorithms for protecting this package and keys are selected, with the help of which the package will be decrypted and its integrity checked. The informational (encapsulated) part of the packet is extracted and decrypted. The integrity of the package is checked based on the selected algorithm.

If an integrity violation is detected, the packet is discarded. The packet is sent to the destination (over the internal network) according to the information found in its original header.

A firewall is a software or software and hardware tool that protects local and individual computers from unauthorized access from external networks by filtering a two-way message flow during information exchange. The firewall is a "cut down" VPN agent that does not encrypt packets and control their integrity, but in some cases, it has several additional functions, the most common of which are the following:

i. anti-virus scanning;
ii. package correctness control;
iii. control of the correctness of connections (for example, the establishment, use, and termination of TCP sessions);
iv. content control.

Software bugs are the bottleneck of any network. Sources of errors in software are specialists – specific people with their characteristics, qualifications, talent, and experience. Most errors are harmless; some can lead to tragic consequences, such as an attacker gaining control of the server, server inoperability, and unauthorized use of resources. Such vulnerabilities are fixed using service packs released regularly by the software manufacturer. Installing these updates is a prerequisite for network security.

Various DoS and DDoS attacks. Denial of Service (DoS) is a special type of attack aimed at bringing a network or server out of service. DoS attacks can use software bugs or legitimate operations, but on a larger scale (for example, sending a huge amount of emails). A new type of Distributed Denial of Service (DDoS) attack differs from the previous one in the presence of a huge number of computers located in a wide geographical area. Such attacks simply overload the channel with traffic interfering with the passage, and often completely blocking the transmission of useful information. Protection against DoS attacks should be based on a firewall. Monitoring and analyzing traffic will allow timely detection of threats and taking of the necessary measures. More reliable protection against DDoS attacks is achieved using a dedicated server. Secure Disk Space securely stores data under the control of data center experts. It provides round-the-clock access to the network. There is a traffic cleaning system as high-quality protection for DDoS attacks, built on the detection of fake packets and their blocking. During a DDoS attack, you can immediately notice anomalous deviations in the plotted curves. At the first symptoms of an attack, it is recommended to contact professional services that protect against such attacks.

Computer viruses, worms, Trojan horses. A computer virus is a type of malicious software that can create copies of itself and intrude into the code of other programs to disrupt the operation of software and hardware systems. Due to the active use of network technologies for data transmission, viruses are increasingly integrated with Trojan components and network worms. Currently, a computer virus uses either email or software vulnerabilities to spread. There are a lot of methods of defense, and among them are the same timely installation of updates, installation of anti-virus software, monitoring tasks and services running in the system, and installing a personal firewall.

Protocol analyzers and listening programs ("sniffers"). This group includes means of intercepting data transmitted over the network. Typically, data are transmitted over the network in the clear, which allows an attacker inside the local network to intercept it. Some networking protocols (POP3, FTP) do not use password encryption, which allows an attacker to intercept them and use them themselves. When transmitting data over global networks, this problem arises most acutely.

A packet sniffer is an application program that uses a network card operating in promiscuous mode (in this mode, all packets received over physical channels are sent by the network adapter to the application for processing). The sniffer intercepts all network packets that are transmitted through a specific domain. Currently, sniffers work in networks on a completely legal basis. With the help of sniffers, you can find useful and sometimes confidential information (for example, usernames and passwords).

You can mitigate the threat of packet sniffing by:

i. Authentication. Strong authentication is the most important way to protect against packet sniffing. By "strong" we mean authentication methods that are hard to bypass. One-time passwords (OTPs) are an example of such authentication.
ii. Switched infrastructure. Another means of combating packet sniffing in a network environment is the creation of a switched infrastructure. If your entire organization uses switched Ethernet, hackers can only access traffic coming in on the port they are connected to.
iii. Anti-sniffers. This anti-sniffing tool is to install hardware or software that recognizes sniffers operating on the network.
iv. Cryptography. This is the most effective means of combating packet sniffing. Although it does not prevent interception and does not recognize the work of a sniffer, it makes this work useless.

IP spoofing occurs when a hacker, whether inside or outside a corporation, poses as an authorized user.

The threat of spoofing can be mitigated by the following measures:

i. Access control. The simplest means of preventing IP spoofing is to choose the right access control.
ii. RFC 2827 filtering. An administrator can stop users on their network from spoofing foreign networks. To do this, you need to reject any outgoing traffic whose start address is not one of your organization's IP addresses [2].
iii. The most effective method of dealing with IP spoofing is the same as in the case of packet sniffing: you need to make the attack completely ineffective. IP spoofing can only function if authentication is based on IP addresses. Therefore, the introduction of additional authentication methods makes such attacks useless.

Application layer attacks can be carried out in several ways. The most common of these is exploiting known weaknesses in server software (Sendmail, HTTP, FTP).

The main problem with application layer attacks is that hackers often use ports that are allowed to pass through the firewall.

Remote attacks would not be carried out if each network connection had a separate communication line, but the infrastructure of public networks does not provide a dedicated channel connection for each network object. An alternative to a dedicated communication channel is the use of secure virtual connections using VPN technologies, a mechanism which is addressed earlier in this chapter. The task of identifying and authenticating users in a distributed network is very important. The security of the information system as a whole depends on the success of its solution. As discussed earlier, the standard methods for compromising users by an attacker are:

i. presenting oneself to a legal user with the assignment of his rights and powers to access the system (for example, a typical "MITM" remote attack);
ii. introduction into the system of an erroneous object pretending to be a trusted object of the system (for example, a typical remote attack "False Network Object").

Because the standard methods of identification and authentication (name/password) in information systems are not sufficient to protect against remote attacks, it is necessary to introduce additional means of identifying objects in the information network and crypto protecting the information transmitted in it.

When creating a virtual channel, cryptographic algorithms with a public key (for example, SSL – Secret Socket Layer) can be used. As mentioned earlier, the main idea is a two-key encryption method in which the encryption key and the decryption key are different from each other, and the latter cannot be determined from the former. The essence of public-key cryptography (or two-key cryptography) is that the keys available in the cryptosystem enter in pairs, and each pair satisfies the following two properties:

i. Information encrypted with one key can be decrypted with another,
ii. Knowledge of one key does not allow one to calculate another.

Therefore, one of the keys can be published. With a published (public) encryption key and a secret decryption key, a public key encryption system emerges. Each network user can encrypt messages using the public key, and only the owner of the private key can decrypt it. When the decryption key is published, the digital signature system is released. Here, only the owner of the secret signing key can correctly encrypt the text (i.e., sign it), and any of the published signature verification keys can verify the signature (decrypt the text).

Protection against the "network traffic analysis" attack. Network traffic analysis refers to a constantly anticipated threat that cannot be eliminated but can be made meaningless to an attacker if strong cryptographic algorithms are applied to the transmitted data stream.

To provide remote authorized access to the resources of information systems, it is not recommended to use the remote access protocols TELNET, HTTP, and FTP, since they do not provide for elementary crypto protection of identifiers (names) and authenticators (passwords) transmitted over the network. The use of secure exchange protocols (such as SSL, TLS, SSH, and HTTPS) will provide secure remote access to the resources of their systems. To transfer confidential information, it is recommended to use virtual communication channels (VPN), the connections of which are provided using cryptographic tools.

Protection against DoS attacks. Today, several companies offer both software and hardware protection against DoS attacks. However, there is no 100% denial-of-service protection for IPv4 in a WAN. This is because IPv4 has no way to control the route of messages. Therefore, it is impossible to provide reliable control over network connections, since an unlimited number of communication channels with a remote object can be occupied by one user, while the user's anonymity is preserved.

However, by following certain rules, you can significantly weaken the DoS attack and reduce its impact on the system under attack. Next are recommendations, the application of which will allow you to protect yourself from DoS attacks to a certain extent.

i. To increase the reliability of the system, use as powerful computers as possible. The greater the number and frequency of processors, the greater the amount of RAM and the more reliable the operation of the network OS will be when a directed storm of erroneous requests to create a connection hits it. In addition, it is necessary to use the appropriate computing power of operating systems with an internal queue that can accommodate a large number of connection requests.
ii. The use of anti-DoS and anti-spoofing functions on firewalls and routers protects the system from overload by limiting half-open channels.
iii. Regular updates of the operating system and antivirus software will help patch a significant number of security gaps in the information system's protection mechanisms.
iv. Using a server cluster allows you to increase the reliability and performance by several times compared to a conventional server.

14.3 SELECTION OF REDHUNT SYSTEM UTILITIES FOR DETECTION OF NETWORK ATTACKS

Attack emulation tools are used to raise awareness of the most well-known attacks that are performed using specific programs. This chapter considers the three basic utilities of the RedHunt system, listed next.

DumsterFire is a tool for creating recurring security events. This makes it easier for the security team to create event chains and set up alerts to infect or attack the system. Attackers can also use the DumpsterFire utility to create bait incidents and distract defenders to support and scale their operations. The utility has its library of modules called "Fires". It is possible to create and add your modules and edit existing ones. DumpsterFire is an easy-to-use console utility designed to test vulnerabilities and attacks on the system as a whole. Thanks to this utility, you can completely simulate a vulnerable operating system. The program shows the attacker's full path, starting with his standard port scan and identifying traces that will allow him to access and control this system in the future. This system is convenient for security administrators when used not as a regular simulator, but as a system for early detection of the threat of unauthorized intrusion.

Nmap is free open-source software for network security research and audit with detection of active network services. Nmap uses many different scanning methods such as UDP, TCP [24], TCP SYN, FTP, ICMP, FIN, ACK, Xmas tree, SYN, and NULL scanning. Nmap also supports a wide range of advanced features, including:

i. determination of the operating system of the remote host using the fingerprints of the TCP/IP stack;
ii. hidden scans;
iii. determination of inactive hosts by parallel ping-scan;
iv. determining the presence of batch filters;
v. scanning using IP fragmentation;
vi. arbitrary indication of IP addresses and port numbers of scanned networks.

Nmap is a console utility. It can be used as a standalone program or as a regular command on the command line (you still need to install it before that). The utility makes it possible to check the connection between different systems within the same common environment. Nmap can also check the status of ports, and if any of the insignificant ports are open, it implements actions to stop their work.

Nmap can also be asked to check the operating system used on the target computer. This information is very useful in identifying vulnerabilities. To use this feature, use the -O option [7].

For example, you can find the operating system used on the target machine with the Nmap -O 172.16.43.156 command (Figure 14.1).

To activate the probe, you must add the -A option. In this case, you can get the following information:

i. service version detection (-sV);
ii. operating system detection (-O);
iii. script scanning (-sC);
iv. tracing (-traceroute).

To perform such a scan, you must enter the command nmap -A 172.16.43.156.

Figure 14.2 shows a summary of the execution of this command.

To view the packets sent by Nmap, you need to scan the 172.16.43.0/24 network. The tcpdump packet capture utility was used for monitoring the sent packets:

tcpdump -nnX tcp and host 172.16.43.150

The IP address 172.16.43.150 belongs to the machine running Nmap. On the same computer, open another terminal and enter the following command:

nmap 172.16.43.0/24

In the tcpdump console, you will see the following (Figure 14.3):

To scan a host with IPv6, use the -6 option before the target IP address. nmap -6 fe80::20c:29ff:fe18:f08. The result of IPv6 scanning is shown in Figure 14.4.

When testing IPv6, you can see that the number of open ports is less than when testing IPv4. This is because not all services on the remote computer support IPv6.

```
Starting Nmap 6.49BETA4 ( https://nmap.org ) at 2024-03-20 20:59 PDT
Nmap scan report for 172.16.43.156
Host is up (0.00021s latency).
Not shown: 977 closed ports
PORT      STATE SERVICE
21/tcp    open  ftp
22/tcp    open  ssh
23/tcp    open  telnet
25/tcp    open  smtp
53/tcp    open  domain
80/tcp    open  http
111/tcp   open  rpcbind
139/tcp   open  netbios-ssn
445/tcp   open  microsoft-ds
512/tcp   open  exec
513/tcp   open  login
514/tcp   open  shell
1099/tcp  open  rmiregistry
1524/tcp  open  ingreslock
2049/tcp  open  nfs
2121/tcp  open  ccproxy-ftp
3306/tcp  open  mysql
5432/tcp  open  postgresql
5900/tcp  open  vnc
6000/tcp  open  X11
6667/tcp  open  irc
8009/tcp  open  ajp13
8180/tcp  open  unknown
MAC Address: 00:0C:29:18:0F:08 (VMware)
Device type: general purpose
Running: Linux 2.6.X
OS CPE: cpe:/o:linux:linux_kernel:2.6
OS details: Linux 2.6.9 - 2.6.33
Network Distance: 1 hop

OS detection performed. Please report any incorrect results at https://nmap.org/
submit/ .
Nmap done: 1 IP address (1 host up) scanned in 3.46 seconds
```

FIGURE 14.1 Finding the operating system on the target machine.

```
Starting Nmap 6.49BETA4 ( http://nmap.org ) at 2024-03-20 14:01 PDT
Nmap scan report for 172.16.43.156
Host is up (0.00021s latency) .
Not Shown: 977 closed ports
PORT      STATE     SERVICE     VERSION
21/tcp    open      ftp         vsftpd 2.3.4
| ftp-anon: Anonymous FTP login allowed (FTP code 230)
22/tcp    open      ssh         OpenSSH 4.7p1 Debian 8ubuntu1 (protocol 2.0)
| ssh-hostkey:
|  1024 60: 0f :cf :e1:c0:5f:6a:74:d6:90:24:fa: c4:d5:6c:cd (DSA)
|  2048 56:56:24:0f:21:1d:de:a7:2b:ae:61:b1:24:3d:e8:f3 (RSA)
23/tcp    open      telnet      linux telnetd
25/tcp    open      smtp        postfix smtpd
|_smtp-commands: metasploitable.localdomain, PIPELINING, SIZE 10240000, VRFY, ETRN, STARTTLS, ENHANCEDSTATUSCODES, 8BITMIME, DSN,
SMTPUTF8

| ssl-cert: Subject: commonName=ubuntu834 base.localdomain/organizationName=OCOSA/statrOnProvinceName=There is no such thing outside US/
countryName=XX
| Not valid before: 2020-04-22T18:38:06
| Not  valid  after : 2020-04-20T18:38:06
|_ssl-date: 2024-02-14T13:18:17+00:00; 35d07h43mlls from scanner time.
53/tcp    open      domain      ISC BIND 9.4.2
| dns-nsid:
|   bind.version: 9.4.2
80/tcp    open      http        Apache httpd 2.2.8 (Ubuntu) DAV/2)
|_http-methods: No Allow or Public header in OPTIONS responce (status code 2000)
|_http-server-header: Apache/2.2.8 (Ubuntu) DAV/2)
|_http-title: Metasploitable2      Linux
```

FIGURE 14.2 Report on the execution of the command with the -A parameter.

```
    22:42:12.107532 IP 172.16.43.150.49270 >172.16.43.156.23: Flags [S],
seq 239440322, win 1024, options [mss 1460], length 0
      0x0000:  4500 002c eb7f 0000 3006 ad2e c0a8 3866  E..,....0.....8f
      0x0010:  c0a8 3867 c076 0017 0e45 91c2 0000 0000  ..8g.v...E......
      0x0020:  6002 0400 4173 0000 0204 05b4            `...As......
```

FIGURE 14.3 Demonstration of tcpdump utility operation.

```
Starting Nmap 6.49BETA4 ( https://nmap.org ) at 2024-03-20 14:16 PDT
Nmap scan report for fe80::20c:29ff:fe18:f08
Host is up (0.00011s latency).
Not shown: 996 closed ports
PORT     STATE SERVICE
22/tcp   open  ssh
53/tcp   open  domain
2121/tcp open  ccproxy-ftp
5432/tcp open  postgresql
MAC Address: 00:0C:29:18:0F:08 (VMware)
```

FIGURE 14.4 IPv6 scan result.

Nmap has already become a massive network exploration inventory. If you add scripting capabilities to this application, it becomes a more powerful tool. With the Nmap Scripting Engine (NSE), users can automate various network tasks, such as checking for new security vulnerabilities in applications, detecting application versions, or other features not available in regular Nmap. The Nmap scanner has already included various NSE scripts in its package, but users can also write their scripts according to their needs.

These Nmap scripts are located in Kali Linux at /usr/share/Nmap/scripts directories. Nmap version 7.70 currently contains 588 scripts. This version of Nmap is included in Kali Linux. There are several command line arguments to invoke NSE [7]:

i. -sC or—script=default – scanning is performed using scripts selected by default;
ii. --script <file_name> | <category> | <directories> – scanning is performed using a script defined in file names, categories, or directories;
iii. --script-args <args> – entry gives script argument. If the auth category is used, an example of such arguments would be a username or password.

Using the default scripts, Nmap can get more detailed information. For example, using four NSE HTTP scripts, we obtain more information about the web servers of the target system.

i. choice of coding technique to encrypt the payload so that it cannot be found by the attack detection system;
ii. exploit execution.

The Metasploit Project is a computer security project that provides information on vulnerabilities in information systems and assists in intrusion testing and the development of attack detection systems. Its best-known subproject is the Metasploit Framework, which is an application for developing and implementing code exploits

```
Starting Nmap 6.49BETA4 ( https://nmap.org ) at 2024-03-20 14:21 PDT
Nmap scan report for 172.16.43.156
Host is up (0.00032s latency).
PORT   STATE SERVICE
80/tcp open  http
| http-enum:
|   /tikiwiki/: Tikiwiki
|   /test/: Test page
|   /phpinfo.php: Possible information file
|   /phpMyAdmin/: phpMyAdmin
|   /doc/: Potentially interesting directory w/ listing on 'apache/2.2.8 (ubuntu) dav/2'
|   /icons/: Potentially interesting folder w/ directory listing
|_  /index/: Potentially interesting folder
| http-headers:
|   Date: Sun, 14 Feb 2016 13:37:43 GMT
|   Server: Apache/2.2.8 (Ubuntu) DAV/2
|   X-Powered-By: PHP/5.2.4-2ubuntu5.10
|   Connection: close
|   Content-Type: text/html
|
|_  (Request type: HEAD)
|_http-methods: No Allow or Public header in OPTIONS response (status code 200)
| http-php-version: Versions from logo query (less accurate): 5.1.3 - 5.1.6, 5.2.0 - 5.2.17
| Versions from credits query (more accurate): 5.2.3 - 5.2.5
|_Version from header x-powered-by: PHP/5.2.4-2ubuntu5.10
MAC Address: 00:0C:29:18:0F:08 (VMware)
```

FIGURE 14.5 Result of executing a command that includes HTTP scripts.

against a remote target computer. The main steps for operating a system based on Metasploit are:

- exploit selection and configuration (code that penetrates the target system using its vulnerabilities);
- additional verification of the system's susceptibility to this exploit;
- payload selection and configuration (code that will be executed on the target system in case of successful penetration).

The main advantage of Metasploit is its modular approach – allowing any exploit to be combined with any payload.

Thus, the Metasploit utility is a database of exploits, often very closely related to the Nmap utility. Hackers record and exploit vulnerabilities and viruses, and specialists create anti-virus programs such as heuristics and behavior blockers actively using this database, which is a utility or program.

14.4 IMPLEMENTATION OF THE PROCESS OF DETECTION OF NETWORK ATTACKS BASED ON THE REDHUNT SYSTEM

The running network attack detection simulation in the DumpsterFire utility demonstrates the actions of an attacker in a compromised system in stages. The attacker opens a URL session on various sites where you can find information about certain exploits or vulnerabilities. There are also sites where an attacker finds common logins and passwords, as well as other information about the purpose of the displayed Figure 14.6.

Figure 14.7 shows the pre-attack activities, namely downloading programs and exploits to carry out the attack. Downloading virus programs directly depends on

```
Igniting Fire:  Websurfing/hacking_sites.py
Using ConfigStr: (None)

Websurfing/hacking_sites: Opening URL session to ExploitDB landing page
Sleeping for 78 seconds to simulate human browsing habits
Websurfing/hacking_sites: Opening URL session to ExploitDB exploits
Sleeping for 13 seconds to simulate human browsing habits
Websurfing/hacking_sites: Opening URL session to ExploitDB Google hacking DB
Sleeping for 71 seconds to simulate human browsing habits
Websurfing/hacking_sites: Opening URL session to SecList FullDisclosure site
Sleeping for 69 seconds to simulate human browsing habits
Websurfing/hacking_sites: Opening URL session to Shodan (systems with default passwords)
```

FIGURE 14.6 Demonstration of the attacker's activity in the system based on the DumpsterFire utility.

```
UTC: 01/25/24 08:00:10  /  PDT: 01/25/24 01:00:10

Delayed Fire ignition detected. Pausing for (HH:MM) 00:09
(Waiting...)

UTC: 01/25/24 08:00:10  /  PDT: 01/25/24 01:00:10

Igniting Fire:  FileDownloads/download_hacking_tools.py
Using ConfigStr:  Downloads/
FileDownloads/download_hacking_tools: Downloading Mimikatz to: Downloads/mimikatz.zip
```

FIGURE 14.7 Simulation of downloading a virus program.

```
Delayed Fire ignition detected. Pausing for (HH:MM) 00:08
(Waiting...)

UTC: 01/25/24 08:17:11  /  PDT: 01/25/24 01:17:11

Igniting Fire:  NetworkScans/nmap_top_80_ports.py
Using ConfigStr:  10.1.0.1-254
NetworkScans/nmap_top_80_ports: Scanning with nmap -Pn -n --open -sT -sV --top-ports=80 10.1.0.1-2
54

Starting Nmap 7.60 ( https://nmap.org ) at 2024-01-25 01:17 PDT
Service detection performed. Please report any incorrect results at https://nmap.org/submit/ .
Nmap done: 254 IP addresses (254 hosts up) scanned in 1445.01 seconds
```

FIGURE 14.8 Simulation of scanning the target workstation.

the sites listed in the previous menu item. In this case, the Mimikatz program was loaded, the purpose of which was to steal user passwords in the selected system.

In the next stage, a simulation is carried out associated with an attack on the target system as a result of its scanning (Figure 14.8). During the scan, you can find information about network services and their vulnerabilities, which can later be used for unauthorized entry.

Then a simulation based on BruteForce technology is performed. A brute force attack is a hacking method that uses trial and error to crack passwords and login credentials. Attackers can use many databases with standard logins and passwords for their purposes. Therefore, the web pages of many global services say that the standard logins and passwords need to be changed. The implementation of this simulation is shown in Figure 14.9.

```
UTC: 01/25/24 08:41:16  /  PDT: 01/25/24 01:41:16

Delayed Fire ignition detected. Pausing for (HH:MM) 00:13
(Waiting...)

UTC: 01/25/24 08:54:17  /  PDT: 01/25/24 01:54:17

Igniting Fire:  AccountBruting/telnet_top_100_defaults.py
Using ConfigStr:  10.1.0.76
UTC 01/25/24 08:54:17 - Attempting telnet connection to: 10.1.0.76
```

FIGURE 14.9 Simulation based on BruteForce technology.

At the final stage, a simulation is performed showing the actions of an attacker after gaining temporary or permanent access to the target system. During this simulation, the attacker tries to collect as much information as possible about the vulnerability of the system. Therefore, he needs to obtain information about the last commands that the user entered in the system, the numbers of the corresponding ports, the IP addresses with which the user was connected in one way or another, the Internet connection, etc. An example of the collected information is shown in Figure 14.10.

To use the Nmap and Metasploit utilities together, you need to perform a scanning process that would allow you to find out more information about the services installed on the target operating system. To do this, use the «nmap -p –sV» command, which scans all open ports and services of the target system. The command's use and the work's result are shown in Figure 14.11.

Therefore, a separate service is bound to each port. In addition, all ports shown in the figure are open. This means that the ports and services installed on the target system are vulnerable. In addition, by going to the Metasploit utility, you can see many exploits related to these services. Most problems are solved by a regular service update. Operating system developers learn about known vulnerabilities in their products only after some time and fix them by releasing regular patches or updated versions of systems.

Upon completion of system testing of a system based on the Nmap utility, the next step in simulating attacks is to use the Metasploit utility, which is a database that contains a large number of exploits. By obtaining information about open ports and related services, as well as versions of the services, the security administrator can simulate an attack on them using the exploit library to assess their vulnerability.

An example of a vulnerable version of a service is the VSFTPD program. This is an FTP service for exchanging data and files between clients, and thanks to its Backdoor Command Execution vulnerability, you can gain unauthorized access to the target system using the Metasploit utility and its module, just created for this vulnerability. After launching the exploit, the attacker, using a backdoor, gains access to the network as an administrator, and therefore can perform any action on the compromised system. The principle of operation of the module is shown in Figure 14.12.

Another example is the exploitation of a VNC server vulnerability, which can only be accessed by guessing a username and password. A special exploit module accesses the database of standard logins and passwords for verification and their

```
Igniting Fire:  OSCommand/os_linux_unix_command.py
Using ConfigStr:  ifconfig; netstat -ant; last; find /home -name '*.bash_history' -exec cat {} \;
OSCommand/os_linux_unix_command: Running OS command => ifconfig; netstat -ant; last; find /home -n
ame '*.bash_history' -exec cat {} \;
ens33: flags=4163<UP,BROADCAST,RUNNING,MULTICAST>  mtu 1500
        inet 192.168.150.14  netmask 255.255.255.0  broadcast 192.168.150.255
        inet6 fe80::a118:aca:15cd:710c  prefixlen 64  scopeid 0x20<link>
        ether 00:0c:29:0f:b7:33  txqueuelen 1000  (Ethernet)
        RX packets 5427  bytes 5980937 (5.9 MB)
        RX errors 0  dropped 0  overruns 0  frame 0
        TX packets 30008  bytes 2343754 (2.3 MB)
        TX errors 0  dropped 0 overruns 0  carrier 0  collisions 0

lo: flags=73<UP,LOOPBACK,RUNNING>  mtu 65536
        inet 127.0.0.1  netmask 255.0.0.0
        inet6 ::1  prefixlen 128  scopeid 0x10<host>
        loop  txqueuelen 1000  (Local Loopback)
        RX packets 313  bytes 23550 (23.5 KB)
        RX errors 0  dropped 0  overruns 0  frame 0
        TX packets 313  bytes 23550 (23.5 KB)
        TX errors 0  dropped 0 overruns 0  carrier 0  collisions 0

Active Internet connections (servers and established)
Proto Recv-Q Send-Q Local Address           Foreign Address         State
tcp        0      0 127.0.0.1:8000          0.0.0.0:*               LISTEN
tcp        0      0 127.0.0.1:9191          0.0.0.0:*               LISTEN
tcp        0      0 127.0.0.1:3306          0.0.0.0:*               LISTEN
tcp        0      0 127.0.0.1:6379          0.0.0.0:*               LISTEN
tcp        0      0 0.0.0.0:80              0.0.0.0:*               LISTEN
```

FIGURE 14.10 Simulation of collecting information about the whole system based on DumpsterFire.

```
To run nmap use the command: nmap
hunter@redhunt:~$ nmap -p- -sV 192.168.126.133

Starting Nmap 7.60 ( https://nmap.org )
Nmap scan report for 192.168.126.133
Host is up (0.0029s latency).
Not shown: 65505 closed ports
PORT      STATE SERVICE     VERSION
21/tcp    open  ftp         vsftpd 2.3.4
22/tcp    open  ssh         OpenSSH 4.7p1 Debian 8ubuntu1 (protocol 2.0)
23/tcp    open  telnet      Linux telnetd
25/tcp    open  smtp        Postfix smtpd
53/tcp    open  domain      ISC BIND 9.4.2
80/tcp    open  http        Apache httpd 2.2.8 ((Ubuntu) DAV/2)
111/tcp   open  rpcbind     2 (RPC #100000)
139/tcp   open  netbios-ssn Samba smbd 3.X - 4.X (workgroup: WORKGROUP)
445/tcp   open  netbios-ssn Samba smbd 3.X - 4.X (workgroup: WORKGROUP)
512/tcp   open  exec        netkit-rsh rexecd
513/tcp   open  login       OpenBSD or Solaris rlogind
514/tcp   open  tcpwrapped
1099/tcp  open  rmiregistry GNU Classpath grmiregistry
1524/tcp  open  shell       Metasploitable root shell
2049/tcp  open  nfs         2-4 (RPC #100003)
2121/tcp  open  ftp         ProFTPD 1.3.1
3306/tcp  open  mysql       MySQL 5.0.51a-3ubuntu5
3632/tcp  open  distccd     distccd v1 ((GNU) 4.2.4 (Ubuntu 4.2.4-1ubuntu4))
5432/tcp  open  postgresql  PostgreSQL DB 8.3.0 - 8.3.7
5900/tcp  open  vnc         VNC (protocol 3.3)
6000/tcp  open  X11         (access denied)
6667/tcp  open  irc         UnrealIRCd
6697/tcp  open  irc         UnrealIRCd (Admin email admin@Metasploitable.LAN)
8009/tcp  open  ajp13       Apache Jserv (Protocol v1.3)
8180/tcp  open  http        Apache Tomcat/Coyote JSP engine 1.1
8787/tcp  open  drb         Ruby DRb RMI (Ruby 1.8; path /usr/lib/ruby/1.8/drb)
35989/tcp open  mountd      1-3 (RPC #100005)
38969/tcp open  status      1 (RPC #100024)
53554/tcp open  nlockmgr    1-4 (RPC #100021)
56202/tcp open  rmiregistry GNU Classpath grmiregistry
Service Info: Hosts:  metasploitable.localdomain, localhost, irc.Metasploitable.LAN; OSs: Unix, Linux; CPE: cpe:/o:linux:linux
```

FIGURE 14.11 The result of scanning all ports and services of the target system based on Nmap.

selection. If the required username and password are found in the database, the exploit shows the correct username and password, which can be used for your purposes. The selection of a login and password by an exploit of the Metasploit utility is shown in Figure 14.13.

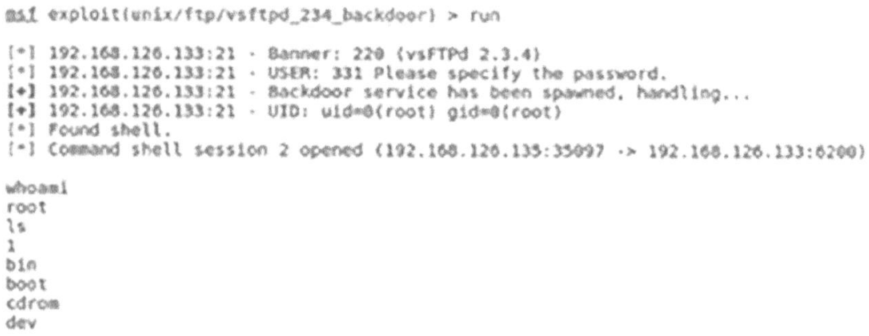

FIGURE 14.12 Using a Metasploit exploit to attack an FTP service.

FIGURE 14.13 Launching an exploit with the selection of logins and passwords of the utility Metasploit.

Thus, the use of a set of RedHunt virtual machine utilities provides an opportunity for a security administrator to get a complete picture of the security threats to his information system, regardless of the operating environment used in it, which allows him to take preventive measures to improve the effectiveness of information system protection as a whole.

14.5 CONCLUSIONS AND FUTURE SCOPE

The simulations of the process of detecting network attacks using the RedHunt virtual machine utilities have shown that this tool is a practical choice for a security administrator and allows you to timely identify threats to an information system and effectively monitor the operating environment in real-time. It is thanks to the utilities of the proposed system, based on which a network attack on the protected object is implemented, that it is possible to neutralize a certain type of vulnerability of the information system or its components, which will prevent the implementation of many types of attacks.

The Kali Linux distribution was chosen because it contains many penetration testing tools, which allow both periodic testing of networks and nodes, as well as corporate network security audits to identify existing vulnerabilities and configuration flaws and close them before they can be exploited by attackers.

During the study, it was found that each system is unique due to the use of different types of rules (signatures) and applications. Such a representation requires in-depth knowledge of attacks and documentation of a specific system from the developer to configure the system itself for monitoring specific (non-standard) applications.

Directions for further research can be aimed at developing network utilities to implement the protection of various types of operating systems from unauthorized interventions and their subsequent integration into the RedHunt system, as well as improving the efficiency of monitoring the information system as a whole to identify various vulnerabilities on its assets, which will improve them.

REFERENCES

[1] Qaddoori, S. L., Ali, Q. I. An In-Depth Characterization of Intrusion Detection Systems (IDS). *Journal of Modern Technology and Engineering*, Volume 6, Issue 2, 2021, pp. 161–188.

[2] Abbas, S. H., Naser, W. A. K., Kadhim, A. A. Subject Review: Intrusion Detection System (IDS) and Intrusion Prevention System (IPS). *Global Journal of Engineering and Technology Advances*, Volume 14, Issue 02, 2023, pp. 155–158. DOI: 10.30574/gjeta.2023.14.2.0031.

[3] Ashoor, A. S., Gore, S. Importance of Intrusion Detection System (IDS). *International Journal of Scientific & Engineering Research*, Volume 2, Issue 1, January 2011, p. 1. ISSN 2229-5518. IJSER © 2010. http://www.ijser.org.

[4] Meena, G., Choudhary, R. R. A Review Paper on IDS Classification Using KDD 99 and NSL KDD Dataset in WEKA. *2017 International Conference on Computer, Communications and Electronics (Comptelix)*, IEEE, Electronic, 1–2 July 2017. ISBN: 978-1-5090-4708-6, Print on Demand (PoD) ISBN: 978-1-5090-4709-3. DOI: 10.1109/Comptelix.2017.8003950.

[5] Kim, A., Park, M., Lee, D. H. AI-IDS: Application of Deep Learning to Real-Time Web Intrusion Detection. *IEEE Access*, Volume 8, 10 April 2020, pp. 70245–70261. Electronic ISSN: 2169-3536. Under a Creative Commons License.

[6] Threat Report, Volume I, Issue 6, 4 March 2015. [Online]. https://www.blacklotus.net/connect/ddos-threat-report/ (date of access: 22.06.2023).

[7] Arbor Networks. Q1 2015 DDoS Report. [Online]. http://www.arbornetworks.com/news-and-events/press-release (date of access: 19.09.2023).

[8] Positive Research 2015. [Online]. http://www.ptsecurity.ru/download/PT_Positive_Research_2015_RU_web.pdf (date of access: 8.11.2015).

[9] Delamore, B., Ko, R. K. L. A Global, Empirical Analysis of the Shellshock Vulnerability in Web Applications. *2015 IEEE Trustcom/BigDataSE/ISPA*, Helsinki, Finland, 2015, pp. 1129–1135. DOI: 10.1109/Trustcom.2015.493.

[10] Mansfield-Devine, S. The Secure Way to Use Open Source. *Computer Fraud & Security*, Volume 2016, Issue 5, 20 May 2016, pp. 15–20. DOI: 10.1016/S1361-3723(16)30046-X.

[11] Symantec. *Internet Security Threat Report (April 2015 Volume 20 v2)*. [Online]. http://www.symantec.com/security_response/publications/ (date of access: 26.03.2020).

[12] Axelsson, S. *Intrusion Detection Systems: A Survey and Taxonomy*, 2000 (retrieved 21 May 2018). https://neuro.bstu.by/ai/To-dom/My_research/Paper-0-again/For-research/D-mining/Anomaly-D/Intrusion-detection/taxonomy.pdf.

[13] Mafra, P. M., Fraga, J. S., Santin, A. O. Algorithms for a distributed IDS in MANETs. *Journal of Computer and System Sciences*, Volume 80, Issue 3, 2014, pp. 554–570; [2] Arbor Networks. Q1 2015 DDoS Report.

[14] Parasram, S. V. N., Samm, A., Boodoo, D., Johansen, G., Allen, L., Heriyanto, T., Ali, S. *Kali Linux 2018: Assuring Security by Penetration Testing: Unleash the full potential of Kali Linux 2018, Now With Updated Tools*, 4th Edition. 2018, p. 448. ISBN 978-5-4461-1252-4.

[15] Muscat, I. Web Vulnerabilities: Identifying Patterns and Remedies. *Network Security*, Volume 2016, Issue 2, 18 February 2016, pp. 5–10.

[16] Allen, L., Johansen, G., Heriyanto, T., Ali, S. *Kali Linux 2 – Assuring Security by Penetration Testing*. Published by Packt Publishing Ltd., 2016, p. 214. ISBN 978-1-84951-948-9.

[17] Vasylyshyn, S., Opirskyy, I., Susukailo, V. Analysis of the Use of Software Baits as a Means of Ensuring Information Security. *2020 IEEE 15th International Scientific and Technical Conference on Computer Sciences and Information Technologies, CSIT 2020 - Proceedings*, Volume 2, 2020, pp. 242–245.

[18] Horpenyuk, A., Opirskyy, I., Vorobets, P. Analysis of Problems and Prospects of Implementation of Post-Quantum Cryptographic Algorithms. *2023 Workshop on Classic, Quantum, and Post-Quantum Cryptography, CQPC 2023, CEUR Workshop Proceedings*, Volume 3504, 1 August 2023, pp. 39–49. ISSN 1613-0073.

[19] Rajagopal, D., Rao, P. An Efficient Intrusion Detection System by Using Behaviour Profiling and Statistical Approach Model. *International Arab Journal of Information Technology*, Volume 18, Issue 1, 2021, pp. 114–124. Department of Computer Science and Applications, Vivekanandha College of Arts and Sciences for Women (Autonomous), India. DOI: 10.34028/iajit/18/1/13. Gold Open Access. ISSN 1683-3198.

[20] Eljialy, A. E. M., Uddin, M. Y., Ahmad, S. Novel Framework for an Intrusion Detection System Using Multiple Feature Selection Methods Based on Deep Learning. *Tsinghua Science and Technology*, Volume 29, Issue 4, 1 August 2024, pp. 948–958. DOI: 10.26599/TST.2023.9010032. Bronze Open Access. ISSN 1007-0214.

[21] Mykhaylova, O., Fedynyshyn, T., Sokolov, V., Kyrychok, R. Person-of-Interest Detection on Mobile Forensics Data—AI-Driven Roadmap. *Conference Paper, CEUR Workshop Proceedings*. ISSN 1613-0073.

[22] Opirskyy, I., Tyshyk, I., Susukailo, V. Evaluation of the Possibility of Realizing the Crime of the Information System at Different Stages of TCP/IP. *2021 IEEE 4th International Conference on Advanced Information and Communication Technologies, AICT 2021 - Proceedings*, Lviv, 21–25 September 2021, pp. 261-265. ISBN 978-166540618-5. DOI: 10.1109/AICT52120.2021.9628936.

[23] Velu, V. K., Beggs, R. *Mastering Kali Linux for Advanced Penetration Testing*, 3rd Edition. Packt Publishing, 2019, p. 540.

[24] Hutchens, J. *Kali Linux*. Network Scanning Cookbook Published by Packt Publishing Ltd., 2014, p. 450. ISBN 978-1-78398-214-1.

[25] Sovyn, Y., Opirskyy, I., Mykhaylova, O. Finding a Bit-Sliced Representation of 4×4 S-Boxes based on Typical Logic Processor Instructions. *2023 Workshop on Classic, Quantum, and Post-Quantum Cryptography, CQPC 2023, CEUR Workshop Proceedings*, Volume 3504, 1 August 2023, pp. 26–38. ISSN 1613-0073.

[26] Wolf, D., Göbel, T., Baier, H. Hypervisor-Based Data Synthesis: On Its Potential to Tackle the Curse of Client-Side Agent Remnants in Forensic Image Generation. *DFRWS EU 2024 - Selected Papers from the 11th Annual Digital Forensics Research Conference Europe*, Munich, Germany, 15 March 2024. DOI: 10.1016/j.fsidi.2023.301690.

[27] Lewis, N., Case, A., Ali-Gombe, A., Richard III, G. G. Memory Forensics and the Windows Subsystem for Linux. *DFRWS 2018 USA—Proceedings of the Eighteenth Annual DFRWS USA*, 15 July 2018. DOI: 10.1016/j.diin.2018.04.018.

[28] Kasim, Ö. An Efficient and Robust Deep Learning Based Network Anomaly Detection Against Distributed Denial of Service Attacks. *Computer Networks*, Volume 180, 24 October 2020, Article 107390. DOI: 10.1016/j.comnet.2020.107390.

15 Secure 5G Network for Monitoring State of Critical Infrastructure Facilities

Roman Odarchenko, Alla Pinchuk,
Igor Zakutynsky, Viktor Hnatiuk,
Oleh Polihenko, and Oleksii Baranovskyi

15.1 INTRODUCTION

The deployment of 5G networks within critical infrastructure offers transformative capabilities, enabling real-time monitoring, control, and decision-making at unprecedented speeds and scales. Key sectors, such as energy grids, transportation networks, financial institutions, healthcare systems, and government services, are becoming more interconnected through the adoption of 5G technology. This interconnectivity enhances operational efficiency and service delivery, making these sectors crucial not only for societal functioning but also for national defense and economic stability. The high data throughput, ultra-low latency, and enhanced reliability of 5G allow for continuous, near-instantaneous data exchange, supporting vital infrastructure systems and enabling rapid responses to potential disruptions or emergencies.

The integration of 5G with advanced technologies like artificial intelligence (AI) and machine learning further enhances these capabilities. AI algorithms can analyze vast amounts of 5G-generated data to identify patterns, anomalies, and trends that were previously undetectable. This enables the prediction of equipment failures, detection of security threats, and optimization of resource allocation, allowing for proactive maintenance and threat mitigation. Such a proactive approach is essential to maintaining the operational stability and security of critical infrastructure, especially in an increasingly complex and unpredictable cyber environment where threats can emerge rapidly.

However, the rapid expansion of 5G also brings significant cybersecurity challenges. The increased connectivity and massive data flows associated with 5G create new entry points for cyber attackers, expanding the potential attack surface. This makes critical infrastructure more vulnerable to a variety of threats such as multifunctional malware, ransomware, botnets, and complex attacks on cloud services and supply chains. Additionally, the use of AI by malicious actors can lead to more sophisticated and hard-to-detect cyber threats. With the development of AI over the

DOI: 10.1201/9781003546153-15

next decade, the scale and impact of these cyber threats are expected to rise significantly, presenting an unprecedented challenge to sectors that are essential to national security and economic stability.

In light of these threats, ensuring a secure and resilient 5G network for critical infrastructure is imperative. Establishing a robust cybersecurity framework, including advanced threat detection, real-time monitoring, and rapid response capabilities, is essential to protect critical assets from potential large-scale disruptions and catastrophic failures. Collaboration between government agencies, private sector stakeholders, and international partners is also crucial for sharing information and best practices. Ultimately, safeguarding public and national interests in an evolving cyber landscape requires a comprehensive approach to security, ensuring that the benefits of 5G technology can be fully realized without compromising the integrity and reliability of critical infrastructure systems.

15.1.1 Key Contributions of the Chapter

The following are the significant contributions of this chapter:

i. *Development of a Secure 5G Network Architecture for Critical Infrastructure.* The proposed architecture includes several interconnected components, such as a Security Module, a traffic collection system, an analytical module, and a management console. They operate at different levels of the 5G network stack, providing comprehensive monitoring, analysis, and detection of cyber threats.

ii. *Integration of the Security Module with Artificial Intelligence and Machine Learning Technologies.* The Security Module implements rule-based algorithms and machine learning methods to analyze network traffic and detect anomalies. This ensures proactive detection of potential threats such as DDoS attacks, spoofing, and packet injection.

iii. *Testing the Proposed Architecture on the 5G Testbed.* The experiments performed on the 5G test platform with simulation of real operating conditions and various types of attacks confirmed the effectiveness of the system. The Security Module demonstrated high accuracy in detecting threats, low latency, and adaptability to new threats.

iv. *Adaptive Training of the Security Module To Improve the Accuracy of Threat Detection.* The use of feedback mechanisms and periodic updates of machine learning models allows the module to continuously improve its detection capabilities, adapting to new types of attacks and changes in network behavior.

15.1.2 Chapter Organization

Section 15.1 presents the introduction, covering 5G's potential for real-time monitoring of critical infrastructure and the cybersecurity challenges associated with protecting these essential systems. Section 15.2 offers the background analysis, where the related literature is analyzed. Section 15.3 identifies the problem statement and research objectives for developing a secure 5G network architecture. Section 15.4 presents the design and functionality of the proposed secure 5G network architecture. Section 15.5 details the development of the Security Module, including its model development approach, data preparation, model selection, multi-layer perceptron architecture, and hyperparameter tuning. Section 15.6 explains the experimental research, covering the design of experiments and analysis of results. Section 15.7 describes the integration of the Security Module into a 5G network monitoring system, including visualization and alerting features. Section 15.8 provides a comparative analysis of anomaly detection techniques for 5G networks. Section 15.9 concludes the chapter.

15.2 LITERATURE REVIEW

The integration of 5G technology into critical infrastructure sectors has been extensively researched, with a primary focus on enhancing network security and addressing emerging cybersecurity challenges. Various studies have proposed methods to improve the security architecture of 5G networks within critical sectors such as energy, transportation, and healthcare.

Several authors have developed frameworks to bolster 5G security in critical infrastructures. In [1], a method is proposed for improving the security of 5G network architecture specifically tailored for the energy sector and other critical infrastructures. The authors introduce a conceptual framework that integrates advanced security mechanisms to protect against sophisticated cyber threats targeting essential services. Similarly, paper [2] discusses enhancing smart grid security through 5G-enabled IoT and edge computing. The authors propose leveraging edge computing to reduce latency and enable immediate detection of anomalies in smart grids, thereby enhancing resilience against cyber attacks.

Addressing the broader cybersecurity challenges in 5G-enabled IoT and critical infrastructures, papers [3–5] provide comprehensive overviews of potential vulnerabilities introduced by the integration of IoT devices with 5G networks. They highlight that increased connectivity and device heterogeneity expand the attack surface, making critical infrastructures more susceptible to cyber attacks. These studies recommend implementing robust authentication protocols, intrusion detection systems, and standardized security practices, emphasizing the importance of industry-wide collaboration to address existing gaps in 5G security measures.

The application of artificial intelligence (AI) and machine learning (ML) techniques in enhancing 5G network security has been explored in several studies. In [6], the authors develop a model for cyber-attack detection and response within 5G networks using machine learning techniques. Their system analyzes network traffic patterns in real-time to identify anomalies indicative of malicious activities. Paper [7] focuses on advancements in software-defined networking (SDN) for 5G security, developing an enhanced reference monitor algorithm for SDN controllers to provide better oversight and dynamic enforcement of security policies. Additionally, paper [8] surveys AI-driven container security approaches for 5G and beyond, exploring AI techniques employed to detect vulnerabilities within container environments, ensuring the protection of virtualized network components.

The impact of 5G technology on communication infrastructure and its security implications is analyzed in paper [9]. The authors discuss how 5G's high-speed connectivity and low latency can revolutionize communication systems but also introduce new security challenges due to increased data flow and network complexity. They emphasize the need for scalable security solutions that do not compromise performance.

The assessment of security Key Performance Indicators (KPIs) for 5G network slices, particularly for special groups of subscribers like emergency services and governmental agencies, is explored in paper [10]. The authors propose tailored security policies and continuous monitoring mechanisms to ensure that these dedicated network segments meet stringent security requirements, given the sensitive nature of the data and services involved.

The functionality of critical information infrastructure cybersecurity networks is examined in paper [11], emphasizing the importance of integrated security systems that combine physical and cyber defenses. Recognizing that attacks may target multiple facets simultaneously, the study underscores the necessity for comprehensive protection strategies.

15.3 PROBLEM STATEMENT

The deployment of 5G networks in critical infrastructure sectors creates both new opportunities and serious challenges for cybersecurity. On the one hand, 5G allows for real-time monitoring and control, which is key to the smooth operation of critical systems. On the other hand, large volumes of data and expanded connectivity create new vulnerabilities that can be exploited by attackers. Existing security tools are not able to effectively counter sophisticated and large-scale cyber attacks targeting critical infrastructures, which threatens stability and national security.

Thus, the aim of this chapter is to provide the possible solution. The following research tasks should be solved:

i. Secure 5G network architecture development.
ii. Security Module development and integration to the 5G network.
iii. Testing the effectiveness of the Security Module on the 5G testbed.

15.4 SECURE 5G NETWORK ARCHITECTURE DEVELOPMENT

Firstly, let's consider the basic architecture of the 5G network. Schematically, the 5G system uses the same elements as previous generations: user equipment (UE), which consists of a mobile station and a USIM (Universal Subscriber Identity Module), a radio access network (NG-RAN), and a core network (5GC), as shown in Figure 15.1.

The main network functionality lies in the fifth generation network core that is shown in Figure 15.2 (TS 23.501).

In Figure 15.2, the user plane, i.e., the network functions (NFs) and elements involved in the transmission of user data, are shown at the lower level, while the upper part of the figure shows all the main NFs of the control plane.

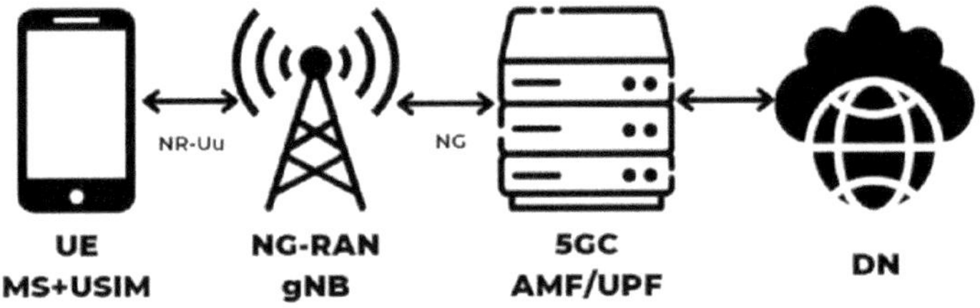

FIGURE 15.1 5G system overview.

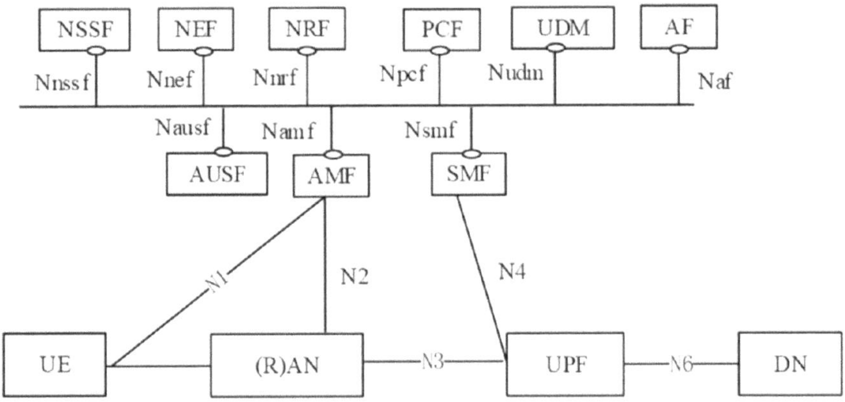

FIGURE 15.2 5GS architecture [12].

Each component of the network core performs its own function [13]:

- *Network Slice Selection Function (NSSF)*: selects a set of network slice elements to satisfy a service request from a UE. When a UE requests registration in the network, the AMF sends a network slice selection request to the NSSF with information about the desired network slice selection. The NSSF responds with a message that contains a list of suitable network slice instances for the UE.
- *Network Exposure Function (NEF)*: provides an interface for external applications to communicate with the 5G network to obtain network-related information in the following categories: monitoring, redundancy, policy/billing management, and analytical reporting.
- *Network Repository Function (NRF)*: allows network functions to register their functionality and discover services offered by other NFs present in the network.
- *Policy Control Function (PCF)*: provides functionality to monitor and manage policy rules, including rules for QoS, charging, and traffic routing. PCF provides end-to-end QoS provisioning with QoS parameters (e.g., maximum data rate, guaranteed data rate, and priority level) at the

appropriate granularity (e.g., per user device, per flow, and per protocol data session [PDU]).

- *Unified Data Management (UDM)*: responsible for access authorization and subscription management. UDM works with AMF and AUSF as follows: AMF provides authentication, authorization, and mobility management services to the UE. AUSF stores data for subscriber authentication, and UDM stores subscriber subscription data.
- *Application Function (AF)*: provides session-related information to the PCF so that the SMF can use this information to manage the session. AF interacts with application services that require dynamic policy management. The AF extracts session-related information (such as QoS requirements) from application signaling and provides it to the PCF to support rule generation. An example is an IP Multimedia Subsystem (IMS) that can interact with the PCRF to request QoS support for VoIP calls.
- *Authentication Server Function (AUSF)*: performs authentication between the UE and the network.
- *Access and Mobility Management Function (AMF)*: receives all connection and session related information from the user equipment (UE) (N1/N2) but is only responsible for handling connection, registration, reachability, and mobility management tasks. All messages related to session management are forwarded to the Session Management Function (SMF).
- *Session Management Function (SMF)*: is responsible for creating, modifying, and terminating a PDU session between a user device and the data network. A PDU session, or simply a session, is a connection between a user device and a data network that provides a PDU connection service. A PDU connection service is a service that enables the exchange of PDUs between a UE and a data network.
- *User Plane Function (UPF)*: user plane functions control the user plane path for PDU sessions. The 3GPP specifications support deployments with a single UPF or multiple UPFs for a given PDU session. The selection of the UPF is performed by the SMF. More details are described in [13].

An analysis of the 5G core network functions shows that while built-in security features like the Authentication Server Function (AUSF) for secure authentication, Unified Data Management (UDM) for subscriber data protection, and Policy Control Function (PCF) for enforcing security policies enhance the network's security, the complexity and expanded attack surface of 5G networks necessitate additional measures, especially, in case of using 5G network in critical infrastructures.

5G networks can be designed in different ways that consist of different additional components. Thus, we propose secure 5G network architecture that can be seamlessly integrated into the existing network of critical infrastructure facilities, while enabling real-time analysis and detection of malicious activities (Figure 15.3). The system consists of several interconnected components that operate at various levels of the 5G network stack to ensure comprehensive monitoring, analysis, and anomaly detection. To ensure the additional layer of security, we also proposed such data transmission mode as *data diode*. In this case, it will be denied to send data from critical infrastructure facilities to the whole network, as it will be allowed just to receive.

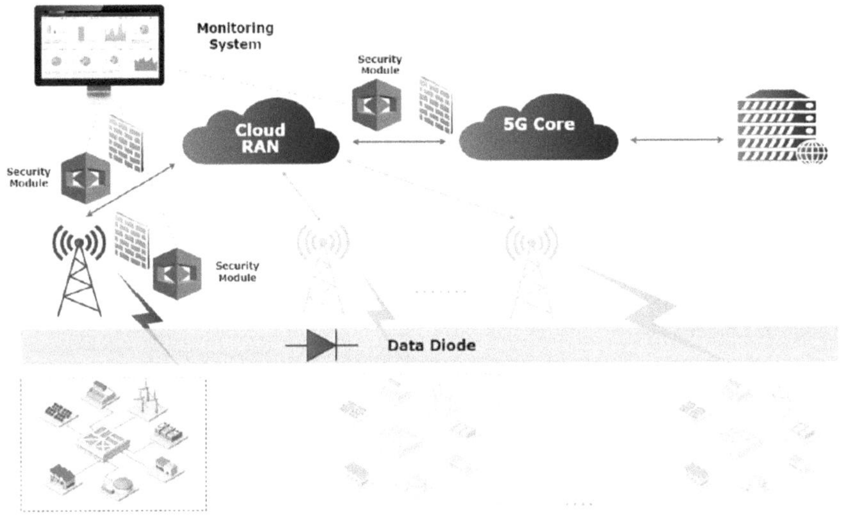

FIGURE 15.3 Secure 5G network architecture.

The primary components of secure 5G network architecture include:

- *Security Module.* A centralized system responsible for the analysis of network traffic data, specifically TCP and UDP packets. It operates by continuously scanning network traffic for anomalies or unusual patterns indicating a potential cybersecurity threat.
- *Traffic Data Collector.* This component captures network traffic data at various points in the 5G network infrastructure. It collects raw data from Radio Access Network (RAN), Core Network (CN), and edges nodes, then forwards it to the Security Module for analysis.
- *Data Analysis Engine.* Embedded within the Security Module, the Data Analysis Engine performs packet inspection and anomaly detection. It uses both rule-based and machine learning (ML) algorithms to identify unusual patterns in network traffic that may indicate a potential threat or an attack.
- *Management Console.* The interface that provides network administrators with insights into the current cybersecurity status of the 5G network. It displays alerts generated by the Security Module and allows for configuration adjustments to meet evolving security requirements.

Basically, it is important to ensure security of the network critical nodes. Thus, to effectively monitor and secure network traffic, the Security Module integrates with multiple levels of 5G network stack:

- *5G CN.* Here, the Security Module monitors data flows within the CN, where high data throughput and complex traffic make it an attractive target for threats/malicious actors.

- *5G RAN.* The Traffic Data Collector component interfaces with the RAN to capture data at the edge, providing early detection of anomalous traffic patterns. This ensures that cyber threats are identified before they can propagate through the CN.
- *Edge Nodes.* By extending traffic monitoring to the edge, it is possible to detect threats at the periphery of the network, ensuring that remote locations are equally secure.

The data processing and anomaly detection workflow in a secure 5G network is designed to identify and mitigate potential cybersecurity threats in real-time, as illustrated in Figure 15.4.

Data collection. The workflow begins with the Traffic Data Collector, which captures network traffic data at various points within the 5G network infrastructure, including the RAN, CN, and edge nodes. It collects raw data, focusing on TCP and UDP packets that are common vectors for cyber attacks.

Data Filtering and Forwarding. The collected raw data are filtered to retain only the relevant TCP and UDP packets. These filtered data are then forwarded to the centralized Security Module for analysis.

Traffic Analysis. Within the Security Module, the embedded Data Analysis Engine performs in-depth packet inspection and anomaly detection. It examines packet headers, payloads, and flow patterns using both rule-based methods and ML algorithms. This combination allows it to identify unusual patterns and deviations from normal network behavior that may indicate potential threats or attacks.

Anomaly Detection. The Data Analysis Engine detects anomalies in real-time by continuously scanning the network traffic for signs of cybersecurity threats. Upon identifying an anomaly, the Security Module generates alerts to notify network administrators of potential issues.

15.5 SECURITY MODULE DEVELOPMENT

The Security Module is the core component of our 5G security framework, designed specifically to detect and respond to anomalous traffic patterns. By analyzing TCP and UDP packets, it can identify unusual behavior that may indicate malicious activity, such as Distributed Denial of Service (DDoS) attacks, packet injection, or data exfiltration attempts.

The general scheme of developed Security Module is shown in Figure 15.5.

Packet Analysis. The Security Module performs detailed inspection of TCP and UDP packets to detect anomalies in network traffic. It examines *packet headers* for irregularities like unusual sizes, sequence numbers, or flags that might indicate manipulation or spoofing. The module also scans *packet payloads* for signs

FIGURE 15.4 The data processing and anomaly detection workflow.

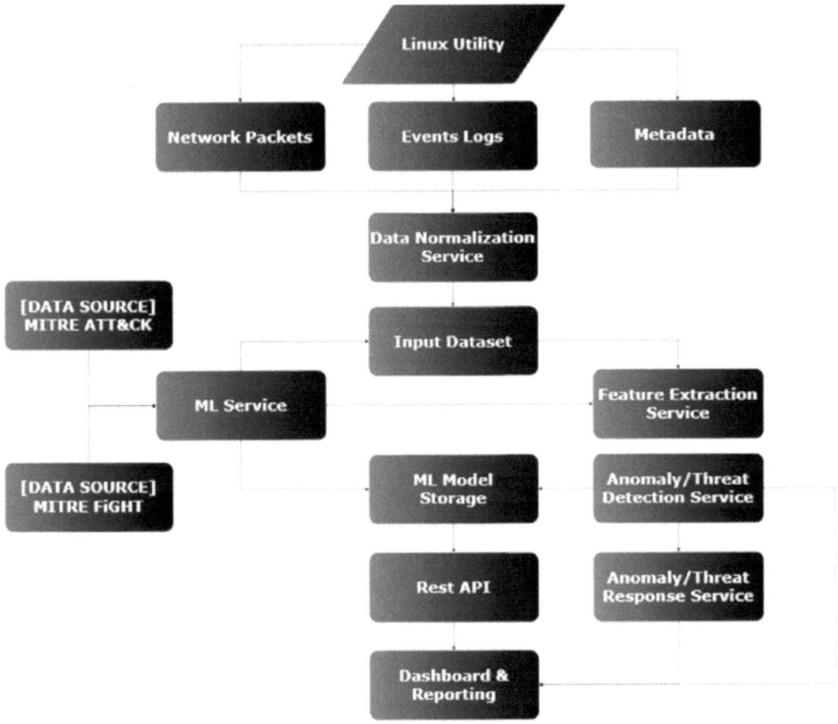

FIGURE 15.5 The Security Module scheme.

of malware or unusual data patterns, triggering further analysis if deviations are detected. Additionally, it evaluates *traffic flow* patterns to identify anomalies such as unexpected volumes of requests from a single source or repeated failed connection attempts. By integrating header inspection, payload analysis, and traffic flow evaluation, the Security Module effectively identifies and mitigates a wide range of network threats targeting critical infrastructure facilities.

Anomaly Detection Techniques. The Security Module employs a multi-layered approach to anomaly detection to effectively identify and respond to a wide range of cyber threats. Initially, it uses *rule-based detection* by applying predefined rules to incoming data packets. This allows for the quick identification of known attack patterns, such as SYN floods or malformed packets, serving as a first line of defense that efficiently blocks common attack types. To detect more sophisticated attacks, the module leverages *machine learning models* trained on large datasets of network traffic. These models can identify subtle deviations from normal traffic patterns, which may indicate previously unseen or emerging threats. By continuously learning from new data, the module adapts to evolving threat landscapes, enhancing its ability to protect critical infrastructure facilities.

Response Mechanism. When the Security Module detects an anomaly, it initiates a response sequence to mitigate potential threats. It begins with *alert generation*, where the module immediately notifies administrators and logs event details for further investigation. If an attack is confirmed, it implements *traffic filtering* to block or reroute malicious traffic, minimizing its impact on network performance. In cases where high-confidence anomalies are detected, the module can initiate *automated mitigation* actions in real-time, such as rate limiting or source blocking, to contain the threat effectively. This proactive response mechanism ensures that potential threats are addressed promptly, maintaining the integrity and availability of the network for critical infrastructure facilities.

Adaptive Learning. The Security Module continuously refines its detection capabilities through adaptive learning. It implements a *feedback loop* where alerts and anomalies are reviewed by network administrators, who label them as false positives or valid threats. This process allows the system to improve its accuracy over time by adjusting detection parameters based on human input. Additionally, the module's machine learning models are periodically *retrained on new data*, incorporating insights from recent threats and evolving network conditions. This ongoing adaptation ensures that the module remains effective against emerging threats and can adjust to changes in network behavior, thereby enhancing the overall security of the critical infrastructure.

15.5.1 Model Development Approach

Basically, the Security Model is the ML model that was developed for network anomaly detection by following a structured approach:

- *Data Collection.* Collecting a large dataset of TCP/UDP traffic from real-world network environments, capturing both normal and attack patterns.
- *Feature Engineering.* Ectracting meaningful features from network traffic data, such as packet size, source and destination IP, protocol type, and packets intervals (Figure 15.6).
- *Model Selection.* Testing different ML algorithms to identify the best model for anomaly detection.
- *Training and Tuning.* Training the selected model using labeled data and fine-tune hyperparameters for optimal performance.

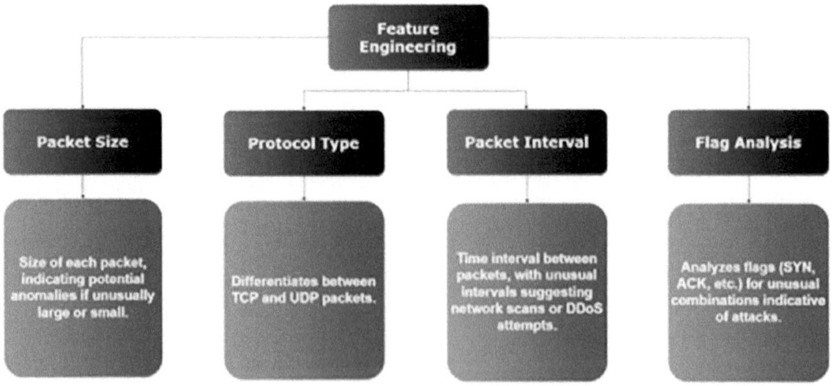

FIGURE 15.6 Feature engineering.

- *Evaluation and Testing.* Evaluation model accuracy, presicion, recall, and other metrics on a test dataset.
- *Visualization.* Visualization of the results to gain insights into model performance and anomaly detection.

15.5.2 Data Preparation

Possible datasets were analyzed in [14]. Our training dataset includes records of TCP/UDP packets captured from a 5G network environment, where each packet is labeled as either "normal" or "anomalous." The dataset includes a mix of real network traffic and synthetic data for rare attack patterns, enabling robust anomaly detection. For model training, we used the CIC IoT dataset 2023 [15], a comprehensive dataset for DDOS attack [16] and own assembled dataset with DDOS emulation. Training dataset structure is shown in Figure 15.7.

The dataset was preprocessed to normalize features and split into training (80%) and testing (20%) subsets. The training data includes both normal traffic and a variety of attack scenarios, such as DDoS, packet injection, and spoofing attacks.

15.5.3 Model Selection

Several ML algorithms were evaluated for anomaly detection:

- *Random Forest.* A versatile model that performs well on tabular data by building multiple decision trees and using ensemble learning.
- *Support Vector Machine (SVM).* Effective for binary classification tasks and detecting anomalies by maximizing the margin between normal and anomalous classes.
- *Neural Network.* A simple multi-layer perceptron (MLP) model was tested for anomaly detection based on the non-linear relationships within network traffic.

FIGURE 15.7 Training dataset.

- *Isolation Forest.* Specifically designed for anomaly detection, Isolation Forest isolates anomalies by constructing random partitions.

All mentioned models were evaluated using various metrics:

- *Accuracy.* Overall accuracy of the model in detecting anomalies.
- *Precision and Recall.* Important for evaluating the model's effectiveness in identifying true positives (actual anomalies).
- *F1 Score.* Harmonic mean of precision and recall, providing a balanced metric for model performance.

The result of testing is listed in Table 15.1 and Figure 15.8.

TABLE 15.1
The Result of Models' Testing

Model	Accuracy	Precision	Recall	F1 Score
Isolation Forest	0.25	0.4523809523809524	0.5714285714285715	0.15873015873015875
Random Forest	0.55	0.55	0.55	0.55
SVM	0.3055555555555556	0.3055555555555556	0.3055555555555556	0.3055555555555556
Neural Network	0.4230769230769231	0.4230769230769231	0.4230769230769231	0.4230769230769231

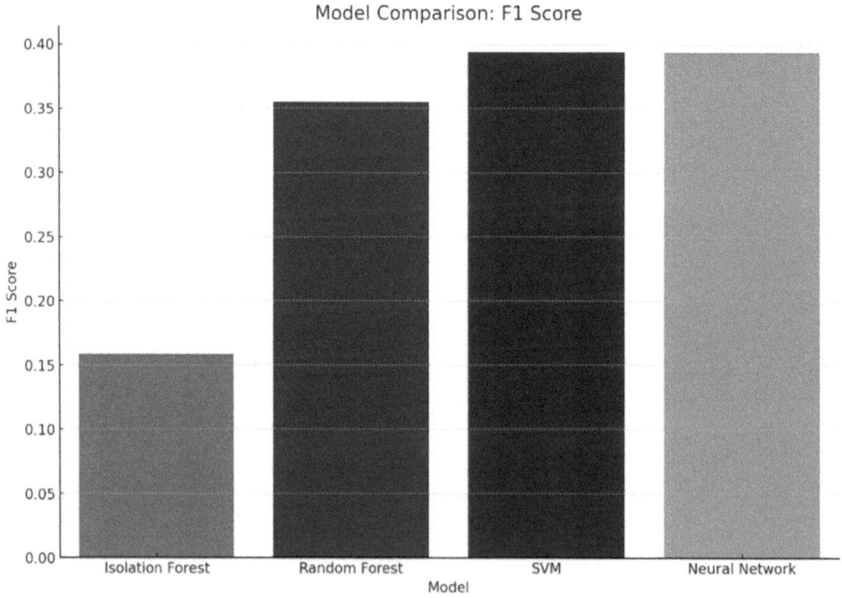

FIGURE 15.8 Models' comparison by F1 score.

After testing these algorithms, the *Isolation Forest* was selected as the primary model due to its high accuracy and efficiency in detecting outliers in network traffic.

15.5.4 Multi-Layer Perceptron Model Architecture

The multi-layer perceptron (MLP) model used for anomaly detection in the secure 5G network efficiently processes network traffic data (Figure 15.9).

It comprises an *input layer* that receives features such as packet size, interval between packets, protocol type, and other relevant metrics.

The model includes two fully connected *hidden layers* with ReLU activation functions, one with 128 neurons and another with 64 neurons, that learn complex patterns in the data to distinguish between normal and anomalous behavior.

The *output layer* consists of a single neuron with a sigmoid activation function, suitable for binary classification, outputting the probability that a network traffic instance is anomalous.

This streamlined architecture effectively balances complexity and performance, enabling real-time detection of cybersecurity threats without compromising the high data throughput characteristic of 5G networks.

15.5.5 Model Training and Hyperparameter Tuning

The general model training is shown in Figure 15.10. The Isolation Forest model was trained on the labeled dataset. Key hyperparameters, including the number of estimators (trees) and maximum depth of each tree, were fine-tuned to improve detection accuracy.

The training process includes several steps:

- *Data Split.* The dataset was split into 80% for training and 20% for testing.
- *Hyperparameter Tuning.* Grid search was used to optimize the model's hyperparameters.
- *Cross-Validation.* The model was validated using k-fold cross-validation to avoid overfitting.

The model was trained using the following parameters:

- Optimizer: Adam (adaptive learning rate optimization).
- Loss Function: Binary cross-entropy.

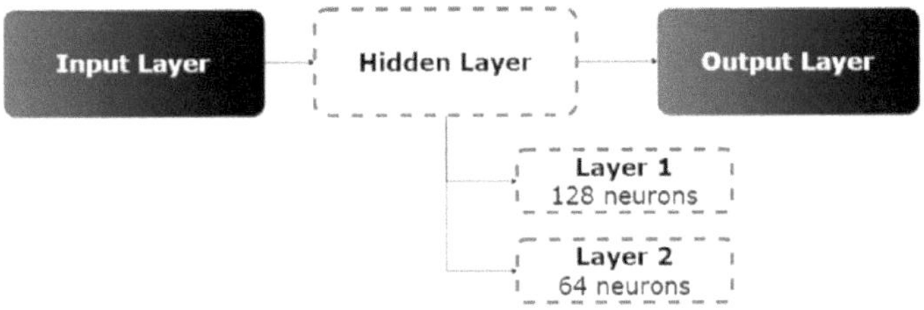

FIGURE 15.9 Multi-layer perceptron model architecture.

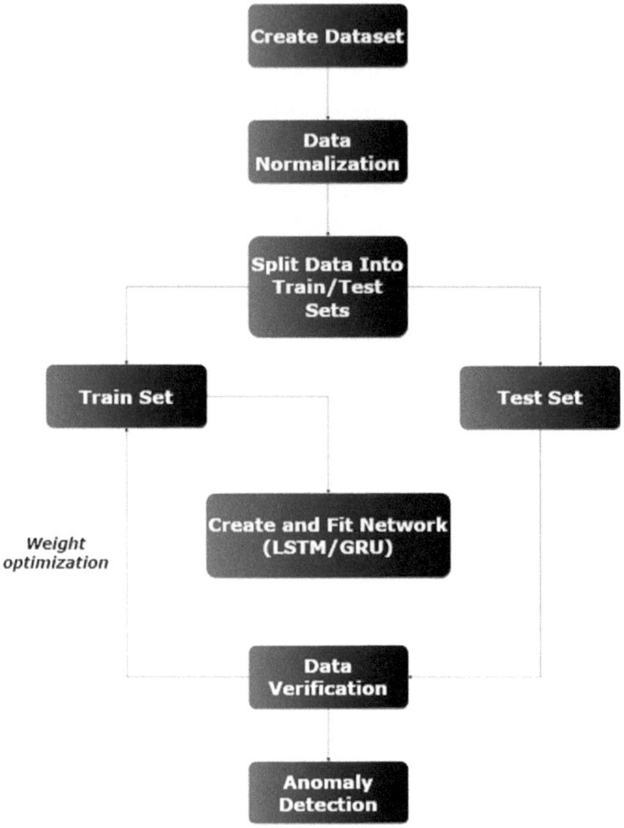

FIGURE 15.10 The model training.

```python
from sklearn.ensemble import IsolationForest
from sklearn.model_selection import train_test_split

# Split data
X_train, X_test, y_train, y_test = train_test_split(X, y, test_size=0.2, random_state=42)

# Define the model
model = IsolationForest(n_estimators=100, max_samples='auto', contamination=0.1, random_state=42)

# Fit the model
model.fit(X_train)

# Predict anomalies
y_pred = model.predict(X_test)
```

FIGURE 15.11 The model training process.

- Learning Rate: 0.001.
- Batch Size: 64.
- Epochs: 50.

Grid search was used to fine-tune the hyperparameters, focusing on learning rate, batch size, and the number of neurons in each layer.

The Neural Network (MLP) outperformed the other models in all key metrics, providing the highest accuracy, precision, recall, and F1 score. Additionally, its inference latency of 12 milliseconds ensures near-real-time anomaly detection suitable for a 5G network environment.

15.6 EXPERIMENTAL RESEARCH

To test the developed solution, the previously deployed 5G network testbed was used. The 5G testbed deployed within the open-source project openairinterface5g, the general network architecture is given in Figure 15.12. The testbed deployment is discussed in detail in [17, 18].

The testbed architecture consists of several key components, including the Radio Access Network (RAN), core network (CN), and user equipment (UE). The RAN was set up with gNodeB element, as the 5G access point, while the core network (5GC) provided all standardized by 3GPP functions.

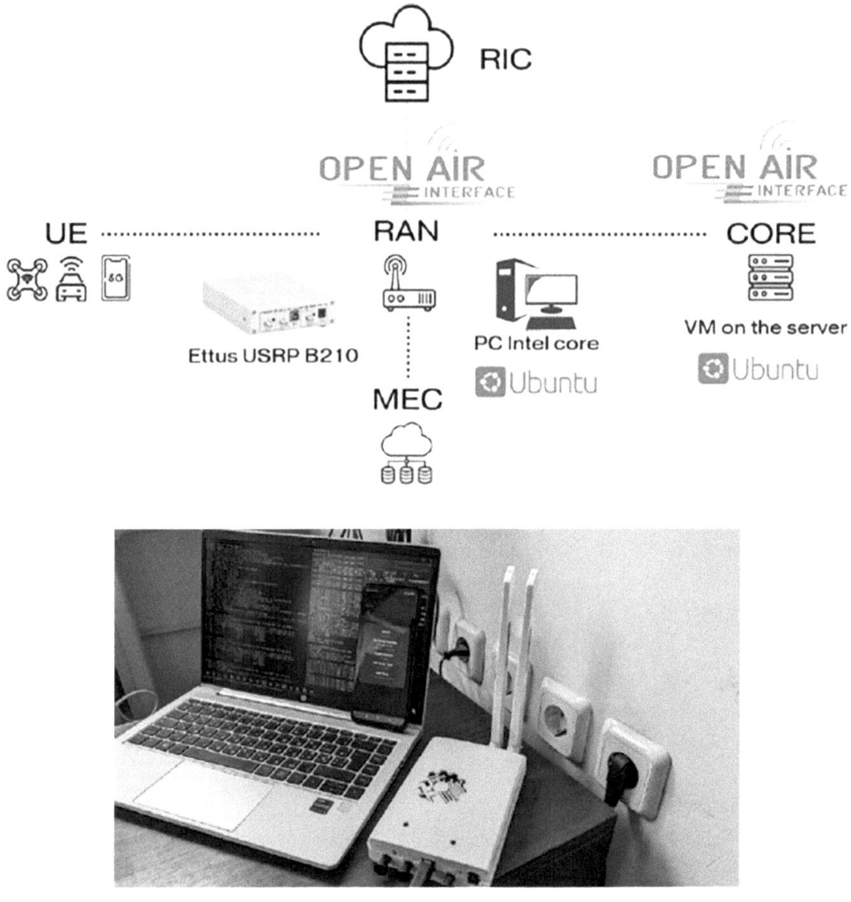

FIGURE 15.12 The 5G network testbed.

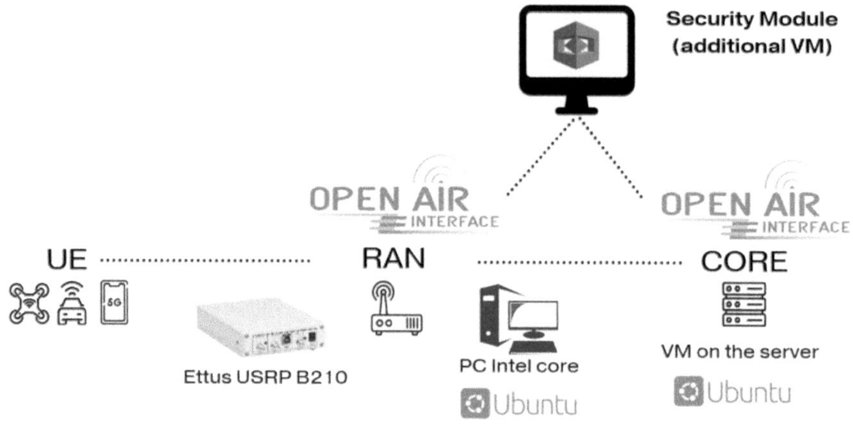

FIGURE 15.13 Allocated Security Module.

The testbed was configured to provide traffic data for both normal operational scenarios and specific attack simulations, including Distributed Denial of Service (DDoS) and packet injection attacks. This setup enabled us to evaluate the Security Module's effectiveness in real-time threat detection.

The Security Module was allocated on an additional virtual machine that has all necessary access rights to the RAN and CN machines, as presented in Figure 15.13.

15.6.1 Experiment Design

The experiment aimed to validate the performance of the Security Module in detecting anomalies and handling diverse traffic patterns. The evaluation metrics included accuracy, detection time, false positive rate, and adaptability to new threats. To conduct a comprehensive assessment, we set up two primary experiment scenarios: normal traffic scenario and attack scenario.

Normal Traffic Scenario. In this scenario, regular network traffic was generated using simulated UEs that connected to the core network and accessed typical services (e.g., web browsing, video streaming, and file downloads). This baseline scenario allowed the Security Module to establish normal traffic patterns, ensuring it could differentiate between expected behavior and anomalous activity. Key metrics recorded were:

- *Throughput.* Average throughput of the network under normal conditions.
- *Latency.* End-to-end latency for typical data requests.
- *False Positive Rate.* Frequency of false anomaly detections in normal traffic.

Attack Scenario. The attack scenario (Figure 15.14) involved the simulation of several common 5G network attacks to evaluate the Security Module's anomaly detection capabilities:

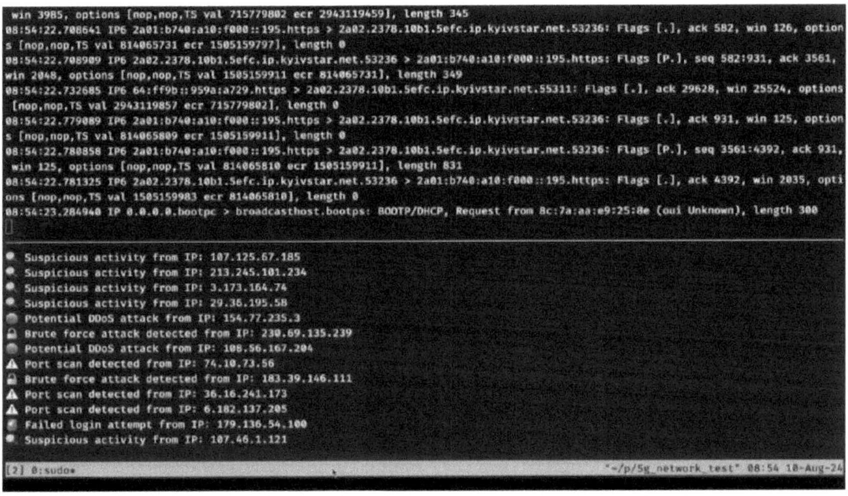

FIGURE 15.14 The attacks scenario.

- *DDoS Attack Simulation.* A high-volume traffic burst aimed at overwhelming the network, simulating a denial-of-service condition. This tested the module's capacity to detect and flag excessive data requests from single or multiple IP sources.
- *Packet Injection Attack.* Simulated injection of malformed or unsolicited packets into the network to assess the module's ability to detect abnormal packet headers and payloads.
- *Spoofing Attack.* Simulation of IP spoofing where fake source IP addresses were used to mimic legitimate devices. This scenario tested the module's ability to identify inconsistent IP patterns or discrepancies in packet metadata.

15.6.2 Results and Analysis

Anomaly Detection Performance. The Security Module was tested on various performance metrics for anomaly detection, including accuracy, precision, recall, and F1 score across both the normal and attack scenarios (Table 15.2).

Real-Time Detection Latency. One of the key factors for effective anomaly detection in a 5G network is the system's ability to detect threats in real-time without impacting user experience. During the experiments, the average detection latency (time taken by the module to analyze and flag anomalies) was recorded:

- *Normal Scenario.* Average latency of 10 milliseconds.
- *Attack Scenarios.* Detection latency remained consistent around 15 milliseconds, even during high-traffic DDoS simulations.

TABLE 15.2
Anomaly Detection Performance

Metric	Normal Traffic Scenario	Attack Scenario (DDoS)	Attack Scenario (Packet Injection)	Attack Scenario (Spoofing)
Accuracy	98.5	96.2	97.3	95.6
Precision	99.1	94.8	96.5	93.7
Recall	97.8	95.2	94.9	94.2
F1 Score	98.4	95.0	95.7	93.9

False Positive and False Negative Rates. False positives (normal traffic flagged as anomalous) and false negatives (missed detections of actual anomalies) were also monitored:

- *False Positive Rate.* 1.2% in the normal scenario, indicating the module's high accuracy in not falsely identifying normal traffic as threats.
- *False Negative Rate.* 2.3% on average across attack scenarios, showing a low likelihood of missing actual threats.

Adaptability to New Threats. The module's adaptability to new and evolving threats was tested by introducing variations in attack patterns mid-experiment. After a brief training period, the module demonstrated enhanced adaptability, effectively detecting previously unseen variations in the DDoS and spoofing attacks. This adaptability is attributed to the module's machine learning algorithms, which leverage continuous learning to improve detection accuracy.

15.7 INTEGRATION AND MONITORING

To ensure the practical application of the developed anomaly detection model, it was integrated into the 5G network monitoring system. The integration aimed to enable real-time visualization, analysis, and alerting of detected anomalies, ensuring comprehensive and actionable network security monitoring.

15.7.1 Integration with the Monitoring System

The chosen Neural Network (MLP) model was integrated into a centralized monitoring system, leveraging the flexibility and extensibility of modern observability tools. The key objectives were to seamlessly incorporate the anomaly detection capabilities into the existing system and to provide meaningful insights to network administrators through visualization and alerts.

System Architecture. The system architecture integrates key components for efficient data processing and real-time anomaly detection in the secure 5G network.

In the *Data Pipeline*, network traffic data (TCP/UDP packets) is continuously streamed from critical points like the Radio Access Network (RAN), core network, and edge nodes to a preprocessing layer. The *preprocessing stage* involves cleaning,

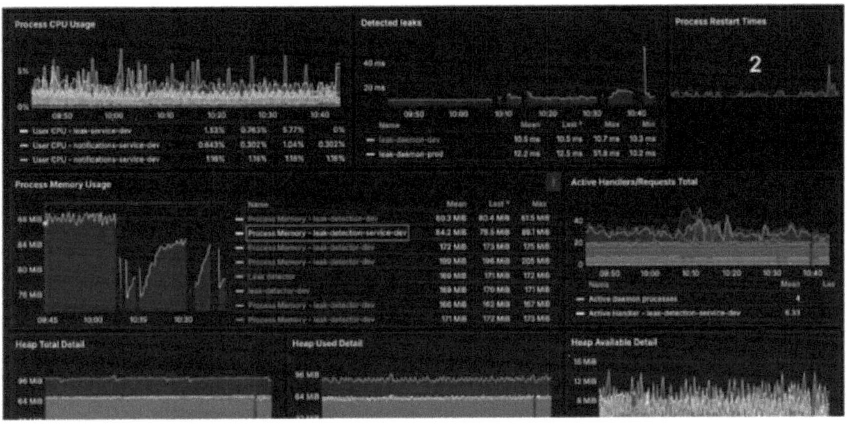

FIGURE 15.15 5G network monitoring system.

normalizing, and converting raw traffic data into feature vectors suitable for the MLP model. The *anomaly detection* component feeds this preprocessed data into the MLP model, deployed as a service, to classify packets as normal or anomalous in real-time.

The *Monitoring Backend* consists of a time-series database (e.g., Prometheus) where detected anomalies and metadata are stored for historical analysis and visualization. *Grafana* is used as the *visualization tool* to display anomaly detection results, providing an intuitive interface for monitoring.

An effective *Alerting Mechanism* is in place, with *threshold-based alerts* configured in Grafana based on detection criteria like sudden spikes in anomaly counts. Alerts are routed through various *notification channels*, email, Slack, and SMS, to ensure prompt action by network administrators.

15.7.2 Visualization in Grafana

Grafana was customized to visualize the results of the anomaly detection module in a way that provided actionable insights.

Dashboard Overview. A dedicated dashboard was created in Grafana, featuring the following panels:

1. *Anomaly Trend Over Time*: a line graph showing the number of anomalies detected per unit time, enabling administrators to identify spikes or trends indicative of potential attacks.
2. *Anomaly Distribution by Type*: a bar chart categorizing detected anomalies (e.g., DDoS, packet injection, spoofing), providing a quick understanding of prevalent threats.
3. *Traffic Health Indicators*: real-time metrics such as packet throughput, latency, and error rates, offering context to the anomaly detections.
4. *Top Anomalous IPs*: a table listing the IP addresses associated with the highest number of anomalies, helping to pinpoint potential sources of attacks.

Grafana Panel Example. A sample Grafana panel setup for "Anomaly Trend Over Time":

- *Query*: data queried from the Prometheus database where anomalies were stored.
- *Visualization*: time-series line graph with color-coded markers for significant spikes.
- *Thresholds*: configured to highlight critical levels (e.g., anomalies exceeding 50 in a 5-minute window).

15.7.3 Alerting Configuration

Alerting was implemented to provide proactive notifications when the Security Module detected critical anomalies.

Alert Conditions. Alerts were configured in Grafana using the following conditions:

- *High Anomaly Volume*: triggered if the number of anomalies exceeds a predefined threshold (50 anomalies within 5 minutes).
- *Persistent Anomalies*: triggered if anomalies are continuously detected for a sustained period (more than 10 anomalies every minute for 30 minutes).
- *Specific Threat Type*: alerts for specific attack types, such as a DDoS or spoofing attempts.

Notification Channels. To ensure timely responses, alerts were routed to multiple channels:

- *Email*: for detailed alert notifications.
- *Slack*: for quick team-wide notifications in the dedicated security operations channel.
- *SMS*: for critical alerts requiring immediate attention.

15.8 COMPARATIVE ANALYSIS OF ANOMALY DETECTION TECHNIQUES FOR 5G NETWORKS

This discussion compares three anomaly detection techniques: the proposed MLP-based solution, the ConvLSTM-based approach [19], and the machine learning-driven cyber-attack detection and response system. The focus is on their performance, adaptability, and scalability within the context of 5G network security.

Performance Comparison. The comparison between the three approaches highlights their strengths and limitations as shown in Table 15.3.

The cyber-attack detection and response system [20] reports a significantly lower accuracy (80.05%). While it excels in integrating detection and response mechanisms, its machine learning approach may require optimization to handle the high complexity of 5G network traffic effectively.

Each solution offers unique advantages depending on the specific requirements of the 5G network. The ConvLSTM-based approach is ideal for scenarios prioritizing accuracy and scalability, while the cyber-attack detection system provides comprehensive threat response capabilities. The MLP-based solution, with its emphasis on

TABLE 15.3
Comparison between the Three Approaches

Metric	Our Solution (MLP)	ConvLSTM-Based Approach	Cyber-Attack Detection and Response System
Accuracy	96.8	99	80.05
Precision	95.7	99	-
Recall	96.3	99	-
F1 Score	96.0	99	-
Detection Latency (ms)	12	Not Reported	24.9
Scalability	Moderate	High	Moderate

low latency and practical integration, presents a balanced choice for real-time applications. Future work could explore hybrid models combining the strengths of these approaches to develop a more robust and versatile anomaly detection framework.

15.9 CONCLUSIONS

The deployment of 5G networks within critical infrastructure presents transformative advantages for real-time monitoring, control, and rapid decision-making, ensuring greater operational efficiency and resilience in essential sectors. Key sectors such as energy grids, transportation networks, financial institutions, healthcare systems, and government services benefit immensely from the high data throughput, low latency, and reliability that 5G networks offer. However, these benefits are accompanied by increased cybersecurity vulnerabilities, which expose critical systems to sophisticated cyber threats.

This chapter presented an architecture of a secure 5G network for monitoring critical infrastructure facilities, providing a high level of protection against modern cyber threats. Experimental results confirmed the effectiveness of the proposed Security Module in real-time anomaly detection within a 5G network environment. Integrated with artificial intelligence and machine learning technologies, the Security Module successfully detected threats in real-time, including DDoS attacks, spoofing, and packet injection. The high accuracy, low latency, and adaptability to new threats demonstrate that the module provides a reliable layer of security without impacting network performance.

Tests conducted at the 5G testbed showed that the average threat detection time does not exceed 15 milliseconds, meeting real-time requirements and not affecting the quality of network service. Additionally, a low level of false positives (1.2%) and missed threats (2.3%) was observed, indicating the high efficiency of the system. However, there were minor increases in latency during high-traffic simulations, suggesting a need for optimization in more congested environments.

The Security Module demonstrated the ability to adaptively learn, allowing it to improve the accuracy of threat detection and respond promptly to new types of attacks. The multi-layered security architecture covering key network elements, including the Radio Access Network (RAN) and Core Network (CN), ensures comprehensive monitoring and protection of all critical nodes of the 5G infrastructure.

Future work could explore the module's performance in a fully deployed 5G network with greater device diversity and additional threat simulations, such as data exfiltration and insider threats. Furthermore, expanding the module's machine learning model with unsupervised learning techniques may further reduce false positive rates, enhancing real-world applicability.

Thus, the developed architecture is a robust and adaptable solution for detecting anomalies in a 5G environment, demonstrating significant potential for deployment in high-security 5G networks. Further research can focus on optimizing the performance of the Security Module and integrating it with other cyber defense tools to increase the network's resilience to sophisticated attacks. Ensuring a secure and resilient 5G network is imperative for protecting critical infrastructure assets from potential large-scale disruptions and catastrophic failures, ultimately safeguarding public and national interests in an evolving cyber landscape.

15.10 ACKNOWLEDGMENT

This work was supported by the Shota Rustaveli National Foundation of Georgia (SRNSFG) (NFR-22–14060).

REFERENCES

[1] Iavich, Maksim, Akhalaia, Giorgi & Gnatyuk, Sergiy. (2022). *Method of Improving the Security of 5G Network Architecture Concept for Energy and Other Sectors of the Critical Infrastructure*. doi: 10.1007/978-3-030-87675-3_14.

[2] Borgaonkar, Ravishankar, Tøndel, Inger Anne, Degefa, Merkebu & Jaatun, Martin. (2021). Improving Smart Grid Security Through 5G Enabled IoT and Edge Computing. *Concurrency and Computation: Practice and Experience*. 33. doi: 10.1002/cpe.6466.

[3] Altaleb, Haya & Rajnai, Zoltán. (2023). Addressing Cybersecurity Challenges in 5G-Enabled IoT and Critical Infrastructures: A Comprehensive Overview. *2023 IEEE 27th International Conference on Intelligent Engineering Systems (INES)*, IEEE, 2023. doi: 10.1109/ines59282.2023.10297774.

[4] Sobrinho, Alvaro, Vilarim, Matheus, Silva, Amanda, Santos, Danilo & Gurjao, Edmar. (2023). *A Systematic Literature Mapping on the Security of 5G and Vertical Applications*. doi: 10.21203/rs.3.rs-3791360/v1.

[5] Zapata, Jannette. (2023). *Security Challenges and Solutions for 5G Networks*. doi: 10.13140/RG.2.2.35696.88326.

[6] Anthony, Kwubeghari, Ezigbo, Lucy & Okoye, Francis. (2024). Modelling of Cyber Attack Detection and Response System for 5G Network Using Machine Learning Technique. *ABUAD Journal of Engineering Research and Development (AJERD)*. 7, 297–307. doi: 10.53982/ajerd.2024.0702.29-j.

[7] Waziri, Jamilu & Omokhuale, Emmanuel. (2022). Development of Enhance Reference Monitor Algorithm for Software Defined Networking (SDN) Controller for 5G Security. *International Journal of Multidisciplinary Research and Growth Evaluation*. 226–241. doi: 10.54660/anfo.2022.3.3.15.

[8] Aktolga, Ilter, Kuru, Elif Sena, Sever, Yiğit & Angin, Pelin. (2023). AI-Driven Container Security Approaches for 5G and Beyond: A Survey. *ITU Journal on Future and Evolving Technologies*. 4, 364–382. doi: 10.52953/ZRCK3746.

[9] Nkrumah, Matt. (2024). The Impact of 5G Technology on Communication Infrastructure. *Journal of Communication*. 4, 43–55. doi: 10.47941/jcomm.1655.
[10] Odarchenko, Roman, Iavich, Maksim, Iashvili, Giorgi, Fedushko, Solomia & Syerov, Yuriy. (2023). Assessment of Security KPIs for 5G Network Slices for Special Groups of Subscribers. *Big Data and Cognitive Computing*. 7, 169. doi: 10.3390/bdcc7040169.
[11] Gorbatov, Viktor, Zhukov, Igor, Kravchenko, Vladislav & Pravikov, Dmitry. (2023). Functionality of the Critical Information Infrastructure Cybersecurity Network. *Bezopasnost Informacionnyh Tehnology*. 30, 27–39. doi: 10.26583/bit.2023.1.02.
[12] Specification #: 23.501. *3GPP Portal*. [Online]. https://portal.3gpp.org/desktopmodules/Specifications/SpecificationDetails.aspx?specificationId=3144.
[13] Overview of 5G Use Cases and Architecture | 3.1 5G Use Cases | InformIT. *InformIT: The Trusted Technology Source for IT Pros and Developers*. [Online]. https://www.informit.com/articles/article.aspx?p=3128834&seqNum=3.
[14] Odarchenko, Roman, Imanbayev, Azamat & Pinchuk, Alla. (2023). Development of the Testbed for Testing Deep Learning Based IDS System for 5G Network. *MoMLeT+ DS*.
[15] IoT Dataset 2023 | Datasets | Research | Canadian Institute for Cybersecurity | UNB. University of New Brunswick | UNB. Date of access: November 13. 2024. [Online]. https://www.unb.ca/cic/datasets/iotdataset–2023.html.
[16] A Comprehensive Dataset for DDOS Attack. Kaggle: Your Machine Learning and Data Science Community. Date of access: November 13. 2024. [Online]. https://www.kaggle.com/datasets/amanverma1999/a-comprehensive-dataset-for-ddos-attack.
[17] Pinchuk, A., Odarchenko, R., Samoilenko, V. & Imanbayev, A. (2023). 5G Network Deployment Based on Open-source Projects: A Comparative Analysis. *2023 IEEE 12th International Conference on Intelligent Data Acquisition and Advanced Computing Systems: Technology and Applications (IDAACS)*, Dortmund, Germany, pp. 596–601. doi: 10.1109/IDAACS58523.2023.10348675.
[18] Pinchuk, Alla & Odarchenko, Roman. (2024). Experimental Studies of 5G Open-Source Network Performance. *International Scientific And Practical Conference Problems of Computer Science, Software Modeling and Security of Digital Systems*. 45–45.
[19] Kumar, S., Kour, V., Sah, R. K. & Misra, R. (2024). Scalable and Accurate Anomaly Detection in 5G Networks with ConvLSTM. *2024 International Conference on Emerging Trends in Networks and Computer Communications (ETNCC)*, IEEE, 2024, pp. 1–7. doi: 10.1109/etncc63262.2024.10767523.
[20] Anthony, Kwubeghari, Ezigbo, Lucy & Okoye, Francis. (2024). Modelling of Cyber Attack Detection and Response System for 5G Network Using Machine Learning Technique. *ABUAD Journal of Engineering Research and Development (AJERD)*. 7, 297–307. doi: 10.53982/ajerd.2024.0702.29-j.

16 Cybersecurity and Resilience in the Data Centres Design in Wartime

Andrii Davydiuk and Vitalii Zubok

16.1 INTRODUCTION

In multi-domain operations, the application of cyber domain measures and their interaction with other domains are of significant importance [1, 2]. A prerequisite for conducting cyber operations is the ability to exploit the adversary's infrastructure to diminish its military potential. This capability can be achieved through both cyber-attacks and physical interventions in the IT infrastructure. During Russia's invasion of Ukraine in 2014, a hybrid approach was employed. The seizure of administrative buildings, server rooms of Internet service providers, and mobile operators provided Russia with a significant advantage in the cyber domain. Unauthorized access to network elements and data leaks facilitated rapid reconnaissance to prepare more sophisticated cyberattacks on unoccupied territories.

Ukraine is facing new challenges, prompting questions about reducing the adversary's capabilities to negatively impact Ukraine's infrastructure. Several approaches can be considered to mitigate such influence. Segmenting network segments through isolation isolates the controlled segment from the hazardous one, but at the same time, it retains users' ability to access services and opportunities for reconnaissance and cyber operations in that direction. During temporary occupation, the adversary does not make fundamental changes to the architecture but quickly reconnects local providers to its own. Another more straightforward approach is the physical destruction of such objects in case of a high risk of data centre or individual server room capture. Evacuation of equipment to more secure areas is considered optimal, leaving only the minimal necessary infrastructure for the population. Considering the preceding, the use of mobile infrastructure arises as a question, which can be quickly deployed and provide trusted access to state services. Such an option is an alternative and effective [3] solution for de-occupied territories and can facilitate the complete evacuation of equipment or its destruction while ensuring minimal service availability for citizens.

In this direction, Ukraine has established the National Center for Reserving State Information Resources (hereinafter referred to as the NC). A key component of this NC is specialized mobile and portable mobile complexes designed for storing

DOI: 10.1201/9781003546153-16

national electronic information resources [4]. These complexes are subject to cybersecurity requirements for critical infrastructure [5].

Such an approach aligns with existing best practices in designing military IT infrastructure [6]. These solutions are based on elevated reliability and security requirements. Meanwhile, the solution is divided into two components: the management container and the functional container.

Given the preceding, there arises a question of ensuring the security and resilience of mobile architectures, which depends on the availability of appropriate power supply and stable, secure network connectivity.

Considering the aforementioned, ensuring the security and resilience of mobile architectures, which depends on the availability of appropriate power supply and stable, secure network connectivity, is a relevant scientific and technical problem. To address it, we will identify the main threats to data centres and consider options for their minimization through the use of mobile architectures.

16.1.1 Key Contributions of the Chapter

The following are the significant contributions of this chapter:

i) A comprehensive analysis of situational response to crisis incidents in data centres has been conducted.
ii) It has been established that the main criterion is to ensure the resilience and continuity of data centre operations.
iii) The approach for assessing the resilience of data centres as critical infrastructure objects during wartime has been presented based on this criterion.
iv) An analysis of the main threats to data centres has been carried out.
v) The approach for the overall assessment of data centre reliability considering the mobile component has been proposed, and a set of applied indicators has been mathematically described.
vi) The method for situational response to security crisis incidents in data centres has been developed in the form of a formal model describing a set of actions.

16.1.2 Chapter Organization

Section 16.2 presents an analysis of the subject area of data centre resilience, including an analysis of normative documents, standards, and scientific publications. Section 16.3 presents an approach to assessing data centre mobility risks. Section 16.4 presents the results and discussion. Section 16.5 concludes the chapter with future direction.

16.2 RELATED WORK

16.2.1 Analysis of the Subject Area for Resilience in the Data Centres Design

Data centres offer clients a range of services for data management using cloud computing technologies, including Infrastructure as a Service (IaaS), Platform as a Service (PaaS), Software as a Service (SaaS), Security as a Service (SECaaS), and more [7]. The use of cloud resources has enabled organizations to swiftly scale their IT infrastructure to meet increased demand and to plan expenditures on IT and cybersecurity. Concurrently, leveraging cloud services allows for substantial financial savings. These factors contribute to the widespread adoption of data centre services. Users of data centres include both governmental and private organizations and critical infrastructure entities, and several governmental bodies either possess or are establishing their own data centres [8].

However, centralizing data in one location creates increasing dependencies on the surrounding IT infrastructure and transforms data centres into critical infrastructure objects, for which ensuring resilience and cybersecurity becomes a top priority. In the conditions of war with the Russian Federation, additional risks arise for the operation of data centres. These risks include issues with power supply, Internet access, service maintenance (specialists, equipment delivery, service centres), missile attacks, enemy occupation of premises and equipment of data centres, and so on.

The question arises regarding the handling of such risks. One of the most effective ways to manage these risks is offshoring. However, this also poses a number of challenges, including significant financial costs, computational capabilities of foreign data centres, bandwidth limitations of data transmission channels, and so on. Another issue is data backup with restricted access, as there is a prohibition on using unprotected data transmission channels during their processing. Additionally, prioritizing information assets in data centres remains a challenge. For instance, the data centre administrator does not have access to the client's logical container (tenant) and cannot determine which information needs to be backed up as a priority within limited time constraints. Furthermore, the question of actions in the event of risks of enemy capture remains unresolved, particularly whether it would be less consequential to destroy the data centre oneself or leave it to the enemy.

All these challenges prompt the need to ensure the resilience of data centres in Ukraine. Within this task, it is advisable to consider information as a specific substance with volume -B_{inf} (TB), which constantly grows at a certain rate - V_{inf}. The data centre infrastructure (computing capacity) serves as a container for this material, the volume B_{dc} whose volume increases at a slower pace V_{dc} than the volume of data.

This approach enables the description of a range of states of resilience to the risk of data loss in the data centre. For instance, a state in which $B_{dc} > B_{inf}$ and $V_{inf} > V_{dc}$ is considered as the stable functioning of the data centre. However, under the conditions of implementing the aforementioned risks of a state of war, there may be situations where $B_{inf} > B_{dc}$ and $V_{inf} > V_{dc}$, which will not allow data preservation and they will be lost. The solution to such a problem may involve procedures for freeing up resources within the data centre or rapidly scaling up resources. Quickly scaling resources in conditions of a state of war is a challenging task considering the lead times for delivering the necessary equipment. Freeing up resources by deleting or transferring data will also take a considerable amount of time. It is also worth noting that it is nearly impossible to predict all the consequences of data loss.

In Ukraine, data centres, taking into account the existing risks and client demands, have begun extensively backing up data abroad [9]. However, the presence of citizens' data abroad may entail additional political and economic risks. A safer approach is to avoid moving sensitive data abroad by relocating it to more secure areas where infrastructure should be available. Of course, for a country to independently build infrastructure, following the example of Switzerland [10] (see Figure 16.1), in the Carpathian Mountains during wartime is an exceedingly challenging task that requires significant resources and time.

Thus, it is advisable to consider the possibilities of public-private partnerships to ensure the resilience of data centre infrastructure, including mechanisms for providing equipment and computational capabilities between data centres to address crises promptly. The mechanisms of such collaboration can be outlined within the framework of the concept of data centre resilience in times of war. This concept should take into account the risks of data centre placement, physical threats, security risks, resource assessments for risk management, and necessary cooperation for resilience.

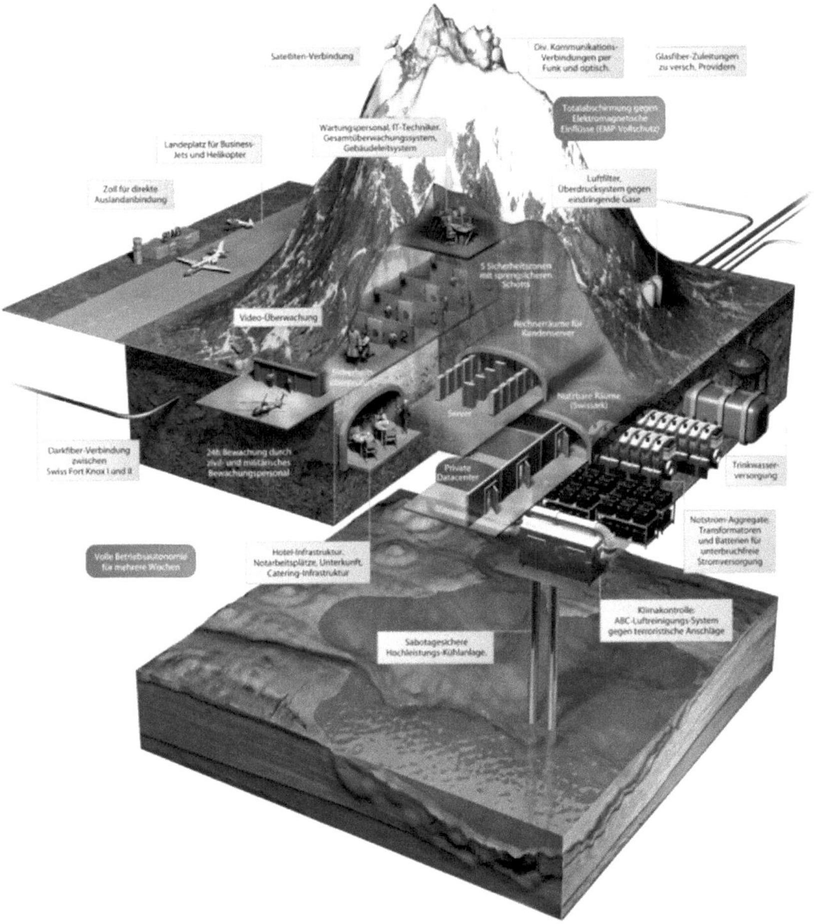

FIGURE 16.1 Structure of Swiss Fort Knox [10].

The concept should serve as the basis for developing evacuation procedures, destruction to prevent capture, personnel reserves, equipment reserves, and equipment relocation with subsequent deployment at an alternate site (such as another data centre) through integration into existing infrastructure.

The experience gained from such procedures could be unique for Ukraine and other countries experiencing armed conflicts, frequent natural disasters, or climatic challenges [11].

Firstly, let us consider the main threats that data centres may face during multi-domain operations.

The assessment of the aforementioned threats is conducted by taking into account the internal and external context of a specific data centre. Based on the analysis of the documents cited in the publication [12], it can be argued that there are requirements for increased reliability of data centres.

TABLE 16.1
The Threats to Data Centres

No.	Risk	Measures for processing
1	Power supply interruptions	Backup power systems
1.1	System downtime	Backup generator systems
1.2	Data loss	Equipment and system maintenance and testing
1.3	Equipment damage	
1.4	Failure of cooling systems	
1.5	Security system breaches (cameras, access control systems, etc.)	
2	Failure of cooling systems	Backup cooling systems
2.1	Equipment damage	Monitoring systems
2.2	System downtime	Technical maintenance and equipment/system testing
2.3	Data loss	
3	Connectivity Issues	Backup connectivity
3.1	Network overload (slowing down speed/blocking data exchange between servers, storage devices, and other resources)	Cybersecurity measures Personnel training
3.2	Network downtime (power supply issues, equipment failures, software errors, cyberattacks)	
3.3	Unauthorized network access (viruses, malware)	
3.4	Bandwidth limitations (exceeding resource demands)	
3.5	Delays and jitter – disruptions in real-time services such as video conferencing	
4	Hardware failures (server failures, data storage and processing devices, networking equipment, and other components)	Technical maintenance and testing of equipment and systems Utilization of backup systems (power supply, hardware components)
4.1	System downtime	Implementation of monitoring systems
4.2	Data loss	Implementation of procedures for rapid replacement (repair) of damaged components

TABLE 16.1 (*Continued*)
Overview of Recent Advancements in S-Box Design and Analysis

No.	Risk	Measures for processing
5	Physical security breaches	Robust security protocols
5.1	Unauthorized physical access	Access control
5.2	Equipment damage	Surveillance cameras
5.3	Employee negligence	Security training for personnel
5.4	Fire	Fire suppression systems
		Technical maintenance and testing of equipment and systems
6	Cybersecurity breaches	Reliable security policies
6.1	Loss of data confidentiality, integrity, and availability	Access control
6.2	Financial losses	Firewalls
6.3	Reputational losses	Encryption
6.4	Failures in critical infrastructure	
6.5	Disruptions in government services	
7	Natural disasters (floods, earthquakes, hurricanes, etc.)	Data and service backup
		Development of recovery plans
8	Human errors (configuration mistakes, maintenance errors)	Control and monitoring procedures
8.1	Physical destruction	Data and service backup
8.2	Data loss	
8.3	Operational disruption	
8.4	Power supply interruptions	Backup power supply
9	Network interruptions	Backup communication channels
10	Cyberattacks	Backup communication channels and implementation of cybersecurity measures
10.1	Violation of confidentiality, integrity, and data availability	
10.2	Disruption of data centre operations	
11	Supply chain disruptions (logistics and resource issues)	Availability of backup and repair kits, clear action protocols
12	Personnel security (staff turnover)	Measures to ensure personnel operation (access channels, secure accommodation)
13	Capture of the data centre by the adversary	Evacuation protocols (if possible), data destruction

16.2.2 Levels of Reliability in Data Centres

According to the Uptime Institute approach [13], the reliability of a data centre is assessed based on tiers, as shown in Figure 16.2. Data centre tiers are a standardized rating system indicating the reliability of data centre infrastructure. This classification evaluates facilities on a scale from 1 to 4, where 1 represents the lowest and 4 is the most effective level. This international data centre rating is provided by the Uptime Institute, an independent organization that determines the level of a facility primarily based on guaranteed uptime, fault tolerance, and serviceability.

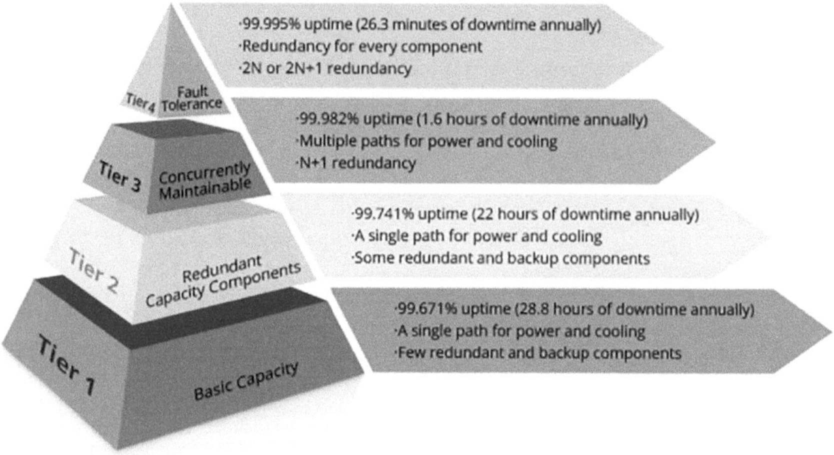

FIGURE 16.2 Levels of reliability in data centres [13].

The evaluation is conducted based on the following criteria:

- Guarantee of availability and uninterrupted operation of the service.
- Levels of redundancy (the process of duplicating critical components and preserving them as backup copies and safeguards in case of planned or unplanned failures).
- Condition of cooling and power infrastructure.
- Experience of personnel and maintenance protocols (including the ability to handle simultaneous repairability).
- Cost of service.
- Operational resilience and the centre's ability to achieve long-term business objectives.
- Time required for the data centre to onboard a new client.
- Tiers of security in data centres.
- Operator neutrality.

The four levels of data centres certified by the Uptime Institute are as follows:

Tier 1: A data centre with a single path for power and cooling without redundant components. This level offers an expected annual uptime of 99.671%.

Tier 2: A data centre with a single path for power and cooling, along with some redundant components. This level provides an expected annual uptime of 99.741%.

Tier 3: A data centre with multiple paths for power and cooling, as well as backup systems that allow personnel to work on configurations without transitioning to autonomous mode. The expected annual uptime for this level is 99.982%.

Tier 4: A fully fault-tolerant data centre with redundancy for every component. This level entails an expected annual uptime of 99.995% [13].

16.2.3 The ISO/IEC 22237 Series of Technical Specifications

Technical specifications of the ISO/IEC 22237 series are dedicated to data centre facilities and infrastructure design and assessment.

Parts 1, 3, 4, and 5 of the ISO/IEC 22237 series specify requirements and recommendations for the design of data centres to meet a given Availability Class. Parts 2 and 6 of the ISO/IEC 22237 series specify requirements and recommendations for the building construction and security systems for data centres.

Determination of the risk and scale of seismic activity should be included as part of the overall risk assessment approach found in ISO/IEC 22237–1. ISO/IEC TS 22237–2 requires a geographical risk analysis which includes seismic activity and relevant mitigation actions but does not identify the specific actions to be applied. ISO/IEC TS 22237–6 addresses external environmental events but does not explicitly list earthquakes or seismic activity within that group of events (other than general vibration) or indicate the specific measures required.

ISO/IEC TS 22237–30 describes earthquake risk and impact analysis. The most recent part of the series is ISO/IEC TS 22237–31. It introduces key performance indicators for data centres' resilience.

The first document of the series introduces and describes four available classes for which data centres can be classified. Following are the high-level descriptions of each rating level.

Availability Class-1: Basic Site Infrastructure. A data centre that has single capacity components and a single, non-redundant distribution path serving the ICT equipment.

Availability Class-2: Redundant Capacity Component Site Infrastructure. A data centre that has redundant capacity components and a single, non-redundant distribution path serving the ICT equipment.

Availability Class-3: Concurrently Maintainable Site Infrastructure. A data centre that has multiple independent distribution paths serving the ICT equipment. From a conformity point of view, it is acceptable to have one distribution path serve the ICT equipment with the second distribution path to be on standby for maintenance purposes. However, most data centres use both distribution paths on a continuous basis. The data centre is required to be concurrently maintainable, meaning that each and every capacity component, including elements/components that are part of the distribution path, can be removed/replaced/serviced on a planned basis without disrupting the ICT capabilities of the end user.

Availability Class-4: Fault Tolerant Site Infrastructure. A data centre which has multiple independent distribution paths serving the ICT equipment which are all active. The data centre allows concurrent maintainability and one (1) fault anywhere in the installation without causing downtime. The data centre must be able to automatically detect a fault, automatically isolate the fault, and to automatically continue operation.

Then, it represents four protection classes for which various areas of the data centre can be classified. For example, the staging area could have a different protection class rating compared to the computer room. At high level they can be described based on access type:

Protection Class-1: A publicly accessed area with no special protection against internal fire. There is no special protection applied against environmental events.
Protection Class-2: Partially restricted areas with fire detection and suppression. Mitigation is applied against environmental events at this class and higher classes.
Protection Class-3: An area which is restricted to specified individuals only.
Protection Class-4: An area which is restricted to specified employees only.

Part 31 introduces simple but sharp definitions for resilience, resilience level, availability, availability tolerance, dependability, failure rate, fault tolerance, reliability, and others. All 22237 series use the term "resilience" to specify the coherence between fault tolerance, determined by the number and the design of supply paths, and the data centre availability.

The document describes three basic KPI categories, or domains for DCI:

- Dependability.
- Fault tolerance.
- Availability tolerance.

Dependability splits on three sub-categories: reliability, availability, and failure rate, so in total there are five KPIs. Each KPI is provided with relevant formulae.

Application of the proposed KPIs is possible at every stage of design and/or operation of the data centre. The application of key performance indicators for DCI fault tolerance depends on the specified operating point (OP). Therefore, the specified OP and DCI load assumptions should always be provided when reporting KPIs.

Each category and sub-category contains either measurable or calculable KPIs. For calculable KPIs, there are metrics which serve as the quantitative indicator data for the calculation of particular KPIs.

There is an important question of how the document transforms a set of calculated or measured KPIs into a quantified resilience level. Short answer: it doesn't.

The document recommends one to pre-define normal resilience level and reduced resilience level depending on different operating points, then define different availability classes to meet different services requirements. Clause 6.6.2 describes the way of setting calculated operational availability as an integral indicator of data centre resilience for a particular availability class. Availability class means some level of power and environment controls within the data centre infrastructure. Operational availability is calculated from measured KPIs:

- Maximum number of single points of failure (SPoF).
- Reporting time interval (years).
- Maximum accepted number of faults per reporting interval.
- Maximum accepted down time per service violation (h).

Operational availability is represented by the coefficient < 1 (e.g. 0.995, 0.9995) which is typical for availability characteristics.

Particular attention should be paid to clauses 6.7.1 and 6.7.2 which describe preparing for resilience analysis and the process of it. Depending on the objectives of the analysis and the applicable resilience data, measurable and non-measurable aspects should be taken into account: failure rates for infrastructure elements, failure models, architecture, environment, human errors, skills of operators, and more. After that, the document proposes some methods derived from other existing standards, e.g. IEC 61078, to calculate the success function and dependability function.

16.2.4 Other Related Documents and Papers

In publication [14], a methodology for assessing the availability of next-generation data centres has been developed. This methodology is based on automatically obtaining the hardware configuration of data centres for evaluation using models of their availability. The proposed methodology utilizes a new standardized API Redfish and corresponding modelling structures. With this approach, we analyzed the advantages of transitioning from traditional data centre infrastructure (referred to as Performance Optimization Data Center (POD) with redundant servers) to a virtual Performance Optimized Data Center of the next generation (referred to as virtual POD (vPOD), consisting of a pool of disaggregated hardware resource data).

However, during wartime, unlikely risks of peacetime, such as physical destruction of data centres or frequent power supply failures, network access problems, and unauthorized access, become more probable. Thus, the realities of war require the development of new approaches to assessing the resilience of data centres. Taking the aforementioned into account, it is expedient to implement Key Performance Indicators (KPIs) in data centre resilience processes. In general, the following basic criteria for assessing data centre resilience can be identified.

1) Mean Time Between Failures (MTBF) – measures the average time between failures in the data centre infrastructure. This helps assess the reliability of components and systems in the data centre.
2) Mean Time to Repair (MTTR) – indicates the average time required for repair or restoration after a malfunction. Lower values of this indicator indicate that the data processing centre can quickly recover from failures, ensuring minimal downtime.
3) Availability (A) – measures the percentage of time during which the data processing centre is operational and accessible. A higher availability percentage indicates a more resilient data processing centre.
4) Redundancy Level refers to the duplication of critical components such as power supplies, cooling systems, and networking equipment.
5) Disaster Recovery Time (DRT) measures the time required for full recovery of operations after a catastrophe or significant outage. A shorter recovery time indicates a more reliable and efficient disaster recovery plan.

6) Data Backup Frequency and Completeness (DBFC) measures how often backup copies of data are created and whether these backups are complete and up-to-date. This metric ensures the ability to recover critical data in case of loss or damage.
7) Energy Efficiency (EF) is an assessment of the energy efficiency of the data centre infrastructure, including cooling systems, servers, and other equipment. This metric is crucial for reducing operational costs and minimizing the environmental impact of the data centre.
8) Security Incident Response Time (SIRT) measures the time required to detect security incidents in data centres and respond to them. A swift response is crucial for mitigating potential threats and minimizing the impact of security breaches.

These indicators can be measured in the following manner.

1. Mean Time Between Failures (16.1) [15]:

$$\text{MTBF} = \text{Total operational time / Number of failures} \tag{16.1}$$

2. Mean Time to Repair (16.2) [16]:

$$\text{MTTR} = \text{Total downtime due to failures / Number of failures} \tag{16.2}$$

3. Availability (16.3):

$$\text{Availability} = \left(\text{Total operational time} - \text{Total downtime}\right) / \text{Total operational time} \tag{16.3}$$

4. Redundancy Level (RL) (16.4) [17]:

$$\text{Redundancy Level} = \left(\begin{array}{l}\text{Number of redundant components /} \\ \text{Total number of components}\end{array}\right) \tag{16.4}$$

5. Disaster Recovery Time (16.5) [18]:

$$\text{DRT} = \text{Time taken to recover from a disaster} \tag{16.5}$$

6. Data Backup Frequency and Completeness (16.6) [19]:

$$\text{Backup Completeness} = \left(\text{Amount of data backed up / Total data size}\right) \tag{16.6}$$

7. Energy Efficiency (16.7) [20]:

$$\text{Power Usage Effectiveness (PUE)} = \text{Total Facility Power / IT Equipment Power} \tag{16.7}$$

8. Security Incident Response Time (16.8):

$$\text{Incident Response Time} = \text{Time taken to detect and respond to a security incident} \quad (16.8)$$

Thus, the basic resilience of a data centre (DR) can be calculated as follows (16.9): [21]

$$DR = \frac{MTTR + A + RL + DRT + DBFC + PUE + SIRT}{7} * 100\% \quad (16.9)$$

By obtaining the indicator of the basic resilience of data centres, it becomes possible to quantitatively assess the effectiveness of implementing resilience and security measures in data centres as critical infrastructure objects. Quantitative assessment of resilience contributes to efficient resource management, which is extremely important in wartime conditions.

16.3 MATERIALS AND METHODS/METHODOLOGY

16.3.1 Mobility Risk Assessment

Risk of capture – assessment of the risk of the data centre being captured by adversaries during transportation. It is advisable to consider factors such as security measures, transportation routes, and potential threats.

Risk of physical destruction – assessment of the likelihood of physical destruction of the data centre during transportation due to accidents, attacks, or natural disasters.

A mathematical model describing the aforementioned components may look as follows:

Risk assessment component (16.10):

$$R = P \times I \quad (16.10)$$

R – overall risk assessment.
P – probability of risk occurrence.
I – impact of risk.

Time required for component relocation (16.11):

$$Tp = f(Tasks) \quad (16.11)$$

Tp – preparation time;

$f(Tasks)$ is a function that addresses tasks related to preparing the data centre for relocation.

The component of resilience indicators (16.12):

$$C = \frac{Operateonal\ Continuity}{Downtime} \quad (16.12)$$

C – resilience coefficient.

Continuity of operation and downtime are quantitatively defined variables representing the uninterrupted operation and downtime during movement.

The mobility risk assessment component (16.13):

$$MR = CR \times PDR \tag{16.13}$$

MR – mobility risk
CR – capture risk
PDR – physical destruction risk

General resilience formula (16.14):

$$R = \frac{R + Tp + C - MR}{N} \tag{16.14}$$

N – it represents normalization coefficients for comparing different indicators for summation.

16.4 RESULTS AND DISCUSSIONS

16.4.1 Approach to Situational Response to Security Incidents in Data Centres

Based on the earlier mathematical formalization, it becomes possible to describe the approach to situational response as a set of the following actions:

Identification and Classification of Threats:

Threat Detection Algorithm: Continuous monitoring and analysis of various threats using sensors, artificial intelligence-driven algorithms, and cybersecurity protocols.

Threat Classification: Classifying threats based on severity, urgency, and impact on the data centre.

Immediate Response to Threats:

High-Level Threat (e.g., physical destruction):

- Instant activation of security protocols.
- Notification of relevant authorities and initiation of emergency response protocols.
- Application of blocking mechanisms to protect critical data and systems.

Medium-Level Threat (e.g., cybersecurity breach):

- Isolation of affected systems while maintaining core functions.
- Activation of backup systems and traffic redirection to secure nodes.
- Initiation of threat analysis and activation of response teams to contain and resolve the incident.

Low-Level Threat (e.g., environmental risks):

- Monitoring and assessment of the situation for potential escalation.
- Initiation of preventive measures without affecting core operations.
- Continuous monitoring and readiness for escalation if necessary.

Real-Time Risk Assessment:

- Assessment of the risk to stay or move based on threat intensity and vulnerability.
- Calculation of the probability of success in movement against the risk of being captured or destroyed during transit.

Dynamic Preparation Time:

- Adjustment of preparation time for movement based on urgency and severity of the threat.
- Prioritization for critical tasks such as data backup, system shutdown, and container protection.

Optimized Mobility Plan:

- Determination of the safest route for movement considering threat scenarios and potential evacuation paths.
- Coordination with relevant authorities or security groups for safe transit.

Algorithmic Decision Support:

- Utilization of AI-driven decision-making algorithms considering risk assessment, historical data, and real-time threat analysis.
- Integration of human decision-makers for critical judgment and re-evaluation capabilities.

Continuous Learning and Improvement:

- Post-threat analysis to evaluate response effectiveness and identify gaps and areas for improvement.
- Updating the resilience model based on observed response and its outcomes.
- Conducting training and simulations to enhance readiness and response strategies.

Such an approach can be described mathematically as follows:

1) Threat reality and impact (TRI) (16.15)

$$TRI = Reality\ threat \times Reality\ impact \tag{16.15}$$

This formula represents the overall quantitative assessment of the threat severity and potential impact on the data centre.

2) Dynamic threat assessment (DTA) (16.16):

$$DTA = f\left(Threats\ identification\right) \tag{16.16}$$

DTA provides a dynamic assessment of threats considering input data from the system and threat detection algorithms.

f(Threats identification) – this is a function that processes real-time threat data and assigns a threat assessment.

3) The adaptive mobility assessment (AMA) (16.17):

$$\text{AMA} = \frac{Probability\ of\ success\ in\ movement}{Risk\ of\ capture\ or\ destruction\ during\ movement} \tag{16.17}$$

AMA – the assessment evaluates the feasibility and risk associated with mobility in response to threats.

The probability of success in movement and the risk of capture or destruction during movement are quantitative values based on threat analysis and historical data.

4) Decision-making component (DMC) (16.18):

$$DMC = Decision\ Support\ based\ on\ AI + Human\ Factor\ Assessment \tag{16.18}$$

DMC combines the influence of AI-driven decision-making algorithms with human judgment to determine an appropriate response strategy.

5) Overall situational response (OSR) (16.19)

$$OSR = \frac{TRI + DTA + AMA + DMC}{H} \tag{16.19}$$

OSR – Overall situational response.

H – Normalization coefficient for standardizing the aggregation of different indicators.

An effective approach to situational response to security incidents in data centres is crucial to minimize damage, ensure rapid recovery, and maintain operational continuity. This approach involves real-time monitoring, swift identification, and containment of threats alongside robust incident response protocols. It ensures data integrity and availability, safeguards against data breaches, and upholds trust in the system's security, thereby protecting sensitive information and supporting uninterrupted business operations.

16.5 CONCLUSIONS AND FUTURE SCOPE

A comprehensive analysis of situational response to crisis incidents in data centres has been conducted. The main criterion has been established as ensuring the resilience and continuity of data centre operations. Based on this criterion, an approach for assessing the resilience of data centres as critical infrastructure objects during wartime has been presented. An analysis of the main threats to data centres has been carried out. Based on these threats, an approach for the overall assessment of data centre reliability considering the mobile component has been proposed, and a set of applied indicators has been mathematically described. Based on the aforementioned mathematical formalizations, a method for situational response to security crisis incidents in data centres has been developed as a formal model describing a set of actions. Further studies are planned to analyze approaches to the engineering design of data centres. Such an analysis should include an analysis of the strengths and weaknesses of such approaches as Design-Bid-Build, Design-Build, Premanufactured/Prefabricated Solutions, and Developer-Delivered. With the emergence of new approaches, such as Construction 4.0, data management will become central and will necessitate new business models for the industry. Beyond the traditional data and information generated during the design and execution of construction projects, substantial amounts of data will be produced by sensors and other CPS systems. The sheer volume, diversity, and the need for rapid processing of this data will require platforms that can interpret and manage it and connect it to existing business platforms. These systems will need to be more than just Big Data or decision-making platforms; they must be matchmaking platforms that offer innovative services and products, linking construction sites with smart factories and facilitating smarter design and use of connected smart buildings (or cities). However, many challenges remain, such as the development of global standards. Resilient data centres are essential for Construction 4.0 as they ensure continuous data integrity, availability, and cybersecurity, minimizing downtime and protecting against cyber threats. They provide the scalability and flexibility needed to handle the vast and growing data volumes, support regulatory compliance, and facilitate secure stakeholder collaboration. By enabling advanced analytics and AI-driven insights, resilient data centres enhance innovation, efficiency, and productivity in construction projects, ensuring seamless operations and real-time decision-making.

REFERENCES

[1] *Allied Joint Publication–3.20 Allied Joint Doctrine for Cyberspace Operations.* (2020). Nato Standardization Office (NSO), 53 p. https://assets.publishing.service.gov.uk/media/5f086ec4d3bf7f2bef137675/doctrine_nato_cyberspace_operations_ajp_3_20_1_.pdf (date of access: 29.03.2024).

[2] Multi-Domain Operations in NATO—Explained. *act.nato.int.* https://www.act.nato.int/article/mdo-in-nato-explained/ (date of access: 29.03.2024).

[3] Mobile Data Center Latest Solution for Military, First Responders - Breaking Defense. *Breaking Defense.* https://breakingdefense.com/2012/07/mobile-data-center-latest-solution-for-military-first-responder/ (date of access: 29.03.2024).

[4] Some Issues Regarding the Functioning of the National Center for Reserving State Information Resources, Resolution of the Cabinet of Ministers of Ukraine No. 311 (2023) (Ukraine). https://zakon.rada.gov.ua/laws/show/311-2023-п#Text (date of access: 29.03.2024).

[5] Approval of General Requirements for Cybersecurity of Critical Infrastructure Objects, Resolution of the Cabinet of Ministers of Ukraine No. 518 (2022) (Ukraine). https://zakon.rada.gov.ua/laws/show/518-2019-п#Text (date of access: 29.03.2024).

[6] Defense & Government. (n.d.). *Thinklogical | A Belden Brand.* https://www.thinklogical.com/defense_government/ (date of access: 29.03.2024).
[7] On Cloud Services: Law of Ukraine Dated February 17, 2022. № 2075-IX. https://zakon.rada.gov.ua/laws/show/2075-20#Text (date of access: 24.04.2023).
[8] On the Implementation of an Experimental Project Regarding the Functioning of the National Center for Reserving State Information Resources: Resolution of the Cabinet of Ministers of Ukraine Dated February 8, 2021. № 94.
[9] Management Understood: War Will Begin. Cloud Provider on Operations During War. *dev.ua.* https://dev.ua/news/gigacloud-support (date of access: 24.04.2023).
[10] MOUNT10—Swiss Fort Knox: Europe's Safest Data Center. MOUNT10—MOUNT10 AG - Das Original Schweizer Online Backup. https://mount10.ch/en/about-us/swiss-fort-knox/ (date of access: 29.03.2024).
[11] On the Approval of the Rules for Ensuring Information Security in Information, Telecommunication, and Information-Telecommunication Systems: Resolution of the Cabinet of Ministers of Ukraine dated March 29, 2006. № 373. https://zakon.rada.gov.ua/laws/show/373-2006-п#Text (date of access: 24.04.2023).
[12] Davydiuk, A. (May 17, 2023). Ensuring Data Center Security in Times of War. *Collection of Materials of the XLI Scientific and Technical Conference of Young Scientists and Specialists of the G.E. Pukhov Institute for Modelling in Energy Engineering of the National Academy of Sciences of Ukraine: Collection of Abstracts*, Kyiv, pp. 139–140.
[13] What are Data Center Tiers | FS Community. (n.d.). *Knowledge.* https://community.fs.com/article/what-are-data-center-tiers.html (date of access: 24.04.2023).
[14] Dzhereliy, D. (2016). Current State of the Regulatory Framework for Designing Data Storage and Processing Centers. *Modern Industrial and Civil Construction*, 12(4), pp. 187–191.
[15] What are Data Center Tiers | FS Community. *Knowledge.* https://community.fs.com/article/what-are-data-center-tiers.html (date of access: 18.12.2023).
[16] Data Center Tiers Classification Explained: (tier 1, 2, 3, 4). (n.d.). *phoenixNAP Blog.* https://phoenixnap.com/blog/data-center-tiers-classification (date of access: 24.04.2023).
[17] Rosendo, D., Gomes, D., Santos, G. L., Goncalves, G., Moreira, A., Ferreira, L., Endo, P. T., Kelner, J., Sadok, D., Mehta, A., & Wildeman, M. (2019). A Methodology to Assess the Availability of Next-Generation Data Centers. *The Journal of Supercomputing*, 75(10), pp. 6361–6385. https://doi.org/10.1007/s11227-019-02852-3 (date of access: 24.04.2023).
[18] Mean Time Between Failures (MTBF) | MTBF Calculation | Fiix. (n.d.). *Fiix.* https://fiixsoftware.com/maintenance-metrics/mean-time-between-fail-maintenance/#:~:text=MTBF%20=%20#%20of%20operational%20hours%20÷,of%20equipment%20is%20125%20hours (date of access: 24.04.2023).
[19] MTBF, MTTR, MTTF, MTTA: Understanding Incident Metrics. (n.d.). *Atlassian.* https://www.atlassian.com/incident-management/kpis/common-metrics#:~:text=MTTR%20(mean%20time%20to%20repair,system%20is%20fully%20functional%20again (date of access: 24.04.2023).
[20] Wang, F., Ramamritham, K., & Stankovic, J. A. (1995). Determining Redundancy Levels for Fault Tolerant Real-Time Systems. *IEEE Transactions on Computers*, 44(2), pp. 292–301. https://doi.org/10.1109/12.364540 (date of access: 24.04.2023).
[21] What is the Difference Between RPO and RTO? Real Meaning. (n.d.). *Data Resiliency Cloud | Fully Managed SaaS Platform | Druva.* https://www.druva.com/blog/understanding-rpo-and-rto (date of access: 24.04.2023).

17 Indexing the State of Military Cyber Defence and Hacktivism in Wartime in Ukraine

Mykola Khudyntsev,
Andrii Davydiuk, and Artem Zhylin

17.1 INTRODUCTION

The beginning of open-armed military aggression of the Russian Federation against Ukraine on February 24, 2022, was preceded by large-scale cyber-attacks starting in January 2022. They were directed at objects of critical information in infrastructure, providers of access to the Internet, telecommunications operators, etc. The number of cyber-attacks on Ukrainian information resources has increased significantly [1]. These cyberattacks aimed to impose panic, lose control of the state and troops, and distort the information space in favour of the enemy. The result of the advantage of the enemy in the information and cyber confrontation may also be direct losses of human resources and equipment of the Armed Forces of Ukraine. At the same time, conducting only cyber defence measures leads to losing initiative and being under constant enemy attacks without the possibility of retaliatory actions. Therefore, there is an urgent question about the transition from cyber protection to cyber defence.

Such a definition of cyber defence indicates only its components but does not provide an opportunity to assess the country's ability to decide the military and political leadership regarding the concentration of forces and means to counter the aggressor in cyberspace. Taking this into account, the work solves the problem of indexing the state (capability) of the country's cyber defence in conditions of martial law.

17.1.1 Key Contributions of the Chapter

The following are the significant contributions of this chapter:

i. The study contains an analysis of the conditions for assessing the state of cyber defence and hacktivism in Ukraine after the beginning of the open-armed military aggression of the Russian Federation, as a comparison of the definition, interpretation and application of the terms of "cybersecurity", "cyber defence", "cyber protection" and "hacktivism", and an analysis of the

DOI: 10.1201/9781003546153-17

state of cyber defence of NATO member states, as part of the main task of the Alliance's collective defence.

ii. A comparative characterisation of the indicators of cyber defence and hacktivism of the existing global cybersecurity indices was carried out.

iii. Possible indicators of the formation of the MCDHI at the national and international levels, including the Ukrainian experience, are proposed in detail.

17.1.2 Chapter Organisation

Section 17.2 presents an analysis of related regulatory documents and works on determining indicators for the formation of indices of the state of cyber defence and hacktivism during war. Section 17.3 presents methods and approaches to identifying and collecting cyber defence indicators. In particular, indicators from Ukrainian legislation, global indicators of cyber security indices and indicators of hacktivism are proposed to form an index of military cyber defence and hacktivism. Section 17.4 presents the results and discussion. Section 17.5 concludes the chapter with future direction.

17.2 RELATED WORK

The Law of Ukraine "On the Defence of Ukraine" stipulates that cyber defence (active cyber defence) measures are carried out in peacetime to protect the sovereignty of the state and ensure its defence capability, prevent armed conflict and repel armed aggression, and repel armed aggression against Ukraine based on the appropriate decision of the president of the Armed Forces of Ukraine, together with other military formations, begin military operations, including conducting special operations (intelligence, informational and psychological, etc.) in cyberspace [2]. It is worth noting that here terms cyber defence and active cyber defence are synonymous. According to the law "On the Basic Principles of Cybersecurity in Ukraine", cyber defence is a set of political, economic, social, military, scientific, scientific-technical, informational, legal, organisational and other activities carried out in cyberspace aimed at protecting the sovereignty and defence capabilities of a state, preventing armed conflict and repelling armed aggression [3]. The term active cyber defence is not present at all. At the same time, according to the Law of Ukraine "On the State Service for Special Communications and Information Protection of Ukraine" (SSSCIP), the SSSCIP performs the task of actively countering aggression in cyberspace [4]. According to [3], active countermeasures against aggression in cyberspace are actions aimed at increasing the level of cyber protection by neutralising cyberattacks of the aggressor state, information and communication systems and networks, as well as the sources of cyber threats and cyberattacks that are used to harm the national security of Ukraine. For a complete analysis, it is also worth considering definitions of the terms cybersecurity and cyber protection. Cybersecurity is the protection of vital interests of individuals and citizens, society and the state in the use of cyberspace, which ensures the sustainable development of information society and the digital communication environment, timely detection, prevention and neutralisation of real and potential threats to the national security of Ukraine in cyberspace. Cyber protection is a set of organisational, legal, engineering and technical measures, as well as measures of cryptographic and technical protection of information, aimed at preventing cyber incidents, detecting and protecting against cyberattacks, eliminating their consequences, restoring consistency and reliability of functioning of communication and technological systems [3].

To avoid uncertainty in the understanding of these terms, let's compare the functions included in them in Table 17.1. The purpose of such a comparative analysis is

TABLE 17.1
Comparison of Terms

	Active cyber defence	Cyber defence	Active countermeasures against aggression in cyberspace	Cybersecurity	Cyber protection
Protect the sovereignty of the state					
Ensure defence capability					
Prevent armed conflict					
Repel armed aggression					
Conduct military operations					
Conduct intelligence special operations					
Conduct informational special operations					
Conduct psychological special operations					
Increase the level of cyber protection					
Neutralise cyberattacks					
Neutralise information and communication systems, networks, sources of cyber threats					
Protect vital interests of individuals and citizens, society and the state					
Detect real and potential threats to the national security					
Prevent real and potential threats to the national security					
Neutralise real and potential threats to the national security					
Prevent cyber incidents					
Detect cyberattacks					
Protect against cyberattacks					
Eliminate consequences of cyberattacks					
Restore consistency of functioning of communication and technological systems					
Restore the reliability of functioning of communication and technological systems					

to identify functional relationships within the framework of the processes described by these terms. On the basis of the identified connections, it will be possible to determine the processes of information exchange and data sets that can be exchanged by the participants of these processes. The description of information connections will contribute to more efficient use of work resources, reduce the likelihood of duplication or incomplete data, and help to identify outdated or incorrect data faster.

Given the results in Table 17.1, cyber defence functions are of a general strategic nature. They do not exclude the possibility of active cyber defence, active countermeasures against aggression in cyberspace, cybersecurity and cyber protection. These functions can be logically grouped as shown in Figure 17.1.

Given the preceding, it is appropriate to define metrics for assessing the state of cyber defence and hacktivism during the war for their possible use in the structure of the state cyber defence index. Proposals regarding the formation (application) of indicators of cyber defence should be based on the analysis of relevant provisions of the legislation of Ukraine and best similar practices.

The law [3] defines that:

Subjects of cybersecurity within their competence shall:

1) implement measures to prevent the use of cyberspace for military, intelligence-subversive, terrorist and other illegal and criminal purposes
2) detect and respond to cyber incidents and cyberattacks and eliminate their consequences;
3) carry out information exchange regarding actual and potential cyber threats
4) develop and implement protective, organisational, educational and other measures in the field of cybersecurity and cyber defence
5) ensure the conduct of information security audits, including at subordinate facilities and facilities belonging to the scope of their management
6) carry out other activities to ensure the development and security of cyberspace.

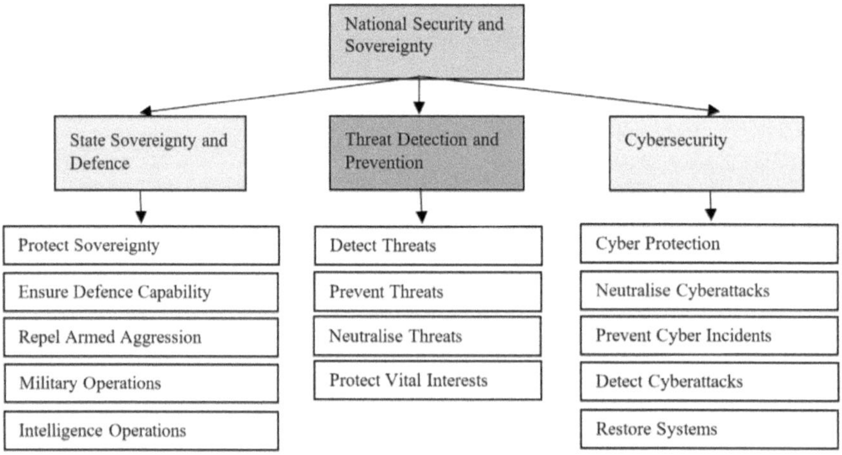

FIGURE 17.1 Logical distribution of functions.

The main military subjects of cybersecurity are SSSCIP, the Ministry of Defence of Ukraine and the General Staff of the Armed Forces of Ukraine, the Security Service of Ukraine.

The SSSCIP ensures the formation and implementation of public policy on the protection in cyberspace of state information resources and information whose protection is required by law, and cyber defence of critical information infrastructure facilities, and exercises state control in these fields; coordinates the activities of other cybersecurity subjects with regard to cyber defence; ensures the establishment and operation of the National Telecommunications Network and the implementation of an organisational and technical model for cyber defence; implements organisational and technical measures to prevent, detect and respond to cyber incidents and cyberattacks and eliminate their consequences; informs about cyber threats and appropriate methods of protection against them; ensures implementation of information security audits at critical infrastructure facilities, establishes requirements for information security auditors and determines the procedure for their attestation (recertification); coordinates, organises and conducts an audit of the security of communications and technological systems of critical infrastructure facilities; and ensures the functioning of the State Cyber Protection Centre, the government's computer emergency response team of Ukraine CERT-UA.

The Ministry of Defence of Ukraine (MOD) and the General Staff of the Armed Forces of Ukraine (GS AFU) shall, with the respective competence, carry out measures to prepare the state to repulse military aggression in cyberspace (cyber defence); carry out military cooperation with NATO and other defence subjects to ensure the security of cyberspace and joint protection against cyber threats; implement measures to ensure cyber protection of critical information infrastructure in conditions of emergency and martial law.

The Security Service of Ukraine (SSU) prevents, detects, suppresses and solves criminal offences against peace and security of humanity that are committed in cyberspace; carries out counterintelligence and operational-search activities aimed at combating cyberterrorism and cyber espionage, and covertly checks the readiness of critical infrastructure facilities for possible cyberattacks and cyber incidents; counteracts cybercrime, the consequences of which may threaten the vital interests of the state; investigates cyber incidents and cyberattacks against state electronic information resources and information, the requirement for protection of which is established by law, and critical information infrastructure; provides a response to cyber incidents in the field of national security [3].

In this way, it is possible to distribute the participation of these subjects according to the functions from Table 17.1 and present this distribution in Table 17.2.

Thus, the basic cybersecurity legislation contains sufficient grounds for the normative and organisational and technical definition of individual indicators of cyber defence (active cyber defence or military cyber defence).

We will also consider the general indicators of cyber defence adopted by the countries of the North Atlantic Alliance. North Atlantic Treaty Organization defined a basic approach to cyber defence [5], according to which cyber defence is part of the main task of NATO's collective defence. In cyberspace, NATO's actions are defensive, proportionate and consistent with international law. Individual allies are

TABLE 17.2
The Military Subjects of Cybersecurity Functions Logical Distribution

SSSCIP
MOD & GS AFU
SSU

	Active cyber defence	Cyber defence	Active countermeasures against aggression in cyberspace	Cybersecurity	Cyber protection
Protect the sovereignty of the state					
Ensure defence capability					
Prevent armed conflict					
Repel armed aggression					
Conduct military operations					
Conduct intelligence special operations					
Conduct informational special operations					
Conduct psychological special operations					
Increase the level of cyber protection					
Neutralise cyberattacks					
Neutralise information and communication systems, networks, sources of cyber threats					
Protect vital interests of individuals and citizens, society and the state					
Detect real and potential threats to the national security					
Prevent real and potential threats to the national security					
Neutralise real and potential threats to the national security					
Prevent cyber incidents					
Detect cyberattacks					
Protect against cyberattacks					
Eliminate consequences of cyberattacks					
Restore consistency of functioning of communication and technological systems					
Restore the reliability of functioning of communication and technological systems					

responsible for their cyber defences, but NATO will serve as a platform for cyber defence consultations, information sharing on cyber threats, sharing best practices and coordinating activities.

The main indicators of strengthening cyber protection in the organisation are:

- exchanging information about threats in real-time through a special platform for exchanging information about malicious software, as well as sharing advanced methods of responding to cyber threats

- support for rapid response teams that can be sent to help allies in solving cyber challenges
- developing objectives for allies to promote a common approach to their cyber defence capabilities
- investing in education and training (in particular, such as the Cyber Coalition).

The NATO Computer Incident Response Team (NCIRC), based at NATO Headquarters Europe in Mons, Belgium, protects NATO's networks by providing 24/7 cyber defence support to Alliance facilities. Experts handle incidents and provide NATO and allied countries with up-to-date analysis of cyber challenges and cyber threats. The NCIRC is part of NATO's communications and information agency that supports NATO's operations in cyberspace, connects NATO's information and communications systems, and secures NATO's networks.

A Cyberspace Operations Center has also been established in Mons (Belgium). The centre supports military commanders with situational awareness to inform Alliance operations and missions. The centre will also coordinate NATO's operational activities in cyberspace, ensuring freedom of action and resilience of military operations against cyber threats.

NATO's Joint Center of Advanced Technologies for Cyber Defence (NATO CCDCOE) in Tallinn, Estonia, is a NATO-accredited research and training centre engaged in education, research and development in the field of cyber defence. The centre provides valuable knowledge on cyber defence issues and organises cyber training with the participation of NATO members and Alliance partners.

The NATO School Oberammergau in Germany provides cyber defence training in support of Alliance operations, strategy, policy, doctrine and procedures.

The NATO Academy of Communications and Information in Oeiras (Portugal) provides training for specialists in the field of NATO cyber defence.

The NATO Defence College in Rome (Italy) promotes the development of strategic thinking on military-political issues, including issues of cyber defence.

Cooperation on cyber defence issues with the specified NATO structures within the framework of practical cooperation is provided for in the Cybersecurity Strategy Implementation Plan of Ukraine (adopted in December 2021).

In March 2022, Ukraine joined the NATO Cyber Center as a country that participates in the work of the centre (contributing participant) due to the country's "invaluable experience in countering cyber-attacks", and in May of the same year, a Ukrainian delegation took part in the meeting of the centre's steering committee for the first time, which took place in Tallinn [6].

The problem of indexing the state of cyber defence is also considered in the special report of the Belfer Center from Harvard Kennedy School [7] (see also the bibliography of the report). The report is devoted to the conception of cyber power in the system of traditional military power and contains the description of two sets of cyber power objectives.

The first (up-level) set includes the next cyber power indicator domains:

- defence and security;
- economic growth and prosperity;
- international power projection.

The second (down-level) set includes the next cyber power indicators:

- surveilling and monitoring domestic groups
- strengthening and enhancing national cyber defences
- controlling and manipulating the information environment
- intelligence gathering and collection in other countries for national security objectives
- amassing wealth and/or extracting cryptocurrency
- extracting IP overseas for commercial gain to enhance domestic industry growth
- destroying and disabling an adversary's infrastructure and capabilities
- defining international cyber norms and technical standards.

Among the works about the research of hacktivism, we note reviews of B. Brady [8] and N.B. Dogan [9] which are devoted to the analysis of electronic civil disobedience and the contextual and conceptual issue of hacktivism. Also, a deep analysis of the methods and parameters of hacktivism, and of comparing hacktivism and cybercrime is contained in the thesis of F. Farmer [10]. The work of M. Husak, M. Lashtovichka, and T. Plesnik [11] is of interest as one of the first studies of the role of hacktivists in repelling Russian aggression against Ukraine in cyberspace.

In general, projects to assess the level of digitalisation and cyber security are constantly developing. For example, the DigWatch team created country profiles based on available indicators [12]. The NCSC-FI developed Kybermittari as a tool that improves the ability of companies, organisations and society at large to prevent cyber threats. Kybermittari is a concrete tool for managers of companies and organisations to control cyber threats better, offering a means to assess critical functions, processes and dependencies. Kybermittari displays the level of cyber risk identification, protection, detection, response and recovery in organisations. It also visualises the maturity level related to the management of the supply chain and external dependencies. What is more, corporate managers can obtain valuable information about their preparations against cyber risks in comparison to the average level in their sector. Kybermittari has been customised for companies and organisations operating in Finland, and it is based on international measurement models for cybersecurity capabilities. The national approach enables the even-handed benchmarking of companies and sectors and defines a shared language for the measurement and development of cybersecurity. The role of NCSC-FI is to support the continuity and long-term use of the tool and to create preconditions for sharing confidential information about best practices, recommendations and reference results in cooperation with critical organisations [13]. A number of other approaches are based on the development of reports on cybersecurity issues. Coalition's Cyber Threat Index 2024 is a comprehensive report with insights on Internet security, cyber risk trends and critical vulnerabilities from the past year [14]. The approach based on the analysis of information operations through the collection and analysis of big data is interesting. The Attak index project team uses open sources, monitoring databases and data sets from online media and social networks [15]. This approach can be useful for establishing cause-and-effect relationships, using the cyber component in information warfare.

17.3 MATERIALS AND METHODS/METHODOLOGY

17.3.1 Ukrainian Legislation Indicators

The world political and military-political situation determined by the Russian aggression against Ukraine demands the urgent development of a system of open (as well as, obviously, confidential, and possibly secret) indicators of the state of military cyber defence and hacktivism of individual countries (states and societies), economic and military-political unions for forming a dynamic and adequate assessment of the capabilities of relevant players in the political and social arenas.

Analysis of the national legislation in the field of cybersecurity for the period from 2016 to 2024 allows determining the following indicators of military cyber defence:

- belonging to the defined strategic goals of the cybersecurity of the state
- availability of strategic tasks and a special defence plan
- conducting defence reviews, reviews of the national cybersecurity system, reviews of the state of cyber protection of state information resources and critical information infrastructure
- conducting joint thematic exercises with relevant divisions of NATO member states
- creation of a military response team to emergency events in cyberspace [16]
- implementation of state support measures [17]
- creation of cyber troops as part of the defence forces [18]
- availability of strategic defence documents, cyber defence plans [19]
- international military-strategic cooperation [20].

The problem of indexing (indicative assessment) of the state of national cybersecurity (including cyber defence) in Ukraine is the first task of the implementation plan of the National Cybersecurity Strategy [16]: to develop a system of indicators of the state of cybersecurity, which will include: basic indicators of the state of cybersecurity, indicators of the development of the National Cybersecurity System and indicators of the state of cyber protection of critical information infrastructure, state information resources and information whose protection is required by law.

17.3.2 Global Cybersecurity Indices

Global cybersecurity indices (or ratings) include regular (periodic) information materials that contain expert, analytical and statistical information on the security status and level of protection of indexing entities (ranking), as well as some indicators regarding the harmful effects of the implemented threats to information security and cybersecurity [21].

Cybersecurity indices are the high-level indicators of the state of cybersecurity or information security of complex telecommunications information systems or ecosystems. Cybersecurity indexes are understood in the sense of quantitative indicators.

Cybersecurity ratings include cybersecurity indices, which are characterised by lists of indexing subjects with the definition of the order place of the subject in that list.

TABLE 17.3
Global Cybersecurity Indices Classification

Group 1 Names	Group 2 Types	Group 3 Categories	Group 4 Access methods	Group 5 Fields
Indices	Global	Reports	Platform	Regulatory
Indexes	International	Expert	Questionnaires	Technical
Ratings	Corporate	Network	Libraries	Marketing
		Data Sets	Applications	
		Financial (Exchange)	Automatic (automated)	
		Combined		

Cybersecurity indices (indexes, ratings) are divided by types, categories, access methods and fields presented in Table 17.3.

Some indices contain features of different groups at the same time, so the proposed classification of cybersecurity indices is conditional.

The definitions for Group 1 are represented in Table 17.3.

Group 2. Global cybersecurity indices include cybersecurity indices, which relate to the assessment (indexing, ranking) of countries on the activities of state institutions. The developers of global cybersecurity indices are usually global and international organisations or well-known research centres. International cybersecurity indices include cybersecurity indices that relate to sectors of the economy, corporations and organisations in different jurisdictions. Also, the international cybersecurity indices include an integrated assessment of countries on individual indicators of cybersecurity, relating to industries (sectors) of the economy, corporations and organisations of certain jurisdictions, including when indexing (ranking) is carried out for a limited number of countries. International cybersecurity indices are usually developed by rating agencies or other expert organisations that specialise in information technology and cybersecurity. Corporate cybersecurity indices include cybersecurity indices that apply to corporations and organisations. Corporate cybersecurity indices are typically generated by manufacturers of technology products and solutions or information technology expert organisations.

Group 3. The cybersecurity indices of the reports category include regular (periodic) materials, which, as a rule, do not contain statistical information and ratings of indexing subjects (ratings) and relate to issues of analysis and assessment of threats, risks, events, incidents, negative consequences and other specialised issues in the areas of information security and cybersecurity, not directly related to the subjects of indexing (rating), evaluation of their activities and security. Expert cybersecurity indices include cybersecurity indices, which are formed and/or confirmed by surveys and/or conclusions of specially involved or self-involved experts. Cybersecurity indices of the network category include cybersecurity indices, which are formed, as a rule, for individual organisations through a multilevel analysis of control information contained in data packets transmitted in packet data networks. Organisations, which usually specialise exclusively in such activities, take part in the collection, processing and analysis of management information. Cybersecurity indices of the data sets category include cyber-security indices, which are formed, as a rule, using automatic visualisation of data (other than the data used in the formation of cybersecurity indices of the network category). If data are directly related to financial (exchange) information, such cybersecurity indices are classified as financial (exchange). The cybersecurity indices of the combined category include cybersecurity indices (indicators, subindexes, domains) to which several other categories can be assigned simultaneously.

Group 4. Platform indices are characterised by the presence of a specialised web platform, an online service for the formation, accounting and processing of data of the corresponding indices. Questionnaires are online or offline forms of the questions and the answers for further completion and expert review. Libraries are updatable indexed sets of documents or files. Applications are custom calculator-type applications that allow calculating the indexing subject score (as a rule, these are cyber risk assessment calculators). Automatic (automated) indices are calculated continuously according to pre-designed algorithms (which can be updated regularly).

Group 5 contains areas of application (fields of use) of indices. In particular, the analyzed indices belong either to the regulatory area (the area of legislation) or are of an applied technical nature (contain indicators of a technical nature), or index marketing information (not of a technical nature).

The subject or object of indexing (rating) is determined separately for each cybersecurity index. In a broad sense, by indexing or rating, we mean any method of evaluation.

The objects of indexing (rating) include:

- activity of indexing subjects (entities, stakeholders) in the field of information security and cybersecurity
- state of information security or cybersecurity of indexing subjects
- the level of protection of indexing subjects from threats (threats)
- certain indicators of information security and cybersecurity, as well as protection against relevant threats
- some indicators regarding the harmful effects of implemented threats.

Indicators of indexing are the certain parameters of the subject of indexing, which are used to describe and evaluate the index. Different cybersecurity indices (indexes) contain from 1 to 50 indicators that belong to the subject or object of indexing (rating) and can be evaluated separately (as a sub-index) or as part of the main index. The list of indicators of indexing is determined separately for each index, which is the basis of the methodology of formation of the corresponding index or rating.

Common methods of indexing (rating):

- examination – definition and expert assessment of indicators of indexing (rating)
- parameterisation – quantitative assessment of indicators of indexing (rating)
- indexing – a method of evaluation, the result of which is a dimensionless numerical indicator (index, score)
- rating – a method of evaluation, the result of which is a natural numerical indicator (number in the rating).

Indicators of military cyber defence and hacktivism are currently not indexed in their pure form in terms of global cyber security indices. The closest in meaning to the military cyber defence index is the National Cyber Power Index (NCPI) [7]. However, individual indicators of existing cybersecurity indices characterise the processes (states) of military cyber defence and hacktivism.

A possible form of cybersecurity assessment is the indexing (ranking) of the subjects on the military cyber defence and hacktivism according to selected indicators. The research materials for the military cyber defence and hacktivism indicators of existing global cybersecurity indices are presented in Table 17.4.

TABLE 17.4
Cybersecurity Indexes with Indicators of Military Cyber Defence and Hacktivism

Index		Editor			Indicator		Total indicators Qty
Name	Abbr.	Name	Abbr.	Country	Name	Type*	
Automate Third-Party Security Rating Platform	A3SRP	Panorays	PNR	USA	Security rating (rating reflects the assessment of domestic security policy from the point of view of a third malicious/hackers party)	H	9
Black Kite Cyber Risk Ratings Platform	BKCRRP	Black Kite Inc.	BKI	USA	Hacktivist shares	H	18
Cyber Exposure Index	CEI	Cyber Intelligence House	CIH	SGP	Identified risks (from hacktivists)	H	3
Cyber Exposure Index	CEI	Cyber Intelligence House	CIH	SGP	Identified risks (from hacktivists)	H	3
Cyber Readiness Index	CRI	Potomac Institute for Policy Studies	PIPS	USA	Defence and crisis response	C	7
Cyber Readiness Index	CRI	Potomac Institute for Policy Studies	PIPS	USA	Defence and crisis response	C	7
Global Cyber Strategies Index	GCSI	Center for Strategic and International Studies	CSIS	USA	Military strategies detailing offensive or defensive military capabilities in cyberspace	C	7

TABLE 17.4 (*Continued*)
Cybersecurity Indexes with Indicators of Military Cyber Defence and Hacktivism

Index		Editor			Indicator		Total indicators Qty
Name	Abbr.	Name	Abbr.	Country	Name	Type*	
Index of Cybersecurity	ICS	Tandon School of Engineering	TSE	USA	Type of attacker (violator), incl. activists (hacktivists) influence on politically or ideologically motivated activities (local or abroad)	H	4
National Cyber Power Index	NCPI	Belfer Centre Harvard University	BCH	GBR	Specialised foreign intelligence activities on national cybersecurity Ability to destroy or disable the information and communication infrastructure and capabilities of the enemy	C	7
S&P Kensho Future Security Index	KSEC UREP	S&P Dow Jones Indices LLC	S&P	USA	Indexes (subindexes) of military systems: space KMARSP, robotics KBOTSP, remote-controlled or unmanned aerial and marine drones KDRONEP, mobile technologies KBORGP, virtual or augmented reality KVRP	C	3
Security Scorecard Ratings	SSR	Security Scorecard Co.	SSC	USA	Exchange of information between hackers (Hacker Chatter)	H	10
Travelers Risk Index Cyber	TRIC	Travelers Indemnity Co.	TIC	USA	Regulatory defence costs/ fines	C	1

* C – military cyber defence, H – hacktivism

17.3.3 Hacktivism and Additional Indicators

The term “hacktivism” does not have established definitions, but hacktivism can be understood as a specific form of public-private interaction using electronic means of resistance, disobedience and countermeasures.

Here are some free (non-normative) definitions of hacktivism:

- (a portmanteau of hack and activism) the use of computer-based techniques such as hacking as a form of civil disobedience to promote a political agenda or social change [22, 23]
- use of computers and computer networks to promote political ideas, freedom of speech, protection of human rights and ensuring freedom of information [24]
- computer hacking (as by infiltration and disruption of a network or website) done to further the goals of political or social activism [25]
- instruments such as information warfare, cultural manipulation and social media hacktivism are being used to achieve foreign policy goals without the use of direct force application [25]
- the act of hacking, or breaking into a computer system, for politically or socially motivated purposes [26].

The analysis of cybersecurity indices with indicators of military cyber defence and hacktivism shows the presence of qualitative and quantitative assessments of the influence of these factors on the relevant indexing indicators. The development and implementation of specialised indices (sub-indices) of military cyber defence and/or hacktivism alongside the indicators of the existing indices included in Table 17.4 will improve the assessment of the impact of these factors on the general state of cybersecurity of indexing subjects.

The analysis of the state of cyber defence under the conditions of Russian open-armed military aggression against Ukraine, as well as the problems of applying the norms of international humanitarian law in matters of conducting cyber defence and hacktivism with the study of relevant indicators, are considered in [27].

As additional open indicators that can be used to index the state (rating of subjects) of military cyber defence and hacktivism, we can offer:

- availability, size and composition of cyber defence forces, as well as special (informational) operations in cyberspace
- the presence and level of maturity of cyber defence technology centres within the cyber defence forces
- composition and number of known groups of hackers (hacktivists)
- composition and number of known special (informational) operations in cyberspace (including in the case of martial law)
- quantitative and analytical indicators of activity (hackability) of participants in social networks, comment threads and other public information resources
- availability of communication channels between entities involved in cyber defence
- availability of data on the enemy's infrastructure.

The mentioned indicators of hacktivism characterise the processes that arose with the beginning of open military aggression, though at the same time, indicators of military cyber defence without significant differences are suitable for use in peacetime as well.

Confidential (sensitive, secret) indicators of military cyber defence must be developed and applied to consider regulatory requirements in the field of information protection.

The indicators considered in this study will form the basis for the objectives of the proposed military cyber defence and hacktivism index (MCDHI). The methodology for determining MCDHI should be based on the existing and tested methodologies for the formation of global cybersecurity indices [28], considering the conducted analysis and the proposed indicators. By the accepted approaches, the compilation (formation) of the index (or rating) takes place according to the following algorithm:

- definition of the subject, requirements for subjects and other parameters of indexing (rating)
- definition of the system (set) of index indicators
- determination of the source and mode of data formation for index indicators (automatic mode – for the Networks, Data Sets, Financial (Exchange) categories, for the rest – non-automatic mode)
- formation of a list (sample) of indexing (rating) subjects
- expertise in the completeness of the system and the weight of indicators
- development of index calculation methods (the existing cybersecurity index calculation methods are analyzed in [28])
- publication of the index and its subsequent versions (releases).

17.3.4 Military Cyber Defence and Hacktivism Index (MCDHI)

MCDHI is the first proposed cybersecurity index built for military cyber defence and hacktivism objectives (indicators) which are mentioned in this study. The MCDHI indicators are determined for the cyber defence (military cyber defence), hacktivism and related spheres (subjects), and consist of:

- Ukrainian legislation indicators
- NATO best practices indicators
- existing global cybersecurity indices
- hacktivism terms indicators
- hacktivism indicators, first used in-wartime
- additional proposed indicators.

The methodology of forming indices (ratings) is based on the methods of expert evaluations, the index method of mathematical statistics, the mathematical theory of ratings and the game-theoretic cooperative resource model [29–33]. A base method for the MCDHI formation and calculation is the method of expert evaluations.

Quantitative evaluation of all considered indicators and numerical calculations for the MCDHI are planned to be carried out in subsequent studies. The effectiveness of the proposed indicator system (objectives) of MCDHI will be determined after conducting numerical calculations.

17.4 RESULTS AND DISCUSSIONS

The study contains an analysis of the conditions for assessing the state of cyber defence and hacktivism in Ukraine after the beginning of the open-armed military aggression of the Russian Federation, as a comparison of the definition, interpretation and application of the terms of "cybersecurity", "cyber defence", "cyber protection" and "hacktivism", and an analysis of the state of cyber defence of NATO member states, as part of the main task of the Alliance's collective defence.

A comparative characterisation of the indicators of cyber defence and hacktivism of the existing global cybersecurity indices was carried out.

Possible indicators of the formation of the MCDHI at the national and international levels, including the Ukrainian experience, are proposed in detail.

The considered and proposed indicators can be used for both peacetime and wartime, but hacktivism indicators were determined specifically for the stage of active hostilities in cyberspace, which coincides with the open (armed) phase of Russian military aggression against Ukraine. The methodology (in particular, approaches to the formation of weighting coefficients of indicators), as well as the results of MCDHI calculations, will have significant differences for peacetime and wartime periods.

The application of MCDHI provides cybersecurity stakeholders, first, the main subjects of the national cybersecurity system, an additional tool for high-level assessment of the state of cybersecurity, cyber protection and cyber defence of the state. For example, cyber defence of data centres is crucial in maintaining the integrity and availability of critical information infrastructure. Military cyber defence plays a pivotal role in safeguarding these centres against myriad threats, including hacktivism. Information security protocols are rigorously applied, leveraging indices and ratings to assess and enhance their effectiveness.

17.5 CONCLUSIONS AND FUTURE SCOPE

The creation of the military cyber defence and hacktivism index (MCDH) increases the effectiveness of planning measures and the distribution of forces and resources of defence (cyber defence, military cyber defence) to repel aggression in cyberspace. Indicators of hacktivism serve as metrics of public activity (hackability) for evaluating measures and consequences of informational and informational-psychological resistance and struggle.

A quantitative (high-level) assessment of the state and processes of military cyber defence will contribute to establishing and improving the state's cyber defence system. The relevant assessments will have a rating nature and may also be open information and available to the public.

Indexing the state of cyber defence (military cyber defence) and hacktivism is one of the most important components of systematic assessment in the field of cybersecurity because of the direct connection with local (microlevel) influencing processes in cyberspace and information space.

REFERENCES

[1] The Government Computer Emergency Response Team of Ukraine, Which Functions as Part of the State Service for Special Communications and Information Protection of Ukraine CERT-UA (Computer Emergency Response Team of Ukraine), Internet Resource. https://cert.gov.ua/articles (date accessed: 24.04.2023).

[2] On the Defense of Ukraine, Law of Ukraine No. 1932-XII (2024b) (Ukraine). https://zakon.rada.gov.ua/laws/show/1932-12#Text (date accessed: 24.04.2023).

[3] On the Main Principles of Ensuring Cyber Security of Ukraine, Law of Ukraine No. 2163-VIII (2024) (Ukraine). https://zakon.rada.gov.ua/laws/show/2163-19#Text (date accessed: 24.04.2023).

[4] On the State Service of Special Communications and Information Protection of Ukraine, Law of Ukraine No. 3475-IV (2024) (Ukraine). https://zakon.rada.gov.ua/laws/show/3475-15#Text (date accessed: 24.04.2023).

[5] North Atlantic Treaty Organization Factsheet, April 2021, Public Diplomacy Division (PDD) - Press & Media Section. https://www.nato.int/nato_static_fl2014/assets/pdf/2021/4/pdf/2104-factsheet-cyber-defence-en.pdf (date accessed: 24.04.2023).

[6] *CCDCOE*. (n.d.). CCDCOE - The NATO Cooperative Cyber Defence Centre of Excellence is a Multinational and Interdisciplinary Hub of Cyber Defence Expertise. https://ccdcoe.org/news/2022/ukraine-to-be-accepted-as-a-contributing-participant-to-nato-ccdcoe/ (date accessed: 24.04.2023).

[7] J. Voo, I. Hemani, S. Jones, W. DeSombre, D. Cassidy, A. Schwarzenbach. (April 2020). *Reconceptualizing Cyber Power, Cyber Power Index Primer Report, China Cyber Policy Initiative*, Belfer Center for Science and International Affairs, Harvard Kennedy School, Cambridge, 18 p. https://www.belfercenter.org/sites/default/files/2020-04/ReconceptualizingCyber.pdf (date accessed: 24.04.2023).

[8] B. Brady. (November 2013). *The Spirit of Hacktivism: An Analysis of Electronic Civil Disobedience and Australian Legislative Responses, Dissertation*, Law School, Adelaide University, 55 p. https://www.academia.edu/9502580/The_Spirit_of_Hacktivism_An_Analysis_of_Electronic_Civil_Disobedience_and_Australian_Legislative_Responses (date accessed: 24.04.2023).

[9] N. B. Dogan. (January 2019). *Contextualizing Hacktivism: The Criminalization of Redhack, CARGC Paper 10*, The Center for Advanced Research in Global Communication, Annenberg School for Communication, University of Pennsylvania, 35 p. https://www.researchgate.net/publication/331373108_Contextualizing_Hacktivism_The_Criminalization_of_Redhack (date accessed: 24.04.2023).

[10] F. Farmer. (March 2022). *Cybercrime vs Hacktivism: Do We Need a Differentiated Regulatory Approach? A Thesis for the Degree of Doctor of Philosophy in Politics*, University of Exeter, 282 p. https://ore.exeter.ac.uk/repository/bitstream/handle/10871/129654/FarmerF.pdf?sequence=2&isAllowed=y (date accessed: 24.04.2023).

[11] M. Husak, M. Lashtovichka, T. Plesnik. (4 May 2022). *Handling Internet Activism during the Russian Invasion of Ukraine: A Campus Network Perspective*, ACM Digital Library. https://doi.org/10.1145/3534566 (date accessed: 24.04.2023).

[12] *Ukraine | Digital Watch Observatory*. (n.d.). Digital Watch Observatory. https://dig.watch/countries/ukraine (date accessed: 24.04.2023).

[13] *Kybermittari - Cybermeter | NCSC-FI*. (n.d.). NCSC-FI. https://www.kyberturvallisuuskeskus.fi/en/our-services/situation-awareness-and-network-management/kybermittari-cybermeter (date accessed: 24.04.2023).

[14] *Download Here: Cyber Threat Index 2024.* (n.d.). Cyber Insurance | Active Insurance & Cybersecurity | Coalition. https://web.coalitioninc.com/download-cyber-threat-index–2024.html (date accessed: 24.04.2023).

[15] *Main Attack Index - Attack Index.* (n.d.). Attack Index - Deflect an Attack Before It Appears. https://attackindex.com/uk/golovna-attakindex/ (date accessed: 24.04.2023).

[16] On the Decision of the National Security and Defense Council of Ukraine Dated May 14, 2021 "On the Cybersecurity Strategy of Ukraine", Decree of the President of Ukraine No. 447/2021 (2021) (Ukraine). https://zakon.rada.gov.ua/laws/show/447/2021#Text (date accessed: 24.04.2023).

[17] On the National Coordination Center for Cyber Security, Decree of the President of Ukraine No. 242/2016 (2021) (Ukraine). https://zakon.rada.gov.ua/laws/show/242/2016#Text (date accessed: 24.04.2023).

[18] On Urgent Measures for State Cyber Defense, Decision of the National Security and Defense Council of Ukraine (2021) (Ukraine). https://zakon.rada.gov.ua/laws/show/n0053525-21#Text (date accessed: 24.04.2023).

[19] About the Implementation Plan of the Cybersecurity Strategy of Ukraine, Decision of the National Security and Defense Council of Ukraine (2022) (Ukraine). https://zakon.rada.gov.ua/laws/show/n0087525-21#Text (date accessed: 24.04.2023).

[20] On Urgent Measures to Deepen Ukraine's Integration into the North Atlantic Treaty Organization, Decision of the National Security and Defense Council of Ukraine (2021) (Ukraine). https://zakon.rada.gov.ua/laws/show/n0047525-21#Text (date accessed: 24.04.2023).

[21] M. Khudyntsev, A. Davydiuk, O. Lebid, O. Trofymchuk, A. Zhylin. (in press). Cybersecurity Indices: Review and Classification, *Proceedings of Selected Papers of the Workshop on Cybersecurity Providing in Information and Telecommunication Systems (CPITS 2021–2),* Kyiv, Ukraine. ISSN 1613-0073. http://sec.picst.org/ (date accessed: 24.04.2023).

[22] M. Yip, C. Webber. (15–17 June 2011). Hacktivism, *The 3rd International Web Science Conference*, Koblenz, Germany, New York, NY, USA. https://doi.org/10.1145/2527031.2527053 (date accessed: 12.10.2024).

[23] G. Mikhaylova. (2014). *The "Anonymous" Movement: Hacktivism as an Emerging Form of Political Participation, A Thesis Submitted to the Graduate Council of Texas State University in Partial Fulfillment of the Requirements for the Degree of Master of Arts with a Major in Sociology*, Texas State University, USA. https://digital.library.txstate.edu/bitstream/handle/10877/5378/MIKHAYLOVA-THESIS–2014.pdf?sequence=1 (date accessed: 24.04.2023).

[24] E. Dalpra. (2021). Hacktivism, *Zeitschrift für kritik - recht - gesellschaft*, no. 1. p. 52. https://doi.org/10.33196/juridikum202101005201 (date accessed: 12.10.2024).

[25] Definition of Hacktivism. https://www.merriam-webster.com/dictionary/hacktivism (date accessed: 24.04.2023).

[26] What is Hacktivism? Cyber Hub (Secure Users & Access), Check Point Cybersecurity Report. (2021). https://www.checkpoint.com/cyber-hub/threat-prevention/what-is-hacktivism/ (date accessed: 24.04.2023).

[27] O. O. Bakalyns'kiy. (27 May 2022). Quantitative Methods of Expert Assessment: Scientific Method, *Development International Humanitarian Law in Matters of Conducting Cyber Defence (in Ukr.) in Cybersecurity of Energy, Scientific-Practical Conference of the G.E. Pukhov Institute for Modeling in Energy Engineering National Academy of Sciences of Ukraine: Materials, PIMEE NAS of Ukraine,* Kyiv, pp. 90–98, 129 p.

[28] M. M. Khudyntsev (general editor), A. V. Zhilin, A. V. Davydiuk. (2021). *World Indices of Cybersecurity: Overview and Formation Methods (Global Report/Catalogue), Monograph*, International Cybersecurity University, G.E. Pukhov Institute for Modeling in Energy Engineering National Academy of Sciences of Ukraine, 240 p. (in Ukr.) ISBN 978-966-136-887-2.

[29] V. P. Novosad, R. G. Seliverstov, I. I. Artym. (2009). *Quantitative Methods of Expert Assessment: Scientific Methodology (in Ukr.)*, NADU, Kyiv, 36 p.
[30] V. Ye. Andriyenko. (1983). *Statistical Indices in Economic Research (in Ukr.)*, Naukova Dumka, Kyiv, 232 p.
[31] V. Ye. Andriyenko. (1990). *Methodology for Building Complex Index Models: Thesis on Degree of Doctor of Economics Sciences: Specialist 08.00.11 "Statistics")*, KINKh, Kyiv, 48 p. https://works.doklad.ru/view/f9k-hB8smOQ/all.html (date accessed: 24.04.2023).
[32] V. M. Romanchak. (2020). Subjective Measurements (Theory of Ratings): Methods of Psychological Research, *Journal of the Belarusian State University. Philosophy and Psychology*, no. 3, pp. 87–98. https://elib.bsu.by/bitstream/123456789/253809/1/87-98.pdf (date accessed: 24.04.2023).
[33] S. Ye. Gorda. (2019). *Methods of Resource-Theoretic Game Analysis of Regional Development Processes, Qualifying Scientific Work on Manuscript Rights, Dissertation for Obtaining the Scientific Degree of Candidate of Technical Sciences in the Specialty 01.05.02 - "Mathematical Modeling and Computational Methods"*, Institute of Telecommunications and Global Information Space of the National Academy of Sciences of Ukraine, Kyiv. https://itgip.org/wp-content/uploads/2019/01/dis1.pdf (date accessed: 24.04.2023).

18 Fast Quantification Methods for Reconfigurable Cybersecurity Systems Using Multi-Pattern Matching

Serhii Hilgurt

18.1 INTRODUCTION AND RELATED WORK

Anomaly detection network security tools, including those based on AI-based approaches such as deep neural networking and others, despite the great progress shown in recent years, still can't provide zero recognition error probability. The consequences of such errors in a critical infrastructure can be catastrophic. That is why the signature-based recognition approach with its mathematically exact matching function is relevant as a basis for building cybersecurity systems such as network intrusion detection systems (NIDS), antiviruses, anti-worms and spam filters.

Signature analysis relies on the use of descriptions of known attacks, called signatures, which include, among other attributes, patterns—fixed consequences of characters (coded by bytes). The intensive flow of input information is compared against the dictionary of patterns during the functioning of the cyber-physical system. Checking each byte of data (network traffic in the case of NIDS) to see if it matches one of hundreds, thousands or even millions of patterns included in the signature database becomes a very resource intensive task [1]. The performance gap between the speed requirements of cybersecurity systems and their software implementation is constantly growing due to sequential execution of instructions on standard processors [2]. To keep up with the required performance, specialized hardware devices are required. Reconfigurable accelerators (RA) built on FPGAs became an appropriate platform for such a purpose because of almost software-like flexibility and near-ASIC performance [3, 4].

The review of the literature demonstrates a wide variety of hardware solutions for multi-pattern matching tasks, using different approaches to building recognizing schemes of various circuitry natures. Figure 18.1 schematically shows the relationships between some approaches to the construction of such schemes,

DOI: 10.1201/9781003546153-18

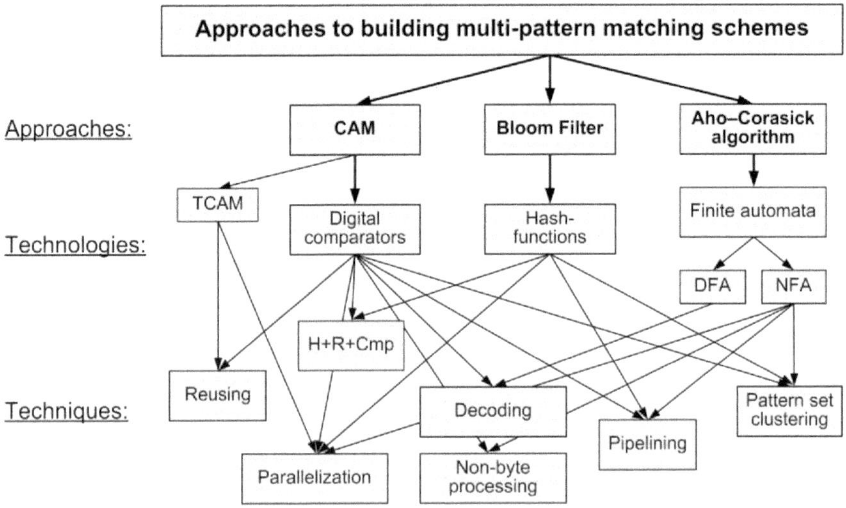

FIGURE 18.1 Approaches, technologies, techniques to building multi-pattern matching schemes.

the technologies they are based on and plenty of techniques to improve their efficiency.

Here CAM—Content-addressable memory; TCAM—ternary CAM; DFA/NFA—deterministic/nondeterministic finite automaton; H+R+Cmp—cascaded matching scheme based on hash-functions, read-only memory and digital comparators. Actually, there are many more elements in this hierarchy of approaches, technologies and techniques, as well as the links between them. For clarity, most of them are not shown in the figure.

Comprehensive analysis of numerous studies from all over the world was performed by the author in [5]. It shows that when building NIDS and other signature-based cybersecurity systems, the following three approaches have shown the best results:

- Content-addressable memory that uses digital comparators as a base [6–8].
- Bloom filter scheme built on hash functions [9–11].
- Aho–Corasick finite automata [12–15].

Each of these approaches has advantages and drawbacks. To increase the efficiency of hardware acceleration, developers offer numerous modifications of the basic schemes for constructing matching circuits. They use various methods, techniques and tricks trying to overcome the shortcomings of each approach. There is an urgent need for a procedure for quantitative assessment of the technical characteristics of each solution in order to work with them systematically and at a high scientific level. Furthermore, the absence of the best solution leads to the need of combining different approaches in one device to maximize the total effectiveness of the resulting scheme. Such a task further requires fast quantification tools that can be included into optimization procedures.

18.1.1 Key Contributions of the Chapter

In this chapter, a method for fast quantification of technical characteristics of reconfigurable components of signature-based cybersecurity systems is proposed. The use of so-called estimation functions allows one to quickly predict the amount of hardware resources that a future reconfigurable device will consume, having a given schematic structure as well as a set of patterns to be recognized by the resulting device.

18.1.2 Chapter Organization

Section 18.2 briefly considers the three most promising approaches to building multi-matching schemes mentioned earlier and some points regarding their FPGA implementation. Section 18.3 discusses the principles of constructing estimation functions using the basic content-addressable memory scheme as an example. An idea of structurally combining different approaches in one device to realize advantages of each of them is concerned in Section 18.4. Experiments to test the proposed method are given in Section 18.5. Section 18.6 concludes the chapter.

18.2 HARDWARE APPROACHES TO MULTI-PATTERN MATCHING

Next, we consider briefly the approaches for building multi-pattern string matching schemes for signature-based cybersecurity systems using FPGAs, such as content-addressable memory, Bloom filter and state machines. Only basic and key modifications of each approach, their main properties and some peculiarities of the FPGA implementation are discussed. All the features of these approaches, as well as their numerous modifications and improvement techniques are thoroughly analyzed by the author in [5] including all references to the correspondent sources.

18.2.1 CAM-Based Approach

Content-addressable memory (CAM) devices were created specifically for solving fast matching tasks. They perform the opposite function in relation to the traditional random access memory (RAM) devices: if the RAM stores the given data at a certain address and finds it by this address, then the CAM, on the contrary, looks up the location (i.e. the address, the number of the cell) of data in the storage device by its content or signals its absence. The high-speed basis of CAM is digital comparators (DC), so later these two names are sometimes used interchangeably.

The simplest way to detect the presence of a suspicious pattern in the data flow is a set of DCs, which compare bytes of the input sequence with all the characters of this pattern (Figure 18.2 a). This circuit has been called the Basic content-addressable memory scheme, or the **BsCAM**.

After providing the input data, the BsCAM circuit is able to output the result very quickly, in fact in one clock cycle. That provides extremely high performance of the

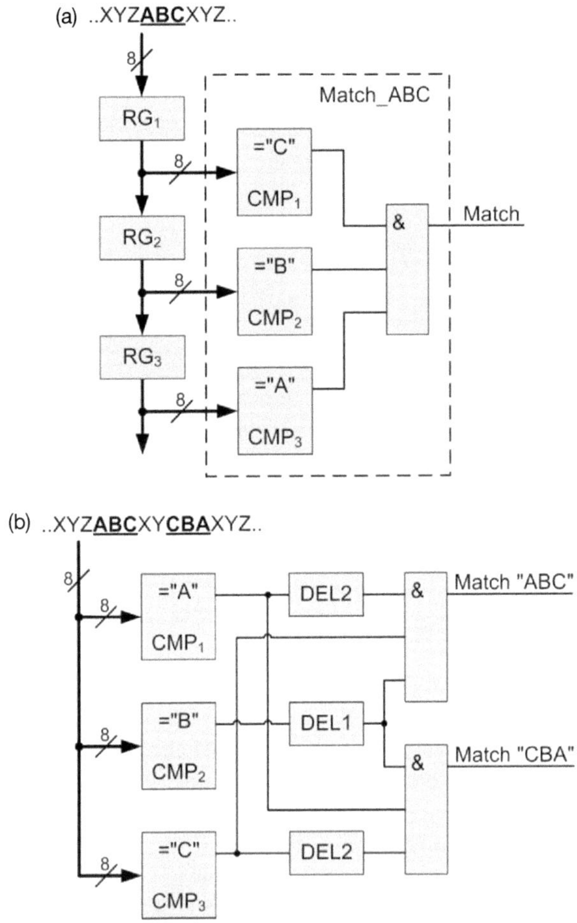

FIGURE 18.2 Recognition by digital comparators: direct (a); DCAM solution (b).

scheme. Its advantage is also the regularity of the structure. The main disadvantage of the scheme is the huge hardware costs: to create it, you need as many DCs as there are characters in the pattern dictionary in total. In addition, multi-input AND gates are needed to join the output signals from comparators.

The hardware costs of the CAM-based recognizing scheme can be reduced by the reuse of DCs. In the extreme case only one DC is allocated for each character, and the resulting match signal is obtained by combining digital delay circuits with the help of AND gates, as shown in the example in Figure 18.2 b. In this figure, DEL1 and DEL2 are the delay circuits for one cycle and two cycles respectively. Such a solution was called the Recognition scheme based on decoded CAM or the **DCAM**, because the full set of DCs actually constitutes a decoder (see links to the correspondent sources in [5]).

A further complexity reduction of the DCAM recognition scheme is possible by using a partial recognition technique, where long patterns are split into shorter

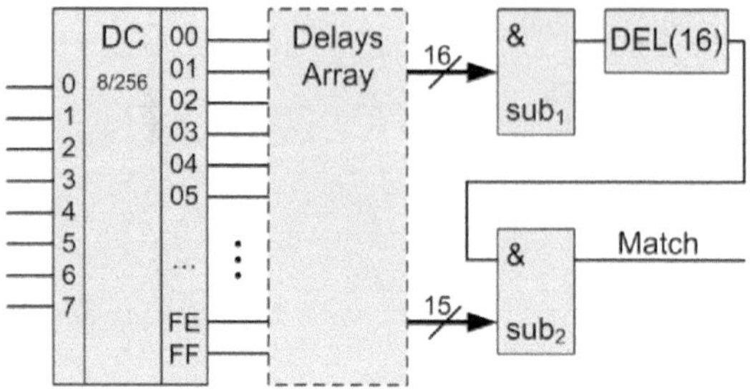

FIGURE 18.3 DpCAM technical solution.

fragments that are matched sequentially. It is enough to delay only the signal of a partial matching instead of using many long-delay circuits for big patterns. Figure 18.3 shows a 31-character pattern recognition scheme built according to this idea. This solution was called the Recognition scheme based on a partially decoded CAM or the **DpCAM** scheme.

The effect of reducing hardware costs due to reuse of DCs also works when using multiple recognition units in parallel (**ParCAM** scheme) to increase performance. Studies show that in this case, using the cost reduction techniques described earlier leads to even higher resource savings than linear growth. That is, CAM schemes on DCs have good scalability by bandwidth.

The survey [5] also considered the use of non-byte data processing, namely circuits based on half-byte comparators (**HbcDCAM** and **ParHbcDCAM** schemes), as well as circuits built using binary decision diagrams (**BCAM** scheme).

It is also possible to reduce the hardware costs by clustering the set of patterns to split the scheme into the corresponding number of smaller sub-schemes.

The fact that the content of the input data does not affect the operation of CAM recognition schemes determines the predictability of bandwidth and consequently makes this approach invulnerable to attacks on cybersecurity systems.

As we can see, the information about patterns is actually "hardwired" into the circuit of the recognition device built on the DCs, which makes it impossible to realize for these schemes the dynamic reconfiguration and selective recognition (switching pattern subsets using a special control signal) features.

18.2.2 Approach Based on Bloom Filter

A Bloom filter (BF) is a digital device that allows for determining whether a certain piece of data belongs to a given set—in particular, whether a given sequence of characters matches one of the patterns included in the pattern dictionary [9].

BF consists of K hash function calculators $h_1(x)$, $h_2(x)$, . . . , $hK(x)$, and a register Rg that contains M bits of memory (Figure 18.4 a).

The Bloom filter functions in two stages: programming and recognition.

Before starting programming, Rg is filled with "zero" values. Then, all n patterns (with a length of W bits) contained in the dictionary are sequentially applied to the inputs of the hash function calculators. For each of them, all K hash functions are

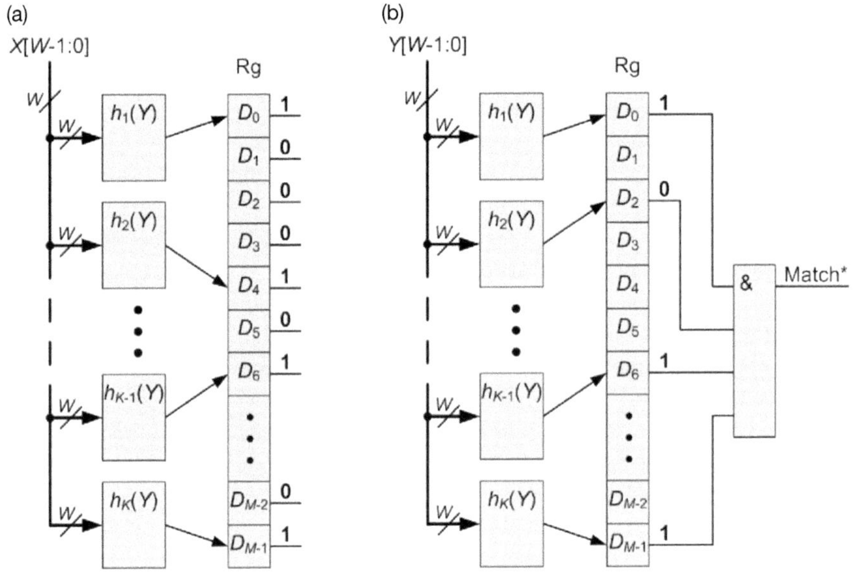

FIGURE 18.4 The functioning of the Bloom filter: programming (a) and recognition (b).

computed, the values of which are interpreted as addresses of Rg cells. The "one" value is written for each of these addresses.

During Bloom filter functioning, a portion of the input sequence of characters (with a length of W bits as well) is fed to its input, and the values of all K hash functions are calculated again (Figure 18.4 b). The resulting numbers address the cells of the Rg. If all the pointed positions contain "ones", it is considered that the entered combination of characters with a certain probability matches one of the templates involved in the BF programming stage. But if at least one hash function points to a cell with a "zero" value, it is guaranteed that there is no match. Therefore, BF functions with some probability of a false positive error of recognition, but without any false negative error. An additional scheme is needed to refine the recognition result. It works slower than recognition itself. It makes performance and hardware costs features worse. It also leads to throughput unpredictability, making the BF vulnerable to attacks on cybersecurity systems.

Unfortunately, the Bloom filter has an important drawback inherent in all solutions using hashing: the size of the input sequence of characters for analysis must be fixed for the given set of hash functions. That is, one BF is able to recognize patterns of the same length only. To overcome this drawback, a parallel structure is built from several BFs for patterns of different lengths. This degrades the hardware cost feature of the scheme, but not the speed.

In general, several BRAM blocks are required to create a BF. The corresponding scheme was called the Full Bloom filter or Large Bloom filter (**LBF**) scheme. But in a majority of practical applications, the so-called mini-BF circuits, which are components of the LBF and contain only one BRAM block, can be used separately to build the recognition module. Let's call such a solution the Simplified Bloom filter (**SBF**) scheme.

The difficulties of building a BF on a FPGA are primarily related to the fact that several hash functions need to simultaneously access the register Rg (Figure 18.4 b). If you implement it on a single storage device (for example, a BRAM block), collisions will occur. The solution consists in dividing the Rg into several storage devices depending on the number of hash functions. For this, it is necessary, firstly, to distribute the outputs of the hash functions between several RAMs, and secondly, to impose additional restrictions on the functionality of the generators of hash functions so that their output range fits into the reduced volume of the memory device. It is proved that such restrictions increase a little the probability of the false positive errors [16]. On the other hand, multiple BRAMs instead of one increase the possibilities of the simplified SBF circuit.

Several BFs can also be combined into a parallel structure in order to increase performance. But unlike CAM, the properties of Bloom filters do not allow for achieving a sublinear law of cost growth, that is, BF does not scale as well as schemes based on CAM/DC in terms of bandwidth.

The classic BF does not allow for removing patterns during operation. If necessary, the Bloom filter with counters or Counting Bloom filter (**CBF**) scheme is used. Such a solution allows for dynamic reconfiguration without stopping the operation of the cybersecurity system.

The process of improving the BF structure continues even today. An example of a recent modification is the Feature extraction Cascaded Bloom Filter (**FeCBF**), a probabilistic data structure organized by cascading multiple BFs in an optimum sequence [17]. This scheme effectively eliminates both false positive and false negative recognition errors, ensuring exact matching at reasonable hardware costs.

18.2.3 Aho–Corasick Finite Automata

Finite automata (FA), also known as finite state machines, are widely used for digital devices design [18]. Classic FA is defined by six elements:

$$A = \{X, Y, S, S_0, f_s, f_y\}, \tag{18.1}$$

where X is a set of input signals, Y is a set of output signals, S is a set of machine automata, S_0 is an initial state of the automaton, *fs* is a function of transition from one state to another, *fy* is an output automaton function. But recently, the machines so-called classifiers are increasingly used [19]. Such an automaton produces an active signal at its output only if a predetermined sequence of symbols (each encoded by several bits) is fed to its input. When such a situation occurs, the classifier jumps to one of the so-called acceptable states [1]. While transitions are made between unacceptable states, there are no active output signals. It is these machines that are used to create signature-based information protection systems. In contrast to the classical FA, instead of the set of output signals Y and the output function *fy*, the automaton-classifier has a set of acceptable states F:

$$A = \{X, S, S_0, fs, F\}. \quad (18.2)$$

So, the classifier is described by five, not by six elements.

The Aho–Corasick algorithm [12] is a classic representative of a tool for multiple string matching. In contrast to single string matching algorithms, it detects several patterns in the input data simultaneously. This algorithm, like the BF approach, also requires a programming stage, at which a corresponding DFA is created from a given set of patterns according to certain rules, and a working stage of recognizing these patterns. Such DFA is called Aho–Corasick finite automaton (AC-FA).

The theory and examples of creating AC-FAs are widely presented in the literature, but the use of this device for signature analysis requires paying additional attention to the transition function fs of the CA-FA. It was proposed to distinguish four types of transitions in such an automaton: *direct* (or goto-transitions), *cross, failure* and *restartable* transitions. Strictly speaking, the restartable type is a subspecies of cross transitions, but due to the peculiarities of the technical implementation, isolating it into a separate type simplifies the handling of the automaton and increases the efficiency of its implementation on the FPGA [20].

The structure of the typical hardware AC-FA implementation (Figure 18.5) is based on the memory unit (MU) which stores the transition table of the automaton [15]. The records of MU contain the "Next state" and "Match vector" fields. The character code from the input sequence is concatenated with the number of the next state extracted from memory. The received value is applied to the address input of the MU and points to the needed line of information. An active bit in a certain position of the match vector indicates the detection of corresponding pattern. The control unit provides the functioning of the device as a whole.

If the implementation of the scheme uses memory external to the FPGA chip (onboard RAM of the reconfigurable accelerator), we will call such a solution the Basic AC-FA scheme with external memory or the **ACRAM** scheme. The solution based

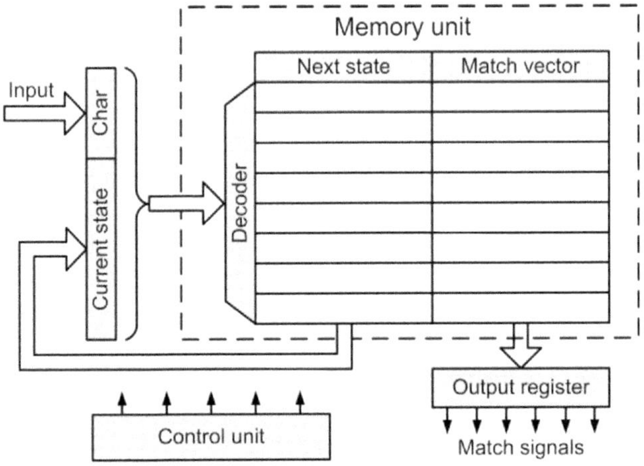

FIGURE 18.5 Aho–Corasick finite automaton structure.

on the internal block memory of the FPGA will be called the Basic AC-FA scheme with block memory or the **ACBRAM** scheme.

The most important advantage of solutions based on AC-FA is the independence of the bandwidth from the volume of the signature dictionary and from the properties of the patterns, in particular, from their lengths, which results in the predictability of the bandwidth. Theoretically, FA accepts one symbol from the input sequence every clock cycle. But if the size of the table becomes too large, and it is necessary to use the external memory, each access to the MU can take several cycles. Furthermore, external memory is slower than internal memory. So, the downside of bandwidth predictability is a relatively low speed, which is also difficult to scale, which reduces the bandwidth scalability of AC-FA.

The main problem that arises when using FPGA for the implementation of AC-FA is the difficulty of effective data exchange with MU. This is especially important for the ACRAM scheme, since the on-board memory of the RA has a fixed structure, while the ACBRAM scheme provides more opportunities due to the flexibility of the BRAM block configuration.

AC-FA requires a modest amount of logic resources to create registers and a control unit. But the MU volume reaches very large values, that is, the approach features high memory resource consumption. An increase in the number of patterns leads to an explosive growth of MU size, i.e. the approach has very poor scalability by the pattern dictionary volume. Therefore, the vast majority of research on the use of AC-FA for cybersecurity systems is aimed precisely at reducing memory consumption and preventing their rapid growth.

Thus, completing a brief review of approaches to the construction of the main matching schemes, we see that each of them has its pros and cons. And none of them is superior to other solutions, at least in the main indicators.

Recent research on hardware implementation of AC-FA based pattern matching can be found in [21].

18.3 USING ESTIMATION FUNCTIONS

Quantitative characteristics of reconfigurable matching components that are necessary when hardware implementing signature-based cybersecurity systems can certainly be found by performing the digital circuit synthesis procedure using the appropriate CAD tool, for example from the manufacturer of the FPGA. But this process consists of several complicated steps, which in some cases lead to unacceptable delays.

The essence of the proposed method for fast quantification of reconfigurable schemes is that for each component of the matching module of the signature-based cybersecurity system, a so-called estimation function (EF) is created. Such a function for a given matching scheme and given pattern set to be recognized by this scheme, calculates estimations of the hardware costs and performance characteristics that this component will possess after synthesis. Taking into account some technical peculiarities of the FPGA implementation allows us to refine the preliminary calculations. Therefore, the proposed method in general case consists of the stage of direct calculation (in the first approximation) and the stage (or several stages) of refining the obtained relationships.

Let's try to find the hardware costs estimation for a device as a normalized sum of all types of FPGA resources spent to build it. In other words, we'll use some conventional unit as a universal estimation value, say, one Conventional Lookup Table (CLT). Suppose, to form a circuit, such FPGA resources are needed as: logics, distributed memory (flip-flops), internal memory of FPGA (BRAM blocks) and built-on RAM of the reconfigurable accelerator used. Then the total resources value required to synthesize the reconfigurable component is:

$$R = L + \alpha F + \beta B + \gamma M, \tag{18.3}$$

where L—amount of FPGA logic resources (number of LUTs), F—amount of distributed memory resources (number of flip-flops), B—amount of block memory (number of BRAMs), M—amount of the RA's on-board memory (Mb), α, β, γ—coefficients of normalization of resources types in relation to LUTs.

Since the matching schemes for the aforementioned approaches are different, the building procedures and the final appearance of the EF will also differ. Nevertheless, the basic principles for creating these functions remain unchanged. To understand them, it is enough to consider EF construction procedure for one of the approaches. This study takes as an example the creation of a resource cost estimation function (RCEF) for the BsCAM recognition scheme discussed earlier.

Since the CAM-based matching circuits do not require memory of any type, expression (18.3) for the BsCAM scheme case simplifies to:

$$R_{\text{BSCAM}} = L_{\text{BSCAM}} + \alpha F_{\text{BSCAM}}, \tag{18.4}$$

where L_{BSCAM} and F_{BSCAM}—the number of LUTs and flip-flops respectively.

Before proceeding to the calculation of resource costs, let's examine more carefully the scheme under analysis (an example presented in Figure 18.2 a). The circuit consist of an 8-bit input pipeline (registers RGi), comparators ($\text{CMP}_1 \ldots \text{CMP}_3$), each of which compares the contents of one of the stages of the pipeline with a certain character, as well as AND gate that combines their outputs.

The collection of comparators represents one of the recognizable patterns. The processed sequence of characters is fed to the input of the device. If a fragment of the sequence matches the sample "ABC" (for this example), an active signal appears at the Match output.

The scheme looks quite simple, but its practical implementation on FPGA leads to certain difficulties. The first problem is as follows. The outputs of the RG_1 register are fed to the comparators corresponding to the last symbol of each pattern of the set, the outputs of the RG_2 register are fed to the comparators of the penultimate symbol of each pattern, etc. Since the signature database of modern security tools can contain a large number of patterns (tens and hundreds of thousands), the load capacity (maximum fan-out value) of the outputs of these registers when synthesized from standard FPGA components becomes insufficient. Also, the length of digital lines connecting a large number of FPGA components leads to signal propagation delays, resulting in a decrease in the digital circuit operating frequency.

To solve this problem, several stages of pipeline circuit are created (Figure 18.6 a), on each of which the output signals are branched into a set of latch inputs of the next stage. This solution allows distributing the RGi registers outputs to an arbitrary number of comparators without decreasing the clock frequency. Only the latency parameter of the circuit is increased.

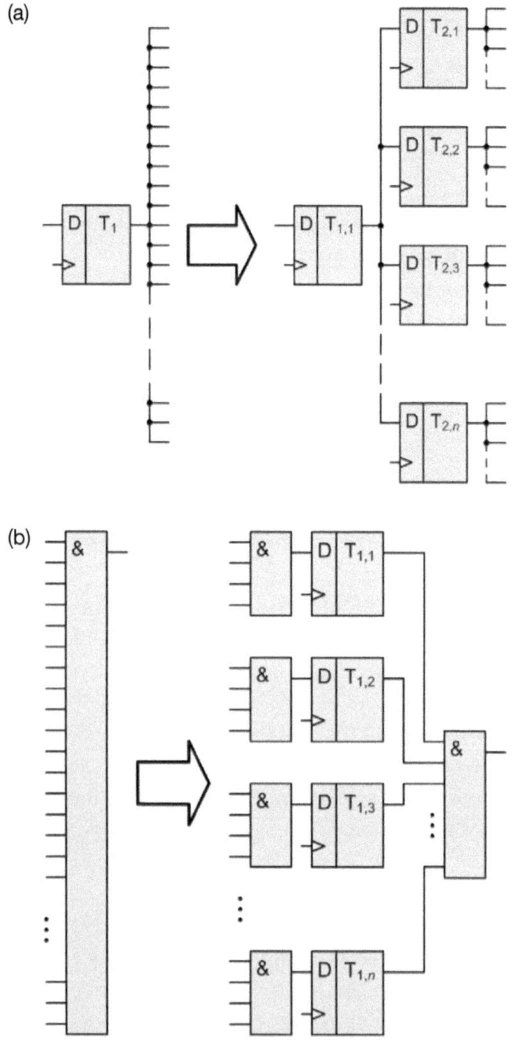

FIGURE 18.6 Solving the problems: fan-out overload (a); multi-input AND gates (b).

Another problem is associated with too many inputs of AND gates, since the length of the patterns can reach dozens of symbols, whereas the LUTs of modern FPGAs, on which these gates are implemented, usually have 4, 6 or 8 inputs. This difficulty is also solved by pipelining (Figure 18.6 b).

Thus, using (18.4), we can find the total amount of hardware resources needed for the basic recognition scheme BsCAM on digital comparators (Figure 18.2 a).

First, let's calculate the amount of logic resources. BsCAM requires LUTs, on the one hand, for synthesizing comparators CMP (see Figure 18.2 a), on the other hand, for creating multi-input AND gate pipelines (see Figure 18.6 b). Therefore, the number of lookup tables required by the BsCAM scheme consists of two corresponding parts:

$$L_{\text{BSCAM}} = L_{\text{CMP}} + L_{\&}. \tag{18.5}$$

BsCAM uses a number of comparators equal to the number of characters that occur in all patterns that the circuit must recognize. The total number Ω of characters in a pattern set is equal to the sum of the products of the length of each pattern and their number in a group of equal length, which is defined in the so-called pattern length distribution function δ_j:

$$\Omega = \sum_{j=m_{\min}}^{m_{\max}} \delta_j \cdot j, \tag{18.6}$$

where $m_{\min}$—the length of the shortest pattern, $m_{\max}$—the length of the longest pattern, δ_j—pattern length distribution function.

A single byte-coded digital comparator requires two 4-input or 6-input lookup tables, or one 8-input lookup table. Let's formalize this moment by introducing a function:

$$\Lambda(x) = \begin{cases} 1, & x \geq 8 \\ 2, & x < 8 \end{cases}, \tag{18.7}$$

where x—the number of inputs that the LUT of FPGA used has. So, the amount of logic resources required to create all comparators for BsCAM scheme is:

$$L_{\text{CMP}} = \Lambda(x) \cdot \Omega. \tag{18.8}$$

And now let's calculate the number of LUTs required to build all the AND logical circuits.

It is easy to check that the total number of x-input LUTs to build a pipelined AND gate for j inputs (see Figure 18.6 b) is equal to:

$$L_j = \left\lceil \frac{j-1}{x-1} \right\rceil. \tag{18.9}$$

As each pattern of length j characters requires Lj LUTs and the number of patterns of length j is equal δ_j, the number of LUTs to form all pipelined AND gates for all patterns is calculated by replacing in (18.6) the current pattern length j by the (18.9):

$$L_{\&} = \sum_{j=m_{\min}}^{m_{\max}} \delta_j \cdot \left\lceil \frac{j-1}{x-1} \right\rceil. \tag{18.10}$$

By substituting (18.8) and (18.10) into (18.5) and taking into account (18.6), as well as the fact that the number x of LUT inputs during calculations the RCEF is a constant, we get the total number of LUTs for the BsCAM scheme:

$$L_{\mathrm{BSCAM}} = \sum_{j=m_{\min}}^{m_{\max}} \delta_j \cdot \left(\Lambda(x) \cdot j + \left\lceil \frac{j-1}{x-1} \right\rceil \right). \tag{18.11}$$

And now let's calculate the number of flip-flops required to build the BsCAM scheme. This amount is equal to the sum of the number F_{RG} of flip-flops needed for the RG-based pipeline (Figure 18.2 a), the number $F_{\text{fan-out}}$ of flip-flops required to build the pipeline for solving the fan-out overload problem (Figure 18.6 a) and the number $F_{\&}$ of flip-flops required to build the pipeline for solving the multi-input AND gates problem (Figure 18.6 b):

$$F_{\mathrm{BSCAM}} = F_{\mathrm{RG}} + F_{\text{fan-out}} + F_{\&}. \tag{18.12}$$

The length of the input RG-based pipeline, along which the stream of recognized characters is advanced, is equal to the longest pattern length $m_{\max}$, and its width is one byte, that is, eight bits. So, the number of flip-flops needed to build it equals to:

$$F_{\mathrm{RG}} = 8 \cdot m_{\max}. \tag{18.13}$$

Calculating the $F_{fan-out}$ number is not a trivial task. Let's consider more closely the load distribution on the input pipeline in the BsCAM scheme (see the Figure 18.7).

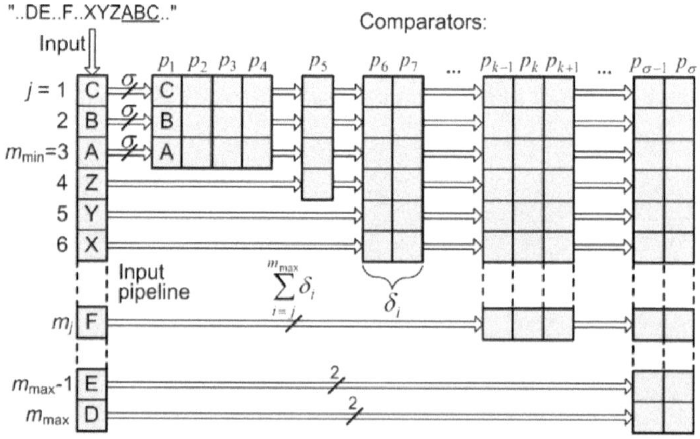

FIGURE 18.7 Distribution of load on the input pipeline in the BsCAM scheme.

Here, the columns made up of squares depict the recognition schemes of all patterns included in the pattern set *P*, made up of comparators.

The signals from the first $m_{\min}$ stages are used to recognize all σ patterns. Starting from the stage $m_{min}+1$ to m_{max} the load is equal to $\sum_{i=j}^{m_{\max}} \delta_i$. The signals from the last stage are used only for recognizing a group of the longest patterns which consists of $\delta_{m\max}$ patterns. Using a formula similar to (18.9) we can find the numbers of flip-flops for the fan-out overload pipelines for every input pipeline output load. Then, we obtain the desired value:

$$F_{\text{fan-out}} = m_{\min} \left\lceil \frac{\sigma - 1}{y - 1} \right\rceil + \sum_{i=m_{\min}+1}^{m_{\max}} \left\lceil \frac{\sum_{i=j}^{m_{\max}} \delta_i - 1}{y - 1} \right\rceil, \tag{18.14}$$

where *y*—the maximum fan-out load property of the FPGA of given RA.

As we can see in Figure 18.6 b every stage of the multi-input AND pipeline has the same numbers of LUTs and flip-flops whereas the last stage hasn't a flip-flop. That is why the numbers $F_{\&}$ of flip-flops required for this circuit is less by 1 than the number $L_{\&}$ of LUTs:

$$F_{\&} = L_{\&} - 1. \tag{18.15}$$

So, substituting (18.13), (18.14) and (18.15) into (18.12), we get the total number of flip-flops in the BsCAM scheme:

$$F_{\text{BSCAM}} = 8\, m_{\max} + m_{\min} \left\lceil \frac{\sigma - 1}{\text{C} - 1} \right\rceil + \sum_{j=m_{\min}+1}^{m_{\max}} \left\lceil \frac{\sum_{i=j}^{m_{\max}} \delta_i - 1}{\text{C} - 1} \right\rceil + \sum_{j=m_{\min}}^{m_{\max}} \delta_j \cdot \left\lceil \frac{j-1}{x-1} \right\rceil - 1. \tag{18.16}$$

Finally, substituting (18.11) and (18.16) into (18.4), we obtain the first approximation R^*_{BSCAM} of the hardware costs for the whole BsCAM scheme (in CLTs).

This result can be refined according to the following considerations. Since each FPGA logic cell simultaneously possesses two types of computing resources—logic and distributed memory—because it contains both LUTs and flip-flops, separate counts of each type's resources lead to imprecise results. Analyzing again the scheme in Figure 18.6 b we can understand that every pair LUT + flip-flop, used when synthesizing it, can be taken together from one logic cell of the FPGA, that is, the amount of resources, calculated in CLT, can be reduced by the value of $F_{\&} \approx L_{\&}$. Therefore, the term $F_{\&}$ can be removed from the first approximation expression R^{*}_{BSCAM}. As a result, we obtain the desired dependence in the second approximation:

$$R^{**}_{\text{BSCAM}} = \sum_{j=m_{\min}}^{m_{\max}} \delta_j \left(\Lambda(x) \cdot j + \left\lceil \frac{j-1}{x-1} \right\rceil \right) + 8m_{\max}$$
$$+ \alpha \left(m_{\min} \left\lceil \frac{\sigma - 1}{y-1} \right\rceil + \sum_{i=m_{\min}+1}^{m_{\max}} \left\lceil \frac{\sum_{i=j}^{m_{\max}} \delta_i - 1}{y-1} \right\rceil \right). \tag{18.17}$$

The obtained result (18.17) is the resource cost estimation function, which provides an estimate of the FPGA resources needed to create the BsCAM scheme, aimed to recognize a set of patterns *P*. As we can see, it contains only variables $\sigma, m_{\min}, m_{\max}, \delta_i$, which are parameters of this set of patterns *P*, and constants *x* and *y*, which are properties of reconfigurable accelerator. The absence of coefficients β or γ in this expression indicates that the BsCAM scheme does not use memory resources. The absence in (18.17) of such parameter of pattern set as self-similarity functions indicates the fact that this scheme does not use the redundancy inherent in the dictionary of signatures, which is the drawback of BsCAM scheme, solved by its numerical.

The example considered for the BsCAM scheme allows an understanding about how estimation functions can be built. Acting similarly, we can obtain RCEFs for any modification of CAM-based matching scheme as well as for schemes of Bloom filter and Aho–Corasick finite automata and their modifications.

Without details, let's present the final expressions for the resource cost estimation function of several more multi-pattern matching schemes.

The RCEF for the DCAM modification of the BsCAM pattern matching scheme in the second approximation can be calculated as follows:

$$R^{**}_{\text{DCAM}} = 256\Lambda(x) + \sum_{j=2}^{m_{\max}} \left(\left\lceil \frac{j-1}{z+1} \right\rceil \sum_{s=0}^{255} \text{NotZ}(\alpha(s,j)) \right)$$
$$+ \sum_{j=m_{\min}}^{m_{\max}} \delta_j \left\lceil \frac{j-1}{x-1} \right\rceil + \alpha \sum_{s=0}^{255} \left\lceil \frac{\sum_{j=2}^{m_{\max}} \text{NotZ}(\mu(s,j)) + \mu(s,j) - 2}{y-1} \right\rceil. \tag{18.18}$$

where *z* is the maximum delay value of the digital delay circuits that can be created on the basis of LUT for given FPGA; NotZ( ) is a zero inequality function; $\alpha(s, j)$ is a so-called first self-similarity function of the pattern set *P*, which is equal to the total number of symbols with the code *s* located in the *j*-th position of all patterns of this set.

The RCEF for the Simplified Bloom filter scheme has such appearance:

$$
\begin{aligned}
R_{\mathrm{SBF}} &= E\left\lceil \log_2 \frac{E\cdot\delta_j}{\ln 2}\right\rceil \left(\left\lceil \frac{8j}{x} \right\rceil + (\alpha+1)\left\lceil \frac{\left\lceil \frac{8j}{x}\right\rceil - 1}{x-1} \right\rceil - \alpha \right) \\
&+ \left\lceil \frac{E}{p} \right\rceil \left(\alpha \left\lceil \log_2 \frac{E\cdot\delta_j}{\ln 2} \right\rceil + \beta + \left\lceil \frac{\left\lceil \log_2 \frac{E\cdot\delta_j}{\ln 2}\right\rceil}{\left\lceil \frac{x-1}{2} \right\rceil} \right\rceil + 4 \right) + \left\lceil \frac{\left\lceil \frac{E}{p}\right\rceil - 1}{x-1} \right\rceil . \qquad (18.19)
\end{aligned}
$$

where E is the factor of false positive recognition, their physical meaning is a power of two, the reciprocal of which is numerically equal to the Bloom filter allowed error probability; j is the length of a pattern to be recognized; x is the number of the inputs of the LUT for given FPGA chip; p is the number of RAM ports.

The resource cost estimation function for the ACBRAM scheme is as follows:

$$
\begin{aligned}
R_{\mathrm{ACBRAM}} &= L_{\mathrm{CU}} + r\left(\left\lceil \frac{\lceil \log_2 r \rceil}{x} \right\rceil + 1 + \beta \right) + w\cdot\left\lceil \frac{r-1}{x-1} \right\rceil \\
&+ \alpha\left(F_{\mathrm{CU}} + w\cdot\left(\left\lceil \frac{r-1}{x-1} \right\rceil - 1 \right) + \left\lfloor \log_2 \left(M_{\mathrm{BRAM}} / w \right) \right\rfloor \right). \qquad (18.20)
\end{aligned}
$$

where L_{CU} and F_{CU} are respectively numbers of LUTs and flip-flops required to create a control device for AC-FA; M_{BRAM}—size (in Kbits) of one BRAM block of the FPGA chip; $r = \left\lceil \frac{B}{1024\left(M_{\mathrm{BRAM}} / w\right)} \right\rceil$—the number of BRAM block required, where B is amount of block memory required for the ACBRAM scheme (in Mbits), which is the sum of the memory amounts for the direct, nross, failure and restartable transitions of the AC-FA: $B = B_{\mathrm{dr}} + B_{\mathrm{cr}} + B_{\mathrm{fl}} + B_{\mathrm{rs}}$; w is the width (in bits) of data stored in BRAM (according to the finite automaton transition memory organization).

Analyzing equations (18.18), (18.19) and (18.20), we can observe that the RCEF expressions can be relatively complex and bulky for some matching schemes. But they mainly require the addition, shift and rounding operations, so don't take much time to calculate them.

Consideration of speed properties is beyond the scope of this publication, although, following the proposed principle, one can successfully find the time characteristics estimation functions.

18.4 STRUCTURAL COMBINING

As mentioned earlier, the absence of a prevailing direction among approaches to the construction of hardware recognition schemes for reconfigurable cybersecurity systems naturally leads to the idea of joining different approaches in one device in order to maximize the efficiency of the resulting scheme. Besides the aforementioned H+R+Cmp scheme, an example of a matching scheme combining a Bloom filter and TCAM [22] can be considered, etc.

In general cases, this idea can be implemented in the form of a structural combining of several matching blocks (MB*i*), built using different approaches, into a single pattern recognition module (PRM) [8]. The set of patterns to be recognized is distributed among the MB*i* in such a way that the advantages of each approach are maximized and the disadvantages are minimized. The highest efficiency is achieved by covering both the partitioning process and the selection of a technical solution for each MB*i* with a single optimization procedure.

The basis of the combination approach is that the patterns contained in the signature database have different properties, in particular, have different lengths and self-similarity. Consequently, the efficiency of processing depends on the approach involved and varies for different pattern groups. So, theoretically, it is possible to choose the most appropriate approaches for each category of patterns.

Another factor in favor of this idea is a fixed set of reconfigurable computing resources on the basis of which cybersecurity systems are built. Using only one recognition approach leads to the situation where some types of resources (for example, LUTs and flip-flops) are used almost completely, while others (external or block memory) are not used at all. As a result, the overall efficiency of the use of available hardware resources is lost.

Structural combining can be used in different ways. MB*i* can be connected in parallel, in series or, in general, constitute a more complex hierarchical structure. Let's consider a simple example—a parallel structural combining—to verify the fast quantification method proposed in this work.

18.5 EXPERIMENTS

Let's assume that PRM of a signature-based cybersecurity system consists of two MBs, joined in parallel. Their inputs are simultaneously fed with a data stream to be checked for malicious content. The task is to split the set of patterns optimally so that the amount of hardware costs necessary to build the entire PRM is minimal.

To achieve the goal, the set of patterns can be sorted by some attribute, for example, by length. The first matching block is synthesizing to recognize those patterns, starting from the shortest one up to some having number *j*. The second matching block is constructing to recognize the rest of the patterns. The sorting also can be fulfilled by the number of patterns of the same length. That is, we assign the largest group of patterns having equal number of characters as the first part of the patterns for recognizing by MB_1. The second part for MB_1 is the closest group in size, etc. A sorting order also can be used, which has the meaning of multiplying the length

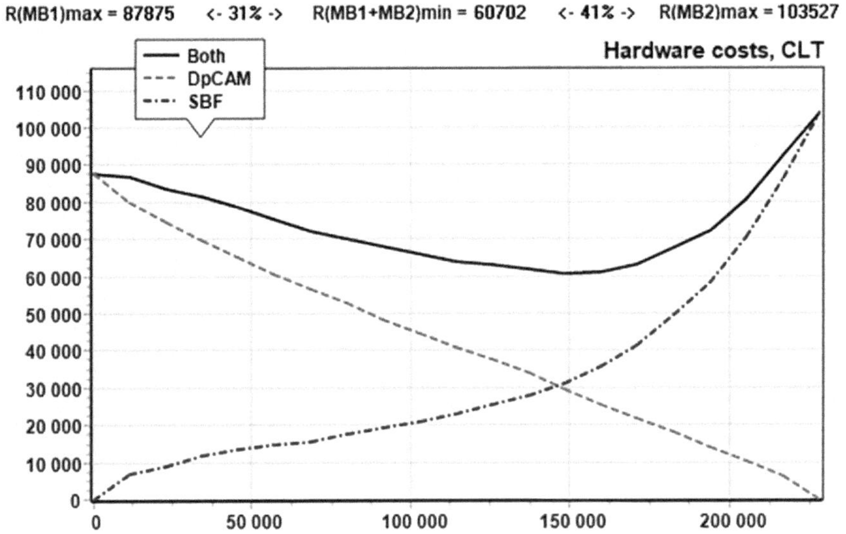

FIGURE 18.8 Parallel combining of BsCAM and LBF matching schemes.

of patterns by their number in the group. Figure 18.8 depicts the results of resource costs minimization under the following conditions:

- Implementation of MB_1—the DpCAM scheme, MB_2—the SBF Bloom filter scheme;
- Order of sorting—by length (ascending);
- The set of patterns is extracted from the "Malware Rules" signature database of the MCBB Suricata NIDS, version 5.0, containing $\sigma = 11355$ patterns in length from $m_{min} = 1$ to $m_{max} = 236$; total amount $\Omega = 228206$ = characters;
- RA type—XUP-VV8 from Nallatech based on the Virtex UltraScale+ VU13P FPGA from Xilinx (now AMD).

The abscissa shows the number of characters in the patterns that are set for recognition by MB_2 as a counterweight MB_1 (the leftmost point means all patterns are recognized by MB_1 and none by MB_2; the rightmost point means vice versa). The ordinate axis shows the hardware costs (in CLT) required to synthesize each of the MBs, as well as to synthesize the PRM that contains both of them. Here the hardware costs value dependence for the MB_1 is depicted by dashed line; for the MB_2—by dot-dash line, and for the PRM—by solid line.

As we can see, the cost curve for PRM has a distinct minimum, at which the whole device has 31% less costs value than the component MB_1 (if it recognizes all the patterns itself), and 41% less than the component MB_2 (if it does).

In practice, a successful parallel combination result like the one shown in Figure 18.8 is rarely obtained. More often, one of the combined blocks gives better

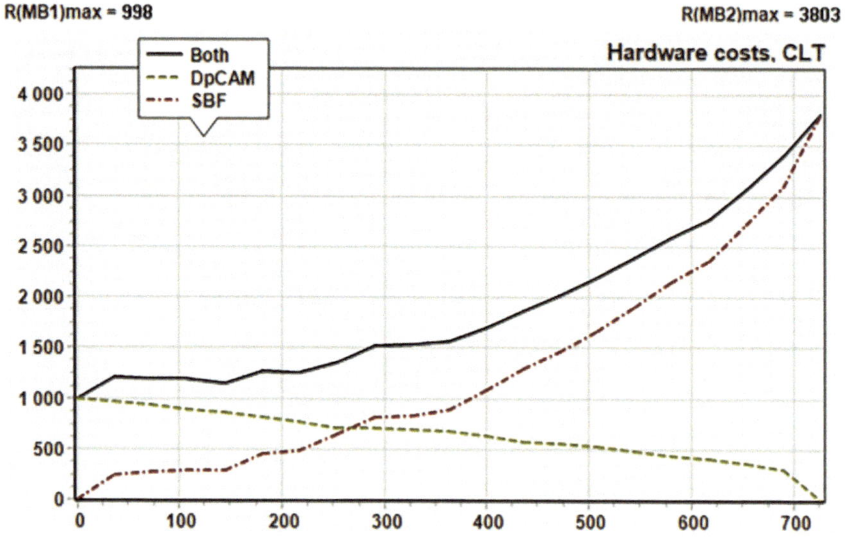

FIGURE 18.9 Unsuccessful result of parallel combining.

values than when combined with another one—for any pattern distribution. Such an example is shown in Figure 18.9.

The same recognition schemes are used here, but other parameters involved are different:

- Order of sorting—of length multiplied by quantity type (descending);
- The set of patterns is extracted from the "Protocol-FTP rules" (group of attacks on web-servers) from the signatures database of another free NIDS Snort version 3.0, containing $\sigma = .97$ patterns in length from $m_{\min}$ = 1 to m_{max} =75; total amount $\Omega = 726$ characters;
- RA type—385A from Nallatech based on the Arria 10 GX 1150 FPGA from Altera (now Intel).

Under such conditions, the cost of creating MB_1 in the extreme case, when it recognizes the entire set of patterns, is several times lower than the cost of creating MB_2 in the case when it recognizes the same set of patterns. As a result, the PRM created by parallel connection of MB_1 and MB_2 is also more expensive across the entire pattern distribution space.

In addition to the situation described earlier, the need to conform the speed characteristics of MBi also imposes restrictions on the possibility of using parallel combining.

But, as experiments show, even if the matching blocks have close resource costs at the extreme points and the same speed parameters, their parallel combination will still not give a positive effect if their cost dependencies on the pattern set content are similar, that is, if the shapes of their RCEF curves are close. To avoid such a situation, for parallel combining, it is necessary to choose those MB*i* for which the dependences of hardware costs on the distribution of patterns mutually differ as much as possible.

Analyzing and summarizing the results of experiments with RCEFs for different situations, it can be formulated the following three conditions for successful parallel combinations of matching blocks for reconfigurable signature-based cybersecurity systems.

Condition 1. The resource costs of MB*i*, which are combined in parallel, should be fairly close in absolute values.

Condition 2. The performance characteristics of parallel connected MB*i* should also be close enough.

Condition 3. The functional dependencies of resource costs on the distribution of patterns in the case of MB*i* parallel combining should differ significantly.

Let's explain the last statement using the preceding example of a successful combination. If you look carefully at the behavior of the curves along the abscissa axis in Figure 18.8, you can pay attention to the fact that falling and rising curves behave differently. The cost plot for the DpCAM scheme is almost linear, while the cost plot for the SBF scheme has significant curvature. It is clear that if both curves behaved in the same way, their sum would not have any extremum.

Figure 18.10 shows a comparison of two hardware cost curves—for the DCAM scheme (modification of the approach based on CAM and DCs) and the SBF scheme (simplified version of Bloom filter). The "Community Ruleset" signature database from Snort sorted by product of length and quantity is used. Here, along the abscissa,

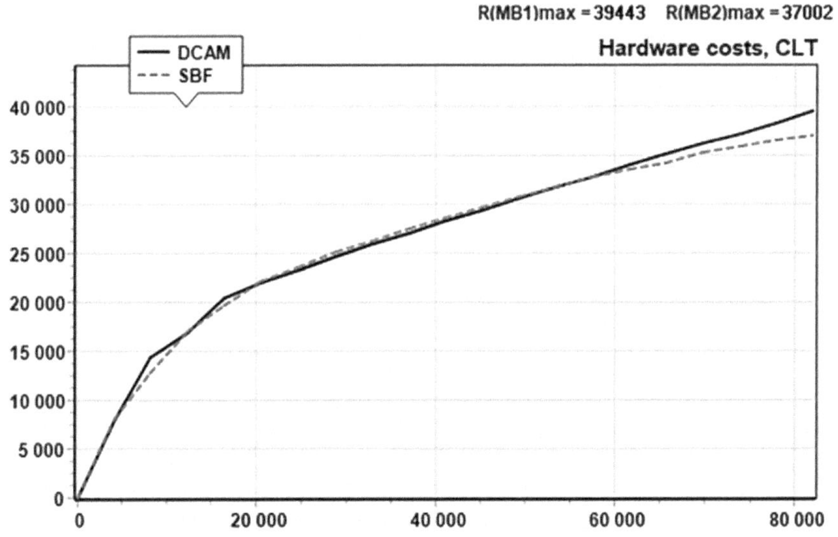

FIGURE 18.10 Comparison of the DCAM and SBF approaches behavior.

the number and content of patterns to be recognized change in the same way for both approaches.

As you can see, the nature of the behavior of both graphs along the entire dimension of variation is almost the same. Sure, their parallel combination will not give a positive effect in the sense of costs reduction despite the closeness of the absolute values, that is, the fulfillment of Condition 1 of a successful parallel combination of matching blocks.

Note that this experimental result disproves the assumption concerning significant behavior difference of recognition schemes built according to approaches of different nature, which was the theoretical basis of the combining methods.

Moreover, also contrary to this theoretical assumption, it turns out that different modifications of the same approach sometimes can differ significantly. In Figure 18.11, under the same conditions, the characteristics of two modifications of the CAM approach are given together.

As you can see, despite the closeness of the internal structure of the DCAM and DpCAM schemes (which are, respectively, decoded and partially decoded modifications of the basic BsCAM scheme, whose internal structures are very similar), they behave significantly differently on the same data set. Therefore, their combination will give a positive effect when combined in parallel.

These facts of discrepancies between theoretical assumptions and real results indicate the importance of conducting experiments during the implementation of this study.

Finally, let's note that Conditions 1–3 stated earlier for efficient parallel combining would be difficult to obtain without using the fast quantification method proposed in this chapter. Otherwise, for each calculated point of each experimental curve, a

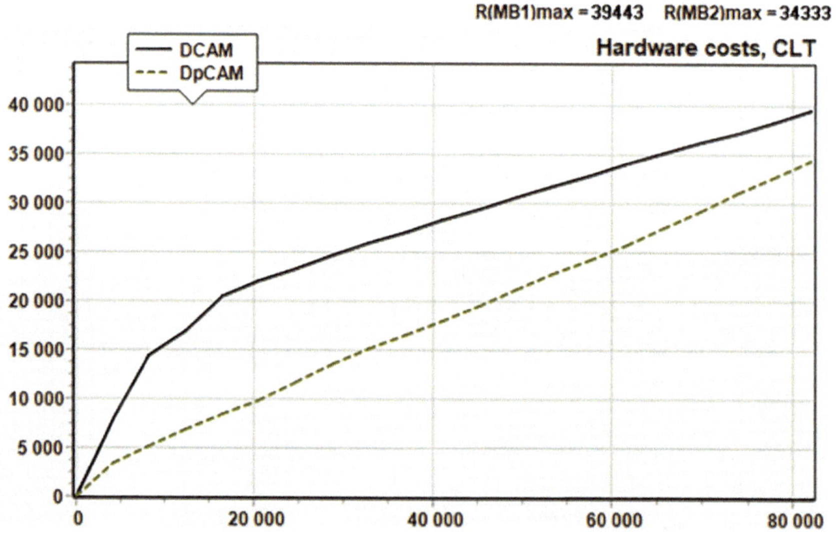

FIGURE 18.11 Comparison of the DCAM and DpCAM modifications behavior.

full, time-consuming digital circuit synthesis procedure using CAD would have to be performed to compile the FPGA design.

18.6 CONCLUSION

A method based on using so-called estimation functions for fast quantification of components of reconfigurable signature-based cybersecurity systems is proposed. The method makes it possible to exclude resource-intensive procedures for synthesizing digital circuits on FPGAs when building complex reconfigurable cybersecurity systems and their components.

An example of the resource cost estimation function building process for simple CAM-based recognition scheme was considered in detail to understand the principles of the estimation function constructing.

The fundamentals of the structural parallel combining technique to maximize the benefits of different hardware matching schemes were discussed.

Experiments to test the proposed method were carried out. In particular, they allowed for revealing three requirements that guarantee successful implementation of the parallel combining technique. For certain conditions, the resulting device provided a hardware costs saving of at least 31% compared to circuits used separately.

REFERENCES

[1] B. Smyth, *Computing Patterns in Strings*. Essex: Pearson Addison Wesley, 2003.

[2] H. Chen, Y. Chen, and D. H. Summerville, "A Survey on the Application of FPGAs for Network Infrastructure Security," *IEEE Communications Surveys and Tutorials*, vol. 13, no. 4, pp. 541–561, 2011, doi: 10.1109/surv.2011.072210.00075.

[3] R. Abdulhammed, M. Faezipour, and K. M. Elleithy, "Network Intrusion Detection Using Hardware Techniques: A Review," in *Proceedings of the IEEE Long Island Systems, Applications and Technology Conference (LISAT)*, 2016, p. 7.

[4] V. Jyothi, S. K. Addepalli, and R. Karri, "DPFEE: A High Performance Scalable Pre-Processor for Network Security Systems," *IEEE Transactions on Multi-Scale Computing Systems*, vol. 4, no. 1, pp. 55–68, January–March 2018, doi: 10.1109/tmscs.2017.2765324.

[5] S. Y. Hilgurt, "A Survey on Hardware Solutions for Signature-Based Security Systems," in *1st International Workshop on Information Technologies: Theoretical and Applied Problems 2021 (ITTAP 2021), CEUR-WS*, vol. 3039, 2021, pp. 6–23, http://ceur-ws.org/Vol–3039.

[6] S. A. Guccione, D. Levi, and D. Downs, "A Reconfigurable Content Addressable Memory," in *Parallel and Distributed Processing, Proceedings, Article; Proceedings Paper*, vol. 1800, 2000, pp. 882–889.

[7] Y. H. Cho, and W. H. Mangione-Smith, "Deep Packet Filter With Dedicated Logic and Read Only Memories," in *12th Annual IEEE Symposium on Field-Programmable Custom Computing Machines, Proceedings, Proceedings Paper*, 2004, pp. 125–134, doi: 10.1109/fccm.2004.25.

[8] I. Sourdis, D. N. Pnevmatikatos, and S. Vassiliadis, "Scalable Multigigabit Pattern Matching for Packet Inspection," *IEEE Transactions on Very Large Scale Integration (VLSI) Systems*, vol. 16, no. 2, pp. 156–166, February 2008, doi: 10.1109/tvlsi.2007.912036.

[9] B. H. Bloom, "Space/Time Trade-Offs in Hash Coding with Allowable Errors," *Communications of the ACM*, vol. 13, no. 7, pp. 422–426, 1970, doi: 10.1145/362686.362692.

[10] S. Dharmapurikar, M. Attig, and J. Lockwood, "Design and Implementation of a String Matching System for Network Intrusion Detection Using FPGA-Based Bloom Filters," in *All Computer Science and Engineering Research, Washington University in St. Louis, WUCSE-2004–12*, March 2004.

[11] S. Geravand, and M. Ahmadi, "Bloom Filter Applications in Network Security: A State-of-the-Art Survey," *Computer Networks*, vol. 57, no. 18, pp. 4047–4064, December 2013, doi: 10.1016/j.comnet.2013.09.003.

[12] A. V. Aho, and M. J. Corasick, "Efficient String Matching: An Aid to Bibliographic Search," *Communications of the ACM*, vol. 18, no. 6, pp. 333–340, 1975, doi: 10.1145/360825.360855.

[13] J. Lunteren, "High-Performance Pattern-Matching for Intrusion Detection," in *25th IEEE International Conference on Computer Communications, Proceedings IEEE Infocom 2006, Proceedings Paper*, vols. 1–7, 2006, pp. 1409–1421.

[14] W. Jiang, Y. H. E. Yang, and V. K. Prasanna, "Scalable Multi-Pipeline Architecture for High Performance Multi-Pattern String Matching," in *24th IEEE International Parallel and Distributed Processing Symposium, IPDPS 2010*, Atlanta, GA, 2010, pp. 1–12, doi: 10.1109/IPDPS.2010.5470374.

[15] C. H. Lin, and S. C. Chang, "Efficient Pattern Matching Algorithm for Memory Architecture," *IEEE Transactions on Very Large Scale Integration (VLSI) Systems*, vol. 19, no. 1, pp. 33–41, January 2011, doi: 10.1109/tvlsi.2009.2028346.

[16] S. Dharmapurikar, P. Krishnamurthy, T. S. Sproull, and J. W. Lockwood, "Deep Packet Inspection Using Parallel Bloom Filters," *IEEE Micro, Article; Proceedings Paper*, vol. 24, no. 1, pp. 52–61, January–February 2004, doi: 10.1109/mm.2004.1268997.

[17] Q.-M. Duong, K.-S. Nguyen, H.-D. Nguyen, X.-U. Dao, A.-T. Do, and Q.-K. Trinh, "FeCBF: A Novel Sub-Optimal Cascaded Bloom Filter Structure Based on Feature Extraction," *IEEE Access*, vol. 12, pp. 67619–67631, 2024, doi: 10.1109/ACCESS.2024.3399062.

[18] H. R. Lewis, and C. H. Papadimitriou, *Elements of the Theory of the Computations*, 2nd ed. Prentice-Hall, 1998.

[19] R. M. Keller, *Computer Science: Abstraction to Implementation*. Harvey Mudd College, 2001.

[20] T. Song, W. Zhang, D. S. Wang, and Y. B. Xue, "A Memory Efficient Multiple Pattern Matching Architecture for Network Security," in *27th IEEE Conference on Computer Communications (INFOCOM), Proceedings Paper*, vols. 1–5, 2008, pp. 673–681.

[21] K. Tashev, I. Durdona, and A. Mokhinabonu, "Comparative Performance Analysis the Aho-Corasick Algorithm for Developing a Network Detection System," in *2022 International Conference on Information Science and Communications Technologies (ICISCT)*, Tashkent, Uzbekistan, 2022, pp. 1–7, doi: 10.1109/ICISCT55600.2022.10146815.

[22] Z. Zhou, and R. Wang, "A 100Gbps Multi-Pattern String Matching Method Based on Bloom Filter and TCAM," in *2024 5th International Seminar on Artificial Intelligence, Networking and Information Technology (AINIT)*, Nanjing, China, 2024, pp. 1034–1039, doi: 10.1109/AINIT61980.2024.10581733.

19 Research and Development of Normalized Link Blocking Models in Secure Traffic Engineering Routing for Programmable Networks

Oleksandr Lemeshko, Anatoliy Persikov, Oleksandra Yeremenko, Amal Mersni, and Maryna Yevdokymenko

19.1 INTRODUCTION

Modern infocommunication networks (ICNs) are complex organizational and technical systems with essential functions to ensure a high Quality of Service (QoS) and network security when transmitting information between different types of users—people, servers, vehicles, etc. These two aspects are key, so more and more technological and protocol solutions for traffic management in the ICN are directly or indirectly considered a set of QoS and network security indicators [1, 2]. For most services, even standards (requirements) are set for the packet transmission rate, the value of the permissible average delay, jitter, packet loss probability, and packet compromise probability [3]. These indicators are diverse and can depend on various traffic characteristics and parameters related to communication equipment and the network as a whole. For instance, improving one or more Quality of Service (QoS) indicators may negatively impact network security, and vice versa.

Therefore, ensuring a high level of QoS and network security requires the systematic and coordinated operation of all traffic management tools, among which routing protocols play a crucial role. Routing protocols must provide end-to-end service, considering the traffic characteristics and functional parameters of network devices and segments, such as bandwidth, utilization, compromise probability, etc. Modern routing protocols operate through continuous periodic or on-demand monitoring of the network's current state. When there are changes in network topology, communication link utilizations, or malicious activity, routing protocols should automatically adjust the set of optimal routes to enhance both QoS and network security. At the

DOI: 10.1201/9781003546153-19

same time, the effectiveness of a routing protocol as a distributed computing program and part of the router or network controller software is directly determined by the type of mathematical model and route calculation method used. The primary requirements for the mathematical foundation of modern and emerging routing solutions include controlled computational complexity, minimal service traffic generation, high scalability, and the ability to maintain a high QoS level and network security by optimizing available resources.

Given the complexity of meeting these requirements within a single theoretical and technological routing solution, no ideal routing solution exists. Scientists and network equipment developers have proposed various routing models, methods, and protocols already being used in practice, depending on the network type, size, available resources, and user requirements for QoS and network security. It is also important to note that routing solutions are continually evolving and being refined at both theoretical and technological levels.

19.1.1 Key Contributions of the Chapter

The significant contributions of this chapter are as follows:

i. The chapter provides an in-depth analysis of existing Traffic Engineering models, methods, and approaches for secure routing. It identifies critical gaps and limitations in current solutions, highlighting the need to improve QoS and security in modern networks.
ii. The chapter introduces an improved flow-based mathematical model designed to optimize secure Traffic Engineering routing under normalized link blocking. This model addresses the challenges of load balancing and enhanced security, offering an innovative approach to routing optimization in networks.
iii. The work thoroughly evaluates the proposed model through numerical research and analysis. The results demonstrate the model's effectiveness, supported by detailed discussions of performance outcomes.

19.1.2 Chapter Organization

Section 19.2 presents an analysis of related work on Traffic Engineering models, methods, and approaches applied to secure routing. Section 19.3 explains the improved flow-based mathematical model for normalized secure Traffic Engineering routing. Section 19.4 focuses on the numerical analysis of the improved secure TE routing model in an infocommunication network. Section 19.5 presents the experimental results and discussion. Finally, Section 19.6 concludes the chapter and highlights the future scope of the research.

19.2 RELATED WORK ANALYSIS

Graph models and combinatorial methods (algorithms) for calculating the shortest path [4, 5], on which most existing IP routing protocols, such as RIP and OSPF, are based, were highly relevant for use in conditions of low computing power of network routers when their performance was tens of packets per second. On the other hand, to take into account the network state, routing protocols generate routing metrics of links (interfaces), which are convolutions, usually weighted sums of various indicators related to the QoS, such as bandwidth, delay, packet loss rate, etc. [6]. Using such metrics has a very indirect effect on the characteristics of the built route. Unfortunately, existing protocols do not explicitly consider the characteristics of packet flows or network security indicators when determining route metrics.

Modern routers and network controllers are ultra-powerful computing systems that operate based on multi-core and multiprocessor architecture and provide packet processing speeds of millions and even billions of packets per second [7]. This computational potential allows for using more complex and efficient mathematical models and routing methods that consider modern network traffic's multi-flow nature and are focused on optimizing routing processes with improved QoS and network security. Therefore, in recent years, scientists worldwide have significantly increased research intensity in developing and improving flow-based models and methods for secure QoS routing [8–14].

Most of the research concerns the development of options for combining QoS and network security indicators in forming routing metrics. That is, depending on the priority level of QoS and network security requirements, the influence of one or the other component in the metrics is enhanced. Another promising direction for improving protocols, mathematical models, and routing methods is to support the principles inherent in the concept of Traffic Engineering (TE) [15–20]. Implementing these principles ensures a balanced use (loading) of the available network resource in the routing process—the bandwidth of the network links and queue buffers on routers. This will prevent a situation where specific segments in the network are underloaded, and some are overloaded, which leads to significant deterioration, primarily in end-to-end QoS indicators, i.e., an increase in delays and packet loss [21, 22].

In developing Traffic Engineering models and methods in the routing field, quite a few attractive solutions have been proposed from the point of view of science and practice, some of which relate to the problems of adapting load-balancing tasks to network security requirements [23–29]. For example, in [27], TE routing solutions are extended to the area of traffic limitation and fault-tolerant routing, considering the network security indicators of edge routers. Papers [2, 28, 29] propose an approach where load balancing in an ICN accounts for the characteristics of traffic and communication link bandwidth but also network security indicators of communication equipment. Within this approach [2, 28, 29], a certain compromise is sought between secure solutions based on the use of single-path routing and QoS solutions based on multipath routing.

Beyond load balancing and optimization, artificial methods like jamming and blocking links or nodes are used to improve network security [2, 27–31]. For example, blocking links or nodes prevents compromised elements from engaging with the network. These techniques play a key role in preserving network security by enabling the system to respond to new threats while minimizing disruption to normal traffic flow.

An effective approach is presented in [30], where a QoS-aware secure routing design for wireless networks with selfish jammers is shown to be rational, stable, distributed, and computationally efficient, achieving optimal transmission security under QoS constraints. A key focus is on using artificial jamming to enhance security, supported by an incentive mechanism that encourages jammers to contribute. A non-cooperative game framework addresses jamming power settings, while a method is proposed to optimize transmission power for security. Path-finding algorithms then solve the routing problem, confirming the scheme's efficiency.

The Load Equalized Traffic Adjustable Routing (LETARP) protocol in [31] reduces traffic in mobile ad hoc networks by redistributing load from blocked nodes to less critical ones, extending network lifespan. Blockage is a major issue in these networks, hindering performance, and load balancing becomes challenging when blockage occurs. LETARP addresses this by using a bi-directional approach to congestion density and link costs to adjust for blockage. The protocol selects routes with lower congestion and longer lifespan for packet transmission, optimizing traffic flow and improving overall network efficiency.

In [2, 27–29], various models were proposed to improve secure routing through Traffic Engineering. These models help reduce the overload on network links with a high probability of compromise by directing more traffic through secure links without overloading them. Different functional dependencies of weighting coefficients on link compromise probability were compared when deriving secure routing solutions.

Therefore, the analysis highlights the importance of a holistic approach to secure routing that combines load balancing, optimization, and artificial techniques. To achieve both security and quality of service, it is essential to implement integrated traffic management solutions that can adapt to changing network conditions while balancing the trade-offs between security and performance. Optimization methods are particularly effective for managing this balance, while artificial techniques add extra layers of security to address emerging threats. These combined strategies create a strong foundation for ensuring both security and performance in modern softwarized network infrastructures.

The flow-based model of TE routing proposed in this work further develops the solutions presented and studied in [2, 28, 29]. The improvements relate to the load balancing conditions and link-blocking model and are focused on the ICN state variant when network equipment, primarily routers and, accordingly, their interfaces (communication links), can be compromised within a specific known range of compromise probability values.

19.3 IMPROVED FLOW-BASED MODEL OF SECURE TRAFFIC ENGINEERING ROUTING

In this section, the notation that is used in the problem definition is explained. A network (SDN data plane) is given by a directed graph $G=(R,E)$, where $R=\left\{R_i; i=\overline{1,m}\right\}$ is the set of nodes and $E=\left\{E_{i,j}; i,j=\overline{1,m}; i\neq j\right\}$ is the set of directed edges representing links between the nodes (network routers). For each edge $E_{i,j}\in E$ (network link) its bandwidth $\varphi_{i,j}$ (packets per second, pps) is defined. It should be noted that the number of edges (links) is determined as the set capacity $|E|=e$.

Let us suppose that in the presented basic Traffic Engineering model, each transmitted flow is unicast with a set of corresponding functional characteristics: K—set of transmitted flows of packets (k ∈ K), s_k—source router, d_k—destination router, and λ^k – kth flow average intensity (pps).

The routing variables $x_{i,j}^k$ need to be calculated to solve the traffic engineering (TE) problem. Each variable corresponds to the portion of the kth flow intensity in the link $E_{i,j} \in E$ that is part of the route.

The following constraints are imposed on the variables when a multipath routing is used [2, 32]:

$$0 \le x_{i,j}^k \le 1. \tag{19.1}$$

The flow conservation conditions are introduced in the model to ensure the routes' connectivity [2, 32]:

$$\begin{cases} \sum\limits_{j:E_{i,j}\in E} x_{i,j}^k - \sum\limits_{j:E_{j,i}\in E} x_{j,i}^k = 0;\ k \in K,\ R_i \ne s_k, d_k; \\ \sum\limits_{j:E_{i,j}\in E} x_{i,j}^k - \sum\limits_{j:E_{j,i}\in E} x_{j,i}^k = 1;\ k \in K,\ R_i = s_k; \\ \sum\limits_{j:E_{i,j}\in E} x_{i,j}^k - \sum\limits_{j:E_{j,i}\in E} x_{j,i}^k = -1;\ k \in K,\ R_i = d_k. \end{cases} \tag{19.2}$$

Additionally, the average packet intensity of the kth flow within the link $E_{i,j} \in E$ can be calculated as follows:

$$\lambda_{i,j}^k = \lambda^k x_{i,j}^k,\ E_{i,j} \in E. \tag{19.3}$$

To estimate the link utilization coefficient, the following expression will be used:

$$\alpha_{i,j} = \frac{\sum\limits_{k\in K} \lambda^k x_{i,j}^k}{\varphi_{i,j}}. \tag{19.4}$$

As shown by the analysis [15–20], to fulfill the requirements of the Traffic Engineering concept, it is necessary to ensure a balanced use of the available network link resource. This is generally implemented by formulating overload prevention conditions [32].

During load balancing in the network to account for the indicators of network security, it is proposed to introduce the following conditions. Assume that each link $E_{i,j} \in E$ is associated with such an important indicator of network security as the probability of it being compromised $p_{i,j}$. The main goal of the proposed solution is to ensure maximum utilization of communication links with minimal probabilities of compromise and vice versa—links with a high probability of compromise $p_{i,j}$ should be loaded minimally or even completely blocked.

Therefore, it is proposed to use an improved load balancing condition [2, 28]:

$$\sum_{k\in K}\lambda^k x_{i,j}^k \le \alpha v_{i,j}(p_{i,j})\varphi_{i,j}, E_{i,j} \in E, \tag{19.5}$$

where α is the additional control variable that numerically determines the upper bound of the network links utilization (under link blocking) and obeys the constraints [28, 32]:

$$0 \le \alpha \le 1, \tag{19.6}$$

while $v_{i,j}$ are the weighting coefficients. The function $v_{i,j}(p_{i,j})$ will be called the link-blocking model for secure routing and load balancing in the ICN. The values of this function indicate what portion of the link bandwidth will be used and what portion will be blocked during the routing process due to the increased probability of link compromise. Works [2, 27, 28] consider the most general case, which in turn must comply with the following boundary conditions

$$v_{i,j} = \begin{cases} 0, & \text{if } p_{i,j} = 1; \\ 1, & \text{if } p_{i,j} = 0. \end{cases} \tag{19.7}$$

If the compromise probability $p_{i,j}$ increases from 0 to 1, the weighting coefficient $v_{i,j}$ should decrease from 1 to 0. The direct dependence of the weighting coefficient $v_{i,j}$ on $p_{i,j}$ will be given by the decreasing function on the whole interval:

$$p_{i,j} \in [0;1]. \tag{19.8}$$

In the same works [2, 27, 28], when studying the processes of secure routing, several possible scenarios of compromising network equipment were considered (Table 19.1), namely:

- the first scenario covered the range of link compromise probabilities from 0 to 0.5 (the risk level is "conditionally low");
- the second scenario covered the range of link compromise probabilities from 0.3 to 0.8 (the risk level is "conditionally medium");
- the third scenario covered the range of link compromise probabilities from 0.5 to 1 (the risk level is "conditionally high");

TABLE 19.1
Matching Compromise Scenarios to Values $p_{i,j}$

First scenario	Second scenario	Third scenario	Fourth scenario
$p_{i,j} \in [0;0.5]$	$p_{i,j} \in [0.3;0.8]$	$p_{i,j} \in [0.5;1]$	$p_{i,j} \in [0;1]$

- the fourth scenario covered the range of link compromise probabilities from 0 to 1 (unpredictable risk level).

In general, expression (19.7) best describes the fourth compromise scenario, which meets the conditions (19.8). In this scenario, insecure links are blocked more heavily so that traffic is directed to more secure areas of the ICN. In the case of other scenarios, for example, the second and third (Table 19.1), a contradictory situation may arise when even the most secure links are blocked, leading to inefficient use of the link resource. Moreover, the traffic from the most secure links will still not be able to be redistributed to insecure links. Therefore, in this work, we propose to modify and clarify conditions (19.7) and (19.8) if the predicted compromise scenario and the bounds $p_{\min}$ and $p_{\max}$ for the link compromise probabilities are known in advance:

$$v_{i,j}(p_{i,j}) = \begin{cases} 0, & \text{if } p_{i,j} = p_{\max}; \\ 1, & \text{if } p_{i,j} = p_{\min}, \end{cases} \tag{19.9}$$

$$p_{\min} \le p_{i,j} \le p_{\max}. \tag{19.10}$$

The value of $p_{\min}$, as a rule, corresponds to the value of the compromise probability of the most secure communication link in the network at the time of calculation. In turn, the value $p_{\max}$ can be determined by the boundary value of the link compromise probability, after which the use of this resource is prohibited. It is clear that, in general, the following expression is true for the successful solution of the secure routing problem

$$0 \le p_{\min} < p_{\max} \le 1.$$

Finally, as the optimality criterion in the problem-solving of the Traffic Engineering technological task, the minimum boundary value α is selected as it was introduced in [2, 32]:

$$\min_{x,\alpha} \alpha. \tag{19.11}$$

The formulation of the Traffic Engineering problem in optimization form with criterion (19.11) and constraints (19.1), (19.2), (19.5) та (19.6) aims to ensure optimal load balancing with minimization of the utilization coefficient of each network link. This optimization problem in multipath routing (19.1) implementation belongs to the Linear Programming (LP) class. This helps improve network performance, time QoS indicators (average packet delay and jitter), and reliability indicators such as packet loss probability.

In the process of further studying secure TE routing in ICN using the proposed model (19.1)–(19.6), (19.9)–(19.11), as an example, we will focus on the use of the blocking model, which, under the modified conditions (19.9), (19.10), is given by the following expression:

$$v_{i,j}(p_{i,j}) = 1 - \left[\frac{p_{i,j} - p_{\min}}{p_{\max} - p_{\min}}\right]^n, \tag{19.12}$$

where n is the control parameter, which is used to adjust the sensitivity of the weighting coefficient $v_{i,j}$ to the values of the link compromise probability $p_{i,j}$. In [22–25], other link-blocking models have been proposed and studied, which can also be modified based on the updated conditions (19.9) and (19.10) using the example of (19.12).

Figure 19.1 shows the dependences of $v_{i,j}(p_{i,j})$ (19.12) for $n \geq 1$ under $p_{\min} = 0.5$ and $p_{\max} = 1$, within which the boundary conditions (19.9) and (19.10) are met.

As shown in Figure 19.1, model (19.12) under $n > 1$ is weakly sensitive to $p_{i,j}$ changes in the region of its minimum values (near $p_{\min}$) and more sensitive to $p_{i,j}$ values in the range of its maximum values.

In the course of the study, three TE routing models were analyzed and compared:

- TE model, which did not take into account the security parameters of the ICN and was represented by expressions (19.1)–(19.6), (19.11) under $v_{i,j}(p_{i,j}) = 1$ [32];
- SecTE model, which took into account the ICN security parameters over the entire range of values of the link compromise probability and was represented by expressions (19.1)–(19.8), (19.11) [2, 27, 28];
- NormSecTE model, which is an improved version of the SecTE model based on the consideration of normalized network security parameters and is represented by expressions (19.1)–(19.6), (19.9)–(19.11).

Three main indicators compared the efficiency of these TE routing models. The first is the upper bound of the network link utilization $\alpha_{\max}$, which was calculated as the maximum of the values characterizing the link utilization coefficients (19.4). The second performance indicator, which determined the network security level, was

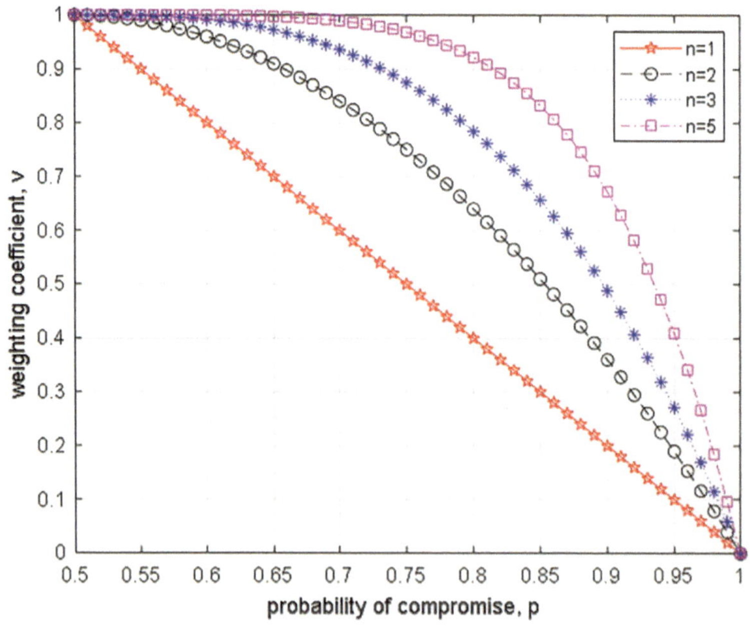

FIGURE 19.1 Visualization of link blocking model (19.12) under $n \geq 1$.

evaluated through the compromise probability of the kth flow packets from end-to-end (E2E) p_{E2E}^{k}, i.e., along the set of used paths. The third performance indicator was the average end-to-end delay of the kth flow packets τ_{E2E}^{k}.

The compromise probability of the kth flow packets in the ICN was calculated using the following formula:

$$p_{E2E}^{k} = \sum_{s \in S^k} \frac{\lambda_s^k}{\lambda^k} p_s, \tag{19.13}$$

where s^k is the set of paths (routes) used to transmit packets of the kth flow between a given pair of network routers; λ_s^k is the intensity of the kth packet flow transmitted by the sth path in the ICN (pps); p_s is the probability of compromising the sth path, which is determined in accordance with the expression

$$p_s = 1 - \prod_{E_{i,j} \in Path_s} (1 - p_{i,j}), \tag{19.14}$$

Where $Path_s = \{E_{i,j}\}$ is a set of network links that form the sth path in the network.

Similarly, the average end-to-end delay of the kth flow packets was calculated as:

$$\tau_{E2E}^{k} = \sum_{s \in S^k} \frac{\lambda_s^k}{\lambda^k} \tau_s, \tag{19.15}$$

where τ_s is the average packet delay along the sth path, which was determined according to the formula

$$\tau_s = \sum_{E_{i,j} \in Path_s} \tau_{i,j}. \tag{19.16}$$

In this work, the value $\tau_{i,j}$ characterizing the average packet delay in the link $E_{i,j}$ was calculated by the formula

$$\tau_{i,j} = \frac{1}{\varphi_{i,j} - \lambda_{i,j}}. \tag{19.17}$$

That is, the link operation model was described by the M/M/1 packet and queue service system.

19.4 RESEARCH OF AN IMPROVED FLOW-BASED MODEL OF SECURE TE-ROUTING IN ICN

Let's demonstrate the features of solving the problem of secure TE routing using the example of the ICN structure shown in Figure 19.2. We modeled the case of routing a single packet flow when packets were transmitted from the first to the fifth router.

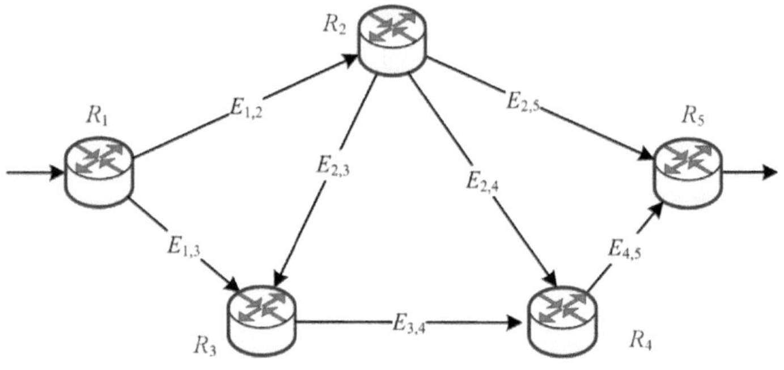

FIGURE 19.2 The variant of the network structure that was studied.

TABLE 19.2
Characteristics of Network Links

Link	$E_{1,2}$	$E_{2,5}$	$E_{1,3}$	$E_{3,4}$	$E_{4,5}$	$E_{2,3}$	$E_{2,4}$
Bandwidth	900	300	400	700	900	800	300
Link compromise probability	0.5	0.9	0.8	0.8	0.5	0.9	0.5

TABLE 19.3
Routes Compromise Probability in a Network

Path	$R_1 \to R_2 \to R_5$	$R_1 \to R_3 \to R_4 \to R_5$	$R_1 \to R_2 \to R_3 \to R_4 \to R_5$	$R_1 \to R_2 \to R_4 \to R_5$
Number	1	2	3	4
Compromise probability	0.95	0.98	0.995	0.875

Therefore, the flow number was omitted in the following section. Table 19.2 shows the bandwidths of the communication links and the probability of their compromise. According to the information about the structure of the ICN (Figure 19.2) and the characteristics of its links, Table 19.3 shows the data on the available routes between the source router R_1 and the destination router R_5, as well as the probability of their compromise.

Therefore, according to the content of Table 19.2, the dependencies presented in Figure 19.1 are relevant to the example under study. Then, Table 19.4 demonstrates the results of the calculations obtained using the three studied models of TE routing at $\lambda = 500$ pps and $n = 2$, i.e., the case of a single packet flow routing was modeled.

In accordance with the features of the network structure (Figure 19.1 and Table 19.3):

- the packet flow rate in the first route (λ_1) determined the flow rate in the $E_{2,5}$ link;
- the packet flow rate in the second route (λ_2) determined the flow rate in the $E_{1,3}$ link;

TABLE 19.4
Comparative Analysis of the Obtained Solutions for Secure Routing and Load Balancing ($\lambda = 500$ pps, $n = 2$)

	TE		SecTE		NormSecTE	
Link	$\lambda_{i,j}$	$\alpha_{i,j}$	$\lambda_{i,j}$	$\alpha_{i,j}$	$\lambda_{i,j}$	$\alpha_{i,j}$
$E_{1,2}$	375	0.4167	406.367	0.4515	406.5421	0.4517
$E_{2,5}$	125	0.4167	53.3708	0.1779	63.0841	0.2103
$E_{1,3}$	125	0.312	93.633	0.2341	93.4579	0.2336
$E_{3,4}$	291.6667	0.4167	235.9551	0.3371	261.6822	0.3738
$E_{4,5}$	375	0.4167	446.6292	0.4963	436.9159	0.4855
$E_{2,3}$	166.6667	0.2083	142.3221	0.1779	168.2243	0.2103
$E_{2,4}$	83.3333	0.2778	210.6742	0.7022	175.2336	0.5841

- the packet flow rate in the third route (λ_3) determined the flow rate in the $E_{2,3}$ link;
- the packet flow rate in the fourth route (λ_4) determined the flow rate in the $E_{2,4}$ link.

19.5 RESULTS AND DISCUSSIONS

Table 19.5 shows the calculated performance indicators for each TE routing model, which characterize the quality of load balancing and aspects related to network security and Quality of Service. A comparative assessment is shown for $n = 2$, corresponding to the results in Table 19.4, and for $n = 3$.

Based on the comparative analysis results (Table 19.5), we can conclude that the TE routing model provides balancing that is focused only on improving QoS indicators, such as the average end-to-end packet delay. The SecTE and NormSecTE secure routing models focus on finding a compromise between QoS and network security. With an increase in the parameter n, these models pay more attention to improving the QoS level. With a decrease in n, the network security parameters are considered more strongly when balancing.

If we compare the effectiveness of the SecTE and NormSecTE models, we can conclude that the replacement of conditions (19.7), (19.8) with (19.9), (19.10) allowed us to account for the security parameters more accurately, i.e., the compromise probability of network links. Using the NormSecTE model, the most secure links were practically not blocked, which made it possible to redirect the load from more insecure communication links to them. Therefore, the routing decisions obtained using the NormSecTE model are still more focused on improving the QoS (average packet end-to-end delay): up to 15% for $n = 2$ and about 11% for $n = 3$ without significantly deteriorating the level of network security (packet compromise probability) in the network: up to 1% for $n = 2$ or $n = 3$.

The increase in network load, i.e., at $\lambda = 600$ pps, naturally led to an increase in the level of network links overload (Table 19.6). This led to a corresponding

TABLE 19.5
Comparative Characteristics of Performance Indicators of Secure Routing and Load Balancing Solutions ($\lambda = 500$ pps)

	$n = 2$			$n = 3$		
Model	α_{max}	p_{E2E}	τ_{E2E} (MS)	α_{max}	p_{E2E}	τ_{E2E} (MS)
TE	0.4167	0.96	7.9	0.4167	0.96	7.9
SecTE	0.7022	0.9368	10.8	0.6383	0.941	9.8
NormSecTE	0.5841	0.9445	9.2	0.5024	0.9498	8.7

TABLE 19.6
Comparative Characteristics of Performance Indicators of Secure Routing and Load Balancing Solutions ($\lambda = 600$ pps)

	$n = 2$			$n = 3$		
Model	α_{max}	p_{E2E}	τ_{E2E} (MS)	α_{max}	p_{E2E}	τ_{E2E} (MS)
TE	0.5	0.96	9.1	0.5	0.96	9.1
SecTE	0.8427	0.9368	16.0	0.766	0.941	12.7
NormSecTE	0.7009	0.9445	11.3	0.6029	0.9498	10.3

increase in the average packet end-to-end delay for all three models. However, the ratio between the packet flows that were sent along different routes did not change, which guaranteed the unchanged compromise probabilities of packets in the network (Tables 19.5 and 19.6) for the corresponding values of the parameter n (19.12).

In this case (Table 19.6), the use of the NormSecTE model allows, in comparison with the SecTE solution, to reduce the average packet end-to-end delay to 30% when $n = 2$ and about 20% when $n = 3$, with a decrease in the packet compromise probability in the network, as in the case of $\lambda = 500$ pps (Table 19.5), to 1%.

The study results of secure routing processes with load balancing confirmed its effectiveness in considering the network state: its topology, flow characteristics, bandwidth, utilization of network links, and the probability of their compromise. This made it possible to orient the resulting routing solutions to reduce the utilization of links with a high compromise probability by redistributing traffic to more secure links. Usually, links that had high bandwidth and a low compromise probability were more heavily loaded.

During the study, several indicators carried out a comparative analysis of the effectiveness of the TE routing models. It has been established that the classical TE routing model [30] always provides the lowest utilization level of network links and, as a result, the best average end-to-end packet delay (19.15). However, this model does not in any way take into account the network security indicators of network elements (links, routers, paths), so the solutions obtained with its help had the worst compromise probability of packets (19.13). The use of SecTE and NormSecTE secure routing models focused on finding a compromise between the QoS and network security indicators (Tables 19.5 and 19.6). At the same time, the proposed improved model of secure TE routing NormSecTE, based on a more accurate consideration of the compromise probabilities of network links, allowed, compared to SecTE, to improve the Quality of Service (average packet end-to-end delay) from 11–15% to 20–30% without a significant (up to 1%) deterioration in the network security (packet compromise probability).

Using the NormSecTE model, it was found that the most secure links were practically not blocked, making it possible to redirect the load from more insecure communication links to them. An increase in network load led to a predictable increase in the average packet end-to-end delay (19.15). However, the ratio between packet flows sent via different routes did not change, which guaranteed the unchanged packet compromise probability (19.13) in the network (Tables 19.5 and 19.6) for the corresponding values of the parameter n (19.12).

19.6 CONCLUSIONS AND FUTURE SCOPE

Traffic management and routing tools are promising areas for developing and improving network security solutions. The latest traffic management and routing solutions should include network performance (bandwidth, delay, and packet loss) and network security parameters that characterize the effectiveness of the network's intrusion detection, vulnerability, and risk analysis systems.

The work improves the flow-based model of secure routing with load balancing in accordance with the Traffic Engineering concept by considering network security parameters in the ICN, which is represented by expressions (19.1)–(19.6), (19.9)–(19.12). Within this model, the solution to the technical problem of secure routing with load balancing in an ICN was reduced to solving an optimization problem with the optimality criterion (19.11) and constraints (19.1)–(19.3), (19.5), and (19.6). In implementing multipath routing (19.1), the formulated optimization problem belongs to the class of linear programming problems, which guarantees the predictable computational complexity of solutions and low requirements for the computing power of devices responsible for solving routing problems—routers, route servers, controllers, etc. The novelty of the proposed model is that it modifies the communication link blocking model (19.12), taking into account the normalized conditions (19.9) and (19.10) instead of (19.7) and (19.8) to prevent a situation where even the most secure links will be blocked, which will lead to inefficient use of the link resource (bandwidth).

The future development of the solutions proposed in this work is seen in the expansion of the set of link-blocking models, which need to be adapted to the normalized conditions (19.9) and (19.10), as was done with the model (19.12). Additional research is needed to analyze the impact of network topology, compromise scenarios, and network load on the comprehensive provision of a given level of network efficiency, both in terms of Quality of Service and network security indicators.

19.7 ACKNOWLEDGEMENT

This chapter was published due to work on the Erasmus+ Project Jean Monnet module "The European experience for enhancing the resilience of critical entities in Ukraine" Project No.: 101085825—ERASMUS-JMO-2022-MODULE.

REFERENCES

[1] Bojović, P. D., Malbašić, T., Vujošević, D., Martić, G., and Bojović, Ž. "Dynamic QoS Management for a Flexible 5G/6G Network Core: A Step Toward a Higher Programmability," *Sensors*, 22, p. 2849, 2022. doi: 10.3390/s22082849.

[2] Lemeshko, O., Yeremenko, O., Yevdokymenko, M., Shapovalova, A., and Baranovskyi, O. "Complex Investigation of the Compromise Probability Behavior in Traffic Engineering Oriented Secure Routing Model in Software-Defined Networks," in Klymash, M., Beshley, M., and Luntovskyy, A. (eds) *Future Intent-Based Networking. Lecture Notes in Electrical Engineering*, vol. 831. Springer, Cham, 2022, pp. 145–160. doi: 10.1007/978-3-030-92435-5_8.

[3] ITU-T Rec. Y.1541. *Network Performance Objective for IP-Based Services*. December 2011, 66 p. https://www.itu.int/rec/T-REC-Y.1541-201112-I/en.

[4] Medhi, D., and Ramasamy, K. *Network Routing: Algorithms, Protocols, and Architectures*. Morgan Kaufmann, San Francisco, CA, USA, 2017.

[5] Gargano, P., and Empson, S. *CCNP and CCIE Enterprise Core & CCNP Enterprise Advanced Routing Portable Command Guide: All ENCOR (350–401) and ENARSI (300–410) Commands in One Compact, Portable Resource*. Cisco Press, 2020, 416 p.

[6] Savage, D., Ng, J., Moore, S., Slice, D., Paluch, P., and White, R. *Cisco's Enhanced Interior Gateway Routing Protocol (EIGRP) (No. rfc7868)*. 2016. https://datatracker.ietf.org/doc/html/rfc7868.

[7] Lei, B., Zhao, Q., and Mei, J. "Computing Power Network: An Interworking Architecture of Computing and Network Based on IP Extension," in *2021 IEEE 22nd International Conference on High Performance Switching and Routing (HPSR)*, Paris, France, 2021, pp. 1–6. doi: 10.1109/HPSR52026.2021.9481792.

[8] Li, C., Liu, Y., Xiao, J., and Zhou, J. "MCEAACO-QSRP: A Novel QoS-Secure Routing Protocol for Industrial Internet of Things," *IEEE Internet of Things Journal*, vol. 9, no. 19, pp. 18760–18777, 1 Oct. 2022. doi: 10.1109/JIOT.

[9] Pathak, A., Al-Anbagi, I., and Hamilton, H. J. "An Adaptive QoS and Trust-Based Lightweight Secure Routing Algorithm for WSNs," *IEEE Internet of Things Journal*, vol. 9, no. 23, pp. 23826–23840, 1 Dec. 2022. doi: 10.1109/JIOT.

[10] Hashem Eiza, M., Owens, T., and Ni, Q. "Secure and Robust Multi-Constrained QoS Aware Routing Algorithm for VANETs," *IEEE Transactions on Dependable and Secure Computing*, vol. 13, no. 1, pp. 32–45, 1 Jan.–Feb. 2016. doi: 10.1109/TDSC.2014.2382602.

[11] Dinesh, K., and Svn, S. K. "GWO-SMSLO: Grey Wolf Optimization Based Clustering With Secured Modified Sea Lion Optimization Routing Algorithm in Wireless Sensor Networks," *Peer-to-Peer Networking and Applications*, vol. 17, pp. 585–611, 2024. doi: 10.1007/s12083-023-01603-9.

[12] Ravi, S., Matheswaran, S., Perumal, U. et al. "Adaptive Trust-Based Secure and Optimal Route Selection Algorithm for MANET Using Hybrid Fuzzy Optimization," *Peer-to-Peer Networking and Applications*, 16, pp. 22–34, 2023. doi: 10.1007/s12083-022-01351-2.

[13] Lozano Domínguez, J. M., and Mateo Sanguino, T. D. J. "Walking Secure: Safe Routing Planning Algorithm and Pedestrian's Crossing Intention Detector Based on Fuzzy Logic App," *Sensors*, 21, p. 529, 2021. doi: 10.3390/s21020529.

[14] Lemeshko, O., Yeremenko, O., and Yevdokymenko, M. "Models and Methods of Secure Routing and Load Balancing in Infocommunication Networks," in Oliynykov, R., Kuznetsov, O., Lemeshko, O., and Radivilova, T. (eds) *Information Security Technologies in the Decentralized Distributed Networks. Lecture Notes on Data Engineering and Communications Technologies*, vol. 115. Springer, Cham, 2022, pp. 225–242. doi: 10.1007/978-3-030-95161-0_10.

[15] Farrel, A. ed. *RFC 9522: Overview and Principles of Internet Traffic Engineering.* 2024. https://datatracker.ietf.org/doc/rfc9522/.

[16] Wang, A., Khasanov, B., Zhao, Q., and Chen, H. *RFC 8821: PCE-Based Traffic Engineering (TE) in Native IP Networks.* 2021. https://www.rfc-editor.org/rfc/rfc8821.html.

[17] Ceccarelli, D., and Lee, Y. *Framework for Abstraction and Control of TE Networks (ACTN) (No. rfc8453).* 2018. https://datatracker.ietf.org/doc/rfc8453/.

[18] Osborne, E. *Extended Administrative Groups in MPLS Traffic Engineering (MPLS-TE) (No. rfc7308).* 2014. https://datatracker.ietf.org/doc/html/rfc7308.

[19] Papneja, R., Vapiwala, S., Karthik, J., Poretsky, S., Rao, S., and Le Roux, J. L. *Methodology for Benchmarking MPLS Traffic Engineered (MPLS-TE) Fast Reroute Pr0tection (No. rfc6894).* 2013. https://datatracker.ietf.org/doc/html/rfc6894.

[20] Awduche, D., Berger, L., Gan, D., Li, T., Srinivasan, V., and Swallow, G. *Rfc3209: RSVP-TE: Extensions to RSVP for LSP Tunnels.* 2001. https://datatracker.ietf.org/doc/html/rfc3209.

[21] Lemeshko, O., Yevdokymenko, M., and Yeremenko, O. "Model of Data Traffic QoS Fast ReRouting in Infocommunication Networks", *Innovative Technologies and Scientific Solutions for Industries*, vol. 3, no. 9, pp. 127–134, 2019. doi: 10.30837/2522-9818.2019.9.127.

[22] Lemeshko, O., and Yevdokymenko, M. "The Method of Hierarchical Inter-Domain Routing in a Software-Defined Telecommunications Network With Ensuring End-To-End Quality of Service", *Innovative Technologies and Scientific Solutions for Industries*, vol. 2, no. 12, pp. 169–182, 2020. doi: 10.30837/2522-9818.2020.12.169.

[23] Patil, M. V., and Jadhav, V. "Secure, Reliable and Load Balanced Routing Protocols for Multihop Wireless Networks," in *2017 International Conference on Intelligent Computing and Control (I2C2)*, Coimbatore, India, 2017, pp. 1–6. doi: 10.1109/I2C2.2017.8321936.

[24] Anjum, M. N., Chowdhury, C., and Neogy, S. "Implementing Mobile Agent based Secure Load Balancing Scheme for MANET," in *2019 International Conference on Opto-Electronics and Applied Optics (Optronix)*, Kolkata, India, 2019, pp. 1–6. doi: 10.1109/OPTRONIX.2019.8862375.

[25] Lazrag, H., Chehri, A., Saadane, R., and Rahmani, M. D. "A Blockchain-Based Approach for Optimal and Secure Routing in Wireless Sensor Networks and IoT," in *2019 15th International Conference on Signal-Image Technology & Internet-Based Systems (SITIS)*, Sorrento, Italy, 2019, pp. 411–415. doi: 10.1109/SITIS.2019.00072.

[26] Xue, P., and Jiang, Z. "SecRouting: Secure Routing for Network Functions Virtualization (NFV) Technology," *IEEE Transactions on Circuits and Systems II: Express Briefs*, vol. 69, no. 3, pp. 1727–1731, March 2022. doi: 10.1109/TCSII.

[27] Lemeshko, O., Yeremenko, O., Yevdokymenko, M., Shapovalova, A., and Lemeshko, V. "Network Security Approach Based on Traffic Engineering Fast ReRoute With Support of Traffic Policing," in *2021 Workshop on Cybersecurity Providing in Information and Telecommunication Systems, CPITS 2021, CEUR Workshop Proceedings*, vol. 2923, 2021, pp. 81–90. https://ceur-ws.org/Vol-2923/paper9.pdf.

[28] Lemeshko, O., Hu, Z., Shapovalova, A., Yeremenko, O., and Yevdokymenko, M. "Research of the Influence of Compromise Probability in Secure Based Traffic Engineering Model in SDN," in Hu, Z., Petoukhov, S., Dychka, I., and He, M. (eds) *Advances in Computer Science for Engineering and Education IV. ICCSEEA 2021. Lecture Notes on Data Engineering and Communications Technologies*, vol. 83. Springer, Cham, 2021, pp. 47–55. doi: 10.1007/978-3-030-80472-5_5.

[29] Lemeshko, O., Yeremenko, O., Yevdokymenko, M., Shapovalova, A., Lemeshko, V., and Persikov, M. "Analysis of Secure Routing Processes Using Traffic Engineering Model," in *2021 11th IEEE International Conference on Intelligent Data Acquisition and Advanced Computing Systems: Technology and Applications (IDAACS)*, Cracow, Poland, 2021, pp. 951–955. doi: 10.1109/IDAACS53288.2021.9660980.

[30] Xu, Y., Liu, J., Shen, Y., Jiang, X., Ji, Y., and Shiratori, N. "QoS-Aware Secure Routing Design for Wireless Networks With Selfish Jammers," *IEEE Transactions on Wireless Communications*, vol. 20, no. 8, pp. 4902–4916, Aug. 2021. doi: 10.1109/TWC.2021.3062885.

[31] Selvan, T., Malathi, P., and Freeda, S. "An Efficient Method for Adjustable Load Equalization for Reducing Traffic in Routing for Mobile Ad Hoc Networks," *Wireless Personal Communications*, vol. 110, pp. 2149–2164, 2020. doi: 10.1007/s11277-019-06834-9.

[32] Seok, Y., Lee, Y., Choi, Y., and Kim, C. "A Constrained Multipath Traffic Engineering Scheme for MPLS Networks," in *International Conference on Communications ICC 2002 (Cat. No.02CH37333): Proceedings of the IEEE International Conference.* IEEE, New York, NY, USA, 28 April–2 May 2002, pp. 2431–2436. doi: 10.1109/ICC.2002.997280.

20 AI-Driven Content Optimization and Generation with Integrated Digital Forensics for Authentic and Secure Media

Oleksandr Kuznetsov, Marco Arnesano, Emanuele Gennuso, Giordano Zannoni, and Agbotiname Lucky Imoize

20.1 INTRODUCTION

The digital revolution has completely changed the face of media and journalism, bringing unprecedented opportunities and overwhelming challenges. At the very front line, the rapidly developing AI technologies have significantly enhanced our ability to create, optimize, and distribute content. Once a fairly straightforward set of practices, SEO techniques have grown into multi-layered strategies that capitalize on AI as a prime driver in achieving the highest state of visibility and engagement with content. This progress of technology, however, equally brings with it a very important caveat. While AI generates and manipulates content with ease, it unfortunately opens the way to let it like wildfire take hold on misinformation, fake news, and ethically questioned content. This situation threatens the integrity of public discourse and an informed democracy's foundations.

AI-generated content will become indistinguishable from humans and continue to blur the line between fact and fiction by challenging our capability for truth-seeking in the digital space. In this respect, it becomes imperative to have a framework that utilizes AI in content optimization and simultaneously verifies the authenticity, ethical integrity, and legality of such content. This becomes all the more significant in the field of journalism premised, as it is, on the inalienable principles of veracity, accuracy, and public interest.

Most of the research into AI-driven content optimization currently focuses on increasing visibility, engagement, and conversion rates. Although these might be relevant indicators from a commercial point of view, they fail to appreciate critical

DOI: 10.1201/9781003546153-20

aspects of content integrity, journalistic ethics, and adherence to the law. A literature gap exists in how AI can be used to generate search engine-optimized content while strictly upholding journalistic standards and adherence to media laws.

Our research tries to fill this gap by proposing an integrated framework that combines AI-driven content optimization with digital forensics techniques and ethical guidelines. It thus addresses a tripartite challenge:

- Optimization of content for maximum visibility and engagement;
- Ensuring the authenticity and factual accuracy of the content;
- Complying with journalistic ethics and having knowledge of the media laws.

By addressing these challenges together, we develop a solution that should be well-grounded ethically and legally, as well as technologically advanced. This is significant since AI-generated multimedia has just become pervasive on all social media and communication platforms.

This is not just an academic concern or an issue to which only probative value can be attached. Rather, this study is of empirical importance to media organizations, journalists, and content producers working in the tumultuous digital media landscape. By providing a framework for creating optimized, genuine, and ethically acceptable content, we'd like to help keep journalistic integrity intact on all digital fronts.

We review the current state of AI-driven content optimization and digital forensics for content verification and propose a new framework considering ethical and legal adherence to these components. We believe that AI will enhance and not compromise the quality and integrity of digital media content in the future.

20.2 LITERATURE REVIEW

The rapid evolution of digital media and search engine technologies has evoked huge interest in studies related to content optimization, search engine optimization, and the interface of these areas with AI and cybersecurity. In this chapter, a review of the literature related to recent contributions made towards such interrelated areas is presented in detail, mentioning major findings and gaps in the existing literature.

Erdmann et al. (2022) [1] offer numerous valuable insights into long-term keyword strategies in SEO. A time series analysis of economic keyword costs in the fashion e-commerce industry demonstrates convergence between branded and generic keywords, challenging conventional wisdom for short-term SEO tactics. This amounts to a longitudinal approach, which most literature in SEO still lacks, focusing primarily on short-term optimization techniques.

Himu et al. (2023) [2] suggest a very different approach to search engine algorithms by incorporating data mining in social networks. Their machine learning system aims to give better results based on user-generated content and opinion mining. This research connects the gap between traditional SEO practices and unstructured data on social media platforms.

Le et al. (2024) [3] highlighted the growing menace of SEO poisoning, especially to SMEs. Their analysis of attack techniques and proposed mitigation strategies, framed within the NIST Cybersecurity Framework, filled an important gap in the literature that had not considered such security implications for SEO.

Lin et al. (2024) [4] propose a fully novel approach to maximizing information spread by optimizing the content. Their simulation framework for human-in-the-loop work allows data-driven optimization of message propagation over social networks by content creators, completing the gap between the creation and distribution strategies of content.

Roumeliotis and Tselikas (2022) [5] provide a rich tutorial on the effective use of SEO techniques and technologies. Their evaluation of different methods for performing SEO gives practical insights to webmasters and covers the demanding need for a structured approach when applying strategies related to SEO.

Scanlon et al. (2023) [6] discuss the possible uses of ChatGPT in digital forensic investigations and their limitations. Their assessment of GPT-4 capability for different forensic use cases reflects opportunities and risks related to integrating large language models in digital forensics workflows.

Sezer Çırakoğlu and Koşaner (2024) [7] discussed the linguistics of high-quality content creation to improve SEO. Their application of Grice's conversational maxims in content optimization provides a novel framework for understanding and improving content quality, addressing the often-overlooked linguistic aspects of SEO.

Tatikonda et al. (2024) [8] have discussed SEO techniques and their role in a digital marketing perspective in broad terms. Their work considers the relationship between SEO and user experience (UX) and underlines the balance necessary between search engines' needs and users' satisfaction. Such valuable opinions on future trends and challenges in SEO give a lot of insight into the evolving landscapes of digital promotion.

While these studies have contributed much towards understanding content optimization, search engine optimization, and related areas, many aspects remain open. More research is required regarding the ethical implications of AI-driven content generation and optimization in view of the growing concern over misinformation and deepfakes. Ensuring veracity through integrating digital forensics techniques into content verification for SEO purposes is an underexplored area, with much potential.

With this in mind, we would like to bring forward a more general framework that closely integrates AI-driven content optimization techniques with digital forensics techniques. This way, both the integrity and authenticity of the content will be further enhanced, while its effectiveness in relation to search engine rankings will remain maintained. This approach contributes to both the theoretical comprehension of content optimization and SEO and practical solutions for the challenges of misinformation and content manipulation in the digital era.

20.3 BACKGROUND: AI-DRIVEN CONTENT OPTIMIZATION AND DIGITAL FORENSICS IN MEDIA

The digitized media landscape is in a radical state of flux propelled by rapid advancements in AI and the growing sophistication of content optimization. This section is supposed to critically explain the theoretical grounding of SEO, AI-generated content, digital forensics in the context of information authentication, and the ethical consideration of the uses of AI in content generation. It's for one of these interrelated areas that we primarily press toward providing a framework within which one might understand a number of the critical challenges and opportunities facing today's modern-day digital content management.

20.3.1 Search Engine Optimization—SEO and Content Optimization

SEO has grown from rudimentary techniques to a multi-faceted art lying at the crossroads between computer science, linguistics, and marketing. Primarily, SEO seeks better visibility and content relevance within SERPs. Such is accomplished by grasping the nuances of the algorithms governing search engines, user behaviors, and content quality metrics.

While modern SEO goes far beyond just placing keywords in strategic locations, a variety of techniques—technical, on-page, and off-page—go toward improving the authority, relevance, and user experience of a website (Figure 20.1). Technical SEO involves optimizing website architecture, improving page load speed, and improving responsiveness on mobile devices. Each of the mentioned factors has grown in significance with each passing day, as search engines like Google have started to include user experience signals into their ranking algorithms in recent times.

On-page optimization can be explained as what one does on each webpage to enable that page to rank higher, driving more relevant traffic. This would include writing compelling meta descriptions, optimizing header tags, and crafting keyword-rich yet high-quality and relevant content. The notion of "relevance" in SEO has become increasingly refined over time as search engines are capable of discerning semantic relationships between words and concepts.

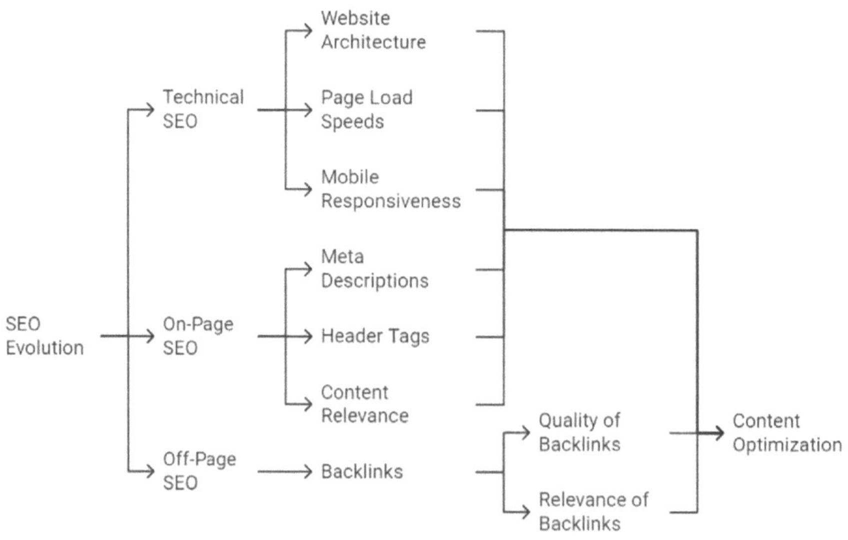

FIGURE 20.1 Evolution of Search Engine Optimization.

This development has implied the emergence of topic clustering and pillar content strategies whereby websites build comprehensive content hubs on particular themes.

As such, off-page SEO generally focuses on establishing the authority of a site through various backlinks from high-authority sources. However, link building has undergone some massive changes in recent years. In fact, today's search engines focus more on the quality and relevance of backlinks, rather than their numbers. This is translating into an upgrowing focus on content-driven link-building methods.

Content optimization is integral to SEO, which refers to the process of creating content and refining it to ensure that the content fully addresses the needs of both users and search engines. These days, content generation and optimization have turned data-intensive, with content developers taking help from Google Search Console or third-party analytics tools that reflect user queries, monitor major performance metrics, and iteratively help them work on their content strategy.

Moreover, the emergence of voice search and mobile-first indexing further complicates the SEO landscape. The need to optimize for natural language patterns and conversational queries creates an additional layer that the content optimizer needs to adapt to for these new search modalities (Krrabaj et al., 2017) [9].

20.3.2 AI-Powered Content Generation

That artificial intelligence has changed content generation is well known; text contexts that were unimaginable up to now have been produced, but this change is, above all, the consequence of the progress made in natural language processing and machine learning, and more precisely, the development of big language models based on transformer architectures Figure 20.2.

These transformer models are the backbone of modern AI content creation and were first proposed by Vaswani et al. (2017) [10], in a seminal work titled "Attention Is All You Need." The models make use of self-attention mechanisms so as to process input sequences. This allows them to capture long-range dependencies in text more effectively than previous recurrent neural network architectures.

With this as the foundation, researchers have been developing more and more advanced models for language. The GPT models and their variants at OpenAI have been considered milestones in this regard. These models are trained on enormous

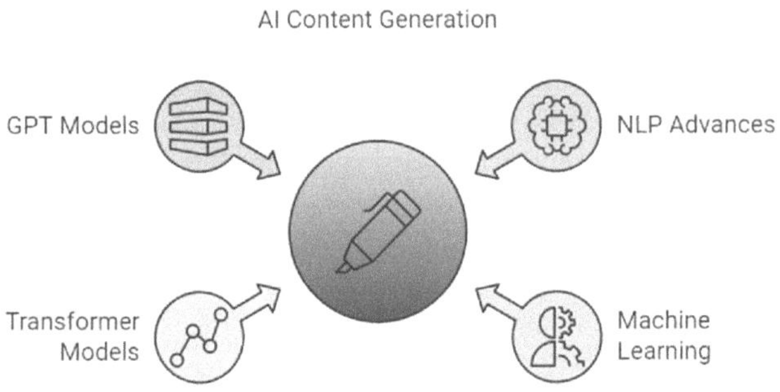

FIGURE 20.2 AI Content Generation.

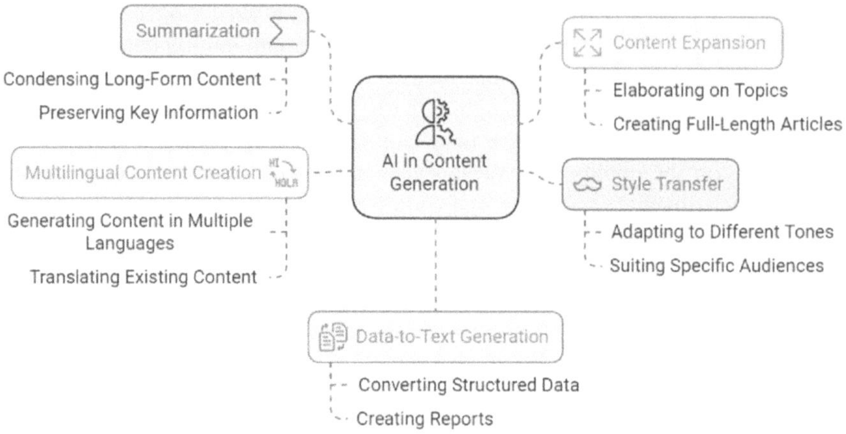

FIGURE 20.3 AI in Content Generation.

corpora of text and are able to generate coherent content that fits contextually in many topics and in numerous styles (Brown et al., 2020) [11].

AI applications in content generation go far beyond the simple production of text. Advanced systems can now do the following: Figure 20.3.

1. Summarization: The process of summarizing long content into concise summaries while maintaining the essential information in the content of Liu & Lapata [12].
2. Content Creation: It involves expanding given topics or outlines into full-fledged articles or reports, as in Zellers et al. (2019) [13].
3. Style Transfer: It is the modification according to various tones or writing styles that best suit the target audiences or purposes (Jin et al., 2020) [14].
4. Content Creation in Multiple Languages: The generation of content in different languages or translating existing content while keeping context and subtlety (Johnson et al., 2017) [15].
5. Data-to-Text Generation: This generation involves the translation of structured data into natural language narratives and hence helps in developing reports or even news articles from raw data [16].

These capabilities have tremendous implications for the workflow of content creation in media organizations. AI-driven tools can contribute to human writers through ideas for drafts, suggestions for improvement, or even research tasks. This also brings up critical questions about the role of human creativity and the potential for misinformation created by AI.

Recent efforts have gone into making AI-generated content both more controllable and interpretable. Techniques such as prompt engineering and fine-tuning allow for more precise control over the output of language models, thus enabling content creators to guide the AI towards desired outcomes more effectively (Keskar et al., 2019) [17, 18].

Despite these developments, AI-generated content still grapples with sustaining coherence over long periods, ensuring factually correct content, and capturing nuances that only human writers bring to bear on complex topics. Indeed, these are challenges that in general fall within the domain of active research related to the generation of natural language.

20.3.3 Digital Forensics in the Context of the Information Verification

While digital forensics is traditionally associated with cybercrime investigations, a new and critical application of digital forensics has been found in the realm of information verification. In a world where misinformation and disinformation continue to pose really insidious challenges, techniques of digital forensics have become an important arsenal in the search for truth in the digital age [19].

This, therefore, is the basic definition that can be named, where the method of digital forensics in information verification involves the approach of scientific methodology to digital evidence to ascertain the authenticity, integrity, and origin of the digital content. A number of ancillary techniques and technologies regarding this are developed for addressing specific aspects of content verification.

Image and video analysis is one of the most important branches involved in digital forensics that deal with such materials. Since manipulated visual content nowadays has become more and more impressive, forensic analysts use a range of techniques for finding evidence of manipulation. The techniques include (Figure 20.4):

1. ELA: This technique examines the compression levels within an image to identify areas that may have been modified [20].

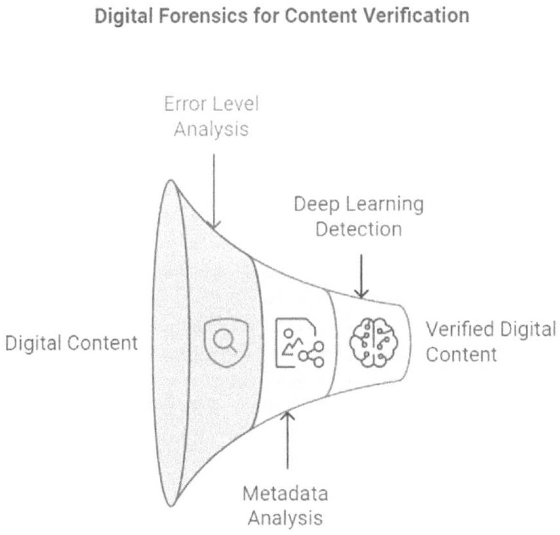

FIGURE 20.4 Content Verification Using Digital Forensics.

2. Metadata Analysis: The EXIF metadata attached to digital images provides information on the capturing device, date and time of capture, possible camera settings, and post-processing of the image (Farid, 2009) [21].
3. Detection Based on Deep Learning: Recent developments in machine learning have made neural networks capable of finding out sophisticated image manipulations; the ones created by the AI-powered tool known as DeepFakes are representative examples of this technology (Rossler et al., 2019) [22].

Digital forensics techniques have evolved to handle such challenges in the realm of text analysis. These methods include:

1. Stylometry: doing statistical analysis of writing style for authorship attribution or to highlight anomalies which could indicate machine-generated text (Stamatatos, 2009) [23].
2. "Facts Extraction vs NLP": Extracting explicit factual claims within texts by applying advanced NLP techniques and cross-checking these against trusted knowledge bases is done (Hassan et al., 2017) [24].
3. Provenance Tracking: methods of tracing the origin and dissemination of information on digital platforms to find sources of misinforming [25].

The use of blockchain in digital forensics opens promising vistas on capabilities for content verification. Blockchain allows the creation of an immutable record of creation and modification of any content; as such, it offers a transparent and tamper-proof chain of custody for digital assets [26].

However, even in these modern days, digital forensics linked to information verification faces several challenges. These include the continuous race between the bad actors taking advantage of AI-powered content generation and technologists who

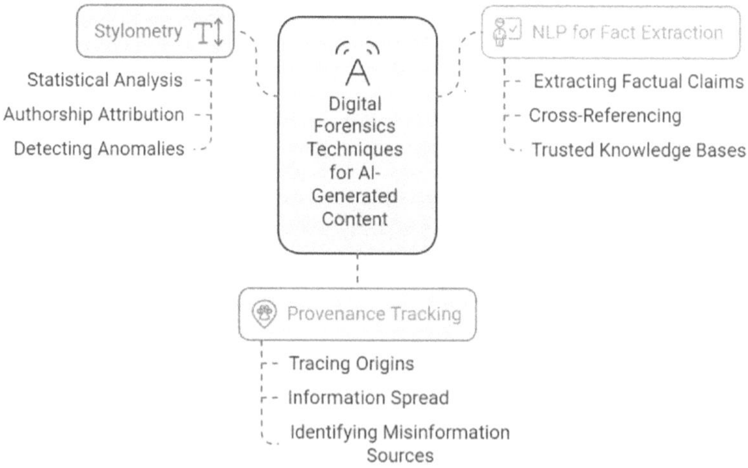

FIGURE 20.5 Digital Forensics Techniques for AI-Generated Content.

come up with methods for its detection, and the volume of digital content produced today presents significant scalability challenges to forensic analysis.

20.3.4 Ethical Considerations around AI Use in Content Creation

AI integrated into content creation has created a serious ethical debate about authorship, creativity, and responsibility in the new digital landscape. To the extent that these systems can produce plausible humanlike text, images, and even video, ethical considerations about the role and function of AI systems have risen to the top of academic and public debate. Figure 20.6.

One of the most critical ethical considerations is that AI-generated content can be used to spread misinformation or disinformation with unprecedented scale. The capability of AI systems to produce great volumes of coherent, seemingly credible content calls into question the integrity of the online information ecosystem. This is furthered by the fact that AI-generated text can be designed to manipulate cognitive biases and emotional triggers, potentially amplifying societal divisions and undermining democratic discourse.

Another important ethics-related issue is that of transparency and disclosure. There is much debate on whether AI-generated content needs to be transparently labeled as such, and if so, exactly how these disclosures may be made. While advocates believe that users have the right to understand where content they are consuming is derived, others argue that such labeling may unfairly stigmatize what really can be equal in quality or higher, as opposed to content created by humans (Diakopoulos, 2019) [27].

Currently, both the issue of authorship and those surrounding intellectual property rights as it pertains to AI-generated content have proven to be quite complex

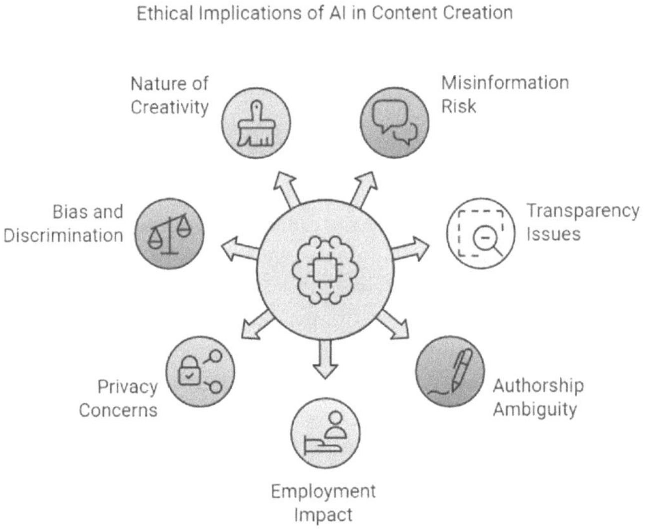

FIGURE 20.6 Ethical Implications of AI in Content Creation.

and remain largely unresolved. Again, there is a question of who owns the rights to AI-generated work: the actual developer of the AI system, the user who prompted this system, or even the AI itself. This has serious implications for copyright law in general and the creative industries (Boyden, 2016) [28].

The other ethical implication is the misemployment of humans in the creative fields that AI content generation may cause. While AI tools enhance human creativity and productivity, there is fear that in the long run, this will result in human writers, graphic artists, and other creative content developers losing their jobs. It calls into question some very basic policy issues in the future of work and the value of human creativity in an AI-dominated landscape (Acemoglu & Restrepo, 2018) [29].

Privacy issues also arise, especially concerning the data on which AI models are trained. Large language models usually have enormous text corpora on which they are trained, containing private or sensitive information. Such data are used without explicit consent, and the ethics in this regard are still debated (Bender et al., 2021) [30].

One of the big ethical issues is the fact that AI-generated content bears the potential for bias and discrimination. Due to the fact that many biases are reflected in training data, AI systems can unintentionally continue or amplify harmful biases in society by generating such content that will marginalize or misrepresent certain groups. This always calls for continued efforts towards increasing diversity in their training data and, therefore, the building of more inclusive AI systems (Mehrabi et al., 2021) [31].

Finally, the use of AI for the creation of content raises very basic questions about the nature of creativity and the value of human expression. As systems of AI develop increasingly sophisticated and emotionally resonant content, society will have to work out what it means for something to be creative, and what part human intuition and experience play in the making of meaningful art and literature (du Sautoy, 2019) [32]. While AI-driven content creation develops further, ethical considerations would be at the forefront of development and implementation. It calls for constant interaction between technologists and ethicists, policymakers, and the public so benefits arising from the utilization of AI in content creation are reaped while harm is possibly mitigated and values of human creativity and authenticity are preserved.

20.4 AI-DRIVEN SEO AND CONTENT OPTIMIZATION

AI-driven SEO and content optimization are fields of research and application within computer science focused on the automated generation of linguistic content by computer systems. Algorithms and language models are put to work by this technology in producing text that can span from the simple automation of repetitive tasks to the creation of highly complex and contextually appropriate content. In this framework, the thesis focuses on automatic text generation, putting particular emphasis on the qualitative and relevant aspects of the content for SEO-oriented uses.

Web content optimization refers to the process of improving websites' visibility through search engines. Online visibility has emerged as one of the top agendas in contemporary business, as it directly affects business opportunities. Content optimization is a crucial activity in the process since search engines evaluate the quality and relevance of a webpage's content before ranking it in the list of search results.

20.4.1 Current Approaches to AI-Driven Content Creation

With continuous development in content generation, AI has ushered in several sophisticated approaches to automating text creation.

These techniques achieve this using various methods, some of which use NLP, while others involve deep learning models. It is because of these techniques that the generated texts have become not only coherent but also contextually relevant. The following section describes some state-of-the-art methodologies practiced in AI-driven content creation and explains their relative strengths and applications.

There are several approaches to automatic text generation, which involve the following methods (Figure 20.7):

- Rules and Models: In this approach, texts are generated using linguistic rules and rule templates according to a predefined set of criteria. This approach is often used to generate texts with fixed structures.
- Statistical Approaches: These are generally based on the statistical analysis of large amounts of already existing texts to generate new texts. This can be done because the language model is trained on data and is, hence, capable of producing more variable texts.

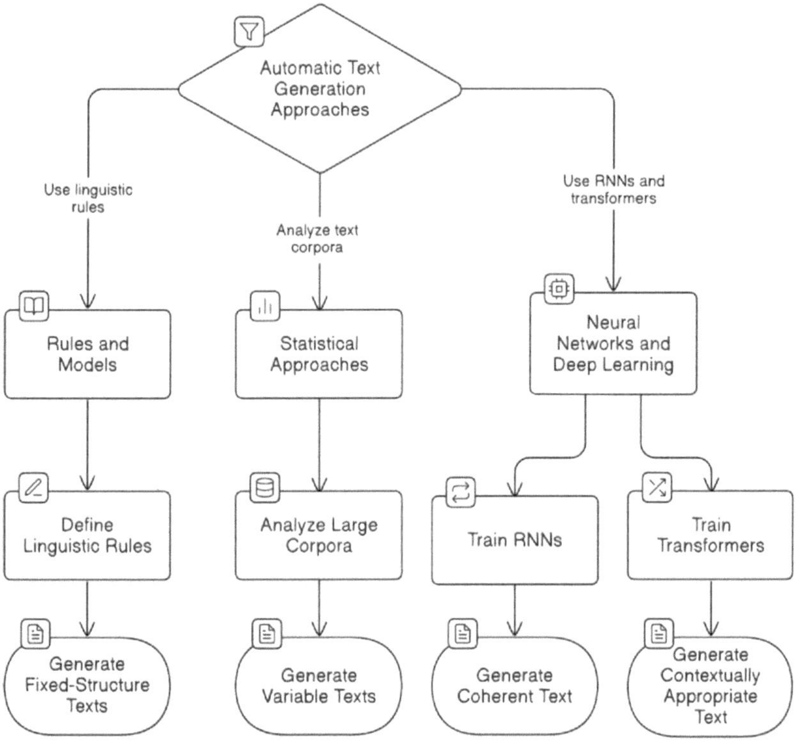

FIGURE 20.7 Automatic Text Generation Approaches.

- Neural Networks and Deep Learning: With paramount importance, neural networks, especially incorporating RNNs and transformer neural networks, have great potential in automatic text generation. These models learn from data and can produce highly coherent texts with great contextual appropriateness.

Approaches toward AI-driven content generation vary in complexity and applicability: Rules and statistics rule for simpler tasks, while neural networks represent the cutting edge in the field, allowing customization and coherence. In any case, the choice among the approaches depends on the peculiarities of the application and on the trade-off between content quality and human management capacity. The three approaches are examined in detail hereafter.

20.4.1.1 Rules and Models

Rule-based approaches are among the oldest ways of text generation. Generally speaking, they construct sentences by using specific grammatical and syntactic structures in accordance with predefined linguistic rules. Approaches based on rules are fully suitable for the creation of a text that presupposes the repetitive and predictable formats, such as business reports, standardized forms, or system messages.

Practical Examples:

- Business Email Templates: Automatic e-mail responses can be achieved using a rules-based system in a business context. As such, one such template would provide an automatic generation of a response to a request for support:
  - Inputs: "Support request for the technical problem."
  - OutPut: "Dear [Customer Name], we got your request regarding [Problem Description]. One of our operators will contact you within 24 hours in order to help you."
- Report Generation: The software might generate financial reports by a predefined structure, automatically filling in new data within a set of standardized sentences. For example, "[Month]'s revenue for the month was [Value] euros, an increase of [Percentage]% compared to the previous month."

These systems are relatively easy to implement, but they are not flexible at all. They can't handle complex contexts or sudden changes in user needs, which in turn further limits their application for creative content generation. Because of that, they are less fit for writing creative or dynamic content with SEO in their focus.

20.4.1.2 Statistical Methods

Approaches to generating text statistically are performed by analyzing a huge dataset of existing texts. They employ techniques, including Markov models and n-grams, in analyzing the probability of the occurrence of one word after another in every sentence. These models look at the regularity and sequence of words to come up with new texts that closely resemble the training data.

Practical Examples:

- n-gram Models: A bigram model, where $n = 2$, could calculate the chance of a subsequent word based on the one before it. For instance, if it had been trained on a sports news corpus, here are example sentences it could generate:
  - Input: "The team has"
  - Predicted Output: "won the match" or "lost the match,"

depending on how frequent these sentences turn up in the training dataset.

- Text Suggestions: Statistical methods may be employed to make sentence completions. For example, if you type "The real estate market," the system may suggest "is growing" if this phrase is common in the training dataset.

This makes these models also tend to reproduce the trends in the data they get trained on. This could make them less creative and innovative, since they tend to repeat some already existing patterns. They also don't capture long-term context that can lead to inconsistent results.

20.4.1.3 Neural Networks and Deep Learning

Neural networks represent a real revolution in the field of automatic text generation, first of all, with deep learning models like RNNs and transformers—high-powered models such as GPT. These models can comprehend and generate texts by keeping track of short- and long-term memory, which makes them especially adapted to handle such complex tasks as SEO content generation, machine translation, and creative writing.

The Practical Examples:

- Genius GPT: GPT is generatively pre-trained transformers that have learned the relationships between words expressed in vast amounts of text data. The output of these models is surprisingly like something written by a human and may change in style and topic.
  - Input: "Write an article on the importance of environmental sustainability."
  - Output: "The topic of environmental sustainability is becoming highly important in our society. By following sustainable practices, it will not only preserve our planet . . .".
- Product Description Generation: The company would be able to use a GPT template to create SEO-optimized product descriptions. Example:
  - Input: "Organic coffee, 500g, intense aroma."
  - Output: "Find our 500g organic coffee with an intense aroma, and high quality. For those seeking a full flavor."

Deep learning models require a lot of data and computational resources; hence, they can be expensive to train. They also sometimes generate contents that appear to be plausible but can contain factual errors; therefore, they need human reviews. Added to that, complex algorithms have low interpretability, making the 'how' and 'why' about their generation difficult to understand.

20.4.2 Comparison between Approaches

Table 20.1 depicts graphically concepts treated in the preceding paragraphs. It compares, for artificial intelligence, three approaches regarding content generation: rules and models, statistical approaches, and neural networks with deep learning. Each method is analyzed for advantages and disadvantages, implementation complexity, hardware, and human resources requirements, its effectiveness and execution times. This representation gives you a synthetic and comparative view of the main characteristics of each approach.

TABLE 20.1
Comparison of Approaches to Content Generation Using Artificial Intelligence

Method/ Approach	Advantages	Disadvantages	Hardware Requirements	Human Resources Requirements	Effectiveness	Times
Rules and Models difficulty: low	Simple to implement, suitable for repetitive and structured texts	Lack of flexibility, not suitable for complex or creative content	Standard computer, no need for GPU; minimum RAM of 4–8 GB	1–2 people (developer and editor)	Average for specific tasks	Short
Statistical Approaches difficulty: medium	Able to generate variable content, suitable for sentence completions and linguistic patterns	Tends to repeat patterns, can produce inconsistent texts over the long term	Computer with advanced CPU; RAM of 8–16 GB	2–3 people (data scientist, editor)	Decent for short texts	Medium
Neural Networks and Deep Learning difficulty: high	High coherence and ability to adapt to the context, suitable for complex contents such as SEO and creative texts	Requires large amounts of data and computational resources, possibility of factual errors	Server with high performance GPU (e.g. NVIDIA Tesla or A100); RAM of 32–64 GB; SSD storage for large data loads	3–5 people (data scientist, ML engineer, editor)	High for complex content	Long for training

20.5 ANALYSIS BASED ON PRACTICAL EXPERIENCE

Figure 20.8 gives an overview of the end-to-end process of the automated form submission system. Users fill up the form and request its submission through the CMS. The latter fetches templates and validates the input data with the assistance of the server application on the backend. On the back, this communicates with a keyword verification service and generative language models like Chat-GPT. It confirms that data has been routed to the CMS and also optionally forwarded as a notification email to the user via an email forwarding server. The system is designed with modularity in terms of integration and parallel processing for efficiency and scalability.

Figure 20.9 presents a diagram on the overall workflow of the creation and management system for contents through forms and artificial intelligence services, like ChatGPT. The project represents practical experience.

The process flow represented has been described as follows (Figure 20.9):

1. User: A user initiates this process by filling out a form in Content Management Systems and then submits it for processing.
2. Content Management System (CMS):
   - The CMS receives the form filled out by the user.
   - After receiving the form, it sends it to Server Application for processing.
3. Server Application: The Server Application forms the core of all architecture and manages a host of services required to process the request. The main functions of the Server Application are:
   - Template Management: The Server Application interacts with a database to pull or administer templates; the application performs the standard Create, Read, Update, Delete operations on such templates.

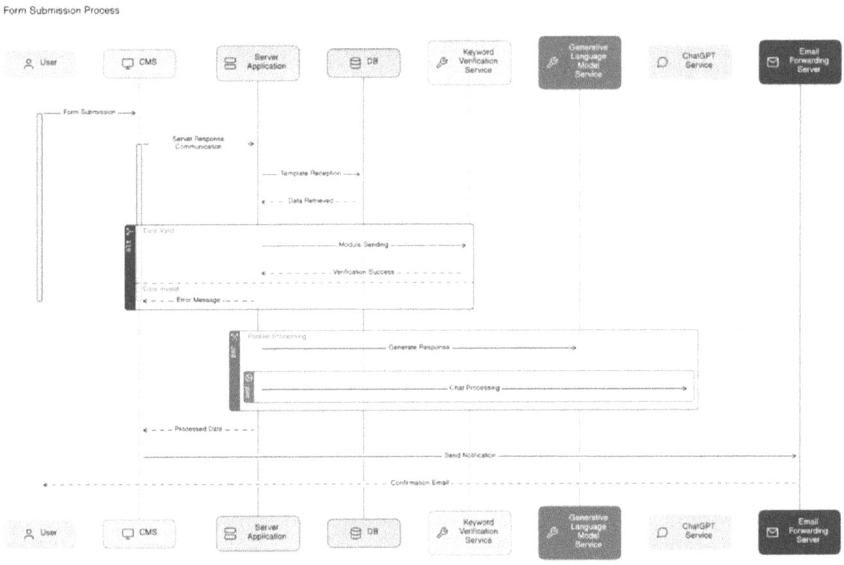

FIGURE 20.8 Automated Form Submission and Processing Workflow.

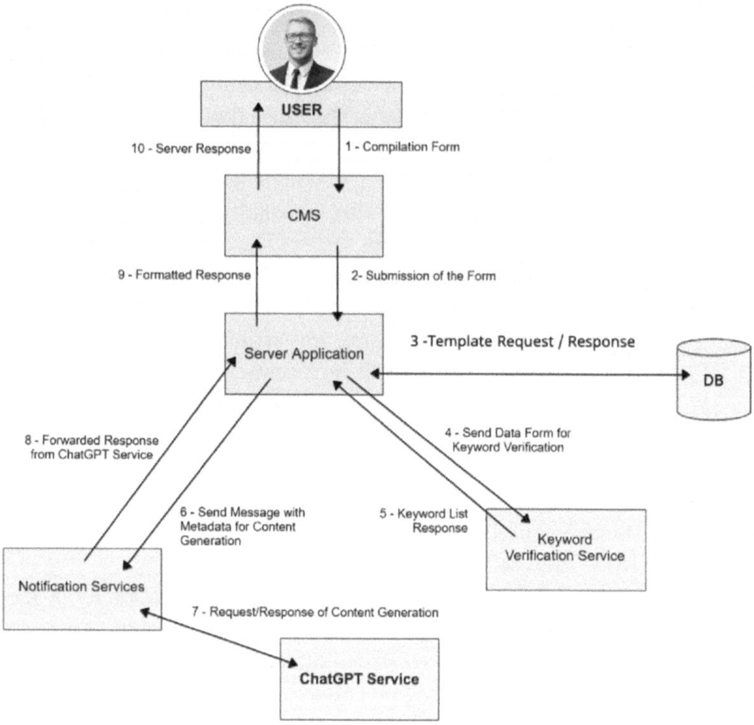

FIGURE 20.9 Workflow of Content Generation and Management System Based on Forms and Artificial Intelligence Services.

- Keyword Verification:
    - The Web Application requests the Keyword Verification Service to verify particular keywords in the content.
    - The Keyword Verification Service processes the request and sends a response back to the Server Application.
- Calling the Generative Language Model Service (ChatGPT):
    - The Server Application initiates the call to the ChatGPT Service with a request for generating one based on the contents of the form filled out by the user.
    - The response is generated by the ChatGPT Service and returned to the Server Application.
- Sending the Response to the Email Forwarding Server: When the response from ChatGPT Service has been received, the Server Application forwards the response to the Email Forwarding Server for subsequent actions of forwarding.

4. Email Forwarding Server:
    - Response from the ChatGPT Service is sent to the email of the user or his friend/recipient through the e-mail forwarding system.

5. Response to the User:
    - Finally, the response reaches the CMS through the Server Application, which again presents that response in front of the user to complete the interaction cycle.

Process Summary:

- The user submits the form via CMS.
- The CMS forwards the form to the Server Application.
- With which the Server Application interacts:
    - and DB for template management;
    - and Keyword Verification Service to check specific keywords;
    - and ChatGPT Service to generate the requested content.
- The response generated is passed to the user through CMS and, where applicable, via the Email Forwarding Server.

This will be a system for automated, personalized responses and content created from user input; it will make use of keyword testing services coupled with sophisticated language models to ensure the content is of the highest quality and relevance. The infrastructure also allows you to manage templates and facilitate feedback via email, thus making the communication process efficient and personalized.

20.6 ANALYSIS OF MAIN TECHNIQUES OF NATURAL LANGUAGE PROCESSING—NLP

NLP stands for natural language processing, which is a subfield of artificial intelligence dealing with giving computers the ability to understand and manipulate human language. Natural-language-processing methods can be divided into two broad categories:

- Language analysis techniques, which deal with understanding the meaning of the text;
- Language generation techniques, which deal with producing text.

The basics of NLP are theoretical and algorithmic, thus providing a way to understand and generate human languages. Key notions include grammatical analysis, part-of-speech tagging, extraction of entities, sentiment analysis, and natural language generation.

The techniques of language analysis can be further decomposed into three subcategories:

1. Text segmentation can be assessed as the division process of text into smaller pieces such as words, sentences, or paragraphs.
2. Grammatical tagging consists in assigning each unit of text its grammatical category: noun, verb, adjective, etc.
3. Semantic analysis, which would involve determining the meaning of words and sentences.

These can further be divided into two categories in the light of techniques adapted for language generation:

- Machine translation, which involves translating text from one language to another.
- Text Synthesis: This may include generating text from non-textual data, like numerical data or tables.

NLP is a fast-growing field, and newer work is being pursued every day. Its applications in various fields have encouraged the development of more and more NLP techniques to make computers more capable of understanding human languages and interact using natural language.

20.6.1 Framework of NLP

Among the different frameworks which can be used to develop an automatic text generation system, there are (Figure 20.10):

- NLTK: The NLTK is an open-source framework for natural language processing. It is among the most popular frameworks and is active, being used by researchers and developers worldwide. Depending on the goals of the developer, NLTK offers a number of libraries and tools for natural language processing that include:
  - Text Processing: Among the functionality with regard to text analysis, it includes tokenization, lemmatization, stemming.
  - Natural Language: This offers the facility to perform natural language processing with NLTK, a library used for translation, natural language understanding, and natural language generation.
  - Machine Learning: NLTK also performs some tasks of training and testing machine learning models on natural languages.

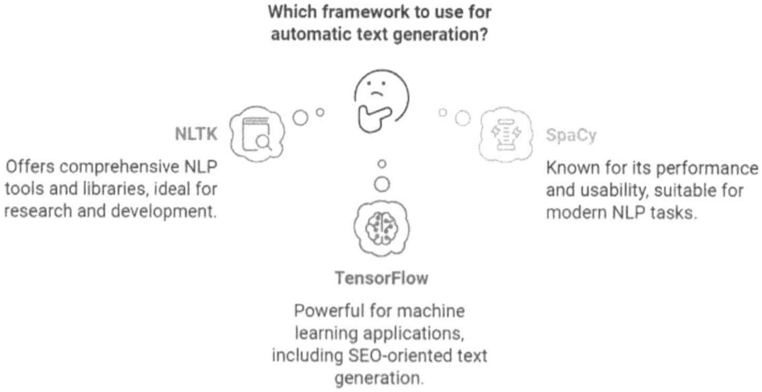

FIGURE 20.10 Frameworks for Automatic Text Generation.

- SpaCy: SpaCy is an open-source framework for natural language processing. It is a relatively new framework, but because of its impressive performance and usability, it already enjoys popularity. Some of the libraries and other tools that SpaCy provides for NLP include:
    - Text Processing: SpaCy can tokenize text, lemmatize and stem it.
    - Natural Language Processing: SpaCy supports a range of functionalities in the field of NLP, including translation, natural language understanding, and natural language generation.
    - Machine Learning: With SpaCy, one can train or test natural language machine learning models.
- TensorFlow: TensorFlow is an open-source framework for machine learning. It is powerful and flexible, therefore finding applications in a variety of uses, which also include SEO-oriented text generation. TensorFlow provides a number of libraries and other tools that make it easy to learn and work with machine learning. These include:
    - Machine Learning Models: TensorFlow has a range of pre-trained machine learning models which one could use for SEO-oriented text generation.
    - Various Machine Learning Algorithms Available: TensorFlow gives you a collection of machine learning algorithms that come in handy for generating SEO-oriented text.
    - In Development Tools: TensorFlow has a set of development tools that can be used for text generation with an approach to SEO.

TensorFlow can be used to generate texts oriented on SEO. For example, it can be used in the following tasks:

- Generate texts that include your target keywords;
- Generate texts that are relevant to the website content;
- Produce readable texts that make sense.

The selection of the most appropriate NLP framework for generating texts oriented on SEO will depend on many criteria, including performance requirements; functionality requirements; developer knowledge and skills. These frameworks allow a set of libraries and tools that can be utilized in the development of automatic text generation systems.

20.6.2 Generative Language Models

A generative language model is a statistical model that can use text generation. The generative language models are trained on a text dataset and are capable of learning relations between words and sentences.

Such generative language models can be used in a number of ways, including but not restricted to the following.

- Creative Text Generation: The generative language model can be used to provide creative text, for example, poems, stories, code, scripts, and so on.
- Translation: It can translate text from one language into another with the help of a generative language model.

- Summary: Generative language models can be used to summarize text in a concise and informative way.
- Answering Questions: Generative language models can be used to answer questions in an informative way.

Some examples of the newest generative language models are (Figure 20.11):

- Calls LLaMA: Large Language Model Meta AI. The Meta Company, previously known as Facebook AI, developed a family of language models, LLaMA, which are supposed to work much more efficiently when smaller in size compared to the classic large models. Improved for accuracy, coherence of generated texts, LLaMA 2, which was released in 2023, positioned itself among the most modern models used both for research and practical applications.
- GPT-4: Developed by OpenAI, GPT-4 is an improvement upon its forerunner, GPT-3, because of its more enhanced ability in generating natural language. It understands texts with a high degree of coherence and better answers to complex questions, therefore providing more context to its output. Applications using GPT-4 range widely, including but not limited to creating SEO content, all the way to computer-aided programming.

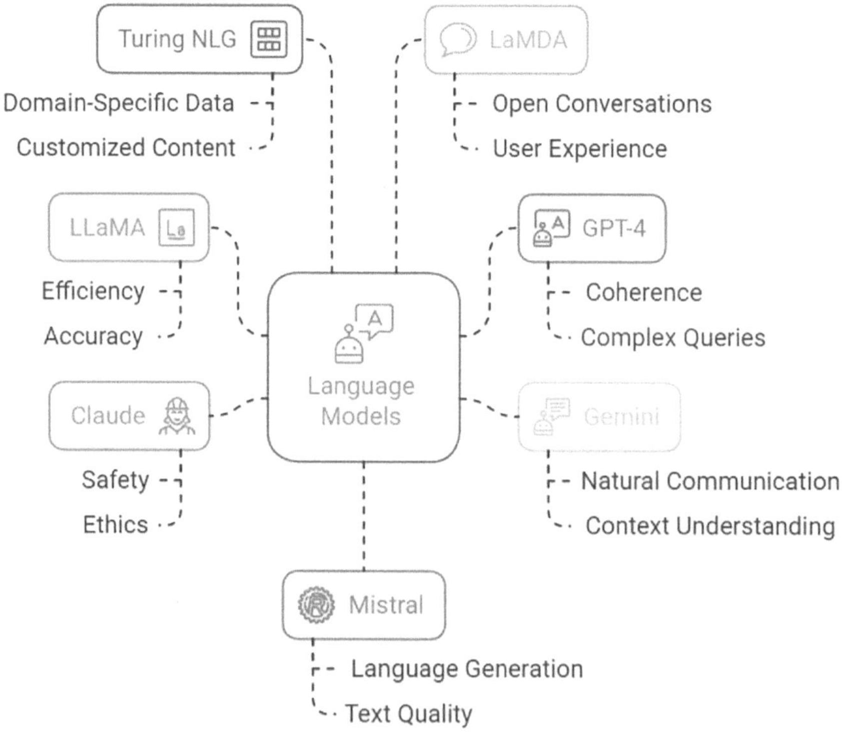

FIGURE 20.11 Examples of the Latest Generative Language Models.

- Gemini (ex-Bard): This is the inner evolution of the Bard model. Google AI designed it to be able to communicate with the user in a much more natural way. With fundamental and deep improvements in the ability both to communicate and understand the context, the model is suitable for different applications, from chatbots right up to sophisticated search engines.
- Claude: Developed by Anthropic, Claude places much emphasis on safety and ethics in AI-related studies. Claude would wish to answer safely and robustly, placing much emphasis on mitigating identity biases, which tend to provide more controlled and reliable responses.
- Turing NLG: Developed at Microsoft, Turing NLG today is one of the more powerful large language models in the market. This is even though it is no longer among the latest. With the capability of ingesting domain-specific data and the generation of customized content, Turing NLG is a very good option for text generation in business issues.
- LaMDA: A Language Model for Dialogue Applications is designed by Google AI to have conversations. It is specially characterized to manage conversations that are open and natural. It is designed to smoothly respond to a wide variety of questions and topics, improving the user experience in chatbots and autoresponder systems.
- Mistral: This rising model got famous due to its deeply capable open-source alternative. While optimizing language generation, it may sacrifice some text quality but remains competitive among newly developed AI models.

With language models improving day by day, new opportunities come to light in the industry for better quality and higher accuracy of the generated events. Models like LLaMA 2 and Gemini are being continuously improved toward achieving higher levels of understanding and interacting with the user. Ethics, on the other hand, considered in models such as Claude show a rising reaction toward using AI responsibly.

20.7 DIGITAL FORENSICS TECHNIQUES FOR CONTENT AUTHENTICITY

Convergence in technologies between artificial intelligence and creative content has thereby drastically changed the digital media landscape today, presenting unparalleled challenges in the processes of verification and authentication. Digital forensics, emerging from its traditional role in cybercrime investigation, is now a pivotal discipline in sustaining content integrity across all digital platforms. This section presents an in-depth review of state-of-the-art forensic methodologies and their uses within media environments today, with a particular focus on identification techniques for artificially intelligent and algorithmically manipulated content.

20.7.1 Overview: Content Verification and Digital Forensics

Digital forensics in content verification represent an advanced junction of computer science, data analytics, and methodology of investigation. In the last years, this has passed through serious changes impelled by the need to counteract greater complexities associated with manipulations of digital content. Modern approaches to forensic resolutions have moved from basic metadata checks via multistep verification systems with the integration of machine learning and distributed ledger technologies.

Modern content verification makes use of a multi-dimensional forensic framework for the checking of digital content integrity. At the center of such a framework, automated analysis tools integrate with human expertise overseers to complete a system capable of detecting overt manipulations to subtle changes that might otherwise remain unnoticed. Source attribution has also evolved from simple device fingerprinting into more sophisticated behavioral analysis and recognition of patterns of creation.

In a similar vein, integrity verification mechanisms also evolve—from traditional hash-based methods to more dynamic ones. Modern systems increasingly rely on continuous monitoring and real-time verification thanks to recent progress in blockchain technology and distributed verification networks. This dynamic verification definitely stands in contrast to the static analysis methods that were supposed to work out-of-the-box for traditional content distribution patterns.

Recent forensic workflows have stressed scalability and automation without losing analytical rigor. Modern forensic systems process large swathes of content in near real-time while maintaining high accuracy levels. This requires developing adaptive analysis frameworks that adjust the level of scrutiny based on content type, distribution context, and risk assessment.

20.7.2 Image and Video Analysis Techniques

Meanwhile, manipulation methods are improving rapidly, and accordingly, their sophistication grows. Modern image and video forensics are based on the synergistic combination of traditional pixel-level analysis with advanced machine learning techniques. The evolution has become particularly crucial with regard to challenges that originate from AI-generated and deeply manipulated content.

Error Level Analysis (ELA) has evolved significantly from its origins in JPEG compression analysis. Contemporary implementations incorporate advanced statistical models that can identify subtle inconsistencies in content creation patterns. These enhanced techniques have proven particularly effective in detecting AI-generated images, where traditional compression artifacts may be absent but other statistical anomalies become apparent under sophisticated analysis.

Similar is the case with metadata analysis, which has moved well away from performing EXIF data analyses. Newer methods take into account the entire digital ecosystem in which the creation and distribution of the content take place, using patterns in device signatures, processing histories, and pathways of distribution. This holistic approach has paid very good dividends, particularly in the revealing of sophisticated manipulation attempts that would retain technical metadata integrity while changing the content.

Integration of deep learning techniques has transformed video forensics, especially on the issue of synthetic media detection. Most modern systems do temporal consistency checking across different dimensions such as motion pattern, lighting conditions, and physical behavior models. This multi-dimensionality has proved strong in identifying sophisticated DeepFake content with more than 95% detection rate in controlled studies.

Recent advances in multi-modal analysis have further increased forensic capabilities. While state-of-the-art systems analyze at the same time visual, audio, and contextual aspects, they can discover incompatibilities that might be imperceptible within a single modality in isolation. This has proved particularly successful in the identification of sophisticated manipulations that are consistent within individual channels but differ in cross-modal relationships.

The integration of blockchain technology presents new dimensions for content authentication. Modern blockchain-based systems go further than mere timestamping, creating extensive audit trails that trace content from creation through distribution. This has especially proven very helpful in establishing content provenance in professional media environments where maintaining authenticity is paramount in building public trust.

These advanced techniques have shown their effectiveness through a number of practical applications, such as large news agencies that have put into practical use some multi-modal analysis systems, which permit verification of the authenticity of content in near real-time, reducing the risk of manipulated media distribution. Conversely, on social media too, sophisticated forensic systems have been deployed that are able to keep track of potentially manipulated content, flagging it before it reaches a wider audience.

20.7.3 Text Analysis and Authorship Attribution Methods

The evolution of digital forensics in terms of text analysis recently gained unforeseen momentum with the appearance of sophisticated language models and AI content. Modern forensic text analysis far exceeds the limits of traditional stylometry, including advanced linguistic analysis, semantic modeling, and recognition of behavioral patterns. Such multivariate analysis now becomes a de facto principle for distinguishing between human-generated and AI-generated content.

Modern systems of authorship attribution use a multitude of sophisticated techniques of computational linguistic analysis based on various textual dimensions. The text is examined not only for the surface stylistic features but also for deep semantic structures, cognitive patterns, and contextual relationships within its framework. It has allowed the identification of those subtle linguistic patterns that often distinguish human writing from AI-generated content because of the integration of neural language models in this regard.

In fact, semantic coherence analysis has now become such a powerful tool in content verification. Modern systems can check the logical consistency and contextual appropriateness of text over long passages, thus finding discontinuities that may prove the generation or manipulation of certain content is artificial. That has particularly proved effective in the detection of the content created by large language models, which may sustain local coherence but usually fails regarding general contextual coherence.

Further development of cross-modal contextual analysis further advanced the text verification capabilities. The modern systems can assess textual content against related media, metadata, and external references, forming a holistic verification framework considering the entire content ecosystem. Indeed, this holistic approach has significantly improved the precision in the assessments of authenticity, especially for intricate multimedia content.

20.7.4 Blockchain- and Distributed Ledger Technology-Based Content Provenance

It has gone from simple applications of mere timestamping to sophisticated systems for tracking provenance. Advanced blockchains will create immutable audit trails that document content creation, modification, and distribution processes [33]. This technological framework is increasingly becoming useful in professional media contexts where the establishment and maintenance of authenticity of content are highly valued.

Distributed ledger technologies allowed the construction of decentralized verification networks that are capable of content authentication across various platforms and jurisdictions. These systems utilize consensus mechanisms within a trusted verification framework devoid of any central authorities. It has further been enhanced by the integration of smart contracts that automate the verification processes, learning from any changing pattern in the same context of the content and its distribution methods.

Recent blockchain scalability advances have overcome most of the limitations that were found in the early versions of the Distributed Content Verification systems [34, 35]. The modern versions can actually handle a high throughput of content transactions with high verification accuracy and fast response time. Specialized content-focused blockchain protocols further improved their efficiency to offer real-time verification even for streaming media and dynamic content.

The integration of zero-knowledge proofs and other privacy-preserving technologies has enhanced the suitability of blockchain-based verification systems for broader adoption.

This way, content creators can keep their confidentiality while providing verifiable authenticity proofs. The capability to do so has proved very useful in scenarios that deal with sensitive or proprietary content (Table 20.2).

20.8 PROPOSED FRAMEWORK: INTEGRATED AI-DRIVEN CONTENT OPTIMIZATION WITH DIGITAL FORENSICS

The increasing sophistication of content manipulation techniques and the growing demand for automated content optimization create a compelling need for integrated systems that can ensure both content effectiveness and authenticity. This section presents a novel framework that seamlessly combines AI-driven content optimization capabilities with robust digital forensics methods, creating a comprehensive solution for modern content management challenges. The proposed architecture addresses the critical balance between content optimization and integrity verification while maintaining scalability and operational efficiency.

TABLE 20.2
Summary Analysis: Technological Comparisons and Recommendations

Technology Category	Key Advantages	Current Limitations	Recommended Applications	Future Development Priorities
Image/Video Analysis	- High accuracy in manipulation detection - Real-time processing capability - Multi-modal analysis support	- Computational intensity - False positives with novel AI techniques	- News media verification - Legal evidence processing - Social media monitoring	- Enhanced GAN detection - Reduced computational requirements - Improved real-time performance
Text Analysis	- Effective stylometry - Deep semantic understanding - Cross-reference capability	- Language dependency - Context sensitivity - Model-specific limitations	- Academic integrity - Journalism - Legal documentation	- Multi-language support - Context-aware analysis - Improved AI detection
Blockchain Systems	- Immutable record keeping - Decentralized verification - Automated processing	- Scalability challenges - Implementation complexity - Resource requirements	- Content licensing - Media archives - Professional publishing	- Enhanced scalability - Reduced energy consumption - Simplified implementation
Multi-Modal Integration	- Comprehensive verification - High accuracy rates - Adaptive analysis	- System complexity - Integration challenges - Resource intensity	- Broadcast media - Social platforms - Security systems	- Improved integration - Enhanced automation - Reduced complexity

20.8.1 System Architecture

The proposed framework employs a microservices-based architecture organized into distinct layers, each handling specific aspects of content processing and verification. This modular approach ensures system flexibility, scalability, and the ability to evolve individual components without affecting the entire system.

20.8.1.1 Core Architectural Components

The system architecture comprises four primary layers (Figure 20.12):

1. Content Processing Layer.
    - Handles initial content ingestion and preprocessing;
    - Implements content classification and routing logic;
    - Manages content metadata extraction and enrichment;
    - Provides format conversion and standardization services.
2. AI Optimization Layer.
    - Executes content optimization algorithms;
    - Implements SEO enhancement processes;

- Manages keyword analysis and optimization;
- Provides readability and engagement optimization.

3. Forensic Verification Layer.
   - Performs real-time content authenticity verification;
   - Implements manipulation detection algorithms;
   - Manages provenance tracking and verification;
   - Provides audit trail generation and management.
4. Integration and Orchestration Layer.
   - Coordinates workflow between system components;
   - Manages system state and transaction integrity;
   - Implements security and access control;
   - Provides API management and external integration services.

Figure 20.12 shows the key architectural components making up the integrated content optimization and verification system. An implementation should be concerned with separation of concerns, keeping strong interaction pathways between layers. IntegrationLayer is the major orchestrator so as to manage workflows between the specialized processing components. The presence of BlockchainService brings cogently into view that this system commits indeed to immutable records of verification and establishing content provenance to rely on.

Figure 20.13 outlines the sophisticated parallel processing of the implementation involved in optimizing and verifying the content. The key capability here is the execution of parallel processes for the system to optimize and verify, reducing latency

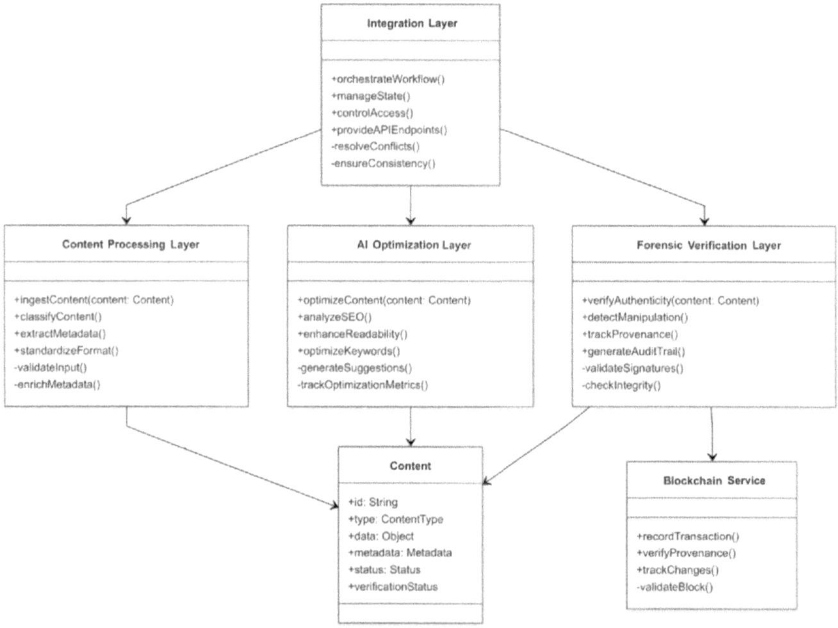

FIGURE 20.12 Core System Architecture Components Diagram.

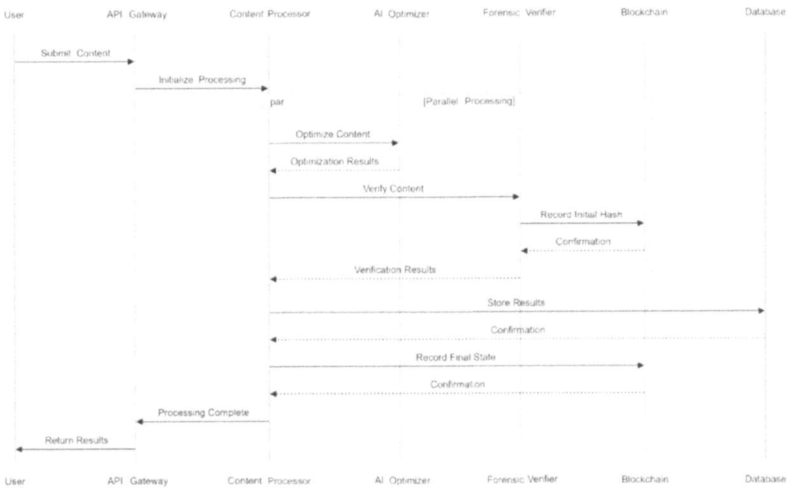

FIGURE 20.13 Content Processing Pipeline Sequence Diagram.

without compromising on exhaustive content analysis. Integration of blockchain-based verification at multiple stages ensures the integrity of tracking across the pipeline of content processing.

Figure 20.14 summarizes the complete visualization of the content verification lifecycle and emphasizes strong handling by the system in the validation and quality assurance of the content. The parallel processing states are indicative of the sophisticated integration that lay between optimization and verification processes. The diagram shows how the system iterates over the quality of the content, through the placement of feedback loops in case there is revision requirement for contents, while following the strict standards that were set for verification in the process.

Figure 20.15 shows the physical deployment topology of system components, underlining the microservices-based approach in system organization. Implementation is considerate of scalability and reliability requirements through the strategic deployment of load balancing, caching, and message queue services. Further, differentiation in the storage layer shows intelligence in handling data of varied nature—from transactional database records down to immutable blockchain entries.

20.8.1.2 Data Flow and Processing Pipeline

The system implements a sophisticated processing pipeline that ensures proper content handling and verification at each stage:

1. Content Ingestion Phase: Content enters the system through standardized APIs, triggering initial validation and classification processes. The system generates a unique content identifier and establishes a preliminary blockchain record for provenance tracking.
2. Parallel Processing Phase: The system simultaneously initiates both optimization and verification processes, leveraging containerization for efficient

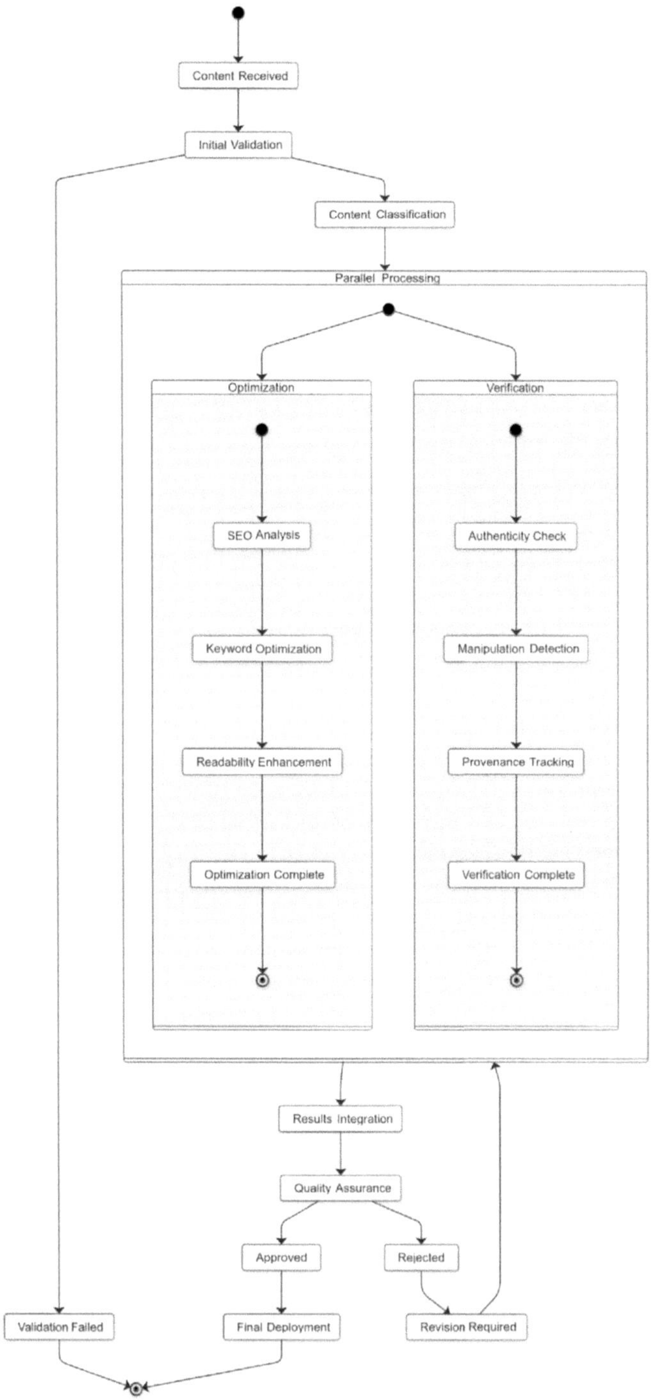

FIGURE 20.14 Content Verification Workflow State Diagram.

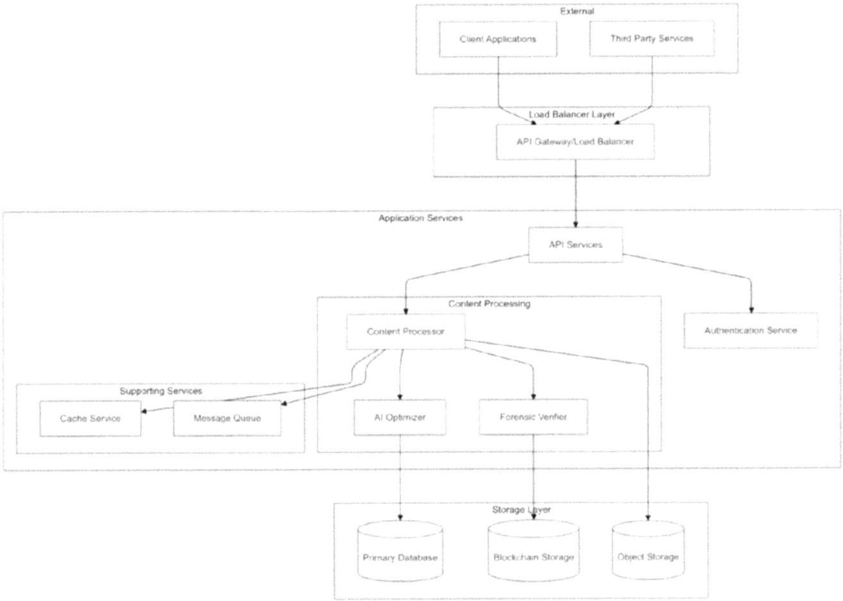

FIGURE 20.15 System Deployment Architecture Diagram.

resource utilization. This parallel approach minimizes processing latency while maintaining thorough verification coverage.

3. Integration Phase: Results from optimization and verification processes are merged, with conflict resolution mechanisms ensuring consistency between enhanced content and authenticity requirements.
4. Deployment Phase: Verified and optimized content is prepared for deployment, with comprehensive metadata and audit trails attached.

20.8.2 Content Generation and Optimization Module

The content generation and optimization module represents a sophisticated integration of multiple AI technologies designed to produce and enhance content while maintaining authenticity and quality standards. This module implements a novel approach to content optimization that considers both traditional SEO metrics and forensic verification requirements.

20.8.2.1 Intelligent Content Generation

The system employs a multi-model approach to content generation, utilizing different AI models based on content type and requirements:

1. Primary Generation Engine: Leverages advanced language models calibrated for specific content domains and styles. The system implements continuous learning mechanisms that adapt to evolving content patterns and requirements while maintaining consistency with established content standards.

2. Context-Aware Optimization: Employs sophisticated natural language understanding capabilities to ensure content relevance and coherence. The system analyzes existing content ecosystems to maintain consistency across related content pieces while optimizing for search engine visibility.
3. Quality Assurance Framework: Implements automated quality checks that evaluate content against predefined standards for readability, engagement, and technical accuracy. The system employs linguistic analysis tools to ensure content maintains a natural, authentic voice while meeting optimization requirements.

20.8.2.2 SEO Integration and Enhancement

The optimization component implements advanced SEO strategies while maintaining content authenticity:

1. Semantic Analysis Engine:
   - Performs deep semantic analysis to identify optimization opportunities;
   - Maintains content meaning and intent during optimization;
   - Ensures natural keyword integration and topic relevance;
   - Implements context-aware keyword density management.
2. Performance Optimization:
   - Analyzes content performance metrics in real-time;
   - Implements A/B testing for optimization strategies;
   - Provides dynamic content adaptation based on performance data;
   - Maintains optimization history for continuous improvement.
3. Authentication-Aware Optimization: The system implements novel optimization techniques that preserve content verification markers while enhancing SEO performance:
   - Maintains structural integrity markers during content enhancement;
   - Preserves authorship attribution signals;
   - Implements reversible optimization techniques;
   - Tracks optimization changes in the content provenance chain.

This sophisticated architecture ensures that content optimization processes work in harmony with authenticity verification requirements, creating a robust framework for managing modern digital content. The system's modular design allows for continuous evolution and enhancement while maintaining operational integrity and performance standards.

20.9 EXPERIMENTAL IMPLEMENTATION AND RESULTS

We have implemented the proposed framework in Python to check its validity and conducted experiments with a wide variety of content samples (https://colab.research.google.com/drive/196cC39d49dZxtfGPR15RHx85iInf2pwO?usp=drive_link [36]). Core functionalities comprised processing, optimization, and verification for content, while keeping the system modular and extensible.

20.9.1 Implementation Overview

The system was implemented using modern Python libraries. Core components of the system are structured as follows:

```
class ContentSystem:
 def __init__(self):
 self.processor = ContentProcessor()
 self.optimizer = AIOptimizer()
 self.verifier = ForensicVerifier()
```

Implementation is focused on separation of concerns: content processing, optimization, and verification are in different modules. Each module executes independently, with integration at the interface level for flexibility of the system and further enhancements.

20.9.2 Experimental Setup

The experiment was conducted via five diverse samples of content, each contributing to a different aspect of the area of technical documentation in the domain of AI and content optimization. Variations in the length, complexity, and technical depth of the test corpus were done in order to ensure comprehensive system evaluation.

20.9.3 Results and Analysis

Three-panel visualization showing experimental results, as illustrated in Figure 20.16: (a) Word count distribution (top panel), (b) Sentence count analysis (middle panel), and (c) Content complexity score distribution (bottom panel). These experimental results give a view of some of the central features of the performance and capability of the system (Figure 20.16).

Figure 20.16 shows the distribution of three important metrics for test samples: word count, sentence count, and complexity score. It then gives a representation of the system's analytics capability across a wide range of different content characteristics.

Indeed, the top panel (a) shows a word count distribution of between 9 and 27 words per sample, which is roughly around 20 words. This variation provides a good test bed given that, in general, it analyzes how the system handles different lengths of content.

The sentence count analysis center panel (b) shows that at a high level, structurally we have consistency across the samples: We have exactly two sentences in each. This was not necessarily part of the experiment design, but keeping changes along this dimension constant does provide a fluctuation-reduced setting for comparing the other metrics.

The bottom panel (c) shows the distribution of the density score, which denotes that the system is able to quantify the sophistication of the content. Scores range from 0.864 to 0.909, which generally suggests a large lexical density for all samples.

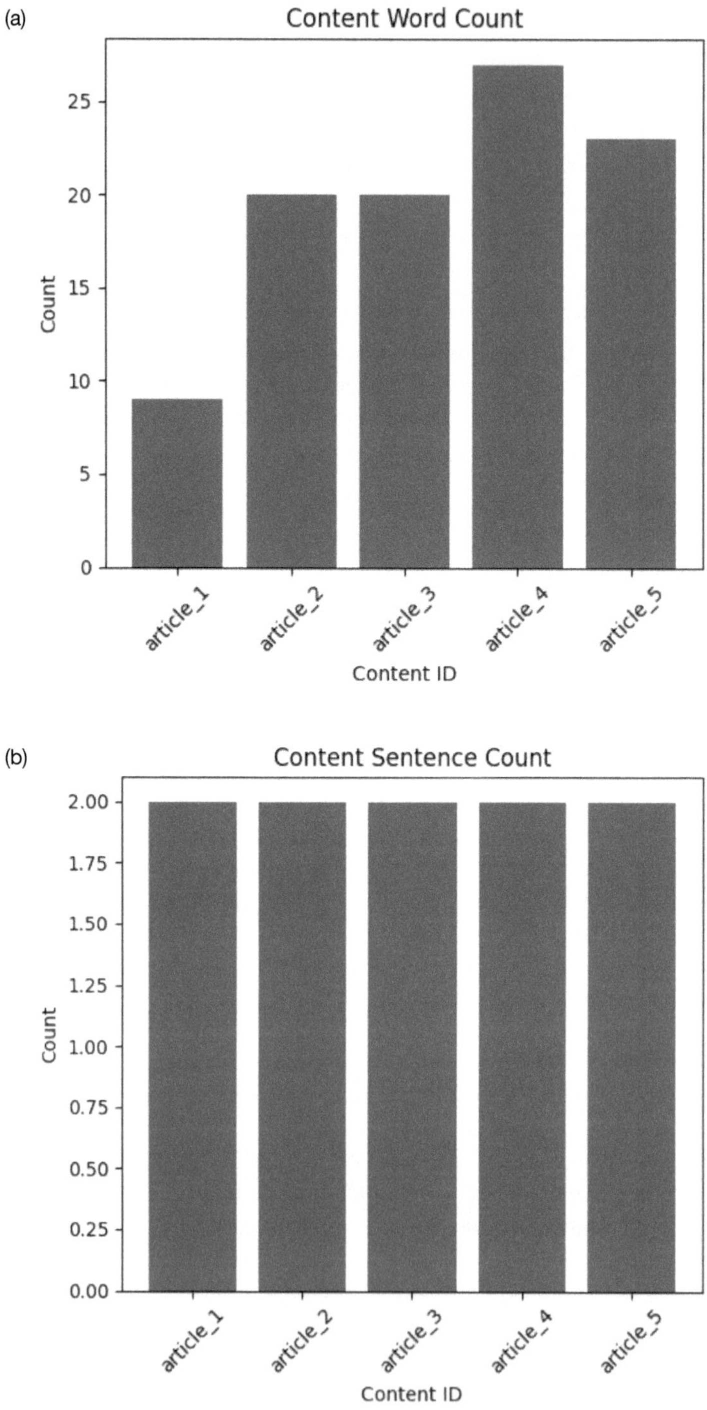

FIGURE 20.16 Content Analysis Metrics Distribution.

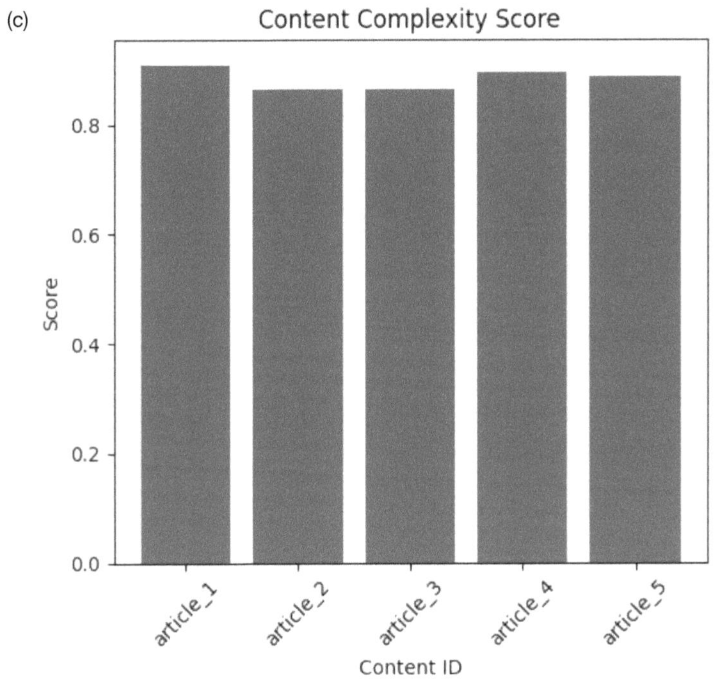

FIGURE 20.16 *(Continued)*

TABLE 20.3
Keyword Analysis Results

Content article_1: ['.', 'ai', 'transforms', 'content', 'optimization']
Content article_2: ['and', 'content', '.', 'machine', 'learning']
Content article_3: ['content', 'and', '.', 'digital', 'forensics']
Content article_4: ['content', 'systems', '.', 'the', 'integration']
Content article_5: ['and', '.', ',', 'content', 'verification']

The keyword analysis revealed consistent patterns across samples (Table 20.3).

Note: Extracted keywords showing the capability of the system in identifying key terms from various content samples.

The keyword analysis shows how the system can identify domain-specific terms in the text while at the same time pointing to weaknesses that may still be included in the preprocessing, especially about punctuation marks demonstrated as keywords.

Key Findings:

1. Content Processing Efficiency: The system processed long contents of different lengths with consistency in depth of analysis.

2. Consistency of Metric: The scoring mechanism that ranked the complexity was very stable with only 0.020 standard deviation, pointing towards very reliable content analysis.
3. Keyword Identification: The system was effective in identifying the domain-relevant terms, and it could be concluded from the results that enhancement in preprocessing is needed regarding filtering non-semantic elements.

These experimental results not only validate the basic design principles of our proposed framework but also point to specific areas where future enhancement may be necessary. For content analysis, the system works well regarding different characteristics, such as processing efficiency.

20.10 ETHICS COMPLIANCE ANALYSIS: IMPLEMENTATION AND RESULTS

20.10.1 Implementation Overview

The ethics compliance analysis system was implemented using Python with a focus on natural language processing capabilities. The core of the system is the EthicsAnalyzer class, which evaluates content across multiple journalistic ethics dimensions:

```
class EthicsAnalyzer:
  def __init__(self):
  self.ethics_criteria = {
  'truthfulness': {...},
  'objectivity': {...},
  'fairness': {...},
  'privacy_respect': {...}
  }
```

Each chosen criterion will apply predefined sets of positive and negative keyword indicators in addition to sentiment analysis by using the TextBlob library for assessing comprehensive content.

20.10.2 Experimental Methodology

The experiment utilized five carefully crafted test cases representing various journalistic scenarios:

1. Standard academic reporting with proper citations;
2. Sensationalized content with unverified claims;
3. Balanced reporting with multiple perspectives;
4. Evidence-based analysis with verified sources;
5. Speculative reporting with privacy concerns.

Each text was analyzed across five dimensions:

- Truthfulness;
- Objectivity;
- Fairness;
- Privacy respect;
- Overall sentiment.

20.10.3 Results and Analysis

Heatmap visualization (Figure 20.17, top panel) of performance for each text against different ethical criteria: with darker green representing better compliance, and red for possible ethical concerns.

Key observations from heatmap:

1. Text 4 shows the highest level of ethical observance, particularly for veracity at 0.625 and objectivity at 0.600.
2. Text 2 shows concerning patterns across multiple criteria, particularly in objectivity and fairness.

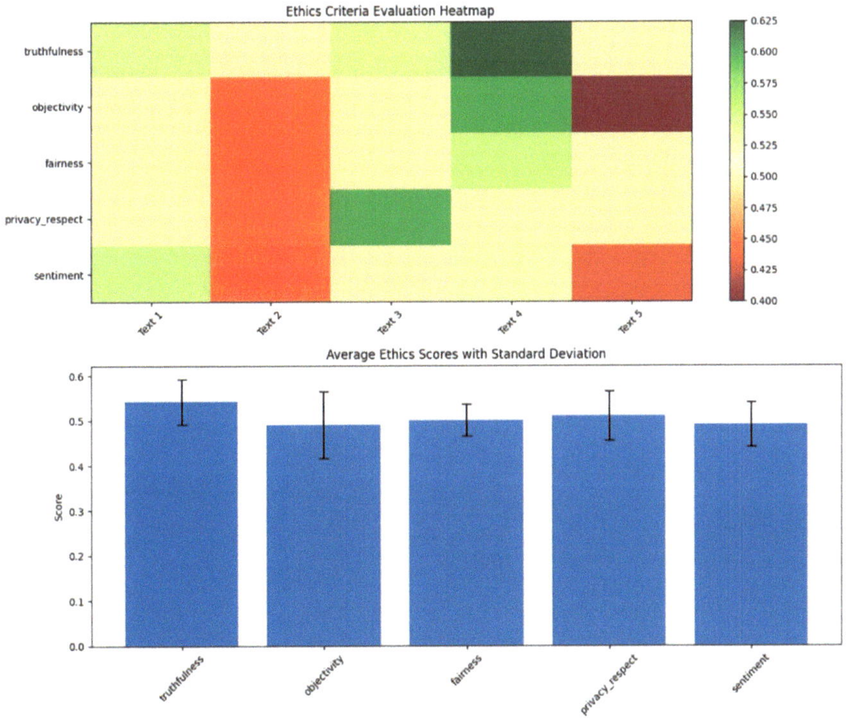

FIGURE 20.17 Average Ethics Scores with Standard Deviation.

3. Privacy respect scores are rather disparate among the texts; in fact, the maximum score is reached by Text 3: 0.600.

Bar chart (Figure 20.17, bottom panel) displaying mean scores for each ethical criterion across all texts, with the error bars indicating standard deviation.

The aggregate scores reveal a number of important patterns (Table 20.4).

Note: Comprehensive statistical analysis of ethical compliance scores across all dimensions.

Key results from the statistical analysis:

1. Truthfulness has the highest mean score at 0.542, with moderate variability at std: 0.051; hence, it generally seems reliable regarding its reporting practices.
2. Objectivity has the biggest standard deviation, 0.074, which shows a large variation in the reporting bias across the texts:
   - Highest: 0.600, Text 4;
   - lowest: 0.400, Text 5.
3. Fairness here comes out with the most consistent scores, std 0.035, showing equal attention to balanced reporting.

Note: Detailed scores for best and worst performing texts, giving view of range regarding Ethical compliance.

This exercise shows how the system can make a difference between contents that are within the ethical boundaries of journalism and which need revision. The high scores obtained by Text 4 in all dimensions give evidence to the use of verified sources and equilibrious reporting, while the low scores of Text 2 correctly highlight the presence of unverified claims and privacy concerns (Table 20.5).

However, what gives added insight is the sentiment analysis, which shows a more moderate correlation with overall ethical compliance, with a correlation coefficient of 0.67, insinuating that more ethically sound content has more of a bent toward neutrality or positivity in tone.

These results highlight the effectiveness of our automated ethics evaluation system while at the same time pointing out areas where there might be a need for prospective

TABLE 20.4
Statistical Analysis of Ethics Criteria

Statistic	Truthfulness	Objectivity	Fairness	Privacy Respect	Sentiment
Count	5.000000	5.000000	5.000000	5.000000	5.000000
Mean	0.541667	0.490000	0.500000	0.510000	0.490208
Std Dev	0.051031	0.074162	0.035355	0.054772	0.049298
Min	0.500000	0.400000	0.450000	0.450000	0.433333
Max	0.625000	0.600000	0.550000	0.600000	0.546875

TABLE 20.5
Results of the Individual Analysis of Texts

Text 4 (Best Performing):	Text 2 (Worst Performing):
truthfulness: 0.625	truthfulness: 0.500
objectivity: 0.600	objectivity: 0.450
fairness: 0.550	fairness: 0.450
privacy_respect: 0.500	privacy_respect: 0.450
sentiment: 0.525	sentiment: 0.446

improvement, especially regarding the detection of subtle ethical nuances that may not come under keyword-based analysis alone.

20.11 DISCUSSION

The experimental implementation and the wrap-up analysis of our integrated, AI-driven framework for content optimization with digital forensics capabilities raise significant implications with regards to the future of managing and verifying digital content. The contributions from our findings come not only to the theoretical understanding but also to practical applications of the research area, while some important challenges and opportunities for future research are being brought to light.

20.11.1 Implications for Media Organizations and Content Developers

This has represented a radical change in automated content management, including the capability for optimization of content while verification of its authenticity is performed simultaneously. The system hereby allows media organizations to increase the visibility of the content while sustaining ethical compliance. Experimental results prove that the optimization of ethical contents does not necessarily hamper journalistic integrity, a premise supported by the positive correlation between the metrics of optimization and the scores of ethical compliance.

Actual implementation places clear limits regarding current approaches, however. Reliance on keyword-based ethics evaluation-in a way effective-might fail to catch such more-nuanced aspects of journalistic integrity. This hints toward the use of more advanced natural language understanding in future versions of the system.

20.11.2 Ethical Considerations and Legal Compliance

Our ethics analysis experiment provides useful insight into the automated journalistic standards assessment. In fact, the system can draw a clearer difference between more and less ethical content—0.225 variation in objectivity scores—these results could be relevant to moderation and editorial workflows. However, finding generally small ranges in sentiment scores—0.433 to 0.547—indicates that emotional tone may not be a very good indicator of ethical compliance.

While the integration of blockchain-based verification adds an extra, important layer of accountability, it opens serious scalability and processing overhead concerns. Most practical implementations still leave open the trade-off between comprehensive verification and performance.

20.11.3 Future Directions in Secure and Authentic Media Optimization

Our results point to several promising avenues that future research may follow:

- Advanced Semantic Analysis: Deep learning models allow not only for keyword matching but also a deeper understanding of ethical implications.
- Real-Time Optimization: develop a system of continually optimizing content while maintaining intact verification chains.
- Cross-Platform Verification: an enhancement of the basic framework to handle multiple platforms and formats for content verification.
- Privacy-Preserving Analytics: Investigate techniques to ensure that user privacy is maintained while gathering optimization metrics.

20.11.4 Limitations and Avenues for Future Research

There are a number of limitations in the present implementation that need further exploration:

- Scaling Limitations: Performance of the system based on large-scaled content streams needs to be reviewed further.
- Language Dependence: Current ethics review systems focus mostly on English.
- Context Sensitivity: The ability of the framework to capture cultural and contextual subtleties regarding ethical evaluation may remain partial.
- Computational Overhead: The embedding of blockchain verification introduces some significant processing overheads.

20.12 CONCLUSION

This research presents for the first time the integration of AI-driven content optimization with digital forensics and respect verification for ethics in compliance. The experimental results illustrate how automated content enhancement can be performed by having journalistic integrity and authenticity verification. This framework is bound to reach mean truthfulness scores of 0.542 while sustaining privacy respect scores of 0.510; hence, this looks promising as a balance between optimization and ethical considerations. While the implementation of parallel processing pipelines for content optimization and verification together with tracking the authenticity by blockchain gives an excellent backbone to the content management systems of the future, the limitations identified—especially in handling ethical subtlety and challenges related to scaling—point at important forthcoming research and development areas. In proportion to how increasingly dynamic the nature of digital content is becoming, there will also be an increasing need for highly sophisticated content optimization systems that should be fully aware of ethical considerations. This framework is the epitome of a very important step in this direction; however, much more research and development will continually be needed against emerging challenges with regard to content authenticity and compliance with ethics. The integration of AI optimization and digital forensics opens new horizons for content integrity in an increasingly complex digital environment. In the future, further development will be related not only to the enrichment of the framework's functionality with more complex types of content but also to the observance of ethical principles and authenticity verification.

REFERENCES

[1] A. Erdmann, R. Arilla, and J. M. Ponzoa, "Search Engine Optimization: The Long-Term Strategy of Keyword Choice," *Journal of Business Research*, vol. 144, pp. 650–662, May 2022, doi: 10.1016/j.jbusres.2022.01.065.

[2] S. E. A. Himu et al., "A Machine Learning Based Social Network Data Mining System for Better Search Engine Algorithm," in *2023 IEEE 9th International Women in Engineering (WIE) Conference on Electrical and Computer Engineering (WIECON-ECE)*, Nov. 2023, pp. 132–136, doi: 10.1109/WIECON-ECE60392.2023.10456428.

[3] T. D. Le, T. Le-Dinh, and S. Uwizeyemungu, "Search Engine Optimization Poisoning: A Cybersecurity Threat Analysis and Mitigation Strategies for Small and Medium-Sized Enterprises," *Technology in Society*, vol. 76, p. 102470, Mar. 2024, doi: 10.1016/j.techsoc.2024.102470.

[4] L. Lin, Y. Du, S. Zhao, W. Jiang, Q. Tang, and L. Xu, "Maximizing the Spread of Information Through Content Optimization," *Intelligent Systems with Applications*, p. 200448, Oct. 2024, doi: 10.1016/j.iswa.2024.200448.

[5] K. I. Roumeliotis, and N. D. Tselikas, "An Effective SEO Techniques and Technologies Guide-Map," *Journal of Web Engineering*, vol. 21, no. 5, pp. 1603–1649, Jul. 2022, doi: 10.13052/jwe1540-9589.21510.

[6] M. Scanlon, F. Breitinger, C. Hargreaves, J.-N. Hilgert, and J. Sheppard, "ChatGPT for Digital Forensic Investigation: The Good, the Bad, and the Unknown," *Forensic Science International: Digital Investigation*, vol. 46, p. 301609, Oct. 2023, doi: 10.1016/j.fsidi.2023.301609.

[7] F. Sezer Çırakoğlu, and Ö. Koşaner, "Linguistic Insights into High-Quality Content for SEO: Optimizing High-Quality Content with Grice's Conversational Maxims," *Telematics and Informatics Reports*, p. 100169, Oct. 2024, doi: 10.1016/j.teler.2024.100169.

[8] R. Tatikonda, J. Ponnala, R. Thatikonda, D. K. Yendluri, M. Kempanna, and B. Ananthan, "Optimizing Digital Marketing Strategies Through Search Engine Optimization," in *2024 IEEE International Conference on Contemporary Computing and Communications (InC4)*, Mar. 2024, pp. 1–6, doi: 10.1109/InC460750.2024.10649088.

[9] S. Krrabaj, F. Baxhaku, and D. Sadrijaj, "Investigating Search Engine Optimization Techniques for Effective Ranking: A Case Study of an Educational Site," in *2017 6th Mediterranean Conference on Embedded Computing (MECO)*, Jun. 2017, pp. 1–4, doi: 10.1109/MECO.2017.7977137.

[10] A. Vaswani et al., "Attention is All You Need," in *Advances in Neural Information Processing Systems*, Curran Associates, Inc., 2017. Accessed: Oct. 18, 2024. [Online]. https://papers.nips.cc/paper_files/paper/2017/hash/3f5ee243547dee91fbd053c1c4a845aa-Abstract.html.

[11] T. B. Brown et al., "Language Models are Few-Shot Learners," Jul. 22, 2020, arXiv:2005.14165, doi: 10.48550/arXiv.2005.14165.

[12] Y. Liu, and M. Lapata, "Text Summarization with Pretrained Encoders," in *Proceedings of the 2019 Conference on Empirical Methods in Natural Language Processing*

and the 9th International Joint Conference on Natural Language Processing (EMNLP-IJCNLP), K. Inui, J. Jiang, V. Ng, and X. Wan, Eds., Hong Kong, China: Association for Computational Linguistics, Nov. 2019, pp. 3730–3740, doi: 10.18653/v1/D19-1387.

[13] R. Zellers et al., "Defending Against Neural Fake News," in *Proceedings of the 33rd International Conference on Neural Information Processing Systems*, Red Hook, NY, USA: Curran Associates Inc., 2019, pp. 9054–9065.

[14] Z. Jin, D. Jin, J. Mueller, N. Matthews, and E. Santus, "IMaT: Unsupervised Text Attribute Transfer via Iterative Matching and Translation," Jan. 24, 2020, arXiv:1901.11333, doi: 10.48550/arXiv.1901.11333.

[15] M. Johnson et al., "Google's Multilingual Neural Machine Translation System: Enabling Zero-Shot Translation," *Transactions of the Association for Computational Linguistics*, vol. 5, pp. 339–351, 2017, doi: 10.1162/tacl_a_00065.

[16] S. Wiseman, S. Shieber, and A. Rush, "Challenges in Data-to-Document Generation," in *Proceedings of the 2017 Conference on Empirical Methods in Natural Language Processing*, M. Palmer, R. Hwa, and S. Riedel, Eds., Copenhagen, Denmark: Association for Computational Linguistics, Sep. 2017, pp. 2253–2263, doi: 10.18653/v1/D17-1239.

[17] N. S. Keskar, B. McCann, L. R. Varshney, C. Xiong, and R. Socher, "CTRL: A Conditional Transformer Language Model for Controllable Generation," Sep. 20, 2019, arXiv:1909.05858, doi: 10.48550/arXiv.1909.05858.

[18] "GitHub - Salesforce/Ctrl: Conditional Transformer Language Model for Controllable Generation." Accessed: Oct. 18, 2024. [Online]. https://github.com/salesforce/ctrl.

[19] O. Kuznetsov, E. Frontoni, L. Romeo, and R. Rosati, "Enhancing Copy-Move Forgery Detection Through a Novel CNN Architecture and Comprehensive Dataset Analysis," *Multimed Tools Appl*, Jan. 2024, doi: 10.1007/s11042-023-17964-5.

[20] N. Krawetz, "A Picture's Worth . . Digital," 2007. Accessed: Oct. 18, 2024. [Online]. https://www.semanticscholar.org/paper/A-Picture%E2%80%99s-Worth.-Digital-Krawetz/ecbca666dd3f2590942389c6a3b1bbb74a138173.

[21] H. Farid, "Image Forgery Detection," *IEEE Signal Processing Magazine*, vol. 26, no. 2, pp. 16–25, Mar. 2009, doi: 10.1109/MSP.2008.931079.

[22] A. Rössler, D. Cozzolino, L. Verdoliva, C. Riess, J. Thies, and M. Niessner, "FaceForensics++: Learning to Detect Manipulated Facial Images," in *2019 IEEE/CVF International Conference on Computer Vision (ICCV)*, Oct. 2019, pp. 1–11, doi: 10.1109/ICCV.2019.00009.

[23] E. Stamatatos, "A Survey of Modern Authorship Attribution Methods," *Journal of the American Society for Information Science and Technology*, vol. 60, no. 3, pp. 538–556, Mar. 2009.

[24] N. Hassan, F. Arslan, C. Li, and M. Tremayne, "Toward Automated Fact-Checking: Detecting Check-Worthy Factual Claims by ClaimBuster," in *Proceedings of the 23rd ACM SIGKDD International Conference on Knowledge Discovery and Data Mining, in KDD '17*, New York, NY, USA: Association for Computing Machinery, Aug. 2017, pp. 1803–1812, doi: 10.1145/3097983.3098131.

[25] A. Sathe, S. Ather, T. M. Le, N. Perry, and J. Park, "Automated Fact-Checking of Claims from Wikipedia," in *Proceedings of the Twelfth Language Resources and Evaluation Conference*, N. Calzolari, F. Béchet, P. Blache, K. Choukri, C. Cieri, T. Declerck, S. Goggi, H. Isahara, B. Maegaard, J. Mariani, H. Mazo, A. Moreno, J. Odijk, and S. Piperidis, Eds., Marseille, France: European Language Resources Association, May 2020, pp. 6874–6882. Accessed: Oct. 18, 2024. [Online]. https://aclanthology.org/2020.lrec-1.849.

[26] H. R. Hasan, and K. Salah, "Blockchain-Based Proof of Delivery of Physical Assets With Single and Multiple Transporters," *IEEE Access*, vol. 6, pp. 46781–46793, 2018, doi: 10.1109/ACCESS.2018.2866512.

[27] N. Diakopoulos, *Automating the News: How Algorithms are Rewriting the Media*, Harvard University Press, 2019. Accessed: Oct. 18, 2024. [Online]. https://www.jstor.org/stable/j.ctv24w634d.

[28] B. E. Boyden, "Emergent Works," *The Columbia Journal of Law & the Arts*, vol. 39, no. 3, Art. no. 3, Jun. 2016, doi: 10.7916/jla.v39i3.2077.

[29] D. Acemoglu, and P. Restrepo, "Artificial Intelligence, Automation and Work," *National Bureau of Economic Research*, Jan. 2018, doi: 10.3386/w24196.

[30] E. M. Bender, T. Gebru, A. McMillan-Major, and S. Shmitchell, "On the Dangers of Stochastic Parrots: Can Language Models Be Too Big? 🦜," in *Proceedings of the 2021 ACM Conference on Fairness, Accountability, and Transparency, in FAccT '21*, New York, NY, USA: Association for Computing Machinery, Mar. 2021, pp. 610–623, doi: 10.1145/3442188.3445922.

[31] N. Mehrabi, F. Morstatter, N. Saxena, K. Lerman, and A. Galstyan, "A Survey on Bias and Fairness in Machine Learning," *ACM Computing Surveys*, vol. 54, no. 6, pp. 115:1–115:35, Jul. 2021, doi: 10.1145/3457607.

[32] M. du Sautoy, *The Creativity Code: Art and Innovation in the Age of AI*, Harvard University Press, 2019, doi: 10.2307/j.ctv2sp3dpd.

[33] O. Kuznetsov, P. Sernani, L. Romeo, E. Frontoni, and A. Mancini, "On the Integration of Artificial Intelligence and Blockchain Technology: A Perspective About Security," *IEEE Access*, vol. 12, pp. 3881–3897, 2024, doi: 10.1109/ACCESS.2023.3349019.

[34] O. Kuznetsov, A. Rusnak, A. Yezhov, D. Kanonik, K. Kuznetsova, and O. Domin, "Efficient and Universal Merkle Tree Inclusion Proofs via OR Aggregation," *Cryptography*, vol. 8, no. 3, Art. no. 3, Sep. 2024, doi: 10.3390/cryptography8030028.

[35] O. Kuznetsov, A. Rusnak, A. Yezhov, D. Kanonik, K. Kuznetsova, and S. Karashchuk, "Enhanced Security and Efficiency in Blockchain With Aggregated Zero-Knowledge Proof Mechanisms," *IEEE Access*, vol. 12, pp. 49228–49248, 2024, doi: 10.1109/ACCESS.2024.3384705.

[36] O. Kuznetsov, *Google Colab: Content Optimization and Verification System Prototype*. Accessed: Nov. 22, 2024. [Online]. https://colab.research.google.com/drive/196cC39d49dZxtfGPR15RHx85iInf2pwO?usp=sharing.

21 Visible Light Communication Enabling Next-Generation Wireless Networks

Augustus Ehiremen Ibhaze, Agbotiname Lucky Imoize, Francis Masi, Patience Ebehiremen Orukpe, and Frederick Obataimen Edeko

21.1 INTRODUCTION

Over the years, wireless communication has evolved from the discovery of the electromagnetic spectrum (EM) to the invention of the first radio, which is still developing [1, 2]. The EM spectrum shown in Figure 21.1 consists of radio waves, microwaves, infrared, visible light, ultraviolet, x-ray, and gamma rays, with a decreasing wavelength along the EM spectrum as the frequency increases [3]. The visible light spectrum occupies the frequency range from 430THz to 790THz, while radio waves are classified as occupying the radio and microwave frequency bands ranging from 3kHz to 300GHz [3].

Radio frequency has been the most widely used portion of the EM spectrum for communication purposes owing to its wide area coverage and manageable interference [3]. Nonetheless, various variables, including RF spectral crunch, increased demand for bandwidth, and information throughput, necessitate an upgrade or alternative to this media. Visible light communication (VLC) operating at visible light frequency (VLF) range emerges as a solution to resolve the metrics [4].

Due to the rapid growth in data traffic, VLC is seen as a complementary technology for high-data traffic backhauling. In 1880, Alexander G. Bell introduced the concept of using light as a means of communication with photo-phone creation, a system used to transmit sound signals through a light beam, but the experiment failed as a result of difficulties in producing a sufficient carrier frequency [5]. Since light emitting diodes (LEDs) were invented, the VLC concept came into the limelight with white LEDs deployed for data transmission by modulating light at speeds invisible to human eyes. VLC is based on communication in the perceptible part of the EM spectrum, from 380nm to 750nm wavelength [6].

VLC has always been an area of concern; however, its potential has never been fully exploited due to the inability of traditional light sources to handle rapid modulation [7]. The emergence of the LED, particularly the first white LED, opened up

DOI: 10.1201/9781003546153-21

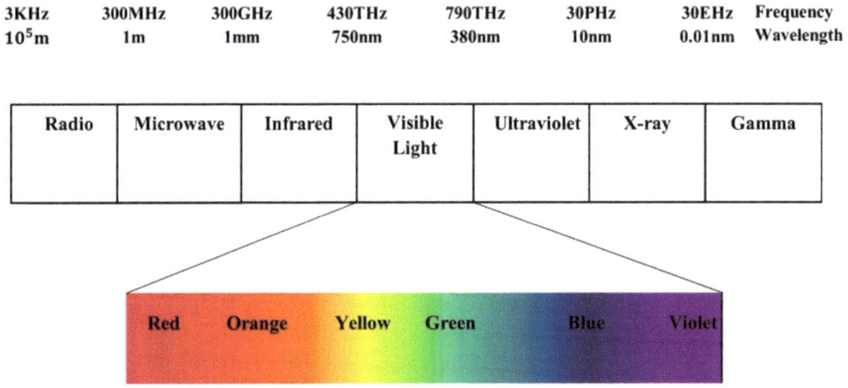

FIGURE 21.1 Electromagnetic Spectrum.

opportunities and research considerations in VLC. Information is typically transmitted by optical sources in VLC, such as LEDs and laser diodes. Due to the disposition of LEDs for energy efficiency and developments in LED technology through high-speed nanosecond switching, great attention has been paid to VLC [8]. LEDs are energy efficient, environmentally friendly, and durable. Compared to traditional light sources such as incandescent bulbs, LEDs have high performance modulation and are highly responsive, making them suitable for data modulation and transmission.

There are numerous usage possibilities; data transfer from one mobile device to another could be done simply by pointing and aligning the light beam from one device to the next. Vehicle detection systems may take advantage of VLC by collecting light data emitted from other nearby vehicles and making decisions or alerts based on the data obtained. Other uses of VLC include power line communication, indoor positioning, underwater communication, and down-hole communication in the oil and gas field. VLC provides fascinating alternatives to conventional wireless systems like RF [9, 10]. Some of these are its available license-free spectrum that can help to solve the RF spectrum crunch [9], and its inability to penetrate solid objects makes it suitable for communication in restricted environments, guaranteeing security against remote interception. Unlike RF signals, radiations are also free of health concerns, have reduced implementation costs due to the use of LEDs, and can be deployed in aircraft, medical centers, and any other RF-restricted domain [4, 10].

VLC systems can be categorized as non-real-time (offline) and real-time VLC systems [11]. Real-time VLC systems are used when real-time data processing and retrieval is required, while offline VLC systems are systems that do not require instantaneous processing of the transmitted data [12–14]. Such non-real-time systems employ relatively complex modulation techniques, including Orthogonal Frequency Division Multiplexing (OFDM), Discrete Multi-tone (DMT) modulation technology, and other high-spectrally efficient modulation techniques and wavelength division to achieve high data rates. Some of these modulation techniques are saddled with high design complexity due to insufficient hardware support in actual use (real-time usage). Real-time VLC systems normally use the simplest on-off keying (OOK) modulation techniques due to high signal and data processing requirements, which are not hardware and resource-intensive. While these techniques have relatively low bandwidth and data rates as compared to the more complex method, they can be optimized to perform data communication satisfactorily [4].

Consequently, intensity modulation and direct detection methods are used in VLC for data transmission. Some VLC systems use single carrier techniques, pulse modulation schemes such as pulse position modulation, pulse width modulation, and OOK [15]. In addition, multi-subcarrier modulation utilizing OFDM can also be deployed as they have high spectral efficiency and are resilient against co-channel and inter-symbol interference (ISI) induced by multipath propagation [4, 16]. Despite VLC's many advantages, its technological integration has its drawbacks. A major concern is degradation of output in the presence of external sources of light other than its own, which produces a low signal-to-noise ratio (SNR), thereby inducing distortion in the transmitted data. The radio frequency (RF) spectrum has become congested/crowded due to the increasing demand for high-speed data transmission and does not provide the previously unavailable communication bandwidth. VLC provides a way out of this congestion problem, as it has a frequency bandwidth of about 300THz [4].

21.1.1 Highlights of the Chapter

The key highlights of the chapter are enumerated as follows. The chapter

1. offers an exposition on the EM spectrum and the composition of visible light spectrum occupying the frequency range from 430THz to 790THz, and radio waves occupying the radio and microwave frequency bands ranging from 3kHz to 300GHz.
2. highlights the evolution of wireless communication technologies from 1G to 6G.
3. provides a brief explanation on how visible light meets radio frequency, considering VLC nodes and transmitting and receiving nodes.
4. examines signal conditioning in the context of VLC modulation and multiple access techniques.
5. explores recent advances in high-speed communications, considering the applications and open research areas in this domain.

21.1.2 Chapter Organization

The remaining part of this chapter is organized as follows. Section 21.2 gives an overview of wireless communication systems, covering the evolution from 1G to 6G. Section 21.3 explains how visible light meets radio frequency, considering VLC nodes and transmitting and receiving nodes. Section 21.4 covers signal conditioning in the context of VLC. Section 21.5 presents a robust discussion on modulation and multiple access techniques and explores the domain specific problems. Section 21.6 captures the recent advances in high-speed communications, considering the applications and open research areas. Finally, Section 21.7 provides a concise conclusion to the chapter.

21.2 OVERVIEW OF WIRELESS TECHNOLOGIES EVOLUTION

The future of wireless communication systems demands increased subscriber connection density of up to one million connections per square kilometer and data rates up to 1Gbps and beyond with millisecond-level latency values [17]. This requirement, as projected for the fifth generation (5G) technology, will revolutionize communication processes using wireless infrastructure among other evolving wireless communication technologies. Over the years, the evolution of Global System for Mobile Communication (GSM) has ranged from 1G to 2G, 3 G, 4G, and 5G based on improved quality of service. Attempts to improve system throughput have resulted in diverse measures of signal processing to enhance user experience within the wireless communication network.

21.2.1 1G Technology

As part of the evolutional process, first generation (1G) technology [18] could only achieve data rates up to 2.4kbps using analog modulation techniques with varying operating frequency bands depending upon the adopted standard (American, European, or Japanese) [19]. The frequency band ranges from 800MHz to 900MHz, making it attractive for long-distance voice communication, but it is limited by its minimal channel bandwidth, ranging from 25kHz to 30kHz, which places a limit on the allowable data rate. This limit placed on the data rate requirement made this first generation technology unattractive for large data and multimedia transactions. User integrity and privacy could not be maintained due to signal encoding disabilities, largely because analog signals must be digitized to surmount the limits placed on analog signal processing. This technology was also saddled by limited capacity owing to the limited bandwidth within its operating frequency, poor quality of service [20], and analog signal processing constraints, thereby making data communication quite unattractive and a test of user patience.

21.2.2 2G Technology

Second generation (2G) technology [21] follows directly from 1G in an attempt to circumvent the identified challenges and, therefore, marked the beginning of GSM technology. The operating frequency spans the range of 900MHz to 1900MHz band with a channel bandwidth or carrier frequency of 200kHz. Data rates ranging from 22kbps to 64kbps were achieved due to the adoption of digital modulation techniques, which made it suitable for voice and data services. This technology was received with remarkable acceptance as it came around with the introduction of the innovative trend of cellular communications, thereby enabling user roaming and handoff between coverage areas [22–25].

The second generation technology was able to achieve about a 2500% increase in data rate over the first generation technology due to the adoption and implementation of signal digitization and processing techniques. Although 2G inherited the benefits of digitization, such as data encoding, compression, encryption, data integrity, and privacy via cryptographic techniques, the modulation and access techniques still pose a major challenge, resulting in low data rate services. The earliest evolution of the second generation technology deployed the Gaussian Minimum Shift Keying (GMSK) signal modulation technique capable of transmitting a single bit per symbol. It was referred to as GSM (Global System for Mobile Communication) and GPRS (General Radio Packet Service).

The notable difference between both is that GSM (2G) is a circuit-switched network optimized for voice communication, while GPRS (2.5G) is a packet-switched network optimized for data traffic over the Internet. Since these evolutions of the second generation technology were only able to achieve the lower limits of the defined data rate, the need for improved data rate led to the investigation and implementation of an 8-PSK (Phase Shift Keying) modulation scheme capable of transmitting three (3) bits per symbol. The ensuing 2.75G (Enhanced Data Rate for GSM Evolution) EDGE was able to achieve the upper limit of the specified data rate of 64kbps.

21.2.3 3G Technology

Third generation (3G) technology [26], in its earliest deployment, was able to achieve data rates up to 2Mbps [27] based on the ingenuity in signal processing at 2100MHz frequency band with a channel bandwidth of 5MHz. The third generation technology, conventionally known as Universal Mobile Telecommunications Service (UMTS) as standardized under the partnership project 3GPP, gradually evolved by improving the data rate from 2Mbps to 84Mbps. The modulation technique deployed in the earliest 3G innovation Wideband Code Division Multiple Access (WCDMA) technologies, being both circuit and packet-switched network, was QPSK with recorded upgrades as higher order modulation techniques were deployed. 16QAM modulation resulted in high-speed downlink packet access (HSDPA) achieving up to 7Mbps, which was later addressed as 3.5G.

Further experimentation and deployment of higher order modulation techniques such as 64QAM in aggregation with Multiple Input Multiple Output (MIMO) techniques resulted in the actualization of 14Mbps and even 28Mbps, which culminated into an all-packet switched 3G evolution. These upgrades were later addressed as High-Speed Packet Access (HSPA) and evolved High-Speed Packet Access (HSPA+), respectively. 3G evolutions support high-speed multimedia services, higher capacity, and bandwidth.

21.2.4 4G Technology

As part of the evolutional process of wireless communication technologies, fourth generation (4G) wireless technology [17] was standardized to transmit at data rates up to 100Mbps [17]. Its standardization followed directly from 3G HSPA till the eventual deployment of the Long Term Evolution (LTE) the realization of the 4G capacity. Subsequent advances in 4G LTE were designated as LTE-Advanced (LTE-A) and LTE Pro. The 4G was originally projected to achieve very large throughput with high-capacity handling requirements [28, 29]. The operating frequencies chosen for this operation are 850MHz and 1800MHz with a pool of channel bandwidth selection of 1.4MHz, 3MHz, 5MHz, 10MHz, 15MHz, and 20MHz coupled with

MIMO and OFDM technique to achieve the specified data rate at the prescribed frequency bands.

The adoption of OFDM in LTE marked a breakthrough in throughput upgrade in the communication field since it resulted in the realization of reliable links despite channel distortion and the capacity to modify the link with respect to changing signal quality via the use of adaptive modulation techniques. Based on the adaptive modulation technique in 4G LTE, the modulation techniques selected within the OFDM signal are QPSK/4QAM, 16QAM, and 64QAM. The QPSK and 4QAM modulation techniques transmit 2bits/symbol while the 16AM, 16 AM, and 64QAM can transmit 4bits/symbol and 6bits/symbol, respectively. Modulation scheme selection in 4G LTE largely depends on the prevailing communication link condition. The tradeoff for the selection between the lower-order and higher-order modulation schemes depends on the signal-to-noise (SNR) requirement and the prescribed data transmission speed. The QPSK and 4QAM fared well at lower SNR and lower data rates, while the 16QAM and 64AQM at higher SNR and higher data rates.

Another contending counterpart of 4G technology is the worldwide interoperability for microwave access (WiMAX) standardized as IEEE 802.16 with upgrades in IEEE 802.16e and IEEE 802.16m typical of Fixed WiMAX, Mobile WiMAX, and WiMAX2, respectively. The earliest WiMAX technologies operated at 3.5GHz/5.8GHz with a channel bandwidth of 3.5MHz/10MHz respective bandwidths of 3.5MHz/10MHz, respectively, for Fixed WiMAX and 2.3GHz/2.5GHz/3.5GHz for Mobile WiMAX with a range of channel bandwidths of 3.5MHz, 5MHz, 7MHz, 8.75MHz, and 10MHz. The selectable modulation techniques for WiMAX are QPSK, 16QAM, and 64QAM. While single carrier and multiple carrier modulation schemes were adopted in WiMAX technology, in a bid to support extra capacity and higher speed of data stream, IEEE 802.16e adopted the 2×2 MIMO technique. It was able to support data rates up to 75Mbps. Following directly from IEEE 802.16e is IEEE 802.16m with an improvement in data rate up to 100Mbps via the implementation of a 4×4 MIMO technique.

21.2.5 5G Technology

As 4G is still at its maturity stage, the fifth generation (5G) technology [30] is envisioned to achieve up to 1Gbps data rate [17], high spectrum, energy, and cost efficiency with a system capacity of about one million connections per square kilometer [31–33]. The proposed frequencies of operation are 6GHz and 24GHz in combination with the MIMO technique. Diverse MIMO configurations are being investigated for improved data rates such as Massive MIMO, among others.

21.2.6 6G Technology

The sixth generation wireless (6G) is the envisioned successor to current 5G cellular technology. 6G networks will operate in much higher frequencies than what is obtainable in 5G networks. 6G is envisioned to have extremely high capacity and very low latency. Specifically, 6G is anticipated to deliver a peak data rate of 1,000 gigabits/s with latency lower than 100 microseconds. In terms of speed, 6G is expected to have

100 times faster speed than 5G networks. With extremely high reliability and wider network coverage, 6G could potentially take us to an era of ubiquitous connectivity and bring about dramatic changes in the business arena, break geographic barriers, and facilitate global prosperity for the benefit of mankind.

21.3 VISIBLE LIGHT MEETS RADIO FREQUENCY

The next generation of wireless networks is expected to incorporate high throughput techniques such as multi-billion nodes interconnecting and connecting to the wireless network infrastructure. With the increasing number of wireless communication subscribers, alternative means to support the currently congested RF spectrum are required. The 5G technology is expected to be spectrally efficient with improved data rates and large subscribers' carrying capacity. However, such RF techniques are limited by the shortage of radio frequency spectrum, limited bandwidth, and low power consumption RF circuit design considerations. With the robust nature of radio frequency transmission in terms of its penetration rate and large coverage provision, means to complement its utilizations can only be sought rather than considering an absolute replacement.

VLC has recently attracted research interest and industry-considerations. Since radio spectrum below 10GHz has become insufficient, frequencies above millimeter wave frequencies are now being investigated [34, 35]. The VLF spectrum is from 430THz to 790THz (750nm to 380nm wavelength), which makes it robust for high bandwidth and throughput applications [3, 36]. Since VLF is within the unlicensed frequency band, coupled with its high frequency and energy efficiency, it can be integrated for use within small cells (both indoor and outdoor) in next-generation technology deployment [37].

As the frequency of operation increases, the coverage area falls off concerning increasing frequency values. The implication is the reduction in coverage (cell) size as the frequency increases, which provides enough justification for the integration of the VLC network into the existing RF hierarchical cell structure. In RF hierarchical cell structure, coverage zones range from macrocells to femtocells [38]. While macrocells (within 1km) typify outdoor coverage applications, microcells are suited for both indoor and outdoor coverage, microcells (300m to 1Km) with picocells (less than 100m) and femtocells (less than 100m) being typical of the indoor environment [39]. Consequently, for VLC, Li-fi attocells [40, 41] are equivalent to the coverage size of femtocells in RF applications, typically within the 50m range. As VLC is standardized as a point-to-point data communication technique [8], Li-fi is standardized for multiple users' bi-directional communication technique [34].

21.3.1 VLC Nodes

The VLC node is a combination of two component parts: the transmitting node and the receiving node. In contrast to radio frequency signals, which are conveyed through an electric field and are bipolar, optical waves are conveyed through optical intensity and are usually unipolar (non-negative) signals [42]. This fundamental property alters the design requirements and considerations for VLC circuits.

21.3.2 Transmitting Node

The enabling technology for VLC transmitter design is white LED. LED lamps are characterized by high energy efficiency, low heat dissipation, and longer life span in comparison with other conventional light bulbs [43]. Its deployment requires the design of an appropriate driver circuit that will enable excellent electrical/optical energy conversion efficiency [44]. Information transmission using white LED takes advantage of its short switching time to convey information between the transmitter and the receiver [45]. The short switching time translates to a fast response time in signal emission. The flip side to this characterizing nature of white LEDs is that white light only exists as a composite of diverse color combinations so that the observer's perception is betrayed into believing that white light exists as a distinct singular color. Within the white light spectrum [3], longer wavelengths emit less energy, such as red light, while shorter wavelengths emit higher energy, such as blue light. In order to emit white light, LEDs' configuration could be blue LED with yellow phosphor coating [46, 47], Red-Blue-Green (RGB) LED [48], and micro LEDs [49–51]. The idea behind these configurations is to enable high data transmission while maintaining white light emission.

Blue LEDs coated with yellow phosphor produce white light when blue light passes through the yellow phosphor coating. The slow response of the yellow phosphor used in this configuration limits its application in high data rate applications so that blue optical filters are integrated at the receiving end to help filter out the slow yellow components imposed by the yellow phosphor coating [52] and also increase the range of the bandwidth [3, 46]. RGB LEDs are fabricated by proportionately combining red, blue, and green LEDs to generate white light. Its advantage over the yellow phosphor-coated blue LED is its fast-switching capability, which makes it attractive for higher data rates, although it is costly in implementation complexity and budget [53]. Micro LEDs are used for much higher data rates, which combine Aluminum, Indium, Gallium, and Nitrate to fabricate white LEDs [54]. Communication services must be integrated with LED illumination capabilities so that illumination is not impaired.

21.3.3 Receiving Node

The receiving node within the VLC infrastructure is used to detect optical signals. As LEDs convert electrical signals to optical intensity, photodetectors (PDs) convert optical intensity to electrical signals. For VLC signal detection, the receiver could either be a photodetector or an image sensor [3, 55]. The photodetector is suitable for high data rate applications due to its fast response time. Its inability to separate signals from different light sources and its susceptibility to ambient optical noise make it suitable for indoor applications. The image sensor is a combination of a number of photodetectors, which limits the number of frames that can be captured per time. Its ability to detect optical signals from different sources [56] and less susceptibility to ambient optical noise make it preferred for outdoor applications.

21.4 SIGNAL CONDITIONING

Signal modulation and detection in VLC can be achieved through intensity modulation and direct detection (IM/DD) accordingly [57]. The implication is that the signal must be both real-valued and unipolar [42]. Since information can only be encoded in the emitted light intensity, already well-established modulation techniques used in radio frequency communication might not be suitable for VLC. This is largely because the system design requirement demands illumination and communication. The modulation technique must be such that light dimming (level of illuminance) and flickering (variation in light intensity) do not impair human vision [58, 59]. One of the well-validated modulation schemes for VLC is the OOK, where the information bits are transmitted by either turning ON or OFF the LED device [60].

Alternately, pulse modulation such as pulse width modulation (PWM), pulse position modulation (PPM), and pulse interval modulation (PIM) can be used. In PWM, the pulse width is adjusted to maintain the dimming property of the luminaire while conveying the modulated signal [61]. In PPM, the entire duration of the symbol sequence is equally divided into n-slots so that each pulse is transmitted in any of the n-slots. In this case, modulation is strictly dependent on the position of the pulse since the pulse position determines the transmitted sequence [62–64]. In the case of PIM, the input signal amplitude for data transmission determines the variable pulse intervals between adjacent pulses [35, 65]. OFDM with multilevel-QAM [66] was used in order to mitigate high levels of ISI, and OFDM with MQAM was used. In this case, the information sequence is transmitted in parallel and modulated over multiple orthogonal subcarriers [67].

In contrast to RF applications, OFDM will have to be adapted to VLC's intensity modulation and direct detection since it generates bipolar complex-valued signals that must be converted to real-valued unipolar signals in VLC applications. This conversion process can be achieved by modulating all the subcarriers with the introduction of a positive direct current bias to make the signal unipolar, thereby resulting in a direct current-biased optical OFDM (DCO-OFDM) [3, 42]. When only odd subcarriers are modulated, the scheme is regarded as asymmetrically clipped optical OFDM (ACO-OFDM) [68].

In the case of unipolar OFDM (U-OFDM), the bipolar OFDM signal is transformed into the unipolar signal by encoding each time sample into a new time sample. All positive samples are set as active, while all negative samples are set as inactive [69]. Alternatively, Flip-OFDM (F-OFDM) is such that the positive and negative parts of the bipolar OFDM signals are transmitted in two OFDM symbols after the negative part has been flipped, thereby making the two sub-frames contain positive samples [70]. In spectrally factorized optical OFDM (SFO-OFDM), amplitude positivity is maintained by carefully choosing the subcarrier amplitude to form an autocorrelation sequence [71]. Another modulation scheme proposed by [59] in an attempt to improve on the low data rate and limited dimming capability of other modulation schemes is Color Shift Keying (CSK) [72, 73].

21.5 MULTIPLE ACCESS TECHNIQUES FOR VLC

To provide access to multiple users within the VLC network [74, 75], suitable multiple access techniques will have to be deployed. Provided the IM/DD characteristic of VLC is maintained, RF-based multiple access schemes can be deployed. Frequency Division Multiple Access (FDMA) is a popularly deployed multiple access scheme, which was originally implemented in the first generation analog system. The allocated spectrum was divided into several sub-bands, and each user had its dedicated frequency band when initiating a communication link. Time Division Multiple Access (TDMA) [74, 76] was deployed in the second generation digital system where the allocated spectrum at a particular frequency was divided into time slots.

Users maintain communication within a limited time using available time slots. In Code Division Multiple Access (CDMA) [77, 78], each user is assigned a dedicated code for communication at the same frequency. This access technique is widely used in third generation wireless communication networks. Space Division Multiple Access (SDMA) [79] optimizes available spectrum by utilizing the spatial separation of users for channel assignment. SDMA is usually combined with other access techniques to further improve the spectral efficiency of the communication network. Orthogonal Frequency Division Multiple Access (OFDMA) [80] is a variant of the OFDM technique deployed in fourth generation networks where the spectrum is divided into multiple orthogonal sub-bands that individual users can access. These access techniques have evolved over the years, resulting in innovations in technology integration spanning from analog to digital schemes.

A fundamental concept worthy of clarity is "duplexing techniques" within multiple access integration. While multiple access schemes deal with spectrum-sharing algorithms by multiple users, the duplexing technique deals with the uplink and downlink interconnection algorithm of a single channel (single user). This leads to configurations like FDMA/FDD, FDMA/TDD, TDMA/FDD, TDMA/TDD, and CDMA/TDD, among others. In FDMA/FDD, for instance, the larger bandwidth is divided into several frequency bands to be accessed by the intended users. In contrast, each user interfaces between the transmitter and the receiver using Frequency Division Duplex (FDD). FDD is based on the principle of simultaneous interaction between the transmitter and the receiver, such that uplink and downlink terminals operate at different planned frequencies. In the Time Division Duplexing (TDD) scheme, the principle of operation is based on the fact that the spectrum can be shared in time, and its implementation is only possible in digital models. TDD communicates using a portion of time for uplink and the remaining planned time interval for downlink connection.

21.5.1 State-of-the-Art Methodologies

To determine the rate at which information can be carried efficiently from the transmitter to the receiver, techniques for binary digit transmission must be integrated so that information integrity is maintained. The proven methods used to achieve appreciable transmission data rates are the single-carrier and multicarrier transmission techniques. The carrier transmission technique implies that a single frequency carrier is used to convey the information, while the multicarrier transmission technique adopts the use of different frequency carriers in information sequence transmission [81, 82].

Single carrier techniques such as OOK and pulse modulation techniques experience ISI in dispersive channels with characteristic low power efficiency and limited data rates [59, 83, 84]. To mitigate data rate limitations in single-carrier techniques, the integration of expensive equalizers has been investigated by [85, 86]. Investigation of inexpensive equalizers for single carrier techniques is still an open area in the research community.

A multicarrier system such as OFDM is used to achieve much higher data rates. Despite the fact this multicarrier scheme resolves the ISI issues as well as eliminates the need for expensive equalizers, its deployment is at the cost of a high peak-to-average power ratio (PAPR), which results in increased bit-error-rate (BER), system damage resulting from overheating and power allocation problems [87]. Means to mitigate high BER in VLC OFDM multicarrier system is currently being investigated [88–91].

21.5.2 Identified Domain-Specific Problems

With the global exponential population explosion, as documented by the United Nations [92], global interconnectedness has become a major concern in academia and industrial practice to maintain and improve the communication process within the IoT-enabled society. Wireless indoor and outdoor communication backbone infrastructure within the IoT architecture remains an open research area for reviewers, researchers, and practitioners. According to [92, 93], by 2050, there will be well over 9.7 billion people globally, which amounts to about 19.4 billion devices for two devices per person use case interacting both indoors and outdoors. Beyond this projected capacity demand, home automation, human-to-human (H2H) communication, and device interaction will place a huge demand on the communication infrastructure globally.

Within a mature IoT infrastructure, well over 1.94 trillion devices will be connected as every device becomes smart. The consideration behind having devices interact wirelessly both indoors and outdoors has resulted in specific problems that are open to further research within the wireless communication domain. The literature identified domain-specific problems in indoor positioning/localization and data rate concerns for next-generation technologies (NGT).

With the increasing expansion of location-based services, indoor location tracking and navigation have attracted huge attention from industry and academia. Indoor positioning has generated such concerns largely because the Global Positioning System (GPS) does not work indoors due to the high level of satellite signal scattering and attenuation within enclosures [94], and also due to the complicated nature of building geometry, human orientation/movement, and the random nature of the propagated signal [95]. For indoor visible light positioning, the methods used as investigated from the literature are triangulation, trilateration, and fingerprinting [96, 97].

Triangulation computes positioning by mapping the reference point under consideration with the relative angles, while trilateration relates the reference point for positioning with several distance measurements with respect to the time difference between the arrival of the signals and the received signal strength [98, 99]. Fingerprinting employs the ideology that every location has a unique signal strength distribution, and its coordinate can result in location-finding [97].

In practical terms, a few researchers have investigated sensor-based solutions to overcome GPS limitations in indoor positioning/localization. The work [100] investigated the use of laser range finders, [101, 102] considered the use of cameras, and [103] used depth-sensing cameras. While the received signal strength indication (RSSI) has been well validated in the literature, they suffer from global accuracy with time so [104] attempted a novel approach to making the environment intelligent rather than the agent. Visible Light Position (VLP) remains an open research area until an appropriate indoor localization technique is developed that can map objects to a particular position.

Data rate improvement in wireless communication cannot be overemphasized, as the evolution of wireless communication technology is predicated on high throughput schemes. As user data rate requests increase, frequency bands capable of providing multi-gigabits per second data rates are being investigated [105, 106]. The basic challenges faced in high data rate wireless communication systems are ISI and low bandwidth modulation schemes [106].

To overcome these challenges, [107, 108] achieved a data rate of up to 40Mbps through pre-equalization at the transmitter while filtering out the slow-response yellowish-phosphor component at the receiver using optical blue filters. [109] improved the data rate to about 80Mbps by integrating complex equalization. Considering the drawbacks of pre-equalization in LED driver circuit design, low emitter efficiency, and high cost, [110] combined pre-equalization and post-equalization to achieve 75Mbps. Up to 230Mbps was achieved by [111] by integrating OOK modulation scheme. Since VLC channel bandwidth is far larger than the LED transmitter modulation bandwidth, this imposes a limit on the transmission rate. Schemes to fully exploit the potential of the VLC spectrum for improved data rate remain an academic problem to solve and a major concern for the industry in terms of deployment.

21.6 RECENT ADVANCES IN HIGH-SPEED COMMUNICATIONS

Although the VLF is an alternative communication band, it remains complementary to the existing radio, microwave, and millimeter wave bands. With the ever-increasing demand for high-speed communication links, the need to explore alternative measures to hasten the attainment of global standardization for seamless wireless communication services cannot be overrated.

In the work of [112, 113], the OOK, a generic subset of Pulse Amplitude Modulation (PAM), was implemented as part of the standardization stride for VLC, now referred to as the IEEE 802.15.7 standard [59]. The major drawback in this earliest implementation was high levels of ISI, which is particular to single carrier schemes since information bits are transmitted over a single wideband channel [114, 115]. In order to surmount the effect of signal degradation due to ISI in the earliest VLC-PAM system, the work [116] proposed an algorithmic implementation of zero-forcing frequency domain equalization for perfect signal reconstruction alongside the single carrier modulation scheme. This proposition took cognizance of the peculiarities of signal processing in the visible light spectrum, being that intensity modulation at the transmitter and direct detection at the receiver are preferred schemes for signal transmission and reception in VLC.

Since the original PAM signal is bipolar, to generate a unipolar PAM signal that will be able to drive the LED transmitter, the bipolar signal is first direct current biased such that the eventual output becomes real-valued and non-negative. Despite the fact that the algorithm proposed by [116] could minimize the ISI effect, the cyclic prefix was added to the unipolar output signal to further mitigate the effect of multipath dispersion. The ensuing output signal was then applied to a digital-to-analog converter to drive the LED transmitter, thereby generating the optical intensity signal required by the photodetector at the receiving end for direct detection. The distorted electrical output was then fed to an analog-to-digital converter before the removal of the cyclic prefix, and discrete Fourier was transformed and equalized.

Finally, the discrete Fourier was transformed to generate the required signal for PAM demodulation. The modulation algorithm in [116] performed satisfactorily under line-of-sight VLC channel conditions, although [117], in earlier work, proposed linear minimum mean squared error estimation of single carrier frequency domain equalization for multipath VLC channel. This algorithm achieved better performance in terms of energy per bit to noise power spectral density and reduced bit error rate. However, the shortfall in the proposition by [116, 117] was that the authors did not consider the effect of LED non-linearity on VLC-PAM systems. In practical systems, the input forward bias voltage of the LED transmitter is non-linear to the output emitted optical power, which is a major deviation from the idealized theoretic notion of linearity.

When the driving voltage of the LED transmitter required to generate the desired current grows beyond predefined threshold limits, the power and voltage-current characteristics exhibit non-linear relationships. This directly impacts the average emitted optical power following directly from the illumination level and ultimately impacts the SNR and achievable data rate for a specified bit error rate. This nonlinearity effect between the current and voltage of the LED transmitter degrades the overall system performance. The works [118, 119] proposed superimposed PAM to mitigate the adverse effect of LED nonlinearity. This approach grouped LEDs to produce different intensities when driven by specified voltages. Since each LED could assume one of two states (ON or OFF) at a given instant, the technique could slightly mitigate the nonlinear effect with a major drawback in implementation complexity since different voltage values drove the group of LEDs. A prior development of group modulation technique to improve the transmission data rate at minimal cost of implementation devised a technique for driving the LEDs using the same voltage source at the expense of illumination control of the transmitter front end [120].

In [83], an orthogonal single-carrier modulation technique was investigated. In this scheme, a single symbol duration is divided equally into a given number of time slots so that only one of the time slots occupied by a pulse is used for data transmission. The pulse position is used to represent the transmitted data rather than its intensity. This technique, therefore, earns its name from its mode of operation, pulse position modulation (PPM). Compared with its PAM counterpart, PPM requires lower average power at the expense of increased bandwidth since a fraction of the pulse duration is activated for data transmission. The implication is a high peak-to-average power ratio (PAPR), which necessitates the need for a much higher peak power at the transmitter since the time slots other than the one used for data transmission are zero over the transmission cycle. Under multipath channel conditions, this proposition was flawed since the transmitting pulse could interfere with the zero-pulse position, thereby resulting in ISI; however, if performed optimally under LoS channel conditions.

The works [121, 122] investigate the effect of maximum likelihood sequence detection, which improved the system throughput and mitigated the effect of ISI. However, high processing delays and system complexity made the scheme impracticable. Then, the impact of decision feedback equalizers (DFE) under multipath constraints was proposed [123]. This model investigated the effect of chip rate, symbol rate, and correcting chip rate decision feedback equalization for ISI mitigation. [124] proposed the minimum mean squared error DFE for ease of implementation since symbol interference occurs each time a chip is in error. In [123], an effort was made to investigate the impact of chip rate and symbol rate zero, forcing DFE to eliminate ISI. Unlike the chip rate version, the symbol rate version integrates a feedback filter to eliminate all prevailing inter-symbol interference, yet it is unable to mitigate intra-symbol interference. Another version of PPM capable of improving the spectral efficiency and, consequently, the throughput is the differential PPM [125, 126]. In this algorithm, the authors devised a scheme that ignores the OFF chip in the presence of the ON chip, which led to a faster transmission rate at the expense of increased power.

In the earlier work by [127], multiple ON chips were transmitted per symbol duration with the major drawback in illumination control. This Multi-pulse PPM achieved an appreciable data rate [128]. According to [59], there is a limit to light illumination perceivable by the human eyes, which necessitates proper lighting constraint mechanisms (flicker, dimming, and chromaticity) for illumination control, signal modulation, and processing. In [129], higher data rates, as well as lighting constraints such as dimming control, were achieved. The import of dimming control is that it directly impacts light illumination and optical power output. Since VLC is meant for illumination and communication simultaneously, dimming and, consequently, the signal-to-noise optical intensity will invariably interfere with the received optical power and, consequently, the signal-to-noise ratio. This necessitates ingenuity in the conceptualization of VLC architecture. The ensuing scheme in [129] was regarded as Overlapping PPM since the transmitted multiple ON chips in different symbols were made to overlap.

Improvement made in [130, 131] led to expurgated PPM, which achieved dimming control and mitigated light flickering by transmitting multiple pulses per symbol duration. Further innovation led to variable PPM, a hybrid of PPM, and pulse width modulation (PWM). This scheme employed PPM for bit encoding while adjusting the width of the pulse by PWM, thereby improving the overall throughput [132]. In the work of [133–135], a variant of QAM, carrier-less amplitude-phase modulation, was investigated. The earliest Carrier-less Amplitude and Phase (CAP) algorithm adopted a signal modulation scheme through orthogonal filters. In this case, two orthogonal filters were used to modulate two sets of data streams multiplexed for transmission. This technique achieved a higher rate but was limited to two users. Further investigation led to using three orthogonal filters to modulate three data streams for three users.

The orthogonal filters were generated by multiplying a root-raised cosine filter with either a cosine or sine function. This algorithm outperformed the earlier scheme in terms of increased throughput, SNR, and increased user access. Despite improvement in system performance over implementation with single carrier schemes [136, 137], there exists a limiting factor at high SNR since the computational complexity grows with increasing throughput, which imposes a huge cost in terms of system design [138]. Attempts to resolve the actualization of higher throughput at minimal computational cost and higher SNR have led to investigating the possibility of adopting multicarrier with OFDM technique in visible light system design [139–141].

21.6.1 Application Areas

VLC on a global scale has gradually received widespread adoption due to its high throughput, secured communication link, and the ability to operate in radio frequency-restricted areas. Light Fidelity (Li-Fi) remains a major application of VLC, which is used for the provisioning of high-speed data transmission in enclosed networks [2]. VLC is a possible replacement for Global Positioning System (GPS) in navigation and indoor localization. Visible light positioning, therefore, finds application in tunnels, mines, hospitals, and airports to name a few, for location finding or tracking [142, 143]. VLC also finds application in high-speed short-range underwater wireless communication [144]. Other notable applications are intelligent transportation [145], healthcare [146], smart cities [147], augmented reality/virtual reality (AU/VR) [148], lighting systems [149] and the Internet of Things (IoT) [150].

21.6.2 Open Research Areas

VLC is an emerging technology with several research gaps due to its potential as a complementary and a possible replacement of traditional communication technologies. With the new entrant 6G technology, VLC may be integrated to enhance effective throughput while supporting applications like immersive augmented reality, IoT, and holographic communication. The research gap lies in the possibility of developing hybrid VLC and radio frequency technologies for data communication. Another possible open research area is the investigation of machine learning adoption in VLC channel estimation, signal detection, and interference mitigation. MIMO VLC-based systems are another area requiring research attention in relation to advanced interference management techniques and beamforming. The need for energy-efficient VLC transmitters that necessitate a tradeoff between optimizing the throughput while minimizing power consumption begs for some research attention. Underwater communication is saddled by radio frequency and acoustic communication limitations, typically low bandwidth and data rates. Consequently, VLC could be deployed for high bandwidth and improved data rate experience by focusing on novel techniques to mitigate light scattering and absorption. Other relevant research areas to be considered are security techniques to mitigate eavesdropping, advanced modulation techniques, and VLC outdoor scenarios, with special consideration for high mobility applications such as vehicle-to-vehicle and vehicle-to-everything communication.

21.7 CONCLUSION AND FUTURE SCOPE

In this chapter, an overview of VLC as a key enabler of next-generation wireless networks is presented. The chapter describes the electromagnetic (EM) spectrum and explains its interrelationship with visible light. In addition, the chapter highlights the evolution of wireless communication technologies from 1G to 6G and offers a clear explanation of visible light meeting radio frequency. Furthermore, the chapter examines signal conditioning and multiple access techniques applicable to VLC. Finally, the chapter examines recent advances in high-speed communications and highlights research directions in this exciting area. The potential of VLC enabling the envisioned 6G wireless networks will require further exploration.

REFERENCES

[1] K. Dilukshan, Z. Fahad, K. Vineetha and R. Parthiban, "LED Based Indoor Visible Light Communications: State of the Art," *IEEE Communications Surveys & Tutorials,* vol. 17, no. 3, pp. 1649–1678, 2015.

[2] A. E. Ibhaze, P. E. Orukpe and F. O. Edeko, "Li-Fi Prospect in Internet of Things Network," in *FICC2020, Advances in Intelligent Systems and Computing*, vol. 1129, Cham, Switzerland, Springer Nature Switzerland AG, 2020, pp. 272–280.

[3] P. H. Pathak, X. Feng, P. Hu and P. Mohapatra, "Visible Light Communication, Networking and Sensing: A Survey, Potential and Challenges," *IEEE Communications Survey & Tutorials,* vol. 17, no. 4, pp. 2047–2077, 2015.

[4] A. E. Ibhaze, P. E. Orukpe and F. O. Edeko, "High Capacity Data Rate System: Review of Visible Light Communications Technology," *Journal of Electronic Science and Technology,* vol. 18, no. 3, p. 100055, 2020.

[5] A. G. Bell, W. G. Adams, Tyndall and W. H. Preece, "Discussion on the Photophone and the Conversion of Radiant Energy into Sound," *Journal of the Society of Telegraph Engineers,* vol. 9, no. 34, pp. 375–383, 1880.

[6] S. Li, A. Pandharipande and M. J. Willems, "Two-Way Visible Light Communication and Illumination With LEDs," *IEEE Transactions on Communications,* vol. 65, no. 2, pp. 740–750, 2017.

[7] L. U. Khan, "Visible Light Communication Applications, Architecture, Standardization and Research Challenges," *Digital Communications and Networks,* vol. 3, no. 2, pp. 78–88, 2017.

[8] S. Rajagopal, R. D. Robert and S.-K. Lim, "IEEE 802.15.7 Visible Light communication: Modulation Schemes and Dimming Support," *IEEE Communication Magazine,* vol. 50, no. 3, pp. 72–82, 2012.

[9] G. Blinowski, "Security Issues in Visible Light Communication Systems," *ELSEVIER IFAC-PapersOnLine,* vol. 48, no. 4, pp. 234–239, 2015.

[10] H. Shin, S. Park, K. Lee, D. Jung, Y. Lee, S. Song and J. Park, "Investigation of Visible Light Communication Transceiver Performance for Short Range Wireless Data Interfaces," in *The Seventh International Conference on Networking and Services*, Venice, Italy, 2011.

[11] C. Han, X. Sun and S. Cui, "Design of 100Mbps White Light LED Based Visible Light Communication," in *IEEE 4th International Conference on Systems and Informatics (ICSAI)*, Hangzhou, China, 2017.

[12] Y. Q. Wang, Y. G. Wang, N. Chi, J. J. Yu and H. L. Shang, "Demonstration of 575M b/s Downlink and 225Mb/s Uplink Bi-Directional SCM-WDM Visible Light Communication Using RGB LED and Phosphor—Based LED," *Optics Express,* vol. 21, no. 1, pp. 1203–1208, 2013.

[13] F.-M. Wu, C.-T. Lin, C.-C. Wei, C.-W. Chen, Z.-Y. Chen and H.-T. Huang, "3.22Gb/s WDM Visible Light Communication of a Single RGB LED Employing Carrier-Less Amplitude and Phase Modulation," in *IEEE Optical Fiber Communication Conference and Exposition and the National Fiber Optic Engineers Conference (OFC/NFOEC)*, Anaheim, CA, USA, 2013.

[14] Y. Wang, X. Huang, J. Zhang, Y. Wang and N. Chi, "Enhanced Performance of Visible Light Communication Employing 512 QAM NSC-FDE and DD-LMS," *Optics Express,* vol. 22, no. 13, pp. 15328–15334, 2014.

[15] Z. Wang, Q. Wang, W. Huang and Z. Xu, *Visible Light Communications: Modulation and Signal Processing*, New Jersey: John Wiley & Sons, Inc., 2017.

[16] T. Komine and M. Nakagawa, "Fundamental Analysis for Visible-Light Communication System Using LED Lights," *IEEE Transactions on Consumer Electronics,* vol. 50, no. 1, pp. 100–107, 2004.

[17] C. Shanzhi, S. Shaohui, W. Yinmin, X. Guojun and R. Tamrakar, "A Comprehensive Survey of TDD-based Mobile Communication Systems from TD-SCDMA 3G to TDLTE(A) 4G and 5G Directions," *IEEE China Communications,* vol. 12, no. 2, pp. 40–60, 2015.

[18] W. H. Bernhard, "Mobile Data Communications in Germany - A Survey," in *5th IEEE International Symposium on Personal, Indoor and Mobile Radio Communications, Wireless Networks - Catching the Mobile Future*, The Hague, Netherlands, Netherlands, 2002.

[19] T. S. Rappaport, *Wireless Communications Principles and Practices, Prentice HAll Communications Engineering and Emerging Technologies Series ed.*, NJ: Pearson Education Ltd, 2002.

[20] W. R. Young, "Advanced Mobile Phone Service: Introduction, Background, and Objectives," *IEEE Bell System Technical Journal,* vol. 58, no. 1, pp. 1–14, 1979.

[21] G. Gu and G. Peng, "The Survey of GSM Wireless Communication System," in *IEEE International Conference on Computer and Information Application*, Tianjin, China, 2010.

[22] B. J. T. Mallinder, "Specification Methodology Applied to the GSM System," in *IEEE 8th European Conference on Electrotechnics, Conference Proceedings on Area Communication*, Stockholm, Sweden, 1988.

[23] D. J. Goodman, "Second Generation Wireless Information Network," *IEEE Transactions on Vehicular Technology*, vol. 40, no. 2, pp. 366–374, 1991.

[24] D. J. Goodman, "Trends in Cellular and Cordless Communications," *IEEE Communications Magazine*, vol. 29, no. 6, pp. 31–40, 1991.

[25] K. S. Gihousen, I. M. Jacobs, R. Padovani, A. J. Viterbi, L. A. Weaver and C. E. Wheatly, "On the Capacity of a Cellular CDMA System," *IEEE Transactions on Vehicular Technology*, vol. 40, no. 2, pp. 303–312, 1991.

[26] T. Halonen, J. Romero and J. Melero, *GSM, GPRS and EDGE Performance Evolution Towards 3G/UMTS*, West Sussex, England: John Wiley & Sons, Ltd., 2003.

[27] D. N. Knisely, Q. Li and N. S. Ramesh, "cdma2000: A Third-Generation Radio Transmission Technology," *IEEE Bell Labs Technical Journal,* vol. 3, no. 3, pp. 63–78, 1998.

[28] W. W. Lu, "Fourth-Generation Mobile Initiatives and Technologies [Guest Editorial]," *IEEE Communications Magazine,* vol. 40, no. 3, pp. 104–105, 2002.

[29] W. W. Lu and R. Berezdivin, "Guest Editorial - Technologies on Fourth-Generation Mobile Communications," *IEEE Wireless Communications*, vol. 9, no. 2, p. 6, 2002.

[30] A. Gohil, H. Modi and S. K. Patel, "5G Technology of Mobile Communication: A Survey," in *IEEE International Conference on Intelligent Systems and Signal Processing (ISSP)*, Gujarat, India, 2013.

[31] S. Chen and J. Zhao, "The Requirements, Challenges, and Technologies for 5G of Terrestrial Mobile Telecommunication," *IEEE Communications Magazine,* vol. 52, no. 5, pp. 36–43, 2014.

[32] S. Kilaru, K. Harikishore, T. Sravani, C. L. Anvesh and T. Balaji, "Review and Analysis of Promising Technologies with Respect to Fifth Generation Networks," in *IEEE First International Conference on Networks & Soft Computing (ICNSC2014)*, Guntur, India, 2014.

[33] J. Gozalvez, "Fifth-Generation Technologies Trials," *IEEE Vehicular Technology Magazine,* vol. 11, no. 2, pp. 5–13, 2016.
[34] H. Haas, L. Yin, Y. Wang and C. Chen, "What is LiFi?," *IEEE Journal of Lightwave Technology,* vol. 34, no. 6, pp. 1533–1544, 2016.
[35] S. Dimitrov and H. Haas, *Principles of LED Light Communications: Toward Networked Li-Fi*, United Kingdom: Cambridge University Press, 2015.
[36] Y. Wang, X. Wu and H. Haas, "Fuzzy Logic Based Dynamic Handover Scheme for Indoor Li-Fi and RF Hybrid Network," in *IEEE International Conference on Communication (ICC)*, Kuala Lumpur, Malaysia, 2016.
[37] M. Kavehrad, "Sustainable Energy-Efficient Wireless Applications Using Light," *IEEE Communications Magazine,* vol. 48, no. 12, pp. 66–73, 2010.
[38] S. O. Ajose and A. E. Ibhaze, "Improvement of GSM Coverage Using Microcell," *International Journal of Electronics Engineering Research,* vol. 4, no. 3, pp. 233–244, 2012.
[39] A. E. Ibhaze, *Radio Frequency Network Planning with Microcell Deployment*, Beau Bassin: LAP LAMBERT Academic Publishing, 2018.
[40] H. Haas, "High - Speed Wireless Networking Using Visible Light," *SPIE, The International Society for Optics and Photonics Newsroom*, vol. 1, no. 1, pp. 1–3, 2013.
[41] C. Chen, D. Basnayaka and H. Haas, "Non-line-of-sight Channel Impulse Response Characterisation in Visible Light Communications," in *IEEE International Conference on Communications (ICC)*, Kuala Lumpur, Malaysia, 2016.
[42] D. Tsonev, S. Videv and H. Haas, "Light Fidelity (Li-Fi): Towards All-Optical Networking," in *Proceedings of SPIE 9007, Broadband Access Communication Technologies*, San Francisco, CA, United States, 2013.
[43] S. Nizamoglu, G. Zengin and H. V. Demir, "Color-Converting Combinations of Nanocrystal Emitters for Warm-White Light Generation with High Color Rendering Index," *Applied Physics Letters,* vol. 92, no. 3, pp. 1–4, 2008.
[44] H.-J. Chiu, Y.-K. Lo, J.-T. Chen, S.-J. Cheng, C.-Y. Lin and S.-C. Mou, "A High-Efficiency Dimmable LED Driver for Low-Power Lighting Applications," *IEEE Transactions on Industrial Electronics,* vol. 57, no. 3, pp. 735–743, 2010.
[45] G. D. Campo-Jimenez, F. J. Lopez-Hernandez and R. Perez-Jimenez, "Modulation Schemes Effect on the Driver Efficiency and the Global Transmitter Energy Consumption," in *IEEE 10th International Symposium on Communication Systems, Network and Digital Signal Processing (CSNDSP)*, Prague, Czech Republic, 2016.
[46] L. Zeng, D. C. O'Brien, H. L. Minh, G. E. Faulkner, K. Lee, D. Jung, Y. Oh and E. T. Won, "High Data Rate Multiple Input Multiple Output (MIMO) Optical Wireless Communications Using White LED Lighting," *IEEE Journal on Selected Areas in Communications,* vol. 27, no. 9, pp. 1654–1662, 2009.
[47] J. Grubor, S. C. J. Lee, K.-D. Langer, T. Koonen and J. W. Walewski, "Wireless High Speed Data Transmission With Phosphorent White Light LEDs," in *33rd European Conference and Exhibition of Optical Communication*, Berlin, Germany, 2007.
[48] K. Cui, J. Quan and Z. Xu, "Performance of Indoor Optical Femtocell by Visible Light Communication," *Elsevier Optics Communications,* vol. 298–299, pp. 59–66, 2013.
[49] C. W. Jeon, H. W. Choi and M. D. Dawson, "Fabrication of Matrix-Addressable InGaN-Based Microdisplays of High Array Density," *IEEE Photonics Technology Letters,* vol. 15, no. 11, pp. 1516–1518, 2003.
[50] C.-W. Jeon, H. W. Choi, E. Gu and M. D. Dawson, "High Density Matrix-addressable AlInGaN-Based 368nm Microarray Light Emitting Diodes," *IEEE Photonics Technology Letters,* vol. 16, no. 11, pp. 2421–2423, 2004.
[51] D. Massoubre, J. McKendry, B. Guilhabert, Z. Gong, I. M. Watson and M. D. Dawson, "Fabrication of Planar GaN-Based Micro-Pixel Light Emitting Diode," in *IEEE LEOS Annual Meeting Conference Proceedings*, Belek-Antalya, Turkey, 2009.

[52] J. Vučić, C. Kottke, S. Nerrete, K.-D. Langer and J. W. Walewski, "513 Mbit/s Visible Light Communications Link Based on DMT-Modulation of a White LED," *IEEE Journal of Lightwave Technology,* vol. 28, no. 24, pp. 3512–3518, 2010.
[53] O. Ergul, E. Dinc and O. B. Akan, "Communicate to Illuminate: State-of-the-Art and Research Challenges for Visible Light Communications," *Elsevier Physical Communication,* vol. 17, pp. 72–85, 2015.
[54] A. J. Shaw, A. L. Bradley, J. F. Donegan and J. G. Lunney, "GaN Resonant Cavity Light-Emitting Diodes for Plastic Optical Fiber Applications," *IEEE Photonics Technology Letters,* vol. 16, no. 9, pp. 2006–2008, 2004.
[55] T.-H. Do and M. Yoo, "Potentialities and Challenges of VLC Based Outdoor Positioning," in *IEEE International Conference on Information Networking (ICOIN)*, Cambodia, 2015.
[56] M. Yoshino, S. Haruyama and M. Nakagawa, "High-Accuracy Positioning System Using Visible LED Lights and Image Sensor," in *IEEE Radio and Wireless Symposium*, Orlando, FL, USA, 2008.
[57] S. Randel, F. Breyer, S. C. J. Lee and J. W. Walewski, "Advanced Modulation Schemes for Short-Range Optical Communications," *IEEE Journal of Selected Topics in Quantum Electronics,* vol. 16, no. 5, pp. 1280–1289, 2010.
[58] S. M. Berman, D. S. Greenhouse, I. L. Bailey, R. D. Clear and T. W. Raasch, "Human Electroretinogram Responses to Video Displays, Fluorescent Lighting, and Other High Frequency Sources," *Optometry and Vision Science,* vol. 68, no. 8, pp. 645–662, 1991.
[59] IEEE802.15.7, *IEEE 802.15.7 Standard for Local and Metropolitan Area Networks–Part 15.7: Short-RangeWireless Optical Communication Using Visible Light,* New York, USA: Institute of Electrical and Electronics Engineers (IEEE), 2011.
[60] G. W. Marsh and J. M. Kahn, "Performance Evaluation of Experimental 50-Mb/s Diffuse Infrared Wireless Link Using On–Off Keying with Decision-Feedback Equalization," *IEEE Transactions on Communications,* vol. 44, no. 11, pp. 1496–1504, 1996.
[61] G. Ntogari, T. Kamalakis, J. W. Walewski and T. Sphicopoulos, "Combining Illumination Dimming Based on Pulse-Width Modulation With Visible-Light Communications Based on Discrete Multitone," *IEEE/OSA Journal of Optical Communications and Networking,* vol. 3, no. 1, pp. 56–65, 2011.
[62] D.-S. Shiu and J. M. Kahn, "Differential Pulse-Position Modulation for Power-Efficient Optical Communication," *IEEE Transactions on Communications,* vol. 8, no. 1201–1210, p. 47, 1999.
[63] C. N. Georghiades, "Modulation and Coding for Throughputefficient Optical Systems," *IEEE Transactions on Information Theory,* vol. 40, no. 5, pp. 1313–1326, 1994.
[64] T. Ohtsuki, "Rate Adaptive Transmission Scheme Using Punctured Convolutional Codes in a Fixed Channel Reuse Strategy with PPM CDMA," in *IEEE GLOBECOM*, Sydney, New South Wales, Australia, 1998.
[65] B. Wilson and Z. Ghassemlooy, "Pulse Time Modulation Techniques for Optical Communications: A Review," *IEE Proceedings J - Optoelectronics,* vol. 140, no. 6, pp. 347–357, 1993.
[66] H. Elgala, R. Mesleh, H. Haas and B. Pricope, "OFDM Visible Light Wireless Communication Based on White LEDs," in *IEEE 65th Vehicular Technology Conference - VTC2007-Spring*, Dublin, Ireland, 2007.
[67] M. Z. Afgani, H. Haas, H. Elgala and D. Knipp, "Visible Light Communication Using OFDM," in *IEEE 2nd International Conference on Testbeds and Research Infrastructures for the Development of Networks and Communities, 2006. TRIDENTCOM 2006*, Barcelona, Spain, 2006.
[68] J. Armstrong and A. J. Lowery, "Power Efficient Optical OFDM," *IEEE Electronics Letters,* vol. 42, no. 6, pp. 370–372, 2006.

[69] D. Tsonev, S. Sinanovic and H. Haas, "Novel Unipolar Orthogonal Frequency Division Multiplexing (U-OFDM) for Optical Wireless," in *IEEE 75th Vehicular Technology Conference (VTC Spring)*, Yokohama, Japan, 2012.
[70] N. Fernando, Y. Hong and E. Viterbo, "Flip-OFDM for Optical Wireless Communications," in *IEEE Information Theory Workshop*, Paraty, Brazil, 2011.
[71] K. Asadzadeh, A. A. Farid and S. Hranilovic, "Spectrally Factorized Optical OFDM," in *IEEE 12th Canadian Workshop on Information Theory*, Kelowna, BC, Canada, 2011.
[72] E. Monteiro and S. Hranilovic, "Constellation Design for Colorshift Keying Using Interior Point Methods," in *IEEE Globecom Workshops*, Anaheim, CA, 2012.
[73] R. Singh, T. O'Farrell and J. P. R. David, "An Enhanced Color Shift Keying Modulation Scheme for High-Speed Wireless Visible Light Communications," *IEEE Journal of Lightwave Technology,* vol. 32, no. 14, pp. 2582–2592, 2014.
[74] J. Lian and M. Brandt-Pearce, "Adaptive M-PAM for Multiuser MISO Indoor VLC Systems," in *IEEE Global Communications Conference (GLOBECOM)*, Washington, DC, USA, 2016.
[75] J. Lian and M. Brandt-Pearce, "MIMO Signal Processing for Multiuser VLC," in *IEEE Photonics Society Summer Topical Meeting Series (SUM)*, Newport Beach, CA, USA, 2016.
[76] M. Biagi, A. M. Vegni and T. D. C. Little, "LAT Indoor MIMO-VLC—Localize, Access and Transmit," in *International Workshop on Optical Wireless Communications (IWOW)*, Pisa, Italy, 2012.
[77] T. Miyazawa and I. Sasase, "Enhancement of Tolerance to MAIs by the Synergistic Effect Between M-ary PAM and the Chip-Level Receiver for Optical CDMA Systems," in *IEEE Global Telecommunications Conference*, Dallas, TX, USA, 2004.
[78] T. Miyazawa and I. Sasase, "Enhancement of Tolerance to MAIs by the Synergistic Effect Between M-ary PAM and the Chip-Level Receiver for Optical CDMA Systems," *IEEE Journal of Lightwave Technology,* vol. 24, no. 2, pp. 658–666, 2006.
[79] Z. Chen and H. Haas, "Space Division Multiple Access in Visible Light Communications," in *IEEE International Conference on Communications (ICC)*, London, UK, 2015.
[80] J. Fakidis, D. Tsonev and H. Haas, "A Comparison Between DCO-OFDMA and Synchronous One-Dimensional OCDMA for Optical Wireless Communications," in *IEEE 24th International Symposium on Personal, Indoor and Mobile Radio Communications (PIMRC)*, London, UK, 2013.
[81] C. U. Ndujiuba, O. Oni and A. E. Ibhaze, "Comparative Analysis of Digital Modulation Techniques in LTE 4G Systems," *Journal of Wireless Networking and Communications,* vol. 5, no. 2, pp. 60–66, 2015.
[82] C. U. Ndujiuba and A. E. Ibhaze, "Dynamic Differential Modulation of Sub-Carriers in OFDM," *Journal of Wireless Networking and Communications,* vol. 6, no. 1, pp. 21–28, 2016.
[83] J. M. Kahn and J. R. Barry, "Wireless Infrared Communications," *Proceedings of the IEEE,* vol. 85, no. 2, pp. 65–298, 1997.
[84] H. G. Olanrewaju, J. Thompson and W. O. Popoola, "Generalized Spatial Pulse Position Modulation for Optical Wireless Communications," in *IEEE 84th Vehicular Technology Conference (VTC-Fall)*, Montréal, Canada, 2016.
[85] P. A. Haigh, F. Bausi, T. Kanesan, S. T. Le, S. Rajbhandari, Z. Ghassemlooy, I. Papakonstantinou, W. Popoola, A. Burton, H. L. Minh, A. D. Ellis and F. Cacialli, "A 20 Mb/s VLC Link with a Polymer LED and a Multi-Layer Perceptron Equalizer," *IEEE Photonics Technology Letters,* vol. 26, no. 19, pp. 1975–1978, 2014.
[86] Y. Celik, R. C. Kizilirmak, N. Odabasioglu and M. Uysal, "On the Performance of SC-FDE Schemes with Decision Feedback Equalizer for Visible Light Communications," in *IEEE 17th International Conference on Transparent Optical Networks (ICTON)*, Budapest, Hungary, 2015.

[87] A. Singh, A. Jain and P. Vyavahare, "A Study of Peak to Average Power Ratio for Different Companding Techniques in VLC-OFDM System," in *IEEE International Conference on Advances in Computing, Communications and Informatics (ICACCI)*, Jaipur, India, 2016.

[88] S. Ding, Y. Zhang, S. Li, J. Liu, R. Shu and Z. Gu, "A Novel PAPR Reduction Method Based on ScaledPTS and Clipping for VLC-OFDM Systems," in *IEEE 16th International Symposium on Communications and Information Technologies (ISCIT)*, Qingdao, China, 2016.

[89] F. B. Ogunkoya, W. O. Popoola and S. Sinanovi, "Pilot-Assisted PAPR Reduction Technique for O-OFDM Using Multiple LEDs in VLC Systems," in *IEEE International Conference on Communications Workshops (ICC)*, Kuala Lumpur, Malaysia, 2016.

[90] K. Ying, Z. Yu, R. J. Baxley and G. T. Zhou, "Constrained Clipping for PAPR Reduction in VLC Systems with Dimming Control," in *IEEE Global Conference on Signal and Information Processing (GlobalSIP)*, Orlando, FL, USA, 2015.

[91] Z. Yu, K. Ying, R. J. Baxley and T. Zhou, "PAPR Reduction for Bit-Loaded OFDM in Visible Light Communications," in *IEEE Wireless Communications and Networking Conference (WCNC)*, New Orleans, LA, USA, 2015.

[92] UN, *News: Population*, United Nations, 29 July 2015. [Online]. http://www.un.org/en/development/desa/news/population/2015-report.html [Accessed 28 February 2025].

[93] J. Manyika, M. Chui, J. Bughin, R. Dobbs, P. Bisson and A. Marrs, *Disruptive Technologies: Advances That Will Transform Life, Business and the Global Economy*, McKinsey Global Institute, May 2013. [Online]. https://www.mckinsey.com/business-functions/mckinsey-digital/our-insights/disruptive-technologies [Accessed 28 February 2025].

[94] G. Hein, M. Paonni, V. Kropp and A. Teuber, "GNSS Indoors Fighting the Fading - Part 1," *Inside GNSS,* pp. 43–52, 2008.

[95] S. Ye, Y. Chen and T. Hu, "Evolutionary Algorithmic Deployment of Radio Beacons for Indoor Positioning," in *IEEE Congress on Evolutionary Computation (CEC)*, Vancouver, BC, Canada, 2016.

[96] L. Yin, X. Wu and H. Haas, "Indoor Visible Light Positioning with Angle Diversity Transmitter," in *IEEE 82nd Vehicular Technology Conference (VTC2015-Fall)*, Boston, MA, USA, 2015.

[97] D.-V. Nguyen, M. E. V. Recalde and F. Nashashibi, "Low Speed Vehicle Localization using WiFi Fingerprinting," in *IEEE 14th International Conference on Control, Automation, Robotics and Vision (ICARCV)*, Phuket, Thailand, 2016.

[98] H. Liu, H. Darabi, P. Banerjee and J. Liu, "Survey of Wireless Indoor Positioning Techniques and Systems," *IEEE Transactions on Systems, Man, and Cybernetics, Part C (Applications and Reviews)*, vol. 37, no. 6, pp. 1067–1080, 2007.

[99] J. Armstrong, Y. A. Sekercioglu and A. Neild, "Visible Light Positioning: A Roadmap for International Standardization," *IEEE Communications Magazine,* vol. 51, no. 12, pp. 68–73, 2013.

[100] M. Montemerlo, S. Thrun, D. Koller and B. Wegbreit, "FastSLAM: A Factored Solution to the Simultaneous Localization and Mapping Problem," in *ACM 8th Proceeding National Conference on Artificial Intelligence*, CA, United States, 2002.

[101] J. Civera, A. J. Davison and J. M. M. Montiel, "Inverse Depth Parametrization for Monocular SLAM," *IEEE Transactions on Robotics,* vol. 24, no. 5, pp. 932–945, 2008.

[102] M. Liu and R. Siegwart, "DP-FACT: Towards Topological Mapping and Scene Recognition with Color for Omnidirectional Camera," in *IEEE International Conference on Robotics and Automation*, Saint Paul, MN, USA, 2012.

[103] P. Henry, M. Krainin, E. Herbst, X. Ren and D. Fox, "RGB-D Mapping: Using Depth Cameras for Dense 3D Modeling of Indoor Environments," in *12th International Symposium on Experimental Robotics*, Berlin, Heidelberg: Springer, 2014, pp. 477–491.

[104] K. Qiu, F. Zhang and M. Liu, "Let the Light Guide Us: VLC-Based Localization," *IEEE Robotics & Automation Magazine,* vol. 23, no. 4, pp. 174–183, 2016.
[105] D. O'Brien, G. Parry and P. Stavrinou, "Optical Hotspots Speed Up Wireless Communication," *Nature Photonics,* vol. 1, pp. 245–247, 2007.
[106] A. T. Hussein and J. M. H. Elmirghani, "Mobile Multi-Gigabit Visible Light Communication System in Realistic Indoor Environment," *Journal of Lightwave Technology,* vol. 33, no. 15, pp. 3293–3307, 2015.
[107] P. A. Haigh, T. T. Son, E. Bentley, Z. Ghassemlooy, H. L. Minh and L. Chao, "Development of a Visible Light Communications System for Optical Wireless Local Area Networks," in *IEEE Computing, Communications and Applications Conference*, Hong Kong, China, 2012.
[108] H. L. Minh, D. O'Brien, G. Faulkner, L. Zeng, K. Lee, D. Jung and Y. Oh, "High-Speed Visible Light Communications Using Multiple-Resonant Equalization," *IEEE Photonics Technology Letters,* vol. 20, no. 14, pp. 1243–1245, 2008.
[109] H. L. Minh, D. O'Brien, G. Faulkner, L. Zeng, K. Lee, D. Jung and Y. Oh, "80 Mbit/s Visible Light Communications Using Pre-Equalized White LED," in *IEEE 34th European Conference on Optical Communication*, Brussels, Belgium, 2008.
[110] L. Zeng, H. L. Minh, D. O'Brien, G. Faulkner, K. Lee, D. Jung and Y. Oh, "Equalisation for High-Speed Visible Light Communications Using White-LEDs," in *IEEE th International Symposium on Communication Systems, Networks and Digital Signal Processing*, Graz, Austria, 2008.
[111] K.-D. Langer, J. Vučić, C. Kottke, L. Fernández, K. Habel, A. Paraskevopoulos, M. Wendl and V. Markov, "Exploring the Potentials of Optica Lwireless Communication Using White LEDs," in *13th International Conference on Transparent Optical Networks*, Stockholm, Sweden, 2011.
[112] D. J. F. Barros, S. K. Wilson and J. M. Kahn, "Comparison of Orthogonal Frequency-Division Multiplexing and Pulse-Amplitude Modulation in Indoor Optical Wireless Links," *IEEE Transactions on Communications,* vol. 60, no. 1, pp. 153–163, 2012.
[113] G. Stepniak, M. Schüppert and C.-A. Bunge, "Advanced Modulation Formats in Phosphorous LED VLC Links and the Impact of Blue Filtering," *Journal of Lightwave Technology,* vol. 33, no. 21, pp. 4413–4423, 2015.
[114] N. Fujimoto and H. Mochizuki, "477 Mbit/s Visible Light Transmission Based on OOK-NRZ Modulation Using a Single Commercially Available Visible LED and a Practical LED Driver with a Pre-Emphasis Circuit," in *IEEE Optical Fiber Communication Conference and Exposition and the National Fiber Optic Engineers Conference (OFC/NFOEC)*, Anaheim, CA, USA, 2013.
[115] X. Li, N. Bamiedakis, X. Guo, J. J. D. McKendry, E. Xie, R. Ferreira, E. Gu, M. D. Dawson, R. V. Penty and I. H. White, "Wireless Visible Light Communications Employing Feed-Forward Pre-Equalization and PAM-4 Modulation," *IEEE Journal of Lightwave Technology,* vol. 34, no. 8, pp. 2049–2055, 2016.
[116] A. Nuwanpriya, S.-W. Ho, J. A. Zhang, A. J. Grant and L. Luo, "PAM-SCFDE for Optical Wireless Communications," *IEEE Journal of Lightwave Technology,* vol. 33, no. 14, pp. 2938–2949, 2015.
[117] K. Lee, H. Park and J. R. Barry, "Indoor Channel Characteristics for Visible Light Communications," *IEEE Communications Letters,* vol. 15, no. 2, pp. 217–219, 2011.
[118] Y. Yuan, M. Zhang, P. Luo, Z. Ghassemlooy, D. Wang, X. Tang and D. Han, "SVM Detection for Superposed Pulse Amplitude Modulation in Visible Light Communications," in *IEEE 10th International Symposium on Communication Systems, Networks and Digital Signal Processing (CSNDSP)*, Prague, Czech Republic, 2016.
[119] J. F. Li, Z. T. Huang, R. Q. Zhang, F. X. Zeng, M. Jiang and Y. F. Ji, "Superposed Pulse Amplitude Modulation for Visible Light Communication," *Optics Express,* vol. 21, no. 25, pp. 31006–31011, 2013.

[120] A. Yang, Y. Wu, M. Kavehrad and G. Ni, "Grouped Modulation Scheme for LED Array Module in a Visible Light Communication System," *IEEE Wireless Communications,* vol. 22, no. 2, pp. 24–28, 2015.
[121] J. R. Barry, "Sequence Detection and Equalization for Pulse-Position Modulation," in *IEEE Proceedings of ICC/SUPERCOMM'94 - 1994 International Conference on Communications*, New Orleans, LA, USA, 1994.
[122] M. D. Audeh, J. M. Kahn and J. R. Barry, "Performance of Pulse-Position Modulation on Measured Non-Directed Indoor Infrared Channels," *IEEE Transactions on Communications,* vol. 44, no. 6, pp. 654–659, 1996.
[123] M. D. Audeh, J. M. Kahn and J. R. Barry, "Decision-Feedback Equalization of Pulse-Position Modulation on Measured Non-Directed Indoor Infrared Channels," *IEEE Transactions on Communications,* vol. 47, no. 4, pp. 500–503, 1999.
[124] A. G. Klein and P. Duhamel, "Decision-Feedback Equalization for Pulse-Position Modulation," *IEEE Transactions on Signal Processing,* vol. 55, no. 11, pp. 5361–5369, 2007.
[125] D.-S. Shiu and J. M. Kahn, "Differential Pulse-Position Modulation for Power-Efficient Optical Communication," *IEEE Transactions on Communications,* vol. 47, no. 8, pp. 1201–1210, 1999.
[126] S. Tiwari, V. K. Jain and S. Kar, "Performance Evaluation of Different Pulse Position Modulation Schemes in Atmospheric Turbulence Channel for Ground-to-Satellite Optical Communication," in *IEEE International Conference on Optical Engineering (ICOE)*, Belgaum, India, 2012.
[127] H. Sugiyama and K. Nosu, "MPPM: A Method for Improving the Band-Utilization Efficiency in Optical PPM," *IEEE Journal of Lightwave Technology,* vol. 7, no. 3, pp. 465–472, 1989.
[128] H. S. Khallaf, A. E. El-Fiqi, H. M. H. Shalaby and S. S. A. Obayya, "Average SER of MPPM Technique Over Exponentiated Weibull Fading FSO Channels Considering Fog and Beam Divergence," in *IEEE 19th International Conference on Transparent Optical Networks (ICTON)*, Girona, Spain, 2017.
[129] B. Bai, Z. Xu and Y. Fan, "Joint LED Dimming and High Capacity Visible Light Communication by Overlapping PPM," in *IEEE 19th Annual Wireless and Optical Communications Conference (WOCC 2010)*, Shanghai, China, 2010.
[130] M. Noshad and M. Brandt-Pearce, "Expurgated PPM Using Symmetric Balanced Incomplete Block Designs," *IEEE Communications Letters,* vol. 16, no. 7, pp. 968–971, 2012.
[131] M. Noshad and M. Brandt-Pearce, "Application of Expurgated PPM to Indoor Visible Light Communications—Part I: Single-User Systems," *IEEE Journal of Lightwave Technology,* vol. 32, no. 5, pp. 875–882, 2014.
[132] T. Ozaki, Y. Kozawa and Y. Umeda, "Variable Multi-Pulse PPM Using New Dimming Control Method for Visible Light Communications," *IEEE International Symposium on Information Theory and its Applications,* pp. 80–84, 2014.
[133] C.-C. Wei, F.-M. Wu, Z.-Y. Chen, C.-T. Lin, Y.-S. Huang, Y.-J. R. Chen and S. Chi, "Indoor VLC System with Multiple LEDs of Different Path Lengths Employing Space-Time Block-Coded DMT/CAP Modulation," *IEEE/OSA Journal of Optical Communications and Networking,* vol. 7, no. 3, pp. A459–A466, 2015.
[134] J. Du, L. Sun, W. Zhang, L. Ma and Z. He, "Recent Progresses of Advanced CAP Modulation for Short Reach Optical Interconnections," in *IEEE Optoelectronics Global Conference (OGC)*, Shenzhen, China, 2016.
[135] K. O. Akande, P. A. Haigh and W. O. Popoola, "On the Implementation of Carrierless Amplitude and Phase Modulation in Visible Light Communication," *IEEE Access,* vol. 6, pp. 60532–60546, 2018.
[136] A. E. Ibhaze, F. O. Edeko and P. E. Orukpe, "A Signal Amplification-Based Transceiver for Visible Light Communication," *Journal of Engineering,* vol. 11, no. 26, pp. 123–132, 2020.

[137] A. E. Ibhaze, P. E. Orukpe and F. O. Edeko, "A Simplified Approach for Single Carrier Visible Light Communication Transceiver Using off-the-Shelf Components," *Applied Research and Smart Technology,* vol. 1, no. 2, pp. 64–70, 2020.
[138] H. Witschnig, A. Koppler, A. Springer, R. Weigel and M. Huemer, "A Comparison of an OFDM System and a Single Carrier System Using Frequency Domain Equalization," *European Transactions on Telecommunications Banner,* vol. 13, no. 5, pp. 519–530, 2002.
[139] A. E. Ibhaze, P. E. Orukpe and F. O. Edeko, "Visible Light Channel Modeling for High-Data Transmission in the Oil and Gas Industry," *Journal of Science and Technology,* vol. 12, no. 2, pp. 46–54, 2020.
[140] A. E. Ibhaze, F. O. Edeko and P. E. Orukpe, "A Novel Adaptive OFO-OFDM Modulation for Visible Light Communication," *Süleyman Demirel University Journal of Natural and Applied Sciences*, vol. 25, no. 2, pp. 269–282, 2021.
[141] A. E. Ibhaze, F. O. Edeko and P. E. Orukpe, "Comparative Analysis of Optical Multicarrier Modulations: An Insight into Machine Learning-based Multicarrier Modulation," *Gazi University Journal of Science,* vol. 34, no. 4, pp. 1016–1033, 2021.
[142] N.-S. Duong, T.-P. Nguyen, Q.-T. Nguyen and T.-M. Dinh-Thi, "Improving Indoor Positioning System Using Weighted Linear Least Square and Neural Network," *International Journal of Sensor Networks,* vol. 41, no. 2, pp. 67–77, 2023.
[143] S. H. Oh and J. G. Kim, "Indoor Positioning by Double Deep Q-Network in VLC-Based Empty Office Environment," *Applied Sciences*, vol. 14, no. 9, p. 3684, 2024.
[144] M. F. Ali and D. N. K. Jayakody, "SIMO-Underwater Visible Light Communication (UVLC) System," *Computer Networks,* vol. 232, p. 109750, 2023.
[145] K. Shaaban, M. H. M. Shamim and K. Abdur-Rouf, "Visible Light Communication for Intelligent Transportation Systems: A Review of the Latest Technologies," *Journal of Traffic and Transportation Engineering (English Edition),* vol. 8, no. 4, pp. 483–492, 2021.
[146] S. Chaudhary, X. Tang and X. Wei, "Experimental Demonstration of 62.5 Mbps VLC Link for Healthcare Infrastructures by Incorporating Limiting Amplifier as an Amplification Scheme," *Microelectronics Journal,* vol. 108, p. 104971, 2021.
[147] V. Georlette, V. Moeyaert, S. Bette and N. Point, "Visible Light Communication Challenges in the Frame of Smart Cities," in *22nd International Conference on Transparent Optical Networks (ICTON)*, Bari, Italy, 2020.
[148] R. Zhang, M. Li, Y. Zhang, J. Xiong and L. Lu, "LiRF: Light-Based Wireless Communications Supporting Ubiquitous Radio Frequency Signals," *IEEE Photonics Journal,* vol. 16, no. 5, 2024.
[149] B. Xu, B. Hussain, Y. Wang, H. C. Cheng and C. P. Yue, "Smart Home Control System Using VLC and Bluetooth Enabled AC Light Bulb for 3D Indoor Localization with Centimeter-Level Precision," *Sensors,* vol. 22, no. 21, p. 8181, 2022.
[150] M. H. Ullah, G. Gelli and F. Verde, "Visible Light Backscattering with Applications to the Internet of Things: State-of-the-Art, Challenges, and Opportunities," *Internet of Things,* vol. 22, p. 100768, 2023.

22 Leveraging the Integrated Decision Model for the Emerging Market of Visible Light Communication

Augustus Ehiremen Ibhaze, Aisha Glory Ibhaze, Agbotiname Lucky Imoize, and Francis Masi

22.1 INTRODUCTION

Wireless communication evolution with the Internet of Things (IoT) and smart technologies at its center has become the mainstay for global technological concerns in academia and the industry. Techno-economic indicators will depend on the eventual flawless deployment of these initiatives. The need for entity/device integration through sensors, actuators, and controllers demands an excellent-performing wireless communication infrastructure even now with the advent of the coronavirus disease (COVID-19) [1]. Despite performance efficiency, the interconnection of numerous wireless sensors will require an optimal high-data rate communication technique that will proffer high-speed data transmission processes. The ideology behind IoT will bring about the storage of large amounts of data, which will be processed and, at some point, transmitted over the communication channel. The exacted intellectual tenacity behind big data/future innovations for large data analytics will be a futile engagement if the said data cannot be intelligently processed, transmitted, efficiently reconstructed, and recovered with minimum probability of error within the shortest possible time [2, 3].

According to [4], IoT is envisioned to interconnect things/everything ranging from home automation to the general environment with such entities as furniture, gadgets, devices, cars, etc., by 2025. As a matter of urgency, this proposes building intelligence into objects, thereby making them smart. The idea behind initiating communication between diverse smart objects will demand an integrated communication approach between the indoor and outdoor wireless environment [5]. To cope with this enormous diversified and interactive wireless channel (indoor/outdoor), a novel approach for a high data rate will be required to cater to the high throughput requirement of the IoT deployment in the global marketplace.

 DOI: 10.1201/9781003546153-22

Within the purview of global population densification [6, 7] asserted that 66 percent of the world's population will reside in urban areas by 2050 as opposed to the 30 percent of the world's population that resided in urban areas in 1950. The implication of this projected densification will pose major concerns in dealing with certain critical issues of combating crime, managing traffic incidences, considering economic growth, and dealing with other cyber-physical issues within smart and connected communities. According to the IEEE Smart Cities Initiative [8], a smart city is characterized by a smart economy, environment, people, mobility, living, and governance; communication between the aforementioned entities must be efficient.

According to [9], a smart city is where traditional networks and services are optimized through enabling technologies. As a matter of concern, developing and deploying efficient enabling technologies such as high throughput techniques—a backbone for the Internet of Things and big data initiative rollout—will have to be implemented as the network bandwidth requirement increases within smart and connected communities. Looking at the space-time constraint of global activities, the transmission data rate will remain a major constraint as multi-billion nodes interact within the communication channel. Measures to improve the transmission data rate will revolutionize the integrated transmission mechanism of the Internet of Things initiative.

With the unprecedented increase of data traffic in recent times, the exhaustion of the radio frequency spectrum has resulted in the frequency spectrum revolution of investigating alternative frequency bands for high data rate transmission within the electromagnetic wave frequency spectrum. One untapped band is the visible light spectrum, which can complement the existing radio frequency-based infrastructure in designing high-capacity networks [10]. Since the frequency band of the visible light spectrum spans hundreds of terahertz, it will be logical to investigate its implementation within the small cell regions in the wireless network architecture, making its integration closer to the user's domain.

Since the United Nations has predicted the global population to exceed 9 billion people by 2050, it, therefore, falls within reason without an iota of doubt that there will be an explosive demand for communication infrastructure as our regular daily living has become dependent on interconnectivity [4, 6]. This invariably will require novel business decision models to cater to the unforeseeable explosion in market forces. Coupled with the larger bandwidth property of the visible light spectrum is the capability for higher data rate applications as the research community attempts to adapt the well-developed radio frequency techniques for visible light communication deployment. A fundamental challenge in processing signals in the visible light spectrum is that the signal has to be valued and unipolar as opposed to radio frequency signals that are complex and bipolar. Therefore, this property of the signal requires some ingenuity in processing and channel estimations since existing ideologies do not apply directly. This, again, is a potential business idea that will open newer businesses built around such initiatives.

Daily generated data is about 2.5 quintillion (2.5 million terabytes), which is expected to exceed 10 exabytes of data (that is, 10 million terabytes by 2050) as the human population threshold exceeds 9 to 10 billion people. This will result in an enormous demand for the existing wireless communication infrastructure, which will invariably underperform in limited system capacity if not optimized. Since technology innovation and convergence are being researched to help ameliorate the impending challenging wireless communication network crunch, measures to provide possible solutions for high-speed data transmission and massive data analytics admixed the existing infrastructure base about future demand are inevitable.

22.1.1 Highlights of the Chapter

The key highlights of the chapter are as follows. The chapter

1. examines the adoption of the integrated decision model for the VLC initiative.
2. discusses the visible light communication integrated decision model.
3. explores the potential of VLC as a means to sustainable development.
4. weighs the economic implications of VLC adoption.
5. explores the policy issues and market penetration of visible light communication.

22.1.2 Chapter Organization

The remaining parts of the chapter are organized as follows.

Section 22.2 dwells on adopting the integrated decision model for the VLC initiative. Section 22.3 covers the visible light communication integrated decision model. Section 22.4 details VLC as a means to sustainable development. Section 22.5 examines the economic implications of VLC adoption. Section 22.6 explores the policy issues and market penetration of visible light communication. Last, the conclusion to the chapter is drawn in Section 22.7.

22.2 Adopting the Integrated Decision Model for the VLC Initiative

Various models have existed, ranging from the ball of mud model to the relational, hierarchical, and now the decision model [11–13]. While business concerns have over the years attempted efficient ways to manage core components of the business environment, diverse entities such as security, workflow, presentation, transaction, base, business intelligence/reporting, databases, and business logic have been managed in an unstructured or structured manner. While the decision model attempted to tease out the business logic model from the ball of mud, which encompasses the entire business components with the business logic inclusive, a novel decision model, the integrated decision model, is proposed in this work.

The underlying reasoning behind the conventional decision model is that it connotes an independent representation of the business logic. This implies that the business logic, which is a set of business rules represented as conditions leading to business decisions, is independent of how the business is executed, the exact location where it is executed, and if the execution process is/or is not automated. Hence, business logic is said to have an exclusive existence, meaning that its business structure is distinguishable from the structure of other models. While the decision model is distinctively based on business logic, the relational model is based on data that could utilize the hierarchical model in data management or the unstructured approach adopted in big data analytics.

The integrated decision model attempts to integrate the execution model into the decision model rather than teasing it out of the business logic. The reasoning behind this integrative process is that the execution process of the business decision is seen as business logic since it encompasses the strategy of getting things done through proper investigation, analysis, and follow-through. How and where the business execution is to take place, and the possibility of automation now becomes a trigger in the business logic in IDM. Looking at the extension of the decision model by integrating the execution phase into the decision logic, it is to be noted that the execution phase, in this case, encompasses the development of the business logic of the uncertainties in the decision model. The potential threats, strengths, weaknesses, and opportunities are decided in this integrated model.

In a proper business domain such as the VLC used as a case study in this proposition, certain execution indicators such as how the markets are changing, the creation of strategies based on market dynamics, and linking of the strategies with operations are seen as pure logic to conclude the decision model. However, a fundamental question in business decisions is how reliable the strategies could be. Notably, strategies are orchestrated to initiate customer preferences while maintaining a sustainable competitive edge and profitability. To guarantee a successful strategy, the way (how) the strategy is to be executed must be taken as an integral part of the decision model for seamless actualization of the business objectives. As much as the relational model deals with data about existing things, the decision model is more concerned with conclusions (facts). In contrast, the integrated decision model makes provision for uncertainties, making it robust against potential vulnerabilities while taking advantage of possible opportunities.

22.3 VISIBLE LIGHT COMMUNICATION INTEGRATED DECISION MODEL

The proposed visible light communication–integrated decision model (VLC–IDM) is structured as shown in Figure 22.1 to ensure seamless market penetration.

The structured IDM depicted in Figure 22.1 highlights the key indicators in the decision model, such as the market analysis business model innovation, risk management, partnership, and implementation strategy. Market penetration analysis for VLC technology is initiated, and the market analysis strategy is executed by conducting a SWOT (Strengths, Weaknesses, Opportunities, and Threats) analysis followed by market segmentation. Notable strengths are increased bandwidth, high throughput, secured network due to the absence of radio frequency interference, and energy efficiency from using LEDs. The weaknesses could be the line-of-sight link limitations and the initial cost of deployment. The opportunities in the market analysis phase are indoor localization or positioning applications, smart lighting, and potential markets in densely populated regions. The threat includes regulatory issues, competing technologies, and market readiness. Given market segmentation, the market segments are

FIGURE 22.1 The structured visible light communication integrated decision model.

classified and specified as possible targets, such as healthcare, finance, smart cities, academia, and other enterprises, among others.

The technology adoption strategy involves the diffusion of innovations and technology acceptance models. The diffusion of innovations model aims to forecast the adoption rate of VLC technology, such as the early adopters and innovators, as well as the tech-savvy and high-security clientele base. The technology acceptance model assesses the ease of use and usefulness of the rollout in predicting the potential acceptance of the VLC technology in the marketplace. The competitive strategic model for VLC penetration is implemented by utilizing Porter's five forces [14] and by conducting an industry analysis. Porter's five forces analyze the possible market dynamics affecting VLC's market penetration. It considers threats to new entrants, such as the complexity of the technology and patent protection rights. The threat of substitution is also considered by considering the likelihood of existing wireless technologies adopting VLC as a substitute in critical applications. The five forces also consider the customer's bargaining power by evaluating the awareness of the businesses, telecommunication service providers, and government relative to the benefits and initial investment cost of VLC technologies.

The fourth point is the supplier's bargaining power by evaluating the role of key component suppliers, especially components like transceivers, LEDs, and signal conditioning devices. The fifth force relates to industry rivalry by assessing the notable competitors in the wireless and VLC technology domains. Consequently, the competitive landscape and market dynamics are further analyzed as critical components of industry analysis to make an informed decision relative to competitive strategy. The business model strategy provides a roadmap for how VLC technology will be developed and marketed. It considers the value proposition regarding high-speed data transmission, enhanced security, and energy efficiency. It details customer segments such as smart cities, enterprises, healthcare, and localization strategies in radio frequency-restricted areas.

The revenue streams relative to infrastructure deployment fees, subscription-based models, and licensing for the manufacturers of smart lighting technologies are equally captured. In a similar vein, the cost structure relative to initial research and development (R & D), customer training, manufacturing, and installation are all considered in the business model. The risk management and migration phase entail implementing risk management strategies that address the uncertainties in market penetration. It encompasses the market, regulatory, and technology risks. While the market assesses technological barriers and market readiness, the regulatory risk demands an understanding of the existing standards and potential regulations around VLC.

Consequently, technology risk considers VLC compatibility with the existing technology infrastructure and potential future shift or technology migration. The partnership and ecosystem development phase combines strategic partnership and platform strategy to drive collaboration and innovation. The strategic partnership is built around research institutes, universities, telecommunication companies, lighting manufacturers, and smart systems providers to trigger innovation and foster a robust VLC ecosystem. The platform strategy leverages open platforms to harvest developers and innovators to develop novel use cases for VLC.

In the simulation and forecasting phase, modeling of the system is used to predict VLC penetration under diverse market conditions. This forms the basis for estimating the expected revenue and market penetration. The foregoing triggers the decision phase to evaluate the outcomes arising from the market analysis, technology model, and risk assessment. Should VLC penetration be viable, the implementation strategy is triggered; otherwise, the strategies are reassessed. In the implementation or execution phase, the VLC technology is rolled out in the targeted segments with continuous monitoring to tailor the strategies based on real-time market forces and feedback.

22.4 VLC A MEANS TO SUSTAINABLE DEVELOPMENT

VLC technology can be classified under the broader category of green technologies since the interfacing signal link is purely visible light. This makes the VLC technology free from environmental pollution and possible health concerns. The integration of VLC technology is geared towards a pragmatic approach to sustainable development in relation to energy efficiency, pollution-free society, and readily available resources [15]. For instance, the transmitters and receivers are low-power consumption devices such as light-emitting diodes (LED) and photodiodes (PD). The LEDs could be deployed for energy-efficient electrification (green energy) and as low-power wireless communication hotspots (green communication) for device connectivity. The limited communication distance of the VLC link makes it suitable for small-cell communication, making it an excellent alternative for 5G deployment. Unlike the currently investigated radio frequency bands for 5G deployment, the visible light spectrum will be a good candidate since the spectrum is free from any known health concerns.

Investigations have been ongoing regarding the health implications of the radio frequency signals of 6GHz and 24GHz for 5G implementation [16]. Although there is no known validation of the health risk posed by 5G technology, common reasoning can adjudge that the proposed densification of numerous closely spaced 5G radio frequency radiators will result in an airwave corroded by microwave frequencies. The question that arises is: what will the impact of this proposed wireless chaotic microwave channel have on living organisms? While this remains an open research area, deploying 5G technology using the visible light spectrum will naturally ameliorate such potential concerns while expanding the capacity and effective throughput of the communication system.

22.5 ECONOMIC IMPLICATIONS OF VLC ADOPTION

Since VLC operates in the license-free band of 430THz to 790THz [17, 18], policy for VLC-based device design and integration will be required such that devices are designed with propriety-based authentication addresses. This will keep the manufacturers in the market as devices must be synchronized using these addresses for connection. This will further revolutionize the device-to-device communication industry as it operates at optimal capacity and transmission speed. A tiered-addressing scheme could be developed that will transcend the device level, the communication coverage level, and the network coverage level. The encapsulation, mapping, and authentication of these addresses will determine whether each tier will be active. Once the device identification is deactivated at the network level, the device will not be able to interact with other devices in its tier within the communication coverage domain. This will invariably generate high-level cyber security concerns as policies and decisions will have to be made regarding the security protocols that guarantee safety across the defined tiers using IDM.

VLC adoption will not only improve the way things are done now but will also open up a wide range of business opportunities, including those in device design, branding, manufacturing, coding, identification/localization, networking, security, system integration, data analytics, billing, and cloud computing. In view of the emerging markets that will ensue in relation to the maturity of VLC integration, the integrated decision model will possibly guarantee a seamless transition in the economic and technology domains.

22.6 POLICY ISSUES AND MARKET PENETRATION OF VISIBLE LIGHT COMMUNICATION

Increased demand for highly secure yet smooth Internet will expand visible light's market penetration. The population of countries such as the United States and Canada continues to grow. Yet, this growth does not detract from their ongoing maintenance and developments in providing high-quality wireless connectivity. As a result, visible light communication would thrive in those locations among other Asian, African, European, Australian, and other American metropolises, requiring a wider frequency range to accommodate a large number of Internet users. According to [19], the VLC market was valued at $454.8 million in 2015 and is expected to grow to $101.30 billion by the end of 2024. VLC will be widely adopted and used in the future in device-to-device, vehicular or vehicle-to-infrastructure, and underwater communication. This entails vehicle-to-vehicle communication as well as traffic signal communication.

The state of the transportation system in the country that wants to adopt it is a factor that will influence this. In general, the transportation system is being upgraded in order to lessen the risks to human life. Therefore, VLC would be adopted for effective transportation communication. VLC's promising characteristics are still restricting its adoption, but as innovation improves, it will be embraced on a greater scale in the coming years. Because LED lighting is becoming increasingly popular, it would be cost-effective to utilize the same lighting to provide high-speed Internet [20]. LED light's intensity is limited, a major policy issue influencing visible light. VLC has been used for more downlink transmission than uplink transmission. Because so much light intensity is still necessary for uplink transmission in VLC, [21, 22] advised that the color temperature of LED light be limited to 3000K. The spectral effectiveness of a color is determined by its temperature. As a result, special developments must be made to lower the inefficiencies of LED light so that VLC can be widely adopted.

22.7 CONCLUSION

An integrated decision model (IDM) has been proposed in this work to enhance the reliability of the core components of business ideologies, including VLC deployment for sustainable development. The integrated model is anticipated to provide a more robust domain for handling critical, anticipated, and unexpected contingencies. The conceptualization of this proposition could be developed into a full-fledged model for businesses and technologies in the emerging technology markets.

REFERENCES

[1] Indranil Chakraborty, and Prasenjit Maity, "COVID-19 Outbreak: Migration, Effects on Society, Global Environment and Prevention," *Science of the Total Environment*, vol. 728, no. 1, pp. 1–7, 2020.

[2] Augustus Ehiremen Ibhaze, Simeon Olumide Ajose, Aderemi Aaron-Anthony Atayero, and Francis Enejo Idachaba, "Developing Smart Cities Through Optimal Wireless Mobile Network," in *IEEE International Conference on Emerging Technologies and Innovative Business Practices for the Transformation of Societies (EmergiTech)*, Mauritius, 2016, pp. 118–123.

[3] Augustus E. Ibhaze, Obinna Okoyeigbo, Uyi A. Samson, Paschal Obba, and Ignatius K. Okakwu, "Performance Evaluation of IPv6 and IPv4 for Future Technologies," in *FICC2020, Advances in Intelligent Systems and Computing*, vol. 1129. Cham, Switzerland: Springer Nature Switzerland AG, 2020, pp. 15–22.

[4] James Manyika et al., *McKinsey Digital*. 2013, May. [Online]. https://www.mckinsey.com/business-functions/mckinsey-digital/our-insights/disruptive-technologies.

[5] Augustus Ehiremen Ibhaze, *Radio Frequency Network Planning with Microcell Deployment*. Beau Bassin: LAP LAMBERT Academic Publishing, 2018.

[6] UN, *News: Population*. 2015, July. [Online]. http://www.un.org/en/development/desa/news/population/2015-report.html.

[7] Houbing Song, Daqiang Zhang, Antonio J. Jara, Jiafu Wan, and Khaled Boussetta, "IEEE Access Special Section Editorial: Smart Cities," *IEEE Access*, vol. 4, pp. 3671–3674, 2016.

[8] R. P. J. RonSchipper, and A. J. GilbertSilvius, "Characteristics of Smart Sustainable City Development: Implications for Project Management," *Smart Cities MDPI*, vol. 1, no. 1, pp. 75–97, 2018. [Online]. http://smartcities.ieee.org.

[9] Saraju P. Mohanty, Uma Choppali, and Elias Kougianos, "Everything You Wanted to Know About Smart Cities: The Internet of Things is the Backbone," *IEEE Consumer Electronics Magazine*, vol. 5, no. 3, pp. 60–70, 2016.
[10] Parth H. Pathak, Xiaotao Feng, Pengfei Hu, and Prasant Mohapatra, "Visible Light Communication, Networking and Sensing: A Survey, Potential and Challenges," *IEEE Communications Survey & Tutorials*, vol. 17, no. 4, pp. 2047–2077, 2015.
[11] Ken Orr, *Putting Data into SOA: Data Virtualization, Data Buses, and Enterprise Data Management.* Cutter Consortium, Business Intelligence, 2009.
[12] Barbara Halle Halle, and Larry Goldberg, *The Decision Model a Business Logic Framework Linking Business and Technology.* Boca Raton, FL, USA: Taylor and Francis Group, LLC, 2010.
[13] S. Misra, M. Maheswaran, and S. Hashmi, *Security Challenges and Approaches in Internet of Things.* Switzerland: Springer International, 2017.
[14] Peter Gratton, "Porter's Five Forces Explained and How to Use the Model," *Investopedia*, 2024. [Online]. https://www.investopedia.com/terms/p/porter.asp [Accessed: 15-October-2024].
[15] Augustus E. Ibhaze, Frederick O. Edeko and Patience E. Orukpe, "A Novel Adaptive OFO-OFDM Modulation for Visible Light Communication," *Süleyman Demirel Üniversitesi Fen Bilimleri Enstitüsü Dergisi (Süleyman Demirel University Journal of Natural and Applied Sciences)*, vol. 25, no. 2, pp. 269–282, 2021.
[16] Antonio Morgado, Kazi Mohammed Saidul Huq, Shahid Mumtaz, and Jonathan Rodriquez, "A Survey of 5G Technologies: Regulatory, Standardization and Industrial Perspectives," *Digital Communications and Networks*, vol. 4, no. 2, pp. 87–97, 2018.
[17] Augustus E. Ibhaze, Patience E. Orukpe, and Frederick O. Edeko, "Li-Fi Prospect in Internet of Things Network," in *FICC2020, Advances in Intelligent Systems and Computing*, vol. 1129. Cham, Switzerland: Springer Nature Switzerland AG, 2020, pp. 272–280.
[18] Augustus E. Ibhaze, Patience E. Orukpe, and Frederick O. Edeko, "High Capacity Data Rate System: Review of Visible Light Communications Technology," *Journal of Electronic Science and Technology*, In Press, 2020b.
[19] Ryan Manuel, "Visible Light Communication Market Growth to Propel Based on Increasing Demand for Wireless Internet Connection Till 2024," *Million Insights.* [Online]. https://www.prnewswire.com/news-releases/visible-light-communication-market-growth-to-propel-based-on-increasing-demand-for-wireless-internet-connection-till-2024-million-insights–300971940.html [Accessed: 04-May-2021].
[20] Market Summary, "Visible Light Communication Market - Growth, Trends, Covid-19 Impact, and Forecasts (2021 - 2026)," *Mordor Intelligence.* [Online]. https://www.mordorintelligence.com/industry-reports/visible-light-communication-market [Accessed: 04-May-2021].
[21] S. U. Rehman, S. Ullah, P. H. J. Chong, S. Yongchareon, and D. Komosny, "Visible Light Communication: A System Perspective—Overview and Challenges," *Sensors*, vol. 19, no. 5, p. 1153, 2019. doi: 10.3390/s19051153.
[22] Environment and Energy, "American Medical Association Warns of Health and Safety Problems from 'White' LED Streetlights," *The Conversation*, 2016. [Online]. https://theconversation.com/american-medical-association-warns-of-health-and-safety-problems-from-white-led-streetlights-61191 [Accessed: 04-May-2021].

23 Advancing Cyber Defense with Artificial Intelligence

State-of-the-Art Techniques and Future Directions

Cristian Randieri and Claudio Tomazzoli

23.1 INTRODUCTION

Today, more than ever, we live in a new era in which digital is revolutionizing how individuals, organizations, and even entire nations operate, creating a dense network of interconnected systems increasingly characterized by efficiency and functionality never seen before [1].

However, as with everything, there is always a downside since this interconnection has also introduced significant vulnerabilities that cannot go unnoticed. These vulnerabilities are characterized by cyber threats that, over time, become increasingly sophisticated and pervasive; that is, they become increasingly capable of hitting critical infrastructures, sensitive data, and individual privacy. Let us take a moment to think about the different types of cyber-attacks—everything from ransomware and phishing scams to more sophisticated threats like advanced persistent threats (APTs) and zero-day vulnerabilities. It is concerning how real and prevalent these risks are becoming. We need to find better and more innovative ways to protect ourselves sooner rather than later. The continuous and incessant proliferation of cyber incidents classified as "high impact" further highlights the limited capabilities and inadequacy of cyber security methods defined as "conventional."

The most advanced attackers are always looking for and using increasingly sophisticated techniques, including obfuscation, polymorphic malware, and social engineering, which are, in fact, capable of evading most of the traditional defenses put in place. Furthermore, we witness continuous growth in the daily volume of security data, creating further challenges for human analysts. They face an increasingly variable and dynamic context, for which the identification of significant patterns and the timely response to threats become increasingly arduous undertakings characterized by increasing difficulty levels. To address these challenges, solutions based on artificial intelligence can be resorted to since machine learning (ML) algorithms, by their very nature, can process and analyze large amounts of data to detect patterns

DOI: 10.1201/9781003546153-23

capable of identifying malicious activities, even in cases where the attack signatures are unknown. In addition, DL excels in recognizing even evolving threats with its pecuniary ability to model complex and hierarchical data realities.

No less, autonomous defense systems based on AI can respond in real-time to attacks, consequently reducing the latency time of the response to the attack and minimizing the potential damage. Although the use of AI in cybersecurity is constantly evolving, it is mandatory to investigate integration because it produces multiple challenges, including the possibility of receiving cyber-attacks on the same AI models. This work aims to explore the latest applications of artificial intelligence in cybersecurity thoroughly.

We want to shine a light on the techniques involved and the various tools and systems research that have been shown to be effective in enhancing cybersecurity measures. Our primary focus will include several key areas of interest:

- Threat detection: leveraging ML and DL for anomaly detection, intrusion prevention, and malware classification;
- Autonomous defense systems: AI-based mechanisms for dynamic threat response and mitigation without human intervention.

In addition to summarizing current progress in this field, this chapter aims to explore emerging opportunities and the most critical challenges. It seeks to shed light on the ethical, technical, and operational considerations involved in the context of AI application in the cybersecurity world while also identifying the gaps in existing research and related practical implementations and discussing future directions for the development of cyber defense systems characterized by greater resilience and adaptability. Finally, our goal is to improve our grasp of how AI and cybersecurity can drive innovation and enhance security in today's world amidst the constantly evolving cyber threats landscape.

23.1.1 Contribution of the Chapter

The escalating sophistication of cyber threats necessitates innovative approaches to ensure robust digital security. This chapter begins with a detailed overview of the cutting-edge methodologies currently most widely used to improve cybersecurity resilience. In particular, we highlight the urgency of adopting AI-based solutions to address the most modern and sophisticated vulnerabilities affecting digital infrastructures, which are increasingly targeted by malicious actors illicitly spreading advanced tools such as malware, ransomware, and botnets. Through this exploration, we aim to give the readers an understanding of the fundamentals underlying the interaction of AI methodologies with the cybersecurity imperatives, delving into various AI paradigms and shedding light on their underlying principles, operational mechanisms, and applications in cybersecurity.

The principal methodologies we have analyzed and proposed include:

1. Supervised learning applications in intrusion detection systems (IDS) and classifying malicious behaviors based on labeled datasets;

2. Unsupervised learning using clustering and anomaly detection techniques to identify previously unknown attack patterns and irregular network activities;
3. Reinforcement learning strategies to develop adaptive security mechanisms that respond to dynamic threat environments;
4. NLP to enhance threat intelligence through automated analysis of textual data, such as phishing emails and hacker communications;
5. DL to leverage neural networks for tasks like advanced malware analysis and real-time threat prediction.

Our discussion addresses and highlights specific use cases, such as ransomware detection and botnet identification, demonstrating AI's practical impact and implications in its capacity to address real-world cyber challenges.

While the integration of AI offers and promises a higher transformative potential, we show how it can present significant challenges. The chapter critically examines data privacy, model interpretability, adversarial attacks against AI systems, and the ethical implications of automated decision-making. We further explore the new opportunities for AI to drive innovation in cyber defense by enabling proactive, adaptive, and scalable solutions that prompt responses to the evolving threat landscape.

In this chapter, we identify pathways for bridging existing gaps in research and practice to advance the application of AI in cybersecurity.

To assess the performance and reliability of AI systems in different computing environments, we also aim to support and foster interdisciplinary collaboration by focusing on real-time AI implementation and developing robust frameworks. These efforts are essential to modernizing the design and building of more resilient digital infrastructures, meaning they can better withstand emerging threats.

Beyond the mere academic contribution, we also aim to provide modern insights for all the stakeholders involved in the cybersecurity ecosystem by addressing ethical, technical, and operational considerations and providing the tools needed to implement AI-driven solutions.

Furthermore, our work aims to identify research gaps and lay the foundation for future innovation, promoting the development of next-generation advanced cyber defense systems.

23.1.2 Chapter Organization

Due to the multifaceted content of our review study, we have made every effort to present this chapter in a very structured manner. In order to make the presentation of the findings as clear as possible, this chapter has been structured in the following manner. We begin with an introductory section that sets the stage for the subsequent exploration by outlining the necessity for advanced methodologies to counter contemporary cyber threats.

Then, we continue with a detailed examination of each AI paradigm through these other sections:

1. The Enabling Techniques section introduces the foundational AI techniques employed in bolstering cybersecurity measures, including supervised

learning, unsupervised learning, reinforcement learning, NLP, and DL. Each technique is discussed in terms of strengths, weaknesses, and potential applications within the context of cyber defense;
2. Application Scenarios delves into the practical implications of integrating AI techniques into contemporary cybersecurity challenges. We explore the role of AI in mitigating real-world threats such as ransomware, phishing, malware, and botnets, drawing upon case studies and research findings to illustrate AI's superior performance compared to traditional methods;
3. Malware Mitigation focuses on using AI to detect and counteract malware, one of the most pervasive cyber threats. It examines the effectiveness of various AI techniques, such as CNNs, RNNs, and LSTMs, in identifying malicious software and discusses emerging malware life cycle modeling trends;
4. Botnet Detection explores the application of AI in detecting botnets, a critical aspect of defending against distributed denial-of-service (DDoS) attacks and other coordinated cyber assaults. We highlight the potential of ML algorithms, anomaly-based detection methods, and DL architectures in recognizing botnet activity;
5. IoT Botnet emphasizes the unique challenges posed by IoT botnets and the necessity for specialized AI-driven solutions to address their complexities. We discuss advanced techniques like linear discriminant analysis (LDA), feed-forward neural networks, autoencoders, and Generative Adversarial Networks (GANs) in detecting IoT-based threats;
6. Cyberattack Reaction Systems explores the role of AI in improving the cybersecurity systems' capacity to react to emerging threats. In this context, we examine the integration of AI-driven intrusion detection systems (IDS), intrusion prevention systems (IPS), and intelligent decision support systems (IDSS) to enable real-time analysis, prediction, and autonomous countermeasure implementation;
7. The Conclusion summarizes our key findings, emphasizing AI's transformative potential in fortifying cybersecurity defenses. We also highlight the importance of continuous refinement, exploration, and responsible deployment of AI-based solutions to address the rapidly evolving threat landscape.

While maintaining the chapter's scientific rigor, we have ensured that the language used is simple and pertinent to benefit the sector's operators and stakeholders.

23.2 ENABLING TECHNIQUES

Modern cyber threats and their evolution are distinguished by several continuously and rapidly evolving factors that characterize them in complexity and frequency [2].

Therefore, there is a growing demand for continuous and modern development of new methods and algorithms that can offer robust yet advanced countermeasures to address threats to digital ecosystems, such as integrating advanced algorithms, threat intelligence, and resilience-focused frameworks.

Many studies have highlighted the importance of these particular approaches that can be adopted to improve digital security and thus be able to promptly respond to emerging challenges in sectors such as smart cities and critical infrastructures. The complexity of modern cyber threats demands more integrated countermeasures to mitigate risks in digital ecosystems [3].

Therefore, exploring the dynamics of evolving cyber threats, including advanced persistent threats (APTs) and AI-based attacks, is crucial to highlight the importance of threat intelligence and advanced mitigation strategies [4]. Innovative and scalable approaches to cybersecurity are also critical in smart cities, where digital technology is deeply integrated into urban services to propose frameworks and countermeasures that align with the dynamic interactions between technological advancements and the urban environment [3].

It is also essential to analyze cyber threats within the context of smart cities, illustrating the need for scalable countermeasures to protect interconnected infrastructures [5]. In this complex scenario, AI has become a new and valid foundation of this shift, integrating modern approaches and technologies that are trying to alter traditional cybersecurity concepts. Such conceptual frameworks, which involve the use of different techniques like ML, DL, and natural language processing (NLP), are critical in this regard.

Therefore, advancing cybersecurity through AI relies on diverse and scientifically intriguing computational techniques that leverage adaptive, predictive, and decision-making approaches to counter increasingly sophisticated threats.

These techniques are essentially based on sophisticated mathematical models and algorithms that allow the rapid processing of huge amounts of data, the detection of anomalies, the classification of behavior, and the optimization of the threat response process.

Figure 23.1 shows the ML process, in which there are two important phases: learning and execution; once the training has been done on known data, the model can be used to obtain the result on new unknown ones.

The following sections aim to explore five of the most critical methodologies of AI landscape technology: supervised learning, unsupervised learning, reinforcement learning, NLP, and DL, each offering unique contributions to safeguarding digital infrastructures.

These paradigms enable one to identify hidden patterns, spot discordant behavior, and self-heal to changing threat environments. Besides the play of such enabling techniques, elucidating their foundational principles and operations to enhance these capabilities, each contributing to the symbiosis between AI methodologies and cybersecurity imperatives, we illuminate pathways to more resilient digital infrastructure. This discourse underscores AI's transformative role and identifies challenges and prospects inherent in deploying these cutting edge solutions within diverse cyber domains.

It is also possible to recognize cyber threats using AI together with metaheuristic algorithms such as genetic algorithms (GAs). These algorithms present an interesting and promising approach in the broader field of AI in an ongoing search for adaptable, scalable, and resilient solutions to increasingly sophisticated attacks.

They offer innovative strategies capable of solving and, therefore, addressing complex optimization problems related to cybersecurity. In essence, GAs are algorithms inspired by the natural principles of natural selection and genetic evolution;

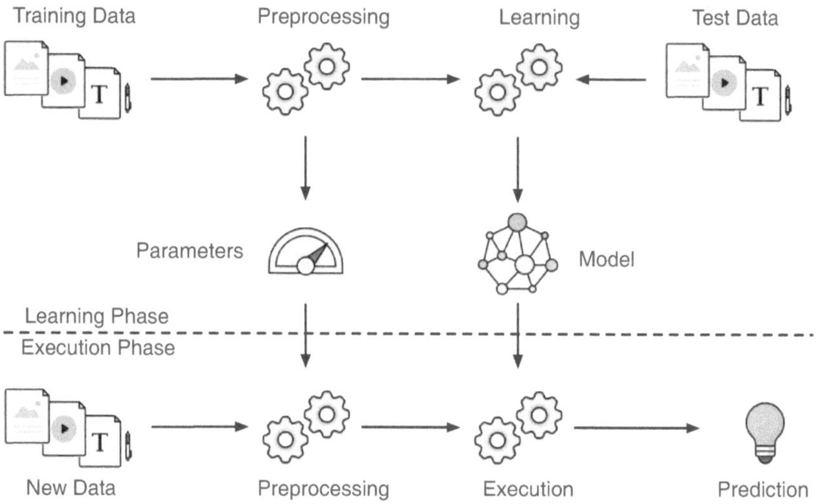

FIGURE 23.1 Diagram showing the machine learning workflow divided into two phases: the learning phase and the execution phase.

they operate through the iterative evolution of candidate solutions [6]. With Selection, Recombination, and Mutation activities, GAs aim to find convergent solutions regarding possible optimal or near-optimal configurations that effectively address emerging threats. Inspired by biological systems, this framework can enhance how we detect, respond to, and prevent cybersecurity threats [7]. It opens up new possibilities for building more resilient security systems.

23.2.1 Supervised, Unsupervised, and Reinforcement Learning

ML algorithms can be broadly classified as unsupervised or supervised, depending on the type of prior information available (or not available) about the data used during the learning process [8]. Unsupervised learning algorithms analyze a dataset containing numerous features (Figure 23.2 exemplifies a clustering output with three clusters over a two feature dataset) and aim to uncover valuable properties of the dataset's structure. In the context of deep learning, these algorithms often seek to learn the entire probability distribution that generated the dataset, either explicitly, as in density estimation, or implicitly for tasks such as synthesis or denoising. Other unsupervised algorithms perform different roles, such as clustering [9], which involves dividing the dataset into clusters of similar examples.

On the other hand, supervised learning algorithms analyze a dataset that includes features, but each example is also associated with a label or target. In practice, while unsupervised learning involves observing multiple examples of a random vector x and attempting to learn implicitly or explicitly the probability distribution p(x) or other properties of interest, supervised learning involves observing multiple examples of a random vector x along with an associated value or vector y (label). The objective in supervised learning is to predict y from x,

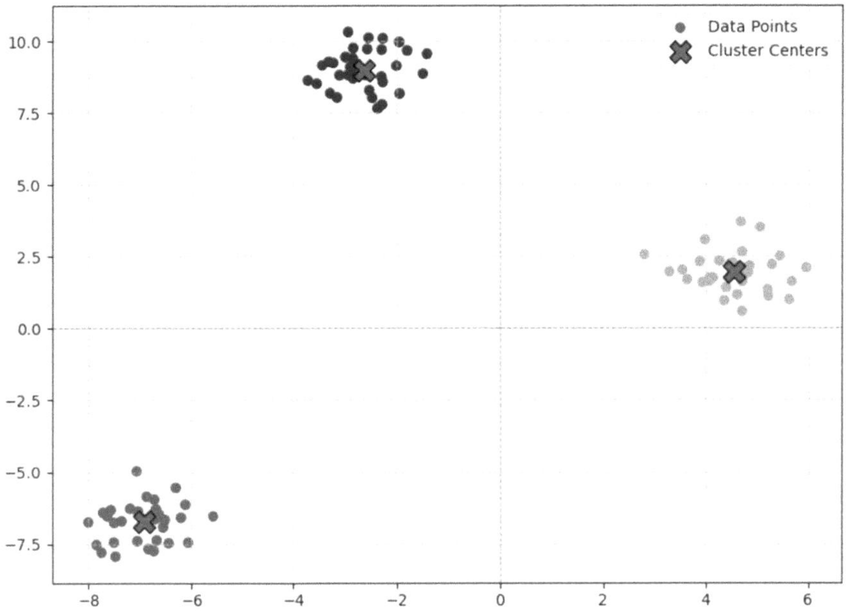

FIGURE 23.2 Scatter plot illustrating an example of unsupervised learning through clustering based on two numerical features.

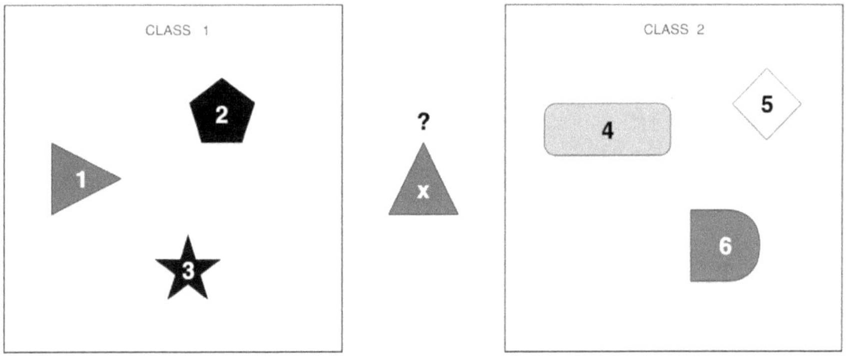

FIGURE 23.3 Diagram illustrating supervised learning for binary classification.

often by estimating p(y|x). Figure 23.3 depicts the most common one: a classificator, whose purpose is to attach a label (the class name) to an item. Supervised learning originates from the idea that the target y is provided as initial input data to the learning system. In contrast, in unsupervised learning, the algorithm must autonomously learn the features and make sense of the data without such initial guidance. Several variants of the learning paradigms described earlier are also possible: Semi-supervised learning: Only part of the dataset is labeled, while the rest remains unlabeled. Multi-instance learning: An entire instance or subset of data is labeled as belonging to or not belonging to a class, but individual members of the subset are not labeled.

Some ML algorithms do not merely analyze a fixed dataset. Reinforcement learning (RL), for example, focuses on determining actions to maximize cumulative reward [10]. It is one of the three fundamental paradigms of ML, alongside supervised and unsupervised learning. RL differs from supervised learning in that it relies on dynamic programming techniques. The primary distinction between traditional dynamic programming methods and reinforcement learning algorithms is that the latter does not assume prior knowledge of a mathematical model. Instead, RL algorithms learn to optimize actions by interacting with an environment, often through trial and error. This makes them particularly suitable for tasks requiring adaptive decision-making under uncertainty.

In addition to reinforcement learning, other ML algorithms provide powerful tools for handling diverse data-driven tasks. Support Vector Machines (SVMs), decision trees, and Random Forests stand out for their versatility and effectiveness in solving classification and regression problems.

Support Vector Machines are supervised learning models primarily used for classification and regression tasks [11]. These models work by finding the optimal hyperplane that maximally separates data points belonging to different classes in a feature space, as sketched in Figure 23.4. Essentially, the SVM algorithm seeks a decision

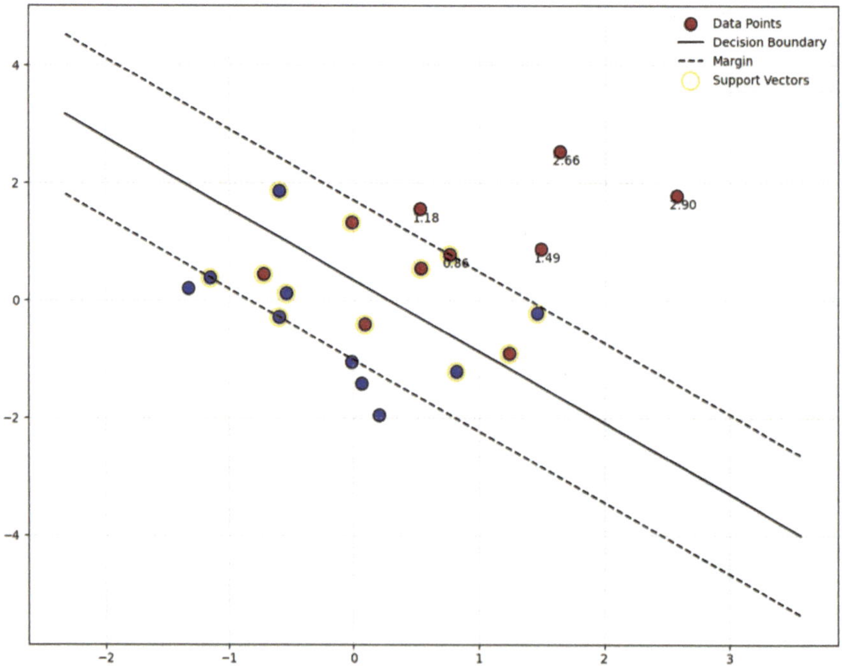

FIGURE 23.4 Scatter plot representing the working of a Support Vector Machine (SVM) decision boundary with margins and distances.

boundary with the largest margin between the classes, improving generalization to unseen data. These models use kernel functions to transform non-linearly separable data into higher-dimensional spaces where a linear separator can be applied. Popular kernel functions include radial basis function (RBF), polynomial, and linear kernels. SVMs are particularly effective in cases where the number of features exceeds the number of samples, making them suitable for applications such as text classification and bioinformatics.

Decision trees (DTs) are intuitive, hierarchical models, well-known for their interpretability and robustness, and are mainly used for classification and regression tasks [12]. A typical decision tree model splits the data into specific subsets based on feature values. Each split aims to reduce the impurity or variance of the target variable in the resulting subsets, providing a visual and precise representation of the entire decision-making process, making them easy to interpret and communicate. They can also handle categorical and continuous data and adapt well to various problems. Decision trees do not assume an underlying data distribution, allowing them to perform well on non-linear relationships. However, these models need to be more balanced, mainly when grown deep without pruning mechanisms.

Random Forests build on the strengths of decision trees by introducing an ensemble approach. This algorithm constructs multiple decision trees during training and aggregates their predictions (e.g., majority voting for classification or averaging for regression) [13]. By averaging the outputs of multiple trees, random forests can reduce overfitting, achieving better generalization compared to individual decision trees. Random forests provide insights into feature relevance by measuring the contribution of each feature to the model's predictive accuracy. The ensemble effect makes the algorithm less sensitive to noise and outliers. Random forests use two levels of randomization—bootstrapping samples to create diverse training datasets and randomly selecting subsets of features for splitting nodes—enhancing diversity among trees.

23.2.2 Natural Language Processing

NLP is a branch of AI focused on enabling computers to comprehend, interpret, and respond to human language in a manner that emulates human communication [14]. NLP has witnessed rapid advancements over the past few decades, driven by the exponential growth of digital data, computational power improvements, and ML techniques innovations. The main characteristic of NLP is its ability to integrate computational linguistics—studying the structure and function of language—with ML and DL models to effectively process and analyze extensive volumes of natural language data [15]. These capabilities are pivotal in machine translation, sentiment analysis, information retrieval, and conversational AI systems. The success of NLP hinges on a combination of linguistic theories and computational techniques. The main components in an NLP pipeline include:

- Text preprocessing: Text preprocessing is the foundational step in NLP pipelines, transforming raw text into a format suitable for analysis. Techniques such as tokenization, stopword removal, stemming, and lemmatization reduce linguistic noise and prepare text for downstream tasks [16]. Additionally, normalization methods address variations in language use, including case sensitivity and spelling inconsistencies.

- Syntactic analysis: This step focuses on understanding the structure of language. Techniques such as part-of-speech tagging, parsing, and dependency analysis enable machines to interpret grammatical relationships within text [17]. Syntax-driven approaches are critical in tasks like machine translation and grammar correction.
- Semantic analysis: Semantic analysis focuses on understanding the meanings of words, phrases, and sentences within a given context. Techniques such as named entity recognition (NER), word sense disambiguation, and semantic role labeling extract contextual significance, enabling computational models to recognize subtle distinctions, including idioms and polysemy, in textual data [18].
- Pragmatics and discourse: Pragmatics extends beyond sentence-level understanding to analyze the contextual factors influencing language use, encompassing speaker intent and implied meanings [19]. Discourse analysis investigates the interrelationships between sentences to elucidate text coherence and narrative progression, which are critical components for document summarization and dialogue systems applications.

23.2.3 Deep Learning

DL can be defined as a subfield of the broader ML field [20] that focuses on leveraging neural network architectures to model complex data relationships and structures. Unlike traditional ML algorithms such as linear regression, which analyzes training data to identify patterns for generalization to similar datasets, DL employs hierarchical layers to capture increasingly abstract data representations. Patel et al. [21] highlight how deep learning models can leverage hierarchical structures to capture complex data patterns, enhancing generalization across diverse datasets. ML algorithms often rely on hyperparameters that are predetermined externally, emphasizing their nature as applied statistics enhanced by computational automation [22, 23]. Discuss the optimization of hyperparameters in ML algorithms, emphasizing the importance of grid and random search strategies for improving model performance and addressing the computational challenges posed by hyperparameter tuning. These characteristics enable ML to estimate complex functions while placing less emphasis on establishing statistical confidence intervals for these functions. ML approaches are broadly categorized into supervised and unsupervised learning, with deep learning advancing both paradigms by overcoming traditional limitations in generalization and computational efficiency. Classic ML algorithms excel in various applications but struggle with inherently complex AI tasks such as speech and object recognition. This limitation stems from the inability to generalize effectively in high-dimensional spaces or solve problems requiring intricate, non-linear mappings. Deep learning can address these challenges by introducing multi-level feature hierarchies, leveraging stochastic gradient descent (SGD) optimization, and employing loss functions tailored to specific tasks.

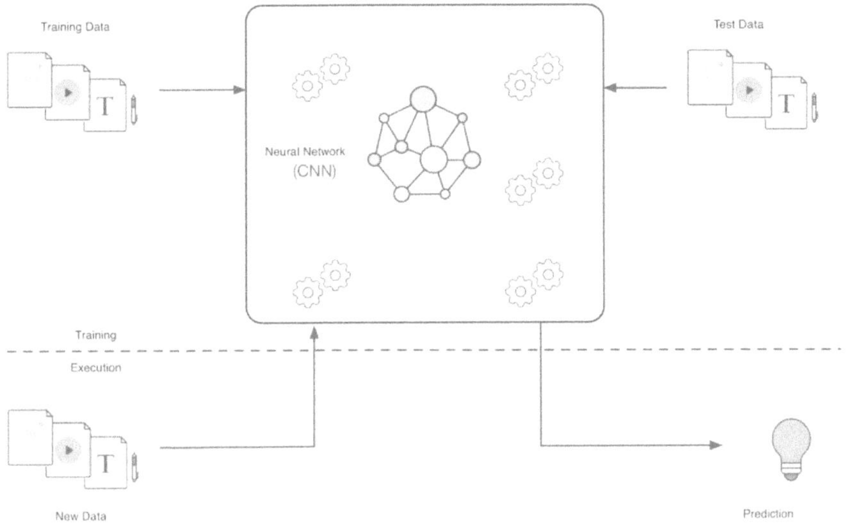

FIGURE 23.5 Deep learning (DL) process, showcasing two phases: training and execution.

Figure 23.5 shows the DL process, which shares training and execution phases with ML but does not need the preprocessing step.

These advancements enable DL algorithms to handle the exponential complexity of modern data sets, including cases where the parameter space far exceeds the size of the training set. ML algorithms require prior assumptions about the target function to generalize effectively. DL incorporates additional structural priors to mitigate overfitting in sophisticated tasks. Unlike many ML approaches that rely on explicit task-specific assumptions, neural networks adopt more generalized hypotheses, enabling broader adaptability. This flexibility is particularly crucial for AI applications where task structures are too complex to be captured by simple periodic properties. The central hypothesis in DL is that data can be modeled as compositions of hierarchical features across multiple levels, offering exponential improvements in efficiency concerning data examples versus representational complexity. A critical concept in ML and DL is manifolds—connected regions representing data distributions in high-dimensional spaces with locally low-dimensional structures. For example, data points representing natural images or speech signals often reside on low-dimensional manifolds embedded in higher-dimensional input spaces. A recent work [24] addresses the challenge of explaining the internal workings of deep learning models, focusing on a geometric and topological perspective. It explores how neural networks represent data internally and how the topology and geometry of the data manifolds evolve through different layers. By learning the underlying manifolds, DL algorithms achieve better generalization while requiring fewer degrees of freedom. This manifold hypothesis is particularly evident in AI tasks involving image, sound, or text processing, where probability distributions are concentrated along these low-dimensional structures. From a broader perspective, the study of ML and DL advances computational capabilities and deepens our understanding of the principles underlying intelligence. By addressing tasks too complex for human-designed algorithms, these fields provide insight into the mechanisms that drive learning and cognition, offering a bridge between computational models and philosophical inquiries into intelligence.

Deep learning uses specialized architectures to effectively handle different data modalities. The most influential in the scientific landscape are convolutional neural networks (CNN), recurrent neural networks (RNN), and long short-term memory (LSTM) networks. Each of these techniques exploits specific structures and patterns in the data. CNNs are particularly well-suited for processing image data [25] due to their ability to capture spatial hierarchies and local dependencies. By employing convolutional layers, these networks extract features such as edges, textures, and more complex patterns as data progresses through successive layers. CNNs' hierarchical structure is the automatic discovery of feature representations, aligning with the manifold hypothesis by concentrating relevant data structures along low-dimensional spaces [26]. This characteristic makes CNNs highly effective in image classification, object detection, and medical image analysis tasks. Adding pooling layers can reduce dimensionality while maintaining essential information and guarantee computational efficiency.

While CNNs excel in spatial domains, RNNs are designed for sequential data, where temporal dependencies and order are critical. Due to their intrinsic characteristics, RNNs are typically adopted to solve specific tasks involving time series, natural language, or other sequential inputs. They access data step-by-step and retain information through their hidden state representations. This iterative mechanism facilitates understanding and predicting sequential patterns by mapping sequences of trajectory-like structures into feature space. One aspect of RNNs that limits their effectiveness in specific applications is that they often need help with vanishing gradients when learning long-term dependencies. To address the limitations of traditional RNNs, LSTMs introduce a more sophisticated memory cell architecture, as shown in Figure 23.6. LSTMs regulate the flow of information using specific components

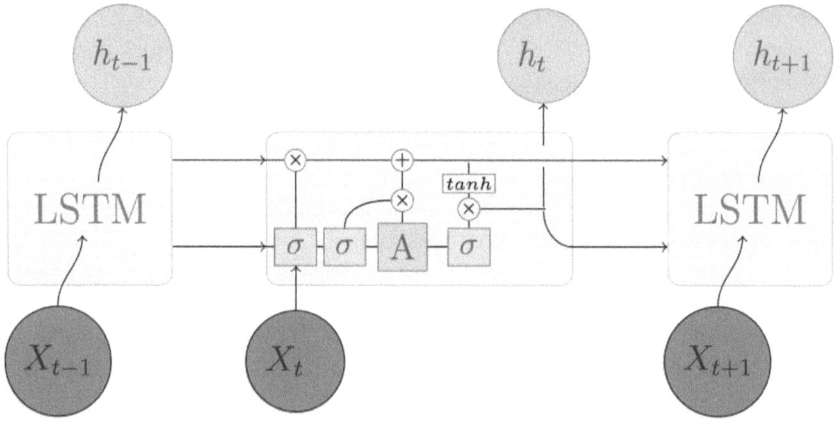

FIGURE 23.6 Structure and workflow of long short-term memory (LSTM) networks, designed for processing sequential and time-series data.

such as input, output, and forgetting gates, allowing them to retain or discard specific details over extended time intervals. This capability makes LSTMs particularly effective for any task that requires long-term context, such as machine translation, speech recognition, and sentiment analysis. LSTMs help the network better understand and recognize patterns over time by keeping important information over longer sequences. This strengthens the link between deep learning and how data structures are understood using shapes and geometry.

The interplay between manifold representations and these neural architectures highlights deep learning's adaptability to align with data's intrinsic structures.

23.3 APPLICATION SCENARIOS

Some of the biggest cybersecurity concerns in today's digital environment include ransomware, phishing, malware, and botnets, which can endanger people, businesses, and vital infrastructures. A wide range of harmful software intended to harm, interfere with, or obtain unauthorized access to systems is called malware.

Phishing uses phony communications to trick people into disclosing private information, which frequently makes it easier for later intrusions to occur.

Critical data are encrypted or locked by ransomware, which demands money to unlock it.

Botnets use networks of hacked machines to carry out coordinated assaults like spam campaigns or distributed denial of service (DDoS).

These more complex attacks combine social engineering techniques and modern technologies to avoid detection. AI provides innovative solutions superior to traditional cybersecurity measures and has gained popularity in the battle against these threats.

AI-powered systems utilize ML and DL to analyze vast datasets, identify patterns, and detect anomalies indicative of malicious activities. For malware detection, AI recognizes obfuscated or polymorphic malware through dynamic and heuristic analyses. Phishing detection systems leverage NLP and behavioral models to identify deceptive content in URLs and email communications. In ransomware mitigation, AI-driven solutions incorporate semi-supervised frameworks and deception strategies, such as decoy files, to detect and isolate attacks.

Similarly, botnet detection uses AI's capacity to examine vast network traffic to spot odd patterns and connections indicative of malicious activity.

The following sections provide specifics on AI use in each of these scenarios.

23.3.1 Threats against Computer Users

Ransomware and phishing are two of the most common cyber threats, taking advantage of digital system weaknesses through malicious software and social engineering. Phishing attacks utilize phony emails or websites to trick users into divulging personal information, and ransomware encrypts important data and demands payment to unlock it. Both threats have become more sophisticated, using cutting-edge strategies to get around conventional security measures and seriously harm people and companies financially and operationally. With ML and DL techniques, AI has become a potent weapon in the battle against these dangers, providing adaptable and dynamic solutions. AI-based phishing detection systems look at URL patterns, metadata, and behavioral characteristics to distinguish between fake and authentic activity. Similarly, AI-driven ransomware detection combines runtime behavior analysis, decoy-based techniques, and anomaly detection to identify and neutralize assaults frequently before significant harm occurs.

23.3.1.1 Phishing

AI has brought advanced, valuable methods that can adapt to evolving threats and has significantly changed phishing detection. Phishing, a dishonest electronic activity that involves posing as a trustworthy entity to perform an attack, is still a global threat.

AI-based phishing detection models have been successfully used: k-nearest neighbors, naive Bayes, decision trees, and random forests have shown to be effective when analyzing features extracted from the content of the message and related links [27, 28].

In order to find dangerous patterns, AI-driven detection techniques primarily analyze URLs, HTTP responses, and content metadata. For example, ML techniques, like the one mentioned earlier, are frequently used to determine if a URL is malicious or legitimate.

These models analyze features such as URL length, special characters, HTTP protocols, and the inclusion of suspicious elements like IP addresses. Such techniques have been demonstrated to improve detection rates significantly compared to traditional methods like denylists, which are limited by their inability to detect new attacks [28, 29].

Advanced ensemble learning models combining multiple ML algorithms have been developed to improve accuracy and robustness. A hybrid model integrating logistic regression, even with simple algorithms such as Support Vector Machine and decision tree, trained on an 11.000 URL dataset, has achieved high precision and recall [29].

By using feature selection and cross-validation approaches, these models can adapt to various phishing patterns. More complicated techniques like DNN can find complex and subtle correlations in data that simpler models may miss [30]. Dynamic ML-based phishing detection systems utilize datasets extracted from repositories like PhishTank and Alexa to train algorithms on phishing and legitimate websites. Features such as the number of special characters, the structure of URLs, and HTML tags are analyzed to develop classifiers that have been shown to be quite effective in predicting phishing attempts. These systems outperform traditional approaches, with reported accuracies exceeding 90% in certain cases [28, 29].

NLP models are also beneficial for phishing detection. NLP-based systems analyze textual content in URLs and related metadata to find linguistic patterns suggestive of phishing. Important keywords that are essential to the detecting process are highlighted using techniques like TF-IDF. Finally, deep learning approaches like CNN and LSTM can be used to identify specialized attacks, named "spear-phishing" attempts [28, 31].

23.3.1.2 Ransomware

Ransomware, software that locks or encrypts victim files to extort money, is a real threat to everyday life for people and businesses worldwide.

The sophistication of ransomware attacks has increased with advancements in social engineering tactics, code obfuscation, and encryption technologies. AI, particularly ML and DL, offers robust solutions for mitigating ransomware by enhancing detection capabilities and enabling adaptive defenses.

Behavior-based detection has advanced with AI's ability to analyze system-level behaviors such as API calls, file operations, and network activities. A recent study highlights that ML algorithms like Random Forest and decision trees accurately distinguish ransomware from benign software, effectively countering obfuscation techniques [32].

When combined with Principal Component Analysis (PCA) in a streamlined process, the accuracy obtained is similar to data-driven solutions [33] while computational complexity is kept to a minimum.

Deep learning techniques, particularly neural networks, are emphasized for their ability to handle large datasets and identify subtle behavioral patterns. Similarly, integrating big data analytics enhances the scalability of detection systems, addressing the evolving complexity of ransomware [32].

ML can help generate adaptive decoy files, strategically planting them across user directories to attract ransomware attacks. This strategy detects ransomware activities early and contains them by triggering automated responses to isolate affected systems. The real-time monitoring of decoy files ensures a high deception rate and minimal data loss, even against sophisticated ransomware variants, and a recent work demonstrated the efficacy of these methods against 20 ransomware families [34].

Dealing with ransomware threats has changed dramatically with the use of DL for detection. Both labeled and unlabeled data may be analyzed by AI systems, which are able to recognize trends in ransomware variants that use encryption and obfuscation.

An example is a deep learning-based semi-supervised framework that integrates runtime behavioral analysis with supervised classifiers, where the deep learning block is used to process unstructured data and identify ransomware behaviors dynamically, feeding the data to a classifier so that the overall performance is higher than any conventional methods [35].

AI-based detection systems still face several obstacles despite these developments. Due to their ability to target memory-only activities and legitimate programs, polymorphic and fileless ransomware variants are becoming increasingly common, which presents substantial challenges for detection using traditional approaches [34].

Additionally, the computational intensity of deep learning models limits their deployment in real-time environments. Adversarial attacks, where ransomware creators counter AI models with evasion techniques, further complicate the development of robust defenses [32].

The future of AI in ransomware detection will focus on capabilities, better integration of big data, and increased resistance against hostile attempts. Innovations that dynamically adapt to ransomware behaviors, such as deception-based tactics and adaptive hybrid models, show great promise.

These methodologies bolster detection accuracy while enhancing the overall robustness of ransomware detecting frameworks [35].

23.4 MALWARE MITIGATION

Examining the progression of distributed denial of service (DDoS) attacks and, in general, of malware effects in the last decade highlights trends in these threats' increasing complexity and frequency, giving evidence of the critical need for flexible cybersecurity strategies [36].

AI has achieved impressive strides in malware mitigation thanks to its sophisticated algorithms and strategies to tackle the growing complexity of cybersecurity threats. Malware is disruptive software that targets specific system weaknesses and can take many forms, such as ransomware, spyware, Trojan horses, and worms. DL techniques such as CNN, RNN, and LSTM have proven to be more accurate and have fewer false positives than classic ML approaches [37].

One of the primary contributions of AI in malware mitigation lies in its ability to rapidly process and analyze large datasets. The best algorithms for these jobs are DNNs, such as CNNs and RNNs, which can spot patterns and anomalies in data that could indicate hostile behavior. CNNs, for example, have been used to convert malware binary files into pictures, allowing for pattern recognition that separates harmful software from benign software [38].

RNNs, particularly those integrated with techniques like Word Vectorization for feature extraction, have demonstrated robust capabilities in detecting malware by analyzing sequences of API calls and other behavioral patterns [39].

Deep learning methods have surpassed traditional ML techniques [40] by addressing limitations such as scalability and adaptability, which are extremely important when dealing with Android malware. Techniques like LSTM networks are specialized in analyzing time-series data to detect subtle, long-term dependencies in malware behaviors. These models enable a dynamic approach to identifying malware; by evaluating performance metrics such as accuracy and F1-score, these DL techniques are the best suited for distinguishing between benign and malicious applications in Android-specific scenarios [41].

Unlike signature-based methods, which rely on predefined patterns, heuristic and behavior-based detection approaches, typical of dynamic deep learning, can generalize from known threats to predict and prevent novel malware. On the other hand, behavioral analysis observes runtime characteristics, enhancing the detection of obfuscated or polymorphic malware that evades static analysis and can provide an automated detection and classification tool for cybersecurity analysts [42].

Malware has also spread to Internet of Things (IoT) devices, as will be discussed in the next section; these appliances are increasingly targeted due to their limited security frameworks. Advanced deep learning architectures, such as Bidirectional Gated Recurrent Unit combined with a CNN model (Bi-GRUCNN), have been applied to detect and classify IoT malware in a platform independent way, achieving robust performance across diverse IoT CPU architectures while minimizing preprocessing efforts across various CPU architectures. Without AI's generalization capabilities, the burden of modern cyber threat counteraction would be extremely, if impossibly, complicated [43].

Moreover, as malware life cycles sometimes mimic disease behaviors, integrating epidemiological models with AI provides a predictive framework for understanding and controlling malware propagation. Models adapt concepts from disease spread to simulate and predict malware dynamics, leveraging infection, recovery, and immunity loss rates to simulate malware spread and suggest defensive strategies for containment [44].

Real-time detection and managing the growing complexity of evasion techniques still need to be improved despite these developments. For example, specific deep learning techniques need much processing power and are vulnerable to zero-day attacks.

Nonetheless, AI's continuous evolution, combined with hybrid approaches that integrate static, dynamic, and heuristic analyses, is gradually addressing these issues [37, 42]. Ransomware, software that locks or encrypts victim files to extort money, is a real threat to everyday life for people and businesses worldwide.

Thanks to developments in encryption, code obfuscation, and social engineering strategies, ransomware assaults have become more complex. Because AI improves detection capabilities and makes adaptive defenses possible, it provides strong options for reducing ransomware, especially ML and DL.

Behavior-based detection has advanced with AI's ability to analyze system level behaviors such as API calls, file operations, and network activities. A recent study highlights that ML algorithms like Random Forest and decision trees accurately distinguish ransomware from benign software, effectively countering obfuscation techniques [32].

When combined with Principal Component Analysis (PCA) in a streamlined process, the accuracy obtained is similar to data-driven solutions [33] while computational complexity is kept to a minimum.

Deep learning techniques, particularly neural networks, are emphasized for their ability to handle large datasets and identify subtle behavioral patterns. Similarly, integrating big data analytics enhances the scalability of detection systems, addressing the evolving complexity of ransomware [32].

Adaptive fake files can be created with ML, and these decoys can then be strategically placed throughout user folders to draw ransomware attacks. This tactic isolates compromised computers by initiating automated reactions, which helps identify and stop ransomware activity early.

The real-time monitoring of decoy files ensures a high deception rate and minimal data loss, even against sophisticated ransomware variants, and a recent work demonstrated the efficacy of these methods against 20 ransomware families [34].

Dealing with ransomware threats has changed dramatically with the use of DL for detection. Both labeled and unlabeled data may be analyzed by AI systems, which can recognize trends in ransomware variants that use encryption and obfuscation.

For instance, a deep learning-based semi-supervised framework might integrate runtime behavioral analysis with supervised classifiers; the deep learning block can be used to process unstructured data and identify ransomware behaviors dynamically, feeding the data to a classifier so that the overall performance is higher than any conventional methods [35].

AI-based detection systems still face several obstacles despite these developments. Due to their ability to target memory-only activities and legitimate programs, polymorphic and fileless ransomware variants are becoming increasingly common, which presents substantial challenges for detection using traditional approaches [34].

Additionally, the computational intensity of deep learning models limits their deployment in real-time environments. Adversarial attacks, where ransomware creators counter AI models with evasion techniques, further complicate the development of robust defenses [32].

The future of AI in ransomware detection will focus on capabilities, better integration of big data, and increased resistance against hostile attempts. Innovations that dynamically adapt to ransomware behaviors, such as deception-based tactics and adaptive hybrid models, show great promise.

These methodologies bolster detection accuracy while enhancing the overall robustness of cybersecurity frameworks [35].

23.5 BOTNET DETECTION

A "botnet" is a network of computers, Internet of Things devices, or smartphones infected by malware and controlled by an attacker to execute coordinated cyberattacks. These compromised computers, known as bots or zombies, can carry out illegal activities such as distributing ransomware, sending spam, stealing confidential information, and overloading servers with traffic in distributed denial-of-service (DDoS) attacks.

The communication infrastructure is essential for operation, with centralized botnets that rely on command-and-control servers to direct operations and decentralized or peer-to-peer systems in which communications between peers are of the essence.

Because they depend on preset patterns or thresholds, which botnets are skilled at evading, traditional detection techniques like rule-based systems and signature-based IDS are ineffective against them.

Therefore, more dynamic methods are needed: ML, anomaly-based detection, and behavioral analysis can identify patterns and anomalies both in system activities and in network traffic, effectively helping recognize the activity of botnets.

Several ML techniques have been fruitfully used, both supervised/unsupervised learning and deep learning.

Using honeypots to collect attack data over SSH sessions safely, a supervised learning (ML) model can be trained to automatically detect future attacks without any signature comparison. The models that have shown their effectiveness while trained with several dozen features such as command usage, session states, and network traffic characteristics are decision trees, Random Forests, Support Vector Machines (SVMs), and Naive Bayes [45]. Even without the help of labeled data, unsupervised learning models can be trained using network traffic features such as packet size and volume through time, identifying shifts that indicate the emergence of new patterns. These patterns can be organized in clusters, thanks to the Hierarchical Agglomerative Clustering (HAC) algorithm, which can subsequently be analyzed for botnet activity, leveraging Euclidean distance metrics to distinguish benign from malicious traffic [46]. Deep learning has recently been effectively applied to botnet detection, with only benign IP network traffic used to build a baseline of typical network behavior. In specific, autoencoder architectures have shown their potential when modified to adhere to network traffic analysis. Autoencoders are neural network models designed to compress data into a lower-dimensional representation and reconstruct it. The reconstruction error indicates how well the input aligns with the learned distribution of routine data. An adaptation of Generative Adversarial Networks (GANs), which incorporates adversarial training to enhance anomaly detection by generating more precise reconstructions of innocent traffic patterns, obtained remarkable results in dealing with this problem [47].

23.6 IOT BOTNET

IoT botnets are malware-infected IoT devices that can be controlled remotely using inherent weaknesses in IoT devices, such as poor authentication systems, hardcoded credentials, and a lack of regular firmware updates. Once infiltrated, these devices are used to carry out distributed denial of service (DDoS) assaults, data exfiltration, and other nefarious operations. Given the diversity of IoT devices and network environments, the detection and prevention of these attacks pose an even higher level of complexity so that traditional ML approach limitations, including lower detection accuracy, high false-positive rates, and computational inefficiencies, fail to be effective when applied to IoT settings.

Advanced techniques combined with deep learning have been devised as a valuable solution for IoT botnet detection. Linear Discriminant Analysis (LDA) is used to capture diverse metrics such as entropy, information gain, flow-based statistics, and correlation between features, which are then fed to a specialized feed-forward neural network [48].

Deep autoencoders, a specialized DNN whose schema is depicted in Figure 23.7, and Generative Adversarial Network (GAN) purposefully built for outlier detection have also proven to be effective against these kind of botnet [49].

23.7 CYBERATTACK REACTION SYSTEMS

Modern society has become increasingly dependent on information technology (IT), and cyber dangers are becoming more widespread and sophisticated. The inability

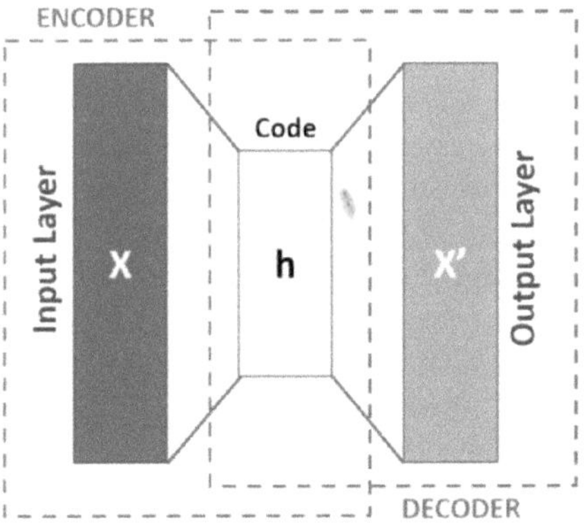

FIGURE 23.7 Diagram of an autoencoder neural network architecture.

of traditional cybersecurity systems to adjust to these difficulties frequently calls for creative solutions like AI.

Cyber threats are constantly changing so that to reduce cyber risk and safeguard digital infrastructure there is the need for proactive and adaptable countermeasures, which AI can provide.

AI addresses the limitations of conventional cybersecurity methods by enabling real-time analysis of vast datasets, detecting patterns, and identifying anomalies indicative of threats. For instance, intrusion detection systems (IDS) and intrusion prevention systems (IPS) integrated with AI can analyze network behaviors, predict attacks, and autonomously implement countermeasures. AI's ability to detect zero-day vulnerabilities through ML models marks a significant leap in the capability to respond to emerging threats [50, 51].

AI integration has been especially beneficial for reactive systems like Intrusion Response Systems (IRS). Thanks to the ability to autonomously choose and implement the optimal countermeasures, these systems minimize response times and the need for human interaction. By analyzing historical data and current threats, AI-driven IRS can recommend optimal strategies to counteract complex and stealthy attacks [51].

Bio-inspired methodologies, such as Artificial Immune Systems (AIS), have introduced a paradigm shift in countermeasure selection. AIS emulates biological immune systems to create adaptive responses to cyber threats, considering countermeasures as "antibodies" that evolve to minimize risks of "infections" while considering features like effectiveness, impact, and cost. These systems employ processes like cloning and mutation to optimize the effectiveness of countermeasures iteratively. Such approaches ensure that responses are tailored to specific threats, enhancing the adaptability and resilience of cybersecurity frameworks [52, 53].

The approach driven by AIS reduces risk while weighing cost, impact, and effectiveness considerations. The countermeasure benefit index, for instance, ranks and assesses responses according to how they might affect assets. This makes it possible to respond to threats precisely and effectively [52]. AIS has proven particularly useful in environments like IoT networks, where the threat landscape is dynamic and unpredictable [50].

AI performance has been improved with optimization techniques like Genetic Algorithms (GA). An AIS-based system enhanced with GA, called AISGA, optimizes input parameters to strike a compromise between risk mitigation and execution speed. AISGA achieves resilient and adaptable responses to cyber threats by iteratively improving solutions during crossover and mutation stages. This approach has demonstrated significant improvements in efficiency and scalability, validating the potential of GA in strengthening cybersecurity strategies [52, 53].

AI has also transformed decision-making in cybersecurity through Intelligent Decision Support Systems (IDSS). Thanks to the Constraint Object-Oriented Logic Program (COOLP), the task of selecting mitigation actions is formalized as a Constraint Optimization Problem (COP). These systems integrate real-time monitoring, planning, and execution to provide cybersecurity teams with actionable recommendations. Automating these processes reduces response times and ensures that countermeasures are optimized for effectiveness and resource efficiency [54].

IDSS framework isolates impacted nodes, applies targeted defenses, and dynamically adjusts network configurations. They are, therefore, important weapons against cyberattacks, and more so on critical infrastructure and industrial control systems. These systems are improved by the incorporation of ontological knowledge and technologies, such as ML and Network Function Virtualization (NFV), which allow for context-aware and nuanced decision-making [54].

Despite the transformative potential of AI in cybersecurity, challenges remain in ensuring transparency, explainability, and reliability.

Research must focus on bridging gaps in autonomous countermeasure strategies and developing systems that align with regulatory and ethical standards [50, 51].

23.8 CONCLUSION

Integrating NLP, ML, and DL techniques presents itself as a highly valid and promising approach to addressing the most modern and contemporary cybersecurity challenges. The success of these techniques depends on multiple factors, including a combination of linguistic theories and computational techniques. Therefore, it is easy to deduce that applying these techniques in cybersecurity has multiple and possible applications of use. For example, AI-based systems use NLP to detect phishing attempts by identifying deceptive content in URLs and email communications. Both ML and DL are widely used for malware detection, ransomware mitigation, and botnet detection, exploiting their specific ability to analyze large amounts of data, identify patterns, and detect anomalies indicative of malicious activity. In addition, it has been demonstrated that random and grid search strategies can improve model performance while addressing the computational challenges posed by hyperparameter optimization. Therefore, the convergence of technologies based on NLP, ML, and DL in cybersecurity represents a significant step forward in progress in the security paradigms conventionally adopted. Thanks to these technologies, it is possible to develop very sophisticated analytical tools capable of identifying patterns, detecting anomalies, and responding to threats even in real-time. In the near future, these technologies will likely be more critical in safeguarding people, businesses, and vital infrastructure from various cyber threats. Future research will focus on continuously refining these techniques, exploring and addressing their limitations with new applications in the rapidly changing cybersecurity landscape.

REFERENCES

[1] S. Okdem. Artificial intelligence in cybersecurity: A review and a case study. *Applied Sciences*, 14(22):10487, 2024.

[2] Ogugua Chimezie Obi, Onyinyechi Vivian Akagha, Samuel Onimisi Dawodu, Anthony Chigozie Anyanwu, Shedrack Onwusinkwue, and Islam Ahmad Ibrahim Ahmad. Comprehensive review on cybersecurity: Modern threats and advanced defense strategies. *Computer Science and IT Research Journal*, 5(2):293–310, February 2024.

[3] Muhammad Fakhrul Safitra, Muharman Lubis, and Hanif Fakhrurroja. Counterattacking cyber threats: A framework for the future of cybersecurity. *Sustainability*, 15(18), 2023.

[4] Masike Malatji, and Alaa Tolah. Artificial intelligence (AI) cybersecurity dimensions: A comprehensive framework for understanding adversarial and offensive AI. *AI and Ethics*, February 2024. DOI: 10.1007/s43681-024-00427-4.

[5] Vasiliki Demertzi, Stavros Demertzis, and Konstantinos Demertzis. An overview of cyber threats, attacks and countermeasures on the primary domains of smart cities. *Applied Sciences*, 13(2), 2023.

[6] Sandeep Katoch, Swapnil S. Chauhan, and Vijay Kumar. A review on genetic algorithm: Past, present, and future. *Multimedia Tools and Applications*, 80(5):8091–8126, 2021.

[7] Ahmed H. Salem, Salah M. Azzam, Omar E. Emam, et al. Advancing cybersecurity: A comprehensive review of AI-driven detection techniques. *Journal of Big Data*, 11:105, 2024.

[8] Raffaele Pugliese, Stefano Regondi, and Riccardo Marini. Machine learning-based approach: Global trends, research directions, and regulatory standpoints. *Data Science and Management*, 4:19–29, 2021.

[9] Hui Yin, Amir Aryani, Stephen Petrie, Aishwarya Nambissan, Aland Astudillo, and Shengyuan Cao. *A rapid review of clustering algorithms*, Swinburne University of Technology, VIC and Australian National University, Canberra, 2024.

[10] Majid Ghasemi, Amir Hossein Mousavi, and Dariush Ebrahimi. Comprehensive survey of reinforcement learning: From algorithms to practical challenges, 2025. https://arxiv.org/abs/2411.18892

[11] Derek A. Pisner, and David M. Schnyer. Chapter 6 support vector machine. In Andrea Mechelli and Sandra Vieira, editors, *Machine Learning*, pp. 101–121. Academic Press, 2020.

[12] Vitor G. Costa, and Cecilia E. Pedreira. Recent advances in decision trees: An updated survey. *Artificial Intelligence Review*, 56:4765–4800, 2023.

[13] Gilles Louppe. Understanding random forests: From theory to practice, 2015. https://arxiv.org/abs/1407.7502

[14] Diksha Khurana, Aditya Koli, Kiran Khatter, and Sukhdev Singh. Natural language processing: State of the art, current trends and challenges. *Multimedia Tools and Applications*, 82(3):3713–3744, 2023.

[15] Jan Sawicki, Maria Ganzha, and Marcin Paprzycki. The state of the art of natural language processing—a systematic automated review of NLP literature using NLP techniques. *Data Intelligence*, 5(3):707–749, 2023.

[16] Christine P. Chai. Natural language engineering: Dvances and challenges. *Natural Language Engineering*, 29(3):509–553, 2023.

[17] A. Chiche, and B. Yitagesu. Part of speech tagging: A systematic review of deep learning and machine learning approaches. *Journal of Big Data*, 9:10, 2022.

[18] Palanichamy Naveen, and Pavel Trojovský. Overview and challenges of machine translation for contextually appropriate translations. *Iscience*, 27(10), 2024.

[19] Rui Mao, Mengshi Ge, Sooji Han, Wei Li, Kai He, Luyao Zhu, and Erik Cambria. A survey on pragmatic processing techniques. *Information Fusion*, 114:102712, 2025.

[20] M. M. Taye. Understanding of machine learning with deep learning: Architectures, workflow, applications and future directions. *Computers*, 12(5):91, 2023.

[21] Ankit Patel, Tan Nguyen, and Richard Baraniuk. A probabilistic framework for deep learning. arXiv preprint arXiv:1612.01936, 2016.

[22] Y. A. Ali, E. M. Awwad, M. Al-Razgan, and A. Maarouf. Hyperparameter search for machine learning algorithms for optimizing the computational complexity. *Processes*, 11(2):349, 2023.

[23] Adnan Masood, and Ahmed Sherif. *Automated Machine Learning: Hyperparameter Optimization, Neural Architecture Search, and Algorithm Selection with Cloud Platforms*. Packt Publishing, Birmingham, UK, 2021.
[24] German Magai, and Anton Ayzenberg. Topology and geometry of data manifold in deep learning, 2022. https://arxiv.org/abs/2204.08624
[25] Sonya Coleman, Dermot Kerr, and Yunzhou Zhang. Image sensing and processing with convolutional neural networks. *Sensors*, 22(10), 2022.
[26] Dulari Bhatt, Chirag Patel, Hardik Talsania, Jigar Patel, Rasmika Vaghela, Sharnil Pandya, Kirit Modi, and Hemant Ghayvat. CNN variants for computer vision: History, architecture, application, challenges and future scope. *Electronics*, 10(20), 2021.
[27] Shouq Alnemari, and Majid Alshammari. Detecting phishing domains using machine learning. *Applied Sciences*, 13(4649), 2023.
[28] Sibel Kapan, and Efnan Sora Gunal. Improved phishing attack detection with machine learning: A comprehensive evaluation of classifiers and features. *Applied Sciences*, 13(13269), 2023.
[29] Abdul Karim, Mobeen Shahroz, Khabib Mustofa, Samir Brahim Belhaouari, and S. Ramana Kumar Joga. Phishing detection system through hybrid machine learning based on url. *IEEE Access*, 11:36805–36810, 2023.
[30] Rami Mohammad, T. L. McCluskey, and Fadi Thabtah. A dynamic selfstructuring neural network model to combat phishing. In *Proceedings of the International Joint Conference on Neural Networks (IJCNN)*, 2016.
[31] Issa Qabajeh, Fadi Thabtah, and Francisco Chiclana. A recent review of conventional vs. automated cybersecurity anti-phishing techniques. *Computer Science Review*, 29:44–55, 2018.
[32] Ibrahim Bello, Haruna Chiroma, Usman A. Abdullahi, et al. Detecting ransomware attacks using intelligent algorithms: Recent development and next direction from deep learning and big data perspectives. *Journal of Ambient Intelligence and Humanized Computing*, 12(9):8699–8717, 2020.
[33] Amjad Alraizza, and Abdulmohsen Algarni. Ransomware detection using machine learning: A survey. *Big Data and Cognitive Computing*, 7(143), 2023.
[34] Gaddisa Olani Ganfure, Chun-Feng Wu, Yuan-Hao Chang, and Wei-Kuan Shih. Rtrap: Trapping and containing ransomware with machine learning. *IEEE Transactions on Information Forensics and Security*, 18:1433–1445, 2023.
[35] Shaila Sharmeen, Yahye Abukar Ahmed, Shamsul Huda, Bari S. Kocer, and Mohammad Mehedi Hassan. Avoiding future digital extortion through robust protection against ransomware threats using deep learning based adaptive approaches. *IEEE Access*, 8:24522–24539, 2020.
[36] Olufunsho I. Falowo, Murat Ozer, Chengcheng Li, and Jacques Bou Abdo. Evolving malware and ddos attacks: Decadal longitudinal study. *IEEE Access*, 12:39221–39237, 2024.
[37] Al-Ani Mustafa Majid, Ahmed Jamal Alshaibi, Evgeny Kostyuchenko, and Alexander Shelupanov. A review of artificial intelligence-based malware detection using deep learning. *Materials Today: Proceedings*, 80:2678–2683, 2023.
[38] Halit Bakir, and Rezan Bakir. Droidencoder: Malware detection using autoencoder based feature extractor and machine learning algorithms. *Computers and Electrical Engineering*, 110:108804, 2023.
[39] Sudan Jha, Deepak Prashar, Hoang Viet Long, and David Taniar. Recurrent neural network for detecting malware. *Computers & Security*, 99:102037, 2020.
[40] S. Vanjire, and M. Lakshmi. Behavior-based malware detection system approach for mobile security using machine learning. In *2021 International Conference on Artificial Intelligence and Machine Vision (AIMV)*, pp. 1–4, 2021.

[41] Manoj Kumar, Sanjay Singh, Urmila Pilania, Gaurav Arora, and Mayank Jain. Lstm-based approach for android malware detection. *Procedia Computer Science*, 230:679–687, 2023.

[42] Amir Djenna, Ahmed Bouridane, Saddaf Rubab, and Ibrahim Moussa Marou. Artificial intelligence-based malware detection, analysis, and mitigation. *Symmetry*, 15(677), 2023.

[43] Rajasekhar Chaganti, Vinayakumar Ravi, and Tuan D. Pham. Deep learning-based cross-architecture IoT malware detection and classification. *Computers & Security*, 120:102779, 2022.

[44] Isabella Martínez Martínez, Andrés Florián Quitián, Daniel Díaz-López, Pantaleone Nespoli, and Félix Gómez Mármol. Malseirs: Forecasting malware spread based on compartmental models in epidemiology. *Complexity*, 2021:Article ID 5415724, 19, 2021.

[45] José Tomás Martínez Garre, Manuel Gil Pérez, and Antonio Ruiz-Martínez. A review of SSH botnet detection in initial stages of infection: A machine learning-based approach. In *H2020 PALANTIR Project Conference Proceedings*, 2021.

[46] Bruno Henrique Schwengber, Andressa Vergütz, Nelson G. Prates, and Michele Nogueira. Learning from network data changes for unsupervised botnet detection. *IEEE Transactions on Network and Service Management*, 19(1):601–613, 2022.

[47] Orestis Kompougias, Dimitris Papadopoulos, Evangelos Mantas, et al. IoT botnet detection on flow data using autoencoders. In *H2020 PALANTIR Project Conference Proceedings*, 2021.

[48] Balaganesh Bojarajulu, Sarvesh Tanwar, and Thipendra Pal Singh. Improved deep max-out for IoT botnet attack detection with LDA based selected feature set. In *2023 14th International Conference on Computing Communication and Networking Technologies (ICCCNT)*, pp. 1–8, 2023.

[49] Orestis Kompougias, Dimitris Papadopoulos, Evangelos Mantas, Antonis Litke, Nikolaos Papadakis, Dimitris Paraschos, Akis Kourtis, and George Xylouris. IoT botnet detection on flow data using autoencoders. In *2021 IEEE International Mediterranean Conference on Communications and Networking (MeditCom)*, pp. 506–511, 2021.

[50] Evangelos Mantas, Dimitris Papadopoulos, Carolina Fernández, et al. Practical autonomous cyberhealth for resilient micro, small and medium-sized enterprises. In *H2020 PALANTIR Project Conference Proceedings*, 2021.

[51] Sergio Bernardez Molina, Pantaleone Nespoli, and Félix Gómez Mármol. Tackling cyberattacks through AI-based reactive systems: A holistic review and future vision. arXiv preprint, arXiv:2312.06229, 2023.

[52] Pantaleone Nespoli, Félix Gómez Mármol, and Jorge Maestre Vidal. A bio-inspired reaction against cyberattacks: AIS-powered optimal countermeasures selection. *IEEE Access*, 9:60971–60996, 2021.

[53] Pantaleone Nespoli, Félix Gómez Mármol, and Georgios Kambourakis. Aisga: Multi-objective parameters optimization for countermeasures selection through genetic algorithm. In *The 16th International Conference on Availability, Reliability and Security (ARES 2021)*. ACM, 2021.

[54] Camilo Correa, Jacques Robin, Raul Mazo, and Salvador Abreu. Intelligent decision support for cybersecurity incident response teams: Autonomic architecture and mitigation search. In *International Conference on Risks and Security of Internet and Systems*. Springer, 2021.

Index